The Complete Handbook of
Coaching

Praise for the book

'Easy to understand and read, *The Complete Handbook of Coaching* provides a comprehensive coverage of the key areas in coaching and is a good introduction to the subject matter. As a single reference it sets the standard for its breadth of coverage of the field of coaching.'

Dr Caroline Horner, Director, i-coach academy

'A fascinating, timely and comprehensive text … This is a great resource for coaches of all persuasions. It is the most comprehensive handbook that I know, and it is one that I expect to cherish for a long time to come.'

Professor David Megginson, Sheffield Hallam University

'This book is the most thorough, comprehensive and accessible overview of key approaches to coaching yet on the market. It is a tour de force in its range and structure, offering both theoretical explanation and practical application, and a must for students and practitioners of coaching alike.'

Dr Janice Russell, Executive and Life Coach, University of Hull

The Complete Handbook of
Coaching

Edited by

Elaine Cox, Tatiana Bachkirova
and David Clutterbuck

Los Angeles • London • New Delhi • Singapore • Washington DC

First published 2010

SAGE Publications Ltd
1 Oliver's Yard
55 City Road
London EC1Y 1SP

SAGE Publications Inc.
2455 Teller Road
Thousand Oaks, California 91320

SAGE Publications India Pvt Ltd
B 1/I 1 Mohan Cooperative Industrial Area
Mathura Road
New Delhi 110 044

SAGE Publications Asia-Pacific Pte Ltd
33 Pekin Street #02-01
Far East Square
Singapore 048763

Library of Congress Control Number: 2009924546

British Library Cataloguing in Publication data
A catalogue record for this book is available from the British Library

ISBN 978-1-84787-542-6
ISBN 978-1-84920-288-6 (pbk)

Typeset by Glyph International, Bangalore, India
Printed and bound in Great Britain by
TJ International Ltd, Padstow, Cornwall
Printed on paper from sustainable resources

Contents

List of Figures and Tables   viii

Foreword   x

List of Contributors   xii

INTRODUCTION   1
Tatiana Bachkirova, Elaine Cox and David Clutterbuck

SECTION I   THEORETICAL APPROACHES   21

1   The Psychodynamic Approach to Coaching   23
     Graham Lee

2   Cognitive Behavioural Coaching   37
     Helen Williams, Nick Edgerton and Stephen Palmer

3   The Solution-focused Approach to Coaching   54
     Michael J. Cavanagh and Anthony M. Grant

4   The Person-centred Approach to Coaching   68
     Stephen Joseph

5   The Gestalt Approach to Coaching   80
     Peter Bluckert

6   Existential Coaching   94
     Ernesto Spinelli

7   Ontological Coaching   107
     Alan Sieler

 8   Narrative Coaching   120
     David B. Drake

 9   The Cognitive–Developmental Approach to Coaching   132
     Tatiana Bachkirova

10   The Transpersonal Approach to Coaching   146
     John Rowan

11   The Positive Psychology Approach to Coaching   158
     Carol Kauffman, Ilona Boniwell and Jordan Silberman

12   Transactional Analysis and Coaching   172
     Trudi Newton and Rosemary Napper

13   The NLP Approach to Coaching   187
     Bruce Grimley

SECTION II   GENRES AND CONTEXTS OF COACHING   201

14   Skills and Performance Coaching   203
     Bob Tschannen-Moran

15   Developmental Coaching   217
     Elaine Cox and Peter Jackson

16   Transformational Coaching   231
     Peter Hawkins and Nick Smith

17   Executive and Leadership Coaching   245
     Jon Stokes and Richard Jolly

18   The 'Manager as Coach'   257
     Andrea D. Ellinger, Rona S. Beattie and Robert G. Hamlin

19   Team Coaching   271
     David Clutterbuck

20   Peer Coaching   284
     Richard Ladyshewsky

21 Life Coaching   297
    Anthony M. Grant and Michael J. Cavanagh

22 Career Coaching   311
    Bruce Hazen and Nicole A. Steckler

23 Cross Cultural Coaching: A Paradoxical Perspective   324
    Geoffrey Abbott

24 Mentoring in a Coaching World   341
    Bob Garvey

SECTION III   PROFESSIONAL PRACTICE ISSUES   355

25 The Future of Coaching as a Profession   357
    David A. Lane, Reinhard Stelter and Sunny Stout Rostron

26 Ethics in Coaching   369
    Diane Brennan and Leni Wildflower

27 Coaching Supervision   381
    Peter Hawkins

28 Coaching and Mental Health   394
    Andrew Buckley

29 Continuing Professional Development for Coaches   405
    Dianne R. Stober

CONCLUSION   417
Tatiana Bachkirova, David Clutterbuck and Elaine Cox

Author Index   422

General Index   429

Figures and Tables

FIGURES

0.1	Four dimensions of coaching	5
2.1	Client example using the ABCDEF model	43
2.2	Depiction of low performance state using the SPACE model	44
2.3	Depiction of high performance state using the SPACE model	45
3.1	The cycle of self-regulation	57
5.1	Cycle of experience as orienting framework	85
9.1	Example of a combination of the developmental lines in an individual	134
12.1	Three-cornered contract	175
12.2	Multiple contracts	175
12.3	Ego-state diagrams	176
12.4	Drama and winners triangles	178
12.5	TA concepts in organizational coaching	180
12.6	Life positions and flow	182
14.1	A Mobius-strip model of SPC	206
15.1	Skills, performance and developmental coaching – an evolution	218
16.1	Four levels of engagement	235
16.2	The coaching continuum	242
23.1	The integral model	327
23.2	Action learning cycle	328
23.3	Identification with own and other cultures	331
23.4	Trait interaction possibilities	332
23.5	Certainty/reflectiveness paradox	333
23.6	Individualism/collectivism paradox	333
23.7	Rafael's communication paradox	336
27.1	The coaching continuum	385
27.2	The seven-eyed model of coaching supervision	387
27.3	The seven modes of coaching supervision	389

TABLES

0.1	Transitions from traditional coaching	3
0.2	The matrix	10
2.1	PRACTICE model of coaching	41
2.2	Example of PITS and PETS for making a presentation	42
5.1	A framework for Gestalt coaching practice	84
9.1	Five stages of development according to Kegan's theory	138
18.1	Behavioural taxonomies	261
19.1	Differences between team leading and team coaching	277
19.2	Team coaching v. team facilitation	278
20.1	Eight stage peer coaching model	287
22.1	Goals, objectives and processes in career coaching	312
27.1	Three main functions of supervision	384
27.2	The CLEAR model	386
28.1	Warning signs of mental ill health	398
28.2	Deciding 'What next?'	402

Foreword

The introductory chapter to this fascinating, timely and comprehensive text includes a full description of its structure and contents, so I will not repeat that here. Instead, I will offer a more personal reaction to the volume and invite you, as reader, to follow the same route.

I think that everyone who reads this book will have a different take on it. Just consider what the three most engaging chapters are for you out of the 29 presented here, and this gives you thousands of possibilities, even before starting to take into account the different things that even two people who chose the same three chapters might take from them. So I am not prioritizing my choice of three chapters as being the best or the most important in the book, or recommending them to you above others. They just happened to chime with *my* preoccupations when I was writing this Foreword.

I was surprised and delighted by John Rowan's take on transpersonal coaching. In contrast to the rest of a field – the transpersonal – filled with hippies (the meadows before Longshaw Lodge in England's Peak District in autumn swarming with people in red bandanas hunting for magic mushrooms is a metaphor that comes to mind) this chapter is full of sound sense and a spirited defence of what is important. From the definition of the two types of transpersonal through to the splendid distinction between 'letting go' and 'letting come', John Rowan is clear, undogmatic and pragmatic about how we ordinary coaches can deal with these heady but crucially important issues.

David Drake's chapter on narrative coaching addresses one of the areas that has been preoccupying me in the past year. His chapter explores how we position ourselves in our inner constructions and our outer interactions, and describes the back story of the narrative approach, with its roots in literary theory, humanism and psychology. He offers a strong and helpful challenge to the lingering behaviourism that hangs round some accounts of coaching like the miasma from a swamp. Drake is a suitable candidate to be the hero that comes to defeat the monster in the swamp – a Beowulf to challenge the Grendel of SMART goals and the Grendel's mother of performativity.

The chapter on cognitive development coaching by Tatiana Bachkirova is preoccupied with meaning-making, and offers the most explicit adult development approach in this volume. It is central to the book because the perspective of the authors here is *au font*, grounded in adult learning. After a helpful and comprehensive review of the theoretical contributions, Bachkirova develops the work of Robert Kegan and relates it to the process of coaching whereby what the client takes as themselves (Subject) can, with the coach's help, become Object, and thus amenable to interrogation or development. These orders of mind are outlined and the theory seems sufficiently complex to embrace significant aspects of experience without being unwieldy.

Integrating what I have learned from these three chapters is about articulating the crucial agendas that Rowan points to, using the tools of Subject–Object transformations explored by Bachkirova, and deepening further my use of stories using frameworks from Drake, not only as tools of diagnosis but also as a means (for myself and for clients) of re-storying and restoring a life.

So, those are my three chapters. Remember, I am not recommending you to pay attention to those three in particular – they are just mine at this particular moment in my development. I suggest that a reading of Part One: Theoretical Approaches – could lead you to choosing your own three perspectives, which you could then seek to integrate into your own practice.

However, for me, the real joy of this book (and the extent to which it has been pulled off is impressive) is the integrative structure which separates perspectives and genres in a fruitful and intriguing way. As well as the theoretical approaches section, there is a series of chapters addressing different contexts and genres and these are comprehensively integrated and cross-referenced with the theoretical approaches chapters. It is rare in any book to have so comprehensive an interaction of different aspects of the authors' meta-model, and for a book of contributed chapters it is almost unprecedented. It is testimony to the clear thinking and thorough briefing of the contributors, making it very valuable to students and more experienced coaches wishing to articulate and develop their own approach – their signature presence. I remember hearing members of the Lindsay String Quartet talking about their long collaboration with the composer Michael Tippett. They asked him about the source of his inspiration for themes and harmonies. However, he was much more interested in structure. I have the sense that the authors of this volume are preoccupied with structure too, and the result is that for us readers, we have a structure which can help us to make sense of what we read, and this structure also gives us tools and ways of thinking that can enrich our own structures in developing our practice.

Some areas of difference between perspectives and genres are exposed; some perspectives are radically emancipatory: concerned with the development of human freedom, in which the agenda, the content and to an extent the process all best belong with the coachee/client. Other contributors acknowledge the coach as being there, in the process of change (coach as participant, not neutral observer); and this is a helpful challenge to those of us who see ourselves as emancipatory and learner-centred. I found the arguments laid out chapter by chapter to be provocative and stimulating, so that I even enjoyed the bits I disagreed with.

I like the mix of those researching and commenting on the part of the field that is the focus of their chapter (e.g. Grant and Cavanagh on life coaching), in contrast with the chapters where the authors are passionate advocates for their method, for example Sieler, who has invented his own brand of ontological coaching, or Clutterbuck, who has presciently developed team coaching as a genre.

This is a great resource for coaches of all persuasions; it is the most comprehensive handbook that I know, and it is one that I expect to cherish for a long time to come.

Prof David Megginson, Sheffield Hallam University, 2009

List of Contributors

Geoffrey Abbott is an Australian executive coach, consultant, researcher, lecturer and author. Geoff is the Director of the Centre for International Business Coaching Pty Ltd. He specializes in coaching in complex international environments and runs international business coaching seminars globally. He has extensive experience in strategic planning as an executive for the Special Broadcasting Service, Australia. Geoff is co-editor of the Routledge Companion to International Business Coaching (Moral and Abbott, 2009) and has numerous articles and chapters on related topics. Geoff's doctorate (from Australian National University) examined the effectiveness of executive coaching in assisting expatriate managers. He is an Adjunct at Macquarie Graduate School of Management in Sydney, lecturing in organizational behaviour, and a guest lecturer at various universities and business schools.

Tatiana Bachkirova is a Programme Director for MA in Coaching and Mentoring Supervision at Oxford Brookes University. She is a Chartered Occupational Psychologist and an experienced coaching supervisor. Her work as an academic involves research, teaching and supervising MA and doctoral students of coaching and mentoring. She is also Co-editor in Chief of *Coaching: An International Journal of Theory, Research and Practice*.

Rona S. Beattie is Professor of Human Resource Development and Head of the Division of People Management and Leadership, Caledonian Business School, Glasgow Caledonian University. Rona's research interests include management development, coaching, mentoring, line management and voluntary sector management.

Peter Bluckert is the Managing Director of PB Coaching, a specialist business and executive coaching consultancy based in the UK. Peter's background and experience in both organizational development and coaching spans over twenty-five years. He is Programme Director on the Masters programme in Business and Executive Coaching with Leeds Met University in the UK and University College Dublin (UCD), Michael Smurfit Business School in Ireland. Peter has published numerous articles on coaching and in 2006 the Open University Press published his book *The Psychological Dimensions of Executive Coaching*. Recently, Peter was nominated to be recognized by the Harvard Business Review as one of the world's top 100 executive coaches.

Ilona Boniwell is programme leader for the first Masters Degree in Applied Positive Psychology in Europe at the University of East London. Her research interests include: psychology of time, eudaemonic well-being and applications of positive psychology to coaching and education.

She founded the European Network of Positive Psychology and is the Vice-Chair of the International Positive Psychology Association. She is the author of *Positive Psychology in a Nutshell* (PWBC, 2006); *Time in Our Lives* (VDM, 2009); and a co-author of *The Happiness Equation* (Adams Media, 2008). She acted as the main consultant for and appeared in the BBC2 series 'The Happiness Formula'.

Diane Brennan is an executive coach and consultant, and works with individuals and organizations in healthcare, science and engineering. She holds a Masters in Business Administration, and the International Coach Federation (ICF) credential of Master Certified Coach. She served as President of ICF in 2008. Brennan is co-editor and contributing author of *The Philosophy and Practice of Coaching: Insights and Issues for a New Era* (Wiley and Sons, 2008). In addition to coaching, she has more than 20 years experience in senior leadership and clinical practice positions within private and publicly traded healthcare.

Andrew Buckley is founder of the mental wellbeing organization Kipepeo, and has been helping individuals and organizations to understand mental health since the mid-1990s. He is a psychotherapist, coach and co-author of *A Guide to Coaching and Mental Health. The Recognition and Management of Psychological Issues* (Routledge, 2006). Andrew is regularly invited to speak at conferences and events on the topic of managing mental-health issues and advocates a simple approach that looks for practical and effective means which will help all concerned.

Michael J. Cavanagh is Deputy Director of the Coaching Psychology Unit at the University of Sydney. He is also the Australian co-ordinating editor for *International Coaching Psychology Review*. Michael has over 20 years experience in facilitating personal, group and organizational change. He has coached leaders and managers at all levels from a diverse range of public and private, national and multinational organizations. Michael leads a team of researchers who have recently won funding to undertake a $3.5million research project investigating leadership development and coaching in high stress workplaces.

David Clutterbuck is visiting professor in the Coaching and Leadership faculty at Oxford Brookes University and also at Sheffield Hallam University. He is the author or co-author of 50 books, of which 12 are on coaching or mentoring. Co-founder of the European Mentoring and Coaching Council, he is a long-standing member of its research committee. He has conducted numerous studies into aspects of coaching and mentoring, including a longitudinal study of developmental mentoring from both mentor and mentee perspectives. He led the creation of the International Standards for Mentoring Programmes in Employment and is Practice Leader at international consultancy Clutterbuck Associates.

Elaine Cox is Head of Research in the International Centre for Coaching and Leadership Development at Oxford Brookes University. While at Westminster College during the 1990s, she was responsible for managing and obtaining significant funding for a range of government and European funded courses aimed at helping adults back into the workplace. During this time she became involved with developing coaching and mentoring initiatives and programmes through pilot projects, such as the Oxford Lone Parent Mentoring Scheme. More recently, Elaine developed and led the MA in Coaching and Mentoring Practice at Oxford Brookes University, and also developed and now leads their Doctor of Coaching and Mentoring programme. She is also the founder and editor of the *International Journal of Evidence Based Coaching and Mentoring* and Chair of the Oxford Brookes Coaching and Mentoring Society.

David B. Drake is Executive Director of the Center for Narrative Coaching based in Sydney and San Francisco. His firm works with organizations to develop coaching strategies, teams, skills and cultures through innovative conversation-based methods. For example, he is currently working with PricewaterhouseCoopers on a systemic multi-year project to develop a coaching-based culture. David pioneered the field of narrative coaching and leads workshops for master coaching professionals around the world (www.narrativecoaching.com). He is the lead editor and contributing author for *The Philosophy and Practice of Coaching: Insights and Issues*, published by Jossey-Bass in 2008 (www.practiceofcoaching.com) and he has written over thirty publications on narratives, evidence and coaching.

Nick Edgerton is an independent Chartered Psychologist providing coaching, counselling and Cognitive Behavioural Therapy (CBT) services from his practices near Woodbridge in Suffolk and Blackheath in London. His consultancy work has mainly been in the provision of coaching, counselling and interpersonal skills courses for public service organizations and the oil and gas industry. He has been Chair of the Counselling Psychology Section of the BPS and was Head of the Centre for Studies in Counselling at the Polytechnic of East London. He is currently developing and presenting courses at the Centre for Stress Management and Centre for Coaching in London.

Andrea D. Ellinger is Professor of Human Resource Development in the School of Human Resource Development and Technology, College of Business and Technology at the University of Texas at Tyler. Her research interests include informal learning in the workplace, evolving managerial roles, coaching, mentoring, organizational learning, and the learning organization concept.

Bob Garvey is a leading academic practitioner in mentoring and coaching. His work is regarded as deeply influential, groundbreaking, original and innovative in terms of both research and practice. In particular, his 'dimensions' framework has proved to be of both practical and theoretical use to communities in which mentoring and coaching take place. His research has directly influenced policy, practice and productivity in a range of organizations in all sectors – corporate, small business, public and the not-for-profit sector. Bob's work has benefited organizations by offering best practice guidance and skills practice; developing knowledge of mentoring and coaching processes and skills; increasing knowledge of scheme design and implementation and providing models and a language with which to discuss mentoring and coaching. He is a member of the European Mentoring and Coaching Council and the co-author of four best selling books and numerous journal articles.

Anthony M. Grant is the founder and Director of the Coaching Psychology Unit at the University of Sydney. He is widely regarded as a founding figure in contemporary coaching psychology. Anthony's background is grounded in the realities of the commercial world. He left school at the age of 15 with no qualifications, beginning tertiary studies in psychology in his 30s. His PhD thesis is one of few about the effectiveness of evidence-based coaching. He has over 50 coaching publications, including the first published randomized controlled study of executive coaching. Anthony is an experienced executive coach and his work has frequently been reported in national and international media.

Bruce Grimley is a successful Coaching Psychologist and neuro linguistic programming (NLP) trainer based in St Ives, Cambridgeshire. His company; Achieving Lives Ltd (www.achieving-lives.co.uk) has been established since 1995 and, through coaching, assists at both organizational and individual levels. Bruce also trains NLP up to Master Practitioner level through Inner Game (www.innergame.co.uk). At present Bruce is undertaking a PhD at Surrey University, researching how coaching relationships within companies can become standard practice.

Robert G. Hamlin is an Emeritus Professor and Chair of Human Resource Development (HRD) at the University of Wolverhampton. He now works as an independent management and organization development consultant, researcher and author. His research is focused mainly on 'managerial and leadership effectiveness', 'managerial coaching effectiveness' and 'mentoring effectiveness' within public, private and third sector organizations. Bob is Honorary Treasurer of the University Forum for HRD and a distinguished Fellow of the Chartered Institute of Personnel and Development.

Peter Hawkins is Chair and founder of Bath Consultancy Group and Honorary President of the Association for Professional Executive Coaching and Supervision (APECS) and a visiting professor in the School of Management at both the University of Bath and Oxford Brookes University. He is an international organizational consultant and executive coach, and author of several books including co-author of *Coaching, Mentoring an Organizational Consultancy: Supervision and Development*, Open University Press 2006. Peter is leader of the Bath Consultancy Group training in Coaching Supervision.

Bruce Hazen has extensive and diverse industry experience as an internal and external management coach and consultant, as a member of corporate staff as well as in line management. He currently coaches professionals on the interface of where their skill and style come together to impel or impede success, and teaches at the University of Portland School of Business: The Three Questions You Must Answer (multiple times) Throughout Your Career. He has a BS in

Industrial and Labor Relations from Cornell University, with an emphasis in organizational behaviour and psychology. In addition, he holds an MS in Clinical Psychology.

Peter Jackson teaches part-time on the Oxford Brookes University postgraduate programme in Coaching and Mentoring Practice as well as running a professional coaching practice. Peter's practice focus is on professional specialists moving into general management. He has research interests in coaching approaches, coaching philosophy, professional and academic development of coaching practitioners and the physical and environmental influences on the coaching process.

Richard Jolly is a Director of the consulting firm, Stokes & Jolly (www.stokesjolly.com) who provide leadership coaching, top team facilitation, management development programmes and assessment selection services for a wide range of professional service and corporate clients. Richard is Adjunct Associate Professor at London Business School, where he teaches several core modules and electives on the topics of leadership, change management and power and politics in organizations, as well as working on a diverse range of company-specific programmes, both in the UK and across Europe, the Middle East and Asia.

Stephen Joseph is Professor of Psychology, Health and Social Care at the University of Nottingham, where he is co-director of the Centre for Trauma, Resilience, and Growth, and an Honorary Consultant Psychologist in Psychotherapy in Nottinghamshire HealthCare NHS Trust. Stephen is a senior practitioner member of the British Psychological Society's Register of Psychologists specializing in Psychotherapy. Stephen's interests are in the person-centred and positive psychological applications to therapy and coaching. He is Co-editor of *Positive Psychology in Practice* (Wiley, 2004), *Person-centred Psychopathology* (PCCS Books, 2005), *Positive Therapy* (Routledge, 2006), and *Person-centred Practice* (PCCS Books, 2007).

Carol Kauffman is Founding Director of the Institute of Coaching at Harvard Medical School. She teaches positive psychology and coaching, and has been a senior supervisor at McLean Hospital for over twenty-five years. Dr. Kauffman has an active executive coaching and supervision practice, and is Chief Supervisor of Meyler Campbell, a UK based business coaching programme. Professor Kauffman is co-editor in chief of *Coaching: An International Journal of Theory, Research & Practice*. The Institute is funding coaching research and creating a global coaching research directory; please contact us to be included (CarolKauffman.com for details).

Richard Ladyshewsky is an Associate Professor at the Graduate School of Business, Curtin University of Technology in Perth, Western Australia. His professional qualifications range from registered physiotherapist and healthcare administrator to educator in leadership and management development. His particular research interests centre around professional development and reasoning in the healthcare sector and leadership development in the higher education sector. He has developed a range of initiatives to promote leadership and learning in these sectors on a national and international level. He uses peer coaching as a central strategy to promote professional and leadership development, and publishes widely on this topic.

David A. Lane is Director of the Professional Development Foundation and contributes to leading-edge research in coaching as well as supervising leading coaches undertaking doctoral research. He is Chair of the British Psychological Society (BPS) Register of Psychologists, specializing in psychotherapy, and convenes the psychotherapy group of the European Federation of Psychologists Associations. His work with the European Mentoring and Coaching Council has been concerned with codes of conduct and standards and kite marking of coach training. Working with the Worldwide Association of Business Coaches, he has researched and developed the standards for the Certified Master Business Coach award. He is a member of the steering group for the Global Convention on Coaching. His contributions to counselling psychology led to the senior award of the BPS for 'Outstanding Scientific Contribution'.

Graham Lee is Managing Director of The Thinking Partnership, and specializes in advising and coaching senior leaders and their teams. With a background in both business and psychoanalysis, he has championed the need to understand the psychology of leaders and their organizations in enabling change, as explored in his influential book, *Leadership Coaching* (CIPD, 2006).

Rosemary Napper is internationally qualified as a trainer and supervisor in the organizational and educational applications of transactional analysis, and is also accredited as a TA 'counsellor', which is the continental European designation for a coach. She is Director of TAworks in Oxford, where she provides five-year part-time training programmes in all applications of TA (www.TAworks.co.uk), she is also President of the International Transactional Analysis Association 2009–2012, and founder member of the International Association for Relational Transactional Analysis. Rosemary has an MA in Education and has written a number of articles and books.

Trudi Newton is a Teaching and Supervising Transactional Analyst, writer, researcher and consultant on learning, working nationally and internationally. She has an active practice supervising accredited coaches in both the Executive and Life coaching fields. Over the last few years she has developed coach supervisor training programmes, one of which is the first (and so far only) such to be recognized by the International Coach Federation.

Stephen Palmer is Founder Director of the Coaching Psychology Unit at City University London and Director of the Centre for Coaching. He is executive editor of *Coaching: An International Journal of Theory, Research and Practice* and co-editor of the *Handbook of Coaching*

Psychology: A Guide for Practitioners (with Whybrow) (Routledge, 2007). He is an accredited executive coach and supervisor and a Chartered Psychologist.

Sunny Stout Rostron is an executive coach and consultant, with a wide range of experience in leadership and management development, business strategy and executive coaching. Sunny is the author of *Accelerating Performance, Powerful New Techniques to Develop People* (Kogan Page, 2002); *Business Coaching Wisdom and Practice, Unlocking the Secrets of Business Coaching* (Knowledge Resources, 2009); and *Business Coaching International* (Karnac, available mid-2009). Sunny is a Founding Director of the Manthano Learning Institute (Pty) Ltd in South Africa; Founding President of COMENSA (Coaches and Mentors of South Africa); a Research Advisor for the Institute of Coaching at Harvard; and one of the founding faculty members of The Coaching Centre (TCC) based in Cape Town which has recently launched a Masters in Executive Coaching at the Da Vinci Institute in Johannesburg.

John Rowan has been working with the transpersonal since the early eighties, and has been described as one of the founding fathers of transpersonal psychology in the UK. He is the author of a number of books, including *The Transpersonal: Spirituality in Psychotherapy and Counselling* (2nd ed., Routledge, 2005). He is on the editorial board of the *Journal of Humanistic Psychology*, the *Transpersonal Psychology Review* and the *Counselling Psychology Review*. He is a Fellow of the British Psychological Society (member of the Psychotherapy Section, the Counselling Psychology Division, the Special Group on Coaching Psychology and the Transpersonal Psychology Section) and a member of the Association for Coaching. His particular workshop interests are creativity, research, the dialogical self, AQAL and the transpersonal.

Alan Sieler is the Director of Newfield Institute, an international coach training, executive coaching and consulting company. Alan leads the Graduate Diploma of Ontological Coaching in Australia and Asia. He has been an executive coach for more than fourteen years, working with corporate clients from fifteen countries. Alan's two volumes of *Coaching to the Human Soul* (Newfield, 2005) have been used in coaching, leadership and organizational change courses at universities in the United States, South Africa and Australia. Major organizations, such as Intel, Hewlett Packard and NASA have also purchased copies of both books for their training departments.

Jordan Silberman began his career as a pianist, and studied at the Eastman School of Music. He has performed at Carnegie Hall in New York City, the Viper Room in Los Angeles and many places in between. Since changing paths in 2002, Jordan has authored and co-authored articles on healthcare communication, psychology, bioethics, pediatric palliative care and proteomics; served as a reviewer for a major health services research journal; chaired a psychology symposium in Hong Kong; completed two provisional patents; and finished three marathons.

His first-authored research has been described in *Prevention*, *Self*, and *Good Housekeeping* magazines; co-authored work has been covered by the New York Times, NPR, CNN, and others. Jordan earned a Masters of Applied Positive Psychology at the University of Pennsylvania, where he was advised by Martin Seligman. He is currently a medical student at the University of Rochester, and he works part-time on psychology projects with Harvard Professor Carol Kauffman.

Nick Smith is a Director of Bath Consultancy Group and has been with them for over twelve years. He is a senior faculty member of Bath Consultancy Group's international modular training programme on the Supervision of Coaches, Mentors and Consultants and supervises executive coaches in a number of organizations. He coaches senior leaders in organizations across public, private and third sector, as well as working as part of BCG's organizational development consultancy. Nick is the co-author of *Coaching, Mentoring and Organizational Consultancy: Supervision and Development* (McGraw-Hill/Open University Press, 2006).

Ernesto Spinelli has gained an international reputation as one of the leading contemporary trainers and theorists of existential analysis as applied to psychology and psychotherapy and coaching. He is a Fellow of the British Psychological Society (BPS) as well as a founding member of the BPS Special Group in Coaching Psychology, and accredited executive coach and coaching supervisor. Ernesto is also a consultant trainer, supervisor and faculty member of the i-coach Academy and Director of ES Associates, an organization dedicated to the advancement of coaching, facilitation, mediation and psychotherapy through specialist seminars and training programmes.

Nicole A. Steckler is Associate Professor of Management in the School of Medicine at Oregon Health and Science University. She holds a PhD in Organizational Behavior from Harvard University. Niki's expertise is in communication and collaboration across disciplines and organizational boundaries. She coaches academic leaders and healthcare professionals on increasing their leadership capabilities and reaching their career goals. Niki has won awards for her teaching excellence; she currently teaches graduate courses on becoming an effective manager, influence and communication skills, and managing people in healthcare organizations.

Reinhard Stelter is Professor of Sports and Coaching Psychology and Head of the Coaching Psychology Unit, Department of Exercise and Sport Science, at the University of Copenhagen, Denmark. He has a PhD in Psychology and is Honorary Vice-President and accredited member of the Society for Coaching Psychology. Reinhard is a member of the managing board of the Danish branch of the European Mentoring and Coaching Council (EMCC), a member of the Research Advisory Board, Institute of Coaching at Harvard Medical School, and author of a Danish bestselling book on coaching. He is also external lecturer at Copenhagen Business

School and Copenhagen Coaching Center. His major research interests are around identity, learning, and coaching on phenomenological, social constructionist and narrative bases.

Dianne R. Stober is the Business Leader for Sentis's North American operations and is a licensed clinical psychologist. Sentis is an international consulting company bringing to heavy industries an innovative approach to psychology in the workplace. Dianne has over 17 years' experience as a clinician, consultant and academic. Prior to her work at Sentis, Dianne was faculty in the Organizational Management and Development graduate program at Fielding Graduate University and also maintained a coaching and consulting practice. She has written a number of articles on coaching and is the co-editor of the *Evidence Based Coaching Handbook: Putting Best Practices to Work for Your Clients* (Wiley, 2006). Dianne has presented and facilitated on coaching internationally, including at the American Psychological Association, the British Psychological Society, the Australian Evidence-based Coaching Conference, and the Harvard Coaching and Positive Psychology Conference among others.

Jon Stokes is a Director of the consulting firm, Stokes & Jolly (www.stokesjolly.com) who provide leadership coaching, top team facilitation, management development programmes and assessment selection services for a wide range of professional service and corporate clients. Jon is a Visiting Professor at Strathclyde University Business School and member of Associate Faculty at Henley Business School. He trained and worked as a clinical psychologist at the Tavistock Clinic in London for over 20 years, where he was Head of the Adult Department. He founded and ran the Tavistock's Organisational Consultancy Service (TCS) for six years.

Bob Tschannen-Moran is President of LifeTrek Coaching International and serves on the faculty of Wellcoaches Corporation. Bob has co-authored two books on coaching, the Lippincott Wellcoaches *Coaching Psychology Manual* (2010) and *Evocative Coaching: Transforming Schools One Conversation at a Time* (2010), and publishes a weekly email newsletter, 'LifeTrek Provisions', with thousands of subscribers in 152 countries. Bob received an undergraduate degree from Northwestern University, a Master of Divinity degree from Yale University, coach training from Coach U, CoachVille, Wellcoaches and FastTrack Coach Training Academy. He is also trained in the practices of appreciative inquiry and non-violent communication. Bob has served as President of ICF Greater Richmond and as Secretary and President-Elect of the International Association of Coaching (IAC) Board of Governors.

Leni Wildflower is the Founder and Director of Fielding Graduate University's Evidence Based Coaching certificate programmes. She holds a doctorate in Human and Organizational Systems and is credentialed by the International Coach Federation (ICF) as a Professional Certified Coach. Dr. Wildflower is a contributing author to the *Sage Handbook of Online Learning* (2009). In addition to her university work, she has worked for over 35 years as a consultant and executive coach in business and not-for-profit agencies.

Helen Williams is a chartered Occupational Psychologist and Principal Consultant with SHL People Solutions. Specializing in management and leadership development and engaging with client organizations across a range of industries, her work involves psychometric assessment and feedback, coaching, facilitation of peer coaching groups and the design and delivery of behavioural change workshops. Helen is a founding member of the BPS Special Group in Coaching Psychology and member of the Association for Coaching.

Introduction

Tatiana Bachkirova, Elaine Cox and David Clutterbuck

Coaching could be seen as a human development process that involves structured, focused interaction and the use of appropriate strategies, tools and techniques to promote desirable and sustainable change for the benefit of the coachee and potentially for other stakeholders. Its popularity is indisputable, and across all economic sectors an increasing number of organizations are commissioning coaches to support their staff at different stages in their careers. Coaching is therefore recognized as a powerful vehicle for increasing performance, achieving results and optimizing personal effectiveness. Because it has proved to be so effective, many companies and government departments invest in internal and external coaching for their employees. The work of independent coaches is flourishing, enabling clients to accomplish their goals, both professionally and personally.

As the field of coaching has developed, existing models of coaching have begun to be applied in wider contexts, used with diverse client groups and with different media. Coaching practitioners come from a variety of professions and often from multi-theoretical backgrounds. They constantly bring new dimensions to the field via the adaptation of concepts, ideas and practical tools developed in their 'home' traditions and through interdisciplinarity. It is possible to meet coaches whose philosophies and practices of coaching would have very little in common, although their aims and purposes may be similar.

In this book, we recognize that coaching is an applied field of practice that has its intellectual roots in a range of disciplines: social psychology; learning theory; theories of human and organizational development; and existential and phenomenological philosophy, to name just a few. This diversity of the field creates exciting opportunities for meaningful interaction and mutual enrichment but there is also the potential for confusion, particularly for novices in the field and for buyers of coaching. Questions that may be asked include: What is the difference between existential coaching and solution-focused coaching? What would a performance coach do differently from a developmental coach? Is it possible to compare psychodynamic coaching with life coaching? Could a Gestalt-trained coach be a good choice in career coaching? Until now, there were no resource books in the field that could help practitioners and other stakeholders to find comprehensive answers to these types of questions. In this book we aim to address this gap by clarifying not only the differences between the theoretical approaches to coaching but also the differences and links between these perspectives in relation to the genres and contexts of coaching.

In this introduction there are three sections. The first section discusses coaching in terms of its identity, definition and role in organizations. In the second section we discuss the knowledge base of coaching and identify adult learning theory as an important theoretical tradition underpinning coaching. In the third section we explain the matrix structure of the book. We conclude with short summaries for each chapter and brief guidance on how to read the book.

I. THE IDENTITY OF COACHING

Discussions about identity usually begin with an historical overview of how the term came into usage and how the meaning has developed over time. According to the Online Etymology Dictionary, the word 'coach' derives from a town called 'Kocs' in northern Hungary, where horse drawn carriages were made. The meaning of coach as an instructor or trainer is purportedly from around 1830, when it was Oxford University slang for a tutor who 'carried' a student through an exam; the term coaching was later applied in the 1800s to improving the performance of athletes.

In the twentieth century, coaching found its way into the workplace, where it was associated with a specific process of education for young recruits. The coach was typically a more experienced employee, often with managerial authority over them. He or she would typically demonstrate a task, instruct them to attempt the same task, observe their performance, and provide feedback based either on their own experience, or a standardized perception of performance. Coach and coachee (usually called trainee or apprentice) would then discuss the feedback and plan how the coachee would approach the task differently next time. In essence, this form of coaching has much in common with instruction. Where instruction and coaching clearly differ in this model is the transition from assignment of task and extrinsic observation (by the coach) to self-managed experimentation and intrinsic observation (by the coachee). We have no reliable information that would allow us to identify what proportion of coaching today fits this approach.

The concept and application of coaching has since mushroomed into a panoply of models and approaches, many of which are more non-directive in nature. The distinction between directive and non-directive approaches is shown in Table 0.1.

Table 0.1:   Transitions from traditional coaching

From	To
Coach requires expertise/knowledge of the task	Coach requires expertise/knowledge of the coaching process
Driven by the coach's agenda, or at best an agreed agenda	Driven by the coachee's agenda
Coachee performance (doing)	Coachee self-actualization (becoming)
Skills acquisition (building knowledge of the task)	Capability development (building insight and self-knowledge as stepping stones to more substantive change)
Meeting standards set by others	Meeting standards set by the coachee

A next step in identifying what coaching is would be to try to provide a definition of it. Coaching books invariably begin with some kind of definition that identifies coaching as a helping strategy, designed to enable people to reach their full potential. It appears, however, that these definitions are not definitive enough to distinguish coaching from its close neighbours – mentoring, counselling and training – as these other forms of helping all make similar claims.

Attempts to define coaching usually try to make it distinctive in terms of ultimate purpose (what it is for?), type of clients (who uses this service?) or process (how it is done?) or a combination of these. In relation to an ultimate purpose coaching is often described as aiming at individual development or 'enhancing well-being and performance' (Grant & Palmer, 2002). These types of definitions are difficult to dispute but they cannot differentiate coaching from counselling or mentoring or even training, because essentially their purposes are the same. The initial attempts (Grant, 2000) to define coaching as designed for the 'mentally healthy' clientele group are now seen as unsatisfactory for many practical and ethical reasons. Attempts to define coaching on the basis of a distinct process are similarly problematic. Not only do they include some characteristics that cannot distinguish coaching from other helping professions, they also include characteristics that are so specific or just desirable, that they cannot be attributed to all the various forms of coaching (Bachkirova, 2007).

We are aware, therefore, that creating a unique identity of coaching is still an unresolved problem. Nevertheless, we believe that readers should be able to see our position in relation to what coaching is. Our working definition is presented in the very first sentence of this introduction. It is not, of course, free from limitations, but we hope the reader will make use of it while reading this book.

Coaching is used in various contexts, sometimes unconnected with the world of work. However, the use of coaching within organizations has given an immense impetus for the development and growth of the field. Therefore we want to give particular attention to coaching in organizations and suggest the role categorization as a reflection of the pragmatic distinctions that we have observed in organizations:

Line manager as a coach   the most difficult and controversial coaching role. Many commentators express doubt as to whether line managers can ever give priority to the coachee's agenda and devote enough time and effort to coach at anything more than a basic level (Ferrar, 2006).

The expert coach   many organizations reward experienced employees at all levels for transferring knowledge and skills to others. It is a core part of effective knowledge management. The coaching skills required in this role are arguably too similar to instruction-giving and agenda of the process is as questionable as it is for coaching by the line manager.

The internal professional coach typically someone from human resources, this individual performs many of the same roles as an external professional. However, they may be constrained by authority structures within the organization (for example, in confronting more senior executives) and may be less able to take an independent perspective.

Coaching role model companies such as Kellogg Europe have equipped some of their senior line managers with relatively advanced levels of coaching skills. Their role is to be role models to other line managers for good coaching practice, and to champion the cause of coaching within the organization.

The performance coach typically this is an external professional coach, who specializes in helping the coachee to focus on and achieve task-specific behavioural change over a relatively short period.

The developmental coach usually an external professional coach, who focuses on the broader, longer-term consolidation of leadership competence. Developmental coaches also tend to have a wider remit that encompasses issues such as work–life balance and the crystallization of life purpose.

II. THE KNOWLEDGE BASE OF COACHING

Many different disciplines and areas of knowledge contribute to the emerging knowledge base of coaching. These include management, education, social sciences, philosophy, and psychology. Within each of these established fields of knowledge there are various schools, traditions and approaches. They contain their own set of assumptions about human nature, how people grow and change and how this process can be facilitated. All of them potentially enrich the knowledge base of coaching. However, their diversity can be confusing, particularly for newcomers to the field. Within psychology, for example there are significant differences among existential and solution-focused traditions or between psychodynamic and transpersonal.

   Coaches who were educated originally in different fields of knowledge and practice and so were trained according to different traditions, may disagree profoundly on their philosophy and their practice of coaching. When adapted to coaching, each of these disciplines and various schools of thought seems to have significantly different assumptions, not just about coaching but even about what is worth exploring and what is not. The intention of this book is to reflect the diversity of the field and to illustrate how a multiplicity of approaches can enrich the knowledge base of coaching. We hope this will also help individual coaches to find their way through this diversity towards their own style of coaching.

At the same time we acknowledge that by introducing such diversity we are taking a risk of appearing over inclusive, particularly to those who, while valuing their own approach, take a very strong stand and reject other approaches. The following is therefore our attempt to make transparent our philosophy and main assumptions in relation to the knowledge base of coaching. An overview of the current literature and research on coaching increasingly shows that coaching has been described and explored in at least four major dimensions (Figure 0.1):

- 'I' – a first person perspective on the coaching process by the coach and/or coachee describing individual experiences of both parties involved
- 'We' – a second person perspective that emphasizes the relationship between the coach and the coachee, the role of language and culture in their interaction
- 'It' – more tangible elements of the coaching process, that are able to be observed by a third party and even measured if necessary, such as particular interventions and tools of coaching, specific behaviours and models
- 'Its' – the systems that are present as a background and an influencing force of the coaching process, such as sponsoring organizations and other social and professional groups.

These dimensions correspond to four quadrants described by Wilber (1996, 2000) as essential perspectives that are important to take into account if we want to understand any phenomenon or event that involves human beings. If we look now at various theoretical traditions that are applied to coaching we can see in what corner of this 'map' they would sit more comfortably and could claim their main influence. Individual coaches may also see where the weight of their coaching approach mainly lies, even if they treat as important all of these dimensions.

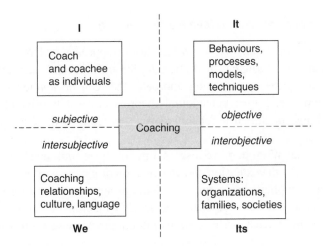

Figure 0.1   Four dimensions of coaching.

For example some coaching approaches in the 'It' corner tend to rely on outcome studies of coaching that are based on data that are observable and measurable. They are looking for effective techniques that can be reliably used in coaching interactions. Other approaches lean towards the 'I' corner, focusing on how individuals experience an event or process such as a coaching encounter. They are looking for individuals' feedback on interventions. Within this corner even standpoints such as the transpersonal or spiritual are valuable as they can deepen understanding of what matters to people in coaching. Approaches that lean towards the 'We' corner emphasize the role of language in the way we interpret events and experiences and the historical and cultural perspectives that have an impact on these interpretations. They, and also those who defend a systemic approach to coaching from the 'Its' corner, are emphasizing how important is an awareness of the complexity of factors that influence the coaching process. They bring to our attention the fact that each author represents a particular cultural and historical perspective and that such a position may differ significantly from country to country and may also change with further development of the coaching field.

Unfortunately, those who position themselves very strongly at some particular standpoint within this structure sometimes reject other perspectives and approaches, thus missing an important angle on the process of coaching. We, however, would like to emphasize the main stance of this overall integral methodological position (Wilber, 2006), which recognizes the value of all dimensions and rejects absolutist claims for the exclusivity of any of them. We believe that the approaches discussed in each chapter can illuminate a particular angle on coaching practice, being sufficiently clear about their philosophical assumptions and ensuring sufficient criticality at the same time. Such an intention allows readers to explore each approach and enables them to decide which, if any, they want to integrate into their own personal model of coaching.

Adult learning theories and their relevance to coaching

In this book, we argue for 'inclusivity' and equality of approaches. However, we want at the same time to emphasize a particular theoretical tradition that in our view underpins coaching practice. Adult learning theory is not an approach that can be applied to coaching in the way that, for example, cognitive–behavioural theories or Gestalt principles can. Rather, it underpins all coaching practice. It is for this reason that we present adult learning theories in the introduction.

The definition of learning that we use is one of three outlined by Knowles, Holton and Swanson (2005: 11): 'the extension and clarification of meaning of one's experience'. This, it seems to us, is the implicit theme for our clients in any coaching encounter. The concept of change, which is at the heart of coaching, is also inherent in the concept of learning. Any discernible change in behaviour or cognitive development suggests that learning has taken place.

The basic principles of three theories of adult learning are presented here in order to reinforce how they underpin the very nature of coaching. The three theories identified are:

A. Andragogy, the theory of adult learning introduced by Malcolm Knowles in the 1970s
B. Experiential learning as propounded by David Kolb (1984)
C. The transformative learning theory of Jack Mezirow (1990).

A. The assumptions and principles of andragogy

Andragogy is concerned with recognizing the inherent characteristics of adults as learners and using these to guide and support learning. Building on work by Lindeman in the 1920s, together with a variety of other theories from across a range of disciplines, Knowles (1978) devised a set of assumptions about adult learning that would contrast it distinctly with the traditional peda-gogical approach to teaching children. These assumptions or principles have come to underpin our views about learning and development and about adulthood. Knowles (1978; Knowles et al., 2005) identified a number of characteristics of adult learners that impact on the way in which they learn or approach learning. Since the 1970s these principles have been assimilated into the learning culture and are now discernible in coaching (Cox, 2006) as the following six main principles:

1. Adults need to know   Working with adults as collaborative partners for learning satisfies their need to know what they will be learning, as well as appealing to their self-concept as independent learners. Therefore, in coaching the agenda always belongs to the coachee, or is carefully negotiated so that ownership is theirs and they know the course of the learning.

2. Adults are self-directed   As a person matures, they become a more self-directed, autonomous human being (Knowles et al., 2005). However, it is recognized that not all adults have full personal autonomy in every situation: learners still exhibit different capabilities and preferences. Nevertheless, adult learning tends to be facilitated rather than directed: adults want to be treated as equals and shown respect both for what they know and how they prefer to learn. This also explains why specific feedback that is free of evaluative or judgmental opinions is a key feature of coaching.

3. Adults have a wealth of prior experience   A mature person accumulates a growing reservoir of experience that becomes an increasing resource for learning and coaches recognize that adults' experiences have a very important impact on their learning. However, as well as being a source of new learning, experience can also act as a gatekeeper, reinforcing mental models and schemas. Therefore, the unlearning process is as important as the learning process. The coach is very well placed to challenge coachees' existing assumptions in relation to new learning or new experiences, thus encouraging both learning and unlearning.

4. Adults learn when they have a need to learn   Adults generally become ready to learn when their life situation creates a need to know or understand, e.g. when they need to cope with a life situation or perform a task. The more the coach can anticipate and understand the client's life situation and respond to readiness for coaching, the more effective their role in coaching will be.

5. Adults are relevancy-oriented   Instead of being interested in knowledge for its own sake, adults frequently seek immediate application of what they learn and are oriented to problem solving. They learn best when there is a need to address a pressing issue. For the coach, this suggests that the client may need to work on immediate problems, as well as longer term, developmental issues.

6. Adults are internally motivated   Adults are generally more motivated towards learning that helps them to solve problems as they see them, or that results in 'internal payoffs' (Knowles et al., 2005: 199). This does not mean that external motivators, such as requests or encouragement from the line manager, do not have relevance, but rather internal needs and values are more powerful motivators. The coach's role then is to help provide the sense of connection between the client's needs and values, and the results of the coaching.

B. Experiential learning

The second learning theory that we identify as underpinning all coaching practice is the theory of experiential learning, first articulated in the philosophy of John Dewey (1910) and later operationalized by David Kolb (1984). Like coaching, experiential learning can be viewed as concerned with technique and process, rather than with content. Kolb differentiates experiential learning theory from rationalist and other cognitive theories of learning that tend to give primary emphasis to acquisition, manipulation and recall, and from behavioural learning theories that deny any role for consciousness and subjective experience in the learning process. He points out that learning is in fact a continuous process that is grounded in concrete experience.

In experiential learning theory an immediate concrete experience is the basis for observation and reflection. The reflections are then assimilated into a 'theory' from which the implications for future action are deduced. The process can take place incidentally or intentionally. According to Kolb, experiential learning is best viewed as a process and should not be seen in terms of outcomes. It is a constructivist theory that suggests that 'ideas are not fixed and immutable elements of thought but are formed and re-formed through experience' (Kolb, 1984: 26). Learning is seen as a dialectic process that integrates experience, concepts and observations in order to give direction to impulse. This would seem to us to be very much in tune with coaching as a process.

C. Transformative learning

Transformative learning involves a deep, fundamental revision to our beliefs, principles, and feelings: it implies a shift of perception that has the potential to alter our understanding of ourselves and others, and our sense of possibilities (Mezirow, 1990). Transformative learning, as Mezirow explains, refers to the process by which we transform our 'taken-for-granted frames of reference (meaning perspectives, habits of mind, mind-sets) to make them more inclusive, discriminating, open, emotionally capable of change, and reflective so that they may generate beliefs and opinions that will prove more true or justified to guide action' (2000: 7). Meaning perspectives are notoriously difficult to change, but do need to be challenged if deep learning is to occur. Sometimes such a challenge occurs spontaneously through life events and is the focus of the client's opening agenda, but often, significant challenge is generated by the coach in order to promote the required learning. The challenge, however, generated, results in a 'disorienting dilemma'.

This dilemma is then followed by discussions of long held beliefs and values. This is one of the most important stages in a transformative coaching situation and involves the critical reflection on the nature and origin of the dilemma. Critical reflection, Mezirow argues, necessitates the suspension of judgment about the truth or falsity of ideas, until a better determination can be made (2000: 13). It is this reflective discourse that is fundamental to transformative learning and leads towards a clearer understanding by tapping experience to arrive at a tentative best judgment. The final stage in the transformative process, following self-examination, is some kind of reorientation that results in deep learning and revised action.

These three adult learning theories provide examples of what we consider to be foundational theories for coaching practice. They are at the heart of all adult learning and development and consequently are at the heart of coaching practices.

III. DESIGN AND STRUCTURE OF THE BOOK

The book consists of three main sections, two of which are presented in the matrix below. The matrix (Table 0.2) illustrates the relationships between theoretical traditions adopted by coaches and the genres and contexts of coaching. Each theoretical approach in the vertical dimension of the matrix is known for its coherent system, which includes background, dominant philosophy and the specific set of processes and tools that coaches use in their practice. At the same time, the same coaches may practice within a variety of contexts, with various categories of clients, under particular conditions and with a specific focus of attention. For example, coaches who consider their approach to be cognitive–behavioural may practice as skills and performance coaches or deliver team coaching; a coach with a distinct person-centred orientation may work as a life coach or career coach. In the same way a transformational coach may be informed by a cognitive–developmental theoretical framework, or an executive coach can be trained in a Gestalt tradition or as an existential coach.

One intention of the book is to make explicit possible links between the theoretical traditions presented and the range of genres and contexts of coaching. That is why each chapter of the book will discuss examples of such combinations, or indicate that some of them are not appropriate. The stars in the matrix indicate that a link is made, whether by the authors of a particular theoretical chapter on the horizontal dimension or by the authors of a genre or context chapter from the vertical dimension. Readers will find the rationale for these links in the respective chapters of the book.

Section 1

Coaching is no longer seen as an atheoretical enterprise that relies only on common sense and an eclectic combination of tools. A number of theoretical approaches in this section describe the

Table 0.2: The matrix

Section 1 Theoretical traditions of coaching	Section 2: Genres and contexts of coaching										
	Skills & Performance	Developmental Coaching	Transformational Coaching	Executive & Leadership	The Manager as Coach	Team Coaching	Peer Coaching	Life coaching	Career Coaching	Cross-Cultural coaching	Mentoring
The psychodynamic approach to coaching	*	*		**		*				*	
Cognitive-behavioural coaching	**	**	**	**	**	**	**	**	**	*	
The solution-focused approach to coaching	**	**		*	*	*	*				
The person-centred approach to coaching	*	**		*		*	**	**	**		*
The Gestalt approach to coaching	*	*	*		*	**		*		*	
Existential coaching	*		*	*				*	*	*	
Ontological coaching	*	*		*	*					*	
Narrative coaching		**			*	*				*	
The cognitive-developmental approach to coaching		**	**			**				*	
The transpersonal approach to coaching	*	*	*	**		**		*	*		
Positive psychology approach to coaching	**	*		*		*		*	*	*	
Transactional analysis and coaching				*	*	*		*	*	*	
The NLP approach to coaching	**	*		*	*	*	*	*	*	*	

various elements of developmental change in individuals that can be successfully adapted for coaching. Elaborate developmental theories usually include essential elements, such as main concepts and assumptions about human nature, obstacles to development and essential processes and dynamics. Therefore, the chapters in Section One follow a common organizational pattern, so that a reader can easily compare and contrast the various models and approaches:

- introduction to the main concepts and assumptions about human nature from within this tradition, including the history of it and the view on conditions for human development
- tasks and goals of the traditions
- essential processes and dynamics involved
- role of the coach and relationship with a client
- methods and techniques for facilitation of change and development
- application to specific coaching genres and contexts that are presented in Section Two of the book, with examples
- evaluation of the tradition
- suggested further reading with annotation
- references

Admittedly not all approaches have sufficient material to fulfil this structure. Some of them are reasonably new fields of knowledge and are in the process of developing the aspects of a comprehensive theory. The specificity of others does not allow expanding on some of these elements. However, readers will be able to discern the most important elements and will be able to compare theoretical approaches. It should be noted that the list of chapters in this section is not exhaustive in terms of all influential traditions in coaching. They are chosen to illustrate the variety of influences on coaching practice and its knowledge base.

1. The psychodynamic approach to coaching

Graham Lee opens this section with a chapter on the psychodynamic approach to coaching. He describes how this rich influential body of ideas can inform coaches in their pursuit for deepening their practice by contributing to awareness about the working of the unconscious. He explains the origin of such terminology as defence mechanisms, transference and countertransference with which coaches currently become more familiar without knowing the background and nature of such phenomena.

This chapter suggests that there is a significant layer in our coaching interactions which is mainly beyond our conscious grasp but may influence individual behaviour or teamwork or organizational dynamics.

2. Cognitive–behavioural coaching

Helen Williams, *Nick Edgerton* and *Stephen Palmer* describe an approach to coaching that aims at enhancing the quality of a client's thinking with the help of skillful interventions by the coach in collaboration with the client. The approach emphasizes the importance of identifying realistic goals and facilitates self-awareness of underlying cognitive and emotional barriers to goal attainment. It aims to equip the client with more effective thinking and behavioural skills.

The chapter introduces a range of different cognitive models, tools and techniques, such as identifying Performance Interfering Thoughts, reframing of the client's cognitions, teaching clients new ways of thinking and a range of behaviour-focused techniques. It illustrates the use of these methods in health coaching in addition to other genres and contexts included in this handbook.

3. The solution-focused approach to coaching

Michael Cavanagh and Anthony Grant describe an approach that is based on the premise that knowing how a problem arose does not necessarily tell one how to fix it. As a very different course of action it aims at assisting the client to define a desired future state and to construct a pathway in both thinking and action that assists the client in achieving that state.

Coaches who use the solution-focused approach rarely offer generic theory-based solutions, instead they are led by 'what works'. The solutions emerge through useful questions framed by the coach, questions that arise as the result of collaborative thinking and the coach's expertise in the coaching process. The essence of the approach is to help clients to develop the skills of addressing any other concerns and goals in a way that has been discovered through this approach.

4. The person-centred approach to coaching

Stephen Joseph presents a person-centred approach as the one that is based on the most important assumption: the actualizing tendency – a tendency of people to develop in a positive and constructive way when the appropriate conditions are present. He emphasizes that it is a biological tendency and not a moral imperative, and he describes six conditions that the coach needs to provide for coaching to be person-centred.

The message that is clear in this chapter suggests that many coaches who describe their coaching as person-centred, particularly those who combine it with other approaches, while emphasizing the importance of the coach–client relationship, may not fully appreciate the depth of the philosophical underpinnings of this approach.

5. The Gestalt approach to coaching

Peter Bluckert argues that the main principles of Gestalt, such as creative adjustment to a changing environment and a paradoxical theory of change, bring a significant contribution to the understanding and practice of coaching. When applied to the coaching process this approach emphasizes the need for clients' moment-to-moment awareness in relation to their experience, external world and blocks to awareness.

Gestalt philosophy implies high responsibility of the individuals for their behaviour promoting active experimentation with reality in order to reach their goals. It invites clients to explore unfinished business that may cause blocks to further growth. The chapter explains why Gestalt practitioners aim to be more faithful to and honouring clients' own words, meanings and subjective experience and to use their own subjective experience when appropriate as part of an authentic dialogue.

6. Existential coaching

Ernesto Spinelli introduces the reader to his version of existential coaching, based on three principles describing the human condition: relatedness, uncertainty and existential anxiety. He identifies the issue of traditional coaching that may be mainly aiming at speedy alteration, reduction or removal of clients' concerns that bring them to coaching. Instead, the focus of existential coaching is primarily on a descriptive exploration of the clients' worldview from the context of their presenting concerns.

The chapter will engage the reader with one of the ways in which to address the tension between certainty and uncertainty by exploring it through the polarities of *meaning* and *meaninglessness*. Such an existential enquiry may help both coaches and their clients to 'own' their experiences, approach, values and beliefs so that their concerns can be more adequately explored.

7. Ontological coaching

Alan Sieler describes ontological coaching as a way of working with individuals in their engagement in three interrelated spheres of human existence. These three spheres are language, emotions and physiology (body posture). The coach attempts to be a catalyst for change by triggering a shift in the coachee's 'way of being' to enable him or her to develop perceptions and behaviours that were previously unavailable.

The process starts from developing a shared understanding of the issue the coachee brings to the conversation, and the desired coaching outcomes. It moves consequently to the coach's interpretation of the coachee's way of being through a set of tools that focus on language, emotions and body, which ensures that learning is embodied and consolidated.

8. Narrative coaching

David Drake makes a convincing case for an approach to coaching in which clients are seen as *narrators* and the coach helps them to identify new connections between their stories, their identities and their behaviours using the narrative material in the session. Working experientially, contextually and transpersonally, the coach enables clients to generate new options and to create new stories of their lives in action.

Narrative coaches invite people to see their stories from different perspectives. They may help them to notice how stories are constructed and even the fact that they are constructed. These stories may reveal clients' limits but also discover other possibilities about who they wish to be in the world. One of the attractions of working with clients' stories is a potential access to hidden aspects of themselves through bypassing the habitual defences that typically become engaged whenever the situations are approached in the usual head-on way.

9.. The cognitive–developmental approach to coaching

Tatiana Bachkirova invites the reader to explore an approach that is based on extensive research studies. Cognitive–developmental theories suggest that people differ in their meaning making capacity, which differentiates one person from another more than do their personality types and preferences. Changes of this capacity occur in a logical sequence of stages throughout the life of the individual. They influence the depth and complexity of what any of us can notice and therefore operate on and change.

Adult development from this perspective is an outcome of internal processes, but can also be further stimulated and facilitated by appropriate support and challenges provided by coaching. Understanding developmental trajectories leaves coaches far better equipped to understand the diverse needs of their clients. It also expands the horizons of the coaches' own development, which plays a significant role in the coaching process.

10. The transpersonal approach to coaching

John Rowan gives an introduction to the approach which recognizes dimensions beyond the personal and implies experiences and values of interconnectedness of all the elements in human systems and between the systems. He starts from clarifying the notion of the transpersonal by considering what it is usually confused with, such as religion, spirituality, new age ideas, and so on. Coaching from the transpersonal perspective is said to enhance awareness of the transpersonal dimension of life and to facilitate the experience of being connected to others in a way that provides feelings of completeness and joy.

The chapter suggests several ways of engaging with various manifestations of the transpersonal, such as creativity. This approach helps to identify what many individuals consider to be essential for meaningful life and work.

11. The positive psychology approach to coaching

Carol Kauffman, Ilona Boniwell and *Jordan Silberman* describe an approach to coaching in which the distinct feature is a consistent shifting of attention away from problems and weaknesses to opportunities and strengths. The positive psychology movement is based on the growing body of psychological research that challenges old models of understanding human development by focusing on pathology.

The reader will find in this chapter a range of coaching interventions that give a taste of working from such a perspective, inviting one to use a language of strength and vision in addition to the language of issues and concerns. Coaches who are interested in this orientation will find good ground for being selective about what to focus their attention on in order to energize and pull people forward.

12. Transactional analysis and coaching

Trudi Newton and *Rosemary Napper* describe this interactional approach to coaching as one that is based on several notions such as the ego states, life scripts and interactional patterns. The important assumptions of Transactional Analysis (TA) are that people make current decisions and select goals and methods of their achievement based on past premises that may no longer be appropriate for their own needs and may not be valid. At the same time people are seen as capable of identifying and changing the foundations of their actions: any individual can 're-decide'.

The chapter suggests several ways in which TA can inform coaching practice by providing a thinking framework and by offering accessible language that can be shared with clients for greater understanding of the motivations, interactions and coaching goals.

13. The NLP approach to coaching

Bruce Grimley presents this approach to coaching as one that assists clients in exploring their reality, which may both enable and hinder them. The NLP approach attempts to identify patterns that represent the way individuals construct their realities in order to control their inner experiences in various environmental contexts.

As coachees are often unaware of these patterns, NLP coaches may decide to bring these into the conscious attention of clients or they may choose to work with these at an unconscious level. The chapter gives an overview of a wide range of the NLP techniques that could be useful for coaches, such as matching and pacing; working with well-formed outcomes and anchoring.

Section 2

Applied contexts, forms or types of coaching are referred to in this Handbook as genres and contexts. Genres are forms of coaching that identify the purpose of the coaching in their title, such as performance coaching, developmental coaching or transformational coaching, while contexts refer to the settings or subject matter of the coaching, such as in 'Manager as Coach' or 'Life Coaching'. Each draws on many additional cross-disciplinary theories that are applied in specific contexts, e.g. management, learning, career development and team building.

Section Two (Chapters 14–24) of the Handbook examines the most common genres and contexts of coaching, including the occasionally more directive type of skills and performance coaching, together with the probably less directive types, such as life coaching, developmental coaching, transformational coaching, executive and leadership coaching and cross-cultural coaching. Chapters set out the history and specific features of each context or genre and discuss the role of the coach and the relationship with the client. Each chapter also includes discussion on the relationship of the type of coaching with the theoretical traditions included in Section One and evaluates its strengths and weaknesses.

Each chapter begins with an overview of the genre or context, giving a little of its history, the goals and tasks involved and examining the role of the coach. Chapters also explain the way in which the coaching relationship develops and the relationship with relevant theoretical traditions. Most chapters include descriptions of models or tools that a coach may use in this setting.

14. Skills and performance coaching

Bob Tschannen-Moran describes the goals and tasks of skills and performance coaching (SPC), suggesting that the agenda for SPC is often determined through external, often organizational, requirements. The focus is on meeting a skills or performance need that may have been identified by the organization rather than the client. Even so, as Bob makes clear, there is a vital need to link the learning need with the coachee's internal desires and ambitions; he argues that there can be no mastery of skills or performance without giving attention to mental, emotional and volitional frameworks, since it is these that govern our performance. SPC is probably the most common form of coaching in an organizational context.

15. Developmental coaching

The integral theme introduced by Bob Tschannen-Moran is continued in Chapter 15, where *Elaine Cox* and *Peter Jackson* explore developmental coaching. In this chapter it is explicitly suggested that many of the different kinds of coaching (from either the theoretical or the contexts/genres dimensions) work towards helping the coachee to develop in some way: there is an element of client development and progress making in all forms of coaching. However, developmental coaching is built on a range of often unarticulated assumptions about individual development and the holistic nature of change that may affect clients. The chapter discusses these assumptions as central to the coaching process and the role of the developmental coach.

16. Transformational coaching

Peter Hawkins and *Nick Smith* explain their conceptualization of transformational coaching, where the aim is to help coachees to make significant change in their life or work, and to make that change speedily. Ideally, they say, this change can be discerned even before a client leaves the coaching room. The authors present the CLEAR process model for facilitating such change. Transformational coaching has applications across coaching contexts, particularly where the need for a meaningful change is pressing.

17. Executive and leadership coaching

In the chapter dealing with executive and leadership coaching, *Jon Stokes* and *Richard Jolly* present an overview of the coaching provided at senior levels in organizations. They explain the challenges that face the executive or leader in relation to developing a strategic perspective, enabling others and balancing the competing forces and interests within the organization.

18. The manager as coach

Andrea Ellinger, Rona Beattie and *Bob Hamlin* look at the particular issues facing the manager who also acts as coach. They identify the need to clarify beliefs about managerial roles and capabilities and about learning processes and learners. In addition, the manager needs to have an awareness of where the opportunities for coaching lie in their everyday managerial work and also what constitute effective and ineffective coaching behaviours in this context. The authors draw on their own considerable research in this area to pull together the issues.

19. Team coaching

David Clutterbuck examines the issues surrounding team coaching. He describes his own definition of team coaching as 'a learning intervention designed to increase collective capability and performance of a group or team, through application of the coaching principles of assisted reflection, analysis and motivation for change'. The contrast in theoretical approach here is between short-term performance orientation and the concept of the team as a learning organism. The importance of team coaching is only just being recognized, although it has always been a vital presence in sport. In work contexts it is now being identified as crucial for team level achievement.

20. Peer coaching
Richard Ladyshewsky describes peer coaching, where emphasis is on reciprocal relationships between colleagues with similar experience and responsibility. The focus is generally on expanding or refining work-based skills and competencies. Rick pulls out a number of important issues that have a particular resonance in this context, including trust and confidentiality.

21. Life coaching
Anthony Grant and *Michael Cavanagh* introduce life coaching as a way of enhancing well-being in a whole life context, rather than as a strategy to increase functionality in the workplace. They describe it as a 'personal values-based, holistic approach to personal change and development', but note that despite its popularity and potential to individuals and society there is a comparative paucity of research into life coaching, which sometimes reflects on its status within the coaching community.

22. Career coaching
In this chapter, *Bruce Hazen* and *Nicole Steckler* describe the particular features and processes of coaching that are specifically designed to enhance career development. Career coaches, they explain, help with the establishment of a 'satisfying marriage of work and current identity where work fits the character, competencies, values and experiences of the coachee'. At the same time, the career coach also seeks to gently disturb the current identity, then design and guide a range of experiments to try and refine or develop that identity to its next stage of actualization.

23. Cross-cultural coaching
Geoffrey Abbott discusses the nature and purpose of cross-cultural coaching, suggesting that the successful management of the differences that occur in cross-cultural contexts consists of managing paradox. Abbott argues that cross-cultural coaching can encourage clients towards synergistic, inclusive approaches to conflicting and confusing challenges and should help them to find clarity and commonality despite the complexity of their situations. Cross-cultural coaching should not marginalize culture and give attention to the 'problem' of cultural differences, rather, as Abbott argues, it should support a homogeneous quest for identification of similarities.

24. Mentoring in a coaching world
In the final chapter of this section, *Bob Garvey* talks about mentoring. He explains how mentoring has a longer tradition than coaching, but that both activities share many of the same practices, applications and values. He suggests that ultimately it depends on our choice of terminology and the meaning associated with that terminology: mentoring and coaching will

mean different things to different people in different contexts. Bob suggests that mentoring is likely to be closely aligned with coaching. The choice of terminology is often based on sector or organizational preference, rather than a distinct divergence in the goals or tasks of practice.

Section 3

Despite the expansion of coaching as a practice, the concept of coaching as a profession is still relatively novel. Since 2000, a variety of bodies have been established that link coaches together and provide access to focused developmental opportunities. They embrace a number of important functions, such as creating standards, which although not enforced are indicators of good practice for coaches and other stakeholders. Collaborations between these bodies in Europe, for example, has created an emphasis on coaching supervision and it is now becoming increasingly difficult to practice at a senior level in employer organizations without evidence of both supervision and appropriate coaching qualifications. There seems to be, however, a long way to go in establishing coaching as a profession. Section Three (Chapters 25–29) attempts to pull together the main strands of activity and the concerns that have to be addressed in a wider discussion around professionalization of coaching.

25. *The future of coaching as a profession*
David Lane, Reinhard Stelter and *Sunny Stout Rostron* examine the prerequisites for an occupation to become a profession and assess where coaching fits within these. They explore the question of whether coaching needs to be a profession and/or whether its being an occupation might suffice, offering a more pragmatic solution to the breadth of coaching philosophy and practice. They also draw a useful distinction between being a profession and acting professionally.

26. *Ethics in coaching*
Diane Brennan and *Leni Wildflower* address the issue of ethics, in the light of both the establishment of ethical codes within all the professional bodies and the increasing collaboration between bodies aimed at harmonizing those codes. Fortunately, the codes are for the most part remarkably similar in concept, even though the precise wording varies.

27. *Coaching supervision*
Peter Hawkins presents an overview of issues around coaching supervision, arguing that coaching without supervision is unethical, in that it exposes clients to potential dangers of which the coach may not be aware. As supervision is also an essential element of the coach's continuing professional development, an absence of supervision can impoverish the quality of reflection-on-practice.

28. *Coaching and mental health*
Andrew Buckley reinforces the issue of client safety by reviewing the relationship between coaching and mental health. The coach with a wide portfolio of clients will inevitably meet

some whose needs extend into the psychotherapeutical. Recognizing these needs and responding appropriately is essential from several perspectives, including the well-being of the client, the reputation of the coach and the reputation of the coaching profession. Coach education in this area is relatively thin, reflecting the lack of clarity in relation to boundaries between coaching and therapy.

29. Continuing professional development for coaches

Diane Stober's review of the state of coach education identifies one of the main reasons for the inadequacy of ethical management, supervision practice and boundary management – the sheer confusion of competing training and qualification providers, each operating from a different and sometimes competing theoretical base and approach. While competence frameworks may help, the establishment of a common knowledge base appears to be a long way off. She argues that only with a substantially expanded evidence base will that knowledge base begin to solidify, and that will require a significant shift in the focus of research away from proving that coaching adds value to investigating the dynamics of relationship effectiveness.

How to read this book

There are a number of ways to read this book. Readers could begin with the chapters on theoretical approaches (Section One) and from there move linearly through the text. Alternatively they may want to pinpoint their particular theoretical or practical approach and so choose a chapter from either Section One or Section Two and pick up links from that first chapter in relation to which theory, genre or context to focus on next. Another way would be to use the matrix as a guide (Table 0.2) and to begin by reading chapters where the starred squares next to their approach are in alignment. Readers who approach the book in this way may find that there are links and associations with theories or practical applications that they had not previously considered.

The following questions may be useful to keep in mind while reading this text:

1. How do you feel when you read the chapter? What resonates with you?
2. What sort of evidence is most persuasive for you?
3. What does your intuition tell you about why you align with the tradition/approach?
4. What is your personal philosophy of change, development and coaching? What helps to formulate it better?
5. How has this personal philosophy been enriched or challenged by what you have read?

REFERENCES

Bachkirova, T. (2007). Role of coaching psychology in defining boundaries between counselling and coaching. In S. Palmer & A. Whybrow (Eds), *Handbook of coaching psychology.* London: Routledge.

Cox, E. (2006). An adult learning approach to coaching. In D. Stober and A. Grant (Eds), *The handbook of evidence based coaching.* John Wiley & Sons.

Dewey, J. (1910). *How we think.* Lexington, MA: Heath.

Ferrar, P. (2006). The paradox of manager as coach: Does being a manager inhibit effective coaching? (Unpublished MA dissertation, Oxford Brookes University.)

Grant, A (2000). Coaching psychology comes of age. *PsychNews, 4*(4): 12–14.

Grant, A., & Palmer, S. (2002). Coaching psychology workshop. Annual conference of the Division of Counselling Psychology, British Psychological Society, Torquay, 18 May.

Knowles, M. (1978). *The adult learner: A neglected species.* Houston, TX: Gulf.

Knowles, M., Holton, E., & Swanson, R. (2005). *The adult learner.* Oxford: Elsevier Butterworth Heinemann.

Kolb, D. (1984). *Experiential learning: Experience as the source of learning and development.* Englewood Cliffs, NJ: Prentice Hall.

Mezirow, J. (1990). *Fostering critical reflection in adulthood: A guide to transformative and emancipatory learning.* San Francisco, CA: Jossey-Bass.

Mezirow, J. (2000). How critical reflection triggers transformative learning. In Mezirow, J., & Associates (Eds), *Learning as transformation.* San Francisco, CA: Jossey-Bass.

Wilber, K. (1996). *Eye to eye: The quest for the new paradigm.* Boston, MA and London: Shambala.

Wilber, K. (2000). *Integral psychology.* Boston, MA: Shambhala.

Wilber, K. (2006). *Integral spirituality.* Boston, MA: Shambhala.

Theoretical Approaches

The Psychodynamic Approach to Coaching

Graham Lee

INTRODUCTION

For more than 100 years psychodynamic thinking has been a highly influential body of ideas regarding the workings of the human mind. This chapter describes the distinctive way in which these ideas can inform the activity of coaching, in particular showing how it provides a method for working with the unconscious, as well as the conscious, factors underlying human behaviour.

The term psychodynamic refers to a broad lineage of models that focus on the role of unconscious processes in human behaviour, and more specifically, on the dynamic relationship between different parts of the mind. Since Freud's (1922) first description of psychoanalysis there have been many developments, some of them building on Freud's ideas and his emphasis on instinctual drives, and others providing quite different formulations. Jung (1956) broke away to develop 'analytical psychology' in which prominence is given to the Self and the role of archetypes; Klein (1988) shifted the focus to the role of fantasy in the earliest stages of a child's development; Winnicott (1971) and many other object relations theorists (Greenberg & Mitchell, 1983) stressed the importance of the relationship between mother and baby in the shaping of mental life; and Bowlby (1988), for a long time disowned by much of the psychoanalytic community, researched the role of the caregiver in enabling the baby to form a safe attachment, and his empirical approach sparked a rich vein of research into attachment theory

(Goldberg, Muir, & Kerr, 1995). These are just some of the leading contributors to a constantly evolving field, which in some areas is now being validated by neuroscientific research into the role of non-conscious processes in emotional development (e.g. Solms, 1996; Schore, 2003).

This chapter provides an outline of how the psychodynamic approach can be used within a coaching context. It offers a perspective on coaching that emphasizes the role of the unconscious and past experience in shaping present ways of relating, whether to oneself or to others. By providing a safe relationship for exploring, naming and integrating difficult feelings, thoughts and memories, the coach enables the coachee to approach new challenges with a greater sense of clarity and authenticity. Following this introduction, I describe the goals and tasks of this tradition with some examples of its application to coaching. Then I illustrate some of the key phenomena on which the psychodynamic approach focuses on, such as holding, defence mechanisms, transference and counter-transference, and their relevance to coaching. Then I compare the psychodynamic approach to other approaches, followed by a discussion of its application in a number of different coaching contexts. Finally, I provide a summary of the strengths and limitations of this approach.

THE RELATIONAL REGULATION OF EMOTIONS

A contemporary psychodynamic perspective views the regulation of emotions (rather than instincts) as lying at the heart of much of human behaviour. As a result of previous relationships, particularly those with our parents or earliest caregivers, we develop distinctive but unconscious strategies for regulating our emotions and for building up a sense of self-identity. These early emotional habits tend to persist into adulthood because they become part of the developing brain's neuronal structure and brain chemistry (Gerhardt, 2004). These unconscious strategies are the engine of what Freud first described as 'the dynamic unconscious', an out-of-awareness part of the mind that shapes how we relate to ourselves and to others.

Defence mechanisms, such as repression, denial and projection, are specific examples of unconscious patterns of emotional regulation that operate to avoid or minimize emotions that are currently experienced as too difficult to tolerate. For example, a coachee might seem to persistently dismiss the importance of his/her feelings, a strategy of denial shaped by early experiences of rejection, which are now limiting the coachee's ability to form collaborative and mutually productive relationships in adulthood. The goal of the coach is essentially to expand the coachee's capacity for emotional regulation, that is, to enable the coachee, through the trust and containment of the relationship with the coach, to revisit difficult emotional territory in a way that is contained, so that the need for defensive strategies is reduced, and in which thinking rather than reacting can take place. By creating a space in which feelings can be experienced and labelled in language, they become phenomena that can be looked at and understood. Such a reworking of inner emotional territory, from disconnected sensations of emotional distress that have to be instantly defended against, to meaningfully connected patterns of experience, is transformative because what was once unconscious has been brought into awareness.

The coach comes to know about the coachee's unconscious emotional patterns in a number of ways. These include understanding how the coachee enacts implicit emotional habits in current relationships, including that with the coach, i.e. the transference, and by noticing and making sense of the feelings and sensations evoked in the coach by the coachee, i.e. the counter-transference. The coachee's past experience is also viewed as a valuable source of information, since it is these experiences that provide the earliest patterning of unconscious processes.

One of the great challenges in working with the unconscious is 'resistance', the denial of observations or links made by the coach that are intended to increase the coachee's awareness. While it is necessary for the coach to work at the border of what the coachee is ready to hear and experience, the coach must constantly notice any signs of resistance and modulate the interaction to maintain a safe 'holding environment'. In the next section we look more closely at how the coach creates and sustains, through relational attunement, a holding environment that loosens resistance, enables the coachee to tolerate difficult and buried emotions, and so develop new areas of awareness and insight.

DISTINCTIVE FEATURES OF THE PSYCHODYNAMIC APPROACH

In highlighting the features that are most distinctive to the psychodynamic approach, it is useful to set them in the context of a more generic coaching process. I would suggest that all coaching uses some version of the following process: Contracting, Assessing, Developing, Implementing, Reviewing, with these stages used fluidly and cyclically, and describing the iterative process that occurs within coaching sessions, as well as providing a macro picture of the overall course of a piece of coaching. The psychodynamic approach operates within this broad, generic process: Contracting to agree the scope, boundaries and purpose of the work, both with the coachee and with any sponsors; Assessing to gather useful information; Developing to move the coachee on in some way; Implementing to translate new learning into new behaviours; and Reviewing to check for progress and ongoing realignment of the approach. With awareness that the work takes place within this generic coaching frame, I will highlight key features of the psychodynamic approach.

Creating a holding environment

The first task in coaching is to set up a way of working with coachees that can be described as a 'holding environment' (Winnicott, 1965); a physical, and perhaps more significantly, a psychological space in which coachees feel safe enough to be open with their thoughts and feelings, to be able to share their anxieties, frustrations, aspirations and deepest hopes. For example when a senior manager was referred to me I was told that he had already met a number of coaches, but there was something about the formality of those initial meetings that had put him off. I guessed that his perception of formality had somehow triggered a sense of 'not being safe'; it had failed to support the psychological experience of a holding environment.

On meeting him I was struck by his formality, a rigid quality that made me feel as if I needed to sit up straight and to be at my most professional. However, rather than responding to this apparent pressure, I read it as telling me about one of his established strategies (or defences) for dealing with anxiety. Although I knew that this initial meeting would need to address the formal aspects of a coaching contract, I realized an experience of 'holding' for him needed to come out of my showing that I could contain his anxiety, and my own, and by my not mimicking his defensive strategy. I commented to him in a warm, gentle, mildly playful way, 'I wonder how we can make this an enjoyable meeting for us both?' His response was to smile, to relax a little, and to say how appealing it would be to have a space to slow down in his frenetic working day. My response, coming out of an intention to contain anxiety, without addressing it too directly at this early stage, had enabled the work to begin. Through this and other responses I sought to foster an atmosphere of neutrality and curiosity, a slower, reflective space in which inquiry, wondering and uncertainty is valued as highly as clarity, focus and decision making. Holding, then, in the psychodynamic sense, is concerned with attending to the non-verbal as well as the verbal elements of coach–coachee interaction, and in particular seeking to identify and respond usefully to the emotional agenda that might be underpinning the coachee's behaviour.

Defence mechanisms

Defence mechanisms, self-protective psychological strategies for dealing with distressing feelings, develop unconsciously in childhood, and later in situations where we perceive that others will not adequately regulate our emotions, or where our emotions will be perceived as socially unacceptable. For example coachees in organizations often use intellectualization as a way of dealing with upsetting personnel issues, projection as a way of blaming another department for organizational failings, and displacement as a way of keeping busy with unimportant details rather than tackling more important but anxiety provoking issues. Sometimes these defences are useful, such as when a doctor puts aside personal feelings of distress in order to deal with the practical issue of providing medical care. However, defences can often become a kind of straitjacket for the coachee's identity. For example a coachee who idealizes others may be defending against negative feelings towards others, but fears that if these feelings are expressed then others may reject the coachee.

In coaching the goal is not so much to name specific defence mechanisms but to recognize when the coachee is enacting an unconscious strategy of emotional regulation; they are a clue that the coachee is in psychological territory that feels problematic or overwhelming. In time, with sufficient holding and with the development of a working alliance underpinned by trust and rapport, the coach is likely to gain some understanding of the underlying emotional agenda, and so gradually move towards exploring the nature of these feelings with the coachee, their origins, their development, and their impact on current behaviour and performance.

Transference

One of the primary tools for gaining access to the coachee's implicit and potentially limiting interpersonal strategies is through the dynamics of transference and counter-transference. Transference refers to the implicit assumptions that we make about others based on our past experiences. If a coachee has experienced frowns from a routinely disapproving parent, he/she may attribute to a frowning coach disapproval that was actually an expression of confusion. If a coachee has experienced a parents' preoccupation with time as somewhat rejecting, then the coachee may experience the coaches' strict management of session times as rejecting rather than appropriately bounded. Transference can refer to any piece of unconscious learning that is applied to a new context, but its impact is most tangible when the transference occurs in relation to the coach, for example with the coachee unconsciously behaving towards the coach as if he/she is the coachee's boss or colleague or parent. Understanding the transference is usually linked to a related concept, that of counter-transference.

Counter-transference

Counter-transference refers to the feelings, bodily sensations, thoughts and behaviours that can be unconsciously evoked in the coach by the coachee. By silently examining these experiences the coach can gain insight into the unconscious concerns of the coachee. For example a coach, discussing in supervision a piece of work she was producing with a Managing Director (MD), reported that she felt useless and ineffective, and that she felt too inexperienced to continue with the work. As the supervision progressed she realized that what she was feeling was not really about her. As an experienced coach she felt confident in her ability, and she had previously worked with several MDs. She realized that the feelings evoked in her were directly linked to the MD's own unacknowledged sense of hopelessness about transforming the organization. Counter-transference experiences of this kind provide the coach with an embodied knowledge of the coachee's unexpressed feelings. This apparently mysterious transmission of unconscious feelings is understood in terms of a further mechanism, projective identification.

Projective identification, a concept originally introduced by Klein, is a process where the unconscious emotional experience of one person can be communicated to the unconscious of another. This occurs through subtle nuances of behaviour, such as facial expressions and modulations in the pace, tone and rhythm of the voice that are processed rapidly, non-consciously, and non-verbally in parts of the human brain that are also linked to our perception of bodily sensations (Schore, 2003). By tuning into bodily feelings and sensations, the coach can experience the coachee's non-conscious signals and so come to learn something about the coachee's disowned emotional state.

Thinking and the good enough coach

Working with counter-transference and projective identification is one of the most challenging aspects of the psychodynamic approach, because disowned feelings of the coachee are unconsciously projected into the coach, and containing these feelings often challenges to the limit the coach's own capacity for emotional regulation. In the example above, the coach's sense of capability had been temporarily disabled by the MD's projection into her of feelings of hopelessness. The coach had lost her capacity to think, and in this state she could not be of use to her coachee. Other coaches, on the receiving end of such projections, may find themselves resorting to neat, intellectual formulations, or providing coachees with practical materials to work on. These responses are defensive manoeuvres by the coach, and their impact on the coachee is usually to reinforce psychological defences.

In my experience, if we are vigilant to them, such disruptions to the coach's thinking are not uncommon (Bion, 1962). The goal for the coach, and I think coaching supervision can be invaluable here, is to find a way to reinstate the capacity to think. The coach needs to operate with a dual mode of attention, to attend to his/her own self-regulatory functioning and at the same time participate fully with the coachee in mutual exploration. The 'good enough coach' – an adaptation of Winnicott's phrase, the 'good-enough mother' – is not someone who always gets this right – rather it is a coach who manages to return him/herself to a state of regulation, having temporarily been overwhelmed. It is probable that the coachee, at an unconscious level, perceives this two-stage process, the rupture in the holding environment, and then the coach's return to a thinking state, and so gains an implicit, experiential knowledge that such feelings can be contained. Working at this level is undoubtedly demanding on the coach, but it lays the ground for a fundamental shift in the coachee's capacity to think about feelings, and clears the way for making more explicit links, such as those between past experiences and their impact on the present.

Making links

Much of the discussion thus far has emphasized the ways in which the coach can pay attention to the non-verbal aspects of the coach–coachee relationship and through such attentiveness create the underpinning conditions for the exploration and potential integration of the coachee's full range of emotional experiencing. However, also central to such integration is the naming of experiences – memories, thoughts, feelings, aspirations – and making links between different aspects of experience such that they are perceived and expressed as part of a more coherent sense of identity and personal narrative. One of the most powerful links that the psychodynamic approach seeks to make is between past and present. In order to do this the coach needs to elicit a detailed biographical history from the coachee, which includes information about the coachee's relationships with parents and other significant people in his/her life. By understanding the nature of the coachee's formative relationships the coach is looking for clues about the kinds of unconscious strategies that the coachee has developed in the past, and which may still be operating in the present.

For example, a coachee feeling unconsciously angry and defiant with his father, who was constantly distracted and distant when the coachee was growing up, had a reputation for being difficult and abrasive with his colleagues, and his career was stalling as a consequence. After working with this man for some time I suggested to him that his difficulties with current colleagues was, in part, an unconscious rerun of his unresolved frustration with his father's lack of attention for him (a transference interpretation). Over several sessions, as we worked through this idea, he was increasingly able to acknowledge its relevance for him. By recognizing the unconscious agenda driving his behaviour he was able to look at his current relationships more objectively, and to discern ways in which he could influence and collaborate with his boss and colleagues more effectively.

Creative living

From the psychodynamic perspective coachees enter coaching with a sense of self that has, to a large extent, been shaped by their experiences and interactions, from earliest childhood through to the present. In areas where a person has experienced attunement and responsiveness from parents and other caregivers, then their capacity to make sense of their array of experiences can be managed and integrated, and their internal sense of security provides the basis for play, vitality and creative living. However, in areas where a person has experienced others as being unable to tolerate their feelings or behaviour, then defensive psychological strategies come into operation, and, persisting through time, these can limit a person's capacity for self-realization. In coaching, by creating a space in which disowned feelings can be tolerated, named and thought about, coachees are able to develop a more integrated sense of self, and so approach their work, and their lives, with an expanded capacity for creative living (Winnicott, 1971).

COMPARISON TO OTHER TRADITIONS

In comparing the psychodynamic approach to other theoretical traditions it is important to emphasize that in practice coaching is often used in an integrative way. Coaches, in contrast to counsellors or psychotherapists, do not typically label their style of coaching in terms of a theoretical tradition, but rather in terms of the contexts in which they offer their services. Coaching, through its evolution, is a more eclectic discipline, drawing on multiple models and techniques. Consequently, the coach whose approach is underpinned by psychodynamic thinking may also use ideas from transactional analysis, Gestalt, cognitive, solution-focused, and any of the other major schools of thought. Having said that, it is useful to recognize key differences between approaches so that the coach can make conscious judgements about why one approach is being chosen over another.

The psychodynamic approach places a coachee's unconscious agenda at the centre of the challenge of enabling change. Many other traditions do share an interest in the unconscious, in some cases because their main proponents were themselves trained and influenced by psychodynamic thinking, such as in transactional analysis, Gestalt, and the transpersonal approach. Indeed, the emphasis in psychodynamic thinking on the intra-psychic domain, the internal and potentially conflictive relationship between different parts of the coachee's mind is echoed in transactional analysis as the ego states of Parent, Adult and Child, in Gestalt with such ideas as the 'top dog' and 'underdog' and in transpersonal work as sub-personalities (Rowan, 1991).

In practice, coaches readily borrow ideas from neighbouring traditions, so a coach working psychodynamically might encourage a coachee to name a part of themselves that is self-critical, which would fit with the transpersonal approach; or the coach might describe that part as a critical superego, which is more consistent with psychodynamic language. Having said all of this, it is the psychodynamic approach that is most consistently focused on unconscious emotional issues as the primary blocks to psychological development. The coach working psychodynamically, perhaps more than in other traditions, will develop quite detailed working hypotheses about the way different parts of the coachee's mind interact and the role that past experience has played in this development. Furthermore, particular emphasis will be given to making sense of the transference–counter-transference dynamics, although in contrast to the more spontaneous approach in Gestalt, the coach will take time to make sense of counter-transference feelings before making any explicit comment to the coachee.

The psychodynamic approach, used in isolation, could be contrasted most with the solution-focused approach and to some extent the positive psychology approach, where the focus is not on problems or underlying unconscious issues but on identifying what has already worked in the past, building upon strengths and finding practical solutions towards realizing goals. However, in my view the psychodynamic approach is most useful when it is allied in a more integrative way with these approaches that emphasize strengths and possibility. The cognitive behavioural approach can also be contrasted to the psychodynamic, in that although it does look at the links between emotions and beliefs and their impact on behaviour, it focuses primarily on what is in conscious awareness.

THE PSYCHODYNAMIC APPROACH IN CONTEXT

In this section I look at the psychodynamic approach in relation to four types of coaching: skills and performance coaching; developmental coaching; executive and leadership coaching; and team coaching.

Skills and performance coaching

Viewed as a method for optimizing performance in organizations, skills and performance coaching has become an established management development intervention. On the face of it the psychodynamic approach does not appear to be the most obvious fit in a context where the emphasis is on fulfilling certain behavioural competency standards. However, in many situations behavioural change cannot be achieved without understanding the underlying issues blocking change.

I introduced the concept of ACE patterns (Lee, 2003), integrated patterns of Actions, Cognitions and Emotions, to make explicit the link between unconscious emotional issues and their impact on behaviour. For example a junior manager who had not managed to improve her presentation skills, despite being sent on various skills development workshops, received a single session of coaching with me. She described how she would freeze when in front of an audience. I asked her to describe this experience of freezing (the Action) in detail, and then to look back through her history for times when she might have first had this experience. She reported that she would freeze like this when seeing her father's blank face as she sought his permission to do something, and went on to describe her deep fear (Emotion) of his disapproval. The link that we made was that she was unconsciously projecting her father's disapproval onto the blank faces of the audience when she made a presentation, and consequently froze with fear. By recognizing this link she could begin to approach presentations less dogged by her unconscious fear of her father's disapproval. This example illustrates that improving performance often requires coachees to increase their awareness of unconscious emotional blocks, and the psychodynamic approach provides an elegant method for making links and raising the coachee's self-awareness.

Developmental coaching

Development coaching is concerned with the development of the individual as a whole. While other types of coaching, such as performance or career coaching, are more focused on enabling the coach to develop in a specific area, development coaching has a broad remit encompassing a coachee's personal life as well as his/her work life. Thus development coaching might explore such areas as overarching purpose, underpinning values, signature talents and strengths, key obstacles, career ambitions, and personal and work relationships. The breadth of the approach means that developmental coaching is likely to draw on a range of theoretical traditions, including that of psychodynamic thinking.

One of the central goals of both developmental coaching and the psychodynamic approach to coaching is to increase awareness, since awareness of self and others is viewed as the foundation for making choices that are consistent with the purpose, values, ambitions and strengths of the coachee. The psychodynamic approach can be particularly useful in this context, because many people find that as life goes on they have gradually lost sight of their core passions and convictions; life has become a series of compromises, diluted ambitions, disillusioned hopes, opportunities avoided due to fear. For example I worked with a senior manager in the pharmaceutical industry whose passion for healing, his core motivation for entering the industry, had been forgotten amid the daily challenge of meeting revenue and profit targets and managing a large sales force. Through an exploration of stories of people he found most inspiring he recalled how much he had enjoyed working in a health centre as a student. He also recalled that his father, a self-made businessman, had disapproved of his altruistic, 'softer' side, and had strongly directed him towards a business career. He realized that his desire for his father's approval had unconsciously influenced his choices over many years. This psychodynamic awareness opened up a much wider exploration of his choices, less constrained by his unconscious desire to please his father.

Although developmental coaching, like psychodynamic coaching, is more focused on raising awareness than on achieving specific shifts in behaviour, an increase in awareness typically leads to a shift in how a coachee thinks and feels, and these deeper shifts are often the key elements that underpin a more enduring shift in behaviour.

Executive and leadership coaching

In executive and leadership coaching, we are usually working with a population of managers who have already achieved a good deal of success in their careers, but whose future development requires them to shift perspective; for example, to augment their technical competence with a more strategic view, or to temper their driving leadership style with greater political awareness and effective influence skills. I have suggested (Lee, 2003) that if managers are to be successful leaders then they need to become authentic, in the sense that they consciously balance their personal needs and convictions with the needs and convictions of their colleagues, whether in their team or the wider organization. Drawing on attachment theory, I have suggested that we routinely come across leaders whose authenticity and consequent effectiveness is limited by their use of unconsciously defensive leadership styles, which I call defiant and compliant leadership. Defiant leadership arises where a manager denies his/her vulnerability or self-doubt by adopting a dominant and dogmatic style, which tends to evoke resistance and frustration in others. Compliant leadership arises where a manager avoids confrontation by too readily fitting in with the needs of others, and so limiting his/her capacity for assertiveness and creativity.

The psychodynamic approach to coaching provides an opportunity for leaders to examine the relational assumptions that unconsciously underpin their leadership styles. The defiant leader, contained by the coach's attunement and resilience, finds a space to look at feelings that have long been banished from awareness, and so finds an opportunity to re-examine the need to be controlling of others. The compliant leader, invited to connect with hidden frustrations, learns to confront others in a useful way and so gains confidence in his/her ideas and their potential value to others. In this way, psychodynamic coaching can provide a rich learning environment for evoking authenticity and increased effectiveness in executives and leaders.

Team coaching

Just as individuals can adopt defensive strategies for managing feelings, groups can also behave in ways that defend against anxiety. Bion (1961) proposed three defensive strategies, called basic assumptions: fight/flight, dependency, and pairing. For example team members, anxious about how to solve a difficult issue, may become distracted and angry with senior management for putting them in this predicament (fight or flight). By blaming others they spare themselves the emotional challenge of taking responsibility and for integrating mixed feelings they may have about their capacity to solve the issue.

Another way the team may manage their anxiety is by idealizing one of the team members (or sometimes the coach), and then relying on them to resolve the challenge facing the team (dependency). While appropriate followership is useful, dependency means that there is a lack of shared initiative and responsibility within the team, and if the idealized leader is not success-ful then dependency can turn to fight or flight in relation to the leader. A further defensive strategy, somewhat similar to dependency, is to rely on a pair within the team to solve the team's difficulties (pairing).

The goal in team coaching is to enable the team to manage itself in such a way that it can focus on its primary tasks, drawing usefully on the skills and talents of all of its members, managing differences effectively, operating with appropriate levels of self-disclosure, building creatively on the contributions of others, and effectively managing the boundary with other parts of the organization. By noticing when the team is resorting to defensive strategies, the coach seeks to understand the nature of the anxiety underlying the defence, and from this aware-ness to decide on an appropriate intervention. This might involve naming the defence in some way, but if the team lacks the resilience to face this observation then the coach might for exam-ple encourage the team to work on a simpler, more manageable task in order to reinstate its sense of its effectiveness.

EVALUATING THE PSYCHODYNAMIC APPROACH

In this last section I consider the strengths and limitations of the psychodynamic approach and finish by discussing the contexts in which this approach can be most usefully applied.

Strengths

The psychodynamic approach opens our minds to the possibility that there is substantially more going on below the surface of coaching interaction than can be seen on the surface. Whether it is in the hidden agendas of an organizational sponsor, the defences of a coachee or the diver-sionary games of a team, the psychodynamic approach provides an unparalleled resource for investigating and making sense of unconscious processes and their role in shaping, and often limiting, the achievement of goals.

Applied to the arena of coaching, this approach usefully emphasizes the importance of managing boundaries, since it is through an experience of 'holding' and safety that coachees can allow their defences to loosen. While coaching is necessarily more flexible than counselling or psychotherapy with regard to the regularity of sessions and the location of meetings, the psychodynamic approach encourages us to recognize that the containment provided by fixed start and end times, a consistent physical environment, and explicit confidentiality, all contribute to an experience of holding, and so make possible a deeper exploration of the coachee's ways of making meaning.

The coach informed by psychodynamic practice will also have a particular appreciation of the role of restraint and silence in one-to-one work. Viewed as a space for thinking more than doing, reflecting more than solving, coachees come to experience the coach's restraint as an invitation to go deeper into oneself, to ask the question ' why', to sit with the discomfort of not knowing, to tolerate distressing feelings, and to discover the transformative potential of awareness.

The psychodynamic approach does, however, set a challenge to coaches to stretch their own developmental capacity for meaning-making, and undertaking one-to-one work with a psychodynamic practitioner is perhaps one of the most powerful ways of promoting that. The task for the coach is to be able to take a meta-perspective on their own implicit biases and defences, and through this process gain a more expansive awareness of self and others. It is the emotional resilience that comes from such self-awareness and integration that provides coachees with the profound experience of psychological containment, and so enables them to visit parts of themselves that have long been disowned.

Limitations

However, the depth of the psychodynamic approach is not always appropriate in coaching. Quite apart from whether coaches feel qualified to move towards unconscious territory, there are many coachees who neither want nor need this style of work. Coachees are often looking for relatively short engagements to help them think through a particular issue, and so favour approaches that focus on the present and the future, without needing to dig into patterns learned from the past. Where coachees have specific goals or a preference for pragmatic solutions, the psychoanalytic question 'why do you want that?' may be less useful than 'what do you want?' and 'how can you get it?'

Furthermore, the psychodynamic approach has the potential to be overly concerned with problems, and so miss the value of focusing on a coachee's strengths. The positive psychology movement has arisen out of the concern that much of psychological theory has come out of the clinical treatment of mental disturbance, which consequently views people as problems to be solved. Psychoanalytic theory must take some responsibility for this problem-centric bias, and coaches drawing on the psychodynamic approach need to be cautious about pathologizing coachees. Valuing and building on strengths, appreciating what is working already, and actively celebrating coachee's achievements are important aspects that can put the psychodynamic approach into a more balanced and constructively useful context.

Best use

The psychodynamic approach brings great depth and insight to the work of coaching, and as such is most appropriate for contexts where coachees are interested in exploring the roots of their meaning-making patterns, or where they feel stuck and are prepared to do what it takes to achieve an enduring shift. Leadership, developmental and team coaching, together with coaching supervision, are the areas that lend themselves most to the psychodynamic frame, and in all of these areas I have witnessed the profound effectiveness of the approach. Having said that, I would reiterate that the effectiveness of coaching often derives from the ability of the coach to flex his/her style, to draw on multiple approaches, and so respond usefully to the changing needs of coachees. The psychodynamic approach used within an integrative coaching framework is a potent method for evoking change.

FURTHER READING

Winnicott, D. (1971). *Playing and reality.* London: Penguin. (Many accessible papers on the shaping role of early experience.)

Freud, S. (1960). *The psychopathology of everyday life.* London: Penguin. (Classic account of the unconscious in everyday life, such as the 'Freudian Slip'.)

Jacobs, M. (2004). *Psychodynamic counselling in action.* London: Sage. (An excellent overview of the psychodynamic approach.)

REFERENCES

Bion, W. (1961). *Experiences in groups.* London: Tavistock.

Bion, W. (1962). *Learning from experience.* London: Heinemann.

Bowlby, J. (1988). *A secure base: Clinical applications of attachment theory.* London: Routledge.

Freud, S. (1922). *Introductory lectures on psychoanalysis.* London: George Allen & Unwin.

Gerhardt, S. (2004). *Why love matters: How affection shapes a baby's brain.* Hove: Brunner-Routledge.

Goldberg, S., Muir, R., & Kerr, J. (Eds.). (1995). *Attachment theory: Social, developmental and clinical perspectives.* Hillsdale, NJ: Analytic Press.

Greenberg, J., & Mitchell, S. (1983). *Object relations in psychoanalytic theory.* Cambridge, MA: Harvard University Press.

Jung, C.G. (1956). *Two essays on analytical psychology.* Cleveland, OH: Meridian.

Klein, M. (1988). *Love, guilt and reparation and other works 1921–1945.* London: Virago Press.

Lee, G. (2003). *Leadership coaching: From personal insight to organisational performance.* London: Chartered Institute of Personnel and Development.

Rowan, J. (1991). *Subpersonalities: The people inside us.* London: Routledge.

Schore, A.N. (2003). *Affect regulation and the repair of the self.* New York: Norton.

Solms, M. (1996). Towards an anatomy of the unconscious. *Journal of Clinical Psychoanalysis, 5*: 331–67.

Torbert, W. (1987). *Managing the corporate dream: Restructuring for long-term success.* Homewood, IL: Dow Jones Irwin.

Winnicott, D. (1965). *The maturational processes and the facilitating environment.* London: Hogarth Press.

Winnicott, D. (1971). *Playing and reality.* London: Penguin.

2

Cognitive Behavioural Coaching

Helen Williams, Nick Edgerton and Stephen Palmer

INTRODUCTION

This chapter focuses on the theory and practice of cognitive behavioural coaching (CBC). First, we endeavour to define and explain CBC, looking back on its history and acknowledging the main proponents of the tradition. Next, we outline the goals of cognitive behavioural coaching, reviewing the features and processes that set CBC apart from other approaches. Finally, we discuss the application of CBC across a range of coaching contexts. This chapter will not be describing the cognitive coaching developed by Costa and Garmston (2002) that has been applied to the teaching profession in the USA.

History and theoretical tradition

Cognitive behavioural coaching (CBC) has been defined as: '*An integrative approach which combines the use of cognitive, behavioural, imaginal and problem solving techniques and strategies within a cognitive behavioural framework to enable coachees to achieve their realistic goals*' (Palmer & Szymanska, 2007: 86).

CBC has largely developed since the 1990s, integrating theoretical concepts and strategies based on cognitive behavioural (Neenan & Palmer, 2001a; Neenan & Dryden, 2002; Edgerton & Palmer, 2005; McMahon, 2006; Palmer & Gyllensten, 2008), rational emotive behavioural (DiMattia & Mennen, 1990; Palmer & Burton, 1996; Neenan & Palmer, 2001b; Anderson, 2002;

Kodish 2002; Palmer & Gyllensten, 2008), problem (D'Zurilla, 1986; Palmer, 1997a, 1997b; Palmer, 2007, 2008), and solution focused approaches and techniques (O'Hanlon, 1998; Palmer, 2008). These were underpinned and informed by social cognitive theory (Bandura, 1986) and goal-setting theory (Locke & Latham, 1990), and by research into solution focused cognitive behavioural coaching (e.g. Grant, 2001; Green, Oades, & Grant, 2006). For further information, see the Special Issue on CBC published by the *Journal of Rational-Emotive and Cognitive-behavior Therapy* (2008: 26, 1–61).

Main assumptions of the cognitive behavioural approach

CBC is based on the premise that '*the way you think about events profoundly influences the way you feel about them*' (Neenan and Dryden, 2002: ix), which in turn impacts upon stress and performance. Aaron T. Beck (1976) described the existence of 'internal dialogue', the critical inner voice in our heads that impacts our self-esteem making us doubtful of our self-efficacy (competence) and self-worth. In the 1950s, Albert Ellis (see 1994) highlighted how emotional disturbance is caused not by the activating event, but by the mediating beliefs about the activating event.

Judith Beck (1995) describes three levels of cognitions: automatic thoughts; intermediate beliefs (attitudes, rules and assumptions); and core beliefs. Both intermediate and core beliefs generally develop in early childhood (Curwen, Palmer, & Ruddell, 2000). Unhelpful cognitive 'schema' can lead to negative automatic 'thoughts' preventing us from achieving our true potential. A number of common errors of processing, better known as cognitive distortions or 'thinking errors', have been identified (see Box 2.1 [Palmer & Szymanska, 2007: 99–100]).

GOALS AND TASKS OF COGNITIVE BEHAVIOURAL COACHING

The main goals of CBC are to:

1) facilitate the client in achieving their realistic goals
2) facilitate self-awareness of underlying cognitive and emotional barriers to goal attainment
3) equip the individual with more effective thinking and behavioural skills
4) build internal resources, stability and self-acceptance in order to mobilize the individual to their choice of action
5) enable the client to become their own self-coach.

Self-awareness

In order to facilitate self-awareness of underlying cognitive and emotional barriers, the CBC coach invites the coaching client to explore the problem or issue they have difficulty with, to

---

Box 2.1   Example thinking errors

- Mind reading/jumping to conclusions: jumping to foregone conclusion without the relevant information, e.g. 'If I don't work overtime I'll get sacked'
- All-or-nothing thinking: evaluating experiences on the basis of extremes such as 'excellent or 'awful', e.g. 'She always arrives late'
- Blame: not taking responsibility and blaming somebody or something else for the problem, e.g. 'It's all her fault. She should have reminded me to post the letter'
- Personalization: taking events personally, e.g. 'If our team presentation is rejected, it's my fault'
- Fortune-telling: assuming you always know what the future holds, e.g. 'I know I'll be made redundant next week'
- Emotional reasoning: mistaking feelings for facts, e.g. 'I feel so nervous, I know this merger will fall apart'
- Labelling: using labels or global ratings to describe yourself and others, e.g. 'I'm a total idiot' or 'As I failed my exam this proves I'm a complete failure'
- Demands: peppering your narrative with rigid or inflexible thinking such as 'shoulds' and 'musts': making demands of yourself and others, e.g. 'He should have made a better job of that project'
- Magnification or awfulizing: blowing events out of all proportion, e.g. 'That meeting was the worst I've ever attended. It was awful'
- Minimization: minimizing the part one plays in a situation, e.g. 'It must have been an easy exam as I got a good mark'
- Low frustration tolerance or 'I-can't-stand-it-us': we lower our tolerance to frustrating or stressful situations by telling ourselves, e.g. 'I can't stand it'
- Phoneyism: believing that you may get found out by significant others as a phoney or imposter, e.g. 'If I perform badly, they will see the real me – a total fraud'.

©Palmer & Szymanska, 2007

Note: Reproduced with permission

---

examine the evidence or lack of evidence that exists in support of their current perspective on the situation and consider alternative perspectives they might generate. The questioning process used is referred to as 'Socratic' questioning, after the philosopher Socrates, and involves the coach asking a series of questions aimed at increasing awareness (Neenan & Palmer, 2001a).

Thinking skills

Thinking skills have been defined as '*methods to help you modify your stress-inducing thinking*' (Palmer & Cooper, 2007: 50). However, thinking skills also enhance performance, and increase coping and resilience. Thinking skills include inviting the coaching client to decide whether their idea or belief is logical, whether it is realistic or empirically correct (does the evidence support or refute it?) and also whether the belief is helpful (McMahon, 2007; Palmer & Szymanska, 2007).

Further thinking skills are captured by the three Ps – Perspective, Persistence and Positive thinking. Coaching clients may gain a realistic perspective by considering the question 'If X were to be true, would it really be the end of the world?', and then deciding how bad a situation really is, as seldom are most situations really the end of the world. A 0–10 rating scale where 10 is very bad can be used to re-evaluate how bad the situation or problem seems. The coaching client may also learn to recognize self-imposed demands or rules, and to replace imperatives with preferences (Ellis & Blum, 1967; Palmer & Cooper, 2007). Given the length of time over which our core beliefs and thinking errors have become established, persistence with new more helpful ways of thinking is of great importance. Clients often reframe realistic and helpful thinking as positive thinking. Coping imagery assists clients in preparing for change (Palmer and Cooper, 2007) (see Section III).

Self-acceptance

Palmer and Cooper (2007: 77) described self-acceptance as holding the belief that '*I'm ok, just because I exist*' and '*I can accept myself, warts and all, with a strong preference to improve myself, even though realistically I don't have to*'. For coaching clients self-acceptance means never globally rating themselves (e.g. good, bad, weak, strong, success, failure), only rating aspects of the self, such as skills or skills deficits, as a global rating cannot capture the complexity and uniqueness of a human being (Lazarus, 1977; Palmer, 1997c). For example a student having just heard the news they did not pass their driving examination may conclude, 'I failed my driving test therefore I am a total failure', while another student in the same scenario chooses to conclude 'I have failed my driving test, but I am ok. It just means I need to improve my driving skills and re-take the test next month'.

SPECIFIC FEATURES, PROCESSES AND THE ROLE OF THE COACH

The dual systems approach underlying CBC enables coach and client to assess what needs to be addressed in coaching: the external, practical or goal-orientated behavioural aspects and/ or the internal, psychological or cognitive aspects to a problem or issue (Neenan & Palmer, 2000). There is no need to focus on psychological aspects if a simple problem-solving model will suffice.

Behavioural models, tools and techniques

The CBC coach may initially discuss the issues with the client and then help the coaching client to develop and prioritize their SMART goals i.e. Specific, Measurable, Achievable, Realistic, Time-bound goal(s), and action plans (Locke & Latham, 1990; Favell, 2004; Schwalbe, 2005). There are a number of action-oriented coaching models used within CBC, for example Wasik's (1984) seven-step model and the PRACTICE model (Palmer, 2007, 2008).

Table 2.1: PRACTICE model of coaching

Steps	Questions/Statements/Actions
1. Problem identification	What's the problem, issue or concern?
	What would you like to change?
	Any exceptions when it is not a problem?
	How will we know if the situation has improved?
	Any distortions? Or can the problem or issue be viewed differently?
2. Realistic, relevant goals developed (e.g. SMART goals)	What do you want to achieve?
	Let's develop SMART goals.
3. Alternative solutions generated	What are your options?
	Let's note them down.
4. Consideration of consequences	What could happen?
	How useful is each possible solution?
	Let's use a 'usefulness' rating scale for each solution where '0' is not useful at all and '10' is extremely useful.
5. Target most feasible solution(s)	What is/are the most feasible solution(s)?
6. Implementation of Chosen solution(s)	Let's implement the chosen solution by breaking it down into manageable steps.
	Now go and do it!
7. Evaluation	How successful was it?
	Use a success rating scale 0 to 10.
	What can be learnt?
	Can we finish coaching now or do you want to address or discuss another issue?

Source: Palmer, 2007, 2008 (reproduced with permission).

PRACTICE is an acronym for a problem-solving and solution focused model that has been used within coaching, counselling, psychotherapy and stress management (Palmer, 2007, 2008). The sequential steps of the PRACTICE model facilitate the coaching conversation and help orientate the client towards understanding the problem, developing realistic goals, selecting feasible solutions and their implementation, and finally reviewing progress. Table 2.1 provides an outline of each step in the model and summarizes key questions that may be used to facilitate discussion.

The early behaviour therapists Joseph Wolpe and Arnold Lazarus (Wolpe & Lazarus, 1966) developed a number of behavioural techniques to assist clients to relax, reduce anxiety and overcome phobias by using progressive relaxation and systematic desensitization. Although these are usually considered therapeutic interventions, a cognitive behavioural coach may use relaxation techniques and encourage clients to develop cognitive and behavioural coping strategies; and to expose themselves in imagination and *in vivo* to anxiety triggering situations, such as giving presentations or chairing meetings, which would not normally be associated with clinical disorders. Personal experimentation is encouraged in a bid to help clients incorporate new and more functional ways of thinking and behaving. Wolpe also introduced the concept and practice of assertiveness training that continues as an important component of CBC (Wolpe, 1973). Behavioural approaches to relaxation (Poppen, 1998) have an important role in CBC. Helping a client breathe well is one method used to help clients manage anxiety and panic tendencies in stressful or high performance situations.

Table 2.2:   Example of PITS and PETS for making a presentation

Performance interfering thoughts (PITS)	Performance enhancing thoughts (PETS)
It's going to go badly	It will be at least okay
I'm terrible at making presentations	Some have gone well, some less well but overall I'm reasonable at making presentations
Visions of being unable to speak and of being laughed at	Visions of making the presentation with a mistake or two, but overall going well
The audience will be bored	How do I know? I haven't even given the presentation yet!

Cognitive models, tools and techniques

There is a range of different cognitive models, tools and techniques, a number of which are covered in this section. Coaching clients may be helped to recognize patterns of unhelpful thinking by first identifying Performance Interfering Thoughts (PITS) in order to generate alternative Performance Enhancing Thoughts (PETS) (Neenan & Palmer, 2001a). Table 2.2 provides an example of the PITS/PETS activity for a coaching client with a fear of making presentations.

The ABCDEF model (Ellis, Gordon, Neenan, & Palmer, 1997; Palmer, 2002; 2009) of the rational emotive behaviour approach allows the coach to facilitate a review of the event that triggers psychological disturbance for the coaching client, in order to identify unhelpful thinking patterns and replace these with more constructive thoughts and behaviours (see Neenan & Dryden, 2002; Palmer & Szymanska, 2007).

The model is based on Albert Ellis's ABC model of emotional disturbance (Ellis et al., 1997), whereby an individual typically assumes a direct link between A, the Activating event or an Awareness of a problem or issue, and C, the emotional and/or behavioural and/or physical Consequence, when in actuality this relationship is mediated by B, the Beliefs and perceptions about the activating event. D is about Disputing or examining the beliefs, while E is about developing an Effective, new response or change in behaviour. The ABCDEF model also includes F, representing a Future focus on personal work goals and the learning from ABCDE – '*what the employee has learnt from the process to ensure that they are less likely to become stressed by a similar event in the future*' (Palmer, 2002: 16). Figure 2.1 depicts an example of the ABCDEF model in use for a coaching client as part of a stress management and prevention programme.

The ABCDEF framework is a model of stress, performance, coping and resilience depending upon its application. In practice goals are developed early on in the process and this is often depicted as G-ABCDEF framework. The coaching client is often shown this model using an A4 landscape, five or six column form, noting down the client's problem, beliefs, consequences, modified beliefs, effective new approach and future focus.

The SPACE model was developed by Nick Edgerton (Edgerton & Palmer, 2005). Its development was influenced by Multimodal Therapy (Lazarus 1989) and the Five Aspect Model described by Dennis Greenberger and Christine Padesky (1995). SPACE is a cognitive behavioural framework revolving around a diagram designed to help individuals become aware of

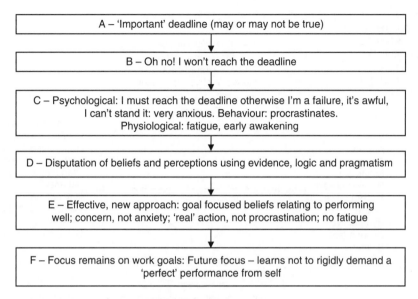

Figure 2.1   Client example using the ABCDEF model.
Source: **Palmer, 2002.**

their dysfunctional patterns, and can be used to plan more effective ways of functioning. SPACE is an acronym for five key aspects of the model, as follows:

S   Social context and Situation
P   Physical & Physiological reaction; for instance low/high arousal, e.g. high heart rate, breathing difficulties, sleep deprivation, fatigue, nausea, tightness in chest, dry mouth, headache, sweating, hormones
A   Action/Inaction; e.g. avoidance behaviours, passive or aggressive behaviours
C   Cognitions; automatic thoughts, attitudes and assumptions, core beliefs
E   Emotions; e.g. anxiety, anger, depression, fear, shame, embarrassment, guilt

The model incorporates a series of nested models of Actions, Cognitions & Emotions (ACE), and with the added dimension, Physical/Physiological (PACE) (Edgerton & Palmer, 2005).

One of the benefits of the SPACE model comes through the deployment of multi-aspect intervention strategies. The coaching client is encouraged to review each of the five areas and to agree how and what they would choose to do differently in each area. Figures 2.2 and 2.3 provide examples of the SPACE model, depicting in turn both low and high performance states.

Lazarus described how '*through the proper use of mental imagery, one can achieve an immediate sense of self confidence, develop more energy and stamina, and tap one's own mind for numerous productive purposes*' (Lazarus, 1984: 3). There is a range of imagery techniques including: Goal imagery (Palmer & Puri, 2006); Motivation imagery (Palmer & Neenan, 1998); Anger reducing imagery (Palmer & Puri, 2006); Coping imagery (Lazarus, 1984; Palmer & Puri, 2006);

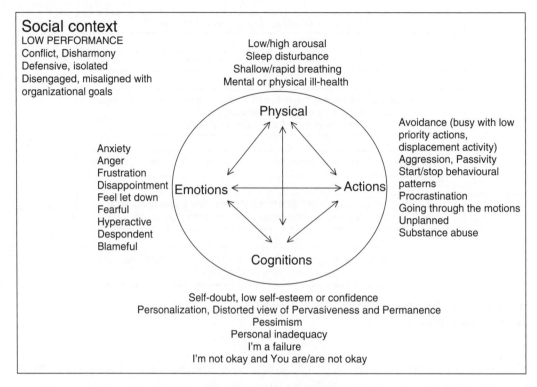

Figure 2.2 Depiction of low performance state using the SPACE model.

Relaxation imagery (Lazarus, 1982; Palmer, Cooper & Thomas, 2003); and Time projection imagery (Lazarus, 1984, 1989; Palmer & Cooper, 2007).

The role of the coach

Neenan & Palmer describe how the cognitive behavioural approach '*is based on a collaborative relationship that helps individuals to focus on problem-solving in a structured and systematic way*' (Neenan & Palmer, 2001a: 17). Through Socratic questioning, active participation and discussion (Roberts & Billings, 1999) the coach supports and challenges the client to achieve heightened awareness, self-esteem, self-acceptance and mobility to act. Through the transfer of the knowledge and skills of cognitive behavioural coaching, the coach is able to facilitate the ultimate goal '*for individuals to become their own coach*' (Neenan & Palmer, 2001a).

It is important to establish a clear contract, both with the coaching client and, where relevant, the line manager or organizational sponsor. This type of 'triad' coaching contract typically includes agreement of objectives of coaching engagement, outcome measurements, feedback

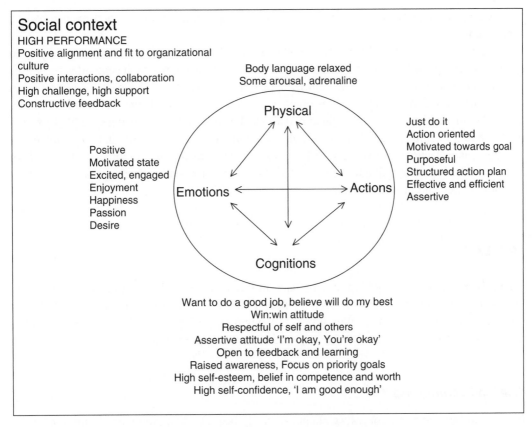

Figure 2.3   Depiction of high performance state using the SPACE model.

procedures and confidentiality, and is best agreed by all parties (McMahon, 2005). It is likely that a set number of coaching sessions or hours will be agreed so that each engagement is clear and purposeful. Lengths of sessions may vary from 30 to 120 minutes, often with a series of six to eight sessions over a time period of four to six months (see Palmer & Szymanska, 2007).

COMPARISON OF TRADITIONS

The CBC approach has a distinct psychological management model at its core, which most coaching clients find easy to learn and adopt. The techniques and strategies are systematically applied depending upon the particular issue the client needs to address.

CBC is a direct approach in that goal-blocking thoughts, feelings and behaviours, and the links between, are identified, examined and then modified. The client is encouraged to put these changes into practice as soon as possible through a series of planned exposures and experiments.

The directness of CBC is in contrast to other approaches such as psychodynamic and person centred coaching, with the Socratic challenges standing out in contrast to the empathic responses that are the hallmark of the person centred approach (Joseph, 2006). Empathy is important in CBC; however, it is not emphasized as much as in the person centred approach and is normally coupled with the direct challenges illustrated above. Person centred approaches are likely to rely on the client eventually challenging him/herself but this can take time and may not occur spontaneously. The use of exposure or behavioural experimentation, combined with cognitive interventions, is another characteristic of CBC that contrasts with other approaches, such as psychodynamic and person centred.

CONTEXTS

Cognitive Behavioural Coaching may be used in the majority of the contexts identified in the book's introduction. It can also be used for health coaching. Wherever a client is disturbing or limiting him/herself by unhelpful thinking, or engaging in self-defeating behaviours that undermine their performance, CBC can be a powerful coaching intervention.

Skills and performance

In skills and performance contexts a client can easily begin to doubt him/herself, thinking: 'I'm not good enough', 'I'm about to fail', and/or 'any moment now my performance will collapse'. Imagery may include others criticizing them and showing disapproval, while anticipated emotions, such as shame and embarrassment, may be experienced and sooner or later their performance will falter or be impaired by avoidance or procrastination. CBC teaches the client to both recognize and correct these self-disturbances.

Life coaching

In life coaching, clients explore their life goals and review their progress against these goals. Often the limiting factor to progress is the client's self-limiting beliefs. The CBC approach would be to recognize that the client is thinking and behaving in ways that are self-defeating or limiting. The client would then be helped to see how they could think about themselves in ways that would enhance their confidence and self-esteem before deliberately engaging in personal experiments designed to develop and enhance confidence to take action towards achieving their life goals.

Developmental

Developmental coaching for executives often focuses on professional and personal transformation within the context of the executive's job and organization (Sperry, 2004). CBC can provide insight into personal beliefs that influence the executive and their team and may block transformation. CBC can facilitate the adult's understanding of their emotions, helping them to comprehend the links between thoughts and emotions, and to learn how to express themselves emotionally and make requests of others in an appropriately assertive manner (Wolpe & Lazarus, 1966; Wolpe, 1973).

Executive and leadership

Executives and leaders in organizations need to be or become skilful in managing their own psychological processes, to manage emotions such as anxiety, frustration and anger, and to maintain an appropriate level of self-confidence without becoming complacent, arrogant or narcissistic. They are more likely to be effective in their roles if they develop high levels of interpersonal, influencing and communication skills. CBC can be helpful in all of these processes as the client learns to become increasingly skilful in managing the interaction between their own actions, cognitions and emotions.

Peer coaching

Peer coaching can come in many forms. For example, within teaching in the UK, peer coaching was set up by the National Union of Teachers on the Teacher2Teacher continuing professional development programme as a collaborative and normally formalized process between two peers to support each other (National Union of Teachers, 2008). It provides a structured framework to provide feedback on each other's work and includes suggestions on informed professional dialogue. This particular approach is on the more behavioural spectrum of coaching, but in other settings the cognitive skills could be introduced. As CBC is a pragmatic and transparent approach, peers can use the theory, models and techniques on each other within peer coaching.

Team coaching

CBC adapts very easily to group settings as it is both insight and skills based with relatively easy to understand theory and models such as the G-ABCDEF, SPACE and PRACTICE as previously described. Depending upon the team concerned, it can be used to enhance performance and manage stress. The coach facilitates the group to look at both team and individual issues. Members can work in pairs when looking at their own particular issues. This has a secondary gain for the organization, as supervisors and managers start to learn how to use cognitive behavioural coaching skills and techniques on themselves, each other and subsequently their own team.

Career coaching

Career coaching can occur across the entire young person and adult spectrum of life. Often, people benefit from career coaching as they make transitions from school to college, from college to work, then from job to job or redundancy to a new career. These transitions are now more prevalent in modern society, as adults are less likely to remain in the same job or even career for a long period of time. The PRACTICE and SPACE models of CBC have been applied to career coaching, for example when a client has been hesitant to make the move from one job to another or to decide upon a new profession.

Coaching and managing

Managers can usefully incorporate coaching strategies and skills into their repertoire. If a manager learns how to apply CBC to him/herself, it puts them in a good place to begin to use the same principles and techniques with their team. If, for example, one of their team is continually late finishing assignments and the manager simply puts the pressure on, it could be counterproductive. A CBC analysis of what is happening might identify a perfectionist demand, either on the part of the manager, the team member or both. Once identified, these demands can be modified to preferential statements and softened to 'good enough', 'fit for purpose', contributing to a learning culture within the team.

Health coaching

Health coaching has been described as '*the practice of health education and health promotion within a coaching context, underpinned by psychological principles, to enhance the well-being of individuals and to facilitate the achievement of their health-related goals*' (Palmer, Tubbs & Whybrow, 2003: 92). Health coaching is now being used within organizational and company settings to help employees tackle health-related issues such as weight control, nutrition, blood pressure, alcohol intake and smoking. This has enabled some American companies to prevent large rises in their annual staff health insurance premiums and demonstrates a noticeable return on investment.

CBC adapts very easily to the field of health coaching (Palmer et al., 2003b; Palmer, 2004). Motivational interviewing is used to engage and motivate clients to address their health-related issues (Miller & Rollnick, 1991). Cognitive behavioural coaching techniques and strategies are often used to tackle psychological blocks to goal achievement by examining the client's Health Inhibiting Thinking (HITs) and then helping them to develop Health Enhancing Thinking (HETs) (Palmer, 2004).

EVALUATION OF THE TRADITION

While the responsibility for change rests at many levels (government, society, organizations and the individual), CBC offers support directly to the individual by equipping them with coping strategies and thinking skills to ready them to achieve their full potential. The applications of CBC are varied, from building confidence and being assertive to tackling blocks to performance such as procrastination, perfectionism and poor time management; reducing unhelpful emotional reactions such as excessive anger or anxiety; or helping to achieve broader life goals.

Palmer and Whybrow (see 2007) researched the prevalence of coaching practices as used by practicing coaching psychologists between 2003 and 2007. They found that cognitive, behavioural and cognitive behavioural approaches were consistently in the top six most popular approaches used. In 2007, the most popular approaches were solution focused and facilitation methods, followed by the cognitive behavioural approach. Each of these methods was reportedly used by over 60% of the coaching psychologist population who completed the online survey.

In 2001, Anthony Grant recommended that researchers investigate whether a '*combined cognitive-behavioural coaching approach [is] effective in helping adults reach "real life" such as establishing businesses or enhancing work performance*' (Grant, 2001: 17). Over the last decade CBC has met this challenge, firmly establishing itself as a coaching practice recognized in its own right. Initially borrowing from the academic and applied research of CBT, there is now a growing body of evidence to directly support the value and effectiveness of CBC.

Anthony Grant has conducted a controlled study comparing cognitive, behavioural and cognitive behavioural approaches to coaching for trainee accountants (Grant, 2001). The follow-up study found '*academic performance increases were maintained only for combined cognitive and behavioural program participants*' (Grant, 2001: 1). In a further controlled study on the effects of a ten-week cognitive behavioural, solution-focused life-coaching group programme, significant increases in goal striving, well-being and hope were found for those receiving coaching, with some of the effects being evident up to thirty weeks later (Green et al., 2006). A study of the efficacy of cognitive behavioural coaching for perfectionism and self-handicapping reported that perfectionism fell and the effect was still evident four weeks later; self-handicapping showed a significant reduction at four weeks (Kearns et al., 2007). Green, Grant, & Rynsaardt (2007) found that solution-focused cognitive behavioural coaching enhanced cognitive hardiness and hope, with significant decreases in depression, in high school students.

Grbcic (Grbcic and Palmer, 2007) developed a stress self-coaching manual for middle managers, based on the cognitive behavioural approach. Four outcome measures were used to measure change: Brief Symptom Inventory (BSI; primary outcome measure); Symptom Assessment-45 (SA45); Coping Inventory for Stressful Situations (CISS); and the Job Stress Survey (JSS). Significant changes were obtained on the BSI (P< 0.001) at post-treatment, as well as on the SA45 (P<0.001), indicating intervention effectiveness regardless of the frequency of work stressors and lack of organizational support. Measures of coping indicated that the intervention increased task, emotion, and distraction-oriented coping styles (P<0.001). No coach, trainer or counsellor was used to teach the self-help approach. This highlights how alternative media may be considered to transfer the benefits usually derived from an actual coach–client relationship.

CBC provides clients with new ways of realizing how they are limiting themselves and their performance. In so doing it helps the client reduce any tendency to blame others or circumstances instead of accepting responsibility for themselves and their own self-disturbing and self-limiting habits. With this new acceptance that 'it's me doing it to myself', comes the realization that 'I can decide to change and become more effective in life'.

As with all coaching models and techniques, cognitive behavioural coaching is only appropriate to use when the coach is CBC trained and is in receipt of supervision, when the coaching contract has been clearly established and the CBC methods explained in non-jargon terms to the coaching client, with their affirmation of interest to pursue this line of enquiry.

CBC will not be necessary where action-oriented models will suffice to generate the desired change in behaviour, and will not be appropriate where the coaching client expresses:

- a need to revisit and address the past, requiring a more psychodynamic approach
- a desire to focus on greater meaning and purpose, where an existential approach will be more aligned to their needs
- an explicit interest in positive psychology and coaching, which may be at odds with the CBC theoretical assumption that negative cognitions and emotions need to be explored in order to be addressed.

Cognitive behavioural coaching is most likely to fail when the coaching client has a clinical disorder or is not accepting either the emotional responsibility for the problems they bring to coaching or the coaching responsibility for taking action (Palmer & Szymanska, 2007).

The following scenarios are examples of when a cognitive behavioural coaching approach may be of most benefit:

- when action models of coaching are not enough to bring about change
- when there is a cognitive or emotional block to achieving full potential
- when current levels of anxiety/avoidance are negatively impacting on performance
- when levels of stress are impacting upon mental and physical health.

CBC provides clients with the conceptual tools to better understand themselves; it also provides vehicles for change through personal experimentation and exposure to situations that previously they may have avoided. Clients will still have to work hard and be vigilant to establish their new ways of thinking and behaving.

FURTHER READING

Neenan, M., & Dryden, W. (2002). *Life coaching: A cognitive behavioural approach.* Hove: Routledge. (This book provides a comprehensive summary of cognitive behavioural models and significant challenges that may be addressed using cognitive behavioural coaching.)

Palmer, S., & Whybrow, A. (2007). *Handbook of coaching psychology: A guide for practitioners.* Hove: Routledge. (This handbook includes a chapter on 'cognitive behavioural coaching: an integrated approach' offering a comprehensive outline of the founding theories, proponents and research of CBC, with descriptions of various CBC models and case examples.)

Peltier, B. (2001). *The psychology of executive coaching: Theory and application.* New York: Routledge. (This book includes a detailed overview of cognitive psychology and cognitive therapy.)

REFERENCES

Anderson, J.P. (2002). Executive coaching and REBT: Some comments from the field. *Journal of Rational-Emotive and Cognitive-Behavior Therapy, 20*(3/4): 223–33.

Bandura, A. (1986). *Social foundations of thought and action: A social cognitive theory.* Englewood Cliffs, NJ: Prentice-Hall.

Beck, A.T. (1976). *Cognitive therapy and the emotional disorders.* New York: New American Library.

Beck, J. (1995). *Cognitive therapy: Basics and beyond.* New York: Guilford Press.

Costa, A.L., & Garmston, R.J. (2002). *Cognitive coaching: A foundation for Renaissance schools.* Norwood, MA: Christopher-Gordon.

Curwen, B., Palmer, S., & Ruddell, P. (2000). *Brief cognitive behaviour therapy.* London: Sage.

DiMattia, D.J., & Mennen, S. (1990). *Rational effectiveness training: Increasing productivity at work.* New York: Institute for Rational-Emotive Therapy.

D'Zurilla, T.J. (1986). *Problem-solving therapy: A social competence approach to clinical intervention.* New York: Springer.

Edgerton, N., & Palmer, S. (2005). SPACE: A psychological model for use within cognitive behavioural coaching, therapy and stress management. *The Coaching Psychologist, 2*(2): 25–31.

Ellis, A. (1994). *Reason and emotion in psychotherapy* (rev. and updated). New York: Birch Lane Press.

Ellis, A., & Blum, M.L. (1967). Rational training: A new method of facilitating management labor relations. *Psychological Reports, 20*: 1267–84.

Ellis, A., Gordon, J., Neenan, M., & Palmer, S. (1997). *Stress counseling: A rational emotive behavior approach.* New York: Springer.

Favell, I. (2004). *The competency toolkit.* Ely: Fenman.

Grant, A.M. (2001). Coaching for enhanced performance: Comparing cognitive and behavioural approaches to coaching. Paper presented at the 3rd International Spearman Seminar, Extending intelligence: Enhancement and new constructs, Sydney. Retrieved 10 November 2008 from http://www.psych.usyd.edu.au/coach/CBT_BT_CT_Spearman_Conf_Paper.pdf.

Grbcic, S., & Palmer, S. (2007). A cognitive-behavioural self-help approach to stress management and prevention at work: A randomized controlled trial. *The Rational Emotive Behaviour Therapist, 12*(1): 41–3.

Green, L.S., Oades, L.G., & Grant, A.M. (2006). Cognitive-behavioral, solution-focused life coaching: Enhancing goal striving, well-being and hope. *Journal of Positive Psychology, 1*(3): 142–9.

Green, S., Grant, A.M., & Rynsaardt, J. (2007). Evidence-based life coaching for senior high schools: Building hardiness and hope. *International Coaching Psychology Review, 2*(1): 24–32.

Greenberger, D., & Padesky, C.A. (1995). *Mind over mood.* New York: Guilford Press.

Joseph, S. (2006). Person centred, coaching psychology – a meta-theoretical perspective. *International Coaching Psychology Review, 1*(1): 47–54.

Kearns, H., Forbes, A., & Gardiner, M. (2007). A cognitive behavioural coaching intervention for the treatment of perfectionism and self-handicapping in a nonclinical population. *Behavioural Change, 24*(3): 157–72.

Kodish, S.P. (2002). Rational emotive behaviour coaching. *Journal of Rational-Emotive and Cognitive-Behavior Therapy, 20*(3–4): 235–46.

Lazarus, A.A. (1977). Towards an egoless state of being. In A. Ellis and R. Grieger (Eds), *Handbook of rational-emotive therapy.* New York: Springer.

Lazarus, A.A. (1982). *Personal enrichment through imagery* (cassette recording). New York: BMA Audio Cassettes/ Guilford.

Lazarus, A.A. (1984). *In the mind's eye.* New York: Guilford Press.

Lazarus, A.A. (1989). *The practice of multimodal therapy.* Baltimore, MD: Johns Hopkins Paperbacks.

Locke, E.A., & Latham, G.P. (1990). *A theory of goal setting and task performance.* Englewood Cliffs, NJ: Prentice Hall.

McMahon, G. (2005). Behavioural contracting and confidentiality in organisational coaching. *Counselling at Work, Spring:* 1–3.

McMahon, G. (2006). Cognitive behavioural coaching: Doors of perception. *Coaching at Work, 1*(6): 36–43.

McMahon, G. (2007). Understanding cognitive behavioural coaching. *Training Journal, January:* 53–7.

Miller, W.R., & Rollnick, S. (1991). *Motivational interviewing.* London: Guilford Press.

National Union of Teachers (2008). The A to Z of peer coaching. Retrieved 12 September 2008 from http://www.teachers. org.uk/resources/pdf/A-Z-peer-coaching.pdf.

Neenan, M., & Dryden, W. (2002). *Life coaching: A cognitive behavioural approach.* Hove: Routledge.

Neenan, M., & Palmer, S. (2000). Problem focused counselling and psychotherapy. In S. Palmer (Ed.), *Introduction to counselling and psychotherapy: The essential guide.* London: Sage.

Neenan, M., & Palmer, S. (2001a). Cognitive behavioural coaching. *Stress News, 13*(3): 15–18.

Neenan, M., & Palmer, S. (2001b). Rational emotive behaviour coaching. *The Rational Emotive Behaviour Therapist, 9*(1): 34–41.

O'Hanlon, W. (1998). Possibility therapy: An inclusive, collaborative, solution-based model of psychotherapy. In M.F. Hoyt (Ed.), *The handbook of constructive therapies: Innovative approaches from leading practitioners.* San Francisco, CA: Jossey-Bass.

Palmer, S. (1997a). Problem focused stress counselling and stress management: An intrinsically brief integrative approach. Part 1. *Stress News, 9*(2): 7–12.

Palmer, S. (1997b). Problem focused stress counselling and stress management training: An intrinsically brief integrative approach. Part 2. *Stress News, 9*(3): 6–10.

Palmer, S. (1997c). Self-acceptance: Concept, techniques and interventions. *The Rational Emotive Behaviour Therapist, 4*(2): 4–30.

Palmer, S. (2002). Cognitive and organisational models of stress that are suitable for use within workplace stress management/prevention coaching, training and counselling settings. *The Rational Emotive Behaviour Therapist, 10*(1): 15–21.

Palmer, S. (2004). Health coaching: A developing field within health education. *Health Education Journal, 63*(2): 189–91.

Palmer, S. (2007). PRACTICE: A model suitable for coaching, counselling, psychotherapy and stress management. *The Coaching Psychologist, 3*(2): 71–7.

Palmer, S. (2008). The PRACTICE model of coaching. *Coaching Psychology International, 1*(1).

Plamer, S. (2009). Rational Coaching: A cognitive behavioural approach. *The Cocahing Psychologist, 5*(1): 12–18.

Palmer, S., & Burton, T. (1996). *Dealing with people problems at work.* Maidenhead: McGraw-Hill.

Palmer, S., & Cooper, C. (2007). *How to deal with stress.* London: Kogan Page.

Palmer, S., & Gyllensten, K. (2008). How cognitive behavioural, rational emotive behavioural or multimodal coaching could prevent mental health problems, enhance performance and reduce work related stress. *The Journal of Rational Emotive and Cognitive Behavioural Therapy, 26*(1): 38–52.

Palmer, S., & Neenan, M. (1998). Double imagery procedure. *The Rational Emotive Behaviour Therapist, 6*(2): 89–92.

Palmer, S., & Puri, A. (2006). *Coping with stress at university: A survival guide.* London: Sage.

Palmer, S., & Szymanska, K. (2007). Cognitive behavioural coaching: An integrative approach. In S. Palmer & A. Whybrow (Eds.), *Handbook of coaching psychology: A guide for practitioners.* Hove: Routledge.

Palmer, S., & Whybrow, A. (2007). Coaching psychology: An introduction. In S. Palmer & A. Whybrow (Eds.), *Handbook of coaching psychology: A guide for practitioners.* Hove: Routledge.

Palmer, S., Cooper, C., & Thomas, K. (2003). *Creating a balance: Managing pressure.* London: British Library.

Palmer, S., Tubbs, I., & Whybrow, W. (2003). Health coaching to facilitate the promotion of healthy behaviour and achievement of health-related goals. *International Journal of Health Promotion and Education, 41*(3): 91–3.

Poppen, R. (1998). *Behavioural relaxation training and assessment* (2nd ed.). London: Sage.

Roberts, T., & Billings, L. (1999). *The Paideia classroom: Teaching for understanding.* Larchmont, NY: Eye on Education.

Schwalbe, K. (2005). *Information technology project management* (4th ed.). Boston, MA: Course Technology.

Sperry, L. (2004). *Executive coaching: The essential guide for mental health professionals.* New York: Brunner-Routledge.

Wasik, B. (1984). Teaching parents effective problem solving: A handbook for professionals (unpublished manuscript). Chapel Hill, NC: University of North Carolina.

Wolpe, J. (1973). *The practice of behaviour therapy* (2nd ed.). New York: Pergamon.

Wolpe, J., & Lazarus, A.A. (1966). *Behavior therapy techniques.* New York: Pergamon.

3

The Solution-focused Approach to Coaching

Michael J. Cavanagh and Anthony M. Grant

INTRODUCTION

All forms of coaching, in one way or another, seek to develop solutions to the issues brought forward by the client. What then is unique about solution-focused coaching? How does it differ from other forms of coaching? This chapter outlines the background and basic tenets of the solution-focused (SF) approach, and examines some core assumptions and processes underpinning it as a methodology for change.

The SF approach to coaching places primary emphasis on assisting the client to define a desired future state and to construct a pathway in both thinking and action that assists the client in achieving that state. It contrasts with other approaches by eschewing much of the problem state definition seen in other traditions. In so doing, the SF approach is situated squarely in a constructivist epistemology – maintaining that events and their meanings are actively constructed in dialogue rather than simply given to us in experience (O'Connell, 1998).

According to SF theorists, the act of spending large amounts of time and effort in articulating a strong definition of the client's problem, deconstructing the chain of cause and effect that led to the current state of affairs, or apportioning blame, is often a waste of time and energy. Indeed, it is often positively counterproductive (Jackson & McKergow, 2007). Knowing how a problem arose does not necessarily tell one how to fix it. Furthermore, proponents of the SF approach suggest that the very act of articulating a causal explanation may serve to constrain the coach and coachee into a frame of reference that limits potential solutions rather than uncovers them (de Shazer, 1994). Hence, the primary emphasis in SF coaching is on defining the desired solution state and potential pathways to get there (Jackson & McKergow, 2007).

History of the solution-focused approach

Like many of the recognized approaches to coaching, the SF approach has its roots in therapy. The foundational work in brief therapy, out of which the SF approach arose, was conducted by Gregory Bateson, John Wicklund, and others at the Mental Research Institute in Palo Alto, California, in the 1960s (Jackson & McKergow, 2007). The solution-focused approach as we have come to know it today was first articulated in the late 1970s and early 1980s by Steve de Shazer, Insoo Kim Berg, and colleagues at the Brief Family Therapy Centre, in Milwaukee Wisconsin, USA. Since then, considerable work has been undertaken in articulating and developing the main tenets of the approach by a host of authors, both at the Brief Family Therapy Centre and at a range of locations around the world (O'Connell, 1998).

According to Berg and Szabo (2005), therapists and researchers at these centres had become dissatisfied with the traditional therapeutic approach, finding that the more clients talked about their problems the more entrenched they would get. Rather than analysing problems, developing diagnoses, uncovering root causes, and prescribing treatment plans based on *a priori* theoretical models of the issue, they began to simply ask questions that focused their clients' attention on building solutions. The key question in developing the approach was 'what works for the client?'

They found that a focus on solution talk, strengths and resources, rather than problem talk, was very effective for a large range of clients. Indeed, there is a growing body of research that shows that solution-focused therapy can be effective for a wide array of problems, including couple counselling (Murray & Murray Jr, 2004), child and adolescent counselling (Corcoran & Stephenson, 2000; Lethem, 2002) and depression (Dahl, Bathel, & Carreon, 2000). There is also research that supports the use of solution-focused coaching in personal coaching (Green, Grant, & Rynsaardt, 2007; Green, Oades, & Grant, 2006; Spence & Grant, 2007), workplace coaching (Barrett, 2004).

Basic assumptions

The SF approach to coaching is distinguished from approaches based on more traditional models of psychological change (e.g. cognitive behavioural and psychodynamic traditions) by two fundamental philosophical and theoretical assumptions.

First, as mentioned above, the SF approach adheres to a constructionist philosophy. It holds that it is the way in which the client (and coach) think and talk about events that constructs those events as problematic. The problem is not something given in reality, but constructed in the discourse between the client and others in the client's world.

Second, the solution-focused approach sees the client as fundamentally capable of solving their problem. That is to say, they already have all they need to create the solution state (Berg & Szabo, 2005; de Shazer, 1988). This conceptualization of the client sees the person as whole and resource-full, rather than as dysfunctional and needy. When taken together these assumptions lead to several key tenets of solution-focused approaches (O'Connell, 1998).

1. **Use of a non-pathological interpretive framework:** Problems are not indications of pathology or dysfunction. Rather they indicate a need to try different perspectives or behaviours.
2. **Client-based expertise:** The idea is that the client rather than the coach is the expert in their own life.
3. **Coaching is about facilitating solution construction:** The coach primarily facilitates the construction of solutions rather than trying to understand the aetiology of the problem.
4. **Focus on client resources:** The coach helps the client recognize and utilize existing resources.
5. **Clear, specific and personalized goal setting:** To assist the client in attaining their preferred future, the articulation of that future state should be clear and behaviourally detailed. Because problems and solutions are constructed by the client, coaching interventions should be tailored to each client.
6. **Action-orientation:** There is a fundamental expectation on the coach's part that positive change both can, and will, occur, and that the work of change takes place primarily outside of the coaching session.
7. **Do what works, and stop doing what does not work:** Allied to the commitment to an action orientation is a pragmatic focus on identifying what is working for the client and amplifying this. Similarly, if an attempt at problem resolution is not working, then stop and try something different.
8. **Change can happen in a short period of time:** Because the client is already whole, change does not require fixing the client. This stands in contrast to the assumption that change must be worked on over a long period of time.
9. **Enchantment:** Borrowed from the work of Milton Erikson, SF approaches suggest that the coaching process be designed and conducted in a way that is attractive and engaging for the client.

CORE CHARACTERISTICS OF SOLUTION-FOCUSED COACHING

The solution-focused approach was developed as a brief intervention. Brevity here is not about limiting the number or length of sessions. Rather, it reflects an intention to do only that which is necessary for the client to achieve movement forward (Berg & Szabo, 2005). Hence, the goals of SF coaching are often narrower or more limited than goals set in other traditions (Berg and Szabo, 2005). The SF approach does not seek to resolve past injuries, uncover and reduce defence mechanisms, rebuild cognitive schemas, or effect character change. Rather, it seeks to uncover with the client his/her own resourcefulness and bring this to bear in the service of the client's goals.

Once the goals have been identified, the SF practitioner seeks to assist the client in identifying the simplest and easiest path to achieving a result that is satisfactory for the client. For example, a coachee might identify that they would like a better relationship with their spouse. The coach would assist the coachee in identifying what a better relationship might look, sound, and feel like – what sort of behaviours, feelings, thoughts and actions might be present in a better relationship. The coach would then work with the client to identify how much of this desired state needs to be present for the coaching to have been successful and the coachee to feel like they are on the way toward their solution.

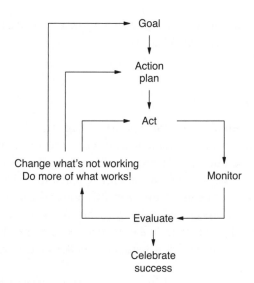

Figure 3.1   The cycle of self-regulation.

Self directed learning

Implicit in the above is the goal of building a capacity for self-directed learning in the coachee. This goal lies at the heart of the solution-focused approach. Self-directed learning seeks to build self-efficacy and self-reliance through the process of discovering personalized solutions to problems, identifying solution steps that work for the individual, assessing effectiveness through feedback, and then altering one's behaviour to maximize the effectiveness of one's attempts to reach the goal. Such a process seeks to elicit a curious, experiential and experimental mindset. Once this learning capacity is activated in service of the client's goal, the expectation of the SF practitioner is that the client will continue to self-regulate and integrate these skills into other aspects of their life.

Self-regulation is thus an important part of the SF approach. Greene and Grant (2003) have graphically represented the process of self-regulation as a simple, iterative cycle of setting a goal, developing an action plan, acting, monitoring, evaluating, and then changing what does not work and doing more of what works (see Figure 3.1). The coach's role is to facilitate the client's journey through this cycle while holding the client's focus on their goal/s.

TECHNIQUES FOR CHANGE IN THE SOLUTION-FOCUSED APPROACH

To enhance and facilitate the development of self-regulatory functioning in the client the SF approach seeks to enhance two types of change – change in the way in which the client views the problem, and the development of behaviours consistent with solution attainment. In other words, the two main tasks of solution-focused coaching are to 'change the viewing' and 'change the doing' (O'Hanlon & Beadle, 1996:11).

1. Changing the viewing

Changing the viewing is central to the SF approach. Clients, when they are focused on the problem or on all the reasons why the problem is difficult to solve, are by definition not looking toward the solution or the resources and steps needed to make the solution real. We know from experience and research that what you focus on grows. When we habitually focus our attention two psychological processes come into play – sensitization and amplification (Barsky, 1992).

Sensitization refers to the process whereby we learn to notice, or become sensitive to, a particular class of stimuli. For example, many parents become sensitized to the cry of their own child; or we might start to notice a particular model of car when we are considering purchasing one.

Amplification refers to the perceptual impact of what we notice. As we pay attention to a particular stimulus, it seems to grow in its importance or impact. Common examples include lying in bed listening to a tap drip or a dog bark. The more we attend to the sound the louder it gets. Of course, it is our perception of the sound that changes, not the volume of sound itself.

Changing the viewing shifts the perceptual cycles of sensitization and amplification from problem to solution. The more we become practised at focusing on solutions, the more solutions we notice and the more obvious they become.

Once the solution state has been clearly identified, and goals for coaching have been established, the task then becomes to marshal the resources needed to achieve the chosen goals. The coaching task at this point is to assist the client in identifying any resources the client has that can be brought to bear in the service of the coach's goal (O'Hanlon & Beadle, 1996).

Solution-focused practitioners have developed dozens of techniques for assisting clients to change the viewing and identify resources. The following techniques are some of the more commonly used.

The Miracle Question   The miracle question is paradigmatic of the SF approach (Berg & Szabo, 2005) In the 'Miracle Question', in which the coach asks 'Imagine that you went to bed tonight, and when you woke up the problem had somehow magically disappeared, and the solution was present ... but you didn't know that the solution had arrived ... what is the first thing that you'd notice that would tell you that the solution was present?'

Scaling   Scaling is perhaps one of the most versatile of the solution-focused techniques. It can be used to: (i) identify where the client currently perceives themselves to be in relation to their goal – 'on a scale of 1 to 10 with ten representing the complete solution, and one representing the problem at its worst, where would you say you are now?'; (ii) clarify fuzzy goals – 'What does an 8 look like, how would you know you were at an 8?'; (iii) identify progress made so far – 'so how come you are at a 4 now – what did you do to get that far?'; (iv) articulate small steps toward the goal – 'so what would be different if you were at a 5, or even a 4 ½?'.

Highlighting resources   The old cliché that every problem contains the seeds of its solution has become a cliché precisely because it has a good deal of truth in it. In this technique the coach listens for hidden and unacknowledged resources, as for example:

> Client: 'The tender was not successful and all the work I put in was completely wasted.'
> Coach: 'Sounds disappointing, but was it a complete waste – what did you learn from the experience?'

Reframing   Reframing is another set of central solution-focused tools. In this set of techniques the coach seeks to reframe the client's statements in a way that opens up possibilities and focuses the client on resources. We often use the following example in workshops.

- Reframing using compliments:

> Client: 'It's far too expensive.'
> Coach: 'It's great that you are concerned about keeping on budget. How can we make it more affordable?'

- Reframing that highlights exceptions:

> Client: 'I really hate my work.'
> Coach: 'It sounds very unpleasant … tell me, which parts of your job are less unpleasant for you?'

- Reframing that clarifies goals:

> Client: 'I really want to improve my leadership skills.'
> Coach: 'So, what does good leadership mean to you?'

- Reframing problems to solutions:

> Client: 'I feel completely lost.'
> Coach: 'So, you'd like to get back a sense of direction and control?'

2. Changing the doing

Changing the viewing is not enough. If the coaching conversation is to be more than an interesting exercise in how we perceive the world, it must result in action. Hence the second major task of SF coaching is to 'change the doing' (O'Hanlon & Beadle, 1996: 11). In this part of the coaching process, the task is to identify patterns of behaviour that support goal attainment, and to change any patterns of behaviour that interfere with goal attainment. This may involve mapping the behavioural sequences present when the problem exists and at times when the solution or part of it is present (O'Hanlon & Beadle, 1996). The client and coach then identify helpful patterns that can be replicated, and these are practised in homework tasks.

Some techniques that can be useful in changing the doing are:

(1) recognizing possibilities by turning presenting problems into springboards for solution construction (Jackson & McKergow, 2007)
(2) asking 'how' questions instead of 'why' questions

(3) generating client-centred multiple options (O'Hanlon & Beadle, 1996)
(4) Using small specific achievable action steps.

An experimental mindset is preferred when it comes to changing the doing. The SF approach makes no prediction about what should be done. Rather, the coach and coachee work together to discover a pathway to success that works for the client, in their context. Hence, identifying what has worked in the past and experimenting with new possibilities are both important. This is consistent with a scientist practitioner model of coaching practice (Cavanagh & Grant, 2006).

The philosophical stance which holds that the client is not broken also encourages the solution-focused coach to change as little as possible (de Shazer, 2005). The old adage 'if it ain't broken, don't fix it' takes the status of core principle in SF coaching (Greene & Grant, 2003). Hence small steps and active engagement in the feedback and evaluation process are important.

THE SOLUTION-FOCUSED COACHING ENGAGEMENT

From the client's perspective, the SF approach is often an attractive and refreshingly strengths-based intervention (Chou, 2007). By avoiding delving deeply into an examination of the client's problems, or searching for aetiological explanations in the client's psychological profile, clients are enabled to experience themselves as healthy and capable, rather than as unhealthy or disabled.

The principal challenge for the coach is taking on the mindset needed for effective solution-focused coaching. Do we really believe in the essential wholeness of the client? Holding the client in this way is not always easy, but it is vital to the solution-focused enterprise – the quality of the working alliance significantly contributes to success (Horvath & Symonds, 1991).

The solution-focused mindset is a challenge for clients too. Some clients are able to clearly articulate exactly what they want to achieve through the coaching. They seem to fall naturally into solution talk. Other clients will more naturally move into problem talk and feel the need to explain the problem in detail. The coach's task is to help the client shift from a problem-focused to a solution-focused mindset as quickly as possible. Sometimes this shift occurs very quickly. However, with heavily problem-saturated clients the coach needs to exercise patience and sensitivity. It is important to meet such clients where they are – and gradually to help shift the conversation toward a more solution-focused frame. Indeed, some clients take a number of sessions before they can start to adopt an SF approach to their difficulties. Nevertheless, failure to reflect empathically the client's experience is likely to lead to a break in rapport which must be mended as the coaching conversation continues.

Many clients oscillate between problem talk and solutions talk, seemingly moving into a positive solution-focused mode only to fall back into the problem moments later. This kind of oscillation can be frustrating for the inexperienced coach wanting to deliver a solution. Here it is important to trust the process and allow the client to explore their thinking while watching in their own time for the seeds of solutions as they emerge. The taking of a 'not the expert' position allows the coach to relax and observe this unfolding creative process. It is the ability to sit with the uncertainty and ambiguity of the coaching process that differentiates the really good coach from the novice.

As the coaching conversation unfolds, the coach is working with the client to build up a picture of their preferred future through reflection and reframing. Scaling can be used to help the client judge their progress in relation to specific goals. As Grant (2006: 85) states: 'Scaling is nearly always an opportunity for the coach to give a compliment. Even if the clients say that they are at a 3 on a 10-point scale, the coach can respond – 'well done – one third of the way there already'.

Like many of the SF techniques, the giving of compliments and reframing must be done from a position of genuine positive regard and desire to really understand and move toward the client's goals. Without this fundamentally respectful stance, SF techniques can appear as superficial and manipulative.

Some solution-focused authors suggest that a hallmark of the SF approach is the use of the miracle question, typically delivered in the first session (de Shazer 1988; O'Connell, 1998). However, we have found that it is often best to ask this question, once the client is ready to shift from an exploratory or deliberative mindset to an implementational mindset (Bayer & Gollwitzer, 2005; Oettingen & Gollwitzer, 2002). The deliberative mindset is characterized by a careful exploring of the pros and cons of potential goals and actions (Carver & Scheier, 1998) and is therefore more likely to produce abstract problem-focused responses to the miracle question. The implementational mindset, on the other hand, is focused on identifying means to change, and is therefore more behaviourally focused and detailed (Bayer & Gollwitzer, 2005). To ask the miracle question while the client is still exploring the problem can result in client confusion, a lack of engagement, and even anger or resentment.

For some clients, the wording of the miracle question can be problematic. They experience talk of miracles as polyanna-ish and silly. For such clients the coach can ask a more concrete variation of the miracle question – such as the Two Videos Question. Here the coach asks the client to imagine two videos playing. One video shows the problem as it is being enacted. The other video shows the preferred outcome being enacted. The client's role is to simply describe the difference between the two.

These questions help the client describe their situation and the solution in concrete behavioural, emotional, and relational terms – i.e. 'who is doing what, how and with whom and what impact does that have?' By describing the solution in this way, both the coach and client are usually able to identify do-able actions that will lead toward the goal.

The miracle question and its variants also help to build the client's capacity for mindfulness. These questions require the client to emotionally disengage from the problem – to step out of the problem, and take a metacognitive position. This metacognitive distance helps to make visible a solution that cannot be seen when we are 'in' the problem. One changes the viewing to change the doing!

Ending the coaching engagement

As mentioned above, the SF approach is designed to minimize intervention. For this reason, contracting for particular numbers of sessions is not entirely consistent with SF coaching. While the coach might ask at the beginning of the engagement about the client's expectation of the number of sessions needed, each session in the solution-focused model is complete in itself (Berg & Szabo, 2005; O'Connell, 1998). Terminating the coaching engagement occurs when the client has met their goal, or feels satisfied that they can move toward it without the coach. Hence, SF coaching typically ends each session with a real question as to whether another session is needed. 'Do we need to meet again, or do you feel like you have done what you needed to do?'

APPLICATIONS OF SOLUTION-FOCUSED COACHING

The SF approach is a methodology that is applicable in a wide range of coaching settings. Because it seeks to work with the client's goals, and begins with the client's perspective, the application across settings is very similar. Nevertheless, it is worth noting some differences in emphasis found in different settings.

Skills and performance coaching

The psychological literature distinguishes between two types of development – horizontal development, or assimilation, and vertical development or accommodation. Horizontal development occurs when a person is able to assimilate new information or new practices into their current worldview. Skills and performance coaching would typically fall into this category of development. In skills and performance coaching, the task is to focus on the development and application of specific knowledge skills and abilities in order to enhance workplace performance or achieve specific organizational targets.

This focus on organizational goals and needs adds some complexity to solution-focused coaching. Often there is congruence between what the organization wants from the coachee and what the coachee wants from coaching. In such cases goal setting within coaching is rather straightforward. However, when there is a mismatch between the coachee's perceived needs and the organization's requirements, then goal clarification becomes critical.

An SF approach to this conundrum is to treat this apparent dilemma as a platform for more solutions (Jackson & McKergow, 2007). For example the coach might bring the issue into the foreground as follows: 'I notice that you would like to achieve X, and at the same time, the organization is requiring that we work toward Y. I wonder what this means for the coaching? Is it possible for us to work toward both targets together, or is one more important for you? Perhaps there are other solutions possible?'

Skills and performance coaching often requires the use of organizational metrics such as 360-degree feedback and other data driven means of assessing performance. Often these metrics lead to a focus on what is missing or undone, rather than what is good or strong about the client's performance. The challenge for the solution-focused coach is to help the client see measurement as feedback in service of their goals. Reframing of feedback and metrics to identify progress and resources is important here.

Developmental coaching

The term developmental coaching has two meanings in the literature. The first refers to holistic development of the client aimed at greater self-actualization and authenticity. The second meaning refers to the notion of vertical development, or accommodation. This type of development requires the enlarging of one's meaning-making to accommodate new goals and practices. In other words, it is the type of development needed when a person's current way of responding to the world needs to change in order to meet the new challenges they are facing (e.g. Kegan, 1994). In both meanings developmental coaching and the solution-focused approach are suited to each other.

There is, however, an inherent tension in the developmental enterprise. The goal of constructing developmental solutions often requires the coach to challenge, at least implicitly, the current worldview of the coachee. For example, let us say a coachee has a goal of dealing with team conflict more effectively, and they are considering an action plan that involves avoiding an aggressive team member. The solution-focused coach might enquire into, and affirm, the client's positive intent, and ask the client to consider any possible unforeseen consequences of their course of action (Berg & Szabo, 2005). Coaching might then consider other options for viewing and acting in the situation that might minimize any potential unintended consequences.

Executive and leadership coaching

Executive and leadership coaching also holds some particular challenges for the solution-focused coach. Typically, executive coaching involves a mix of skills, performance, and development coaching, and generally proceeds as does most SF coaching. Unlike other areas of SF practice, executive coaching often involves the identification of a coherent personalized model of leadership and the competencies that support it.

A second area of difference is that leaders and executives often present in coaching with goals that need others to change behaviour. However, a basic assumption in the SF approach is that change is not something we can determine for others. When a client has a strong need to change another person's behaviour, the SF approach calls for questioning that assists the client in making their view of the situation explicit and tangible, exploring alternate views, and identifying what the client can do to influence self-directed change in the other person, rather than repeating past unhelpful strategies like simply insisting that the other person change.

As in all SF coaching, clear identification of the desired outcome is important. Similarly, identifying positive intentions and providing support for trying new ways of seeing and dealing with the situation are likely to be useful. The coach might use a number of techniques to assist the client to focus on what is do-able and what works. For example, the coach might ask the client to recall conversations that seemed to be effective in helping the target person modify their behaviour, or enquire with the client as to what might be going on for the target person, and how the client might check this out. Encouraging the client to experiment with different types of change conversations with the target person often leads to successful outcomes.

EVALUATING THE APPROACH: AGENCY, CAUSATION AND EMERGENCE

Perhaps the greatest challenge facing the solution-focused coach is to let go of causal problem-focused explanations as a foundation of practice. Given that most of us have had a life-long education based on deterministic principles and scientific method, this is not always an easy task.

The lack of causal reasoning in the SF approach has led to claims that it is a superficial intervention (e.g. Ellis, 1997). Some authors have suggested that for coaching to be truly effective, a 'deeper' approach is necessary (e.g. Berglas, 2002; Kilburg, 2004). The idea that an approach is superficial or deep is interesting. In our experience, the extended discussion of causes can take place with little or no positive change in the person's sense of self, worldview or behaviour. In what sense then is such an approach deemed to be 'deep'? Conversely, the construction of a preferred future, and the identification of hitherto untapped personal resources can have profound impacts on the person's worldview and sense of self, and can issue in significant behavioural change.

Of course, there are times when the solution-focused approach is not appropriate. Some clients may have causal stories about their situation which form a central and protected part of their worldview. Similarly, when clients have deeply felt needs to explore aetiology, attempting then to shoe-horn them into a methodology that feels incongruent is likely to be counterproductive. Our experience suggests that such clients will often respond favourably to a well-presented rationale for the SF approach. However, if they do not, then referral, or use of an alternative methodology is indicated. To force a solution-focused perspective onto an unwilling client runs counter to the core principle of respecting the client.

The solution-focused approach has sometimes been called a theory-free methodology. Diagnostic explanations run counter to the idea that the client is the expert in their lives and the solution is within them awaiting discovery. The coach does not need any expert knowledge about the client's problems, beyond asking the right questions to unlock the client's solutions (e.g. de Shazer, 1988). However, this cannot truly be the case. In order for the coach to ask the right questions, the coach must have at least an implicit theory about the issue, and a theory about what kind of question will best help the client articulate a solution. If the coach really had no expert knowledge or skills, or no theory about how best to help the client, then it is hard to understand why the client would employ the coach in the first place (see Held, 1996 for a detailed discussion of these issues).

Is the coach then the real expert in coaching? Complexity theory teaches us that outcomes are an emergent property of the system, and not the sole responsibility of any single part of the system (Lewin, 1993). As a complex adaptive system, the outcome of the coaching engagement emerges from the complex interaction of the coach *and* client together (Cavanagh, 2006). In other words, the solution is radically co-created by both client and coach.

When viewed from this perspective, expert-centric views of coaching which suggest that the coach 'adds value' either by providing expert knowledge, or by their ability to view the client's system from a more objective perspective, are fundamentally flawed. Similarly, overly simplistic understandings which suggest that the client is the 'expert' in the coaching session are also distorted.

The idea that the solution lies within the client, and the coach's role is merely to facilitate the client in discovering what they already have within them, is a useful metaphor for helping coaches develop an attitude of curiosity and facilitation. The SF project requires the coach to take the beginner's mind. The catch cry 'Ask, don't tell' is often used to encourage this attitude. Yet experience shows that sometimes no matter how long we ask, the solution does not emerge, because it is not 'in' the client.

Our experience as coaches, and as coach educators, suggests that both the simplistic client-centric approach and the expert-centric approach are often more about managing the coach's anxiety and encouraging a open mindset in the coach, than that they are reflective of what actually happens in effective coaching sessions.

Valuing the tensions

There is an inherent important tension between the different expert knowledge bases brought to the session by the coach and client. The creativity of the SF approach relies on this tension; for it is out of the interaction between the two understandings that creative solutions are born. Hence, tension should not only be valued, but also actively sought and nurtured and, where necessary, managed (Stacey, 2000). Rush to closure on this tension stifles creativity. Too much tension between the understandings brought by coach and client is also counterproductive, and usually indicates one or other of the parties have stopped being open to alternate views.

Solution-focused coaches do spend a lot of time asking. But the questions they ask are not atheoretical. Rather, they are informed by implicit and explicit hypotheses about what is going on for the client. Similarly, effective coaches often do tell. They educate their clients. They share their mental models, and direct their clients' attention toward solutions. Good coaches can and do allow their domain specific knowledge to come into play, but they do so in such a way as it becomes a resource in service of the client's goal. In other words, their questions remain genuinely curious, and their telling respectful and timely.

FURTHER READING

Greene, J., & Grant, A.M. (2003). *Solution-focused coaching: Managing people in a complex world.* London: Momentum Press. (An easy-to-read primer on solution-focused coaching and management which cites relevant research and is illustrated throughout with real-life case studies.)

O'Hanlon, B., & Beadle, S. (1999). *A guide to possibility land: Fifty-one methods for doing respectful brief therapy.* London: Norton & Co. (While written with therapeutic cases in mind, this little book is a gold mine of solution-focused methods. An excellent resource that is easily translated to fit the coaching context.)

Berg, I., & Szabo, P. (2005). *Brief coaching for lasting solutions.* London: Norton & Co. (An excellent and practical overview from some of the pioneers of the solution-focused approach. The authors describe a range of techniques in detail with engaging case studies and examples.)

REFERENCES

Barrett, F. (2004). Coaching for resilience. *Organization Development Journal, 22*(1): 93–6.

Barsky, A.J. (1992). Amplification, somatization, and the somatoform disorders. *Psychosomatics, 33*(1): 28–34.

Bayer, U., & Gollwitzer, P. (2005). Mindset effects on information search in self-evaluation. *European Journal of Social Psychology, 35*: 313–27

Berg, I., & Szabo, P. (2005). *Brief coaching for lasting solutions.* London: Norton & Co.

Berglas, S. (2002). The very real dangers of executive coaching. *Harvard Business Review, June*: 87–92.

Carver, C.S., & Scheier, M.F. (1998). *On the self-regulation of behavior.* Cambridge: Cambridge University Press.

Cavanagh, M. (2006). Coaching from a systemic perspective: A complex adaptive conversation. In D. Stober & A.M. Grant (Eds), *Evidence based coaching handbook* (pp. 313–54). New York: Wiley.

Cavanagh, M., & Grant, A. (2006). Coaching psychology and the scientist-practitioner model. In S. Corrie & D. Lane (Eds), *The modern scientist practitioner* (pp. 146–57). London: Routledge.

Chou, Yu-Chen. (2007). A study of the effects and therapeutic factors of a solution-focused parenting group. *Bulletin of Educational Psychology, 39*(1): 1–21.

Corcoran, J., & Stephenson, M. (2000). The effectiveness of solution-focused therapy with child behavior problems: A preliminary report. *Families in Society, 81*(5): 468–74.

Dahl, R., Bathel, D., & Carreon, C. (2000). The use of solution-focused therapy with an elderly population. *Journal of Systemic Therapies, 19*(4): 45–55.

de Shazer, S. (1988). *Clues: Investigating solutions in brief therapy.* New York: Norton & Co.

de Shazer, S. (1994). *Words were originally magic.* New York: Norton & Co.

de Shazer, S. (2005). *More than miracles: The state of the art of solution-focused therapy.* Binghamton, NY: Haworth Press.

Ellis, A. (1997). Response to Jeffrey T. Guterman's response to my critique of his article 'A social constructionist position for mental health counseling'. *Journal of Mental Health Counseling, 19*(1): 57–63.

Grant, A.M. (2006). Solution-focused coaching. In J. Passmore (Ed.), *Excellence in coaching: The industry guide* (ch. 5). London: Kogan Page.

Greene, J., & Grant, A.M. (2003). *Solution-focused coaching: Managing people in a complex world.* London: Momentum Press.

Green, L., Oades, L., & Grant, A. (2006). Cognitive-behavioral, solution-focused life coaching: Enhancing goal striving, well-being, and hope. *The Journal of Positive Psychology, 1*(3): 142–9.

Green, S., Grant, A., & Rynsaardt, J. (2007). Evidence-based life coaching for senior high school students: Building hardiness and hope. *International Coaching Psychology Review, 2*: 24–32.

Held, B.S. (1996). Solution-focused therapy and the postmodern: A critical analysis. In S.D. Miller, M.A. Hubble & B.L. Duncan (Eds), *Handbook of solution-focused brief therapy.* San Francisco, CA: Jossey-Bass.

Horvath, A.O., & Symonds, B. (1991). Relation between working alliance and outcome in psychotherapy: A meta-analysis. *Journal of Counseling Psychology, 38*(2): 139–49.

Jackson, P., & McKergow, M. (2007). *The solutions focus: Making coaching and change simple* (2nd Ed.). Bristol: Nicholas Brealey Publishing.

Kegan, R. (1994) *In over our heads: The mental demands of modern life.* Cambridge, MA: Harvard University Press.

Kilburg, R.R. (2004). When shadows fall: Using psychodynamic approaches in executive coaching. *Consulting Psychology Journal: Practice & Research, 56*(4): 246–68.

Lethem, J. (2002). Brief solution-focused therapy. *Child & Adolescent Mental Health, 7*(4): 189–92.

Lewin, R. (1993) *Complexity: Life at the edge of chaos.* London: Phoenix.

Murray, C.E., & Murray, T.L., Jr (2004). Solution-focused premarital counseling: Helping couples build a vision for their marriage. *Journal of Marital & Family Therapy, 30*(3): 349–58.

O'Connell, B. (1998). *Solution-focused therapy.* London: Sage.

Oettingen, G., & Gollwitzer, P. (2002). Turning hope thoughts into goal-directed behavior. *Psychological Inquiry, 13*(4): 304–7.

O'Hanlon, B., & Beadle, S. (1996). *A field guide to possibility land: Possibility therapy methods.* London: BT Press.

Spence, G.B., & Grant, A.M. (2007). Professional and peer life coaching and the enhancement of goal striving and well-being: An exploratory study. *Journal of Positive Psychology, 2*(3): 185–94.

Stacey, R.D. (2000). *Strategic management and organisational dynamic* (3rd ed.). Harlow: Pearson Education.

4

The Person-centred Approach to Coaching

Stephen Joseph

INTRODUCTION

The aim of this chapter is to provide a guide to person-centred coaching. The chapter will help readers to identify and clarify the philosophical underpinnings of the person-centred approach, the goals and tasks of the person-centred coach, how it relates to other forms of coaching, and contexts in which it is useful.

History and theoretical tradition

The person-centred approach was originally developed by Carl Rogers. Rogers began to develop the person-centered approach during the 1940s and 1950s. Person-centred (or client-centred, as it was known then) refers to the philosophical stance that people are their own best experts. The person-centred approach was seen as an alternative to the then dominant models in American psychology of behaviourism and psychoanalysis, and as such became aligned with the third force in psychology, that of humanistic psychology. Today, Rogers is best remembered for his books *Client-Centered Therapy: Its current practice, implications and theory* (1951) *and On becoming a person: A therapists view of psychotherapy* (1961), both of which have been reprinted numerous times and remain in print and widely read. The person-centred approach is an established psychological tradition supported by over fifty years of research and theory (see Barrett-Lennard, 1998; Kirschenbaum, 2007).

The term person-centred approach is used deliberately to signify that this is an *approach*, not a set of techniques. The person-centred approach can be applied to a range of contexts, from one-to-one settings, in small groups, in community settings, or as applied to social policy (Barrett-Lennard, 1998). In terms of one to one practice, Carl Rogers introduced the term counselling but he might equally well have used the term coaching, because in person-centred practice these terms are interchangeable. The current use of these two terms reflects the prevalent medical model ideology, but person-centred practice is not based in the medical model and so there is no conceptual distinction between coaching and therapy. The practitioner adheres to the same philosophical principle of respecting the self-determination of the other, whether they are practising as a coach or as a therapist. Unlike other therapeutic approaches, person-centred practice is not concerned with 'repairing' or 'curing' dysfunctionality, and never adopted the 'diagnostic' stance of the medical model in which the therapist is the expert. Like coaching, the focus of person-centred counselling has always been to facilitate the self-determination and full functioning of the client.

MAIN ASSUMPTIONS OF THE PERSON-CENTRED APPROACH

The theoretical foundation stone of the person-centred approach is the *actualizing tendency*. The actualizing tendency is defined as a universal human motivation resulting in growth, dev4lopment, and autonomy of the individual (Rogers, 1959, 1963). It is a biological tendency, not a moral imperative. The metaphor most often used to convey this theoretical principle is how an acorn has the potential to develop into an oak tree, and given the right nutrients from the soil, the right balance of sunlight and shade, it will grow to its fullest potential as an oak tree. But given a lack of nutrients from the soil, the wrong balance of sunlight and shade, its potential as an oak tree will be only partially fulfilled. Thus it is with people, person-centered theory suggests. The term *self-actualization* in person-centred terminology therefore refers to the process of becoming, which can be either in a positive, socially constructive direction or a negative, socially destructive direction, depending on the social environment.

The person-centred approach to helping is based on the above theoretical framework, i.e. that people are intrinsically motivated to grow and develop in the direction of becoming more optimally functioning, when the right social environmental conditions are present. The aim of the client-centred coach is to create facilitative social–environmental conditions, within the context of the coaching relationship, that will enable the client to evaluate experiences organismically, which, put more colloquially, is to hear one's own inner voice:

individuals have within themselves vast resources for self-understanding, and for altering their self-concepts, basic attitudes, and self-directed behaviour; these resources can be tapped if a definable climate of facilitative psychological attitudes can be provided. (Rogers, 1980: 115)

Rogers (1957a: 96) described six facilitative relationship conditions that he held were necessary and sufficient for positive therapeutic change.

1. Two persons are in psychological contact.
2. The first, whom we shall call the client, is in a state of incongruence, being vulnerable or anxious.
3. The second person, whom we shall call the therapist, is congruent or integrated in the relationship.
4. The therapist experiences unconditional positive regard for the client.
5. The therapist experiences an empathic understanding of the client's internal frame of reference and endeavours to communicate this experience to the client.
6. The communication to the client of the therapist's empathic understanding and unconditional positive regard is to a minimal degree achieved.

Rogers believed these conditions to underlie *any* therapeutic personality change, and thus believed that they must be in operation in any successful helping relationship.

GOALS AND TASKS OF PERSON-CENTRED COACHING

The ideas first associated with the person-centred movement underpin the practice of many coaches. Palmer and Whybrow (2006) found that the majority of coaching psychologists describe themselves as facilitational (67.9%) rather than instructional (17.4%), and that the person-centred approach is one of the most frequently used approaches to coaching. Indeed, although coaching is a new professional movement, the development of coaching and the origin of many of the ideas can be traced back to the humanistic tradition of psychology (Grant, 2008).

Originally, Rogers used the term *non-directivity*, before introducing the term person-centred. The concept of non-directivity has been prone to misunderstanding, with some commentators claiming that it is impossible to have a non-directive relationship. However, this has been clarified by Grant (2004), who distinguished between *principled* non-directivity and *instrumental* non-directivity. Whereas principled non-directivity refers to the therapist's ethical values of non-interference and respect for the self-determination of the other and is itself the goal of the therapist, instrumental non-directivity refers to a set of behaviours applied by the therapist to achieve a particular goal, such as building rapport. Person-centred approaches are founded on principled and not instrumental non-directivity. This serves as the guiding principle for client-centred practice, which in essence is simply the principled stance of respecting the self-determination of others (Grant, 2004).

> Client-centered therapists make no assumptions about what people need or how they should be free. They do not attempt to promote self-acceptance, self-direction, positive growth, self-actualization, congruence between real or perceived selves, a particular vision of reality, or anything....*Client-centered therapy is the practice of simply respecting the right to self-determination of others.* (Grant, 2004: 158)

Person-centred psychology is not a set of therapeutic techniques but an attitude based on the theoretical stance that people are their own best experts (Joseph, 2003; Levitt, 2005). As Brodley (2005) wrote:

> The non-directive attitude is psychologically profound; it is not a technique. Early in a therapist's development it may be superficial and prescriptive – 'Don't do this' or 'Don't do that'. But with time, self-examination and therapy

experience, it becomes an aspect of the therapist's character. It represents a feeling of profound respect for the constructive potential in persons and great sensitivity to their vulnerability. (2005: 3)

The implication from principled non-directivity is that reflective listening constitutes the majority of responses from the coach:

Client. I don't know, it's like we don't connect anymore, we don't talk, it's not like it was, she says that everything is ok and that she loves me, but I don't feel loved. I don't know what to do.

Coach. You feel stuck, not knowing, she says she loves you, but you don't feel loved. You look frightened as you say that.

Client. Do I? … I suppose I am, I don't know what to do, if she leaves me, I'll … I'll, I don't know …

Coach. You feel frightened, and when you think about this you are … lost?

Client. Abandoned, I don't know if I could cope …

Coach. You don't know if you could cope …

Client. … I know I could cope, but I don't want to go through that, I can't face it, but I know that I'll get through in the end (sighs) … I can't carry on like this either, I can't cope with this …

Coach You are really struggling to manage what's happening right now in your life, all the confusion … you don't want to separate but you know that you will be able to get through it if you have to … is that it?

Client Yes … I've got to look after myself …

In this example of life coaching, the coach is staying with the client's agenda. The coach does not introduce new material, nor prompt the client about how to think about the content of what they say, or what direction to go in. In reflecting to the client that they seem frightened, the coach is staying with what the client is bringing, and in doing so helps the client to become more aware of how they are feeling. It is hard on paper, and with such a snapshot example, to convey the complexity and depth of the relationship that develops between the coach and the client. Reflective listening is not a passive process, it requires attention to all that is said, and all that is not said, and it requires the coach to choose on the basis of their empathic understanding as well as their own congruence in that moment what to reflect on. Reflective listening, when skilfully done, and in the context of an empathic, congruent, positively regarding and unconditional relationship encourages the client to verbalize further, to explore issues in more depth, to be challenged, to reach new insights, and ultimately to be more equipped to make new choices in life.

COMPARISON OF TRADITIONS

There are a variety of other approaches to coaching, and although person-centred coaching has features in common with many of them; such as the shared focus on the relationship with psychodynamic approaches; the client's perceptions with the cognitive approach; the agency of the client with solution focused coaching; the present experiencing with Gestalt coaching; the lack of rigid techniques with existential coaching; the emphasis on optimal functioning with positive psychology; all of these other approaches generally adopt the view that some form of directivity is necessary in the coaching session. The person-centred approach is unique in its adoption of principled non-directivity.

A further distinction is that the person-centred approach adopts a unified and holistic focus on both the negative and the positive aspects of human functioning (Joseph & Worsley, 2005; Joseph & Linley, 2006a). The person-centred approach does not make a distinction between people in terms of their level of psychological functioning, because the process of alleviating distress and dysfunction is the same as that for facilitating well-being and optimal functioning. Psychological functioning is defined in relation to the extent to which self-actualization is congruent with the actualizing tendency (Ford, 1991). When there is greater congruence, greater well-being and more optimal functioning result; but when there is less congruence, greater distress and dysfunction result (see Wilkins, 2005). The development of different terminology, i.e. counselling versus coaching, to describe people at different points on the spectrum of psychological functioning, reflects the pervasive medical model conception that helping people in distress is different from helping people achieve well-being. It must be emphasized that the way in which professional organizations have developed to deal with people at different points on the spectrum ultimately reflects a social construction of human functioning grounded in a medical model and an illness ideology. From the person-centred perspective there is no boundary between coaching and counselling. Thus, person-centred coaching is the same activity requiring the same theoretical base, the same skills, and high level of personal development as required for person-centred counselling. There is no meaningful theoretical distinction from the perspective of the person-centred approach between the process of coaching and that of counselling. In essence both require principled non-directivity within the context of a facilitative relationship.

But this is not to say that an observer would not notice any difference between person-centred coaching and person-centred counselling. Quite simply, what terms we use will determine what clients we work with. If the public understanding is that counselling is about looking back in life at what has gone wrong, whereas coaching is about looking forward to what can go right, different people with different issues will be attracted to counselling than to coaching. Thus, although the task of the person-centred counsellor or coach is the same in either case – to stay with the person and to facilitate the person's process of self determination – at the level of content the sessions would be different, simply because clients are more likely to bring different material to counselling compared to coaching.

SPECIFIC FEATURES, PROCESSES, AND THE ROLE OF THE COACH

A brief fictional example of an exchange during a life coaching session was used above to illustrate the principle of non-directivity (see also Joseph & Bryant-Jefferies, 2008). Life coaching is probably the most obvious arena in which person-centred coaching is applicable. The person-centred approach does not prescribe what the client should do, because it is grounded in the meta-theoretical assumption that people have an inherent tendency toward growth, development, and optimal functioning. The task of the coach is to trust the client to find his or her own direction in life, to hold an attitude of principled non-directivity towards others, and to be a person who is able to maintain an empathic, congruent, and positively regarding stance towards the other.

Thus it is that person-centred coaching, more so than other approaches that emphasize the techniques of the coach, emphasizes the successful formation of a collaborative relationship (Stober & Grant, 2006; O'Broin & Palmer, 2008), and the coaches' attributes – their authenticity, emotional literacy, and so on – factors which are thought to be important in determining coaching effectiveness (Fillery-Travis & Lane, 2008), as with counselling and psychotherapy (Duncan & Miller, 2000; Wampold, 2001; Bozarth & Motomasa, 2005).

In practice, the person-centred coach strives to understand both the content of what the client is saying and the process they are working through, reflecting back their understanding to the client so that the client has a mirror to his or her experiencing in that moment. This helps the client to hear their own inner voice, to go deeper into their process and become aware of new material that was previously at the edge of their awareness. But at no point does the coach direct the client as to how they ought to be experiencing; his or her role is only to offer the relational conditions within which the client's own process will direct the session.

As noted above, person-centred coaching is not defined by the use of techniques, but by the relationship that develops. However, there is no prohibition of the use of techniques per se. There has been much theoretical and practical development in the world of client-centred therapy over recent years (see Sanders, 2004), ranging from the classical client-centred approach to therapy (Merry, 2004); this with its principled role of going with the client at the client's pace, through to more process-directed approaches (Worsley, 2001, 2004), and motivational interviewing, which has its roots in the person-centred approach (Passmore & Whybrow, 2008). What is different about the person-centred way of working is that the techniques, when they are used, become an expression of the meta-theoretical assumptions of person-centred theory (see Joseph & Linley, 2006b). It is not the fact that the coach uses a particular technique or assessment device that is the issue, but *how* they use it. In the above session the coach may introduce the use of various techniques, but the important thing is that they do not violate their principled non-directivity. For example the coach may think it appropriate to offer the suggestion that the client could explore their coping style, perhaps suggesting an appropriate self-help book on the topic, or suggesting to the client that they complete a psychometric test in order to gain insight into their coping style. The coach may choose to offer this because in their judgment they think they have information that the client does not and which could be useful to the client.

Thus, the person-centred coach can draw on and offer to the client various cognitive-behavioural, multimodel, solution-focused, and systems theory techniques (see Kauffman & Scoular, 2004). Cognitive-behavioural psychology, for example offers a wealth of techniques that can be helpful to people in learning about themselves and in exploring the relationship between thoughts and feelings, and learning how what we say to ourselves can hold us back from achieving our goals (Neenan & Palmer, 2001). But two different coaches can use the same techniques in very different ways indeed; one taking the lead as expert, the other assuming that the client is the expert and following their lead.

Contracting

Life coaching is usually funded by the client him/herself. However, contracting is still important, particularly in relation to boundary issues and what should or should not be included in the coaching agenda. Also, as we have seen, attention needs to be paid to the role of influential others, the client's system, and circles of influence. The main question faced by the person-centred coach is 'Whose agenda am I addressing?' It has to be the client's agenda, and boundaries must be set clearly in place when the contract is with an organization. Issues could arise from lack of clarity in contracting or lack of alignment between client and organizational goals. Issues to be considered in relation to person-centred coaching include understanding the client system and particularly influential others who may undermine the coaching process. Confidentiality may also be an issue within an organization. Unless otherwise agreed, it would be usual for details of the coach–client relationship to remain confidential, and when such details are shared with the organization it would be at the agreement of the client, who would in most cases be given the opportunity to discuss the report and to agree with the coach that it provides a fair representation.

CONTEXTS

The person-centred approach is most obviously applicable to life coaching. Often, client's come knowing that they want to change the direction of their lives, but are struggling to hear their inner voice about the best way to move forward. The person-centred coach can help the person think through relationship choices, managing stressful situations, and so on. Person-centred coaching is ideally suited for the exploration of values, beliefs and assumptions.

As such, the person-centred approach is also well suited to career coaching and helping individuals to discover what they really want to do in their working lives and develop a strategy to achieve it. Where this is most suitable is with clients who have the relevant information but are struggling to choose their direction. A further area of applicability is mentoring in which the person-centred approach serves to build up self-direction.

But the skills of the person-centred coach are also applicable to a wide range of contexts. The person-centred approach, because of its grounding in the idea of intrinsic motivation, is also useful to developmental work in which the client is interested in making new decisions, understanding their values and beliefs, becoming authentic or discovering new purpose. This can be appropriate in an organizational context, although one issue of relevance to person-centred coaches is that because of their principled stance of non-directivity, and going with the client's direction, it becomes less appropriate when commissioned by organizations that have particular goals in mind for the client. The person-centred coach will always stay with the agenda of the client, and this can be problematic if they are employed by an organization whose goals are different from those of the client.

The same issue is pertinent in executive and leadership coaching where often the focus is on organizational performance. Insofar as the client is also focused on organizational aims, the person-centred coach will stay with that agenda, but they would not see it as their task to stay with that agenda if the client's agenda shifted. This may seem a disadvantage, and certainly it would be in terms of organizational performance requirements, such as learning new analytical and business skills. What can result, however, is that clients move away from their organizational agenda towards a more personal agenda in a way which is actually beneficial to them in terms of self-understanding and developing social and emotional skills, which in turn has a knock-on effect in terms of decision making and the ability to relate to others, which can benefit the organization.

Person-centred coaching is least appropriate to peer coaching, simply because of the depth of personal awareness and psychological mindedness needed by the coach, as well as their attitude of principled non-directivity. Without appropriate experience and training in person-centred theory and practice it is difficult for colleagues to be able to work together effectively in this way. Reflections on current practice, and sharing experiences, can easily spill into advice giving, which although appropriate at times, needs to be done in the context of principled non-directivity. But some basic training grounded in person-centred constructs, such as reflective listening and empathic understanding, can be useful to increase the effectiveness of peer coaches using other approaches; but it would be misleading to call this person-centred as it lacks the full philosophical depth of the approach.

Person-centred coaches come from a variety of backgrounds and although some are able to offer skills and performance coaching related to their own expertise, generally person-centred coaching does not set out to achieve goals against set performance criteria. Where it can be particularly useful however is in the group learning context, in which experienced person-centred coaches can facilitate group interaction in such a way that the group members are better able to focus on identifying their goals and finding ways of working to achieve these, and to consider their shared values and discuss what is important to them.

EVALUATION OF PERSON-CENTRED COACHING

Within western culture, mainstream psychological approaches adopt medical model-based approaches in which the therapist or coach is expert. In contrast, the person-centred approach requires the ability of the coach to adopt a non-directive attitude in which the client knows best. Thus, the person-centred approach is often seen as limited because people may come seeking help expecting the therapist or coach to take the expert role. As a result some people find the person-centred approach frustrating, as they are not given solutions to their problems and helped to formulate their difficulties from the medical model perspective. Similarly, some coaches also find the approach limited. There is no one version of what coaching is. Coaching, like counselling, is divided down the middle on the issue of directivity, with some emphasizing the role of the coach as expert-advice giver and others advocating the 'ask not tell' approach (Grant, 2008). But it is no use to argue over which of these is right. Certainly there are some contexts in which people want simply to learn new skills, and directive coaching from an expert is called for; then there are other contexts in which what is to be learned is deeper self-understanding and self-determination. In these latter contexts, how one chooses to work with other people is a matter of philosophical principle. As Schmid (2005) wrote:

> Non-directivity is thus a matter of basic beliefs. People who think that directivity is necessary in therapy and counsel-ling have a different image of the human being, a different concept of how to deal with knowledge and a different ethical stance from those who work with their clients on the basis of non-directiveness. Since it is of no use to argue over beliefs (they precede acting, thinking, and science), there is no way to say who, ultimately, is right. (Schmid, 2005:82)

The emergence of the coaching movement has served to reinvigorate interest in the person-centred approach. As mentioned previously, many coaching practitioners describe themselves as using a person-centred approach, and certainly the general ethos of the person-centred approach, that clients are the best experts on themselves, is one that is readily accepted by the coaching community. Grant (2008), for example argues that coaching should be collaborative and client-centred. But it is probably true to say that many who do describe themselves as using the person-centred approach, particularly those who combine it with other approaches, do so in a watered down way in which they may emphasize the quality of the coach–client relationship as being important, but do not fully appreciate the depth of the philosophical underpinnings of the approach.

The person-centred approach provides a robust theoretical system for defining and under-standing psychological process – including both those that limit and those that enhance the person. Traditionally person-centred psychology has been conceptualized as part of the wider humanistic psychology. But in recent years, there has been a new field of research and practice, referred to as positive psychology (Seligman & Csikszentmihalyi, 2000). Like person-centred psychology (Rogers, 1957b), positive psychologists are interested in the 'good life', arguing that mainstream psychology has been overly concerned with distress and dysfunction at the expense of well-being and optimal functioning. The idea that human beings have an inherent tendency toward growth, development, and optimal functioning has become a focus for theory and research within the new movement of positive psychology (Joseph & Linley, 2006b), and offers an alternative vision to that of the medical model for how we might socially construct what it is to be human.

The strongest support for this comes from self-determination theory (SDT). SDT is a more contemporary organismic theory of human motivation and personality functioning, developed over the past 30 years, that also emphasizes the central role of the individual's inner resources for personality development and behavioural self-regulation (Deci & Ryan, 2002; Ryan & Deci, 2002). In accord with person-centred theory, SDT views the person as an active growth-oriented organism, attempting to actualize his or her potentialities within the environment in which he or she functions. The organismic tendency toward actualization is seen as one pole of a dialectical interface, the other pole being the social environment which can be either facilitating or inhibiting of the person's synthesizing tendency (Ryan & Deci, 2002; Deci & Vansteenkiste, 2004; Vansteenkiste & Sheldon, 2006). Similarities between person-centred theory and self-determination theory have been obscured by the differences in terminology and separate research trajectories, but on examination there are such close similarities between these approaches that the extensive research evidence from SDT can be read as providing evidence consistent with person-centred theory (Patterson & Joseph, 2007). Thus, when we examine this weight of theory and evidence we see a real rapprochement between positive psychology and the person-centred approach. Sheldon and Elliot (1999) wrote:

> along with Rogers (1961), we believe that individuals have innate developmental trends and propensities that may be given voice by an organismic valuing process occurring within them. The voice can be very difficult to hear, but the current research suggests that the ability to hear it is of crucial importance for the pursuit of happiness. (Sheldon & Elliott, 1999: 495)

Previously, I have argued that the distinction between counselling and coaching implicitly condones the medical model view (Joseph, 2006). As already emphasized, the person-centred perspective provides a unitary way of working with clients along the spectrum of functioning. Within the person-centred perspective, regardless of where the person starts, coaching can be valuable to all. This is not a new idea within person-centred practice. As Shlien, one of the founders of person-centred psychology, said in a talk originally given in 1956:

> if the skills developed in psychological counselling can release the constructive capacities of malfunctioning people so that they become healthier, this same help should be available to healthy people who are less than *fully* functioning. If we ever turn towards positive goals of health, we will care less about where the person begins, and more about how to achieve the desired endpoint of the positive goals. (Shlien, 2003: 26)

Person-centred coaching is based on the philosophical assumption that the client is their own best expert and has an intrinsic motivation towards growth, development, and optimal functioning, and that this will be given expression when the client's psychological processes are trusted and encouraged in the context of a facilitative person-to-person relationship.

FURTHER READING

Joseph, S., & Linley, P.A. (2006). *Positive therapy: A meta-theory for positive psychological practice.* London: Routledge. (In this book, we discuss the alternative meta-theoretical paradigm of person-centred theory and how it can provide the underpinning to positive psychology, therapy, and coaching.)

Rogers, C.R. (1959). *A theory of therapy, personality, and interpersonal relationships as developed in the client-centered framework.* In S. Koch (Ed.), *Psychology: A study of a Science: Formulations of the person and the social context* (Vol. 3, pp.184–256). New York: McGraw-Hill. (This is the most sophisticated theoretical statement of the person-centred tradition in which Rogers attempted to show how the approach was applicable to a range of contexts, setting out in detail the theoretical propositions that remain the core of the approach today.)

Rogers, C.R. (1980). *A Way of Being.* Boston, MA: Houghton Mifflin Co. (This book brings together some of Rogers's personal and philosophical writings. As such it provides a good introduction to the later writings of Rogers and the wider applications of the person-centred approach, including to contexts that we would today recognize as coaching.)

REFERENCES

Barrett-Lennard, G.T. (1998). *Carl Rogers' helping system: Journey and substance.* London: Sage.

Bozarth, J.D., & Motomasa, N. (2005). Searching for the core: The interface of client-centered principles with other therapies. In S. Joseph & R. Worsley (Eds.), *Person-centred psychopathology: A positive psychology of mental health.* Ross-on-Wye: PCCS books.

Brodley, B.T. (2005). About the non-directive attitude. In B.E. Levitt (Ed.), *Embracing non-directivity: Reassessing person-centered theory and practice in the 21st century* (pp. 1–4). Ross-on-Wye: PCCS books.

Deci, E.L., & Ryan, R.M. (2002). Self-determination research: Reflections and future directions. In E.L. Deci & R.M. Ryan (Eds.), *Handbook of self-determination research* (pp. 431–41). Rochester, NY: University of Rochester Press.

Deci, E.L., & Vansteenkiste, M. (2004). Self-determination theory and basic need satisfaction: Understanding human development in positive psychology. *Ricerchedi di psicologia: Special issue in positive psychology, 27:* 23–40.

Duncan, B., & Miller, S. (2000). *The heroic client: Doing client-directed, outcome informed therapy.* San Francisco, CA: Jossey-Bass.

Fillery-Travis, A., & Lane, D. (2008). Research: Does coaching work? In S. Palmer & A. Whybrow (Eds.), *Handbook of coaching psychology: A guide for practitioners* (pp. 57–70). London: Routledge.

Ford, J.G. (1991). Rogerian self-actualization: A clarification of meaning. *Journal of Humanistic Psychology, 31:* 101–11.

Grant, A.M. (2008). Past, present, and future: The evolution of professional coaching and coaching psychology. In S. Palmer & A. Whybrow (Eds.), *Handbook of coaching psychology: A guide for practitioners* (pp. 23–39). London: Routledge.

Grant, B. (2004). The imperative of ethical justification in psychotherapy: The special case of client-centered therapy. *Person-Centered and Experiential Psychotherapies, 3:* 152–65.

Joseph, S. (2003). Client-centred psychotherapy: Why the client knows best. *The Psychologist, 16:* 304–7.

Joseph, S. (2006). Person-centred coaching psychology: A meta-theoretical perspective. *International Coaching Psychology Review, 1:* 47–55.

Joseph, S., & Bryant-Jefferies, R. (2008). Person-centred coaching psychology. In S. Palmer & A. Whybrow (Eds.), *Handbook of coaching psychology: A guide for practitioners* (pp. 211–28). London: Routledge.

Joseph, S., & Linley, P.A. (2006a). Positive psychology versus the medical model. *American Psychologist, 61:* 332–3.

Joseph, S., & Linley, P.A. (2006b). *Positive therapy: A meta-theory for positive psychological practice:* London: Routledge.

Joseph, S., & Worsley, R. (2005). A positive psychology of mental health: The person-centred perspective. In S. Joseph & R. Worsley (Eds.), *Person-centred psychopathology: A positive psychology of mental health* (pp. 348–57). Ross-on-Wye: PCCS Books.

Kauffman, C., & Scoular, A. (2004). Toward a positive psychology of executive coaching. In P. A. Linley & S. Joseph (Eds.), *Positive psychology in practice* (pp. 287–302). Hoboken, NJ: John Wiley & Sons.

Kirschenbaum, H. (2007). *The life and work of Carl Rogers.* Ross-on-Wye: PCCS Books.

Levitt, B.E. (Ed.). (2005). *Embracing non-directivity: Reassessing person-centered theory and practice in the 21st century.* Ross-on-Wye: PCCS Books.

Merry, T. (2004). Classical client-centred therapy. In P. Sanders, *The tribes of the person-centred nation: An introduction to the schools of therapy related to the person-centred approach* (pp. 21–44). Ross-on-Wye: PCCS Books.

Neenan, M., & Palmer, S. (2001). Cognitive behavioural coaching. *Stress News, 13:* 15–18.

O'Broin, A., & Palmer, S. (2008). Reappraising the coach-client relationship: The unassuming change agent in coaching. In S. Palmer & A. Whybrow (Eds.), *Handbook of coaching psychology: A guide for practitioners* (pp. 295–324). London: Routledge.

Palmer, S., & Whybrow, A. (2006). The coaching psychology movement and its development within the British Psychological Society. *International CoachingPsychology Review, 1*: 5–11.

Passmore, J., & Whybrow, A. (2008). Motivational interviewing: A specific approach for coaching psychologists. In S. Palmer & A. Whybrow (Eds.), *Handbook of coaching psychology: A guide for practitioners* (pp. 160–73). London: Routledge.

Patterson, T.G., & Joseph, S. (2007). Person-centered personality theory: Support from self-determination theory and positive psychology. *Journal of Humanistic Psychology, 47*: 117–39.

Rogers, C.R. (1951). *Client-centred therapy: Its current practice, implications and theory.* Boston, MA: Houghton Mifflin.

Rogers, C.R. (1957a). The necessary and sufficient conditions of therapeutic personality change. *Journal of Consulting Psychology, 21*: 95–103.

Rogers, C.R. (1957b). A therapist's view of the good life. *The Humanist, 17*: 291–300.

Rogers, C.R. (1959). A theory of therapy, personality, and interpersonal relationships as developed in the client-centered framework. In S. Koch (Ed.), *Psychology: A study of a Science: Formulations of the person and the social context* (Vol. 3, pp.184–256). New York: McGraw-Hill.

Rogers, C.R. (1961). *On becoming a person.* Boston, MA: Houghton Mifflin.

Rogers, C.R. (1963). The actualizing tendency in relation to 'motives' and to consciousness. In M. R. Jones (Ed.), *Nebraska Symposium on Motivation* (Vol. 11, pp. 1–24). Lincoln, NE: University of Nebraska Press.

Rogers, C.R. (1980). *A way of being.* Boston, MA: Houghton Mifflin.

Ryan, R.M., & Deci, E.L. (2002). An overview of self-determination theory: An organismic dialectical perspective. In E.L. Deci & R.M. Ryan (Eds.), *Handbook of self-determination research* (pp. 3–33). Rochester, NY: University of Rochester Press.

Sanders, P. (2004). *The tribes of the person-centred nation: An introduction to the schools of therapy related to the person-centred approach.* Ross-on-Wye: PCCS Books.

Schmid, P. (2005). Facilitative responsiveness: Non-directiveness from anthropological, epistemological and ethical perspectives. In B.E. Levitt (Ed.), *Embracing nondirectivity: Reassessing person-centered theory and practice in the 21st century* (pp. 75–95). Ross-on-Wye: PCCS Books.

Seligman, M.E.P., & Csikszentmihalyi, M. (2000). Positive psychology: An introduction. *American Psychologist, 55*: 5–14.

Sheldon, K.M., & Elliot, A.J. (1999). Goal striving, need satisfaction, and longitudinal well-being: The self-concordance model. *Journal of Personality and Social Psychology, 76*: 482–97.

Shlien, J.M. (2003). Creativity and psychological health. In P. Sanders (Ed.), *To lead an honourable life: Invitations to think about client-centered therapy and the person-centered approach* (pp. 19–29). Ross-on-Wye: PCCS Books.

Stober, D.R., & Grant, A.M. (2006). Toward a contextual approach to coaching models. In D. R. Stober & A. M. Grant (Eds.), *Evidence based coaching handbook: Putting best practices to work for your clients.* Hoboken, NJ: Wiley.

Vansteenkiste, M., & Sheldon, K.M. (2006). There's nothing more practical than a good theory: Integrating motivational interviewing and self-determination theory. *British Journal of Clinical Psychology, 45*: 63–82.

Wampold, B.E. (2001). *The great psychotherapy debate: Models, methods, and findings.* Mahwah, NJ: Lawrence Erlbaum.

Wilkins, P. (2005). Person-centred theory and 'mental illness'. In S. Joseph & R. Worsley, (Eds.). *Person-centred psychopatholgy: A positive psychology of mental health* (pp. 43–59). Ross-on-Wye: PCCS Books.

Worsley, R. (2001). *Process work in person-centred therapy.* Basingstoke: Palgrave.

Worsley, R. (2004). Integrating with integrity. In P. Sanders, *The tribes of the person-centred nation: An introduction to the schools of therapy related to the person-centred approach* (pp. 125–48). Ross-on-Wye: PCCS Books:

5

The Gestalt Approach to Coaching

Peter Bluckert

INTRODUCTION

While practitioners from a clinical background will be familiar with Gestalt from the therapeutic arena (Gestalt therapy), what may be less well known is the increasingly coherent body of theory and practice relating to applications of Gestalt at the organizational level.

This chapter describes the key aspects of the Gestalt theoretical tradition and then sets out an emerging conceptual and methodological framework for a Gestalt coaching approach.

The theoretical tradition

Gestalt coaching finds its theory and practice from three places: Gestalt therapy and Gestalt psychology where the primary focus has been on individuals; and more recent applications of Gestalt to wider systems such as couples, families, teams and organizations.

It should be noted that Gestalt therapy is not simply a direct extension of Gestalt psychology. The pioneers of Gestalt therapy absorbed several philosophical and psychological traditions. The period from the 1950s to the 1980s, and particularly the earlier years when much of the influential work was done, was for many a time of deep questioning and dissatisfaction with the status quo. There was a fervent desire for change and an optimistic belief that it could happen. Those early founders, such as Fritz and Laura Perls and Paul Goodman, confronted the Freudian-based psychoanalytical establishment and embraced the radicalism of the time.

They sought their influences not only from psychoanalysis and Gestalt psychology but also from field theory, existential philosophy and the humanistic therapy movement of the time. In 1951, Perls, in collaboration with Goodman and Hefferline, published the seminal Gestalt text: *Gestalt Therapy: Excitement and Growth in the Human Personality*, 'the cornerstone of the Gestalt approach' (Latner, 1992: 15).

Gestalt psychology dates back to the early twentieth century and was developed in Germany by Max Wertheimer, Wolfgang Köhler and Kurt Koffka who were interested in the nature and structure of perceptual experience. They challenged the belief that there is an 'objective reality' and instead sought to understand how we make sense of our experience, moment by moment, against the background of the field which includes our current mental models and historical experience. They believed that people actively strive to impose order and meaningful wholes on what they see and experience. Indeed, the German word Gestalt, which does not easily translate into English, most approximates to words like pattern, shape, configuration, or meaningful organized whole.

From field theorists such as Kurt Lewin the concept of interconnectedness was adopted – that people exist as part of an environmental field, and behaviour can only be understood in relation to that field. An important implication here for organizational consultants, facilitators and coaches is that *you* cannot be outside of the field. The notion of the neutral, independent practitioner exerting no influence or impact on the system you are working with is rejected in the field perspective. The intervener may not be a member of the group, team or system but as Perls, Hefferline, and Goodman (1951: xi) said, 'the whole determines the parts'; if you are part of the field it impacts you and you impact it.

The existential philosophy roots come from Kierkegaard, Sartre and Heidegger with their themes of personal responsibility, freedom and authenticity. In relational terms Buber's philosophy of dialogue based on I–Thou connection, taken later into the therapeutic relationship as the dialogical method, was also influential. Phenomenology, which grew out of existentialism, advocates the value of staying as closely as possible to actual, raw, here-and-now data, rather than interpreting or judging it. In fact, Perls called Gestalt the 'psychology of the obvious'.

Description, says Clarkson (2004: 4), is more important than interpretation. What this looks like in practice is an emphasis on descriptive rather than evaluative feedback and a more faithful reflection and honouring of the coachees' own words, meanings and subjective experience. It calls on the coach to be observant of the body language and energetic presence of their client, fully attend to emotional needs as they arise and be aware of the contact issues within the relationship. Intrinsic in this approach is that the coach needs to focus on his/her own subjective experience and share this appropriately as part of an authentic dialogue. This sharing of the coach's interior and exterior world in the service of the client is known as *the use of self*.

The Gestalt perspective of human functioning

Gestalt is a needs-based approach to understanding human functioning and behaviour. Through effective self-regulation people gratify needs and eliminate tensions. At the physical level this is self evident. As a need, such as hunger emerges, it becomes an increasingly dominant *figure* against the background (*ground*) of that person's other experience. This produces a state of temporary imbalance until that need is met, when it then dissipates with a consequent with-drawal of interest and energy. This process was first described in Goldstein's (Hall & Lindzey, 1957) research where he offered the concept of *organismic self-regulation.* According to Goldstein there is a biological law of balance inherent in human nature and we are programmed to move towards the best form possible to find that balance.

Melnick and Nevis (2005) acknowledge the contribution that Goldstein's work made to our understanding of self-regulation as primarily a physiological process focusing on self preserva-tion, but differentiate it from another important Gestalt concept, *creative adjustment.* This is the notion that we are always seeking to do the best we can in any given circumstances to meet our needs, find solutions to our problems, achieve our goals, and derive satisfaction from our lives. Through creative adjustment Melnick and Nevis (2005: 22) suggest that 'change can happen quickly and permanently'.

Gestalt applications to organizations

The earliest applications of Gestalt within the organizational context are ascribed to Wallen and Nevis. Beginning in 1959, they used awareness-raising techniques within sensitivity training groups for managers. This work can be seen as a forerunner of today's workshop-based emo-tional intelligence programmes.

Nevis went on to play a leading role in the application of Gestalt principles to management and organizational development, setting up the Organization Development Center at the Gestalt Institute of Cleveland in the USA, along with Carter, Lukensmeyer, Hannafin and Siminovitch, and writing the seminal text on the subject, *Organizational Consulting: A Gestalt Approach* (1987). Elsewhere and throughout the world there have been a growing number of Gestalt organizational practitioners who have taken their own Gestalt styles into process consultancy, team development, mediation and one-to-one consultation. In recent years, some of these have rebranded their one-to-one work as executive coaching.

My own applications of Gestalt to organizational consultancy began in the early 1980s through leadership and personal development programmes and since then it has been my primary psychological frame of reference for team development, executive coaching and the training and development of coaches and OD consultants (Bluckert, 2006).

MAIN ASSUMPTIONS AND BELIEFS

Underpinning all Gestalt-based work is the following set of core assumptions and beliefs:

- Gestalt practitioners believe that *people are always doing the best they can.* (Melnick & Nevis, 2005: 13). This belief emanates from the Gestalt perspective of resistance as a meaningful and healthy act when understood from the position of the so-called resistor. Indeed, the Gestalt concept of *creative adjustment* is founded in the belief that people make the best decisions and alter behaviour towards the best outcomes available *within* the external constraints and their own perceptions of what is possible at that time. With this in mind Gestalt can be seen as a positive psychology.

- The Gestalt theory of change, the *paradoxical theory of change* (Beisser, 1970), states that change occurs when one is fully in contact with 'what is', the truth of our experience, rather than trying to be different or disowning parts of ourselves. We must become our truth first before we can move from it. In translating this for the coach, Siminovitch and Van Eron (2006: 52) say, 'A fundamental intervention in Gestalt coaching is to sharply focus attention on what already exists for the client in the present, with the paradoxical result of initiating a profound experiential shift towards something new'. As a consequence of this theoretical perspective the skills and methods are used to support the client to get in contact and stay in contact with 'what is'. *Contact,* a core construct in Gestalt, is defined by Stevenson (2004: 5) as 'the psychological process whereby I allow myself to meet my self (as in memories and imagination); to meet a person, group, or organization; or to meet the environment: a sunset … and I can most effectively make such contact by staying present-centred'.
- A fundamental premise of all Gestalt-based work is that through heightened *awareness* people can more readily organize themselves into new ways of seeing, choosing and acting. Out of this awareness we energize ourselves and take actions that lead to the achievement of important goals. In completing these cycles we assimilate learning as well as gain closure around issues. Implicit in this assumption is that our actions may not lead to our desired results and therefore we may not attain our goals if they are based on impoverished awareness.
- Individual behaviour cannot be fully understood without reference to its context. Each context and situation contains its own dynamic, requiring the coach to appreciate systems and levels beyond the individual. This is known as the *field perspective.*
- The power of *unfinished business* not only drains energy, focus and motivation but also holds us back from fulfilling our potential and seeking out the new possibilities existing in our current situation. Worse still, our unfinished situations may block us from even opening ourselves to the awareness of those possibilities.
- The exploration of here and now, immediate experience, provides opportunities for learning and growth. This accounts for the classic Gestalt question, 'What are you aware of now?'.

THE DEFINING FEATURES OF A GESTALT APPROACH

As Saner (1999: 6) puts it 'one of the distinguishing features of Gestalt is its emphasis on the role that awareness plays in achieving effective behaviour and a healthy way of life'. Gestalt focuses on the individual's (or system's) experience in the present moment, the environmental context or 'field' in which this takes place and the self-regulating adjustments people make as a result of the overall situation. The Gestalt coach is interested in how their client meets or fails to meet their needs and assists them to better understand their own process, especially their habitual thinking and behavioural patterns. This emphasis on awareness as the change agent means that the Gestalt coach needs to learn to be an 'awareness expert'.

Carter (2004) identifies practitioner identity and the effective use of self as the key determinants of the master practitioner. To this I would add the capacity to use the Cycle of Experience (Figure 5.1) as the orienting framework for appreciation of process issues and as the basis for intervention decisions.

For the coachee to experience the support they require for deeper, reflective work, the coach also needs the capacity to build trust, respect and connection. It is generally acknowledged that

Table 5.1:   A framework for Gestalt coaching practice

Defining features	Guiding theoretical perspectives
A. A focus on *the need-fulfilment process* – how we satisfy (or not) needs, achieve closure around issues, assimilate learning and achieve desired goals	• The Cycle of Experience • Interruptions to contact
B. A focus on *how to use self*	• Presence and the intentional use of self as instrument of change
C. A focus on *the coaching relationship*	• Authentic dialogue

the nature and quality of the coaching relationship is a critical factor in successful coaching outcomes.

With these notions in mind I now offer a framework for Gestalt coaching practice, whether or not this is practised in the organizational context (Table 5.1).

A. The need-fulfilment process

The cycle of experience as the orienting framework

The Cycle of Experience is the Gestalt model for understanding how we satisfy (or not) our needs and achieve closure around issues. It is the primary orienting framework for a Gestalt-oriented coach providing a reference point for tracking what Siminovitch and Van Eron (2006: 53) call 'the natural and ongoing experiential processes of need-fulfilment at any level of system'. It equally helps the coach identify when and where people and systems may be stuck, providing clues as to where and how to intervene. The Cycle of Experience is typically represented as a staged process (Figure 5.1), beginning with sensation, moving through awareness and energy mobilization to action and contact, producing resolution, closure and withdrawal of interest.

For the most part people complete Cycles of Experience in an easy, uncomplicated way, especially when it comes to meeting their physical needs. I qualify this with the words 'for the most part' because even at the physical level we do not always engage in a healthy flow. Sometimes, for very good reasons, we go without sufficient food, sleep, exercise or relaxation. We cut corners with ourselves.

Self evidently the process can be far more complex at the social, emotional and spiritual levels. A very common emotional 'figure' in the workplace is the issue of inclusion, yet many people go through prolonged periods of feeling devalued, ignored or sidelined by a boss or the organization. When this happens their energy can be stuck on a negative focus and lead to self-defeating activity. This is what is known as an unfinished situation or 'unfinished business'.

Interruptions to contact   So, what gets in the way of completing cycles? The following *interruptions to contact* are sometimes presented as forms of unconscious resistance but may be more usefully understood as aspects of creative adjustment. From this perspective there

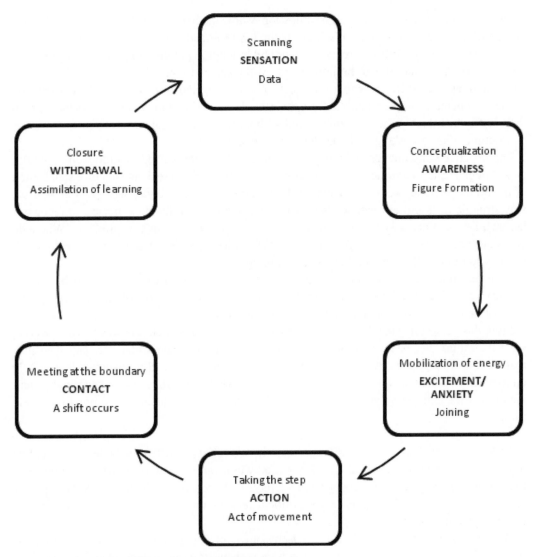

Figure 5.1 Cycle of Experience as orienting framework.
Source: **Adapted from Siminovitch and Van Eron (2006).**

is a positive dimension although they can also limit our capacity to make strong, lasting and authentic contact.

Gestalt theory identifies four major interruptions to contact – *introjection, retroflection, projection and confluence.* Presented as a list they could be seen as separate psychological processes, yet they connect and interrelate in complex and important ways, particularly introjection and retroflection, which have marked relevance for the coach.

Introjection refers to the process of 'swallowing' whole the beliefs, attitudes, values and edicts of significant others. This especially happens in early life and many of these introjections are useful, even necessary. When parents tell their children not to put their fingers into an electrical power socket they want this to be introjected. At the societal level, there are countless norms which nations need their citizens to introject to hold it together – driving on the correct side of the road being a simple example. Companies seek to instil certain values and behaviours in their staff which they want to be introjected without too much argument. Customer service is an example of this; working to the leadership agenda is another.

The negative consequences of introjection occur when internalized 'shoulds' and 'should-nots', 'oughts' and 'ought-nots' prevent people from being able to seek and achieve satisfaction of important personal needs. The young girl who grows up with the message 'put others first', may struggle to assert her own needs in adult life. She may hardly allow herself to recognize her own needs. When asked by her coach, 'What is it you want from your life?' or 'Where do you want your career to go?' this woman is likely to look perplexed and reply 'I really don't know. I don't often think about those kinds of things'.

A far-reaching implication of introjection is that we can never fully know how much, or little, of what we think and believe about the world is undigested material from our pasts – a recycling of other people's views, opinions and mental frameworks.

From this perspective the developmental aspect of coaching is about the coachee discovering what they think and believe, what they want from their work and wider life, and who they really are and want to be. As they proceed on their journey they will probably decide to hold on to much of what they introjected, but from the knowledge that they have taken it out, examined it and made it their own. They may equally cast off or re-evaluate some previously held truths.

Retroflection means to turn inward upon oneself. We retroflect when we believe it would be unwise, even dangerous, to speak or act out what we inwardly wish to say or do. We perceive that there is simply too little support and safety to do otherwise. In the workplace people retroflect to protect their careers or for political reasons on such a regular basis that it can become a habit, a behavioural norm.

Working in the organizational context coaches are confronted with examples of retroflection on a regular basis. Whether their work is with individuals, training groups, teams, departments or the entire system they cannot avoid retroflection. Bottling up of unexpressed views and feelings may simply be part of the human condition and may be the best we can come up with in many situations. We may wish to avoid hurting the other person, it may just be a bad time, or the individual is simply unavailable to deal with directly. Retroflection of different or challenging views may be the wisest course of action when there is a real question of what is safe to share in a given context.

However, there are consequences of habitual retroflection. Turning inward what perhaps needs to be expressed outwardly can have serious effects on our health and well-being and diminish the quality of relationships. Instead of being easy and comfortable in the other person's company we either minimize contact, because it's too difficult, or stay in superficial connection.

While retroflection clearly impacts at the individual and relationship level it can also have a critical impact on organizational performance. Individual team members are often caught up in a culture of retroflection where people go through the motions of teamwork and collaboration but at a deeper, more significant level keep their real thoughts, opinions and feelings to themselves. They also withhold their energy and commitment and some never fully join the enterprise of which they are part. Given these dynamics it is vital that coaches operating in corporate environments understand the nature of organizational relationships if they are to intervene effectively.

B. How to use self

Presence and the intentional use of self as instrument of change

From a Gestalt perspective coaches inevitably bring their presence into the coaching situation. The more relevant questions are about how well they understand their presence and what it evokes in others, to what extent it is grounded and integrated, and whether the coach can bring flexibility and intentionality to it.

Presence is not the same as charisma or style which can certainly be aspects of presence but only go part of the way towards capturing it. Our presence emanates from our ways of being and acting in the world. It contributes to whether we attract and interest others; it can also be a critical factor in distancing them or putting them off. It is the source of the coach's capacity to influence and equally it can explain lack of impact. For example the coach may not be filling their place and space in a room, perhaps coming through too timidly. This may be due to shutting parts of themselves off from a belief that they don't belong in that arena. The result can be a severe loss of power and the coach may look back with disappointment and regret that they didn't establish their presence sufficiently strongly to have impact.

Siminovitch and Van Eron (2006: 51) unpack the notion of presence and practitioner identity in the following way: *life experiences; an intellectual repertoire; particular skills or strengths as well as weaknesses or vulnerabilities; spiritual values and beliefs; and physical presence itself.* Presented in this way it is clear that everyone brings their presence whether or not they are seen by others as charismatic.

From a practitioner perspective we now need to return to the issue of how much we know about our presence and how to use it in the service of the coachee. As argued elsewhere (Bluckert, 2006: 107), this emphasises the critical importance of self development in the journey towards coaching excellence. The coach with less developed awareness won't always understand their impact and may need to learn how to use different aspects of self – soft and hard, loud and quiet, strong and mild – to become a more finely tuned instrument of change. One of the best ways coaches can gain that deeper appreciation of their presence is through an active process of seeking feedback from the widest range of sources – colleagues, clients, trainers and fellow workshop participants on development programmes. As the coach begins to understand their presence they can develop more assurance and creativity in their interventions.

The nature of those interventions will depend on what the coach believes will be most valuable at the time. The Cycle of Experience, the key orienting model of the Gestalt coach, indicates that much of the early work which establishes the safe foundations for developmental work lies at the awareness raising stage. Learning the art of raising awareness is therefore a core competency.

In setting out his main activities of a Gestalt practitioner, Nevis (1987: 57) offers two important pointers to working at the awareness stage of the Cycle:

- Attend, observe and selectively share observations of what you see, hear and feel.
- Attend to your own experience (feelings, sensations, thoughts, etc.) and selectively share these, thereby establishing your presence in doing so.

These direct the coach to what they are noticing in their coachee or client system, in themselves, and the relationship between. The term 'selectively share' is important here and is where the finer art of coaching applies. Well-timed, skilful articulation of observations is the stock-in-trade of the highly accomplished coach. Clumsy, ill-timed interventions can risk the safety, trust and confidence so vital to the working alliance.

Bringing intentionality to coaching interventions also has a tactical dimension. In the early stages of a coaching relationship the presence which most lends itself to awareness raising can be evocative in nature – one which is softer, quieter, milder and leaning towards support. On some occasions and with some coachees this approach may not always be enough or what is valued. A more provocative presence may be necessary. It can be important in these circumstances to alter one's energetic presence in order to match the different energy of the coachee.

C. The coaching relationship

Authentic dialogue

We shouldn't underestimate the importance of the coach–coachee relationship in determining coaching outcomes. The relationship is the vehicle through which the coachee stretches and challenges themselves, goes to their learning edge and, with support, stays there long enough to deepen awareness and learn something. The importance of establishing and maintaining a contactful, trusting connection makes it one of the primary challenges for any coach.

From a Gestalt perspective the responsibility for building this lies with both parties and the nature of the connection has certain defining features. The Gestalt coach is asked to put themselves into the relationship and be fully present with all that this means in terms of not only their strengths and skills but also their flaws and vulnerabilities. The Gestalt coaching presence requires what Yontef (2002: 18) describes as '*authenticity, transparency, and humility*'.

Starting from this position the Gestalt coach strives to develop a particular quality of interaction grounded in inclusion, collaborative partnership, strong contact and a commitment to dialogue. The coach is encouraged to learn the messages from relational Gestalt therapy, and from relational therapy in general, of the importance of compassion, kindness, empathy and humility. The Gestalt coach works as much from their heart as from their head and gut.

However, this emphasis on supportive, empathic behaviours doesn't simply mean 'being nice'. There is a time when the most supportive thing a coach can do is to bring a tough, challenging presence. Coachees can be complex, confusing, frustrating, irritating and downright ingenuous. Sometimes they will criticize and blame the coach when the responsibility for the issue lies primarily with them. There will be occasions when it seems impossible to reach and make connection with the coachee. These are the times when the coach's commitment to 'unconditional positive regard' will be most severely tested. The clue here is in the word authenticity; to be authentic requires honesty. When the coach steps too far back from that he/she will not be fully present or available to engage in genuine dialogue.

Implicit in the Gestalt relational approach is the notion that the coach as well as the coachee will be potentially changed by the work undertaken together. The coach should expect to be moved and impacted by the process. The coachees' story, their struggles, their joys and their pain will touch you and remind you of your own. The very nature of the dialogue requires this openness to meeting at the boundary, where the coachee may never have been before, especially in the professional environment.

Dialogue moves beyond discussion when what Buber referred to as the I–It relationship is transformed into I–Thou connecting. When we are related to as an 'It' we feel like an object. The coachee could be talking to anyone. When we are related to as 'Thou' we experience our personhood. The contact becomes more real, immediate and interesting.

The challenge then for the Gestalt coach is to get into contact with their coachee, work with the emerging process, and let go of the need for certainty and control. This involves what Yontef (2002: 18) calls 'surrendering to the between', that which is co-created by both coach and coachee. Allan and Whybrow (2007: 136) describe how the

> attention to the relationship and the spirit of enquiry means that something new can emerge that was not in the minds of either party when the dialogue started. It is in this potentially very creative way that something completely appropriate for the current situation is generated.

It is here that we capture the essence of Gestalt: that the *whole can be greater than the sum of the parts*.

If the coach is genuinely engaged in the experience there will be learning and growth available for them also. If the coach stays firmly in control and is unable to surrender to the 'in-between' then opportunities for learning will be missed and the message to the coachee is that coaching is a one-way learning process. For sure, many senior executives will not respond well to this.

The implications of the Gestalt relational approach may present as intriguing and exciting with the possibility of a high level of practitioner satisfaction. That much is undoubtedly true but the approach can look equally daunting. To be appropriately transparent to others and present oneself in a genuine manner requires a good deal of personal courage as well as comfort in one's own skin. It may seem far easier and safer to adopt a quasi 'doctor–patient' relationship and hide behind the protection of the expert role.

This traditional 'helper-helped' model will also be nearer to what many coachees expect from their coaching engagement, at least in the first instance. Coachees often assume that the coach will take charge and provide the direction for the coaching. The Gestalt approach can therefore seem at odds with their expectations.

All this probably points to the best-fit coaching clients for a Gestalt approach. They are likely to be relational and reflective by nature with a healthy interest in their interior as well as exterior worlds, have a strong sense of their inner authority and not be overly needy of structure and certainty.

APPLICATIONS OF GESTALT COACHING

In a very real sense Gestalt principles and methods underpin all coaching and mentoring practice whether delivered by externals or internals in organizations, conducted with teams or individuals, designed to address performance or developmental agendas, or offered in the wider life context. This is because *all good coaching and mentoring is based on raising awareness as the starting point for learning and change*. In that sense any and every coach can benefit from a certain amount of Gestalt training and Gestalt-based coaching can be used in all coaching contexts.

That said, there are reasons why some contexts will be more appropriate than others. The manager as coach, being asked by his/her company to adopt more of a coaching style of management, will at best receive no more than a short training in coaching skills, usually two to five days in duration. It will probably focus around a model such as GROW and involve a limited amount of practice. The internalizing of a Gestalt informed conceptual and methodological framework in such a short developmental timeframe is unrealistic and is therefore rarely used in this context. We should not fail to notice however that the R in GROW stands for Reality and is the equivalent to the 'What is' in Gestalt. The Gestalt contribution to coaches using the GROW model would be to raise awareness more fully before rushing to Options.

The best-fit contexts for a Gestalt coaching approach are *executive/leadership coaching, developmental coaching, team coaching and life coaching*. Coaches operating in these contexts often bring previous relevant training and development, which prepares them for working in this way. A significant proportion of executive coaches and some life coaches come from psychological, psychotherapeutic, or counselling backgrounds where they may have already undertaken a primary or secondary level of Gestalt education.

These four coaching contexts also tend to give the coach longer to work with their coachee or client system (team). This is important to the Gestalt coach because it provides the opportunity to more deeply understand the coachees' process, gain a better sense of their habitual behavioural and ideational patterns, and explore how these serve them well and how they interfere with the achievement of their goals. This is equally true in the team context where suboptimal group dynamics, team norms and behaviours may be blocking high performance.

EVALUATION OF THE THEORY

The key strengths lie in the optimism, directness and power inherent in the Gestalt approach. Organizational life, indeed life in general, forces people to address an increasing level of complexity and chaos. Leaders and managers often experience prolonged periods of anxiety from living life in the executive fast lane. They have to dig deep into their capacity to self-support. This can challenge their capacity to stay optimistic, positive and healthy. They can get stuck in negative spirals for prolonged periods yet hardly appreciate the effect on their own well-being, let alone on their colleagues and close ones. The freeing up of that energy, releasing the person from being trapped in unfinished business or redundant ways of seeing and acting can be nothing short of liberating and life-enhancing.

To work in a Gestalt way the coach needs to adopt a positive, optimistic, supportive stance and offer what Siminovitch and Van Eron (2006: 51) call 'a safe arena where vulnerability, strong emotions and failure can play themselves out in the service of learning and growth'. Finding such a place for deeper reflection and self disclosure is rare for business leaders who typically believe that they must remain self-contained and on guard.

Nonetheless, the Gestalt method will be countercultural for some coachees. The deceptively simple yet immensely profound notion that awareness itself leads to change, and that change happens just by paying attention to 'what is' rarely forms part of a coachees' mental models. Executives may be sceptical of it and impatient to see proof. If they don't see it quickly they can lose interest and commitment. Some managers and leaders operating in fast-paced, numbers-driven business environments may not be the natural client group for Gestalt coaching. Awareness-focused work may seem just too slow for them. This type of client also tends to see results only in terms of tangible outcomes and benefits. If the session hasn't produced a concrete action plan then it may be dismissed as too esoteric or subtle.

In corporate life, executive coaches are often labelled in either of two ways by their clients – white coats or suits. Gestalt coaches with a strong therapeutic background but less consultancy experience can be in danger of confusing the boundaries between therapy and coaching. There are occasions in coaching when the coachees' presenting issues could suggest a therapeutic response. Well-trained and supervised coaches become aware that in these moments, despite any glaring therapeutic issues facing them, they need to resist the clinical invitation.

Though the Gestalt coach may sometimes need to step back from more intensive personal growth work, the Gestalt approach nevertheless offers great scope for satisfaction in the role. The emphasis on Presence and the Use of Self as Instrument invites the coach to bring themselves more fully to what they do. This is not a method that asks the coach to fit into a mould or to learn a set of tools and techniques to operate on someone else. From a Gestalt perspective the coach is the instrument of change.

With this comes the hard and disciplined part. If coaches are going to intentionally use presence to intervene more effectively, then they have to understand more about who they are and what they bring to the coaching encounter. The critical issue here is the self-development work that this requires. While many coaches recognize this and proactively search out the kinds of places that provide a vehicle for their own learning and growth there are those who back off from the journey. The Gestalt approach may not appeal to them because they can see that it takes a long time, and perhaps some pain along the way, to gain mastery.

Gestalt theory is an eclectic mix of old and new concepts and beliefs. It draws on philosophy, psychology and humanistic psychotherapy to create a broad canvas onto which the practitioner can bring their own unique style and creativity. Because Gestalt is not formulaic or prescriptive the approach is always in a state of emergence as new generations make their own mark in response to the ever-changing field and the contexts in which they work.

What has been important to me about Gestalt is that its philosophical principles draw on deep wisdom that transcends time and speaks to a set of truths that I recognize for myself. In translating those into my own practice as a consultant and coach I find they speak also to others.

FURTHER READING

Bluckert, P. (2006). *Psychological dimensions of executive coaching.* London: Open University Press. (The only coaching book which focuses on the application of Gestalt principles and methods to the executive coaching context.)

Nevis, E.C. (1987). *Organizational consulting: A Gestalt approach.* New York: Gestalt Institute of Cleveland and Gardner Press. (The definitive book on how Gestalt can be applied to organizational consulting.)

Perls, F.S., Hefferline, R.F., & Goodman, P. (1951). *Gestalt therapy.* New York: Julian Press. (The 'bible' of Gestalt therapy and an essential read for all those wanting to gain a fuller appreciation of Gestalt.)

REFERENCES

Allan, J., & Whybrow, A. (2007). Gestalt coaching. In S. Palmer & A. Whybrow (Eds.), *Handbook of coaching psychology.* London and New York: Routledge.

Beisser, A.R. (1970). The paradoxical theory of change. In J. Fagan & I.L Shepherd (Eds.), *Gestalt Therapy Now* (pp. 77–80). New York: Harper and Row.

Bluckert, P. (2006). *Psychological dimensions of executive coaching.* London: Open University Press.

Carter, J. (2004). Carter's cube and a Gestalt/OSD toolbox: A square, a circle, a triangle, and a line. *OD Practitioner,* Special Issue *36*: 4.

Clarkson, P. (2004). *Gestalt counselling in action.* London: Sage.

Hall, C.S., & Lindzey, G. (1957). *Theories of personality.* New York: John Wiley and Sons.

Latner, J. (1992). The theory of Gestalt therapy. In E.C. Nevis (Ed.), *Gestalt therapy: Perspectives and applications.* New York: Gestalt Institute of Cleveland and Gardner Press.

Melnick, J., & Nevis, S.M. (2005). The willing suspension of disbelief: Optimism. *Gestalt Review, 9*: 10–26.

Nevis, E.C. (1987). *Organizational consulting: A Gestalt approach.* New York: Gestalt Institute of Cleveland and Gardner Press.

Perls, F.S., Hefferline, R.F., & Goodman, P. (1951). *Gestalt therapy.* New York: Julian Press.

Saner, R. (1999). Organisational consulting: What a Gestalt approach can learn from Off-Off Broadway Theater. *Gestalt Review, 3*: 6–21.

Siminovitch, D.E., & Van Eron, A.M. (2006). The pragmatics of magic: The work of Gestalt coaching. *OD Practitioner, 38*(1).

Stevenson, H. (2004). *Paradox: The Gestalt theory of change* (unpublished paper). Retrieved from www.cleverlandconsulting-group.com.

Yontef, G. (2002). The relational attitude in Gestalt therapy. *International Gestalt Journal,* 25(1): 15–35.

6

Existential Coaching

Ernesto Spinelli

INTRODUCTION

All human beings share various existential qualities or 'givens' of existence: we experience our existence through our bodies and within conditions of time and space; we struggle with and are sustained by the possibilities and limitations of the meanings we construe about any and every facet of our lives; and we maintain hopes and plans and expectations within the uncertainty and insecurity of lives whose inevitable movement is towards death. At the same time, *how* each of us gives expression to these 'givens' remains unique (Cohn, 1997; Jacobsen, 2007).

Existential coaching explores the primary concerns of coaching – namely, those matters related to professional, managerial and leadership development and performance – from the perspective of the above givens as expressed and lived by individual clients, be they persons or organizations. In general, it is concerned with the life dilemmas that arise as a consequence of changes and circumstances in a broadly organizational context and which impact upon personal and interpersonal relations both within that context and beyond it.

Existential coaching is best understood and practised as a predominantly descriptively focused investigative enterprise. Rather than be primarily concerned with the alteration, reduction, removal or resolution of presenting concerns, existential theory suggests that the coach's principal task is to assist clients in focusing upon their presenting concerns in ways that contextualize them more adequately, within their *worldview* – which is to say, the whole range of beliefs, values, attitudes, assumptions, affects and behaviours that make up, maintain and identify their 'way of being'. Further, existential coaching proposes that clients' concerns are not to be seen as obstacles to the maintenance of the current worldview, but rather as consequential expressions of it. From this perspective, therefore, the issues brought to coaching cannot be dealt with as separate from the whole being who presents them.

Overall, existential coaching adopts a position that is well summarized by the coaching theorist, Peter Bluckert: 'Many … coaches begin with a strong tendency to look for the solution to the client's problem in the external reality – the outer game. They eagerly race towards a practical set of actions before fully understanding the complexities of the issue in the first place' (Bluckert, 2006: 48). As this chapter will seek to clarify, existential coaching contributes to the development of the profession by illuminating many of these complexities and providing coaches with various means with which to work, in ways that may best benefit their clients.

KEY ASSUMPTIONS OF EXISTENTIAL THEORY

Existential theory has no single founder or authoritative source (Yalom, 1980; Cooper, 2003). Nonetheless, its multitude of manifestations agree upon a number of key foundational principles. As has been argued elsewhere (Spinelli, 2007), three of these principles are pivotal in delineating existential theory's stance toward the human condition and, as well, are particularly pertinent to existential coaching practice.

a. Relatedness

At its simplest, the principle of relatedness argues that all attempts to understand or make sense of any being – ourselves included – on its own or in isolation is far too limiting and inadequate. Rather, all beings express themselves through and are shaped by an interrelational grounding or context. All beings are always *beings-in-relation*.

Existential theory's stance toward the principle of relatedness challenges a persistent assumption held by Western culture in general: that the person is a self-contained unit, understandable within his or her own set of subjectively-derived meanings and behaviours. From the standpoint of relatedness, the problems and concerns presented by coaching clients can no longer be seen as being solely their own, in any exclusively individualistic sense. Our particular ways of relating impact upon all other ways of relating and *vice versa*.

In sum, from an existential perspective, human existence reveals 'the total, indissoluble unity or interrelationship of the individual and his or her world … in the truest sense, the person is viewed as having no existence apart from the world and the world as having no existence apart from persons' (Valle & King, 1978: 7).

b. Uncertainty

The second principle espoused by existential theory argues that if all of one's reflective experience and knowledge of self, others and the world in general arises through and within relatedness, then what is revealed is an inevitable and inescapable *uncertainty* or incompleteness in any and all of our reflections.

This uncertainty is not just about the realization that the unexpected can and does occur in our lives. Rather, uncertainty also permeates what appears as the predictable or habitual in our lives. We can never fully know with complete and final certainty what and how the world will be, or others will be, or even 'I' will be, in any given set of circumstances. At any moment, any and every aspect or dispositional quality that makes up a being's worldview may be opened to challenge, reconsideration or dissolution. Common statements such as 'I never thought I would act like that', or 'she seemed to turn into someone I didn't know', or 'I just can't make sense of what's going on in the world any longer' point us to positions that at least temporarily acknowledge the inevitable uncertainties of being.

c. Existential anxiety

Existential theory argues that humans are 'meaning-making' beings. We *interpret* the world via the human process of constructing meaning of those 'things' or events which impinge themselves upon our experience and with which we are in relation. However, if all of our meaning-making is both relationally-derived and uncertain, then it becomes evident that no meanings we construe can ever be said to be final, complete or closed to further possibility. Instead, because they always remain open to the possibility of novel definitions, all our attempts at meaning-making ultimately confront their definitional openness or *meaninglessness.*

Existential anxiety refers first to the uneasy experience accompanying the awareness of the ultimate incompleteness or openness of all our meanings – including, of course, all of those meanings that serve to define and maintain 'the self'. Second, existential anxiety also refers to the inevitable unease and insecurity that arises when we attempt either to deny, or claim to have resolved, the dilemma of meaning – not least, for example when we 'capture' self (and other) into fixed categories, typologies, characteristics and the like.

Existential theory argues that anxiety permeates *all* reflective experience. However, rather than being only or necessarily a debilitating, disruptive or problematic presence that must be reduced or removed, this anxiety can also be stimulating, can put us in touch with our sense of being alive, and is the source to all creative and original insight and decision making. The dilemma raised by existential anxiety is not so much *that* it is, but rather *how* each of us 'lives with' it.

Taken together, these three basic principles give shape to a view of human development that, unlike many others adopted by coaches, rejects any simple uni-directional perspective or 'growth-model'. Instead, it places human beings within a far more open-ended – and hence uncertain – trajectory whose focus and direction cannot be set or maintained by the individual alone. Rather, what developmental possibilities emerge are always sourced within an interrelational context, remain uncertain and will always provoke some felt sense of unease.

ESSENTIAL PROCESSES AND DYNAMICS

Following on from the above summary of its key principles, it can be seen that existential theory highlights the human experience of an ever-present tension between certainty and uncertainty, between the demand for a fixed and final truth and being 'true to' what presents itself to our lived experience. One useful way to explore this tension is through the polarity of *meaning* and *meaninglessness*.

As was proposed above, a primary characteristic of being human is that we are meaning-making beings. Our encounters with the unknown or uncertain – or broadly speaking, with what is labelled initially as meaningless – provoke the quest to discern (or construct) their meaning (Spinelli, 2005, 2007). Equally, we typically protect ourselves against instances of, or confrontations with, meaninglessness, by adopting rigid stances toward – or *sedimenting* – many of our lived meanings so that they become inflexible 'truths' or dogmas impervious to experiential data that may challenge or contradict them. Each one of us develops a 'life project' (Sartre, 1956) – which includes our goals, our values, our ways of understanding and responding to the expected and the unexpected in our lives – that reveals how, as individuals, we have found means to 'navigate' our way through the inevitable polarity of meaning/meaninglessness.

The worldview can be seen to be a dynamic expression of this life project in that it reflects and contains our attempts to come to terms with polarities such as meaning/meaninglessness. Just as the meaning components of the worldview provide us with the experience of security, certainty, stability, identity and predictability, the worldview possibilities of change, growth and novel possibilities can only occur through our openness toward meaninglessness. Tensions between meaning and meaninglessness can be disturbing and debilitating. However, they are also the means to our creativity, discovery, playfulness and imagination.

If we think of meaning/meaninglessness as complementary end-points along a continuum, each of us can 'locate' him or herself at some point along that continuum. One way of considering the dilemmas presented by coaching clients is to view them as life challenges that have provoked a location disturbance along a polarity continuum (May, 1994). This (usually) temporary sense of dislocation can be experienced as either stimulating or disquieting. Those challenges that we experience as stimulating suggest our willingness to dislocate ourselves from a particular point in our existential continuum and to explore those possibilities that are likely to lead to some sort of relocation. Alternatively, those challenges that provoke increasing levels of disquiet and disorder suggest that the person's response to existential dislocation is one that seeks to avoid or deny that challenge and thereby return or remain at the point in the continuum where he or she currently locates him or herself.

Considering this stance from a coaching standpoint, what on the surface may appear to be the same source of challenge, conflict or disturbance for a person or an organization may not actually be so, since it is only by considering the relationship between that challenge and any particular worldview that the specific impact of that challenge can be discerned.

All challenges threaten the security brought about by having placed oneself along the contin-uum of a currently-maintained polarity. Existential theory argues that in order for the coach to assist clients as adequately as possible, it is critical to clarify just how that sense of security has been disturbed and what sort of disturbing impact is being experienced by the client's worldview.

For example in some instances the client's presenting issues arise from challenges to the worldview that reflect a gap or *dissonance* between one or several rigid or sedimented meanings and the actual experiences of being that disconfirm, or contradict those meaning stances. For example:

a) Arthur insists that he is a team player and an excellent listener, but has been confronted with statements from his team that present him as a bully who is often uninterested in views and concerns raised by others.
b) An organization presents itself as a leader in change but is deeply resistant to novel possibilities in management.

The above examples reveal dissonances between sedimented meanings and lived experience. From the focus point of meaning/meaninglessness, they reveal a dislocation along that polarity. This disturbance can only be adequately resolved through relocation along the continuum. Dynamically speaking, this involves a temporary step into meaninglessness so that a more adequate and effective meaning might emerge. For example:

a) Arthur accepts that his view of himself as always being a team player and an excellent listener is inadequate. Instead, it is more accurate for him to state that he would like to be so and that in the eyes of others he can be seen to be quite the opposite.
b) The organization acknowledges that its view of itself as a leader in change is currently inadequate and sets about reorganizing its management structure so that it is more in keeping with its philosophy.

However, coaching issues may arise under a second, and quite differing, set of circumstances. In this case, the experience of existential dislocation is provoked by challenges that are *consonant* with the client's continuum location. Rather than reveal a lack of fit, or tension, between contradictory or competing meaning-derived stances, the source of disturbance lies in unexpected or undesired expressions of previously unforeseen or insufficiently considered consequences of the currently-maintained worldview. For example:

a) Joanna insists that she is always blunt and honest in her corporate evaluations, and this makes her feel alone, isolated and unappreciated by others.
b) An organization presents itself as a leader in change and this limits the number of desirable managers who will work well within it or who are willing to remain associated with it.

The above examples reveal a tension that arises within a meaning stance that 'fits' or is conso-nant with the worldview. In other words, the presenting issues *arise from* or are consequential expressions of having located oneself along a particular continuum. From the focus point of meaning/meaninglessness, they reveal unexpected or undesired consequences of maintaining, or being consonant with, a particular location along that polarity. This disturbance cannot be properly resolved through relocation along the continuum. Rather, what is required is a temporary step into meaninglessness that will permit the acceptance of previously unconsidered, unexpected and uneasy consequences that emerge simply by locating oneself along a polarity continuum. For example:

a) Joanna realizes that she places a critical value upon her blunt honesty, and while this does not alter her experience of aloneness, isolation, lack of appreciation by others, she discovers a resoluteness that she did not previously appreciate.

b The organization explores its own attitude to change by investigating what it is about its identity, ethos or structure that may be hampering its quest for suitable managers. In doing so, it adjusts the various ways by which it seeks out suitable managers.

Existential coaching argues that it is essential to discern whether any client's presenting issues reveal either dissonant or consonant tensions, since each expresses quite differing concerns. This difference is missed by many coaches who tend to assume that their clients' issues are always and only expressions of dissonance. As a consequence, their interventions may, at best, be unhelpful and, at worst, may provoke far greater disturbances for their clients.

In addition, through its assumption of a foundational interrelatedness, existential theory argues that it is important for coaches to recognize that a change in any *one* aspect of the world-view will alter the *whole* of it (Ihde, 1986; Spinelli, 2005). As such, the consequences of any step taken toward the resolution of either dissonant or consonant issues cannot be known in advance. What we do know is that what might appear in theory to be a minor shift can have dramatic repercussions that may well be undesirable, unexpected and ultimately more debilitating than the initial presenting conflict. For example:

a) Armand realizes that he has always had great difficulty in developing a close friendship bond with other men. Through coaching, he decides to alter this and joins an 'Iron John' type men's group. In doing so, he achieves his desired goal but also experiences unexpected consequences. He finds himself sexually attracted to a number of men with whom he has become close. How will this affect Armand's marriage? How will it affect Armand's sense of himself in terms of sexual orientation? Or his sense of himself in general? How will it affect his relations with his wife? His children? His friends?

b) An organization decides that it is time to change its logo. It does so and is satisfied with the predicted results in that the logo provokes positive perceptions both within the organization and from its customer base with regard to various desirable identifying features. At the same time, however, such shifts in perception have an unexpected and not always desirable impact. For instance, they extend to ways in which management meetings are conducted, in employees' sense of belonging to and responsibility for the organization and in the rise of different demands and expectations from its customer base.

Such examples, which are by no means unusual, highlight existential theory's advocacy of coaches adopting a cautious stance in their desire, or indeed, insistence, to promote change. Once again, any coach-directed tampering with the presenting issues without sufficiently understanding their relatedness to the client's worldview might well create far greater distress and unease in living than did the original presenting problem.

ROLE OF THE EXISTENTIAL COACH IN THE COACHING RELATIONSHIP

Overall, the existential coach's primary role lies in the attempt to *be with* and *be for* the client. In *being with* the client, existential coaches seek to give expression to their respect for, and acceptance of, their client's worldview as it presents itself in their current encounter. In *being for* their clients, existential coaches express their willingness to attempt a challenging, non-judgmental descriptively-focused exploration of that worldview.

In this dual aim, they seek first to disclose, together with their client, the underlying, often implicit and inadequately acknowledged values, beliefs, assumptions, attitudinal stances and their accompanying affective and behavioural components which infuse and maintain the client's worldview. And second, through such explorations, they attempt to illuminate the presenting concerns and issues within the context of that worldview, so that whatever it may be that is being challenged, of or within that worldview, can be clarified and considered.

At the heart of this enterprise lies the attempt to ensure their clients' experience of 'being heard' accurately so that in turn clients may begin to hear their own statements more accurately and honestly. This predominantly receptive stance requires on the part of the coach the abdication of such security that comes with assumptions such as directing change or of 'the expert's' superiority of knowledge and status. Further, the adoption of this stance and attitude removes from coaches much of their professional mystique as well as a good deal of the power that may come with it.

For many coaches, this aspect of existential coaching is likely to be deeply challenging. Rather than focus upon the wisdom of knowledge and authority, the wisdom associated with existential coaching can be seen to be that of un-*knowing* (Spinelli, 1997, 2007). Un-knowing refers to that attempt on the part of the coach to remain as open as possible to that, and only that, which presents itself in the relationship. As such, it expresses the attempt to treat the seemingly familiar, assumed to be understood or understandable, as novel, unfixed in meaning, and, hence, accessible to previously unexamined possibilities. The attempt to 'un-know' directs both the coach's and the client's primary focus to remain on 'what is there' as opposed to 'what once might have been there' or 'what may one day be there'. Further, it challenges the technical authority of the coach as well as the client's own demands to be the recipient of that authority.

Although the stance of un-knowing adopted by existential coaching may, for some coaches, seem unusual or even antithetical to the coaching enterprise, recent views expressed by coaches from differing traditions are in close agreement. For example Graham Lee, an expert in leadership coaching, has written that 'the creation of a learning space depends on a particular quality of the coach that we might describe as "not knowing" ... the coach's capacity for openness, reflection, questioning, wondering and entertaining possibilities ... a willingness to stay with the uncertainties without reaching prematurely for fact or reason' (Lee, 2003: 63).

In adopting this stance of un-knowing, the whole focus of existential coaching centres upon what is taking place *directly* between coach and client. This focus serves to expose and clarify *in the immediacy of the current coaching relationship* the self-same interrelational issues that clients experience within their wider world relations. In other words, from the standpoint of existential theory, the coaching relationship is seen to be the 'microcosm' which both explores and expresses the 'macrocosm' of the client's currently-lived experience (Cohn, 1997; Spinelli, 1997, 2001; Strasser & Strasser, 1997). This view is only just beginning to be addressed by coaching in general. Coaches have tended to be somewhat reluctant, if not unwilling, to bring explicitly this key assumption within existential coaching into their discourse and interventions with their clients. Nonetheless, this reluctance in focusing upon those factors that highlight the immediacy of the coaching relationship has recently been challenged by the coaching theorist, Peter Bluckert, who has written: 'the very dynamics occurring in the coaching relationship may be a mirror image of clients' experiences in their workplace relationships and they may be completely unaware of it' (Bluckert, 2006: 48).

TASKS AND GOALS OF EXISTENTIAL COACHING

Unlike the majority of coaching perspectives that focus upon broadly positive, self-actualizing possibilities for each client, existential coaching recognizes and gives equal emphasis to the divided stances, aims and aspirations that may well exist as competing values and beliefs held by them. In general, existential theory argues that the client's experience of 'what and how it is for me to exist' is rarely entirely complete, coherent or consistent. Instead it reveals 'a complex combination of opposites, some reconcilable, others incapable of being resolved or harmonised' (Cherniss, 2006, as cited in Gray, 2006: 21).

While by no means dismissive of problem- or solution-focused interventions, existential coaching urges patience and caution in providing such without first considering the impacting concerns and issues being presented in relation to the specific worldview of the client. Not to do so might well generate unhelpful solutions that do not sufficiently address the primary concerns being raised for that particular client. Equally, although the solutions provided may well minimize or remove presenting problems, the very removal or reduction of such may bring to light far more disquieting concerns. In other words, presenting problems, issues and concerns are often 'not just' problems – they are also attempted solutions, whose purpose is to protect and maintain the worldview from far more disturbing challenges.

Paradoxically, existential coaching argues that beneficial change may best emerge via the very process of assisting clients to 'stay still' so that they can better explore, evaluate and come to terms with their currently-lived worldview and its experiential consequences.

METHODS AND TECHNIQUES FOR FACILITATION OF CHANGE

Existential coaching neither embraces nor dismisses any particular method or technique available to coaches so long as the technique serves the primary enterprise of a descriptively-focused exploration of the client's worldview from the contextual focus of the client's presenting concerns. Nonetheless, this focus on descriptive exploration requires coaches to develop specific attitudes and skills designed to assist descriptively-focused enquiry. Two such approaches can be briefly summarized:

a) The phenomenological method

One particularly useful and powerful way to assist the coach in becoming attuned to the client's worldview as it expresses itself is to apply what has become known as *the phenomenological method* of investigation. This method can be most easily summarized by highlighting three pivotal 'steps' (Ihde, 1986; Spinelli, 2005, 2007).

Step one: Bracketing
This first step urges coaches to set aside their initial biases and prejudices, to suspend expectations and assumptions – in short, to *bracket* all presuppositions regarding the client as far as is possible. Instead, coaches are encouraged to attune their focus to 'what presents itself as it presents itself' so that the client's currently lived worldview can be more adequately disclosed and, in turn, so that any subsequent reconstructions of it will fit its meanings and values.

Step two: Description
The second step enjoins coaches to: 'describe, don't explain'. Rather than attempt to immediately analyse or transform the client's concerns on the basis of the coaches' preferred theories or hypotheses, the step of description urges them to remain initially focused on that information which arises from a concretely-based descriptive exploration of the client's worldview. The focus of this step centres more on the elaboration of the 'what and how' of a client's experience than it does on the explanation of its 'why'.

Step three: Horizontalization
The third step further advises coaches to avoid placing any unsubstantiated hierarchies of significance or importance upon the client's statements of experience, and instead to treat each as initially having equal value. It proposes that coaches avoid jumping to conclusions as to what really matters to the client or, indeed, what it may be that the client is seeking to address and resolve. In essence, horizontalization reminds coaches to treat the import and significance of all statements made by clients as being initially unknown to them.

Even from this very brief summary, it should be apparent that each 'step' in the phenomenological method is, more accurately, a particular point of focus rather than an entirely independent activity that can be wholly distinguished from the remaining two. Equally, any attempt to carry out the phenomenological method will reveal the impossibility of its fulfilment. Even so, while coaches may be unable to achieve complete bracketing, pure description or total horizontalization, they are certainly capable of attempting each with increasing adequacy and, by so doing, are likely to become more aware of any number of unintended and undesirable biases that dominate their investigations. What is more, this self-same act of bias recognition can invoke for the coach a greater degree of caution in adhering too closely or uncritically to the immediate prejudices that he or she may have imposed upon the investigation from its earliest stages.

b) Descriptive questioning

An extension of the phenomenological method that has been proposed by the present author emphasizes a form of enquiry designed to clarify a client's experience from the standpoints of its *embodiment, metaphorical equivalence* and *narrational parallels* (Spinelli, 2007).

Viewed existentially, many statements made by clients regarding their experiences of someone or of some event (such as 'I'm depressed', 'I'm so angry', 'I'm not sure what to do' and so forth) *suggest* a clear and understandable meaning but are descriptively far too abstract and detached from the client's lived experience of them. Descriptive questioning provokes a more descriptively adequate set of statements regarding the experience and, by so doing, re-awakens their felt experience in the immediacy of the coaching relationship. In general, descriptive questioning concerns itself with the attempt to clarify clients' relations to their felt experience so that these are more adequately 'owned' by or accessible to them. A brief example should clarify each of these descriptive focus points.

Alice, a senior manager in an international organization, has come to coaching because she wants to explore future directions for her career. She states that she 'feels blocked' and can see nothing in her future that excites or stimulates her.

From the standpoint of *embodiment*, descriptive questioning assists Alice in locating her experience of 'feeling blocked', either in parts or the whole of her body. For instance: 'Where, if anywhere, in her body does she experience "feeling blocked"?' What, more precisely, is that feeling? What effect does it have upon the whole or parts of her body? Does it provoke particular statements and emotions?'

From the standpoint of *metaphorical equivalence*, descriptive questioning urges Alice to explore what the experience of 'feeling blocked' is *like* for her. For instance: 'If it were like a shape, an object, a sound, a colour, a song, a statement and so forth, what would it be?'

From the standpoint of *narrational parallels,* descriptive questioning encourages Alice to focus on stories or narratives from her own, or others' (including fictional others') lives that capture the experience 'feeling blocked' in order to bring a narrative focus to her attempts at description.

APPLICATION TO SPECIFIC COACHING CONTEXTS AND GENRES

It can be argued that the existential approach is amenable to every form of coaching, since all of the concerns relevant to coaching, from career and performance issues to matters of leadership and managerial development or transformation, are most usefully explored when considered in relation to the specific context of a person's overall stance and outlook to self, others and life in general. Nonetheless, the approach is particularly useful when working with issues of transition or progression and advancement in work, where dilemmas are often about reconstituting identity, regaining meaning at work, or dealing with lost possibilities and legacy. In addition, existential coaching may be especially valuable when working with clients who find themselves at a crisis point in their lives, who have come up against a loss of meaning or direction, or who are attempting to cope with sudden and dramatic changes in a variety of professional or personal circumstances. Similarly, those clients who enter a foreign culture or who are members of a minority group within a dominant organizational or cultural ethos may find existential coaching to be of particular worth.

In general, those clients who value the reflective, exploratory and challenging qualities of existential coaching are likely to most benefit from it. It is equally likely, however, that some clients will struggle with its emphasis on descriptive exploration rather than prescriptive change or goal-setting.

EVALUATION OF EXISTENTIAL COACHING

Overall, existential coaching's emphasis on 'being qualities' and meaning exploration, as opposed to the development and refinement of the coach's 'doing' skills and repertoire, runs counter to current dominant assumptions and emphases within coaching as a whole. Whether this divergence will eventually prove to be its greatest strength or weakness remains to be seen. Even so, while it is undoubtedly less focused upon providing the means for immediate shifts in specific behaviours and performance, its concern to extend clients' understanding of their stance to life and how this stance impacts upon their behaviour is as likely to provoke performance-focused change as is any other model of coaching.

What direct research evidence currently exists for the effectiveness of existential coaching is extremely limited. In part, this is likely due to the currently small number of coaches who have trained sufficiently to practise this approach. Equally, its philosophical assumptions reveal a decidedly different set of principles from those of dominant empirical models regarding what constitutes evidence and how such may be examined (Spinelli, 2005). Whether these principles can be 'translated' in order that they may be examined and tested within the criteria set by dominant perspectives also remains, as yet, uncertain.

Having said this, clients' self reports related to the outcomes associated with this approach are generally highly positive and emphasize the felt sense of a greater congruence with lived experience and through this, a greater clarity regarding aims, values and identity. Within the context of executive and transformational coaching, clients have reported improvements in managing complexity, ambiguity and anxiety as well as a greater degree of personal and inter-personal responsibility.

While it can stand as a model of coaching in its own right, the descriptive focus that is so central to existential enquiry can assist coaches from whatever orientation or model to consider more adequately and more clearly their own stance, and to recognize how they may be confused or uncertain about various basic principles or practices that their model espouses. In short, existential enquiry can assist both coaches and their clients in 'owning' their experiences, approach, values and beliefs so that their concerns can be more adequately explored.

Some coaches have argued that the existential perspective emphasizes a self-serving individualism that might damage both individuals and organizations (Peltier, 2001). As this chapter has sought to highlight, this view is a serious misreading of existential theory in that it distorts one of its key principles. Rather than foster an individualistic ethos that separates self from others, or the client from his or her life and work conditions and relations, the existential approach asserts the necessity to acknowledge and place oneself in an interrelational context. In coaching, this relational perspective emerges in various ways, such as the encouragement of a stance toward responsibility that is relationally-attuned rather than solely individually focused.

Following on from this last point, it is the view of the present author that in locating itself within a predominantly organizational context, coaching (however unwillingly or inadvertently) is also adopting a relationally-attuned or interrelational perspective akin to that which lies at the heart of existential thought and practice. While an increasing number of coaches and coaching trainers have sought to demonstrate that it is this very same interrelational assumption that provides a baseline grounding in the clarification, challenge and attempted resolution of the issues being brought by coaching clients (Sieler, 2003), the revolutionary impact of this perspective has not yet been sufficiently addressed nor considered. Existential coaching is currently at the forefront of such explorations and, in the long term, this may well turn out to be its most significant contribution to the advancement of the coaching profession.

FURTHER READING

There exists, at present, very little literature on existential coaching – a situation that hopefully will be rectified in the near future. However, many of the central ideas and practices that would inform existential coaching have been elaborated in writings dealing with existential psychology and therapy. Among these, I would recommend the following to interested readers:

Jacobsen, B. (2007). *Invitation to existential psychology.* Chichester: Wiley.

Spinelli, E. (1997). *Tales of un-knowing: therapeutic encounters from an existential perspective.* London: Duckworth.

Spinelli, E. (2007). *Practising existential psychotherapy: The relational world.* London: Sage.

van Deurzen, E. (2001). *Existential counselling and psychotherapy in practice.* London: Sage.

Yalom, I. (1980). *Existential psychotherapy.* New York: Basic Books.

These texts have been noted by reviewers as particularly clear and accessible accounts of existential theory. In addition, all provide examples from general life and professional practice to which many coaches can connect both personally and professionally.

As well as the above, I would highlight three books in particular which, while not strictly within the existential tradition, address similar views and concerns within a specific coaching context.

Bluckert, P. (2006). *Psychological dimensions of executive coaching.* Berkshire: Open University Press.

Senge, P., Scharmer, C.O., Jaworski, J., & Flowers, B.S. (2005). *Presence: An exploration of profound change in people, organizations, and society.* New York: Currency.

Sieler, A. (2003). C*oaching to the human soul: Ontological coaching and deep change.* Blackburn, Victoria: Newfield Australia.

Peter Bluckert's writings are informed by the Gestalt tradition and emphasize the critical significance of the coaching relationship itself. Alan Sieler's advocacy of a being-focused (ontological) approach to coaching raises numerous perspectives that resonate with existential theory and practice. His focus on embodiment is particularly relevant. Peter Senge and his associates have produced an exceptional and eloquent text that should be read by all coaches. Their idea of *Presence* – that is to say, the interconnectedness between the whole and its parts and the influences of change in the latter upon the former – addresses a crucial existential theme in a manner that is particularly relevant and accessible to coaches.

REFERENCES

Bluckert, P. (2006). *Psychological dimensions of executive coaching.* Berkshire: Open University Press.

Cherniss, J. (2006). Introduction to *Political ideas in the romantic age: Their rise and influence on modern thought* by I. Berlin. Princeton, NJ: Princeton University Press.

Cohn, H.W. (1997). *Existential thought and therapeutic practice.* London: Sage.

Cooper, M. (2003). *Existential therapies.* London: Sage.

Gray, J. (2006). The case for decency. *New York Review of Books,* LIII(12): 20–2.

Ihde, D. (1986). *Experimental phenomenology: An introduction.* Albany, NY: State University of New York.

Jacobsen, B. (2007). *Invitation to existential psychology.* Chichester: Wiley.

Lee, G. (2003). *Leadership coaching.* London: CIPD.

May, R. (1994). *The discovery of being.* New York: Norton.

Peltier, B. (2001). *The psychology of executive coaching: Theory and application.* New York: Brunner-Routledge.

Sartre, J.P. (1956). Being and nothingness: An essay on phenomenological ontology (trans. H. Barnes). London: Routledge.

Sieler, A. (2003). C*oaching to the human soul: Ontological coaching and deep change.* Blackburn, Victoria: Newfield Australia.

Spinelli, E. (1997). *Tales of un-knowing: Therapeutic encounters from an existential perspective.* London: Duckworth.

Spinelli, E. (2001). *The mirror and the hammer: Existential challenges to therapeutic orthodoxy.* London: Sage.

Spinelli, E. (2005). *The interpreted world: An introduction to phenomenological psychology* (2nd ed.). London: Sage.

Spinelli, E. (2007). *Practising existential psychotherapy: The relational world.* London: Sage.

Strasser, F., & Strasser, A. (1997). *Existential time-limited therapy: The wheel of existence.* Chichester: Wiley.

Valle, R.S., & King, M. (1978). *Existential-phenomenological alternatives for psychology.* Oxford: Oxford University Press.

Yalom, I. (1980). *Existential psychotherapy.* New York: Basic Books.

7

Ontological Coaching

Alan Sieler

INTRODUCTION

This chapter introduces an ontological approach to coaching. The theoretical basis, premises and methodology of ontological coaching are outlined and examples that demonstrate the applicability of the ontological methodology to organizational coaching and life coaching are provided. Ontological coaching is also contrasted with other approaches to coaching and an evaluation made of its strengths, benefits and weaknesses.

Ontology is the study of being, in particular the investigation of the nature of human existence (Honderich, 1995). There are four interrelated components of the theoretical basis of ontological coaching. Heidegger's phenomenological analysis of being (Heidegger, 1962, 1971, 1999), supported by Gadamar's approach to hermeneutics (Gadamer, 1994), forms a major philosophical cornerstone of ontological coaching. Maturana's biology of cognition (Maturana and Varela, 1980, 1987) comprises the second part of ontological coaching's theoretical basis, with the work of Wittgenstein (1958), Searle (1969, 1979) and Austin (1973) in the philosophy of language being the third component. The fourth component is provided by philosophical investigations of the body, in particular the writings of Merleau-Ponty (1962) and Dewey (1929).

Flores integrated of the ideas of Heidegger, Gadamer, Maturana and Searle (Winograd and Flores, 1986) to form an initial body of knowledge, now known as Ontology of the Human Observer (Sieler, 2003).

THE THEORETICAL BASIS OF ONTOLOGICAL COACHING

From his empirical research on the neurophysiology of vision, Maturana (Maturana et al., 1958, 1968; Lettvin et al., 1968) demonstrated that the structure and activity of the nervous system, not events in the world, is the critical factor in the formation of reality, a phenomenon he named *structural determinism*. Maturana's research conclusion is aligned with Heidegger's argument, that humans are interpretive beings, not simply rational beings that operate in an objective world, demonstrated in his presentation of listening as *already listening*, which is the pre-understanding or existing frames of meaning that people bring to the situations they encounter.

Maturana and Heidegger each emphasized the self-referential nature of being. Maturana identified *autopoeisis* (self-production) to be the fundamental mechanism of living systems, as they continually ensure the maintenance of their self-producing capacity. Heidegger contended that humans are always oriented to the world by what they care about, engaging in 'concernful activity' to address what matters for them, i.e. their *concerns*.

Heidegger and Maturana also emphasized the interactive nature of human existence. For Heidegger the essence of being is being-in-the-world (Dasein), being immersed in the activity of everyday living, learning how to adjust to and skilfully cope with the requirements of life in our dealings with others and technology. Maturana claims that cognition is primarily an interactive phenomenon. Because of the plasticity (changeability) of the nervous system, biological entities continually perturb or influence the structure of one another's nervous systems, which Maturana refers to as *structural coupling*. Such change is not a direct cause-and-effect phenomenon because the structure of the nervous system modulates the effects of interactions.

Along with philosophers of language, Heidegger and Maturana highlighted the centrality of language in the formation of reality. Maturana used the expression 'languaging' to highlight language as a process that 'brings forth a world' and for Heidegger 'language is the house of being'. Following work by Wittgenstein and Austin that demonstrated that (i) language is a fundamental form of human activity and (ii) words create effects in the world (Wittgenstein, 1958; Austin, 1973), in the theory of speech acts Searle identified specific ways that language generates reality (Searle, 1969, 1979).

Maturana and Heidegger also recognized the emotional and somatic dimensions of everyday living. Maturana regarded conversation as the basic unit of human interaction, consisting of the 'braiding' of language and emotions, involving dynamic body postures (Maturana, 1988: 48–9). Heidegger claimed that we comport ourselves towards the world, with moods being indicative of our orientation to life and what we care about. We are always in a mood, with a continual challenge to be the master of our moods (Heidegger, 1962).

Nietzsche captured the pivotal role of the body when he wrote, 'Our most sacred convictions are … judgements of our muscles' (Nietzsche, 1968: 173). Merleau-Ponty's in-depth analysis of the body, positioning perception as a somatic phenomenon (Merleau-Ponty, 1962), as well as the philosophy of Dewey (1929), gave philosophical substance to Nietzsche's expression.

Within the theory that underpins Ontological Coaching at least five premises can be identified.

1. Humans exist in three interrelated domains of language, emotions and body; what takes place in people's lives occurs in these domains.
2. The dynamic interplay between the three existential domains of language, emotions and body shapes perception and behaviour, and can be equated to the structure of the nervous system.
3. Humans are self-referencing beings: how the world is viewed and engaged with is always relative to what is important or deeply matters in the world of the individual, i.e. his or her concerns.
4. Humans are relational and conversational beings interacting with the world from their existential domains to take care of concerns.
5. Change occurs through the domains of language, emotions and body being perturbed to generate new meaning.

GOALS AND TASKS OF ONTOLOGICAL COACHING

In ontological coaching the dynamic interplay between language, emotions and body is referred to as the *Way of Being*. The essential goal of the coach is to be a catalyst for change by respectfully and constructively triggering a shift in the coachee's way of being to enable him or her to develop perceptions and behaviours that were previously unavailable, all of which are consistent with what the coachee wants to gain from coaching.

A primary responsibility of an ontological coach is to manage his or her own way of being in the coaching conversation. The only place he or she can coach from is their own way of being, which will affect how (i) acutely they observe the specifics of the coachee's way of being and (ii) they facilitate potential shifts in the coachee's way of being. For example prior to a coaching appointment with a senior executive in a major finance corporation, a coach recognized feeling intimidated by the coachee, being anxious and having negative thoughts about being equal to the task of coaching someone so senior in the organization. He could not shift feeling intimidated merely by changing his thoughts, so focused on his body and breathing, adopting a posture and breathing pattern from which he felt competent and confident, practising this as he walked to the appointment and maintaining it during the conversation.

A critical task for the coach is to create a safe environment for inquiry, learning and discovery through a deeply respectful professional relationship with the coachee. This means regarding the coachee as a *legitimate other.* Two challenges in maintaining a safe environment are: (i) respectfully initiating a different and potentially sensitive direction in the conversation; and (ii) the coach not being too attached to his or her ideas of where the conversation 'should go'.

For example a coachee identified improving self-confidence as the key coaching issue. The coach assessed that the coachee had a negative view of herself (referred to as a core negative self-assessment in ontological coaching) that she was not aware of. The coach said, 'Sometimes we get in our own way by having one or more negative opinions about ourselves without knowing this. I'm wondering if you would like to explore whether you do have a negative view of yourself which is holding you back?'

The main benefit of ontological coaching is enabling the coachee to observe and shift aspects of their own way of being beyond the coaching and therefore enhance their behavioural flexibility for future challenges. For example supporting the coachee to confidently and constructively express her thoughts in business meetings, the coach asked three questions when exploring her future action.

> How will you cue yourself to notice what is happening in your thinking, emotions and posture during the meeting? How exactly will you make the necessary adjustments that will allow you to say what you want to – will it commence with your breathing and posture or with different thoughts? How will you take the posture, breathing, moods and thoughts to other areas of your life?

THE PROCESSES AND FEATURES OF ONTOLOGICAL COACHING

The process of engagement between the ontological coach and coachee revolves around (i) shared understanding of the issue(s) the coachee brings to the conversation and desired coaching outcomes and (ii) the coach's interpretation of the coachee's way of being that underpins his or her issue(s).

Clarifying issues and outcomes is central to the contracting arrangement between coach and coachee. In organizational coaching the coachee's manager may also be part of the contracting and evaluation process, as illustrated in the following example. After a conversation with Stella and her line manager, the following coaching outcomes were identified.

1. First and foremost, greater self-confidence and an enhanced sense of self-worth
2. To be more able to deal with, and express, how she is feeling, rather than keep it inside and get to a breaking point
3. To not to take things personally, which is associated with becoming more resilient
4. To have a more strategic mindset, and not be as operationally oriented – to be able to stand back and observe the bigger picture
5. To express her point of view clearly and firmly in meetings, including having another perspective on senior people present at the meeting
6. To delegate and not be caught up in completing the details of various tasks – to know the deliverables required, where they fit in the larger scheme of things, and to delegate to others in the team
7. Through delegation to gain more from the variety of specialized expertise within her team.

The coach also ensured there was a shared understanding with Stella's manager about observable changes in Stella's behaviour that would be evidence of the fulfilment of the coaching outcomes. These were:

- 'doing less doing', with her team doing much of the detailed work
- asking the appropriate questions – ones that indicated a strategic focus, such as 'How does this relate to the business objectives?'
- being prepared to express well-thought-out 'push-back' or alternative opinions in meetings, especially where more senior personnel were present
- by coping effectively with setbacks, rather than getting down or despondent and dwelling on what 'went wrong', she would move forward to different issues.

After three 90-minute conversations Stella declared she had gained what she wanted from the coaching, rating her self as 8–9 out of 10 on the issues she presented for coaching, compared with 2–3 at the commencement of coaching. Her manager agreed with Stella's assessments stating, 'The coaching has been a very worthwhile investment'.

An important part of the process of ontological coaching is how the coach uses his or her interpretations of the coachee's way of being. Decisions are continually being made about what interpretations are likely to be most relevant and beneficial for the coachee. Part of working respectfully with the coachee consists of a combination of:

- asking questions to affirm if the interpretations are relevant; for example 'What would you say is your mood about this situation? Would it be fair to say that this is a negative mood?'
- presenting distinctions for the coachee to consider; for example 'My guess is that you are experiencing a mood of resentment about this situation. Can I explain what I mean and see if you agree?'

An indispensable part of this process is the coach being open and flexible. Sometimes the conversation may move in a certain direction but not proceed far because it does not 'connect' with the coachee, or he or she does not give permission to proceed further. This is why it is essential that the coach is not attached to his or her interpretations and provides the emotional context for the coachee to decline to respond to the coach's initiative. Ontological distinctions are only useful if they 'hit the mark' and speak to something significant for the coachee, providing a new insight or perspective.

The main features of the methodology of ontological coaching will now be outlined, with coaching examples in each of the three domains of language, emotions and body provided to illustrate the application of the methodology.

Language

One of the premises of ontological coaching is that language generates reality. The coach listens for how the coachee is explicitly and implicitly using language, as well as how he or she is not using language. An ontological coach is specifically listening for the following aspects of language: underlying concerns; basic linguistic acts (renaming of speech acts), including core assessments; types of conversations; and cultural–historical narratives.

Underlying concerns and core assessments are the hidden sides of coachees' language, that is, what exists in their listening that is not being articulated. Every issue for coachees is underpinned by something that matters to them – a concern. Heidegger emphasized that although we are always taking care of concerns, we rarely articulate what our concerns are. It can be especially revealing for coachees to understand what is behind their issue. Some specific questions can be helpful to assist them:

- What is at stake for you here?
- What is missing that is important for you?
- What is not being taken care of that matters to you?

The effect of such questions could be illustrated with an example of working with Helen. Her speciality in a pharmaceutical company is sales management; however, eight months prior she was transferred to an unfamiliar marketing management role, and provided with little support to learn the skills and knowledge for her new role. She seemed good-natured about the experience, saying that was part of corporate life, yet the coach assessed she had been putting on a 'happy face' to herself and the company. Asking how she felt about the way she had been treated by the company revealed that she was upset, as tears welled up. Exploration of underlying concerns through the question 'What wasn't taken care of that deeply mattered to you?' resulted in Helen recognizing that her dignity as a person had not been respected. The theme of taking care of her dignity was primarily explored through the domain of moods and emotions and is outlined in the next section.

The utilization of basic linguistic acts, derived from Searle's set of speech acts (Searle, 1969) is a major feature of the coaching methodology, these being: assertions, declarations, assessments (a subset of declarations), requests, offers and promises. An example illustrates the utilization of some of these acts in coaching conversations.

Jake's work team in the oil industry was consistently well short of meeting its weekly targets for the production of different lubricant products, resulting in delays in customer deliveries. Coaching with Jake and the planner who issued the weekly schedule enabled them to see that the weekly schedule was a *request* and that by not discussing the schedule Jake implicitly accepted it and was making a *promise* or commitment to deliver the weekly target. As a result of the coaching Jake and the planner met every week to discuss the forthcoming schedule to ensure explicit agreement about the weekly target, which is a particular type of conversation called 'conversation for the coordination of action'.

Core assessments are the fundamental beliefs and values people have about themselves, others, their situations in life and the world in general. They are central to how humans function as linguistic beings, providing an 'internal reality' from which the world is observed. A negative core assessment acts like a prison, closing off possibilities and restricting participation in different aspects of life. While these assessments do not 'announce themselves' the coach can discern their likely presence.

Moods and emotions

Moods are subtle, enduring and pervasive emotions, continually influencing perception and behaviour. Ontological coaching utilizes a framework entitled 'Some Basic Moods of Life' (Sieler, 2007), which provides interpretive structures of eight moods. These interpretative structures consist of four components:

(i) how the mood can be created
(ii) the typical linguistic or narrative structure
(iii) the behavioural predispositions
(iv) the likely postural configuration that reflects the embodiment of the mood.

The coach listens for the language of moods as well as observing their somatic manifestation in the coachee's postural configuration.

Returning to the coaching example with Helen in the pharmaceutical company, the coach noted that in the realization that her dignity had not been taken care of, Helen had mentioned that the situation was not fair, given her hard work and success in the sales role. An assessment of not being treated fairly is part of the language of the mood of resentment, which is often subtle yet persistent and pervasive anger. Helen was not comfortable with saying she was angry but she could see how she continually had this feeling of being 'put upon' that had not gone away, that she was resentful and her enthusiasm and energy for her work had been dampened.

In the previous example of coaching Stella on the key issue of lack of confidence, she agreed that she lived with a mood of anxiety, which is persistent background fear of things going badly and of not being able to deal with them. The behavioural manifestation of anxiety is consistently being alert for threats and engaging in protective behaviour to avoid the harm that accompanies perceived threats. For Stella, a consistent fear and threat was that others were making negative judgments about her work; consequently she worked long hours at the office and at home to 'cover all bases' in order to ensure she had anticipated and prepared a response to potential criticism.

The domain of the body

The importance of the somatic domain is that it is where the embodiment of change takes place. One procedure that can be highly effective in taking care of concerns and in diminishing the restrictive effects of core negative assessments is the use of the linguistic act of *declaring,* in which specific words are spoken from a body posture and with a voice tonality (indicative of emotional state) that are congruent with the words.

This could be illustrated with an example of coaching Stephen, a highly regarded manager who had been offered the role of Chief Operating Officer in a fast-growing telecommunications company. Despite his excellent record as a manager, Stephen lived from the core negative self-assessments of 'I'm not good enough' and 'I'm not worthy'. After he realized there was no substance to these assessments he was invited to stand and make a declaration. An important part of this procedure is for the coach to (i) suggest and negotiate an appropriate brief statement that will be spoken and (ii) ask coachees to notice how they speak, inviting them to self-assess whether there is congruence between their words, voice tonality and how they are holding their body.

The coach then invites coachees to self-adjust to be more congruent, after which the coach seeks permission to make suggestions. Stephen and the coach worked with the declaration 'I am a legitimate, worthy and competent person, and I am a learner'. Stephen spoke his declaration nine times and despite his strong scepticism about the value of this process was surprised about the noticeably positive difference he felt about himself, which he described as being more solid and assured. He subsequently accepted the role of Chief Operating Officer.

There are three important issues for ontological coaches to continually keep in mind if they are to maintain a constructive relationship with the coachee:

1. *An emotional orientation of humility, and not arrogance.* The coach becomes arrogant by being too attached to his or her own ideas, forgetting that these ideas are interpretations, and falls into the trap of 'knowing' the best direction for the conversation. The coach is always a learner, privileged by the coachee's willingness to be coached and has the responsibility to be at his or her resourceful best, being flexible in how to use his or her expertise for the benefit of the coachee.
2. *Recognizing that the coach does not directly cause change but is a catalyst for change.* As was presented at the beginning of the chapter, a basic principle of the biology of cognition is that change primarily occurs from within the nervous system, as a result of the system being perturbed by an external agent. All a coach can do is perturb the coachee's nervous system and be a trigger for activating a more resourceful way of being. The artistry of ontological coaching is to know how and when to constructively perturb the coachee's way of being.
3. *The courage to be 'respectfully firm'.* There may be occasions when coachees appear to avoid an aspect of their way of being that the coach considers important. In extreme cases, coachees may take over the conversation. It is essential that the coach respectfully maintains his/her authority and is not put 'off balance' by the coachees' behaviour. The ontological coach needs to respectfully share his/her observation/interpretation of the coachees' behaviour, seek his/her response and inquire if there is permission to explore the issue not being addressed.

ONTOLOGICAL COACHING COMPARED WITH OTHER COACHING GENRES

Ontological coaching differs from other coaching traditions in three main ways.

*   explicit focus on way of being
*   equal importance of the three existential domains of language, emotions and body and their dynamic interrelationship in change
*   explicit application of unique concepts and models, such as basic linguistic acts, concerns, identification of specific moods and the narrative and somatic structures of each mood, and the significance of working with postural shifts as the means to the embodiment of a different way of being.

Unlike many other theoretical approaches to coaching covered in this book, ontological coaching does not have a psychological basis. An ontological approach to coaching is grounded in philosophy (as is existential coaching) and the biology of cognition. Unlike psychologically oriented coaching traditions (for example psychodynamic and cognitive-behavioural approaches), ontological coaching is not based on the concept of mind but on the concept of being or, more explicitly, way of being.

Ontological coaching goes beyond Descartes's conception of being human as 'I think, therefore I am'. From an ontological perspective, human cognition is more than thinking. To consider humans only as thinking beings runs the risk of focusing on the domain of language and not explicitly attending to the equally important domains of emotions and body in the facilitation of learning and change. Although other coaching traditions are attentive to the importance of emotions (for example psychodynamic and cognitive-behavioural approaches, Gestalt, NLP, positive psychology) and the body (Gestalt, NLP), ontological coaching's methodology is unique in the explicit integration of language, emotions and body.

While all other coaching traditions work in the domain of language, ontological coaching is differentiated from other traditions by (i) the explicit premise that language generates reality and (ii) the unique techniques that operationalize this premise. The main linguistic techniques of ontological coaching are the:

- application of a unique approach to listening as a critical part of language and its central role in generating reality
- utilization of the model basic linguistic acts to facilitate shifts in speaking and listening
- application of a typology of conversations
- moving beyond the subtle, yet powerful, negative affects of cultural–historical narratives.

While ontological coaches are not body therapists, their focus on the importance of shifts in postural habits and related muscular tension distinguishes ontological coaching from most other approaches to coaching. This is because change occurs in the nervous system and the role of the body in this process cannot be ignored. Somatic shifts are essential to consolidate shifts in the linguistic and emotional domains, and indispensable for sustainable change.

THE APPLICABILITY OF ONTOLOGICAL COACHING

Ontological coaching is applicable to the entire range of coaching contexts and genres covered in Section 2. In reflecting on the coaching engagements with Stella, Helen, Jake and Stephen it can be seen that the genres of skills and performance coaching, leadership coaching and developmental coaching were covered. The relevance of ontological coaching to the manager as coach, executive coaching and cross-cultural coaching is evident in the following examples.

Executive coaching

Working relationships between senior executives and members of the board are critical for the company's future. Sometimes decisions can leave a residue of negativity that persists and compromises relationships, with important business conversations not happening.

As Managing Director of a medium-sized, family-owned bus building company employing 200 people, Giovanni had experienced a significant breakdown with a decision by the Board of Management. They had overruled Giovanni and brought in consultants to look at the company's manufacturing process. Although the consultants had completed their work, and the board's decision had been made more than eight months prior to the coaching conversation, Giovanni said that the decision 'still sticks in my gut'. Giovanni agreed with the coach's interpretation that he was still in a mood of resentment with the board. He did not want to leave the company, yet continually felt negative towards board members, which was 'not helping me or the company'.

Part of the structure of resentment is continuing to fight against, and not accept, what has happened and cannot be changed. Giovanni agreed this was exactly what he had been doing. He said, 'I was professionally slighted by that decision – it was as if I didn't know and all my experience counted for nothing. My thinking has been continually preoccupied with what was done and how I disagreed with it'. Through the conversation he began to more fully appreciate the damaging consequences of his mood and stated, 'It really is time I put this behind me'. The coach worked with Giovanni to facilitate small yet important shifts in his posture to ensure that he no longer held remnants of resentment. This allowed him, through requests, to initiate conversations with members of the board, including the future chair, that had not been happening. In a follow-up coaching session, Giovanni reported on a marked improvement in the quality of his conversations with the future chair, and how much more relaxed and better he felt within himself.

Cross-cultural coaching

The increasingly globalized world of business presents new challenges to ensure effective communication between personnel with diverse cultural backgrounds across different locations. Different cultures reflect different ways of being. Each culture provides a frame of meaning and associated assumptions about how to understand and behave in different situations. Business performance and productivity is built on people working together effectively (coordinating action) reach objectives, which is underpinned by shared meaning. Ensuring there is shared meaning in business communication can make a significant difference to the operation of a team.

Susan leads a risk team in a major bank, with the members of her team being in Australia and India. Her communication with the members of the team in India is via email and telephone, the latter including phone conferences. Susan was frustrated that her colleagues in India seemed to agree about tasks to be done but did not complete them; i.e. they had made promises (commitments) that they did not keep, engendering lack of trust.

Working from the ontological perspective that listening is meaning and is the crucial factor in communication, the coach explored the general hypothesis that Susan had assumed a shared understanding that did not exist between herself and team members in India. Cultures can be viewed as forms of deep listening, consisting of core assessments, social norms and practices, and cultural narratives that subtly inform members of a culture how to perceive and respond to situations. Within the general hypothesis the coach tested the relevance of two specific hypotheses to the communication breakdown Susan was dealing with. The first hypothesis was that 'saving face' is a significant part of Asian cultures that can result in the cultural practice of saying 'yes' when the listener does not understand. The second hypothesis was related to the influence of gender relationships, specifically males regarding themselves as being superior to females, which in Susan's situation may be the male members of her team in India not accepting her authority as manager and therefore not accepting her ideas, suggestions and requests.

Susan's acceptance of the possible relevance of the above two cultural influences, which included not being resentful of their existence, was the basis for the inclusion of a communication strategy in phone conversations with her colleagues in India. The strategy was to ensure explicit shared understanding of tasks to be completed and the availability of relevant resources in a manner that was not offensive. Conversationally, the implementation of the strategy was as follows.

> Thank you for our discussion. I'd like you to help me out here if you could – I'm not sure if I have done a very good job making clear what I'd like done. Could you please tell me your understanding of what you will be doing from our discussion and don't worry if it is not accurate because it was probably me not being clear enough in the first place.

This was followed by ensuring there was explicit shared understanding of the availability of relevant resources for the tasks to be completed. The coach emphasized the importance of being genuine in her requests, reflected in her voice tonality, which was indicative of her emotions and body posture being congruent with her words.

EVALUATION

While ontological coaching has the capacity to provide significant value across all genres and contexts for coaching, it is important to be mindful of some key considerations that, if not attended to, can act as constraints and limitations of this coaching methodology.

- Some coachees may be reluctant to explore the domains of emotions and body. The essential task of the ontological coach is to respect the boundaries of the coachee and to work skilfully in the area of language to generate shifts in perspectives and behaviour, which may spontaneously produce emotional and somatic shifts.
- Ontological coaches are not psychotherapists or body therapists. The coach has a fundamental responsibility to know his/her own coaching boundaries and not go beyond these. This is a critical aspect of the coach managing his/her own way of being in the coaching conversation. Boundaries are defined by the coach recognizing his/her levels of comfort and knowing his/her competence.
- Technical proficiency in the coaching methodology is not sufficient. The coach always coaches from life experiences, which can provide an invaluable experiential 'feel' for the challenges the coachee is dealing with. For example coaching in the business world requires a sound general understanding of the nature of organizations, the nature of leadership and managerial responsibility, and daily life in the workplace.

With the above considerations in mind, a number of strengths of ontological coaching can be identified:

- The coaching methodology is based on substantive and coherent theory of human perception and behaviour that provides a viable alternative approach to psychology for facilitating sustainable behavioural change.
- Working in the three domains of language, emotions and body provides the coach with the flexibility of multiple areas of engagement. The coach can recognize when the opportunities for learning and change have become

exhausted in one domain and seek permission to focus on another domain. For example new insights and behavioural shifts can open up for the coachee in the domains of moods and the body that are not possible while the conversation remains in the language domain.

- The role of the body in coaching ensures learning is embodied and consolidated.
- Ontological coaching offers a uniquely powerful way of intervening in organizational dynamics and culture. It provides an in-depth framework for positioning human interaction as a core business discipline and practice.

The general benefit of ontological coaching is that coachees experience shifts in their way of being, enabling them to become a different and more powerful observer of themselves, others and how they can constructively engage in the world. The coaching not only supports the coachee to deal with the problematic issues that were presented for coaching, but also positions them to be more resilient and adaptable for dealing with future problematic circumstances.

Ontological coaching is beneficial across a wide range of coaching contexts and genres because it deals with the fundamental ways people understand themselves, the world and what is possible for them in life. The coaching methodology facilitates the emergence of new perspectives as the basis for the development of expanded ways of thinking and increased behavioural flexibility, all of which have become so essential in increasingly unpredictable and uncertain times.

FURTHER READING

Sieler, Alan (2003). *Coaching to the human soul: ontological coaching and deep change,* Vol. I. Melbourne: Newfield Australia.

Sieler, Alan (2007). *Coaching to the human soul: ontological coaching and deep change,* Vol. II. Melbourne: Newfield Australia. (Volumes I and II of *Coaching to the human soul* are the detailed exposition of the methodology and theoretical underpinnings of Ontological Coaching. Volume I covers the specifics of the linguistic basis of the coaching methodology. The focus of Volume II is the emotional domain, which includes an extensive coverage of the model Some Basic Moods of Life. Both volumes provide a wide range of coaching examples and practical activities.)

Winograd, T., & Flores, F. (1986). *Understanding computers and cognition.* Reading, MA: Addison-Wesley. (While the orientation of this book is the design of computer-based systems that facilitate human work and interaction, it provides a worthwhile introduction to the ideas of Heidegger, Maturana and Searle that comprise the theory behind ontological coaching. Flores and Winograd position ontology as a contribution to the emergence of a new intellectual paradigm that is new ground for rationality, which combines traditional rational thinking with intuitive–interpretive thinking.)

REFERENCES

Austin, J.L. (1973). *How to do things with words* (2nd ed.). Cambridge, MA: Harvard University Press.

Dewey, J. (1929). *Experience and nature.* La Salle, IL: Open Court.

Gadamer, H-G. (1994). *Truth and method* (2nd ed., Rev.). New York: Continuum.

Heidegger, M. (1962). *Being and time.* Trans. J. Macquarie and E. Robinson. San Francisco, CA: Harper.

Heidegger, M. (1971). *On the way to language.* Trans. P. D. Hertz. San Francisco, CA: Harper.

Heidegger, M. (1999). *Ontology – the hermeneutics of facticity.* Trans. J. van Buren. Bloomington, IN: Indiana University Press.

Honderich, T. (Ed.). (1995). *The Oxford companion to philosophy.* Oxford: Oxford University Press.

Lettvin, J.Y., Maturana, H.R., McCulloch, W.S., & Pitts, W.H. (1968). What the frog's eye tells the frog's brain. In W.C. Corning & Martin Balaban (Eds.), *The mind: Biological approaches to its functions* (pp. 233–58). New York: John Wiley.

Maturana, H.R. (1988). Reality: The search for objectivity or the quest for a compelling argument. *Irish Journal of Psychology, 9*(1): 25–82.

Maturana, H.R., & Varela, F. (1980). *Autopoeisis and cognition: The realization of the living.* Dordrecht: Reidel Publishing.

Maturana, H.R., & Varela, F. (1987). *The tree of knowledge: The biological roots of human understanding* (Rev. ed.). Boston, MA: Shambala.

Maturana, H.R., Uribe, G., & Frenk, S. (1968). A biological theory of relativistic colour coding in the primate retina. *Arch. Biol. Med. Exp., 1*: 1–30.

Maturana, H.R., Lettvin, J.Y., McCulloch, W.S., & Pitts, W.H. (1958). Anatomy and physiology of vision in the frog. *Journal of General Physiology, 43*: 129–75.

Merleau-Ponty, M. (1962). *Phenomenology of perception.* Trans. C. Smith. London: Routledge and Kegan Paul.

Nietzsche, F. (1968). *The will to power.* Trans W. Kaufman & R.J. Hollingdale. New York: Vintage.

Searle, J.R. (1969). *Speech acts: An essay in the philosophy of language.* Cambridge: Cambridge University Press.

Searle, J.R. (1979). *Expression and meaning.* Cambridge: Cambridge University Press.

Sieler, A. (2003). *Coaching to the human soul: Ontological coaching and deep change,* Vol. I. Melbourne: Newfield Australia.

Sieler, A. (2007). *Coaching to the human soul: Ontological coaching and deep change,* Vol. II. Melbourne: Newfield Australia.

Winograd, T., & Flores, F. (1986). *Understanding computers and cognition.* Reading, MA: Addison-Wesley.

Wittgenstein, L. (1958). *Philosophical investigations* (3rd ed.). Englewood Cliffs, NJ: Basil Blackwell and Mott.

8

Narrative Coaching

David B. Drake

INTRODUCTION

Narrative coaching works with coachees at three primary levels: (1) drawing on narrative psychology to understand and connect to the *narrator*; (2) drawing on narrative structure to understand and elicit the material in the *narrated stories*; and (3) drawing on narrative practices to understand and harvest the dynamics of the *narrative field*. The goal is to help coachees to forge new connections between their stories, their identity, and their behaviours in order to generate and embody new options in these three domains. This approach is instinctual given the ancient and cognitive disposition for stories and it is timely given the need for a deeper, more complex understanding of change. Overall, narrative coaching entails a mindful, experiential, and holistic approach to helping coachees shift their stories about themselves, about others, and about life itself in order to create new results.

A brief backstory

In her marvellous history of the narrative turn in the social sciences, Czarniawska (2004) provides an overview of the three main fields that fed into narrative analysis and studies: literary theory, humanities, and psychology. The literary study of narratives focused on an analysis of texts. For example Burke (1969) put forth his Pentad as the central elements in a narrative: 'what was done (*act*), when and where it was done (*scene*), who did it (*agent*), how he did it (*agency*), and why (*purpose*)'. Bruner's (2002) use of *coda*, the meaning and implications of stories, can be seen as a sixth element. With the rise of literary hermeneutics came an interest in the analysis of interactions of the text and the reader and the subsequent attention to power and discourse.

With the movement into the humanities (e.g. political science, sociology and anthropology), a broader understanding of stories emerged as central to the very fabric of individual and collective life and a frame for a contextual understanding of action. For example phenomenologists such as Berger and Luckmann (1966) and anthropologists such as Geertz (1978) provide important insights into the processes by which we narrate our socially constructed experience. As part of this process, individual stories are viewed within larger cultural narrative frames and forces. Of particular importance for narrative coaching in this regard is Campbell's (1973) work on the heroic journey, van Gennep's (1960) work on rites of passage, and Turner's (1969) work to extend this model into broader cultural life. They provide a theoretical and sociohistorical frame for understanding and guiding change with coachees.

William James was a seminal figure in bringing narrative frames to psychology. James (1927) made the distinction between the *I* (the subject) and the *Me* (the object) – a distinction carried forward as the *self-as-knower* and the *self-as-known* (Hermans, 2004) and the *author* and the *actor* (Mancuso & Sarbin, 1983). This dialectic reflects the ongoing tensions for people in negotiating their narrative identity over time – moving between presenting identities that are socially acceptable and functional and embodying identities that are authentic and consistent with how they see themselves. Coaches would do well to more fully engage the broader humanities as a way to better understand the relational and social nature of both identity and behaviour as they work with their coachees. Adding these systemic elements to coaching yields more sustainable change for clients.

Much of this work was brought together by narrative therapy founders Michael White and David Epston (White, 1988; White & Epston, 1990) who advocated for the deconstruction of dominant narratives, the externalization of problems, and the valuation of 'unique outcomes' or 'exceptions' (Hewson, 1991) in a person's life as contradictions to internalized dominant narratives. Taking this work into coaching, coaches can help coachees to explore alternative territories and possibilities in and for their life by stepping outside their conflation of self with story and external narrative with internal experience. This is useful for coachees because, as Schank (1990) noted, we often see our lives in terms of 'pre-established, well-known stories that can obscure the ways in which our actual situation differs from the standard story' (Schank, 1990: 147).

ASSUMPTIONS OF A NARRATIVE APPROACH

The stories that people tell about their lives are of considerable importance in coaching. The primary assumption here is that there is an intimate connection between the ways in which people see themselves, the ways they narrate their daily life, and the ways in which they behave. Stories are the perfect avenue for exploring these connections because the images they bring to the surface provide material that is indicative of opportunities for inner development and a resource for changing external behaviour. For example in talking with a client about her plan to move, I asked her to visualize who would be living in the house with her. While exploring this image with her through drawing out related stories, she soon recognizes that the 'house' is also a metaphor and an opening for bigger choices about how she wants to live.

This narrative approach presumes that coachees are continually clarifying, claiming and convincing others of their identity through *positioning* (Davies & Harré, 1990) themselves in both their internal constructions and their external interactions. Narrative coaching helps coachees to recognize their common nature and implications of their patterns as seen in their stories and to enhance their positional repertoire (Hermans, 2004) in order to increase the options that are available to them. However, in order for new stories or new relations between stories to take hold in a coachee's life, they must build on elements of familiar stories in order to 'scaffold' their ascendance (Drake, 2008; Gergen & Gergen, 2006).

In relation to narrative structure the dynamics of conflict are key in helping coachees sort out their positional preferences (Drake, 2008). Nothing moves forward in a story except through conflict and, in fact, the conflict is the axis on which the story turns and the cauldron for its resolution. In narrative coaching, the purpose is not to 'resolve' conflicts but rather to increase coachees' capacity to engage with stronger interpersonal and transpersonal forces and transcend them at a higher level. In narrative coaching, the goal is to help coachees move into the heart of their conflicts to discern what they truly want and how to harness the energies there to achieve it. This is important because a person's true character is revealed in the choices they make under pressure (McKee, 1997) and is what propels them toward a resolution.

ESSENTIAL PROCESSES AND DYNAMICS

Narrative coaching presumes that: (1) identity is situated; (2) growth is liminal; (3) discourse is powerful; and (4) *re-storying* is possible. Together, they represent a novel approach to coaching that moves beyond modernist assumptions, linear development models, extroverted goal orientation, and lingering biases toward behaviourism. The focus shifts from the coach and coaching methodologies to the coaching relationship and the stories constituted there.

Identity is situated

Rather than analysing the past or planning for the future, narrative coaching focuses largely on the dynamics in the present as coachees share their stories. As such, there is a bias for working with what IS in contrast to a tendency in coaching to move quickly to what COULD BE. In part, this is about honouring the fact that coachees use their stories to define, develop, and deploy connections between their 'situated selves' (Ochs & Capps, 1996) as part of an ongoing dialectic between themselves and their environments. These stories, and the identities and behaviours associated with them, need to be witnessed and respected before they can be changed. The role of the coach then is to invite coachees to stand fully in the truth of their experience as the first step in their developmental journey.

Coachees' stories are powerful resources in coaching because they make visible their otherwise invisible identity processes, their 'theory of events' (Foucault, 1965), and thereby shed light on their dance between narrative, identity, and performance (Eakin, 1999; Mishler, 1999). This can be seen in the coachee who gained important new insights into his level of stress through exploring his stories about routinely helping others – and fears of what happens when you don't – (narrative), his familial identity as the hyper-responsible oldest son (identity), and his tendencies to micromanage others at work (performance). A narrative approach to coaching can begin with any of the three dimensions to get at the core issues and to identify alternative ways of being in the world, e.g. this coachee learned to delegate as one who wants to mentor others and is informed by stories of those who served him.

Growth is liminal

Coachees use *emplotment strategies* (Hermans & Kempen, 1993; Mattingly, 1994) to make sense of and choices about their experience as a means to define their identity, community, values, etc. These strategies operate largely at nonconscious and somatic levels, but they can be made conscious and malleable through coaching. Therefore, narrative coaches track the ways in which coachees organize their stories, e.g. which events are included, which themes they organize around, which characters are portrayed as significant, and which voices are privileged in the telling (Botella & Herrero, 2000). It is particularly useful to listen for what is missing – the gaps and, the thresholds (Drake, 2007) – where coachee's typical emplotment strategies have broken down or are no longer working. It is in these liminal, in-between spaces where growth most often occurs.

This is often the case because people form stories in response to disruptions in the canonical state of their world. Their goal in telling stories is to resolve the discrepancies between what they expected and what actually happened – what Bruner (1990) called 'breaches of the commonplace' – and to integrate the resulting disorder and return the situation back to 'normal'. However, a frequent outcome of effective coaching is the creation of a new 'normal' for clients. For example a workshop participant started with a story about how his firm poorly handled the departure of a close colleague. 'It was not supposed to be this way' in his view. Drawing on a phrase he had used, I asked him if this was ultimately about a direct challenge to his values. In agreeing, he recognized that it had raised doubts about his decision to seek partnership. He seemed torn between wanting to return to his 'normal' story about the firm in order to ease his disquiet and recognizing that his role as a new leader in the firm would require new stories about himself, about leadership, and about the firm.

Discourse is powerful

Narrative coaches help coachees examine their assumptions about reality through a deep engagement with their stories. In the process, their preconscious schemas and conceptual frames – the *macronarratives* (Angus, Levitt, & Hardtke, 1999) that shape how they live their lives – come to light. This is important because experiences that are not consistent with coachees' preferred self-stories are not deemed significant and are often invisible (White, 1988). If coachees are to adopt new behaviours or attain new results, they must embody an identity and discourse from which to do so and from which the desired behaviours naturally arise. If they are to sustain this new identity, they need to regularly enact these new behaviours – and the stories that go with them. Working with coachees' stories helps them lift the internalized restraints that keep them from noticing the critical exceptions to their current self-descriptions that could be used to scaffold a new way of being in the world.

Therefore, a key task is to introduce to coachees the distinction between their traditionally *available narratives* and their latent *potential stories* (Drake, 2007). Available narratives are drawn from the vocabulary and grammar, plot lines and historical conventions, beliefs and norms of their cultural systems, and go on to inform the stories that coachees construct to understand their experiences and live their lives (Freedman & Combs, 1996). As people begin to recognize the limitations inherent in their available narratives, they can create more distance from these narratives, see them more clearly, and surface other 'selves'. As alternative stories become available, other 'sympathetic' and previously neglected aspects of the person's experi-ence (and the related discourse) can be expressed (White & Epston, 1990) and embodied. Narrative coaching enables people to reframe and reposition themselves relative to their available narratives and to bring more of their potential stories to life.

Re-storying is possible

'Re-storying' is the process of creating a new alignment between one's identity, stories, and behaviours in order to *be* and to behave in new ways. It involves raising coachees' awareness of their current narrative patterns (and the sources and consequences) through working with the narrative material that emerges in the sessions as openings for new possibilities – new stories waiting to be midwived. In order for these kinds of shifts to occur, coachees first need to loosen their *narrative grip* on the past, present, and/or future (Boscolo & Bertrando, 1992) to create the space for new stories about themselves and others. In order to do so, narrative coaches often use experiential and imaginal activities to help coachees break the ossified bonds that have historically held them in the same stories.

Narrative coaches do this by helping coachees discern what they are trying to accomplish with the stories they currently tell (and for whom). In doing so, they come to terms with their hopes and fears as well as their habitual narrative genres and roles, i.e., victim or hero. As McKee (1997) asks, 'What does the coachee want that, if you gave it to her, would stop the story?' 'What value is at stake in her life at this moment?' The answer, the object of their desire, is often found where people must face their greatest fear or challenge, answer their most essential ques-tion, or make their hardest choice. However, as we often see in coaching, their 'holy grail' may not be the one they were originally seeking. For example I was asked to coach a key contributor in a manufacturing company to help her address some critical relational and performance issues. Her initial stories were of anger at her employer and her colleagues. However, through exploring her story more fully she was able to reframe the issue as one in which she felt her professional passions and values had been compromised as the company had grown significantly. What she wanted ultimately was the chance to leave with dignity and the courage to return to the work she loved. In the end, she left the organization, moved to a new city and found a new job where she could thrive again – and the organizational players gained as well in releasing her and reflecting on how much the culture had indeed changed over the years.

THE ROLE OF THE NARRATIVE COACH AND THE RELATIONSHIP

> [One's] role is correspondingly delicate. It may still not be, though, 'to change [their] story, for this is to deny it; it is, rather, to expand and deepen the story, thus releasing the energy bound within it.' (Houston, 1987: 99)

A narrative approach emphasizes real-time attention to facets of coachees' experience and narration in seeking points of leverage to support coachees' development, e.g. stories about eating dinner, empty moving boxes, a childhood mentor, and a dream of riding a boat down the river) that serve as portals to larger themes. For example the above stories led to the following, respectively: major lifestyle changes and early retirement; acknowledgment of anticipatory grief for an ill wife; a platform to celebrate and extend a new direction in business; and breaking a long-held pattern in work relationships and a new job. This approach requires a shift from thinking about a story as a fixed commodity transmitted from one person to another to thinking about a story as a co-created dynamic between the coachee and the coach. A key role for the coach is to create the container in which these processes become possible.

In order to do so, narrative coaches provide both an interpersonal structure, e.g. a safe space in which to tell the whole story and a narrative structure, for example using Bruner's (1990) notions of *landscapes of action* and *landscapes of consciousness,* to help coachees fully engage and explore their stories. Otherwise, coachees' stories devolve into mere chronicles and the process degrades into an abstract analysis – neither of which is productive in coaching. While recognizing this human need for a sense of order and a plot to live by (Hillman, 1983), it is also important that these structures remain in the background as a source for potential questions, rather than in the foreground as expectations to which coachees and their stories must conform.

As a result, narrative coaches take a *decentred* position and role in coaching conversations and remain cognizant of the balance of power. In doing so, they honour the knowledge of coachees about their lives and their primary status as authors of their lives (White, 2000). A narrative coach is generally off to the side somewhat from the coachee, such that they make room for the narrative work to occur in the field as it emerges between them. It also provides a visual cue for the coach in remembering to attend to the stories along with the person telling them. In my practice, I often make extensive use of my hands to *hold* and work with this space, e.g. holding up two story elements, one in each hand so to speak, and drawing the coachee's attention to what might connect them in the middle. A light yet disciplined touch is required by coaches to remain in a decentred position and fully trust the process rather than moving to the centre and trying to be 'helpful' through changing their coachees' stories.

A critical discipline therefore is for coaches to stay as much as possible in *storytime* and *storyspace* as they unfold in working with coachees and the narrative material. The focus here is on the story as it is being told in the here and now. In doing so, coaches continually bring coachees back into their present experience in order to connect the proverbial 'dots' and provide a more solid basis for change. For example, stories about the past and future are explored through such questions as, 'When have you been here before?' and 'When might you be here again?'; the answers are brought back into the moment by asking such questions as, 'What are you thinking/feeling about X right now?'

In an earlier work (Drake, 2008) based on the well-known opening for children's fables, three dimensions of working in the present with coachees were identified. *Once upon a time* is about helping coachees be fully present as the narrator while creating a trusting space in which to do so. *Twice upon a time* is about advocating for the full story to emerge so that as much of the narrative material is available for the conversation. *Thrice upon a time* is about the field that is created in a coaching conversation between the coach, the coachee, and the narrative process where the coachee can reframe or rearrange the narrative material in order to gain a new perspective, sense of self, or options for action. These three dimensions reflect the interest in identity, narrative and behaviour, respectively, in coaching. These three dimensions are reflected in one of the classic narrative coaching processes, as can be seen in the following:

(1) an issue or goal is presented
(2) an invitation is made to tell the story about it, and other related elements or stories are elicited
(3) any themes or patterns are tracked
(4) a guiding image or metaphor is identified that seems to be at the heart of the issue
(5) this image is worked within the conversational 'field'
(6) a resolution occurs – often in ways that transcend the original polarity or issue.

An example can be seen in this coaching interaction: (1) Presenting issue: 'We just moved'; (2) Stories: Description of the move; (3) Themes: Smaller space, giving away; (4) Guiding image: Boxes in the kitchen; (5) Image in the *field*: Unpacking the boxes; and (6) Threshold and resolution: Recognition of anticipatory grief about the implications of the reason for the move.

PRIMARY GOALS AND TASKS

Listening as a method for change

A key goal in narrative coaching is to search for elements in a coachee's stories that are 'amenable to challenge, redefinition, or alternative interpretation so that a new definition of the problem can emerge' (Coulehan, Friedlander, & Heatherington, 1998: 18). One of the core skills in doing so is deep and generative listening based in a commitment to presence, mindfulness, and attention. In addition to working with the words of their coachees' stories, narrative coaches are fully present to the coachee as the narrator, remain mindful of their own impact on the story formation, and pay close attention to the nuances of what is said (and not said) in their interchanges. They listen in some unique ways, particularly to the nonverbal and nonrational elements of their coaching conversations.

Listening this way reaches coachees at multiple levels as a means to connect to the whole person, open up a wider range of material for coaching, and enrich the narrative field on the coachees' behalf. In this sense, listening can be seen as a 360° experience and not a dyadic transaction. A key role for coaches then is to 'invite people to see their stories from different perspectives, to notice how they are constructed (or even that they are constructed), to note their limits and influences, and to discover other possibilities' (Freedman & Combs, 1996). It is about helping coachees notice the differences between the stories they are telling and the stories they are living as well as to identify narrative 'data' from their lives that will support an alternate view of who they are and how they want to be in the world. For example I invited a coachee who looked longingly off into space after stating his issue to verbalize the untold story that was playing in his mind — and to use the feelings of grief which emerged to identify the next steps he needed to take.

The *Narrative Diamond*™ model (Drake, 2007) is used to teach this work and deepen the practice of listening. The underlying presumption is that the characters, objects, and events that appear in our stories are systematically related to the other figures in ways that are important to explore. As such, coaches listen carefully for what is said, not said, wants to be said, and is being said differently in order to gain a deeper understanding of these relationships. This aligns with the notion of *dialogical space*, wherein 'new relationships are established between existing story parts or new elements are introduced' (Hermans, 2004: 175) and narrative researchers who study how people 'locate characters in their stories in relation to one another and in relation to themselves' (Riessman, 2002) and how they position and 'reposition these characters … within a constantly moving interpersonal field' (Anderson, 2004: 317).

Working with coachees' stories and the characters in them, beyond their ego's reach, is powerful because it gives them access to aspects of themselves which are often hidden yet in motion in their psyche. This is important because development generally occurs for coachees outside their habitual plot lines and their psyche's defences. Narrative coaches support this process through listening in a way that is active yet nondirective, nonattached yet generative. A key skill in this regard is to listen simultaneously at multiple levels within the field and to the stories themselves. In this way, narrative coaches are truly 'active' in their listening as they are, paradoxically, both fully engaged and wholly nonattached in helping their coachees to discover and step into a new story of and with their life.

COMPARISONS AND APPLICATIONS

Narrative coaching is based in a unique philosophical stance and a distinct set of methodologies. At the same time, it shares commonalities with other theories and approaches to coaching: (1) the inter-personal nature of the coaching process and the role of conflict as found in the psychodynamic approach; (2) the genuine empathetic presence and commitment to self-actualization and self-determination as found in the person-centred approach; (3) the emphasis on in-the-moment awareness and experimental actions, coachees' language, and expectations of self-responsibility as found in the gestalt approach; (4) an interest in phenomenological methods, unlocking sedimentation, and issues of what IS as found in the existential approach; (5) the values around interconnectedness and spirituality as found in the transpersonal approach; and (6) the willingness to work across all domains of experience, e.g. language, emotions, and physiology, as found in the ontological approach.

Narrative coaching at work

Developmental coaching: A narrative approach helps coachees draw new connections between their personal stories and the collective stories in which they are embedded. A narrative approach can be particularly useful in working with coachees at turning points in how they want to present themselves and/or be seen by others. For example a coachee who had been promoted to VP of Engineering traced his career trajectory in order to make better sense of the difficulties he was experiencing in his new role. We identified the three stages of his career as 'expert, manager and leader', and we explored his stories about himself in each one and the stories others had of him as he advanced. In comparing these stories, he recognized that, in large part, he still saw himself and acted from an old role – particularly as the 'expert' – and he needed to let go in order to step more fully into his new role.

Team coaching: Teams are often caught between organizational demands, client expectations, and personal agendas as they seek to fulfil their mission. A narrative approach to working with teams helps them to surface and sort through their individual and collective stories as a way to address conflict, align their purpose, or shift their patterns of engagement. For example in taking a narrative approach in coaching the IT teams in a health care organization to provide better customer service, they were invited to collectively construct a model of the flow of a key system, visit several sites to see their technology in action, and gather user stories from their stakeholder groups. The essence of shifts that resulted were captured by one participant who reframed his story from 'I want to be left alone to build servers' to 'people depend on me in order to serve our patients'.

Manager as coach: A narrative approach can be used to help managers and leaders understand what is meaningful to them, relinquish the self-imposed burden to have all the answers, and find a healthy balance between being appreciative in growing people and assertive in managing performance. In my work with a global professional services firm, leaders and coaching champions were invited to share stories of their 'experiments' in bringing coaching to bear in new ways in meeting the needs of their teams. As these stories have spread, there have been noticeable shifts in the openness to learning, engagement with coaching, clarity around roles in coaching, and the overall vibe in many of the teams. Coaching is no longer seen primarily as the formal, obligatory, and generally unidirectional sessions dutifully done a few times a year, but rather as the natural, invitational and mutual way all conversations are framed and all business gets done.

EVALUATION

A key focus over the past seven years has been the theory building and process development that have been essential in creating the philosophical foundations and applications for this method. Much of the research that has informed narrative coaching to date has been drawn from efforts in related fields such as narrative psychology and narrative medicine. Narrative approaches are ideal for helping at key turning points when they are in between stories. They can also be used to underpin behaviour change and goal achievement (Hart, 1995) by making connections between internal schemas and external actions and between personal stories and cultural narratives. Narrative coaching seems to works best with coachees who have (1) a comfort with silence and self-reflection; (2) a willingness to work at emotional, metaphorical, and nonrational levels; (3) an astute awareness of and ability to articulate their experience; and (4) the necessary ego strength to be able to self-disclose through their stories.

Obviously, this approach is more challenging if any of the above four conditions are not present in the coach and/or coachee. Also, while narrative approaches often lead to important insights as a platform and frame for change, they are philosophically non-directive and they may need to be augmented with other methods when coaching requires a more directive or tactical approach. Another concern stems from the ties to narrative therapy and its emphasis on issues of power, oppression, and justice. This can be a challenge for narrative coaches who are sensitized to these issues but may be engaged with coaches or organizations who are not. Lastly, given the social and cultural basis for stories, both as identity and discourse, this approach to coaching must be done with a high level of awareness in order to remain as 'clean' and clear as possible in the process.

CONCLUSION

The roots of narrative approaches to coaching can be seen as a movement from *text* to *context* to *subtext*, a progression that was accelerated by the rise of postmodernism and the shift from 'stories-as-objects' to 'stories-in-context' (Boje, 1998). It is a process that focuses on narrative identity, growth at the thresholds, the power of discourse, and the possibilities for new stories. It is based in a commitment by narrative coaches to (1) be mindful and compassionate; (2) listen deeply and respectfully; and (3) engage courageously and fluidly with the stories in the conversational field.

In *thinking narratively* (Drake, 2007) in a coaching conversation, coaches place more emphasis on generating experiences and less on rushing to interpretation, meaning, or action. It does not matter which stories coachees choose to share first; narrative coaches trust that coachees will begin at the level at which they are ready and the critical themes will be forthcoming. Therefore, the aim is to create a rich narrative field, notice what appears, remain connected even in silence, actively engage with the narrative material as it emerges, and trust that any one story or set of stories is a portal into the larger issues at play for coachees in reaching their 'object of desire'. At the same time, narrative-based coaches know that any story told in a coaching session, even if it has served as a transformational vehicle in that setting, must survive the 'retellings' if coachees are to sustain the changes they have begun.

As such, the narrative coach helps coachees to connect their personal stories with the social contexts from which they came and to which they will return in new ways – both in the session itself and in crafting experiments based on their work together. A narrative approach to coaching is a powerful method for helping coachees to (1) become more aware of their own stories, (2) recognize how these stories shape their identity and behaviour at both conscious and unconscious levels, (3) understand that these stories are personally and socially constructed, and (4) be more authorial in aligning their stories with identities and actions that would enable them to authentically embody a new way of being in the world. Overall, it is a present-focused, nondirective and experiential approach more than one that is future-focused, action-oriented and goal-driven. Ultimately, people can only see as far as their stories will take them, and they can only act as far as their stories will back them.

FURTHER READING

Freedman, J., & Combs, G. (1996). *Narrative therapy: The social construction of preferred realities*. New York: Norton and Co. (This excellent introduction to narrative therapy features a good blend of theoretical and practice considerations. As a way to understand its similarities and differences relative to a narrative approach to coaching.)

McKee, R. (1997). *Story: Substance, structure, style and the principles of screenwriting*. New York: HarperCollins. (The master when it comes to understanding screenwriting; he brings together a classic literary knowledge with a sound knowledge of contemporary culture in providing a deep resource on narrative structure.)

Schank, R.A. (1990). *Tell me a story: A new look at real and artificial memory*. New York: Charles Scribner's Sons. (Reading this book was pivotal for me as I studied how to create better transfer of learning and more sustainable change in developing managers and leaders. An educator, he writes with a sound grasp of the research on schemas and other core concepts from cognitive science, but does so from a starting point of the mind as a storyteller.)

REFERENCES

Anderson, T. (2004). 'To tell my story': Configuring interpersonal relations within narrative process. In L.E. Angus & J. McLeod (Eds.), *Handbook of narrative and psychotherapy: Practice, theory, and research* (pp. 315–29). Thousand Oaks, CA: Sage Publications.

Angus, L.E., Levitt, H., & Hardtke, K.K. (1999). The narrative processes coding system: Research implications for psychotherapy practice. *Journal of Clinical Psychology, 55*(10): 1255–70.

Berger, P.L., & Luckmann, T. (1966). *The social construction of reality*. New York: Doubleday.

Boje, D.M. (1998). The postmodern turn from stories-as-objects to stories-in-context methods. *Research Methods Forum*. Retrieved 7 January 2006, from http://www.aom.pace.edu/rmd/1998_forum_postmodern_stories.html.

Boscolo, L., & Bertrando, P. (1992). The reflexive loop of past, present and future in systemic therapy and consultation. *Family Process, 31*: 119–30.

Botella, L., & Herrero, L. (2000). A relational constructivist approach to narrative therapy. *European Journal of Psychotherapy, Counselling & Health, 3*(3): 407–18.

Bruner, J. (1990). *Acts of meaning.* Cambridge, MA: Harvard University Press.

Bruner, J. (2002). *Making stories: Law, literature, life.* Cambridge, MA: Harvard University Press.

Burke, K. (1969). *A grammar of motives.* Berkeley, CA: University of California Press.

Campbell, J. (1973). *The hero with a thousand faces.* Princeton, NJ: Princeton University Press.

Coulehan, R., Friedlander, M.L., & Heatherington, L. (1998). Transforming narratives: A change event in constructivist family therapy. *Family Process, 37*: 17–33.

Czarniawska, B. (2004). *Narratives in social science research.* London: Sage.

Davies, B., & Harré, R. (1990). Positioning: The discursive production of selves. *Journal for the Theory of Social Behavior, 20*(1): 43–63.

Drake, D.B. (2007). The art of thinking narratively: Implications for coaching psychology and practice. *Australian Psychologist, 42*(4): 283–94.

Drake, D.B. (2008). Thrice upon a time: Narrative structure and psychology as a platform for coaching. In D.B. Drake, D. Brennan & K. Gortz (Eds.), *The philosophy and practice of coaching: Insights and issues for a new era* (pp. 51–71). San Francisco, CA: Jossey-Bass.

Eakin, P.J. (1999). *How our lives become stories.* Ithaca, NY: Cornell University Press.

Foucault, M. (1965). *Madness and civilization: A history of insanity in the age of reason.* New York: Random House.

Freedman, J., & Combs, G. (1996). *Narrative therapy: The social construction of preferred realities.* New York: Norton and Co.

Geertz, C. (1978). *The interpretation of cultures.* New York: Basic Books.

Gergen, M.M., & Gergen, K.J. (2006). Narratives in action. *Narrative Inquiry, 16*(1): 112–21.

Hart, B. (1995). Re-authoring the stories we work by: Situating the narrative approach in the presence of the family of therapists. *Australian and New Zealand Journal of Family Therapy, 16*(4).

Hermans, H.J.M. (2004). The innovation of self-narratives: A dialogical approach. In L.E. Angus & J. McLeod (Eds.), *Handbook of narrative and psychotherapy: Practice, theory, and research* (pp. 175–91). Thousand Oaks, CA: Sage Publications.

Hermans, H.J.M., & Kempen, H.J.G. (1993). *The dialogical self: Meaning as movement.* San Diego, CA: Academic Press.

Hewson, D. (1991). From laboratory to therapy room: Prediction questions for reconstructing the 'new-old' story. *Dulwich Centre Newsletter, 3*: 5–12.

Hillman, J. (1983). *Healing fiction.* Woodstock: Spring Publications.

Houston, J. (1987). *The search for the beloved: Journeys in sacred psychology.* Los Angeles, CA: Jeremy P. Tarcher.

James, W. (1927). *Psychology: Briefer course.* New York: Henry Holt.

McKee, R. (1997). *Story: Substance, structure, style and the principles of screenwriting.* New York: HarperCollins.

Mancuso, J.C., & Sarbin, T.R. (1983). The self-narrative in the enactment of roles. In T.R. Sarbin & K.E. Scheibe (Eds.), *Studies in social identity* (pp. 233–53). Westport, CT: Praeger.

Mattingly, C. (1994). The concept of therapeutic 'emplotment'. *Social Science Medicine, 38*(6): 811–22.

Mishler, E.G. (1999). *Storylines: Craftartist's narratives of identity.* Cambridge, MA: Harvard University Press.

Ochs, E., & Capps, L. (1996). Narrating the self. *Annual Review of Anthropology, 25*: 19–43.

Riessman, C.K. (2002). Analysis of personal narrative. In J.F. Gubrium & J.A. Holstein (Eds.), *Handbook of interview research* (pp. 695–710). Thousand Oaks, CA: Sage.

Schank, R.A. (1990). *Tell me a story: A new look at real and artificial memory.* New York: Charles Scribner's Sons.

Turner, V. (1969). *The ritual process: Structure and anti-structure.* New York: Aldine Publishing Co.

van Gennep, A. (1960). *The rites of passage.* London: Routledge and Kegan Paul.

White, M. (1988). The process of questioning: A therapy of literary merit? In M. White (Ed.), *Collected papers* (pp. 37–46). Adelaide, SA: Dulwich Centre Publications.

White, M. (2000). *Reflections on narrative practice: Essays and interviews.* Adelaide, SA: Dulwich Centre Publications.

White, M., & Epston, D. (1990). *Narrative means to therapeutic ends.* New York: Norton & Co.

9

The Cognitive–Developmental Approach to Coaching

Tatiana Bachkirova

INTRODUCTION

The cognitive–developmental approach is based on research studies that suggest that people differ in ways that could not be explained by personality types, learning styles or personal preferences, all of which are usually seen as relatively stable for each individual. This approach suggests that people differ not only from other people but also undergo significant changes in themselves, for example in the way they make meaning of their experiences. The changes of these capacities occur in a logical sequence of stages throughout the life of the individual. They influence the depth and complexity of what each individual can notice and therefore operate on and change. This development can be further stimulated and facilitated by appropriate support and challenge within the coaching process. Understanding developmental trajectories may help coaches to be better equipped to address the diverse needs of their clients.

This chapter opens with a short history of the approach; it is followed by a discussion of its main assumptions and suggested applications for coaching. It will be compared with other theoretical traditions useful for coaching. Examples will be provided for applying this approach to different coaching contexts and genres with an evaluation made of its strengths and limitations.

A brief history of the tradition

Three major areas of research gave rise to principal strands within this approach.

- The first strand began with the important work of Jean Piaget (1976). It emphasizes developmental changes in reasoning and meaning-making which extend, for example to moral reasoning (Kohlberg, 1969); intellectual development (Perry, 1970); reflective judgment (King & Kitchener, 1994); and 'orders of mind' (Kegan, 1982, 1994).

- The second strand is ego-development, with its origins in the research of Jane Loevinger (1976, 1987). It focuses on the development of self-identity and the maturity of interpersonal relationships and has been further extended to include post-autonomous ego development by Cook-Greuter (1999, 2004) and action logics by Torbert (1991); Torbert & Associates (2004).
- The foundation of the third strand is the research of Clare Graves (1970) into levels of existence, which was later extended into 'worldviews' and 'values' by Beck and Cowan (1996) and is known as 'Spiral Dynamics'.

There are other theories and research findings that suggest that other aspects of personal development also occur in sequential stages, for example, emotions (Goleman, 1995), needs (Maslow, 1954) and spiritual awareness (Fowler, 1981). These aspects will be called here 'developmental lines' as suggested by Wilber (1999). All these studies are conducted in the tradition of developmental structuralism, which looks for patterns that connect specific psychological phenomena. According to this approach, individual characteristics are emergent, coming into being in a predictable and sequential way.

The continuing contribution of Ken Wilber (1999, 2000, 2006) to this approach is difficult to overestimate. He pulls together many theories and research findings relevant to this approach, creating a compelling picture of integral individual development that incorporates a range of developmental lines. Discussing the findings of these studies, he emphasizes various milestones of growth and development in each developmental line, calling them 'stages of consciousness'. With each successive stage or level the qualities of the previous stage remain as properties of the new stage. Therefore, with each new stage, a person can use anything learned in a previous stage and so becomes more flexible, integrated and more capable of functioning within a changing world that is also becoming more complex.

MAIN CONCEPTS AND ASSUMPTIONS

Each of the above studies identifies different stages in the developmental lines they study. As in map making, the way to divide and represent the territory is somewhat arbitrary – it is not important 'how you slice and dice development' (Wilber, 2006).

However, some common patterns can be identified in the various ways suggested for 'slicing the developmental pie'. According to one of the patterns, development proceeds from the 'pre-conventional level', which is simple and is focused only on the needs of the ego, to the 'conventional', which could be seen as focused on the individual's environment and the people who are close to them. It then proceeds to the 'post-conventional level', which is more complex and includes 'concern about the whole world'.

Stages take considerable time to develop and cannot be 'skipped', because each is built upon the previous one, and in a particular way. Wilber (2006) calls this '*holarchy*', which is similar to the relationship between atoms, molecules, cells and whole organisms. Holarchy implies that it is not possible to go from atoms to cells 'skipping' molecules. Each developmental line (cognitive, emotional, moral, etc.) is unfolding in the same way but at a different pace for each particular person. This means that someone could be, for example, at the highest stage intellectually, the lowest stage morally and somewhere in the middle interpersonally.

This, of course, makes the topic of overall development of individuals very complex. Wilber suggests that

> although substantial empirical evidence demonstrates that each line develops through these holarchical stages in an invariant sequence, nonetheless, because all two dozen of them develop relatively independently, overall growth and development is a massively complex, overlapping, nonlinear affair, following no set sequence whatsoever. (Wilber, 1999: 291–2)

Figure 9.1 represents a snapshot in time of how an individual's development might look if we were able to measure each developmental line.

This representation, however abstract and tentative, could be useful in dispelling the myths of the simplicity of categorizing people and the validity of quick conclusions about their overall level of development. This may also indicate the futility of attempts to use one line for describing the level of development in another.

At the same time representations of developmental lines, whether linear or spiral, create a natural curiosity about the relationship between the lines: which line is more 'important'? Is there a central line or is there one yardstick against which all of them could be measured? Cook-Greuter (1999), for example, makes a case for an essential connection between the cognitive and ego-development lines, because 'it is the ego whose main function is to generate

Figure 9.1   Example of a combination of the developmental lines in an individual.

coherent meaning' (Cook-Greuter, 1999: 14). Some of the researchers who studied particular developmental lines assumed that theirs was the central characteristic of individual growth (Wilber, 2000).

There are also a number of controversies about the role of the cognitive line. Wilber (2006), for example, describes several propositions that attempt to explain the role of cognition in relation to all other lines. One of them suggests that the cognitive line could be a special one. Growth in the cognitive line is necessary but not sufficient for growth in other lines. After all, one has to be aware of something in order to act on it, need it, value it, etc. Another explanation suggests that the yardstick is consciousness *itself*. If consciousness is defined as 'the degree of openness or emptiness' it could be said to serve as the 'shared altitude' along which all development lines move. As such it is not a line itself but a 'space' in which lines arise and the 'more phenomena in that line that *can* arise in consciousness, the higher the level in that line' (Wilber, 2006: 68).

It is important to notice that Wilber defines cognition as 'the capacity to take perspectives'. He even suggests that cognitive development could be measured in terms of the number of others with whom you can identify and the number of perspectives you can take. This again creates a parallel between consciousness and cognitive development. With this wider understanding of cognition, the description of this approach as 'cognitive–developmental' could legitimately stay as such, in spite of its apparent focus on only one developmental line. This is also the reason why Kegan's (1982) theory, which explores 'orders of mind' and represents a cognitive developmental line, is a good one to use in this chapter as an example of the cognitive–developmental approach in the context of coaching.

GOALS AND TASKS OF THIS THEORY/TRADITION

It is important to notice that cognitive–developmental theories were not developed for coaching or any other kind of developmental intervention. The purpose of the research behind them was to:

- understand human nature
- explain the differences between people
- describe what constitutes 'development' when significant changes in individuals are noticed
- design measures for identifying the stages of development in individuals.

The task of influencing these kinds of changes was secondary. It could even be said that the idea of actively influencing development is contentious with some different authors. In my view the main goal of the cognitive–developmental approach, as in fact of any other approach to coaching, is to facilitate the process of making specific changes that are chosen by the client. For example psychological support is very important when an individual is facing transition or a new developmental task and that is what all coaches are aiming to provide.

What 'a developmentally-minded' coach may bring into this and what is crucial for the quality of this support is, according to Kegan, a presence of someone 'who can see, recognise, and understand who the person is and who he or she is *becoming*' (Kegan, 1982: 260) (emphasis added*)*.

At the same time and in some specific cases, when clients have an explicit interest in a wider task of overall individual development, cognitive–developmental coaches are better placed than others to support them. In order to do this:

- It is useful to identify what developmental lines are the most important for the coaching task and where along the continuum of these lines a person may be.
- Coaches have to be sufficiently aware of the mechanism of change and transition between the stages in order to provide the client with appropriate support and challenge.
- Coaches have to be aware of their own stages of development in order to reflect on their own role in the coaching process and the dynamics of the coaching relationship.

The knowledge of this approach is also important for coaches because it draws attention to their own development and enriches their capacity for reflection and effective interaction with others. With each new stage they reach they become more capable of taking a number of perspectives on situations and of understanding more people (Bachkirova & Cox, 2007). They are, thereby, able to articulate, influence and change more critical situations in the coaching process.

Kegan's theory and specific features of the coaching process

Kegan's theory suggests that, as human beings, we have two tendencies that are rarely in perfect balance. The first is to differentiate ourselves from the environment and others, to be autonomous. The second tendency is to be included, to belong. The adaptive requirement of human nature is to pursue both differentiation and integration. Therefore the development of any organism is a balancing act in which one constantly negotiates 'the self' in relation to 'the other'. At the same time, within oneself, there is a continuous process of recognizing and differentiating elements of self that were previously so integral to the self that they could not be noticed. The shift from what is perceived to be self (subject) to something that can be seen as elements of self (object) allows a new way of differentiating oneself from and relating to others. It could be said that these shifts initiate new ways of seeing the world, oneself and other people, creating new opportunities for autonomy and relatedness.

Before we discuss the important periods of relative stability (that Kegan calls 'orders of mind') between the shifts, it is useful to give some examples of the mechanism of change from subject to object, because it is an important process that coaching can usefully influence.

Things that are Subject in Kegan's theory can prompt us to action but cannot be observed or reflected on. We cannot stand back and take a look at them because we are embedded in them. On the other hand, things that are Object for us are 'those elements of our knowing or organizing that we can reflect on, handle, look at, be responsible for, relate to each other, take control of, internalize, assimilate, or otherwise operate upon' (Kegan, 1994: 32). It has been said that to be Subject is to 'see with' rather than to 'see through' (Drath, 1990). A good example is 'cultural blindness' as described by Drath (1990: 486), who suggests that

> we see with our culture-bound norms and expectations, accept them as given, and cannot examine them for what they are – that is, we cannot see through them. Our cultural heritage is something we are, not something we have. The culture holds us; we are embedded in it and cannot rise above it.

A cognitive–developmental shift, however, is possible when we become aware of culturally determined differences and the distance they create from others. Such understanding could make cultural influences an Object, opening up new ways of seeing ourselves and of relating to others.

It is natural, therefore, that the more individuals can take as Object, the more complex their worldview becomes, because they can examine and act upon more things. The mechanism of the shift from Subject to Object could be considered as an essential element of coaching. It is one of the functions of coaches to watch for the re-absorption of insight in the client and to help build *psychological muscle* in order to hold something out from a person as an Object. As Berger and Fitzgerald (2002: 31) say: 'one of the most powerful interventions coaches can provide is simply help to keep critical insights alive for their clients'.

Here is an example from the coaching process. In his new role of head of department a client received feedback suggesting that his way of one-to-one communication with people made some of his staff uncomfortable. He asked his coach to help him to respond to this feedback, which he found puzzling. They explored this feedback together with the coach's own observations of his interactions with her and others. It appeared that the coachee's style involved unusually long pauses that people perceived as withdrawals. These apparently made those colleagues who were more self-conscious than others feel insecure. The client was not aware of this. His style was so much a part of who he was that he could not reflect on the effect of it on other people. As the result of coaching, his style from being Subject has gradually changed into Object, leading to the client's increased ability to notice it and modify it when necessary.

Kegan (1982) suggests that the shift from subject to object happens in relation to some crucially important elements of self in a similar way to the above example. When this happens it leads to a significant change in people, transforming the way they make meaning of their experience and how they relate to other people. He calls the five periods between these significant changes 'Orders of Mind' through which people evolve. Table 9.1 is created mainly on the basis of his work (1982) with additional contributions from further research and publications by Berger and Fitzgerald (2002) and Cook-Greuter (1999).

Kegan (1982) advocates that the development process is a combination of internal and external factors for each individual, but can be stimulated and facilitated by appropriate support and challenge, for example from within the coaching process. Even if development is not an explicit agenda for the coaching engagement, Berger and Fitzgerald (2002) claim that the cognitive–developmental approach has much to offer, particularly with regard to issues of mismatch between the complexity that the client role may require and his/her own order of mind. They suggest different strategies for supporting clients when there is such a misfit.

Table 9.1: Five stages of development according to Kegan's theory

Stage	Subject	Object	Cognitive style	Self	Others	Conscious preoccupation	Inclusion/separation balance
1	Impulses, perceptions	Reflections (sensing, moving)	Pre-operational simplicity	Emerging ego through ownership of what is 'mine'	Exist for fulfilment of their needs	Safety and gratification of basic needs	More of inclusion

Children act on impulse. They are subject to perceptions, so if perception changes the world also changes. They cannot imagine that others may have different opinions of the same things. They cannot hold ideas in their mind for long and need to be reminded of the rules.

Stage	Subject	Object	Cognitive style	Self	Others	Conscious preoccupation	Inclusion/separation balance
2	Needs, interests, wishes	Impulses, perceptions	Concrete operational, black and white thinking	Single concrete features, emergence of 'agent', 'I am what I want'	Competing for goods and power, and can see through me	Gaining advantages and protecting oneself	More of separation

With the ability to control impulses comes a sense of freedom and power, therefore those at this stage are now synonymous with their needs and wishes. They can see that others also have wishes and interests that may clash with theirs. They feel that they have to protect themselves and are concerned with power over them. They are self-centred and see others as helpers or barriers to getting what they want and follow rules mostly to avoid punishment.

Stage	Subject	Object	Cognitive style	Self	Others	Conscious preoccupation	Inclusion/separation balance
3	The interpersonal, mutuality	Needs, interests, wishes	Ability for abstract thinking and self-reflection	Self is defined in terms of internalized expectations of important others	Others are divided on the inner circle who provide values and identity and those who are outside it	Social acceptance, status and prestige, moral 'shoulds and oughts'	More of inclusion

At this stage the person *has* needs, not *is* his/her needs, so others are understood as also having needs. They are no longer a means to his/her ends and can subordinate their needs to something greater. However, they *are* now their relationship. Expectations of others are so important that this may cause difficulties in making decisions and give rise to issues of self-esteem. They may feel torn apart by the conflict between important others. Kegan believes that people in the Third order feel 'in over their heads' much of the time.

4	Authorship, identity, psychic administration, ideology	The interpersonal, mutuality	Can see multiplicity and patterns, critical and analytical	Strong ego with interest in deep self-understanding. Awareness of self-deception	Capable of understanding others and of having true empathy. Can build meaningful relationships	Achievement of long-term personal goals according to inner standards. Pursuit of truth	More of separation

A person at this stage is someone who now *has* the relationship. This implies a self that may exist outside of relationship with others, with a sense of autonomy and identity. People at this stage are able to examine various rules and opinions and mediate between them. They can feel empathy for others and take their views into consideration, but at the same time are not torn apart by the views of others – they have their own system with which to make decisions. They are self-motivated, self-evaluative. They can create their own rules and fight for them but may not be the best diplomats, because their way of doing things may be too important to them.

5	Inter-individuality, inter-penetrability of self-systems	Authorship, identity, psychic administration, ideology	Systems view and meaning-making as interpretation. Tolerance of ambiguity. Change from linear logic to holistic understanding	Integration of all aspects of self including shadow. Capacity for interdependent self-definition	Others are also self-systems. Respect for uniqueness and development	Individuality and self-fulfilment. Immediate present. Intense relationship	More of inclusion

At this stage a person becomes someone who *has* identity and can explore his/her own self-system. Learning about the limitations of their own inner system they recognize the limitation of *having* an inner system. Looking across their inner systems they can see similarities in what look like differences. They are less prone to black and white thinking and apply fewer dichotomies and polarities in their evaluations of the world.

Here is an example of how a coach may support a client at a Third order of mind whose role has Fourth order expectations. This coaching engagement may easily take place if the client has been successful in a previous role and is promoted to a new, more complex one. It could also happen because of a change in the nature of the job or with a request from a boss who wants the client to take more responsibility for decision making or for the ownership of the process. The client may feel overwhelmed by these expectations. He may have the abilities to meet the demands, but the Fourth order complexity of his new role may require him to evaluate and prioritize these demands without the guidance of a third party. The client may be strained and resentful towards his boss for not providing him with enough direction. The boss, on the other hand, being at the Fourth order of mind, expects the client to take the initiative and becomes frustrated with him when he is reluctant to do so.

Berger and Fitzgerald (2002) suggest that a developmentally-oriented coach can support a client at the Third order of mind by, for example:

- helping to identify and articulate the expectations that are causing strain and confusion
- exploring with the client what sources of information or judgment might be available to support their decision making
- helping the client to craft a decision-making process
- identifying ways to have constructive discussions with bosses and/or peers
- reframing any sense of defeat and failure that the client might feel into a developmental opportunity.

This approach allows the coach to recognize the specific challenges of clients who are moving towards a different level of complexity. For example the challenge for people changing from the Third to the Fourth order is to question the infallibility of external guides and to trust their internal, self-authored guide. However, the challenge of people who move from the Fourth to the Fifth order, in contrast, is to question the infallibility of their own self-authored system and to help them see the need to transcend their reliance on their own system (Berger & Fitzgerald, 2002). Berger (2006) also suggests ways of identifying key strengths, blind spots and areas of growth for clients at each stage, and comments on pitfalls that coaches may face with these client groups.

It has to be said that the cognitive–developmental approach is also known for the complexity of its theory and particularly for its labour-intensive measurements used to identify developmental stages. Lahey and associates (1988) developed the subject–object interview (SOI), which is used for the assessment of 21 gradations within Kegan's orders of mind. It requires 60-90 minutes of recorded interview and a highly skilful scoring of the transcript. There is also the Washington University Sentence Completion Test used to measure Loevinger's (1976) stages, which has been updated by Cook-Greuter (2004) as the Leadership Development Profile (LDP). Laske (2006a, 2006b) uses SOI together with some additional instruments for the assessment of the development of coaches.

The cognitive–developmental approach does not imply the use of specific tools and techniques of coaching or counselling. It implies careful consideration of the appropriateness of all tools and techniques that different approaches might offer to each level of development of clients. The actual helping process could be described as an artful balance of support and challenge appropriate for each stage of development. The crucial part of it is the active engagement of all skills and abilities of developmentally-minded coaches in addressing the work and life tasks of their clients. This approach also emphasizes the importance of the personal growth of practitioners themselves (Bachkirova & Cox, 2007). It is the coach as a person, rather than the application of particular techniques or methods, that makes a difference in coaching practice.

COMPARING THIS THEORY/TRADITION

This approach differs from others in terms of its main philosophical assumption about human nature. Traditional psychoanalysis, for example takes a more sceptical view of human development at the individual and collective levels, while humanistic psychology works on the assumption of unlimited potential for the growth of each individual. According to the developmentalists an individual *may* progress through the various levels, but equally may go into reverse, while humanity itself is always moving forward.

The cognitive–developmental approach was not originally developed for counselling as were most other approaches. Therefore it has no stake in claiming any particular psychological 'territory' as, for example cognitive-behavioural or transpersonal approaches do. Instead, development can be seen from any angle (emotional, rational, behavioural, etc.) and any other approach to coaching is valued as contributing to the overall developmental process.

At the same time it could be said that the focus of this approach is on vertical rather than horizontal changes. The latter changes, such as in skills, performance, specific behaviours and level of confidence, can occur as a result of coaching or just through exposure to life. However valuable these changes are, not all of them will contribute to the developmental shifts in which this approach is interested. In his earlier writings, Wilber (1979) suggested that some psychotherapeutic approaches are better suited than others to the issues that particular developmental stages may deal with, indicating a sort of ladder of therapies. This logic may be similarly applied to coaching approaches.

RELATIONSHIP WITH CONTEXTS AND GENRES OF COACHING

There is an obvious connection between the cognitive–developmental approach and *developmental coaching,* which is concerned with holistic changes in the person. If clients are dealing with important dilemmas or transitions in their lives (a theme that often occurs in developmental coaching) the cognitive–developmental perspective may help coaches and clients to understand that this transition may be not just an adjustment to the environmental changes but also an internal process that has specific features. This can be helpful for clients as it will help them to understand what they are going through and to see the specific landmarks of this process.

For *transformational coaching* some specific pointers may be given from the cognitive developmental perspective as to what may constitute a transformation and under what circumstances it is likely to happen. The cognitive–developmental approach may offer a different explanation of the state of being 'stuck' and of why the coach may not be able to promote a transformation in the client. Clients who appear stuck in the Third order may have a need to stay attached to an important group or organization and may refuse to question anything that shakes their belief system. Other clients may be stuck in the Fourth order of mind because they feel comfortable, confident and in control in their lives there. The cognitive developmental approach may also be useful when there is a need to integrate a person's transformational experience with a relevant self-frame or worldview. Very often these experiences fade because there is no framework that offers 'order', 'explanation', a sense of progression – in short, a meaning – to their experiences.

In relation to *team coaching*, this approach makes clear why group work is sometimes difficult. For example when individuals, at different levels of development, are intensely involved in the same process, the chances of serious misunderstandings are numerous. However, opportunities for expected and unexpected growth may also be present. Cognitive developmental theories may help to explain the reasons for disagreements and conflicts. They may also help coaches to find an overall perspective which allows for the integration of the different needs of individuals into the value system of the team.

The coach's own level of development is also important. To be most help to the client the coach should be able to recognize where the client is on the developmental line. As has been said already, people find difficulty in recognizing levels of development higher than their own and consequently may not be optimally helpful as coaches in such cases. At the same time it could be argued that within certain coaching genres, for example skills coaching, such a discrepancy is less important.

EVALUATION OF THE APPROACH AND CONCLUSIONS

For the evaluation of this approach I would like to consider two aspects of it that cause unease in some coaches. There are also some warnings for those who might be overzealous in using this approach without sufficient appreciation of its complexity. Starting with the latter, it is important to emphasize that the nature of development as discussed in this chapter is a complex process that involves a combination of known and unknown, internal and environmental factors. The shift from one stage to another may even take years to be noticed and recognized. In addition, the theory, once understood, may be so attractive to some coaches that it seduces them into using it inappropriately, designing and suggesting interventions to 'move' clients from one stage to another. The main danger of this approach is that it may create the illusion that significant developmental shifts can be induced by sufficient motivation and effort. It may also distract coaches from attending to other concerns of the client which may actually be more relevant to them and have greater urgency.

Therefore, I would agree with Berger's warning about hasty judgments of developmental stages, particularly in organizational contexts (2006) and about simplistic interpretations of this theoretical perspective. A useful reminder of this is also the following concern of Kegan himself: 'amongst the many things from which a practitioner's clients need protection is the practitioner's hopes for the client's future, however benign and sympathetic these hopes may be' (1982: 295).

At the same time, we do see again and again that the coaching process, even if it aims at specific and pragmatic goals, provides important conditions for potential developmental shifts in individuals. By engaging with the presenting task, coaches inevitably evaluate a fit between the existing capabilities of the client and the complexity of a task. This prompts them to create appropriate conditions for a developmental shift if necessary and it may well happen. However, coaching engagements do not need to aim at such shifts to be successful. Coaching is an ideal means through which to facilitate individual development in all shapes and forms.

Keeping in mind this positive stance, let us address the point of unease that coaches sometimes express in relation to this approach. They are concerned that it implies a judgment about the level of development that a client or coach represents in their behaviour, going against an implicit characteristic of coaching as non-judgmental. This is a sensitive and complex issue which needs to be considered carefully.

Yes, developmental approaches, by the very fact of presenting developmental scales, imply judgments, but similar judgments are made on an everyday basis for all sorts of reasons which are fairly justified. What has to be taken into consideration is the purpose of the judgment and the validity of it. The purpose of judgment in coaching is to facilitate a better fit between the environment and the individual's capacity for dealing with it, which is done in the best service of the client. The validity of the judgment is based on the quality of the theory and supporting data, which is impressive, but also on the quality of the actual assessment.

This leaves us with the second point of unease related to the issue of instruments of assessment for coaching needs. In order to know the stage of development of the client, coaches seem to have two options. One obvious option is to use independent assessments of the client's stage through specific instruments such as the SOI or LDP, which are available, but quite expensive additions to the coaching itself. If coaches are hoping to add such instruments to their tool kits, they have to be aware that they are complex and time-consuming, particularly for scoring and interpretation. It is also advisable to know that, in spite of the reasonable inter-rater reliability amongst highly trained scorers, which is statistically sufficient for research purposes, the probability of error in individual cases is still high.

Another assessment option is for the coach to rely on an 'educated guess'. However imperfect it may sound I would not dismiss and may even advocate this option if at least two conditions are fulfilled. The first condition is that the coach is developmentally-minded and sufficiently knowledgeable of this approach to recognize the meaning-making that the client is applying to various themes, even if the coach makes this judgment 'on behalf of one stage over another' (Kegan, 1982: 292). The second condition is that the coach him/herself is constantly and actively engaged in the developmental process and, ideally, is further along the line of development than the client.

Why do I believe that such judgment is better for coaching than relying on formal instruments? First of all, the coach's judgment of the client's stage will then remain a tentative one and they will not necessarily voice it. (With the use of instruments the temptation to see their results as 'truth' is much higher.) Second, in my view, coaching is valuable when coaches give respectful attention to the voices of *all* the client's states and stages and not only to 'the centre of developmental gravity'. Having a healthy doubt about the client's stage would help to keep the coach's attention fresh and open to these voices. And, finally, I believe that a place for a grain of mystery should be always kept in coaching, which is, to some extent, as much a mysterious process as the development itself.

FURTHER READING

Berger, J., & Fitzgerald, C. (2002). Leadership and complexity of mind: The role of executive coaching. In C. Fitzgerald & J. Berger (Eds.), *Executive coaching: Practices & perspectives* (pp. 27–58). Palo Alto, CA: Davies-Black. (This chapter describes the essence of the approach and gives practical examples of using some of the ideas in executive coaching.)

Cook-Greuter, S. (2004). Making the case for developmental perspective. *Industrial and Commercial Training, 36*(7). (Very clear and comprehensive article that explains the main tenets and applications of the approach to an organizational world.)

Kegan, R. (1994). *In over our heads.* London: Harvard University Press. (This is an original work of Kegan and is an excellent introduction to his theory.)

REFERENCES

Bachkirova, T., & Cox, E. (2007). A cognitive developmental approach for coach development. In S. Palmer & A. Whybrow (Eds.), *Handbook of coaching psychology:A guide for practitioners* (pp. 325–50). London: Routledge.

Beck, D., & Cowan, C. (1996). *Spiral dynamics.* Oxford: Blackwell.

Berger, J. (2006). Adult development theory and executive coaching practice. In D.Stober & A. Grant (Eds.), *Evidence based coaching handbook: Putting best practices to work for your clients.* Chichester: John Wiley.

Berger, J., & Fitzgerald, C. (2002). Leadership and complexity of mind: The role of executive coaching. In C. Fitzgerald & J. Berger (Eds.), *Executive coaching: Practices & perspectives* (pp. 27–58). Palo Alto, CA: Davies-Black.

Cook-Greuter, S. (1999). Postatonomous ego development: Its nature and measurement. (Doctoral dissertation, Harvard Graduate School of Education at Cambridge, MA.)

Cook-Greuter, S. (2004). Making the case for developmental perspective. *Industrial and Commercial Training, 36*(7).

Drath, W. (1990). Managerial strengths and weaknesses as functions of the development of personal meaning. *Journal of Applied Behavioural Science, 26*(4): 483–99.

Fowler, J.W. (1981). *Stages of Faith.* New York: Harper & Row.

Goleman, D. (1995). *Emotional intelligence.* New York: Bantam Books.

Graves, C. (1970). Levels of existence: An open system theory of values. *Journal of Humanistic Psychology,* Nov.

Kegan, R. (1982). *The evolving self: Problem and process in human development.* London: Harvard University Press.

Kegan, R. (1994). *In over our heads.* London: Harvard University Press.

King, P.M., & Kitchener, K.S. (1994). *Developing reflective judgment: Understanding and promoting intellectual growth and critical thinking in adolescents and adults.* San Francisco, CA: Jossey-Bass.

Kohlberg, L. (1969). *Stages in the development of moral thought and action.* New York: Holt, Reinhart and Winston.

Lahey, L., Souvaine, E., Kegan, R., Goodman, R., & Felix, S. (1988). *A guide to the subject-object interview: Its administration and interpretation.* Cambridge, MA: Harvard University, Graduate School of Education, Laboratory of Human Development.

Laske, O. (2006a). From coach training to coach education. *International Journal of Evidence Based Coaching and Mentoring, 4*(1, Spring): 45–57.

Laske, O. (2006b). *Measuring hidden dimensions: The art and science of fully engaging adults.* Medford, MA: IDM Press.

Loevinger, J. (1976). *Ego development: Conceptions and theories.* San Francisco, CA: Jossey-Bass.

Loevinger, J. (1987). *Paradigms of personality.* New York: M. H. Freeman.

Maslow, A. (1954). Motivation and personality. New York: Harper.

Perry, W.G. (1970). *Forms of intellectual and ethical development in the college years.* New York: Holt, Rinehart and Winston.

Piaget, J. (1976). *The psychology of intelligence,* Totowa: NJ: Littlefield, Adams & Co.

Torbert, W. (1991). *The power of balance.* Newbury Park, CA: Sage.

Torbert, W., & Associates. (2004). *Action inquiry: The secret of timely and transforming leadership.* San Francisco, CA: Berret-Koehler.

Wilber, K. (1979). *No boundary.* Boston, MA: Shambhala.

Wilber, K. (1999). *One taste: The journals of Ken Wilber.* Boston, MA: Shambhala.

Wilber, K. (2000). *Integral psychology.* London: Shambhala.

Wilber, K. (2006). *Integral spirituality.* Boston & London: Integral Books.

10

The Transpersonal Approach to Coaching

John Rowan

INTRODUCTION

The transpersonal is a level of consciousness where we admit that we are spiritual beings with a soul and a spirit. As we know from the work of Ken Wilber (2000), it is usual to distinguish between the pre-personal, the personal and the transpersonal. The personal is the ordinary everyday consciousness with which we are all familiar; the pre-personal is all that comes before that in the process of pre-natal and child development, and is well described in developmental psychology generally (Wilber, 2000); and the transpersonal is that which genuinely goes beyond the personal into the realm of the sacred, the numinous, the holy, the divine. It has often been pointed out that society helps us to develop out of the pre-personal into the personal, and even helps us through the early development of the personal into the mature ego that is favoured in our society generally. Society does not, however, help us on into the transpersonal. That is something for each person to initiate and take responsibility for.

Since the founding of the *Journal of Transpersonal Psychology* in 1969, and the formation of the Association for Transpersonal Psychology (ATP) in 1972, the transpersonal has been studied scientifically, and in 1996 the British Psychological Society (BPS) founded the Transpersonal Psychology Section, which publishes the peer reviewed *Transpersonal Psychology Review*. This and the publication of a variety of books (e.g. Cortright, 1997; West, 2000; Wilber, 2000; Ferrer, 2002; Rowan, 2005), have made the subject respectable and well-based.

Examining the boundaries of the transpersonal should help to clarify the concept further.

The transpersonal is not the extrapersonal

A distinction has been drawn by Alyce and Elmer Green (1986) between the extrapersonal and the transpersonal. The point is that the extrapersonal can sometimes be a gift that the person has. It can simply be a wild talent, perhaps present from an early age. The whole range of the paranormal comes in here, as representing the extrapersonal.

The transpersonal is not the same as the right brain

There is a lot of interest these days in the two halves of the brain, and it is often said that our civilization neglects the right brain and overstresses the left brain. There may be something in this, and there is no wish here to pour cold water on the whole idea, but it is important to make the point that to locate the transpersonal in the right brain is a mistake. It is a mistake because it necessarily lumps the transpersonal with the pre-personal.

The transpersonal is not New Age

There is a good deal of interest these days in New Age, and in my travels I have seen whole sections of bookshops, and even whole bookshops, devoted to it. But the general attitude of New Age seems to be undiscriminating, and even to be against the whole idea of discrimination.

The transpersonal is not religion

The transpersonal is to do with personal experience, which may or may not be expressed in religious terminology. If it is expressed in some religious way, it is just as likely to be some little-known religion such as paganism, animism, polytheism or pantheism, as one of the more socially recognized religions. In other words, the transpersonal is a realm of personal discovery, not something which one joins.

The transpersonal is not the spiritual

Even more importantly, the word spirituality is used so vaguely and generally that we have to question its value. There can be 'pre-personal' spirituality (which includes fundamentalism and is often fear-based), personal spirituality (which produces all kinds of good works and human-itarian missions) and transpersonal spirituality. In the early 1970s Roberto Assagioli described the transpersonal as

> a term introduced above all by Maslow and by those of his school to refer to what is commonly called spiritual. Scientifically speaking, it is a better word; it is more precise and, in a certain sense, neutral in that it points to that which is beyond or above ordinary personality. Furthermore it avoids confusion with many things which are now called spiritual but which are actually pseudo-spiritual or parapsychological. (Assagioli, 1991: 16)

I think this is a very important point, because the word 'spiritual' is beginning to be used much more these days as a catch-all, which could obscure the kinds of distinctions I am making here.

Within the transpersonal Within the transpersonal, there is an important distinction to be made, which I think is most clearly put by Wilber (2000). Transpersonal 1 is variously called the

Subtle, the realm of the soul, the superconscious, the heart centre, the intuitive mind, the psychic centre, the *antaratman* and so forth. Its distinguishing feature is that it shows forth the divine in the form of symbols and images, which are accessible and reasonably familiar to all. So it is the realm of archetypes (Shadow, Anima, Puer, etc.), deities, nature spirits, standing stones, wells, trees, rivers and so forth – all things which are accessible to all of us, and which point to the divine if approached in the right way. It is the realm of compassion of a deeply emotional kind. In coaching it is the realm of linking – a psychological connection with another person where the usual boundaries seem to fall away (Rowan, 2005).

Transpersonal 2 is the further stage of transpersonal development, where we are able to give up all symbols and images, all the comfortable distinctions and divisions, and move into the deep ocean of spirituality, where there are no signposts and no landmarks. This is variously called the Causal, the overmind, the bliss mind, the pure self, formless mysticism, the witness, cessation, the Void, Big Mind and so forth (Wilber, 2000). This is less often used in coaching, because it is much harder to attain, and therefore rarer as a resource.

However, Transpersonal 1 can be used quite readily, because it is more accessible and more coaches have had some experience of it, particularly if they have been through psychosynthesis training, where much attention is paid to it. Sir John Whitmore, for example has used ideas from psychosynthesis a good deal – ideas such as sub-personalities, guided imagery and the super-conscious (Whitmore & Einzig 2007). In what follows, I give examples of how it can be used in coaching.

Conditions for human development and obstacles for development in this tradition

The transpersonal tradition is devoted to the idea of development, and holds that we are all on a path of psychospiritual development whether we know it or not and whether we like it or not (Wilber, 2000). At the same time it recognizes that at the extreme point of development the whole idea disappears because it holds that the central part of a person was never born and will never die. This is part of the mystical tradition that we have named as Transpersonal 2. This tradition recognizes that people go through stages in their lives when predictable issues have to be faced and dealt with. What we do not do is to ascribe much importance to them except as illusions to be seen through. In fact, from a transpersonal point of view, the whole object of therapy is to get rid of illusions and false assumptions. Similarly with coaching; what holds people back is not the facts of their situations, but the false assumptions they make about them. As Mark Twain once said, 'It is not the things we don't know that hold us back, it is the things we do know for sure that just ain't so!'

One of the main illusions, which has to be faced and dealt with, is the false belief that we are determined by our previous experiences. The word that is unfortunately too often used for this is 'conditioning', and this is believed in as a real entity with its own fixed laws. From a transpersonal point of view, conditioning may well apply to rats and other organisms, but not to the human soul, which is unconditioned. This is certainly so at the level we have called Transpersonal 1, where we are more inclined to say that 'Wounds are for healing'.

However, there is an interesting contribution which has been made by Whitmore (2002). He suggests that people in business and elsewhere have two forms of development, which can get separated with unfortunate results. One is everyday development, which is objective, quantitative, psychological, out there – mainly concerned with what we have named as the personal: material things and socially approved achievements. He says that many people act as if this were all there is. The other is transpersonal development, which is more qualitative, aspirational, spiritual and mainly concerned with the inner world. He suggests that we look at these as two dimensions at right angles to each other. The horizontal dimension he calls the psychological/quantitative and the vertical dimension the spiritual/qualitative. This gives us a graphic space where we can plot the position of a given person at a given time. If a person were balanced between these two, we would get a neat diagonal line on such a graph, showing equal progress along both dimensions. But what so often happens is that a person, let us say a businessman, crawls along the bottom of the graph, paying much attention to the psychological/quantitative – or in other words, his work – but none or a minimal amount to the spiritual/qualitative. (Of course it would also be possible, if less common in our society, to pay attention only to the spiritual/qualitative dimension, and be equally unbalanced in that way.) But what may happen then is that the person hits a crisis of meaning. This very often takes the form of a break of some kind, forcing the person to rethink their whole life. It can then be a wake-up call, leading the person to take up coaching, for example as a way out. 'When we hit the crisis wall, we tend to bounce back in shock and into temporary confusion and performance regression for a while, but we are at the same time pulled upwards toward the ideal eventually to discover a more balanced path' (Whitmore, 2002: 123). This can then lead to increased wisdom in leading our life in a less one-sided and unbalanced way.

This means that people who come into transpersonal coaching as clients have often hit this wall. 'This crisis was typically associated with mid-life, but we are now seeing it among many younger people too' (Whitmore & Einzig, 2007: 126). In transpersonal coaching we are able to recognize such moments and help clients to use better maps of their world. Such development is not the gradual increase in ability which we found earlier on the path, but rather a step-function change, involving the rejection of much that we took for granted at earlier ages. It is here that the transpersonal can become important, as giving us the guideposts needed for the next phase of our development.

However, spiritual leaders often go wrong at this point in trying to help the person. They try to take the person straight to the highest realms of spirituality, instead of respecting the developmental path. Here Ken Wilber (2000) is a much better guide for people who need sustainable development. He recognizes that there are stages along the way which it is better to respect. The transpersonal is also a part of the journey in which there are no short cuts.

ESSENTIAL PROCESSES/DYNAMICS

From a transpersonal point of view, there are no fixed processes or dynamics, because everything is fluid and open to change all the time. It is a truly experimental point of view, which simply says – 'Let's try it and see'. Taking nothing for granted is easy at the level of Transpersonal 1, because we can now see that nothing is absolutely true. However, there is one theory which turns out to be particularly helpful at this stage. It is called 'Theory U' and it comes from the book *Presence* (Senge, Scharmer, Jaworski, & Flowers, 2005).

The idea is that in transpersonal work we are continually trying to engage with the creativity of the client. Our job is very often to help the client to bring out his or her latent creative spirit. One of the ways in which we can do that is by using Theory U. This postulates seven stages we have to go through with the client. We explain to the client that when we get to Stage 4, the full surge of his or her own creativity will come into play, because there is nothing getting in the way. Stages 1 to 3 are all about clearing out false or unnecessary assumptions, which do in fact get in the way.

Stage 1:   *Suspending*. Here we take the client's problem, opportunity or other issue and stand back from it. The slogan at this point is 'observe, observe, observe'. The coach encourages the client to disengage from any usual or predictable way of seeing the world. It involves seeing our issue as if from a distance. It also involves unhitching our perception, so that it is not grabbed by events in the usual way. Patience is important at this stage, because the client is probably being asked to do something new.

Stage 2:   *Redirecting*. This involves going down a level, so to speak, into the depths of our psyche. We can then begin to see from the whole, instead of the usual close-up vision, which is more partial. 'Retreat and reflect' is one slogan here. Funnily enough, this is actually more familiar for many people. One technique which I have used here is to ask the client to take the beliefs or assumptions which are getting in the way and simply 'lay them aside for the moment', like a package on the sofa or floor, which sounds quite unthreatening.

Stage 3:   *Letting go*. In order to get here, we have to continue to spot and give up any false assumptions that we have been holding on to, perhaps unaware. Here the coach can be of great use in encouraging the client to let go further than he or she would normally. The great enemy of the voice of creativity is the voice of judgement, and the coach can encourage the client not to listen to this voice. And so we arrive at the deepest part of the U. It is a kind of cleared space. We are now able to be genuinely present for the first time.

Stage 4:   *Letting come*. Now it is possible to allow something new to come in. This is something which was not envisaged at any earlier stage: it is radically new. It is truly creative. We have put aside anything that might get in the way of something genuinely fresh to come in. We are allowing what seeks to emerge. We welcome and admit it to the space we have cleared.

Stage 5: *Crystallizing.* Now comes the part where the new discovery has to become more sharp, more clear, more detailed. This is where the practical issues have to be dealt with. This is a very important part of the process; we are now coming up from the depth of the U.

Stage 6: *Prototyping.* Even more concrete and practical, we now try out definite experiments and trials. We try many different angles in order to get the best result possible. This is realizing the rough prototypes we came up with in the first place. And we are seeing them as living microcosms, rather than as mere instrumentalities. The coach can be very helpful at this point, again encouraging the client to persevere. 'Act swiftly, with a natural flow' is one slogan here.

Stage 7: *Institutionalizing.* Here we are finding the way to put resources behind what we have discovered, so that it may find its place in the world. This is the most practical and out-ward-looking part of the process.

We can see, therefore, that in transpersonal work we are not only 'listening for the large life' (Williams and Menendez, 2007), we are also listening for the deep life. It is certainly possible to say, with Dave Ellis, that 'coaching gives the opportunity to think what they've not thought, say what they've not said, dream what they've not dreamt, and create what they've not created' (Ellis, 1995).

Imagery

However, the main tools of the transpersonal coach are intuition and imagery. At the level of Transpersonal 1, intuition has become the main way of thinking, the main platform for interact-ing with the client and imagery is our main tool. Instead of saying 'What happened in that meeting with your boss?' we might say – 'When you imagine that meeting with your boss, what is the image that comes to mind?' And we then allow that answer to sink in to our consciousness and evoke a response in us. We enter into the imaginal world using our intuition.

Again, if a client has a problem with something or somebody, we can ask – 'If that … turned into an animal, what would that animal be?' And if the person answers – 'A rat' – the next ques-tion is – 'How do you feel about rats?' This often leads to more insight into the nature of the problem. If the client produces an image spontaneously, we might become interested in what archetype it represented: at this level archetypes become very real. The anima and the animus, for example can be very much worthwhile exploring, as strongly affecting perception of a person or event (Woolger, 1990).

Dreams are not often mentioned in relation to coaching, but at this level dreams can be very useful in throwing light on everyday issues. The point of this is to undermine the client's taken-for-granted way of seeing the world, and question radically the assumptions that are holding them back. This questioning also affects the issue of goals. Sometimes the client's goals are just as dubious as any of the other assumptions which may be holding them back.

ROLE OF THE COACH AND RELATIONSHIP WITH A CLIENT

From a transpersonal point of view, the role of the coach is that of a companion along the way. There is no assumption of expertise, or leadership, or superiority in any way. It is more like a wise companion on a journey, who does not argue about the way, does not criticize any mistakes, encourages the weary, witnesses the struggles, does not really offer anything but a presence that is nourishing and warm.

The relationship is undemanding, supportive, realistic, truthful, observant and continually offering to go into different dimensions with the client. Williams and Menendez (2007: 152) say that 'The power of a strong collaborative relationship cannot be underestimated'; but the transpersonal relationship goes further than that – it opens up a space in which both client and coach can coexist, in a deeply spiritual way. As Whitmore and Einzig (2007: 122) say, the client may be seen by the coach in the light of 'Here is a soul who has challenges and obstacles to overcome on her journey through the university of life. This is another such learning opportunity'.

It is these other dimensions that make the difference between a transpersonal coach and some other kind. The coach might say: 'What does your soul say about this?' This would be an invitation to enter the Subtle realm (Transpersonal 1), as might be the simple question: 'What image does that bring to mind?' Even a basic question like: 'Who would know the answer to that? Fact or fiction, past or present?' would be likely to take the client into the subtle realm. The subtle realm allows for the possibility that the answer to a problem might lie outside a person, rather than inside them. It allows for the possibility of inspiration.

And when we come to Transpersonal 2 (if we ever do) all the symbols and images and archetypes disappear, and we are left with no signposts and no handrails and no landmarks. This can sometimes be accessed by such a simple question as: 'What would an impersonal witness say about this?' More commonly, the invitation would be to go to a place where there are no problems, and look at the issues from there. Suppose we dropped all the labels such as: 'This is a problem'. 'This not the way it should be'. 'This is hurtful'. What if the situation just *Is*? From the phrase 'This is wrong', we simply drop the word 'wrong'. This is a different dimension, and not every client is ready for this. But with the right person, at the right moment, it can hit a unique button not accessible by other means. This is quite different from the subtle, although both are within the transpersonal.

The transpersonal coach is both a rock and a serpent. At the subtle level, he/she is a serpent, wriggling round obstacles and not being stuck with a rigid answer to anything – a 'feminine' presence that encourages the client to work round so-called problems and not take anything for granted. At this level nothing is absolutely true, so it is easy to see other possibilities than the ones first presented. At the causal level the transpersonal coach is like a rock, with an unswerving solidity that makes the client feel supported in an unwavering way, with a steady compassion that does not fall short.

To understand the rock better, consider the Christian hymn which goes – 'Rock of Ages, cleft for me, let me hide myself in thee'. At the subtle level this is the ability to use the coach as a resource, to take advantage of the deep solidity of the coach. At the causal level it becomes the ability to become the rock oneself. Instead of depending on the rock, one may turn into the rock. The transpersonal coach can see both possibilities, and is not stuck with just one of them.

At a more prosaic level, the coach can simply call on the value of imagery. In the DVD of Whitmore and Einzig (2008), where the latter is coaching a client from the local government field, the coach deliberately encourages the client to bring up an image of a safe place, a place of peace and nourishment, for example. This is used later to help solve a problem for the client. And it is also clear from this example that the coach is really in there with the client, joining with the client in a common endeavour. The transpersonal coach is not an impartial observer, but a real participant in the action, risking his or her own presence in the act.

TASKS AND GOALS OF THE TRADITIONS

The main goal of the transpersonal coach is to enable clients to disengage from whatever beliefs are holding them back from their higher or deeper possibilities. In the transpersonal approach, the human mind is seen as infinite, and the human soul is divine, but most clients are not open to this perspective.

The task for the coach is to enable clients to work at the level most appropriate for them. It is said in therapy that some clients need glue, while others need solvent. This is also true in coaching. Some clients need help in consolidating their previous gains and finding more applications for what they know already. Other clients need help in getting rid of false assumptions and false trails, and finding new directions. Some clients need a combination of both – discovering for example the best ideas on negotiation, so as to yield the optimal result for all the parties involved. From a transpersonal perspective, everyone is right, and the trick is to enable the client to discover that, and to use such insights productively. Unlike New Age approaches, transpersonal coaching has a place for the negative, and recognizes that destruction has a value alongside creation, and is indeed part of the same process.

In fact, the kind of thinking found at the transpersonal level of functioning is very interesting in itself. It operates according to the laws of what Wilber calls vision-logic, and what others have called dialectical logic. It has also been called second-tier thinking. First-tier thinking is limited by the either/or: if I am right the other guy is wrong. In second-tier thinking I can be right and the guy who disagrees with me can be right too. Another way of putting this is to say that in second-tier thinking we start to see the value of paradox. The screen saver on my computer says: 'Of course it matters. Of course it doesn't matter. Of course it matters. Of course it doesn't matter' and so forth, endlessly. If I hold only 'of course it matters', I can get weighed down by responsibilities. If I hold only 'of course it doesn't matter', I can be irresponsible and unreliable. But if I hold both, in suspension so to speak, then I am properly responsible but not weighed down by that.

The transpersonal approach adopts a sceptical attitude to the concepts of goals and tasks. At lower levels such ideas are very useful and indeed inevitable, but at the transpersonal levels there is a radical questioning of such notions. People often come into transpersonal coaching at moments of crisis: 'It is the individual's ability to live through and be transformed by the crisis [from base metal to gold as in the alchemist's crucible] that differentiates the leader from the rest' (Whitmore & Einzig, 2007: 129).

This is not the language of goals and tasks – it is the language of transformation, and the language of the transpersonal: 'Having clear outcomes at the outset is one thing, but this type of work is much more organic and can often meander, diverge and reconnect as the client gains understanding of the next step on their change journey' (Coldman, 2007: 10).

In transpersonal coaching, in other words, we are more concerned with opening out possibilities than with finding answers to problems.

METHODS AND TECHNIQUES FOR FACILITATION OF CHANGE AND DEVELOPMENT

The transpersonal tradition is rich in techniques, because it is so open to creativity. Techniques are invented or modified in virtually every session. There is a particularly strong emphasis on imagery, as the imagination is seen as the best entry point for transpersonal insights. Very often there is much more trust in images than in words. Whitmore and Einzig have made the point that all the techniques of psychosynthesis are useful in transpersonal coaching (Whitmore & Einzig, 2007). Psychosynthesis is of course a well-established discipline in psychotherapy, and has made an impact wherever it has been used.

One of the most important techniques pioneered by psychosynthesis and often mentioned by Whitmore, for example is based on the idea that people are multiple rather than always just single. He uses the word sub-personalities to introduce this idea, but more recently the term I-positions has been found to carry fewer possibilities for misunderstandings and reification (Hermans, 2004).

Some coaches have told me that they cannot use the idea of I-positions in their work because they work on the phone and cannot see the client move about. But this is a false belief. I have certainly said to a phone client – 'See if you can imagine that woman sitting in a chair near you. Move the chair if it makes it easier. As you see her sitting there, how would you describe her?' That went all right, and I then went on to ask her to talk to the other person, and say all the things she really wanted to say. From there it was only a step to say – 'Now switch over and sit in the other chair and be her'. And this dialogue then carried on until a useful terminus was reached.

More important than any of these techniques, however, is the recognition that we are dealing here with a very specific level of consciousness, and that no-one will be able to use such methods convincingly if they have not had at least a glimpse of this level of consciousness, which Wilber (2000) calls the subtle, Hillman (2006) calls the soul, and which Cortright (2007) calls the psychic centre. Transpersonal work is not just about using certain methods, but also of adopting this central outlook. And one way of attaining this state of consciousness is mindfulness (Passmore & Marianetti, 2007).

Some people are very reluctant to admit that they have a soul. There are many ways to get round this. One is simply to rename it: such terms as 'higher self', 'inner teacher', 'wise being', 'psychic centre' or even just 'heart' may be enough to make this acceptable. Another way is to use the concept from transactional analysis of the 'nurturing parent': it is not often realized that this concept contains most of the elements necessary to the soul. Like the soul, it is often neglected, and only needs to be brought into action by paying attention to it. Another way is to ask the client to think of someone they would really trust to have the answer or give understanding: I have had Sir Alex Ferguson, Sherlock Holmes, Aldous Huxley and many others standing in for this role. Simpler still is to ask the client to think of a stranger from another land who has been everywhere and seen everything, and has become very wise. What would this character say about the question?

Another technique is to ask the client to imagine something ideal and removed from the current scene. Williams and Memendez (2007) call this 'stepping into the future', and Whitmore and Einzig (2007) call it 'what makes your heart sing?' The client is asked to bring this to life as if it is happening now. When this has been done, the client is asked – 'What year, what month is it now?' When this has been answered convincingly, the next question is – 'What happened in the previous year to make that possible?' And so we go backwards until the present is reached, whereupon the client is asked to take the first step forward and see what that feels like.

APPLICATION TO SPECIFIC COACHING CONTEXTS AND GENRES

There seems little to be said about application of this approach to various genres and contexts of coaching. There are a few pioneers, such as Whitmore, who experiment in introducing the elements of transpersonal work in leadership coaching and in team coaching, but no research-supported publications are available that can give a reasonable review of such attempts. It could be argued that any context or genre of coaching (performance coaching, career coaching, life coaching) may have a transpersonal dimension in it if the mindset of the coach includes this dimension. However, this is yet to be proven. The developmental or transformational coach may have a particular interest in this approach.

EVALUATION OF THE TRADITION

The transpersonal tradition is so undeveloped in comparison with most of the other approaches to coaching that it is relatively hard to conduct a systematic or evidence-based evaluation of it. However, there is now a well-developed tradition of transpersonal research, and it is only a matter of time before it is applied to coaching (Heron, 1996; Bentz & Shapiro, 1998; Braud & Anderson, 1998). One piece of research confirmed that intuition was highly cultivated in transpersonal therapists (Cameron, 2004). Instead of intuition being a chancy and momentary thing, the transpersonal coach relies heavily on intuition; it is the main way in which they think. This is quite a new way of experiencing intuition, but of course it takes time to build up the kind of trust which enables such things to emerge. Similarly, with the kind of deep empathy we have called linking, there is a kind of union with the client, and some say that an energy flow can be detected (Rowan & Jacobs, 2002; Cameron, 2004). Tobin Hart (1997) talks about this kind of transcendental empathy quite convincingly.

It is obvious, however, that the transpersonal approach is not for everyone. It suits best people who are creative and open to new ideas. It also suits people who have taken some steps in their own psychospiritual development, sufficient to have opened their eyes to the power of the imagination. Such people are more common nowadays, because we have gone beyond the old Jungian statement that such interests are only for the second half of life. Younger people are now waking up to the potential of the transpersonal in their lives.

FURTHER READING

Rowan, J. (2005). *The transpersonal: Spirituality in psychotherapy and counselling* (2nd ed.). London: Routledge. (Gives the basic structure of the transpersonal, and warns against many of the most common errors in this area. Extensive material on actual practice.)

Senge, P., Scharmer, C.O., Jaworski, J., & Flowers, B.S. (2005). *Presence: Exploring profound change in people, organizations and society.* London: Nicholas Brealey. (A ground-breaking book which is very readable and well presented.)

Whitmore, J., & Einzig, H. (2007). Transpersonal coaching. In J. Passmore (Ed.), *Excellence in coaching.* London: Kogan Page. Useful statement of the original ideas behind transpersonal coaching.

Wilber, K. (2000). *Integral psychology.* Boston, MA: Shambhala. (Ideal text on the transpersonal, giving all the research data on which his model is based.)

REFERENCES

Assagioli, R. (1991). *Transpersonal development.* London: Crucible.

Bentz, V.M., & Shapiro, J.J. (1998). *Mindful inquiry in social research.* Thousand Oaks, CA: Sage.

Braud, W., & Anderson, R. (Eds). (1998). *Transpersonal research methods for the social sciences: Honoring human experience.* Thousand Oaks, CA: Sage.

Cameron, R. (2004). Shaking the spirit: Subtle energy awareness in supervision. In K. Tudor & M. Worrall (eds.), *Freedom to practise: Person-centred approaches to supervision.* Ross-on-Wye: PCCS.

Coldman, D. (2007). Beyond results: When clients seek deeper understanding. *Bulletin of the Association for Coaching, 10:* 9–11.

Cortright, B. (1997). *Psychotherapy and spirit: Theory and practice in transpersonal psychotherapy.* Albany NY: SUNY Press.

Cortright, B. (2007). *Integral psychology: Yoga, growth and opening the heart.* Albany, NY: SUNY Press.

Ellis, D. (1995). *Falling Awake*, available from http://www.fallingawake.com/showBookStore.asp

Ferrer, J. (2002). *Revisioning transpersonal theory: A participatory vision of human spirituality*. Albany, NY: SUNY Press.

Green, E.E., & Green, A.M. (1986). Biofeedback and states of consciousness. In B.B. Wolman & M. Ullman (Eds.), *Handbook of states of consciousness*. New York: Van Nostrand Reinhold.

Hart, T. (1997). Transcendental empathy in the therapeutic encounter. *The Humanistic Psychologist, 25*(3): 245–70.

Hermans, H.J.M. (2004). The dialogical self: Between exchange and power. In H.J.M. Hermans & G. Dimaggio (Eds.), *The dialogical self in psychotherapy*. Hove: Brunner-Routledge.

Heron, J. (1996). *Co-operative inquiry*. London: Sage.

Hillman, J. (2006). *The soul's code*. New York: Bantam.

Passmore, J., & Marianetti, O. (2007). The role of mindfulness in coaching. *The Coaching Psychologist 3*(3): 131–7.

Rowan, J. (2005). *The transpersonal: Spirituality in psychotherapy and counselling* (2nd ed.). London: Routledge.

Rowan, J., & Jacobs, M. (2002). *The therapist's use of self*. Buckingham: Open University Press.

Senge, P., Scharmer, C.O., Jaworski, J., & Flowers, B.S. (2005). *Presence: Exploring profound change in people, organizations and society*. London: Nicholas Brealey.

West, W. (2000). *Psychotherapy and spirituality*. London: Sage.

Whitmore, J. (2002). *Counselling for performance* (3rd ed.). London: Nicholas Brealey.

Whitmore, J., & Einzig, H. (2007). Transpersonal coaching. In J. Passmore (Ed), *Excellence in coaching*. Kogan Page.

Whitmore, J., & Einzig, H. (2008). Transpersonal coaching DVD. London: Association for Coaching.

Wilber, K. (2000). *Integral psychology*. Boston, MA: Shambhala.

Williams, P., & Menendez, D.S. (2007). *Becoming a professional life coach: Lessons from the Institute for Life Coach Training*. New York: Norton.

Woolger, R.J. (1990). *Other lives, other selves: A Jungian psychotherapist discovers past lives*. Wellingborough: Crucible.

11

The Positive Psychology Approach to Coaching

Carol Kauffman, Ilona Boniwell and Jordan Silberman

INTRODUCTION

Positive Psychology Coaching (PPC) is a scientifically-rooted approach to helping clients increase well-being, enhance and apply strengths, improve performance, and achieve valued goals. At the core of PPC is a belief in the power of science to elucidate the best approaches for positively transforming clients' lives. The PPC orientation suggests that the coach view the client as 'whole', and that the coach focus on strengths, positive behaviours, and purpose. These, in turn, are used as building blocks and leverage points for coachee development and performance improvement. The positive psychology movement has developed the theoretical and research foundations for PPC, and provided an arsenal of models and interventions that are invaluable for coaching practice. The present chapter is designed to provide an applicable overview of PPC, and to help coaches find specific ways in which PPC can be utilized to optimize the effectiveness of their coaching practices.

Positive psychology arose largely from a shift in the interests of many academic psychologists. Before the recent shift within the field of psychology, most psychologists focused on ridding the world of mental illness, while paying little attention to the enhancement of positive mental health. Although some psychologists researched well-being before the official launch of positive psychology in 1998, these early investigations pale in comparison to the 2000 articles, chapters, and books that are now published annually on positive psychology (Diener, 2007).

Both positive psychology and coaching philosophy are inconsistent with interventions that are disproportionally or inappropriately driven by pathology-focused medical models. Linley and Harrington (2005) note that coaching involves a focus on the positive aspects of human nature, and on inspiring growth and change. Gable and Haidt (2005) suggest that 'positive psychology is the study of the conditions and processes that contribute to the flourishing or optimal functioning of people, groups, and institutions'. This definition encompasses much of what one would hope to observe in any coaching engagement. Indeed, coaching has been described as a 'natural home' for positive psychology, suggesting that coaching is an ideal vehicle through which the science of positive psychology can be applied.

With its origins in academia, it is not surprising that the scholar–practitioner model has been implicitly integrated into PPC (Grant, 2006). A recent definition of coaching psychology suggests that it is 'grounded in established adult learning or psychological approaches' (Palmer & Whybrow, 2005), alluding to the scientific underpinnings that are becoming an increasingly integral part of coaching practice. Positive psychology coaches attempt to weave the 'straw' of research into the 'gold' of artful coaching.

This chapter explores the processes and tools of positive psychology coaching. It describes positive psychology theories, and explores how they can impact the approach taken toward the client, the issues focused upon, and the co-construction of coaching relationships. Specific interventions are discussed, with an eye toward the kinds of goals that clients bring to their sessions. In this way, we explore how positive psychology can inform the process as well as the content of coaching.

GOALS AND TASKS OF THIS THEORY/TRADITION

Before describing the goals and tasks of PPC, it is helpful to explore the importance of interventions designed to increase well-being. We now know that we can reliably increase life satisfaction and other measures of psychological well-being (Boniwell, 2008; Kauffman, 2006; Seligman, Rashid, & Parks, 2006; Seligman, Steen, Park, & Peterson, 2005), and that interventions designed to do so may provide measurable benefits that extend far beyond simply 'feeling good'. A recent meta-analysis of more than 350 studies indicates that, although 'feeling good' is a temporary experience, positive emotion can help build enduring personal resources. Positive emotions enhance cognitive, affective, and physical resilience, and broaden our repertoire of thoughts and behaviours (Fredrickson, 2001). Hundreds of studies have reported associations between positive emotion and tangible outcomes such as higher wages, customer satisfaction, creativity, big-picture thinking, physical health, quicker cardiovascular recovery, and work engagement (Lyubomirsky, King, & Diener, 2005).

These benefits may give rise to a frequently-observed positive upward spiral. The increased positive affect that clients tend to experience often leads to a broadening and building of their thought–action repertoires. This fosters big-picture thinking and creativity, and gives clients access to a wider range of choices. These benefits may then help clients achieve goals, over-come challenges, and perform more effectively. Achieving goals, overcoming challenges, and performing effectively, may in turn boost positive affect, inciting the next iteration of the upward spiral toward improved performance and life satisfaction.

In addition to promoting positive affect, another significant goal of PPC is *directed purpose-ful change*. This is facilitated in part by employing successful transition models. All significant models of change in human behaviour distinguish between several stages, including pre-contemplation, contemplation, preparation, action, and maintenance (Prochaska, Velicier, Rossi, & Goldstein, 1994). The coach assists the coachee through the change process, providing challenges and support that are appropriate for the coachee's current stage of change. As we will see below, interventions based on hope psychology provide important insights for facilitating change. Here we emphasize that focusing on what is 'right' with a person reduces resistance throughout the change process. Applying positive psychology interventions to promote well-being, helping clients achieve the tangible benefits of well-being, and facilitating lasting change, are some of the many goals of PPC.

PPC AND THE GROW MODEL

Perhaps the most ambitious positive psychology initiative has been the development of the *Values in Action Institute Inventory of Strengths* (VIA-IS) (Peterson & Seligman, 2004), a care-fully developed classification of character strengths. After consulting with numerous experts, Peterson and colleagues identified 24 strengths of character that are valued by most of the world's cultures. These qualities include critical thinking, humour, spirituality, hope, and many others. The VIA-IS is a 240-item self-report questionnaire that assesses these character strengths, each categorized within six virtues (Dahlsgaard, Peterson, & Seligman, 2005). Virtues are defined as 'the core characteristics valued by moral philosophers and religious thinkers', while character strengths are 'the psychological ingredients' – i.e., processes or mechanisms – that define the virtues (Peterson & Seligman, 2004). The five highest strengths are often referred to as 'signature strengths', which are celebrated and exercised frequently. The VIA survey is available free of charge online (www.AuthenticHappiness.org), and provides a list of top strengths.

The following exemplifies how positive psychology tools like the VIA can be integrated into coaching models in common use. Many coaches use the 'GROW' model as a way to struc-ture the coaching session. This model incorporates the coachee's *goals*; the *reality* of the coachee's current circumstances, resources, and obstacles; the *options* available for moving toward a goal; and the *will/way forward*, that is, the personal importance of a goal that ignites the coachee's motivation and the specific action steps needed for goal achievement (Whitmore, 2002).

The VIA has facilitated a new approach to this process. One frequently used PPC exercise involves finding ways in which coachees can apply their strengths to achieve desired outcomes. The coach might describe the process to the client using an image similar to the following: 'Visualize yourself on one side of a gap, with the goal on the other side. Now, let's construct bridges over that gap. Let's consider your top five strengths, and see how each one can be used to connect you to what you truly want to be'. If the client's top strength is curiosity, we would begin there. For example, we might encourage a CEO to use his or her creativity to improve products that have been profitable in the past. The coach and coachee then develop an action plan, a road map for traversing the aforementioned bridge. The coachee is then asked to create another bridge based on his or her second-highest strength, and to repeat the process until five bridges have been developed. This step-by-step process integrates the VIA with established coaching approaches for translating brainstorming into action. This approach can easily be translated into an unstructured, emergent process. When coaching in the 'options' phase, for example, the coach might use knowledge of strengths to ask powerful and inspirational questions that reveal a broader range of choices. Such questions can be as simple as: 'how can you use your strengths in this situation?'

PROCESSES AT PLAY IN POSITIVE PSYCHOLOGY COACHING

The following section explores how a positive psychological orientation influences assessment, coach expectations, and the coaching relationship.

Assessment Positive Psychology Coaching offers a clear and articulate assessment of the coachee's strengths, orientation toward well-being, life satisfaction, and potential routes to peak performance. There is a wide array of empirically supported assessments available, some of which have been tested on nearly 1,000,000 participants. These include the VIA inventory, the 'satisfaction with life scale', the 'meaning in life questionnaire', and many others. Additional measures are available for the assessment of optimism, hope, career self-efficacy, positive emotion, and many other positive constructs (Lopez & Snyder, 2003). They are helpful with a wide range of clients, from those whose performance is merely adequate to those who have achieved the highest levels of performance.

Expectations and coaching orientation It is known that an instructor's expectations of a student powerfully affect student performance. Teachers who genuinely believe that their students have great potential are more likely to have students who perform well on objective measures of academic success (Rosenthal & Jacobson, 1968). Similarly, a body of research on 'affective priming', suggests that expectation has a tremendous impact on client functioning. When people are informed that they or their group generally do poorly on a task, performance declines. In contrast, groups or individuals who are told that they perform well tend to do better than those who expect themselves to do poorly (Cooperrider, Whitney, Stavros, & Fry, 2003). Positive psychology coaches seek to harness this 'Positive Pygmalion' effect; it is crucial that coaches identify reasons to genuinely believe in the potential of their clients.

The Coaching Relationship   Although research has not been conducted within the coaching context, the psychotherapy literature clearly suggests that the relationship is a key ingredient in successful outcomes (Horvath & Bedi, 2002). A positive psychological approach is highly congruent with the Co-active Coaching model proposed by Whitworth, Kimsey-House, and Sandahl (1998). They emphasize an egalitarian approach in which coaches engage in active listening, powerful questioning, designing actions, goal setting, and managing accountability.

Another important role of the coaching relationship is achieving an optimal balance between positive and negative. It is important to note that, contrary to misperceptions, positive psychologists do not endorse unbridled positivism. The field advocates a shift to a greater focus on the positive, but does not ignore negative issues or emotions that warrant attention. This approach is based in part on a solid foundation of research. Fredrickson and Losada (2005) have demonstrated that high performing teams are characterized by a ratio of positive to negative emotions of approximately three (positives) to one (negative). Negative emotions encountered in such teams include criticism, anger, and anxiety. PPC involves a coaching relationship in which there is a productive ratio of positive to negative emotions and interactions; coaching relationships should not, by any means, be relentlessly positive. The evidence suggests, in fact, that ratios of positive to negative exceeding 11:1 give rise to performance that is just as poor as the functioning associated with excess negativity (Fredrickson & Losada, 2005). When investigating this phenomenon, performance of businesses was operationalized to include parameters such as customer satisfaction, profitability, and team members' performance reviews. PPC puts this research into practice by structuring the coaching encounter as an active synthesis of support and challenge, addressing both positive and negative emotion and experience.

EXAMPLES OF POSITIVE INTERVENTIONS THAT CAN BE INTEGRATED INTO AN ONGOING COACHING PROCESS

The following section provides a brief description of several evidence-based interventions that are often used in PPC. They are described as stand-alone exercises to be completed without the help of a coach, in part because this is how they have been tested in large studies. In practice, however, these tools are often offered as part of the ongoing coaching process, integrated into powerful combinations of interventions (Kauffman, 2006).

Positive emotion about the past

Three good things One of the most powerful and well-studied of all positive psychology interventions is also one of the simplest. The instructions are straightforward. Every night, just before going to sleep, write down three things that went well during the day. This deceptively simple exercise has been shown to increase happiness and decrease depressive symptoms for at least six months (Seligman et al., 2005). The exercise may feel too simple-minded to be useful, but it is important to remember that studies have clearly demonstrated the remarkable effectiveness of this simple intervention.

Variants of this exercise have also been scientifically investigated, always with promising results. If the coachee feels that a meeting has been disastrous, for example, the coach might simply ask the coachee to name three things that went well with their project today. The coach might then ask what the client did to make those positive things happen. By no means would the coach minimize negative aspects of the meeting; he or she would simply try to cultivate a ratio of positivity to negativity that is likely to promote success. Another variant is useful when unfinished business causes people to lose sleep. Rather than ruminating about problems that have arisen or may arise, it is useful to ask, 'When was I at my best today?' Clients often remember positive events that they would otherwise have overlooked (Sheldon & Lyubomirsky, 2004).

Gratitude visit For many people, the gratitude visit exercise can be genuinely 'life changing'. Instructions for this exercise are as follows. Think of a person to whom you feel gratitude for something he or she has done in the past. Draft a concrete and well-written letter to this person, describing what the person did and how it affected your life. Next, call this 'gratitude recipient', and arrange to meet with him/her. When you meet, stand or sit in front of the person and read your letter aloud. Both individuals generally find this experience to be extremely meaningful (Seligman, 2002). This exercise can also be adapted for the work setting. If a manager is angry at an employee, and feels an impulse to counterproductively chastise the employee, then it may be helpful for the manager to identify things the employee has done that inspire feelings of gratitude. Doing so may reveal a more balanced picture of the individual in question, defuse anger, and set the stage for faster resolution of the problem.

Positive emotion about the present

Savouring Noticing and savouring life's pleasures, both those that are subtle and those that are spectacular, can powerfully enhance well-being. According to Bryant and Veroff (2007), 'people have capacities to attend, appreciate, and enhance the positive experiences in their lives'. Coaches can encourage clients to find specific positive experiences in their daily lives, and focus intentionally on these experiences. This technique might be considered a specific type of mindfulness skill, and is an excellent way to help busy executives slow down and manage stress. Research has shown that positive emotions arising from this technique can buffer one from stress and lead to quicker cardiovascular recovery after difficult experiences (Fredrickson, 2006; Tugade & Fredrickson, 2004).

Positive emotion about the future

Best possible future self   This exercise is similar to the coaching technique of 'futuring', and is similar in spirit to the 'miracle question'. Coachees are asked to imagine that everything has gone the way they wanted, and that all goals have been realized. They are asked to vividly imagine this future. Coachees can do this as homework, typically during a period of approximately four weeks. This exercise enhances optimism and helps elucidate priorities and goals. It is hardly surprising that an increase in happiness usually follows from this exercise.

Engagement

Using your strengths in a new way   This exercise involves choosing a top strength, and applying it in a new way, every day, for one week. On the first day, the client simply identifies situations in which signature strengths are already in action. Clients then brainstorm new ideas, identifying novel approaches to applying their strengths (see case example of Antonia, described below). Clients may also find it helpful to identify ways in which they can apply their strengths to improve or make the most of a trying situation. To ameliorate public speaking anxiety, for example, clients might apply their gratitude, love of learning, or capacity to love. This may help them focus on their core strengths or values, and find the energy and resolve necessary to move forward effectively.

Applying strengths proved invaluable for Antonia, an executive coach, who referred frequently to other coaches. Unfortunately, these referrals were not reciprocated, and Antonia could not afford to lose business. Her top strengths were teamwork and authenticity. When being coached herself, Antonia was challenged with the following questions: 'You use your teamwork to serve others, but why not also apply your teamwork strength to help those who count on you for support?'; 'What about "Team Antonia?"'; 'How can you use this strength on behalf of the people to whom you are most responsible, including yourself?'

As a reflexive giver, Antonia demonstrated a novel application of her teamwork strength. She needed a few strong reflections, and repeated exploration of this positive challenge, as she defaulted to helping others at her own expense. However, because we were harnessing an established strength, this orientation soon led to a cascade of new possibilities that she could contemplate. She realized that she was largely the author of her own dilemma. As a result, Antonia was better able to find ways in which she could apply her strength of authenticity to attract more clients. This process could then be integrated into the GROW model for translating insight into action and accountability.

COMPARISON WITH OTHER THEORIES

PPC is deeply influenced by a number of psychological paradigms, while other paradigms have not been incorporated into the positive psychology movement. For example, PPC has a great deal in common with humanistic psychology. Both orientations focus on developing talents, building self-efficacy, and moving individuals toward self-actualizing goals.

The cognitive–behavioural model currently influences PPC far more than psychoanalytic perspectives. This may reflect the academic origins of positive psychology, and the shift from psychoanalytic to cognitive–behavioural approaches that has occurred in academia during the past few decades.

USE OF POSITIVE PSYCHOLOGY COACHING IN VARIOUS GENRES

The following describes how positive psychology theories and tools may be particularly useful when applied within specific coaching genres such as life coaching, performance coaching, executive coaching, and team coaching.

Life coaching

Empirically-validated positive psychology interventions can be invaluable in the context of life coaching. The approaches and research of self determination theory (SDT) and self-concordance theories (SCT) are particularly informative. SDT (Ryan & Deci, 2000) postulates the existence of three inherent universal needs, or basic psychological nutrients.

- Autonomy: the need to choose what one is doing, being an agent of one's own life
- Competence: the need to feel confident in doing what one is doing
- Relatedness: the need to have human connections that are close and secure, while still respecting autonomy and facilitating competence.

SDT asserts that satisfaction of these needs enhances motivation and well-being, and that deficiencies of these needs undermine effective functioning and well-being. These needs, moreover, may inspire progression from extrinsic to intrinsic motivation, thus enabling individuals to feel more self-determined. Self-determination, in turn, is associated with higher self-esteem, improved weight loss management, success in alcohol treatment programmes, work enjoyment, and other positive outcomes (Ryan & Deci, 2000).

PPC applies self-determination theory in many ways. The coach supports the client's autonomy by enabling clients to make their own decisions. Coaches may also help clients achieve or enhance competencies by guiding them through the applications of strengths, and by identifying evidence supporting the use of these strengths. Finally, relatedness is encouraged when the coach expresses empathy, demonstrates understanding, and finds ways to help clients enhance their existing relationships. Interventions such as the 'random acts of kindness' technique (Lyubomirsky, 2008) are also frequently used, in part to help satisfy the client's relatedness needs.

SCT, like SDT, is applied frequently in the context of life coaching. The coach helps the client ensure that his/her goals are self-concordant (i.e., based on fundamental human needs), inspired by lifelong passions, and consistent with core values. Both working toward and achieving these goals is likely to enhance well-being.

Skills and performance coaching

Many PPC theories and tools can be useful in the context of skill and performance coaching. These include theories of flow and peak performance states, theories of explanatory style, interventions such as the 'best possible future self' exercise, and many others. For the present discussion, we focus on an area of positive psychology that is particularly important for skill and performance coaching: cognitive hope theory.

Contrary to common misconceptions, hope is more than 'wishful thinking'. Rick Snyder and Shane Lopez, the leading researchers on hope theory, have carefully elucidated and defined the construct of hope. According to this cognitive theory of hope, the construct is comprised of two aspects: 'waypower' and 'willpower'. Waypower is a process that involves identifying goals, and finding ways to achieve goals despite obstacles. Willpower involves a general belief in one's own ability to achieve goals (i.e., 'agency beliefs') (Snyder, et al., 1991). Pathways thinking (i.e., generating several feasible routes toward a goal) is crucial; the first pathway toward a goal that is considered or attempted may not be the best path available. If the primary pathway is unavailable, a hopeful person will find an alternate route (Snyder, 2003).

Research suggests that a hopeful disposition yields many benefits. Hope inhibits handicapping and self-deprecatory thoughts, as well as negative emotions. Hopeful people focus more on disease prevention, and hopeful athletes exhibit better athletic performance. In fact, up to 56% of the variance in females' athletic success can be attributed to hope (Curry, Snyder, Cook, Ruby, & Rehm, 1997). Hope may also promote academic achievement, and is one of the strongest predictors of overcoming adversity (Snyder, Rand, & Sigmon, 2002).

PPC builds on both aspects of hope, in order to help clients improve their performance. During coaching sessions, agency and pathways thinking are often described as WILL power and WAY power. Both are essential for successful performance. Self-efficacy, which is very similar to agency thinking, is crucial for behaviour change; self-efficacious individuals are more likely to make an initial decision to change, generally devote greater effort to achieving change, and persevere longer in the face of adversity (Bandura, 1994). While many coaches address agency beliefs in a way that is consistent with research literature, few take full advantage of this rich body of scientific findings. We know, for example, that an individual's prior successes are the most powerful source of self-efficacy, followed by vicarious experiences (e.g., observing the success of another person whom you believe has similar skills). Maddux (2002) suggests that 'imaginal' experiences (e.g., imagining ourselves or others behaving effectively in hypothetical situations) can also boost self-efficacy. Verbally persuading individuals of their efficacy, in contrast, is only occasionally successful (Bandura, 1994).

Executive coaching

According to positive psychology research, top performers have very specific goal-setting habits. It is often assumed that these individuals set high goals, while low achievers set low goals. However, evidence suggests that top achievers know their capabilities, and set goals that are only slightly above their current performance levels (Latham, 2000). Conversely, low achievers are unaware of their ability levels, and often set goals that are unrealistically ambitious. Top achievers also set goals based on their strengths, building their personal and professional lives on these personal assets. They learn to recognize and develop their talents, find roles that suit them best, and creatively invent ways to apply their talents and strengths when necessary.

Assessing and applying strengths can serve many purposes beyond enhancing well-being. Knowledge of strengths can be used to re-craft jobs, negotiate development challenges, construct teams on the basis of complementary strengths profiles, and build better relationships with colleagues and superiors. These types of applications often play a central role in executive coaching.

Team coaching

PPC also lends itself well to team coaching for businesses and organizations. One development in positive psychology is the study of organizational dynamics that produce exceptional outcomes. Cameron, Dutton, and Quinn (2003) have proposed that this process depends largely on positive emotions that are contagious, and that broaden our repertoires of thoughts and behaviours (Fredrickson, 2003). They assert that positive emotions give rise to a wide range of desirable organizational behaviours, such as creativity, tolerance of failure, and transformational leadership. These outcomes, in turn, promote further positive emotions. PPC can be used to help teams capitalize on this knowledge of positive group dynamics. Positive psychology coaches help teams identify and build on positive emotions through investment in high quality connections and relationships (Dutton & Heaphy, 2003), random acts of kindness (Lyubomirsky, 2008), and other strategies.

EVALUATION OF THE THEORY/TRADITION

Positive psychology and PPC, in contrast to traditional approaches, explicitly focus on character strengths, well-being, and the things that make life worth living. Coaching and positive psychology are natural allies in their explicit concern with enhancement of optimal functioning and well-being, their challenge of traditional assumptions about human nature, and their use of a strengths-based approach to performance improvement. As an applied tradition, PPC serves a dual function. On the one hand, it provides a context in which the scholarly ideas of positive psychology can be applied and evaluated. On the other hand, it enables practitioners to understand how the sound base of theory and research provided by positive psychology can give rise to successful intervention and change.

Some may wonder if the benefits of PPC arise simply from being reassuring, caring, and kind to clients. These are certainly important aspects of any therapeutic relationship, including positive psychology coaching, but PPC cannot be reduced to these 'non-specific' factors. Positive psychology coaching is a complex confluence of science and art. Coaches utilize a variety of highly developed and evidence-based coaching tools to help clients achieve optimal performance.

When focusing on the positive, the potential exists for lack of balance; insufficient attention may be devoted to negativity, or to deeper, underlying issues (Popovic & Boniwell, 2007). One of the greatest emotions scholars, Richard Lazarus (2003: 94), challenges the implicit message of separation between positive and negative, arguing that they are two sides of the same coin: 'God needs Satan and vice versa. One would not exist without the other. We need the bad, which is part of life, to fully appreciate the good. Any time you narrow the focus of attention too much to one side or another, you are in danger of losing perspective'. The realities of life and coaching most often fall between positive and negative extremes. If the psychology of the past made the major mistake of focusing on the negative – often at the expense of the positive – is positive psychology not making the same mistake by allowing the pendulum to swing in the opposite direction? An informed PPC practitioner can draw on work in post-traumatic growth and resilience (Tedeschi & Calhoun, 2004) as well as meaning and benefit-finding (Baumeister & Vohs, 2002), but this may not be enough to equilibrate the aforementioned pendulum to a position along the positive–negative spectrum that is optimal for a given client.

Finally, positive psychology has been criticized for adopting an exclusive focus on the individual, and thereby placing responsibility for happiness squarely at the individual level (Held, 1999). This may sound noble, but it may also give rise to an unintended conclusion: victims of unfortunate circumstances can be blamed for their own misery. Instead of acknowledging the socioeconomic forces that may have contributed to an individual's psychological struggles, we may implicitly and unintentionally highlight an individual's failures to exhibit the necessary optimism, strength, virtue, and willpower to be happy despite challenges. Held (1999: 980) writes:

> In my own experiences as … a clinical psychologist, I have repeatedly noticed that some people seem to feel guilty, defective, or both when they can't feel good. They sometimes apologize for not being able to smile in the face of adversity, as if they were committing an act of treason by feeling and acting unhappy.

This appears to reflect an unspoken cultural mandate, which holds that unhappiness is intolerable and should therefore be abolished. The mandate may paradoxically decrease subjective well-being, the very condition it is designed to enhance. For some people who face trying circumstances, it may be possible to apply the tools of positive psychology in order to improve psychological well-being. For others, doing so is simply infeasible. It is crucial that coaches do not imply, even unintentionally, any culpability in those whose circumstances have made it difficult to achieve lasting happiness.

In conclusion, we have argued that PPC is a constructive coaching tradition that combines the very essence of coaching with a robust theoretical and empirical base. As coaches begin to apply the approach they may find that the dichotomy between positive and negative is somewhat misleading; it is rare for coaches to focus exclusively on either positive or negative issues. We call for a balanced approach to positive psychology coaching that moves away from ideological biases on either side, an approach that combines positive psychological science with coaching intuition to positively transform the lives of coaching clients.

FURTHER READING

Peterson, C. (2006). *A primer in positive psychology.* New York: Oxford University Press. (This textbook of positive psychology provides a lucid overview of the field, as well as exercises to help readers develop an experiential understanding of positive psychology principles.)

Haidt, J. (2005). *The happiness hypothesis: Finding modern truth in ancient wisdom.* New York: Basic Books. (An enjoyable and extremely well-written introduction to the positive psychology field that interweaves positive psychology theory with ancient wisdom.)

Boniwell, I. (2006). *Positive psychology in a nutshell.* London: PWBC. (A student-friendly and balanced introduction to the positive psychology field that is both concise and thorough.)

REFERENCES

Bandura, A. (1994). *Self-efficacy.* In V.S. Ramachaudran (Ed.), *Encyclopedia of human behavior* (vol. 4, pp. 71–81). New York: Academic Press.

Baumeister, R.F., & Vohs, K.D. (2002). The pursuit of meaningfulness in life. In C.R. Snyder & S.J. Lopez (Eds.), *Handbook of positive psychology* (pp. 608–18). New York: Oxford University Press.

Boniwell, I. (2008). *Positive psychology in a nutshell.* London: PWBC.

Bryant, F.B., & Veroff, J. (2007). *Savoring: A new model of positive experiences.* Mahwah, NJ: Lawrence Erlbaum Associates.

Cameron, K.S., Dutton, J.E., & Quinn, R.E. (2003). *Positive organizational scholarship.* San Francisco, CA: Berrett-Koehler.

Cooperrider, D., Whitney, D., Stavros, J., & Fry, R. (2003). *Appreciative inquiry handbook.* San Francisco, CA: Berrett-Koehler.

Curry, L.A., Snyder, C.R., Cook, D.L., Ruby, B.C., & Rehm, M. (1997). The role of hope in academic and sport achievement. *Journal of Personality and Social Psychology, 73*(6): 1257–67.

Dahlsgaard, K., Peterson, C., & Seligman, M.E.P. (2005). Shared virtue: The convergence of valued human strengths across culture and history. *Review of General Psychology, 9*(3): 203–13.

Diener, E. (2007). Myths in the science of happiness, and directions for future research. In M. Eid & R. Larsen (Eds.), *The science of subjective well-being* (pp. 493–514). New York: Guilford.

Dutton, J.E., & Heaphy, E.D. (2003). The power of high-quality connections. In K.S. Cameron, J.E. Dutton & R.E. Quinn (Eds.), *Positive organizational scholarship: Foundations of a new discipline.* San Francisco, CA: Berrett-Koehler.

Fredrickson, B. (2006). The broaden and build theory of positive emotions. In M. Csikszentmihalyi & I. Csikszentmihalyi (Eds.), *A life worth living: Contributions to positive psychology.* New York: Oxford University Press.

Fredrickson, B.L. (2001). The role of positive emotions in positive psychology: The broaden-and-build theory of positive emotions. *American Psychologist, 56*(3): 218–26.

Fredrickson, B.L. (2003). Positive emotions and upward spirals in organizations. In K.S. Cameron, J.E. Dutton & R.E. Quinn (Eds.), *Positive organizational scholarship: Foundations of a new discipline.* San Francisco, CA: Berrett-Koehler.

Fredrickson, B.L., & Losada, M.F. (2005). Positive affect and the complex dynamics of human flourishing. *American Psychologist, 60*(7): 678–86.

Gable, S., & Haidt, J. (2005). What (and why) is positive psychology? *Review of General Psychology, 9*(2): 103–10.

Grant, A. (2006). A personal perspective on professional coaching and the development of coaching psychology. *International Coaching Psychology Review, 1*(1): 12–22.

Held, B. (1999). The tyranny of the positive attitude in America: Observation and speculation. *Journal of Clinical Psychology, 58*(9): 956–91.

Horvath, A.O., & Bedi, R.P. (2002). The alliance. In J.C. Norcross (Ed.), *Psychotherapy relationships that work: Therapist contributions and responsiveness to patients.* New York: Oxford University Press.

Kauffman, C. (2006). Positive psychology: The science at the heart of coaching. In D. Stober & A. M. Grant (Eds.), *Evidence based coaching handbook: Putting best practices to work for your clients* (pp. 219–54). Hoboken, NJ: John Wiley & Sons.

Latham, G. (2000). Motivating employee performance through goal setting. In E.A. Locke (Ed.), *Handbook of principles of organizational behavior* (pp. 107–19). San Francisco, CA: Blackwell.

Lazarus, R.S. (2003). Does the positive psychology movement have legs? *Psychological Inquiry, 14*: 93–109.

Linley, A., & Harrington, S. (2005). Positive psychology and coaching psychology: Perspectives on integration. *The Coaching Psychologist, 1*(1): 13–17.

Lopez, S., & Snyder C.R. (2003). *Positive psychological assessment: A handbook of models and measures.* Washington, DC: American Psychological Association.

Lyubomirsky, S. (2008). *The HOW of happiness.* New York: Penguin Press.

Lyubomirsky, S., King, L., & Diener, E. (2005). The benefits of frequent positive affect: Does happiness lead to success? *Psychological Bulletin, 131*(6): 803–55.

Maddux, J.R. (2002). *Self-efficacy: The power of believing you can.* In C.R. Snyder & S.J. Lopez (Eds.), *Handbook of positive psychology* (pp. 277–87). New York: Oxford University Press.

Palmer, S., & Whybrow, A. (2005). The proposal to establish a special group in coaching psychology. *The Coaching Psychologist, 1*(1): 5–12.

Peterson, C., & Seligman, M.E.P. (2004). *Character strengths and virtues: A handbook and classification.* Washington, DC: American Psychological Association.

Popovic, N., & Boniwell, I. (2007). Personal consultancy: An integrative approach to one-to-one talking practices. *International Journal of Evidence-based Coaching and Mentoring, 5*: 24–9.

Prochaska, J.O., Velicier, W.F., Rossi, J.S., & Goldstein, M.G. (1994). Stages of change and decisional balance for 12 problem behaviours. *Health Psychology, 13*(1): 39–46.

Rosenthal, R., & Jacobson, L. (1968). *Pygmalion in the classroom: Teacher expectation and pupils' intellectual development.* New York: Holt, Rinehart, & Winston.

Ryan, R.M., & Deci, E.L. (2000). Self-determination theory and the facilitation of intrinsic motivation and well-being. *American Psychologist, 55*: 68–78.

Seligman, M.E.P. (2002). *Authentic happiness.* New York: Free Press.

Seligman, M.E.P., Rashid, T., & Parks, A. (2006). Positive psychotherapy. *American Psychologist, 61*(8): 774–88.

Seligman, M.E.P., Steen, T., Park, N., & Peterson, C. (2005). Positive psychology progress: Empirical validation of interventions. *American Psychologist, 60*(5): 410–21.

Sheldon, K.M., & Lyubomirsky, S. (2004). Achieving sustainable new happiness: Prospects, practices, and prescriptions. In P. A. Linley & S. Joseph (Eds.), *Positive psychology in practice.* Hoboken, NJ: John Wiley & Sons.

Snyder, C.R. (2003). On the trail of the elusive 'false' hope phenomenon. Paper presented at the 2nd Annual Positive Psychology Summit, Washington, DC., October.

Snyder, C.R., Rand, K.L., & Sigmon, D.R. (2002). Hope theory: A member of the positive psychology family. In C.R. Snyder & S.J. Lopez (Eds.), *Handbook of positive psychology*. New York: Oxford University Press.

Snyder, C.R., Harris, C., Anderson, J.R., Holleran, S.A., Irving, L.M., Sigmon, S.T., et al. (1991). The will and the ways: Development and validation of an individual differences measure of hope. *Journal of Personality and Social Psychology*, *60*(4): 570–85.

Tedeschi, R.G., & Calhoun, L.G. (2004). Posttraumatic growth: Conceptual foundations and empirical evidence. *Psychological Inquiry, 15*(1): 1–18.

Tugade, M.M., & Fredrickson, B.L. (2004). Resilient individuals use positive emotions to bounce back from negative emotional arousal. *Journal of Personality and Social Psychology, 86*(2): 320–33.

Whitmore, J. (2002). *Coaching for performance*. Boston, MA: Nicholas Brealey.

Whitworth, L., Kimsey-House, H., & Sandahl, P. (1998). *Co-active coaching*. Mountain View, CA: Davies-Black.

12

Transactional Analysis and Coaching

Trudi Newton and Rosemary Napper

INTRODUCTION

Transactional Analysis (TA) is known for its philosophy about how people can relate to themselves, others and the world, a philosophy colloquially referred to as 'I'm OK, you're OK'. This apparently simple statement combines an awareness of being in the world with others as independent but connected human beings ('I am, you are') with a belief in a positive aspiration to trust and respect each other and ourselves (Sills, 2007). Building on this, TA presents a theory of human development and communication and a meta-language or meta-perspective that allows a critique of various models, including TA itself.

The aim in this chapter is to describe how TA can inform coaching practice through providing a valuable thinking framework for the coach and by offering an accessible language to be shared with clients for greater understanding of the motivations, interactions and outcomes explored or experienced in the coaching conversation.

Eric Berne, the originator of TA, developed a system that is available to clients through an easily understood language; he was opposed to the elitism and obscuring terminology of the psychoanalytic profession (Stewart, 1992). As a psychiatrist and psychoanalyst in the USA during the 1950s and 1960s he observed the behaviour of clients towards himself and other people, in everyday life and in therapeutic groups. According to Berne, intentions, beliefs and early decisions could be inferred from the observations (by the client and/or the group as well as by the therapist) and checked out, thus presenting opportunities for change. Berne also developed a systemic theory of organizations (Berne, 1963) which takes account of organizational culture, leadership, and the dynamics between these and the individuals and groups within organizations.

True to its colloquial tradition, TA has three straightforward key principles that derive from its value base.

- Everyone is OK (I'm OK, you're OK and they're OK) – belief in the worth and dignity of all people, mutual- and self-respect.
- Everyone can think – and therefore find solutions to solve problems.
- Anyone can change – their behaviour, thinking or feeling (if and when they so choose).

These principles form the base of open communication and a contractual process which is essential to TA practice. Its theoretical ground includes understanding causes, working from an ethical, values-based position and enabling behavioural change. It is also a very practical approach, presenting people with the opportunity to change while respecting their decision about how and when they want to do so.

Since Berne, TA has developed in both theory and practice. It is now widely used in organizational consultancy, team development and education, as well as being a particular approach in psychotherapy and counselling. The creative locus has moved from the USA to Europe, and current writing shows the breadth of outlook within the TA community, embracing psychodynamic, humanistic, cognitive–behavioural perspectives and positive psychology (Allen, 1997; Summers and Tudor, 2000; Sills & Hargaden, 2002).

PROMOTING AUTONOMY – THE AIM OF TA COACHING

The overall goal of TA-based work is change and autonomy, described by Berne (1964) as an awareness (of self and others), spontaneity in relationships, and the capacity for intimacy. Autonomy is variously clarified as cure, or as liberation, self-determination, independence and interdependence. The autonomous person makes his or her own decisions, thinks independently, knows how to avoid psychological games and *scripty* behaviours and is able to express an authentic self and to be fully available to others.

TA 'tools' – concepts, models, metaphors and diagrams – aim to promote autonomy by encouraging people to update old strategies or acquire new ones for interacting, problem solving and achieving goals. People recognize, relate to and integrate the models for themselves. These offer everyone a means to conceptualize their lived experience – of conflict, empathy, inspiration, emotion. Through the coherence of the models and the connections they make with them, individuals are able to make sense of their experience in new ways. Both coach and coachee can recognize their own patterns of thought, feeling and behaviour and bring into the coaching space how these affect the work they are doing together and how they might illuminate personal and professional dilemmas. The coach becomes an instrument in the work as well as an enabler.

THEORY AND PROCESS IN WORKING WITH A TA
APPROACH TO COACHING

Contracting is at the heart of the approach. The TA-literate coach will be aware of the multiple contracts involved in any coaching relationship and sets out at the start to keep these as clear as possible – and to check the contract whenever anything seems to go awry. The first step is always to clarify what the contract is. Contracting happens at several levels.

- First is the administrative (Berne, 1966) or procedural (Hay, 2007) level – concerning *what* the coach and client will do together – how often? face-to-face or by phone? agenda and purpose? who pays and how much? how many sessions? for how long each time?
- This is supported by the professional (Berne, 1966) or implied level – how will these two (or more) people work together, how will they relate, what competencies and experience do they each bring, how will they establish trust and purpose?
- 'Beneath' these lies the psychological level of the contract, which is where the outcomes are determined (Berne, 1966). This concerns the 'messages' which we unconsciously send to others about our beliefs and how we 'really' see the coaching process. Will we aim to get the coach 'on our side' against the boss or organization? Will we hold onto our unconscious belief that nothing will change? Are we out to prove that 'coaching won't work for me'? All these beliefs might be held, entirely or partially out of awareness, by the client, by the coach (am I up to this?), or by a third party (he's not right for the job but we'll try coaching and that won't work so we'll get rid of him). For the coaching to be successful this 'secret' or hidden level needs to be addressed – perhaps by asking 'what concerns do you have about coaching?'; how will I know if this isn't working for you?; if we have a problem how will we deal with or recover from that?' These, and similar questions, help to bring any potential difficulties into the open, as does clarity about the administrative and professional levels.

Time spent on good contracting is never wasted, although it can be time consuming. The aim of all involved parties knowing what they are here to do, trusting each other to do it, and working towards real, testable outcomes establishes the ground for effective coaching. Even though the psychological level of the contract may be positive from the start it still needs to be brought into awareness.

Not only is contracting multi-level, it is also multifaceted. English (1975) first described the three-cornered contract, between practitioner, client and organization (see Figure 12.1).

Often there are other parties to the contract. An individual client may have implied contracts with a manager, HR, colleagues; the coach may have contracts with associates or the partnership that employs them; the organization may be committed to coaching for everyone, and so on (see Figure 12.2).

Awareness of all these influencing relationships, and the potential impact on the contract between coach and client, even drawing them out visually, is a great tool at the start of a coaching relationship. The equilateral triangle represents a situation where all expectations and responsibilities are clear. If the triangle becomes distorted, so that some parties are psychologically closer and others more distant (Micholt, 1992), the coach can ask 'what do we need to do to get the contract back to a healthy place?' A useful question to ask when training new coaches and in coach supervision is 'what is the contract?' Often coaches reply that they didn't have

Figure 12.1 Three-cornered contract.

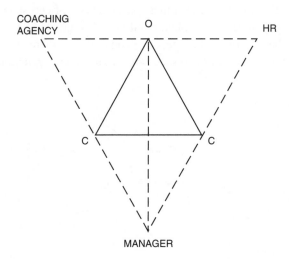

Figure 12.2 Multiple contracts.

a satisfactory three-way meeting before starting the work. The question generally causes recognition of what is going wrong – and how it can be put right.

Clear contracting implies an equal, OK–OK connection between coach and client. This is fundamental to a TA approach, and also a good definition of coaching. The 'OK' model indicates an 'I'm OK, you're OK' relationship as between two people; however, Berne's original writing (1962) suggests 'real' OK-ness involves an attitude to everyone – '3-D OK-ness', as Davidson (2007) described it – 'I'm OK, you're OK and they're OK'. Maintaining this OK frame can be a challenge – and a quick way to check that we are 'on track' in problem solving. People (and thus organizations) sometimes behave in not-OK ways. When this happens it needs to be addressed. But the OK-ness model is also about attitude – how do we each relate? We have a useful intervention in asking – how will we get back to an OK place?

Having made a clear contract and established and modelled an OK relationship, there are some concepts that TA coaches will have in mind while listening to and working with clients.

Working with ego states

The most central concept of TA is ego states, also known as Parent, Adult and Child (PAC). The three ego states (more accurately, sets of ego states) comprise the structure of our personality, and their content is unique to each of us. We all began to develop them when we were very small and continue to update them throughout our lives as we gain new information. The subjective aspect of our experience, and our self-actualization, becomes our Child set of ego states; our probability estimating and objectivity forms our Adult set; and our relationship to others, and our imitation and modelling of them, becomes our Parent set of ego states, which may include things derived from many different people around us (see Figure 12.3).

Just as there are these three categories of 'content', so there are three corresponding categories of functioning – *structural* ego states are 'what is there'; *functional* ego states are how

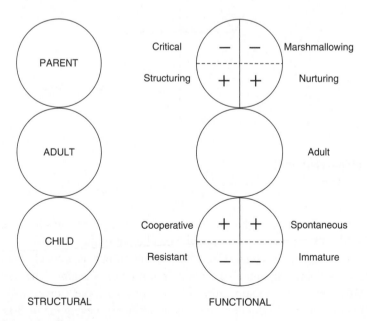

Figure 12.3   Ego-state diagrams.

we use that. How we act in relation to others, our interactions and communication can be described as modes of behaviour and can be positive or negative – the latter may be the result of lack of learning or of awareness of options or strategies. So, we might positively structure or negatively criticize, supportively nurture or insincerely 'marshmallow', account for all factors, cooperate with others or resist them, be creative and spontaneous or childishly immature. The aim is to respond appropriately from a positive mode (Temple, 2004).

Alert coaches will be constantly mapping the flow of energy between ego states through use of language, voice tone or body language – and checking out hunches. They might choose to share thinking with the client (I have a sense that someone in your head is telling you that), or ask a question (is that a real belief?) to maintain a present-centred dialogue. They might teach the basic PAC model to a client, or use it to reflect on the session afterwards and raise their own awareness of what happened in any discordant moments, and consciously choose a healthier ego state next time.

It has to be said that the ego-states concept, although probably the best known, is sometimes the least well understood. For instance there is a belief that people should use adult functioning whenever possible. However, real optimal behaviour means using a balance of the five positive ego-states modes, accounting for appropriateness to the situation.

Transactions, games and script

The next group of concepts (transactions, games and script) can be used to describe what happens between the coach and client. Transactional analysis explores our observable interactions and the modes of behaviour that we derive from our ego states. By monitoring and diagnosing transactions between people we have a great resource to identify how we see ourselves and others, how they might see us, how we 'block' or sabotage our intentions and how we might transact differently to gain a different result.

One of the ways of doing this – and with perhaps the most useful model in the process of TA coaching – is to become aware of the roles of Persecutor, Rescuer and Victim in the drama triangle (see Figure 12.4). This model (from Karpman, 1968) is an elegant way of mapping the positions we take in psychological game playing. Games are ineffective interactions that follow old, familiar patterns and lead to negative outcomes (Berne, 1964). We become involved in games when we feel in need of strokes (recognition) and play from our preferred position of helplessness (V), over-helpfulness (R) or harassment (P); as we play out our personal aspect of transference and/or countertransference in the relationship, transacting in old familiar ways as we 'see' others in particular roles. Coaches can learn their own triggers and somatic signals that tell them that they have been subtly invited to Rescue: 'How can I help you solve this?' Persecute: 'I wish you'd get on with it', or compete with the client for the Victim role: 'I don't know what to suggest'.

When coaches realize that they have been caught in this game (or the client does) they have several techniques for getting back to effective work. One option is to talk about it

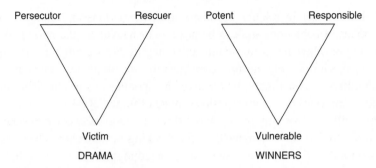

Figure 12.4   Drama and winners triangles.

(what happened there?) and use it as material rich in information that the client and coach can access. Another option is to think back to the contract and identify what behavioural changes might be needed and what changes in perception of self and others might accompany them. A third and incredibly freeing option is to switch to the winners triangle (Choy, 1990) and swap rescuing for responsiveness, persecution for potency and victim-hood for vulnerability.

The clue to moving from game playing to authenticity is to recognize the truth behind the game roles: people do have real problems for which they have not yet learned the strategies to solve; people are genuinely and appropriately concerned about others welfare and can offer support without taking over; and people can be assertive about what they can and cannot do without 'pushing' or blaming others (Napper & Newton, 2000).

Re-decision

Coach and client are engaged together in a co-creative process, rewriting, or re-deciding, part of the client's personal narrative. Every time we become involved in a game we reinforce early decisions about who we are and how OK we are. These decisions, along with the beliefs we have arrived at about how the world works, form our personal story or life script, our childhood meaning-making, which will include some parts that are limiting or even harmful. Every time we challenge these beliefs, recognize a game we play and decide to do something different, action OK–OK transactions, we write part of a healthier story for ourselves. We do this in relationship, not alone (Cornell, 1988; Summers & Tudor, 2000; Newton, 2006). This 're-storying' is done in partnership – coaches might also update their own script stories while paying attention to their client's.

As coaching nears its end the coach will be aware of the importance of contract completion and will check that there is sufficient time to fill any gaps, finishing positively (strokes), and allowing time for review, acknowledging achievements and sadness for a profound relationship coming to an end, as well as looking forward to new goals and pastures.

TA AND SOME OTHER TRADITIONS

A feature of the versatility of TA is the way it has both drawn on and connected to a number of other approaches during its history. It originally grew out of Eric Berne's learning as a psycho-analyst and his extensive reading of the British object relations school; the focus on the intra-psychic within TA is essentially psychodynamic. The structural ego-state model provides 'maps', in the Parent ego state revealing the introjected part-objects, and in the Child ego states denoting self-objects. One criticism of TA is that these diagrams can in themselves reify the theory and take away from the uniqueness of the individual as we look for theoretical patterns. When they are seen as the useful metaphors that they are, ego-states concepts make the intra-psychic more available for discussion and facilitate identification of patterns in the inter-psychic.

The 'humanistic' school is generally regarded as the natural home of TA, alongside person-centred and Gestalt approaches. These share a belief in the value of the individual and their potential for wholeness. Some differences appear when we look at the focus of the TA approach through contracting, for instance, and in confronting game playing and ulteriors by challenging or crossing the transaction. While TA provides a coherent theoretical framework for understanding individuals, groups and systems, Gestalt provides a valuable methodology 'borrowed' by TA. Three-chair work, for instance, can be used in TA coaching as well, to explore intra-psychic conversations between the Parent, Adult and Child ego states; or to investigate motivations to Persecute, Rescue or be a Victim.

The emphasis on life script as a key concept in TA makes an important link with Narrative and Constructivist approaches. Life script is not a once and for all decision but an ongoing process of telling and re-telling our personal stories, co-creating new narratives in the present to replace the unhelpful narratives of the past (Allen & Allen, 1997; Summers & Tudor, 2000; Newton, 2006).

There are also developing connections that TA is keen to explore. Emergent theory in TA (Allen, 2007; Barrow, 2007; Newton, 2007) focuses on health and thriving as something we can promote through applying well-tested ideas about healthy communication and relationships, together with knowledge gained from research into brain development (Gerhardt, 2004). TA can also draw on positive psychology, although the emphasis in 'positive psychology–transactional analysis' is different from traditional TA in that the latter is often pathology oriented. For instance, the traditional 'tombstone' question is designed to reveal limiting script beliefs, whereas the health-oriented 'write your own obituary' task reveals strengths that people may often not realize.

CONTEXTS FOR TA COACHING

The contexts in which a knowledge of TA can inform coaching are many: life coaching (enabling clients to understand how they 'block' themselves through ineffective strategies and

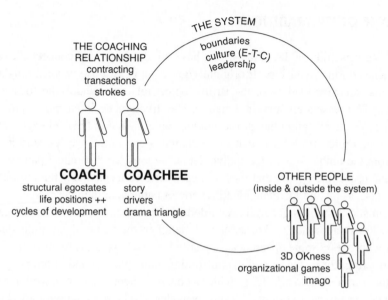

Figure 12.5   TA concepts in organizational coaching.

offering ways of changing these patterns); executive coaching (accounting for organizational culture and multiple relationships in a work context); team coaching (how different working styles benefit or inhibit a team); and parent coaching (a model of child development and strategies for change).

The diagram in Figure 12.5 shows the complexity of relationships involved when coaching and some of the TA concepts to be borne in mind by the coach in a coaching relationship, its context and related systems. Some of this can be shared with the client. The following stories describe, first, coaching with a team and their manager; and second, an example of career coaching in a cross-cultural context.

Coaching teams and managers in an organization

The first two case-studies are connected. A public sector organization shifting from a directive management style to a coaching approach to management asked external coaches to work with a team and the team manager.

A long-standing manager, Dave, had been referred for coaching as he showed signs of stress. He agreed with the new approach, yet found it difficult to engage in it with his team and was uncertain about his authority. The HR Director joined for a three-way meeting once Dave and the coach had explored the professional and psychological contract for working together. As a result there was agreement to provide coaching for Dave's team to enable them to get to grips with the impact of organizational changes on their roles. The following illustrates how two coaches shared similar TA models with manager and team.

Management coaching

The coach working with Dave used the template of functional ego states; he found having a map in his mind helpful. The Parent ego state is concerned with being in charge and providing both structure and nurture. Clarke and Dawson (1998) suggest that this can be thought of as a high-way with two clear 'lanes', the negotiable and the non-negotiable. This helped, for instance, to differentiate a manager using the (negotiable) coach approach, e.g. to provide the boundaries around a team member goal-setting for themselves, and providing (non-negotiable) direction, e.g. with health and safety compliance.

In addition to being in charge, the coach manager needs to take account of what is happening (Adult), co-operate when staff take charge of a piece of work, and be spontaneous and think outside the box (+ Child). This model proved extremely valuable to Dave, who shared it at a team coaching to explain his role and range of styles. Three months later, at the next three-way meeting, he reported feeling much less stressed; the stand-off style of conflict within the team lessened, communication increased, and attitudes to the senior leadership function within the organization became much more positive. Eventually, he reflected to his coach how she had modelled for him, without comment, these different ways of being in charge in their relationship.

Team coaching

The second coach spent time exploring with the team the psychological level of the contract, by telling and inviting stories about how things held in mind and not expressed can cause ongoing rumblings or even explosive conflicts – and how organizational change often triggered thoughts and feelings that could lead to tricky interactions. She followed this with interactive input on 'OK-ness' linked to the fight, flight, freeze instinctive responses (Figure 12.6), giving and invit-ing examples from the team.

The value of the positive OK–OK (flow) position was evident to the team. Also evident was the difficulty of holding this when someone else invited you to respond to their negative position – 'I'm not OK and You're not OK' tries to get others to join in moaning; the 'I'm not OK You are' person goes looking for an 'I'm OK and You're not' person to prove them right (and vice versa!). Ideas emerged among the team for how to work together better, which one member turned into posters for their offices.

The other part of the team coaching explored Schmid's (2006) roles theory. A 'role' is a coherent system of attitudes, feelings, behaviour, perspectives on reality and the accompanying relationships. This suggests that personality is constructed through all the role relationships we have ever been in; these cluster into four arenas: Personal (e.g. sister, friend, school-kid);

```
          − +          + +
       I'm not OK     I'm  OK
       You're OK     You're OK

        FLIGHT         FLOW

       Passenger     Participant
    ─────────────┼─────────────
          − −          + −
       I'm not OK     I'm  OK
      You're not OK  You're not OK

        FREEZE         FIGHT

        Prisoner      Protester
```

Figure 12.6   Life positions and flow.

Professional roles (areas of expertise such as planner, outreach, designer); and Organizational roles, including leader, manager, trade union representative, plus all sorts of major and minor ways of representing the organization's policies and practices both internally and externally (Schmid, 2006). The fourth arena, Community roles (e.g. neighbour, voluntary worker), was later added by Mohr (2006).

Each person made a personal chart for each arena; sharing these facilitated new appreciation of each other and helped everyone clarify their own and each other's current roles. The organizational arena proved fascinating for the team who had never before differentiated times when they and their manager represented the organization, regardless of professional expertise and opinion. What also became apparent for everyone was how miscommunication can happen and how one role area can contaminate or exclude another – when being a parent interferes with working arrangements and others' workloads, or taking work home impacts on family life. The team identified the need for 'contracting' so as to clarify boundaries and give everyone concerned a chance to say what is on their mind, prior to making decisions about what to do.

This work with the team was useful for Dave in clarifying that his role is primarily organizational, and his job is to carry and inspire his team with the organization's purpose and values, and enable them to maximize their own potential and contribute to the organization's whole.

Cross-cultural career coaching

The following case-study illustrates both an approach to career change and overtly cross-cultural work. Using script as an internal reference point the coach was able to work sensitively with difference while acknowledging the recognition and shared values between coach and client that formed a sound basis for working together.

Marsha, a black woman, made a private approach to a coach, a white woman, about her career. She felt in a rut in a private sector managerial post but did not know what she wanted to do instead. Surfacing the psychological level of the contract proved important – why had she chosen this person as a coach? What impact might their different cultures and ethnicities make? It turned out that Marsha admired the coach's entrepreneurship in setting up a coaching business, and that she wasn't sure whether race and cultural differences would help or hinder; however there was agreement that these could be raised by either. Without explaining TA ideas of script the coach asked Marsha to tell her what had been her favourite story around the ages of five to seven. The intention was multiple: to find if there were any kernels of unrealized dreams that might contribute to career decisions, to check on levels of optimism and idealism, and to invite the resources of creativity, intuition and imagination of the Child ego state via positive memories.

The traditional folk story that Marsha told involved a little girl going on a long journey that was very hard work, meeting up with a wicked witch and a wise woman along the way. Marsha had forgotten the purpose of the girl's journey and found it hard to imagine the ending. Rather than asking 'powerful questions', a TA approach considers whether to make the intention behind a query evident by expressing the thought behind the question. The coach wondered aloud about the parallels between the story and what Marsha had already shared about her current situation. Marsha's response was a 'light-bulb' moment of realization, which illuminated the possibility of stepping out of this frame of reference into 'a different story' – one that she made up in the present.

As the story-making frame seemed useful, Marsha agreed to make up lots of stories and look for others that appealed in films, books, and the media. The themes that emerged were: to use her hands in making things, being independent, and providing a service to black women – combining a positive psychology framework of 'the pleasurable, engaged and meaningful life' with TA ideas about life-script. Marsha decided that a portfolio career beginning with one day a week while reducing her well-paid employment time might be a fulfilling experiment. She set up a small business making greetings cards for the Afro-Caribbean community, volunteered as a mentor for women setting up their own businesses and gradually shifted to a three-day week, employing others to help make the cards. A critical moment occurred when the coach was able to say: 'being black is one of your unique strengths – it's OK to build on it!'

EVALUATION

The TA approach provides coaches with useful thinking frameworks. Coaching itself, like TA, uses the Adult ego state through direct questioning and by promoting autonomy, accountability and straight communication. By looking out for ego-state shifts, drama triangle roles, familiar patterns of transacting and unconscious script beliefs the TA-literate coach gains invaluable information to feed back to the client to facilitate getting 'unstuck' or understanding difficulties.

All this may lead the reader to think that TA as an approach is overly structured. Although this may appear true, in fact the TA coach holds the models and concepts in an internal, integrated framework that informs and enriches the use of self in the coaching relationship. The TA coach will be modelling a positive, respectful, attentive and optimistic attitude derived from the philosophy and principles of TA and will demonstrate all positive modes of behaviour as the 'integrating Adult' (Temple, 2004) maps the flow of transactions. The TA coach will show a readiness to change and willingness to be influenced by clients in their co-creative dialogue. They will be potent and present in the here-and-now.

Another characteristic feature of the TA coach is the ability to share important ideas with clients in a straightforward and comprehensible way. Familiarity with the models and experience of their value and impact creates a common language to enhance the coaching conversation and move to outcomes.

Limitations

At the same time a recurring challenge for TA is being seen as superficial or 'too easy'; a continuing theme since Berne's time – confusing a straightforward, clear-cut language with an unsophisticated approach (Stewart, 1992), or use of simple language with risk of reifying concepts into concrete 'things' instead of explicable metaphors. Many writers on psychotherapy traditionally used complex terms to describe phenomena which are in fact easily recognizable; Berne used language that is *simpler* than his ideas (Stewart, 1992). Basic to a TA approach is the belief that a problem being serious does not automatically mean solving it will be complex or difficult.

Some clients may be resistant to the overt use of TA, seeing it as simplistic and unappealing in its colloquialism, even threatening in its directness and candour. Some may be invested in unproductive behaviours which may indicate a 'fixed' frame of reference which is better worked through via a counselling or psychotherapy relationship. Using TA can unexpectedly bring out clients' underlying needs, which may feel inappropriate in coaching, or not understood; the coach must be aware of the triggers and indicators for each client.

Coaches with some TA knowledge may struggle at first to apply it, and to introduce TA concepts without being directive. Those who want to add TA to their toolkit need to be willing to practice 'talking TA' (for instance in supervision), and above all to apply the learning to themselves before sharing it with clients.

And finally, a serious challenge for TA coaching is that in spite of having such riches available, TA has no clear methodology for coaching – or TA practitioners have not yet developed one.

Strengths of TA

TA can be most useful as an internal, analytic tool that works fast and accurately for an experienced coach; it can also be invaluable in creating a shared language with clients. This makes it particularly helpful for coach supervision – the coach who never mentions a TA idea to clients can still find it a powerful means of self-supervision and reflection on practice as well as a basis for discussion with a supervisor (Hay, 2007; Newton & Napper, 2007).

Three key features underpin this usefulness: TA practice is based on observable evidence of patterns of behaviour, thinking and feeling; these link to internal dynamics that are significant for the client and/or the coach; attention to the contract keeps the focus on positive problem solving.

After 60 years, the work of Eric Berne continues to develop well into the present. Today, we have a very flexible system that can be used in many ways to enable people to empower themselves. Whatever is the main approach of the coach, TA-literacy will help to combine their own creativity with their selection of useful tools to provide a safe, structured space, offer support and encouragement, take account of multiple perspectives, work cooperatively with others, and, above all, enjoy!

FURTHER READING

Napper, R., & Newton, T. (2000). *Tactics – transactional analysis concepts for all trainers, teachers and tutors + insight into collaborative learning strategies.* Ipswich: TA Resources. (This book illustrates a potential of TA to inform the adult learning process. It provides an introduction to the central TA theory for people without TA knowledge who are engaged in facilitating learning (such as coaches). It will be also useful for experienced transactional analysts to consider TA ideas in relation to design of learning strategies and interventions.)

Stewart, I., & Joines, V. (1987). *TA today.* Nottingham: Lifespace Publishing. (This book provides a clear overview of currently accepted foundations of TA theory from a cognitive perspective in a counselling and psychotherapy context. There are learning activities threaded through the text which bring alive the psychological theory.)

Hay, J. (1996). *Working it out at work.* Watford: Sherwood Publishing. (People who want a straightforward approach for understanding everyday difficulties find this a useful and very readable book to grapple with the dynamics of the workplace. It is aimed at those who do not want an academic perspective, but want to have a basic grasp of ideas in relation to change.)

REFERENCES

Allen, J.R. (2007). Permission, protection and mentorship: Their roles in psychological resilience and positive emotions. In K. Tudor (Ed.), *The adult is parent to the child: Transactional analysis with young people* (pp. 204–16). Lyme Regis: Russell House.

Allen, J.R., & Allen, B. (1997). A new type of transactional analysis and one version of script work with a constructivist sensibility. *Transactional Analysis Journal,* 27(2): 89–98.

Barrow, G. (2007). Wonderful world, beautiful people: Reframing transactional analysis as positive psychology. *Transactional Analysis Journal,* 37(3): 206–9.

Berne, E. (1962). Classification of Positions. *Transactional Analysis Bulletin,* 1(3): 23.

Berne, E. (1963). *The structure and dynamics of organisations and groups.* New York: Grove Press.

Berne, E. (1964). *Games people play.* New York: Grove Press.

Berne, E. (1966). *Principles of group treatment*. New York: Grove Press.

Choy, A. (1990). The winners triangle. *Transactional Analysis Journal,* 20(1): 40–6.

Clarke, J.I., & Dawson, C. (1998 [1989]). *Growing up again* (2nd ed.). Center City, MN: Hazelden.

Cornell, W. (1988). Life script theory: A critical review from a developmental perspective. *Transactional Analysis Journal,* 18(4): 270–82.

Davidson, C. (2007). ... and they're OK. In K. Tudor (Ed.), *The adult is parent to the child: Transactional analysis with young people* (pp. 188–97). Lyme Regis: Russell House.

English, F. (1975). The three-cornered contract. *Transactional Analysis Journal,* 5(4): 384–5.

Gerhardt, S. (2004). *Why love matters: How affection shapes a baby's brain*. London: Brunner-Routledge.

Hay, J. (2007). *Reflective practice and supervision for coaches*. Maidenhead: Open University Press.

Karpman, S. (1968). Fairy tales and script drama analysis. *Transactional Analysis Bulletin,* 7: 39–43.

Micholt, N. (1992). Psychological distance and group interventions. *Transactional Analysis Journal,* 22: 4.

Mohr, G. (2006). Dynamic organizational analysis. In G. Mohr & T. Steinert (Eds.), *Growth and change for organizations: Transactional analysis new developments* 1995–2006 (pp. 79-101). Pleasanton, CA: International Transactional Anaysis Association.

Napper, R., & Newton, T. (2000). *Tactics – transactional analysis concepts for all trainers, teachers and tutors + insight into collaborative learning strategies*. Ipswich: TA Resources.

Newton, T. (2006). Scripts, psychological life plans and the learning cycle. *Transactional Analysis Journal,* 36(3): 186–95.

Newton, T. (2007). The health system: Metaphor and meaning. *Transactional Analysis Journal,* 37(3): 195–205.

Newton, T., & Napper, R. (2007). The bigger picture: Supervision as an educational framework for all fields. *Transactional Analysis Journal,* 37(2): 150–8.

Schmid, B. (2006 [1994]). Role concept, transactional analysis and social roles. In G. Mohr & T. Steinert (Eds.), *Growth and change for organizations: Transactional analysis new developments 1995–2006* (pp. 32–61). Pleasanton, CA: International Transactional Analysis Association.

Sills, C. (2007). A nice synchronicity. *The Script,* 37(6): 3.

Sills, C., & Hargaden, H. (2002). *Transactional analysis: A relational perspective*. London: Routledge.

Stewart, I. (1992). *Eric Berne.* London: Sage.

Stewart, I., & Joines, V. (1987). *TA today.* Nottingham: Lifespace Publishing.

Summers, G., & Tudor, K. (2000). Co-creative transactional analysis. *Transactional Analysis Journal,* 30(1): 23–40.

Temple, S. (2004). Update on the functional fluency model in education. *Transactional Analysis Journal,* 34(3): 197–204.

13

The NLP Approach to Coaching

Bruce Grimley

INTRODUCTION

Neuro-linguistic programming (NLP) does not have an explicitly articulated theoretical foundation. Despite this, however, most coaches routinely make use of the models that have been developed by NLP practitioners. NLP is thus acknowledged as a practical discipline, where utility, rather than theoretical elegance, is foremost.

Increasingly, authors such as Linder-Pelz and Hall (2007) are beginning to identify the psychological theories that are central to NLP and argue that it is proper to recognize NLP's roots in established psychological strands. The University of Surrey has recognized this gap and in July 2008 hosted the first international neuro-linguistic programming research conference. A close reading of the literature reveals that in fact there are a host of psychological concepts that underpin NLP, many of which have been independently tested.

This chapter begins by exploring NLP's inception and its links to behaviourism and cognitivism. It then examines the language and operating principles of NLP before looking at the approach in relation to a coaching context.

Origins of NLP

NLP began in the early 1970s at the University of Santa Cruz when Richard Bandler contacted John Grinder, an associate professor of linguistics, and was invited to attend a Gestalt workshop with the aim of observing the self-taught expertise of Fritz Perls and developing a model

(Bostic St Clair & Grinder, 2001). One of the main assumptions here, and the one which underpins NLP, was that whoever we are and whatever we do, there is a consistent internal ordering and structuring of our perceiving, thinking, feeling and behaving. By modelling the processes and patterns used by experts, such as Perls and Virginia Satir, consistent results could be obtained. This is made clear in one of the earliest books on NLP: 'Neuro-Linguistic Programming is the discipline whose domain is the structure of subjective experience. It makes no commitment to theory, but rather has the status of a model – a set of procedures whose usefulness, not truthfulness is to be the measure of its worth' (Dilts, Grinder, Bandler, & DeLozier, 1980). Thus it is our own ordering and structuring of the world that achieves results.

From a psychological perspective these assumptions are shared with constructivist psychology. The NLP coach assumes that coachees' internal processes are psychologically channelled by the way in which they anticipate events (Kelly, 1963), and this anticipation is a function of their experience in the world and the maps they have consequently built. Explicitly, the link to a constructive perspective with NLP is made through Korzybski (1933, 1994): 'A map is not the territory it represents, but if correct, it has a similar structure to the territory, which accounts for its usefulness'.

Behavioursim and cognitivism

The eclectic nature of NLP continues in that not only is it constructivist in nature but it also has much in common with behaviourist psychology. Like behaviorism, NLP does not insist on an archaeological, depth approach that explores past events and feelings. Neither does it call for a conscious understanding on the part of the individual undergoing the change. Rather, much of the work is done through classical conditioning. NLP calls this process anchoring, and extends associations to both internal mental and external events. When these associations are individually made in the presence of emotional arousal, they form rudimentary, sensory based templates and synesthesias that form the basis of our experience and our individual creation of meaning. This gives birth to emotional memories that are not represented in the cortical areas of the brain in a coherent and narrative way.

Paradoxically, even though NLP may align itself with behaviourist psychology it is also very different in that, unlike behaviourism, NLP is very interested in what goes on inside the brain. It therefore has a basis in cognitive psychology. It is interested in how individuals create their maps of the world. It is also interested in language.

The result of Grinder's modelling of Perls and Satir was the Meta Model (Bandler & Grinder, 1975a, 1976). When Grinder came out of the 'know nothing state' (a form of deep trance identification used for modelling), and began to analyse the linguistic patterns produced through the modelling process he immediately recognized the similarity with transformational grammar: Bostic St Clair and Grinder (2001) confirm that the single most pervasive influence in NLP is the paradigm that was current in linguistics at the time of the creation of NLP.

Transformational grammar suggests that sensory experience is transformed into conscious understanding through language, and often the language we use deletes and distorts aspects of the original experience. Language also represents the many unconscious generalizations from early experiences to other similar experiences, so that the maps we bring to novel experience sometimes distort that experience based upon previous learnings. In coaching, precise meta-model questions assist the coachee in understanding the nature of their distortions, deletions and generalizations. Once they do this, they are then in a position to alter hitherto unconscious assumptions which they have been carrying about with them, and which formed the basis of behaviour in a particular context.

The Milton Model

Another early NLP exemplar was the psychiatrist Dr Milton Erickson. Bateson, who was mentor to both Bandler and Grinder, suggested that he would be worth modelling. The model that was developed has come to be known as 'The Milton Model' (Bandler & Grinder, 1975b; Grinder, DeLozier, & Bandler, 1977). The assumption Erickson had concerning people was that they already had the resources to make their desired change, however, these resources were often located unconsciously, and they did not know how to access them. Erickson's work was characterized by an approach called utilization, which advocated accepting and amplifying the client's process for therapeutic change.

The essence of change from the Milton Model perspective is that the client's reality is self-generated through unconscious circular processes. These self-reflexive processes can result in either expanded circles of autonomy if the personal reality is appreciated, or vicious circles of unchanging patterns if the 'reality' and its commensurate experience is not valued and is actively resisted. The process of utilization thus encourages the client to value and appreciate all their experience, and with such acceptance comes change.

TASKS AND GOALS

The goal of NLP coaching is to maximize clients' resourcefulness and increase the choice they have in a given context. In order for individuals to develop it is useful from an NLP perspective if they can begin to appreciate how they create their own reality and thus their own possibilities as well as limitations. One popular saying within the NLP community is 'there are no resistant clients … only inflexible coaches'. From an NLP perspective then, whoever comes to coaching, irrespective of whether they share NLP presuppositions or not, should be amenable to personal development of some kind. The NLP coach will have the acuity to notice the structure of their experience and how they consistently repeat their self-defeating patterns. The coachee often is unaware of these patterns, and whether the NLP coach decides to bring them to the conscious attention of the coachee or whether they work with their client at an unconscious level is of secondary importance.

The key to NLP coaching therefore is to develop and increase self awareness to the extent that the coachee recognizes that, whenever they are stuck, it is only because of the way they are construing the world. Their inner powers of thought and emotion, and outer powers of language and behaviour, can be configured in a variety of ways. Through developing self awareness these coachees can then understand what it is that needs to change in order to move on. The array of models and techniques of NLP coaching can benefit coachees in achieving the task of creating autonomy rather than dependence on the coach. As they begin to value their experiences, rather than deny them, they learn to appreciate them as a resource through which they can be developed effectively.

ESSENTIAL PROCESSES AND DYNAMICS

Using the main pillars of NLP; Outcome, Acuity, Flexibility (O'Connor & Seymour, 1995), the NLP coach focuses on three main questions: Does the client know specifically what they want? Can they keep their senses open so they know what they are presently getting? Do they have the flexibility to keep changing till they get what they want? Many coaches will see an overall similarity here with the GROW model (Goal, Reality, Options, Will/Wrap up).

NLP recognizes that in order for desired change to occur, the conscious mind does not really need to be involved. Flexibility within the coaching client can often be accomplished in a covert way. In order to address the ethical objections that could arise from such an approach, the NLP coach will act in at least two ways. During their initial contracting they will make it clear that their coaching style operates in this way, in order to diminish the amount of resistance and speed up the coaching process. Depending upon their style they would obtain written consent to such an approach or at least verbal consent from the coachee. Second, the NLP coach will only work in a process-oriented way. What this means is that no content is introduced by the coach. This is important because often a coachee will request coaching at challenging times in their life and so may be more suggestible than usual and amenable to subtle introductions of content from the coach.

An example of the introduction of content would be:

> Client: 'I feel really angry about that'
> Coach: 'and I guess that means you are pretty frustrated too?'

The association between anger and frustration, even though well documented in the psychology literature, may not have even been there for this particular client before the coach introduced it.

Bostic St Clair and Grinder, (2001: 198–9) summarize what they believe to be the core NLP processes:

1. The Meta Model is designed to verbally challenge the mapping between first access to the outside world through our senses and our linguistically mediated mental maps.

2. Operations define over-representational systems and their sub-modalities.
3. Reframing patterns, so that representations are placed in a different cognitive structure.
4. Anchoring, so that undifferentiated groupings of representations are brought together for purposes of integration.
5. The Milton model, where representations are shifted using linguistically mediated maps without the need to map those representations into the client's conscious understanding.

ROLE OF THE COACH AND RELATIONSHIP WITH A CLIENT

NLP coaching is a very fluid process which starts with the establishment of rapport and the coach uses this rapport to facilitate the natural process of change. This is done by working at the *level of process*. If the client is using visual predicates in their language then the coach will match that visual process by choosing visual predicates oneself. If the coachee's language is punctuated with generalizations then so will the coach's language. In this way, essentially the coach is saying: 'I am like you'. As people tend to like people who are like them, a natural rapport is then built up. Without rapport the coach cannot proceed. Once rapport is established, the coach is in a position to assist the coachee in establishing well-formed outcomes. At this stage the coach is operating as a sounding board for the coachee. Using the Meta Model, questions can be asked to ensure the outcome can indeed be tested and verified so that the coachee knows that he or she has been successful.

At this stage the NLP coach is often required to be supportive. When evidence of limiting beliefs appear, for example metaphor can be used to unconsciously provide a resourcefulness to be drawn on at a later time. Because NLP coaches work 'underneath the radar' so to speak, very often coachees will recognize that change is happening in their life but would not know why. They may not even attribute it to the coaching process and may put it down to the variable of time and natural resourcefulness kicking in, and may rationalize that the coaching was not even necessary. This is characteristic of the very fluid and flexible approach that arises from NLP coaching.

METHODS AND TECHNIQUES FOR FACILITATION OF CHANGE AND DEVELOPMENT

NLP is replete with coaching strategies/techniques which have been developed since the 1970s. In this section we will look briefly at nine different techniques:

1. Matching and pacing

Matching is a rapport-building technique involving feeding back the behavioural patterns of the person being coached. It is recognized that people who are really 'getting on' are almost in a dance. If one person touches their ear, often within a few minutes the other person will match with a hand to face gesture of some kind. Similarly, pacing is feeding back the cognitive patterns of the person being coached. If for example the coachee talks exclusively about the future and does so using abstract language, then those are the patterns fed back to them by the coach.

Critics of NLP sometimes suggest that matching and pacing is being false or incongruent. However, NLP practitioners see these as building bridges so that the map of the coachee can be more fully appreciated. It has to be said that coaches can match or pace someone who is quite different from them, but it will require more effort than matching and pacing someone who is similar. Matching and pacing is the precursor for leading. A very good indicator as to whether or not the coach is matching and pacing effectively is when they do something differently from how the coachee usually does it, and after a time lag, the coachee follows them.

2. Leading

The purpose of leading is to widen coachees' repertoires and to provide them with greater choice in their life. In order to know what set of skills or state they require, coaches must of course have established what their coachees' well-formed outcome is. For example, if they wish to network more effectively, and during the establishment of rapport the coach has noticed that the coachee is moving away from undesirable situations rather than moving towards desirable ones, the following dialogue might be useful:

> Coach: You have told me how you would rather stay in and have other people contact you, and you have also let me know about the anxiety you feel in talking to others about what you do. However, try to see yourself and your business, which is important to you, in five years' time. If you stay in waiting for others to make the move, imagine what that does for your bank balance. Looking at yourself in this situation from that place in five years' time, what could be the first thing you do now to make a difference?

Assuming agreement concerning well formed outcomes has been established, the 'away from' pattern would be activated by this dialogue; the coachee being supported by the coach will naturally be led into a process whereby they search for the most appropriate action in the immediate present to change their situation. This leading process however, would not be effective if the matching and pacing were not present, and during the rapport building process the appropriate cognitive filters had not been picked up on in order to be fed back to the coachee.

3. Well-formed outcomes

To make progress the coachee needs to know what it is they want and NLP approaches can support how they do this in a number of ways that ensure that success is maximized.

a) Stated in the positive

First, a coachee's outcome has to be formulated in positive terms. This is because if it is stated in the negative ('I don't want to be commercially isolated') then in order for them to process this outcome, they have to have in their mind the idea of being commercially isolated; this will be a psychological barrier to what they wish. According to the Coue's (1923) law of reversed effect, the harder one tries to do something the less chance one has of succeeding. This is because whenever the imagination and the will are pitted against each other, it is the imagination that wins the day (Kroger, 1977). If coachees have to process and represent to themselves the experience of being commercially isolated, then, however hard they attempt to use their conscious mind to become otherwise, they will behave in a manner conducive to being commercially isolated. Brooks (1922), who was Coue's student, took the idea further, suggesting that every idea of the conscious mind may become accepted by the unconscious. From there it would be transformed into reality and therefore become a permanent element in life. This works in a similar way to the Pygmalion effect, where expectations influence the outcome in the direction of those expectations without any conscious awareness. Ideally, the outcome needs to be stated in the positive at a conscious level so that it may be supported by the unconscious mind with an equally positive belief and intention.

b) Sensory based

Making a goal 'sensory based' is similar to using the measurable and specific items in the well known SMART acronym. If outcomes are stated in vague abstract language, then it is not possible to imagine achieving the outcome. The goal of being successful tells us little until we break it down into specific sensory-based language which can be unequivocally understood and, most importantly, assimilated by the unconscious mind of the coachee. Evidence from experimental psychology comes from the Encoding Specificity principle (Tulving & Thompson, 1973 [as cited in Smith, Morton, & Oakley, 1998]). Internal and external cues present during the encoding of material are represented in the resulting memory traces. If such cues are present during retrieval then retrieval will be enhanced. Conversely, there is a reduction in retrieval when the encoding context is removed. This is a bit like the home advantage in sports competition. The cues which make up the context during encoding are all sensory based. In addition, the coach encourages coachees to retrieve their well formed outcomes regularly and test whether or not they are moving towards them, ensuring that they are defined within a context which is sensory based.

c) Chunk size

In another comparison with SMART, chunk size would be most similar to the Achievable and Realistic items. 'Changing the world for the better', for example is a vague aim, but it is also a very large chunk. Even though this outcome may be possible, in order to generate action the outcome needs to be of sufficient chunk size to enable coachees to proceed immediately in the present. Conversely, if they are fully capable and confident, but lack motivation, it is beneficial for them to 'chunk up', so that their specific actions can be related to higher, more abstract ideals and beliefs that drive their behaviour through an association with their personal values.

d) Ecology

Ecology does not really have a counterpart in the SMART model. It refers more to emotions. When setting well-formed outcomes, it is important that there are no verbal or non-verbal 'buts'. It is also important that the outcome is in line with the coachees' believes, values and identity. When checking for ecology, one might find that the outcome is good but the timing is wrong. One might also find while the outcome fits with personal beliefs, values and identity, there is a lack of confidence concerning capability. Sometimes, what prevents a successful ecology check is that coachees might feel that while they are gaining something by achieving their outcome, it is at the expense of losing something of value. It would be important then to revise the well formed outcome to include what is being left behind. As can be seen, setting outcomes is important to the beginning of the coaching process; however, it can also be a change process in itself.

e) Time frame

The time frame assists in motivating the coachee to develop a structure within which to work. If there is no time frame then often a consistent reply is 'yes, I am working on this' – ad infinitum. A time frame assists in developing priorities: 'what is important at *this time* of my life?' or 'what do I need to work on *now*?'

f) Ownership

Those with an internal locus of control often fare better than others according to the stress literature (Cooper, Sloan, & Williams, 1988). When setting outcomes, it is important that the coachee owns the outcomes. For example getting a pay rise is not in your control. However, achieving your targets this year and accepting an invitation to the boss's barbecue could well be.

4. Meta Model

The Meta Model is the first model of NLP. It consists of 13 syntactic patterns in human speech along with the appropriate challenges. Questions assist a coachee to elaborate a hitherto impoverished map of the world, resulting in much greater choice.

A coach for example may facilitate change through the use of who, when, what, where, and how questions. In this way the coachee would recover much 'lost' information during the coaching process and have a richer, more elaborated map of their world as a result. This consequence puts the coachee in the position of having more choice. If 'everyone hates me' is challenged, and he/she arrives at the realization that in fact only their spouse hates them, then they immediately come to the realization that many people can now be approached, as it is only their spouse who hates them and not everyone else. Further Meta Model questions such as 'how do you know your spouse hates you?' may assist them to recognize that in fact their spouse does not hate, but loves them!

5. Milton Model

Just as the Meta Model uses language in order to challenge sentences which are not well formed and thus help represent the deep structure of reference experience, so conversely the Milton Model uses language in an ill-formed way with the purpose of overloading the conscious mind, so as to access the unconscious processes: 'You are sitting down in that chair and can begin to relax now'. The coachee cannot deny they are sitting in a chair; however the conjunction 'and' is used to link this irrefutable truth to a suggestion. The Milton Model uses the principle of utilization whereby the coachee's model of the world is maximally used, by accepting it, matching it, and pacing it. Because the nature of Milton Model language patterns is such that they are ill-formed, the conscious mind becomes overloaded, and access to the unconscious mind becomes possible. The utility of this is, as observed by Brooks (1922), if an idea is accepted by the unconscious mind it becomes a part of 'reality'. However, to accept something consciously is to accept it only analytically and for consideration.

6. Metaphor

Another Milton Model technique for the NLP coach is the use of metaphor, which has the effect again of bypassing the conscious mind. Just as humans replace objects with words, so too, using metaphor, the coach can replace the coachee's problem with another problem, within which lies a solution. A well-created metaphor will bypass the analytical mind and be accepted by the holistic mind of the unconscious, becoming a 'reality' for coachees, altering their experience and therefore their thinking, feeling and behaviour.

7. Anchoring

Anchor formats in NLP were developed by Bandler and Grinder as a result of modelling Erickson's style. They found that Erickson would use particular cues as post-hypnotic triggers to help a person change their internal state at some time in the future. If someone is, for example consistently irritated by another's behaviour it may be they have been anchored. Whenever this behaviour occurs they move into this predictable state. Anchoring is a natural phenomenon and is similar to classical conditioning (Dilts & DeLozier, 2000). Whereas in classical conditioning the conditional stimulus and conditional response were always external, anchoring formats have been generalized in NLP, and are used for internal events, too. In coaching therefore, the thought of giving a presentation can be anchored to a feeling of relaxation within the whole body.

8. Logical levels

The relevance of the logical levels model is that it overtly introduces the concept of systems thinking. The idea of logical levels was developed by Dilts (1990) and is loosely borrowed from the concept of logical types formulated by Whitehead and Russell (1910) and used by Gregory Bateson (1972). According to the model there are six levels (spirit; identity; beliefs and values; capability; behaviour; and the environment). Each level synthesizes, organizes and directs the class of activity at the level below it. So changing something at a higher level will necessarily change something at a lower level; however, change at a lower level would not necessarily change the element above.

At an individual level there is a recognition that no behaviour stands alone. In order to understand a behaviour effectively one needs to understand where this behaviour occurs, when it occurs, how it occurs, what are the beliefs which underpin such behaviour, what values drive such behaviour, who would engage in such behaviour, and of what such behaviour is a part in the wider sense of shared and common behaviour. The logical levels model is thus a very useful content framework for exploring coachees' current maps of the world. With it they can understand how they are producing the results they are currently obtaining. This is a useful first stage in facilitating change at a particular level to obtain maximum leverage in the individual system.

9. Eye-accessing cues

In the film 'The Negotiator' the actor Samuel Jackson tells fellow hostages that he knows a group member is lying, because his eye movements went up and to the right when he spoke rather than up and to the left. The empirical evidence for the NLP design of eye-accessing cues seems very mixed. Eye movements may be related to several undefined sources of variance, and as a general rule the eye accessing cues posited by Dilts et al. (1980) need to be calibrated to each individual coachee. If every time the coachee talks about a particular problem they look down and to the right, and they do this consistently, according to the NLP model they are accessing a kinesthetic internal representation. Theoretically, they would respond much more quickly and accurately to the question 'and how do you feel about that?', compared with the questions 'how do you see that?' or 'how does that sound to you?'

Case study

Verna has requested coaching to help her cope with occupational stress. She had got to the point when she would have a panic attack if she met anyone from work. As rapport was built, she was encouraged to redevelop a reference experience (or anchor) of being very relaxed outside of work. This strategy for relaxation was made explicit in terms of sequencing representational systems and eliciting the sub-modalities. As Verna had a background in engineering and electronics, she enjoyed the 'small chunk' work of understanding how her own system was systematically put together.

The next stage involved systematic exploration of the difference between Verna's Meta Programmes (loosely speaking the NLP term for personality), and those explicit in the organization. Certain triggers were identified that made her 'run' a very different programme.

In comparing these programmes Verna was able to see how she was literally creating different experiences for herself. She called these insights 'Condor moments'. By the sixth session Verna was automatically representing herself as a much more relaxed professional when talking and engaging with people at work. To secure this result the old stress strategy was visualized and then replaced by the new relaxation strategy.

EVALUATION

NLP is at a stage where evaluation of its methodology is largely anecdotal. However, there is movement currently to evaluate NLP in a much more robust way, both quantitatively and qualitatively. Many of the increasingly empirical studies of NLP can be found at the website http://www.nlp.de/cgi-bin/research/nlp-rdb.cgi. These are mainly student dissertations and thus characterize well the present state of research into NLP. However, Tosey and Mathison are conducting one of the first funded, university-based research projects into NLP. The project started in November 2005. For those interested in the evaluation of NLP using qualitative paradigms as well as quantitative, the project can be found at http://www.nlpresearch.org/

The current state of research into the use of the NLP approach in coaching is weak and will not impress those who have a need for evidence. It also may not be the best approach for clients who wish to be kept fully informed as to what is going on and who wish to work overtly in a step-by-step fashion. NLP coaches often use many of the described skills working simultaneously at engaging the conscious mind in order to communicate with the unconscious mind where facilitative change occurs. Finally, as NLP is an approach that emphasizes the need to work at the level pattern and process, clients who wish for in-depth conversations concerning the content of their situations may find NLP coaches unsuitable for them. At the same time, consistent interest in this approach seems to support the view that clients do benefit from it.

APPLICATION TO SPECIFIC COACHING CONTEXTS AND GENRES

Currently, NLP coaching is used in almost every coaching context, and this reflects the flexibility of the approach. Having an affinity with behaviourism, it is ideally suited to skills and performance coaching, and with its underlying philosophy of personal responsibility for the maps which govern our experience, it can easily be used within the context of developmental coaching. NLP coaching, which has the consistent theme of systems thinking supporting its presuppositions and change techniques, is well-suited to executive and leadership coaching. At an individual level, perspectives can be challenged and developed. At an organizational level the systemic nature of interactions between and within departments and divisions can readily be represented and then developed using NLP coaching. This is increasingly important, as Peter Senge (1990) points out: system thinking allows organizations to focus on the cause rather than the symptoms and provide long-term solutions rather than short symptomatic quick fixes.

As NLP coaching puts such emphasis on rapport, many life coaches find its personable paradigm well buttressed with a richness of philosophy and techniques. This allows them to develop their coaching style effectively and without constraints on their own personality. If a coach has a preference for detail, they will enjoy coaching using the Meta Model. Alternatively, a coach who prefers to look at the bigger picture will enjoy making use of the Milton Model in their coaching approach. Coaches who deal with cross-cultural issues find NLP coaching very useful because the Meta Model assists clients in developing an awareness of their own cultural values, beliefs and attitudes. It shows how these can be effectively represented in differing cultural contexts in an elegant manner. The Meta Model is specifically useful for assisting such clients to examine their own unexplored assumptions and stereotypes about the behaviours of those in other cultures.

When coaching in a specific competency is called for either in an executive or managerial role, NLP is ideal because of the emphasis on integration of the skills into an unconsciously competent format. For instance anchoring is something that consistently and naturally occurs; one cannot avoid anchoring. The NLP coach is simply a professional person who is aware of the ubiquitous nature of such a process and will use it in an ethical way. This means that integration of NLP coaching skills into an executive or managerial role is seamless and does not create resistance in those being coached. Often, issues of fit come to the fore in both team and career coaching. NLP places great emphasis on goal setting and creating frames that work for individuals and teams; however, it also places an equal emphasis on the mind–body system and the need for ecology and congruence in the lives of those who seek to work as part of a team or to develop their career.

FURTHER READING

Dilts, R., & DeLozier, J. (2000). *Encyclopedia of Systemic Neuro-Linguistic Programming and NLP New Coding*. NLP University Press. (A major work in two volumes, covering everything in NLP.)

DeLozier, J., & Grinder, J. (1987) *Turtles all the way down*. Grinder and Associates. (A chance to experience the 'Spirit of NLP' in this record of a five-day NLP seminar on prerequisites to personal genius.)

Bandler, R., & Grinder, J. (1979). *Frogs into Princes*. Real People Press. (A transcript from a live seminar. Divided into three main sections from three separate days: sensory experience; changing personal history; reframing.)

REFERENCES

Bandler, R., & Grinder, J. (1975a). *The structure of magic* 1. Palo Alto, CA: Science and Behaviour Books.

Bandler, R., & Grinder, J. (1975b). *Patterns of the hypnotic techniques of Milton H. Erickson, MD* (Vol. 1). Cupertino, CA: Meta Publications.

Bandler, R., & Grinder, J. (1976). *The structure of magic* 2. Palo Alto, CA: Science and Behaviour Books.

Bateson, G. (1972). *Steps to an ecology of mind.* Chicago, IL: University of Chicago Press.

Bostic St Clair, C., & Grinder, J. (2001). *Whispering in the wind* (p. 142). Scotts Valley, CA: J&C Enterprises.

Brooks, C.H. (1922). *Practice of autosuggestion.* New York: Dodd, Mead, and Co.

Cooper, C.L., Sloan, S.J., & Williams, S. (1988). *Occupational stress indicator management guide.* Windsor: ASE.

Coue, E. (1923). *How to practice suggestion and autosuggestion.* New York: American Library Service.

Dilts, R.B. (1990). *Changing belief systems with NLP.* Capitola, CA: Meta Publications.

Dilts, R., Grinder, J., Bandler, R., & DeLozier, J. (1980). *Neuro-linguistic programming* (Vol. 1) *The study of the structure of subjective experience.* Capitola, CA: Meta Publications.

Dilts, R., & DeLozier, J. (2000). *Encyclopaedia of systemic neuro-linguistic programming and NLP new coding.* Scotts Valley, CA: NLP University Press.

Grinder, J., DeLozier, J., & Bandler, R. (1977). *Patterns of the hypnotic techniques of Milton H. Erickson, MD* (Vol. 2). Scotts Valley, CA: Meta Publications.

Kelly, G.A. (1963). *A theory of personality: The psychology of personal constructs.* New York & London: Norton.

Korzybski, A. (1933). *Science and sanity: An introduction to non-Aristotelian systems and general semantics.* Lancaster, PA: International non-Aristotelian Library.

Korzybski, A. (1994) *Science and sanity: An introduction to non-Aristotelian systems and general semantics* (5th ed., p. 58). Englewood, NJ: Institute of General Semantics.

Kroger, W.S. (1977). *Clinical and experimental hypnosis* (2nd ed.). Philadelphia, PA: Lippincott, Williams, and Wilkins.

Linder-Pelz, S., & Hall, M. (2007). The theoretical roots of NLP-based coaching. *The Coaching Psychologist, 3*(1): 12–17.

O'Connor, J., & Seymour, J. (1995). *Introducing NLP neuro-linguistic programming.* London: Thorsons.

Perls, F. (1973). *The Gestalt approach and eye witness to therapy.* Ben Lomond, CA: Science and Behavior Books.

Senge, P.M. (1990). *The fifth discipline. The art & practice of the learning organization.* London: Century Business.

Smith, C.H., Morton, J., & Oakley, D. (1998). An investigation of the state-dependency of recall during hypnotic amnesia. *Contemporary Hypnosis, 15(2):* 94–100.

Tulving, E., & Thompson, D.M. (1973). Encoding specificity and retrieval processes in episodic memory. *Psychological Review, 80:* 352–73.

Whitehead, A.N., & Russell, B. (1910). *Principia mathematica.* Cambridge: Cambridge University Press.

Genres and Contexts of Coaching

14

Skills and Performance Coaching

Bob Tschannen-Moran

INTRODUCTION

Skills and Performance Coaching (SPC) is, perhaps, the original and most common genre of coaching: assisting someone to learn how to do something better.

As children, after teaching ourselves to walk and talk, we were taught by others using a combination of two processes: instruction and incentives. These significant others told us what to do and how to do it correctly. They may also have offered incentives, such as rewards, compliments, or punishments to get us to do the work and master the domain.

Although it is not uncommon for these same processes to be used with adults, especially when it comes to training and knowledge transfer, research by educators and psychologists (e.g. Knowles, Holton, & Swanson, 2005) has documented the limitations of this approach. Adults, it is argued, return to that inner toddler when it comes to learning: we seek to figure things out for ourselves, for our own reasons, in our own way, on our own schedule, and with our own resources. For SPC to be effective, therefore, it needs to take these and other adult-specific factors into consideration.

GOALS AND TASKS OF SPC

The goal of SPC is to improve someone's skills and performance in a particular domain of human functioning. Unlike other forms of coaching, the scope and success of which may be entirely defined and determined by the coachee, SPC often involves meeting external requirements established by others. Even when the desire to improve skills and performance is intrinsically motivated, aspects of the project are still extrinsically referenced. An athlete does not improve performance, for example, without knowing the rules of the game; neither does an actor improve performance without the response of the audience. So, too, with engineers and surgeons: there is no way to improve skills without invoking the laws of physics and the standards of their professions. When it comes to SPC, then, coaches are assisting people to improve their handling of such requirements.

To achieve the goal of skills and performance improvements, SPC has seven tasks.

1. *To cultivate motivation.* The motivational task is to shift people from aversive motivators, such as fear and disgust, to attractive motivators, such as hope and competence. A clear and compelling vision of performance mastery, what is wanted rather than what is not wanted, is critical to continuous skills and performance improvements.
2. *To expand awareness.* What is happening right now? What really matters? When things work well, what do they look, sound, and feel like? Assisting coachees to attend to such matters, in the moment and without judgment, facilitates what Gallwey (2008) calls 'natural learning'. A clear and accurate appreciation of the present moment – what is happening rather than what is not happening – is also important for skills and performance improvements.
3. *To build self-efficacy.* Beyond the field of right and wrong lies the confidence that we can initiate and sustain performance improvements. SPC enables coachees to play in that field through verbal persuasion, somatic awareness, vicarious learning, and mastery experiences (Bandura, 1994, 1997).
4. *To frame opportunities.* Skills and performance improvements require understandings and environments that support movement, innovation, and resilience. Coaching assists coachees to frame and develop such opportunities.
5. *To design experiments.* 'Nothing is as dangerous as an idea', writes Chartier, 'when it is the only one you have' (as cited in O'Hanlon & Beadle, 1997: 31). The operational task is to generate and test out multiple ideas for skills and performance improvements instead of getting wedded to a single course of action.
6. *To structure repetition.* It is not enough to implement a new idea or strategy once. Skills and performance improvements take practice and SPC therefore assists coachees to persevere while implementing new behaviours in engaging and fulfilling ways.
7. *To savour success.* SPC strives to assist coachees to experience and celebrate mastery in their desired areas of performance improvement. Quick wins build self-efficacy and long-term success.

FEATURES, PROCESSES, AND ROLES

SPC involves a number of features, processes, and roles:

Identifying a learning need with intrinsic value
The first challenge of SPC is to connect external performance requirements with internal desires and ambitions. Until and unless coachees want to learn something for their own good reasons, the process of coaching will revert to instructions and incentives. Interviewing coachees as to what and how they want to learn is the start of SPC.

Listening to understand and support
Because SPC works with external performance requirements, extending empathy is another one of its essential processes. The route to performance mastery is filled with thrills and agonies, each of which requires supportive, emotionally-intelligent understanding.

Discovering capacities, strengths, and resources
Another challenge of SPC is to shift coachees from a problem-solving to a strengths-building focus. Expanding on what people already know and do well is a more effective and enjoyable way to learn. To facilitate change, therefore, SPC investigates assets more than deficits.

Observing examples of successful accomplishment
More than other forms of coaching, SPC requires a clear picture of successful accomplishment. What does it look like to do something well? Instead of describing this to coachees, SPC gets coachees to discover it for themselves through observation and exploration.

Formulating a vision of personal mastery
SPC also gets coachees to envision themselves performing at higher levels of mastery. It is one thing to observe others; it is another thing to imagine following in their footsteps. Through visualization exercises and other creative activities, SPC assists coachees to move from mimicking to personal anticipation, appropriation, adoption, and assimilation.

Brainstorming innovative designs and strategies
The process of generating multiple possibilities for skills and performance improvements without regard to their value, feasibility, or desirability is an essential process of SPC. Since there is no way to predict which strategies will prove most effective for any given person to actually realize his or her vision, SPC encourages coachees to experiment with different approaches and contexts.

Practising and refining new behaviours
The biggest challenge of SPC is often to keep people moving forward over time. Both advances and setbacks can stall the process of behaviour change, as people become either satisfied or discouraged. The role of SPC is to align internal understandings and external environments so that coachees persistently make adaptive choices and sustain new behaviours.

Celebrating improvement
The old adage, 'Nothing breeds success like success', speaks to a key source of self-efficacy in generating performance improvement. SPC therefore assists coachees to experience quick wins and to appreciate their accomplishments before moving on to new goals and possibilities.

Repeating these steps for continued improvement
Skills and performance improvement is neither a linear nor a terminal process; it is ongoing and iterative with unanticipated loops, twists, and turns. SPC assists coachees to become fully engaged with the spiral dynamic of continuous performance improvement.

These features, processes, and roles are reflected in many SPC models. The Inner-game coaching model, launched by Gallwey, revolves around three conversations which enable coachees to fully engage with and enjoy the process of learning and performance improvement – conversations for awareness, choice, and trust (Gallwey, 2000). Two of Gallwey's disciples, Alexander (Alexander & Renshaw, 2005) and Whitmore (2003), popularized the GROW model (Goals, Reality, Options and Wrap-up or What You Will Do) set in the context of Awareness and Responsibility. More recently, Cox (2006) has developed a model explicitly tied to adult learning theories that goes by the acronym of IMPACT (Identify Life Chapters, Make Sense of Transitions, Plan, Act, Consider, and Track) while Corcoran (2005) proposes an 'integrative strengths-and-skills building model' as a collaborative approach to change. All of these models view and work with coachees as creative, capable, and competent agents of their own learning and growth.

A mobius-strip model of SPC

To illustrate and advance the features, processes, and roles of SPC, I have developed a Mobius-strip model of the coaching process that revolves around two conversations, Story and Strategy, facilitated by Empathy and Inquiry (Figure 14.1). Each will be considered in turn.

Story

Coaching begins when coachees share their stories. These stories reflect the sense coachees make of their experience. They are never the experience itself; they are rather an attempt to understand, value, and shape the experience in ways that make sense and guide future actions.

Figure 14.1   A Mobius-strip model of SPC.

Since coaching works with the stories coachees tell, both to themselves and to others, it is possible to change everything in the twinkling of an eye. Tell a new story and we get a new experience. That is especially true when we begin to work with the attributions of cause and effect that are explicit and/or implicit in most stories (Loehr, 2007: 4). Coaches listen for those attributions, since they illuminate a coachee's path of development. For example:

- What is the overarching theme? Does it lie more with danger or opportunity?
- Where is the locus of control? Does it lie more with the coachee or with others?
- What is the language of capacity? Does it lie more with skills or resources?
- How is the objective defined? Does it lie more with metrics or morale?
- What is happening with energy? Is it emptying out or filling up?
- What is happening with values? Are they being honoured or compromised?
- What is happening with needs? Are they being met, denied, or sacrificed?

There is no end to the attributions we can listen for and find, since there is no end to the stories coachees tell. The secret is to listen mindfully, without judgment or haste. It is tempting to rush through the story part of the process in order to get to strategy. We want a fix, and want it fast. But visions, goals, and strategies based on unappreciated stories often generate unhappy results. Instead of skills and performance improvements, we get more of the same. Instead of learning and growth, we get stuck in the muck. Listening is a key work of SPC.

Empathy

Although empathy has long been recognized as a critical part of therapy it is not often talked or written about in the context of SPC. Yet empathy has much to do with skills and performance improvements. The voice in the head is the judgmental gremlin that gets in the way of perform-ance. Until that voice receives empathy, both from self and others, progress is impaired.

When listening to coachee stories, it is important to distinguish between pity, sympathy, and empathy. Pity is feeling sorry for someone, which does not foster change. Sympathy is sharing someone's feelings, which can lead to advising, rescuing, and defending behaviours. Empathy, the respectful, no-fault understanding and appreciation of someone's experience, is an orienta-tion and practice that fosters radically new change possibilities.

Empathy does this by shifting focus from particular strategies to universal needs. Most of the stories people tell are about the strategies that either did or did not work. That is, in fact, why they tell the stories: because they are feeling good or bad about something. Often, however, they misattribute their feelings to the strategies themselves rather than to the underlying needs. As a result, they get caught up in a self-defeating cycle of interpretations, judgments, criticisms, and diagnoses (Rosenberg, 2005: 52 ff.).

To express empathy, coaches can use the Nonviolent Communication model originally developed by Rosenberg (2005). Upon hearing a story, coaches can notice and reflect back the coachee's feelings and needs in ways that release tension, facilitate calm, and expand awareness. To do this effectively requires fluency in the language of authentic feelings and universal human needs (d'Ansembourg, 2007). Noticing and mirroring are two more key features of SPC.

Inquiry

Inquiry without empathy is interrogation. That is why SPC moves from Story to Strategy through Empathy and Inquiry. Once coachees feel safe and heard at the level of their feelings and needs, they become open to exploring new ways of looking at themselves and what they are doing. Such openness generates alternative stories and, in turn, alternative strategies.

When it comes to improving skills and performance, adult learning theories and growth-fostering psychologies suggest that appreciative, strengths-based inquiries are more effective and empowering than analytic, deficits-based inquiries. Given that many if not most stories are told from a deficits-based framework, it is immediately reorienting to ask open-ended, strengths-based questions, such as:

- What would success look like? What else would it look like?
- What's working with your approach? What else is working? What else?
- What talents and abilities are serving you well? What else?
- What's the best thing that's happening now? What else?
- What fills you with energy and hope? What else?
- What enables you to do as well as you are doing? What else?
- What is the positive intent of your actions? What else?
- What resources do you have available? What else?

The point of such inquiries is to elevate the focus, self-efficacy, resourcefulness, and where-withal of coachees. The more focused coachees are on their problems, deficits, and limitations, the less likely they are to imagine and pursue new possibilities. Appreciative, strengths-based inquiries turn that around. They remind coachees that they have what it takes to learn what they want to learn.

They also remind coachees that stories of hardship, difficulty, frustration, and failure do not represent the whole story. The point of asking 'What else?' on multiple occasions is to raise awareness to other ways of telling the story. Knowing that in every situation something is always working, no matter how bleak or discouraging things may appear, coaches can be courageous in their inquiries to find high points worth celebrating.

In addition to discovering the best of what is, coaches can also ask what the best might be. This can be done either directly ('If you could wave a magic wand and make any three wishes come true, wishes that would infuse you and this situation with energy and life, what would they be?') or indirectly ('If a miracle happened tonight to make these problems disappear, what would be the first thing you would notice when you woke up in the morning?'). Either way, the point is to prime the pump with a compelling vision before moving into strategy. Such inquiry and imagination are two more key works of SPC.

Strategy

When coachee stories are listened to and reframed properly, through empathy and inquiry, strategies for skills and performance improvements often emerge organically from the coachees themselves. Little or no instructions or incentives are required. Instead, once coachees become detached from both the fear of failure and their own illusions as to what is or should be happening, they become fearless in the pursuit of that which will enable them to learn and grow.

The key in SPC, then, is for coaches to avoid reintroducing judgmental frames as to how things are to be done 'correctly' or even 'better'. Strategies are experiments and there is no telling how they will turn out. What works for one person may not work for another. Strategies are best developed, therefore, as games to be played and learned from rather than as blueprints, plans, and prescriptions to be followed.

Brainstorming is a useful tool for developing such learning strategies, especially when coachees and coaches take turns coming up with possible ideas. Basic protocols for brainstorming include:

- setting a minimum number of possibilities to generate
- setting a time limit to keep things moving rapidly
- withholding judgment or evaluation of possibilities
- encouraging wild and exaggerated possibilities
- letting no possibility go unsaid
- building on the possibilities put forth by others
- combining and expanding possibilities.

A central question around which to brainstorm is 'What could I pay attention to that would improve my skills and performance in this situation?' This makes learning both self-directed and enjoyable: by getting coachees to identify what is important, without telling them what to do, they are nudged to make new choices and to try new behaviours with a minimum of resistance. The nonjudgmental focus enables the voice in the head to get out of the way.

Whatever gets generated through brainstorming, SPC assists coachees to winnow through the options and to implement action strategies in incremental timeframes. Small, manageable changes that rapidly give people an experience of improvement and success do much to bolster coachee self-confidence and learning over time. These successes can then be celebrated, while setbacks can be appreciated, as new grist for the coaching mill. Brainstorming, experimenting, and appreciating are key works of SPC that keep the process moving forward.

Case study

Jack was frustrated, confused, and anxious. As a 63-year-old probation officer, Jack wanted nothing more than to do his job well and to retire with full benefits in a few years' time. Yet day after day, week after week, Jack found himself procrastinating on some of the most important aspects of his work: writing and filing reports on a timely basis. His desk was filled with piles of paper, he was missing deadlines, and his boss had given him an ultimatum: get on top of things, or else. 'You better not lose this job,' his wife implored at one of their increasingly tense moments. Perhaps coaching could help.

During Jack's initial session he shared with me the story of how far behind he had got with his paperwork, how overwhelmed he was by the work, and how ashamed he felt to be a procrastinator. 'This is all my fault,' he said ruefully, 'and I'm not getting any younger. Whether I retire here or get fired, it will probably be my last best job.' I reflected back his concern, but not his attribution of blame. I reflected back his anxiety, but not his fatalism. Instead, I guessed that his concern and anxiety might be surfacing because of his very real needs for contribution and security. I could hear the air slowly release over the telephone. 'It's important for me to do a good job,' he said, 'you heard that right. I just wish it wasn't such a struggle.' 'So you also need ease and assistance,' I said. At that, the tension let up even further.

I asked him to tell me a story about the best contribution he ever made as a probation officer. He choked up as he told me about his relationship with Kevin, a teenager who was on the edge of throwing his life away. He visited Kevin after hours and saw him through the process of getting off probation. 'That's the best,' Jack said, 'when someone like Kevin actually makes it clean rather than ending up with a long prison sentence, or worse.' 'That's quite a contribution,' I observed, 'it's almost like you saved somebody's life. I can hear what it means to you in your voice.'

From that simple, values-oriented, strengths-based inquiry, Jack started to shift from a storyline of failure and being overwhelmed to one of meaningfulness and purpose. He also began to connect the dots, all on his own, between paperwork and contribution. In an instant, he no longer saw paperwork as busywork; he suddenly saw it as an integral part of his contribution. 'I'm going to figure this out,' he said, 'I'm going to learn how to do this. For the first time in my life, I'm going to stop procrastinating.'

Week after week we brainstormed ideas and ran experiments: throwing everything on his desk into boxes for immediate gratification; noticing and logging what his office looked like at the start and end of each day; inviting his wife over for an office clean-up party; finishing all paperwork on Wednesdays; or reviewing his notes in the car before leaving a client location. He would start every coaching conversation with new stories as to what was happening and how he was feeling. As the stories came out, we would go through the same process of empathy and inquiry on the way to strategy.

This process also quickened an awareness of new needs. He noticed how tired he felt, for example, because his needs for rest and play were not being met. 'How can I take any time off,' he exclaimed, 'when my office is such a wreck! I have to work all the time just in case someone wants something and I'm the only one who can find it – which sometimes takes me several hours.' He also felt frustrated because his need for interdependence was not being met. 'I'm not the only one who is falling behind,' he said, 'and I'm really not sure how to streamline my reporting.' 'Where could you go with those concerns?' I asked. 'I could talk with my boss about both,' he replied, 'perhaps I could show him a report to get his feedback on the essential elements.' 'Would you be willing to summarize that feedback in the form of a checklist that you could share with me?' I asked. Jack happily agreed.

Two weeks later Jack was beaming at the start of our call. 'You'll never guess what happened,' he bragged. 'You got the clean-office award!' I laughed. 'Not yet,' he said, 'but people are talking. I had those conversations with my boss, and with his boss. We talked about the need for a succession plan and they agreed to hire two more probation officers. In addition, my boss circled the information he wanted on my reports. I've been writing way too much! No wonder I was falling behind. Now my reports are getting easier and soon we'll be able to distribute the work better in the office. I feel like a new man.'

'You sound like a new man,' I reflected back with sincere enthusiasm. 'I *am* a new man,' he said, 'I took a half day off work last week to go to the dentist. And I've started walking in the morning with my son's dog. I'm just more relaxed and even my boss has noticed the difference. He complimented me recently and asked me to handle something when he was going to be out of the office. It wasn't six weeks ago that he was avoiding me and not giving me work. Even other people have noticed the difference. Things have really turned around.'

The breakthroughs this coachee achieved and the progress he made were due to the raised awareness he had as to the connection between his feelings, needs, and strategies. Instead of dealing directly with 'his problems' of procrastination and organization, we used his awareness and stories of contribution to step above the fray and to generate new possibilities for getting help and streamlining his reporting. That shift made all the difference and his competence and self-efficacy grew and enabled him to learn how to meet the tasks at hand and to take better care of himself in the process.

DISTINCTIONS BETWEEN SPC AND OTHER COACHING GENRES

Hall and Duval (2004a) have identified three domains of coaching: performance coaching assists people to make incremental changes in their behaviours, skills, actions, and results; developmental coaching assists people to make evolutionary changes in their thoughts, feelings, beliefs, and other mental-emotional frameworks that govern performance; transformational coaching assists people to make revolutionary changes in the frames of mind that govern purpose, intention, direction, and vision (Hall & Duval, 2004a: 22). At its best, the Mobius-strip model of SPC works in all domains. Indeed, there is no way to achieve performance mastery without attending to the mental-emotional frameworks and volitional frames of mind that govern performance.

Although the three domains of coaching reflect different layers of depth, there is significant overlap between them when it comes to methodology. All coaching, for example involves listening, connecting, exploring, and discerning (Story, Empathy, Inquiry, and Strategy). All coaching also relies on the motivation, awareness, and expertise of the coachee more than of the coach. Coaching is an evocative and empowering process, whether the goal is incremental, developmental, or transformational improvements.

Of the genres identified in this *Handbook*, SPC is related highly to Executive and Leadership Coaching, Peer Coaching, Cross-cultural Coaching, the Manager as Coach, and Mentoring.

That is because those five genres also aim to develop the technical and/or people skills of coachees in particular areas of human endeavour. The Manager as Coach and the Mentoring genres both share the problem of introducing a significant power differential into the coaching relationship; this can make it difficult to implement the model of SPC presented in this chapter. Peer coaching minimizes the power differential but may suffer from problems with confidentiality and coach training. Executive and Leadership Coaching as well as Cross-cultural Coaching both tend to utilize trained, professional, external coaches who can easily use and adapt the Mobius-strip model of SPC to their purposes.

SPC AND ITS RELATIONSHIP TO THEORETICAL APPROACHES

At its best, SPC draws heavily upon the work of adult-learning theorists and growth-fostering psychologists.

Adult-learning theories

When Gallwey first published *The Inner Game of Tennis* in 1974, it was a call to limit the use of instructions and incentives in coaching due to their often debilitating impact on the internal dynamics that make for optimum skill development and performance improvement. Ironically, he noted, the more important the stakes in terms of the external requirements and reinforcements, the more instruction distracted people from their own 'natural learning' style (Gallwey, 2008: 22).

Although Gallwey's first book marked a turning point for athletic coaching and is frequently hailed as a milestone in the modern coaching movement (particularly after the publication of *The Inner Game of Work*, in 2000), his Inner-game principles are inextricably tied to research and practice in adult education and learning theories dating back more than a century. Lindeman (1926) and Knowles (1950) were two of the early pioneers in this field and the characteristics of adult learners, highlighted by Knowles in particular, help to explain why instructions and incentives so often interfere with high performance.

Instructions come with an implicit 'should' as to what is to be done and how it is to be done, undermining autonomy and self-direction. Adding incentives only makes this worse. Instructions also build more on the experience base of the coach than of the coachee, which may or may not be viewed as relevant and workable in the eyes of the coachee. They imply that there is a 'right' way to do something, while extrinsic incentives feel more like enforcement than support. In short, the use of instructions and incentives violates much of what has been learned when it comes to adult education and learning theory. Gallwey (2000, 2008) was right when he asserted there must be a better way to learn. The Mobius-strip model of SPC takes those considerations into account.

Growth-fostering psychologies

At the same time as educators were studying adult learning to improve informal education programmes, psychologists were seeking to understand and improve the dynamics of growth-fostering relationships. Building on controlled laboratory experiments (Watson, 1913; Pavlov, 1927), behaviourism surfaced as a way of explaining human behaviour in terms of external stimuli and reinforcements without reference to internal thoughts, feelings, or needs (Skinner, 1950, 1953). Since behavioural scientists observed that modifying the repercussions of a behaviour led to behaviour change in both animal and human subjects, behaviourism focused on modifying antecedents and consequences in order to promote human learning and growth. Consequences ranged from rewards and punishments to achievement and failure.

In contrast to the core assumptions of behaviourism, other psychologies and approaches emerged that gave priority to the subjective and field dynamics of human functioning. These psychologies include many schools of thought and a wide variety of therapeutic orientations. Traditions that impact most directly on the Mobius-strip model of SPC include constructivism, humanism, cognitive-behavioural therapy (CBT), social-cognitive theory, relational-cultural theory, gestalt therapy, neuro-linguistic programming (NLP), solution-focused therapy, appreciative inquiry (AI), motivational interviewing, and positive psychology. Although there are many differences between these traditions, the following recognitions cut across disciplines.

- People are inherently creative and capable.
- Learning takes place when people actively take responsibility for constructing meaning from their experience (either confirming or changing what they already know).
- The meanings people construct determine the actions they take.
- Every person is unique and yet all people have the same universal needs.
- Empathy, mutuality, and connection make people more cooperative and open people up to change.
- People don't resist change; they resist being changed.
- The more people know about their values, strengths, resources, and abilities the stronger their motivation and the better their changes will be.

These recognitions challenge the presuppositions of behaviourism and provide yet another framework for calling into question the use of instructions and incentives in SPC. Although it is tempting to tell people how to do things better, to make them practise, and to reward their progress, such approaches fail to inspire and leverage the best of human learning and functioning. Indeed, they can just as easily undermine motivation, provoke resistance, usurp responsibility, rupture relationships, ignore reality, discourage risk-taking, limit imagination, and restrict results (Kohn, 1999). They may 'work' in the short run (if 'work' is understood as compliance) but they seldom work in the long run (if 'work' is understood as mastery) and they rarely generate significant improvements, at least not until they are abandoned in favour of self-directed learning.

These recognitions also explain why the Mobius-strip model represents such a promising model for SPC. When the coaching process assists coachees to explore their stories with empathy and inquiry, rather than with evaluation and interrogation, it produces freedom, stimulates curiosity, elevates self-efficacy, and leverages latent competencies in the service of desired outcomes. Such coaching sets aside the notion of there being one 'right' way to do something; it rather invites coachees to become fully engaged in the process of discovering their own unique strategies for skill and performance improvements without suffering the stress of having to do things 'correctly'.

AN EVALUATION OF SPC

Human learning and growth is a natural process that can be facilitated as well as impeded by the intervention of others, including coaches. The more coaches tell their coachees what to do, how to do it, and why to do it, the more resistance gets triggered and the less learning takes place. It may be usual and customary to give instructions and provide incentives, but these approaches can be counterproductive to skills and performance improvements.

Taking this into account, effective SPC assists coachees to find their own path and get out of their own way in the service of desired outcomes. Through cultivating motivation, expanding awareness, building self-efficacy, framing opportunities, designing experiments, structuring repetition, and savouring success, coaches enable coachees to progress more easily and effectively than when they are left to their own devices. That is because people tend to be our own worst enemies when we are not performing as we would like. We pressure ourselves into doing things 'right' and 'get down' on ourselves as if our very identities depended upon the outcome. These dynamics tend to immobilize people and make things worse.

SPC can break that juggernaut through empathy and inquiry, effectively freeing coachees to play with alternative strategies rather than to push for perfect performance. This requires fluency on the part of coaches in the languages of empathy and inquiry, as well as attentiveness to the stories being told. Through listening, noticing, exploring, experimenting, and enjoying the process of discovery, coachees can learn to take their skills and performance to ever higher levels of mastery.

In conclusion, SPC stands on the shoulders of adult-learning theories and growth-fostering psychologies developed since the late 19th century. Although many SPC models have been developed, they share much in common with the Mobius-strip model presented here, especially the use of vision and awareness to stimulate self-directed learning on the part of coachees. This process can be understood as a dance between Story and Strategy set to the music of Empathy and Inquiry.

FURTHER READING

Gallwey, W.T. (2008). *The inner game of tennis: The classic guide to the mental side of peak performance.* (Originally published in 1974, this book makes the case for 'natural learning' with a minimum of instructions and incentives.

To encourage 'natural learning', Gallwey discusses the value of nonjudgmental awareness, creating images, letting things happen, and relaxed concentration. His 2000 book, *The inner game of work*, is also useful in relation to coaching.)

Senge, P.M. (2006). *The fifth discipline: The art & practice of the learning organization.* (With a nod to Gallwey, Senge further describes how to optimize the learning process. The book has helpful chapters on personal mastery, mental models, shared vision, and team learning.)

Hall, L.M., & Duval, M. (2004a, 2004b); and Hall, L.M. (2007). *Meta-coaching:* Vols I–III. (With frequent references to Gallwey's *Inner Game*, these books on coaching change, conversations, and self-actualization, and present a detailed discussion of how to unleash people's creativity and natural ability to learn.)

REFERENCES

Alexander, G., & Renshaw, B. (2005). *SuperCoaching: The missing ingredient for high performance.* London: Random House.

Bandura, A. (1994). Self-efficacy. In V.S. Ramachaudran (Ed.), *Encyclopedia of human behavior* (Vol. 4, pp. 71–81). New York: Academic Press. (Reprinted in H. Friedman [Ed.]. [1998]. *Encyclopedia of mental health.* San Diego, CA: Academic Press.)

Bandura, A. (1997). *Self-efficacy: The exercise of control.* New York: W.H. Freeman.

Corcoran, J. (2005). *Building strengths and skills: A collaborative approach to working with coachees.* New York: Oxford University Press.

Cox, E. (2006). An adult learning approach to coaching. In D.R. Stober & A.M. Grant (Eds.), *Evidence based coaching handbook: Putting best practices to work for your coachees* (pp. 193–217). Hoboken, NJ: John Wiley & Sons.

d'Ansembourg, T. (2007). *Being genuine: Stop being nice, start being real.* Encinitas, CA: PuddleDancer Press.

Gallwey, W.T. (2000). *The inner game of work: Focus.* New York: Random House.

Gallwey, W.T. (2008 [1974]). *The inner game of tennis: The classic guide to the mental side of peak performance.* New York: Random House.

Hall, L.M. (2007). *Meta-coaching:* Vol. III *Unleashed! A guide to your ultimate self-actualization.* Clifton, CO: Neuro-Semantic Publications.

Hall, L.M., & Duval, M. (2004a). *Meta-coaching:* Vol. I *For higher levels of success and transformation.* Clifton, CO: Neuro-Semantic Publications.

Hall, L.M., & Duval, M. (2004b). *Meta-coaching:* Vol. II *Coaching conversations for transformational change.* Clifton, CO: Neuro-Semantic Publications.

Kohn, A. (1999). *Punished by rewards: The trouble with gold stars, incentive plans, A's, praise, and other bribes.* New York: Houghton Mifflin.

Knowles, M.S. (1950). *Informal adult education.* New York: Association Press.

Knowles, M.S., Holton, E.F., & Swanson, R.A. (2005). *The adult learner* (6th ed.). Amsterdam: Elsevier.

Lindeman, E. (1926). *The meaning of adult education.* New York: New Republic.

Loehr, J. (2007). *The power of story: Rewrite your destiny in business and in life.* New York: Free Press.

O'Hanlon, B., & Beadle, S. (1997). *A guide to possibility land: Fifty-one methods for doing brief, respectful therapy.* New York: Norton.

Pavlov, I.I. (1927). *Conditioned reflexes:* An investigation of the physiological activity of the cerebral cortex (trans. G.V. Anrep). London: Oxford University Press.

Rosenberg, M.B. (2005). *Nonviolent communication: A language of life.* Encinitas, CA: PuddleDancer Press.

Senge, P. (2006). *The fifth discipline: The art & practice of the learning organization.* New York and London: Doubleday Business.

Skinner, B.F. (1950). Are theories of learning necessary? *Psychological Review, 57*(4): 193–26.

Skinner, B.F. (1953). *Science and human behavior.* New York: Macmillan.

Watson, J.B. (1913). Psychology as the behavourist views it. *Psychological Review, 20:* 158.

Whitmore, J. (2003). *Coaching for performance: GROWing people, performance and purpose* (3rd ed.). London: Nicholas Brealey Publishing.

15

Developmental Coaching

Elaine Cox and Peter Jackson

INTRODUCTION

Development is widely understood to mean growth and change over time and so coaching that is described as developmental would aim to support the coachee to make the changes necessary to grow and mature. In this chapter, however, we define development not just as change; we consider that it must involve progress and expansion of some kind. As Sugarman (2000: 3) confirms, development is a concept that centres on a value-based notion of improvement. So, inherent in developmental coaching is an assumption of movement from where the client is now to where he or she wants to be, whether that is in relation to making practical changes in the work environment, making changes in response to emotional pressure or making changes in levels of understanding and responses to the world around them. To be developmental the coaching also has not merely to focus on problem solving but also ensuring that client capacity is built through that problem solving.

In much of the coaching literature developmental coaching is described in human capability and potential terms. For example Sperry (2002: 142) sees developmental coaching as recognition by the coach or manager of an employee's skills and potential, and the provision of opportunities to develop or use those skills in the course of their work.

Developmental coaching can therefore be viewed as a natural progression from skills and performance focused coaching. Coaches working across a whole spectrum of contexts have realized that as people enhance their skills and performance they also develop as people. As their functioning improves so their confidence and self efficacy improves and they learn more about themselves. Accordingly, developmental coaching could be seen as a progressive step in

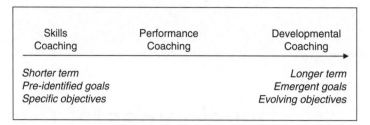

Figure 15.1   Skills, performance and developmental coaching – an evolution.

the provision of coaching; from skills coaching (e.g. sport, technical mastery of aspects of work) through performance coaching (e.g. organizational, career or other aspirational goals), to developmental coaching (e.g. the growth of the whole person to be all that he/she can be). This progression is depicted in Figure 15.1, where we illustrate the movement from what might be seen as the external, behavioural coaching offered by the skills and performance coach to a more constructivist, developmental approach, which, as well as addressing immediate needs, takes a longer term, more evolutionary perspective.

Berman and Bradt's (2006: 245) definition also recognizes the longer time element of developmental coaching. They submit that the intervention tends to be 'relatively long-term (usually more than six months), and emphasizes personal rather than technical or business issues'.

In the next section we provide some theoretical background to developmental coaching. This is followed in Section 2 of this chapter by a discussion of the goals and tasks of developmental coaching; in Section 3 we explore specific features of the process, including contracting and the role of the coach. Towards the end of the chapter we compare developmental coaching with other coaching approaches and stress its relationship with theoretical approaches. We conclude by identifying some of the limitations and benefits of this genre.

BACKGROUND TO DEVELOPMENTAL COACHING

Knowles, Swanson and Holton (2005: 220) confirm that adults do not become adults in an instant and that a developmental process is involved. However, they claim that adult development theory, which might be expected to shed light on the developmental process, is currently little more than an array of untested theories and models. The theories fall into three main categories:

1. physical changes – e.g. theories of maturation and ageing, such as those discussed by Schaie and Zanjani (2006)
2. cognitive or intellectual development – theories such as Perry's (1970) or Kegan's (1994), discussed by Bachkirova in Section 1 of this volume

3. life-span development (theories such as Erikson's (1974), or Levinson's (1978), which are based on social role perspectives).

Sugarman (2000: 3) too has described the imprecision surrounding the term 'development', suggesting that no matter how much data could be collected about an individual life it would still not enable us to define what is meant by the term unless we were to say that 'whatever happens across the life span is what constitutes development'. However, as Sugarman suggests, this negates the idea of development enhancing interventions (such as coaching) since there could be no judgement as to what would be better or preferable: from this viewpoint, she argues, 'any life course is as good (or as developed) as any other, there are no grounds for attempting to influence it'.

Sugarman (2000) goes on to describe how attempts have been made to define development empirically by reference to norms that suggest that certain aspects or stages of development may be expected to happen to the majority of people during their life. In Erikson's (1974) theory, for example there are eight stages of development which unfold as we go through the life span. Each involves the resolution of a crisis. According to Erikson, this crisis is a turning point involving increased vulnerability and enhanced potential. The more a crisis is successfully resolved, the healthier our development will be. For other researchers development is an adaptive response to new priorities and opportunities through the lifespan. Levinson's studies suggest that the (male) life cycle is composed of a series of age-related developmental periods: childhood and adolescence; early adulthood; middle adulthood and late adulthood. Between each of the periods are transitions, such as the mid-life transition, which provide developmental opportunities. Levinson also believed that there are transitional periods in late adulthood and argued that 'as long as life continues, no period marks the end of the opportunities, and the burdens of further development' (Levinson, 1978: 244).

These models, however accurate and useful they seem, have been criticized for discouraging individuality and exceptionality: any concentration on life as a series of stages implies a form of mechanical predictability that seems curiously at odds with the dynamics of change and individual variability. It could be argued that it is impossible to fully capture the considerable complexity of the tasks and processes involved in adult development. As Kolb (1984: 138) notes, 'The paths of development can be as varied as the many systems of social knowledge'. By extension, we would argue that any particular model of development is a partial perspective and cannot reflect the range of developmental opportunities evident in coaching practice.

ASSUMPTIONS

The developmental coaching perspective is built on a complex worldview that assumes that the world is unitary and interactive and that it is itself a developing organism. At the heart of this lies the belief that man is adaptive: people are seen as active organisms that have free will, rather than as merely reactive creatures. Knowles et al. (2005: 24) suggest that individuals who accept this perspective tend to 'emphasize the significance of processes over products and qualitative change over quantitative change'. They also tend to emphasize the importance of the role of experience in constructing, facilitating or inhibiting the course of development.

This constructivist worldview is also evident in much coaching literature. For example following Kolb (1984), Hunt and Weintraub (2004: 42) claim that the underlying assumption of developmental coaching is that employees will learn more when pursuing goals that they have defined, rather than goals defined by others. There is a substantial body of evidence to support the view that self-directed learning results in better outcomes than learning based on demands for compliance to the goals of others (see Knowles et al., 2005). From this it can be deduced that responsibility is also an important issue. Coaching is founded on an understanding of the individual as responsible for their own development (i.e. is self-directed) and that their learning derives from tackling their own problems and solutions.

GOALS AND TASKS OF THE DEVELOPMENTAL APPROACH

Merriam and Clark (2008: 29) suggest that the goal of development is unclear. They ask:

> Is it to achieve an end point, such as self-actualisation (Maslow, 1970), or a fully integrated ego (Loevinger, 1976) or a more permeable and inclusive perspective (Mezirow, & Associates 2000)? Or as Riegel (1973) and others see it, is development dialectic in nature, a function of the 'constant interaction of the person and the environment' (Tennant & Pogson, 1995: 199) with no end point?

In developmental coaching, we suggest, the goal is much clearer: the client agenda is paramount and it is clients' goals that prevail. This suggestion builds on the premise that we all construct our own perspectives of the world based on individual experiences and perceptions; taken with the questions posed by Merriam and Clark above, it would imply that any developmental coaching intervention needs to be holistic and client centred. It needs to involve not merely helping clients to achieve their full potential at work or improving their performance in specific areas, but also enabling them to make conscientious decisions, understand their values and beliefs, take appropriate risks or discover their purpose. This experience may well lead them to considerations outside the immediate concern of skills, performance or advancement within the prevailing organizational frame.

Hunt and Weintraub (2002: 5) define developmental coaching as an interaction between two people, often a manager and an employee, aimed at helping the employee learn from the job in order to promote his or her development. The process they describe involves the coachee being encouraged to reflect on current work challenges and to self-assess his/her performance. The ultimate aim is for the employee to recognize and address the gap between perceived achievement and expected achievement. Developmental coaching, they argue is always driven by the individual's agenda, rather than the organization's agenda. So it would appear that even in the organizational setting the value judgement under-girding the desired improvement can be that of the coachee.

In an attempt to explain the goals of the developmental approach, we asked ourselves why we refer to it as 'developmental'. We found two answers. Firstly, the term 'developmental coaching' is intended to reflect something of the experience that is being created for the client. Whether the trigger for coaching is presented as a performance issue, a project issue or a career issue, the aspiration is to facilitate some *progressive* and *permanent* change. By *progressive* we mean a change that takes the client, over a period of time, to some kind of enrichment of their engagement with their personal, social and career context. By *permanent* we mean that the solution should extend beyond the presenting trigger and create some greater, sustainable capacity in the client. The second answer reflects the core belief that the capacity of the system in which the client sits (organization, family, society) is itself enhanced by the individual's capacity and so the changes initiated have a secondary developmental capacity beyond the client's immediate situation. In summary, we see the goal of development as being a widening of the client's perspective and enhanced ability to engage with the world.

These two arguments for using the term 'developmental' have implications for the way in which the coach works. For example it seems an inevitable consequence that learning sits at the centre of the relationship, and that it is a concept of learning specifically related to the experience of the individual, hence it is constructivist and experiential. There is a close parallel here with the concept of Process Consultation (Schein, 1987, 1998). Schein (1987: 30) argues that a Process Consultation approach will 'increase the likelihood that the immediate problem will be solved, but, even more important, the client learns the skills of problem solving so that he or she can continue to solve problems after the consultant leaves'. So, one of the main tasks is to ensure some ongoing improvement in the coachee's ability to respond to future events.

THE ROLE OF THE COACH AND RELATIONSHIP WITH CLIENTS

In the absence of a single theoretical framework, the concept of development (and particularly the *progressive* outcome) may be problematic. Although we can argue that it is only the client's perspective that matters, the evaluation of such a situation is both subjective and contextual, in that the client may perceive an improvement differently at different times. Similarly, the possibility of the coach taking a longer-term perspective than the client at a particular point in time could be considered a heavy responsibility and a luxury that does not sit well with the other principles of this approach to coaching. Put simply, it is not for the coach to decide that something will be good for the client 'in the end' just as it is not for the coach to decide where 'the end' is, or if there is such a thing at all. This dynamic creates a greater role for the ongoing process of contracting and re-contracting, of asking permission, of challenging by consent. A coach should not necessarily see this as a constant topic of conversation, but it should be a constant concern.

The ambiguity of the concept of 'progress' means that contracting, especially the triangular contract with organizational sponsors, should be approached as far as possible on the level of process and shared understandings rather than specific outcomes and measures. Acknowledging current debates about return on investment, we realize this is an unfashionable formulation that may appear impracticably purist. In practice, however, it need not be. Taking a developmental approach does not mean taking the individual's side at the expense of the organization. It does imply that attention is given to the individual and the sponsor (possibly facilitated by the coach) sharing an understanding of their respective needs and aspirations. There will be times where there is insufficient overlap between these aspirations; in such cases the facilitation of progress for the individual may mean their leaving the organization. If this possibility is unacceptable to the organization then a developmental approach may not be the most suitable. The contracting process can therefore, in some cases, be a significant help in moving an unsatisfactory situation forward. It also sets up a level of communication that is likely to support the ongoing development of the individual within the management processes of the organization. Most managers appreciate the benefits that a three-way contracting process can bring and tend to have a more open attitude towards outcomes as a result.

The attitude that expresses itself in contracting – essentially the negotiation of the purpose of the coaching intervention – is also reflected in the progress and the relationship. There are many characteristics of the developmental coaching relationship that are common to most if not all non-directive approaches, including the emphasis on the client's agenda, their ability to seek and implement solutions, and the avoidance of advice giving. From a developmental perspective, however, any experience of problem solving is equally a learning opportunity for the client. Hence the developmental coach is perhaps less concerned with the immediacy of the presenting problem and may be even more wary of the urge to 'help out'. The coach is more likely to rely on his or her 'presence' to support their clients and may have to help them to hold an uncomfortable level of uncertainty. This can be difficult and coaches must constantly question their own motivation to intervene and the extent to which they may be becoming enrolled in the dynamics of the client's system. In earlier work, Jackson (2005) identified a typology of coaching genres. Developmental follows what he calls a 'flexible personal methodology' evidenced by an interest in the use of the relationship with the coach as the developmental influence. In this genre there is an emphasis on mutual exploration rather than on targets or performance measures.

It follows that developmental coaching is humanist and person-centred in outlook. It has much in common with the Rogerian belief in the human orientation towards self-development. Yet it must be acknowledged that there are likely to be more procedural elements than in person-centred counselling. In parallel to the way that the stakeholding is shared between coachee and sponsor through the triangular contract with the coach, the agenda in development coaching is balanced between the behavioural/performance outcome and the human potential outcome. That is to say that unconditional positive regard does not have centre stage as it does with person-centred counselling by virtue of the fact that this is coaching. Systemic demands on the individual are the occasion and objective (however the individual eventually decides to deal with them) and development is the solution. It may well be the case that developmental coaching is practised by those whose preference in the field of therapy would be for the humanistic approaches. Developmental coaching may also be organizationally sponsored, not simply as an employee support or benefit, but as a means to organizational ends: there is recognition of the individual's development occurring within the organizational context with which it interacts.

In terms of activities there may be a wide variation in the choice of techniques and tools, and indeed a wide variation in the range of attitudes to their use among coaches. There is a tendency to focus more on the relationship as developmental rather than the use of procedural techniques (Jackson, 2005). Hence the developmental coach will tend to reflect on process, avoid questions of content, and embrace ambiguity as ways of enriching the developmental relationship. Procedural tools where used may focus on the learning process, for example reflective and observational logs, experimenting with problem solving or communication patterns that are less preferred by the client (e.g. in terms of Myers-Briggs, Kolb or other typologies). Direct challenge is used with caution and is likely to be focused on process as there is otherwise a risk that it may mask an unacknowledged desire in the coach to lead the client's agenda or solutions. With an emphasis on presence and on the client's own processes, sessions may be marked at times by a quiet, contemplative atmosphere.

In keeping with the outlook described in the discussion of contracting above, clients tend to describe outcomes in terms of what has been learnt *beyond* the presenting topic. For example 'I feel more able to deal with things' (presenting topic: project management); 'I'm communicating more effectively with people inside and outside work' (presenting topic: career). As a consequence of the emphasis on process, clients also report a sense of feeling understood, or that the coach has unusual insight.

From the above it could be inferred that any opportunity the coach takes to widen the coachee's perspective and transform the way he or she thinks will lead to development. However, there are a number of widely used models of developmental coaching that can support the process. In what follows we compare Goodman's developmental coaching process with the more familiar GROW model (West & Milan, 2001) in order to examine how coaching processes can enhance development.

Goodman's (2002: 138) developmental coaching process involves four steps that have their basis in research in the adult learning and development field:

1. asking for meaning
2. building a new perspective
3. creating a bridge
4. developing action.

The first step, asking for meaning, involves asking questions that enable both the coach and the client to arrive at a deep understanding of the issue or dilemma that the client is facing. For the developmental coach, what Mezirow & Associates (2000: 22) would call 'disorienting dilemmas' are an important sign that the client is ready to make some significant and possibly developmental shift. The dilemma could suggest that the current way of making meaning is inadequate. A full understanding of the issue therefore not only helps the coach to understand the problem, but it also provides possibly a first chance for the client to tell their story and undertake some reframing of the issue. Once understanding is achieved; the client's perspective of the dilemma is laid out for examination and the way is open for alternative perspectives or readings of the story to be proposed. Goodman describes how the coach must first validate the client's current construction of the situation, but once the client feels safe and 'held' then new angles can be explored.

Step 2 involves the overt introduction of new perspectives and new options which open up choices for the client. It is here that we begin to see how the GROW model has parallels with this developmental coaching process. 'Asking for meaning' serves the same function as the reality check that is the 'R' part of GROW and 'Building a new perspective' corresponds to the exploration of Options (the 'O' in GROW). The exploration of options helps the client's understanding of the different forces that influence the dilemma.

Step 3, 'Creating a bridge', is a vital process that is not explicitly addressed in GROW, but according to Goodman helps to 'minimize the client's sense of loss by identifying and retaining some aspects of the old behaviour' (Goodman, 2002: 145–6). By reflecting on past fears and relating these to the nature of the challenge ahead, clients are enabled to move forward with a sense that their new options or perspectives have connection and relevance to their (previously articulated) reality. A similar strategy was advocated by William Perry and is well described in Kegan (1994: 277–8).

In step 4, which involves developing action, there is a direct correspondence with the 'W' in the GROW model (Will). At this point in the process a plan is developed that details what the client will do to implement change and, vitally, the coach helps the client to rehearse that change. Once more the holding environment is important: Goodman emphasizes that 'asking the client to envision the change before implementing it can increase his or her sense of control' (Goodman, 2002: 150).

HOW IS THIS GENRE DIFFERENT?

It could be argued that all coaching approaches are in some way developmental. Coaches make the assumption that when they work with the whole person it is developmental coaching, but few use that term in order to describe their work. Most choose to use a term that describes either the target audience for their coaching: executives, leaders, teams, peers; or the context in which they are coaching: life coaching, career coaching or cross-cultural coaching. A quick look at the other chapters in this handbook confirms this. The focus for coaching is on how to help clients deal with or remove the obstacles to growth and to facilitate the conditions that are conducive to their fulfilment. It therefore follows that development, whether overtly stated or not, is an integral part of all coaching contexts and genres.

However, we have identified four specific genres for discussion: transformational coaching; skills and performance coaching; the manager as coach; executive and leadership coaching.

Transformational coaching

We would argue that transformational coaching is in fact a type of developmental coaching, since it too is concerned with helping the client to think and act differently in response to a dilemma. However, it proposes that developmental change can be achieved quite quickly or even that it can be manufactured. Consequently, developmental coaching differs in one significant regard from the model of transformational coaching in that it holds that development is a gradual, organic, even a lifelong process. Development is not instantaneous or even discernable – it has been argued that development sometimes takes years or even decades (Berger & Fitzgerald, 2002; O'Connor & Lages, 2007) – so a short-term coaching relationship may only be a small part or a small phase in the client's developmental journey: just one ingredient in the client's developmental 'stew'.

Skills and performance coaching

Skills and performance coaching is an effort to maximize a client's contribution to the organization (or to their sport) by measuring performance as objectively as possible, providing feedback, and developing strategies to improve performance. Developmental coaching, on the other hand, is an intervention aimed at developing a client's internal *capacity* to meet his/her own goals. Thus in developmental coaching there is less direct emphasis on external goals.

The manager as coach

Similarly, developmental coaching is normally different from the kind of coaching that managers undertake. A manager may necessarily need to be guided by organizational goals to try and address, for example an employee's poor performance. The focus would naturally be on skills and performance to meet organizational objectives. These may conflict with the employee's own developmental agenda.

Executive and leadership coaching

O'Connor and Lages (2007: 230) have argued that developmental coaching is important for supporting leaders, since at higher levels of development 'people construct their world and understand differently; they are able to think more systemically, make finer distinctions and see the world as a bigger place, because they are not so identified with parts of their own ego'.

However, developmental coaching is also quite different from executive and leadership coaching in that it does not necessarily include an organizational focus. In both executive and leadership coaching a systemic perspective is important in order to align the coaching with the client's role in the organization. Frequently, it is this alignment which is under scrutiny. Although examination of the systemic relationship is a form of development, there may sometimes be an over-emphasis on organizational needs that could potentially conflict with the client's own developmental agenda.

RELATIONSHIP WITH THEORETICAL TRADITIONS

Developmental coaching, as we have seen, turns out to be more theoretically grounded than other genres; or to be more accurate it is multi-theoretically grounded. Indeed, it could be argued that each coaching approach involves the development of the client from its own perspective and so every theory is a theory of developmental coaching. However, for the purposes of this chapter we have chosen just four linking theoretical approaches: person-centred; cognitive–behavioural; narrative; and cognitive–developmental.

The person-centred approach

The person-centred approach is the most obvious candidate for alignment with developmental coaching. Rogers's construct of the actualizing tendency is grounded in the belief that human beings have an inherent tendency or motivation towards growth and development, with the fundamental qualities in human nature being viewed as those of growth, process and change. In Rogers's theory, 'man is an actualizing process' (Van Belle, 1980: 70). It follows, therefore, that people are their own best experts. Horney (1950) also highlights 'the struggle toward self-realization', suggesting that if obstacles to growth were removed, we would naturally develop into all that we were capable of becoming. This theory underpins the way person-centred coaching works – to examine obstacles in the client's agenda. Similarly, the developmental coach may work with these concerns through identifying values, encouraging reflexivity and challenging inconsistencies and limiting assumptions.

The cognitive–behavioural approach

The cognitive–behavioural approach also shares many of the aims of developmental coaching: to facilitate self awareness through an exploration of internal dialogue and automatic thoughts; the development of sustainable thinking skills; and the imperative to look at different perspectives. The focus is also on sustaining results over time: neither approach expects a 'quick fix' for the client. Developmental coaches may also draw on specific cognitive–behavioural techniques such as the exploration of the client's beliefs and the consequences of holding those beliefs if they have been unproductive in the past.

The narrative approach

Developmental coaching involves the in-depth exploration of client issues and so cannot help but draw on a narrative approach. The development of stories and accounts are important, particularly at the beginning of the developmental relationship. However, although clients are experts in their own lives, they do tend to focus on particular aspects of the account and downplay others. In addition, recounted sets of events are just one explanation, and developmental coaching, like narrative, recognizes that these are just one story.

The cognitive–developmental approach

The cognitive–developmental approach to developmental coaching involves unequivocal engagement with adult development theory, such as that propounded by Kegan (1982, 1994), which claims that that there are patterns of maturation in adulthood that involve the achievement of increasingly higher (and measurable) levels of self-awareness and cognitive capacity. The theory posits, therefore, that behaviour can be understood, explained and even predicted, as adults make progressive developmental changes through the lifespan (Lucius & Kuhnert, 1999; O'Connor & Lages, 2007).

In forms of coaching where this theory is made explicit, coach and client are both familiar with the theories that might guide an overt movement towards a higher level of development. Coaching with such an explicit focus on movement towards higher levels or stages of cognitive, emotional and ego maturity differs significantly from the developmental coaching approach described in this chapter, since it overtly uses a developmental framework to guide the coaching endeavour (for an example, see Bachkirova & Cox, 2007).

Laske's (2008) work, which he describes as 'evidence-based developmental coaching', is another example of an overtly theoretically guided approach. His emphasis is on facilitating an understanding of current levels of development as identified by a number of measures derived from developmental theories. Laske draws heavily on the work of Kegan (1982, 1994), Basseches (1984) and Jaques (1994) to create a constructive developmental framework for guiding adult development. He argues that 'not only the coachee (client), but the coach as well, is naturally engaged in a journey across the life span that determines his or her Frame of Reference' (Laske, 2008: 78).

Some developmental coaches may find that Laske's synthesis of developmental models and its explicit use as a framework transgresses the content/process boundary that particularly defines developmental coaching as described above. It takes some of the content agenda away from the client. It may be seen to imply that some levels of maturity are intrinsically better than others, with the danger then, as Brookfield (2000: 124) recognizes, that we make 'the explicit judgement that some states of being are better than others'. There is nonetheless something to be gained from it. As is the case with many such systematic models it may provide a framework which helps the client express and describe their own developmental aims; if it is helpful for the client to be able to say that they would like to demonstrate, in Kegan's (1994) terms, a more characteristically 'Level 4' way of making sense of their world, then it may not matter whether the coach feels that 'Level 4' is a valid theoretical construct or not. Similarly, it may provide a way of opening useful enquiries ('what would it look like if you were looking at this in a Level 4 way?') And finally, it may provide the coach with a framework for helping the client's investigation. The important thing here is that the model need not be held to be right for it to be useful.

Interestingly, Laske (2008) has argued that all behavioural coaching, of whatever persuasion, has developmental foundations, and that all adults have what he calls 'developmental intuitions'. What they lack, he claims, is only a methodology and notation for using them professionally. Laske is emphasizing here the inherent human tendency towards growth and development, and reinforces Sugarman's (2000) claim that the values underpinning the concept of development precede all empirical observation.

BENEFITS AND LIMITATIONS

As we have seen, developmental coaching is a genre of coaching where the primary purpose is not to address one specific area of a client's work or life, but to help them to achieve personal growth which will assist in a variety of different areas of their life and in the development of flexibility in their responses to their environment. Developmental coaching therefore has a much broader remit than some other forms of coaching. Developmental coaching is concerned with helping people to perform in response to an altered way of conceptualizing the world. However, it does also focus on the presenting problem as the driver for change. In developmental coaching therefore, there is a fine balance between seeing the problem as need and seeing it as opportunity – the presenting problem provides the immediate driver for finding a solution, but also, inherently, the opportunity to develop beyond that solution.

The strengths of developmental coaching lie in the support provided for the client to grow and change. Clients are encouraged to explore work and life issues from a perspective of future efficacy and efficiency, not merely in relation to short-term solutions. Developmental coaching therefore is aimed towards permanent change.

The limitation of developmental coaching is, as discussed earlier, the lack of an overarching theory to guide its practice. We have shown how many theories have some relevance for this genre, but that no one theory can be invoked. This has three significant consequences: first, it makes it difficult and complex for the coach when looking for the evidence-base to guide their practice. Second, it places a high degree of responsibility on the coach to ensure that the client understands and is a willing participant in the developmental approach, over and above other options available. Finally, because of its less procedural, more personal approach, it places a greater responsibility on the coach to examine and explore their own responses to the coaching experience through supervision.

FURTHER READING

Flaherty, J. (2005). *Coaching: Evoking excellence in others.* Oxford: Elsevier Butterworth Heinemann. (Describes a coaching process that is inherently developmental.)

Sugarman, L. (2000). *Life-span development.* Hove: Psychology Press. (A wide range of developmental concepts and theories are described.)

O'Connor, J., & Lages, A. (2007). *How coaching works.* London: A. & C. Black. (A distillation of coaching that takes best practice from a range of approaches.)

REFERENCES

Bachkirova, T., & Cox, E. (2007). A cognitive-developmental approach for coach development. In S. Palmer & A. Whybrow, *Handbook of coaching psychology.* London: Routledge.

Basseches, M. (1984). *Dialectical thinking and adult development.* Norwood, NJ: Ablex.

Berger, J., & Fitzgerald, C. (2002). Leadership and complexity of mind: The role of executive coaching. In C. Fitzgerald & J. Berger (Eds.), *Executive coaching: Practices & perspectives* (pp. 27–58). Palo Alto, CA: Davies-Black Publishing.

Berman, W., & Bradt, G. (2006). Executive coaching and consulting: Different strokes for different folks. *Professional Psychology: Research and Practice, 37*(3): 244–53.

Brookfield, S. (2000). Transformative learning as ideology critique. In J. Mezirow & Associates (Eds.), *Learning as transformation.* San Francisco, CA: Jossey Bass.

Erikson, E.H. (1974). *Dimensions of a new identity.* New York: Norton.

Goodman, R. (2002). Coaching senior executives for effective business leadership: The use of adult developmental theory as a basis for transformative change. In C. Fitzgerald & J. Berger (Eds.), *Executive coaching: Practices & perspectives* (pp. 135–53). Palo Alto, CA: Davies-Black Publishing.

Horney, K. (1950). *Neurosis and human growth.* New York: Norton.

Hunt, J., & Weintraub, J. (2002). *The coaching manager.* London: Sage.

Hunt, J., & Weintraub, J. (2004). Learning developmental coaching. *Journal of Management Education, 28*(1).

Jackson, P. (2005). The development of a five-dimensional typology of approaches used by independent UK coaching practitioners. *International Journal of Evidence Based Coaching and Mentoring, 3*(2).

Jaques, E. (1994). *Human capability.* Falls Church, VA: Cason Hall.

Kegan, R. (1994). *In over our heads.* London: Harvard University Press.

Kegan, R. (1982). *The evolving self: Problem and process in human development.* London: Harvard University Press.

Knowles, M.S., Swanson, R.A., & Holton, E.F. III. (2005). *The adult learner: The definitive classic in adult education and human resource development* (6th ed.). Oxford: Elsevier

Kolb, D. (1984). *Experiential learning.* Englewood Cliffs, NJ: Prentice Hall.

Laske, O. (2008). Mentoring a behavioural coach in thinking developmentally: A dialogue. *International Journal of Evidence Based Coaching and Mentoring, 6*(2).

Levinson, D. (1978). *The seasons of a man's life.* New York: Knopf.

Loevinger, J. (1976). *Ego development: Conceptions and theories.* San Francisco, CA: Jossey-Bass.

Lucius, R., & Kuhnert, K. (1999). Adult development and the transformational leader, *Journal of Leadership Studies, 6*(1/2): 73–85.

Maslow, A.H. (1970). *Motivation and personality* (2nd ed.). New York: Harper & Row.

Merriam, S.B., & Clark, M.C. (2008). Learning and development: The connection in adulthood. In C. Hoare (Ed.), *Handbook of adult development and learning.* New York: Oxford University Press.

Mezirow, J., & Associates (2000). *Learning as transformation.* San Francisco, CA: Jossey-Bass.

O'Connor, J., & Lages, A. (2007). *How coaching works.* London: A. & C. Black.

Perry, W.G. (1970). Forms of intellectual and ethical development in the college years. New York: Holt, Rinehart and Winston.

Riegel, K. (1973). Dialectic operations: The final period of cognitive development. *Human Development 16*: 346–70.

Schaie, K.W., & Zanjani, F. (2006). Intellectual development across adulthood. In C. Hoare (Ed.), *Handbook of adult development and learning.* New York: Oxford University Press.

Schein, E. (1987). *Process consultation* (Vol II): *Lessons for managers and consultants.* Reading, MA: Addison-Wesley.

Schein, E. (1998). *Process consultation revisited: Building the helping relationship.* Reading, MA: Addison-Wesley.

Sperry, L. (2002). *Effective leadership.* New York: Brunner-Routledge.

Sugarman, L. (2000). *Life-span development.* Hove: Psychology Press.

Tennant, M., & Pogson, P. (1995). *Learning and change in the adult years.* San Francisco, CA: Jossey-Bass.

Van Belle, H. (1980). *Basic intent and therapeutic approach of Carl R. Rogers.* Toronto: Wedge.

West, L., & Milan, M. (2001). The reflecting glass. London: Palgrave MacMillan.

16

Transformational Coaching

Peter Hawkins and Nick Smith

INTRODUCTION

Transformational Coaching enables coachees to create fundamental shifts in their capacity through transforming their way of thinking, feeling and behaving in relation to others. It is our contention that this is achieved through focusing on the shift that needs to happen live in the room so that a sustained change takes place, beyond the coaching session.

Transformational Coaching sits at one end of a spectrum of coaching (Hawkins & Smith, 2006) and is distinguished by four key elements:

1 *Shifting the meaning scheme*

The ability to help clients change their 'meaning schemes' (specific beliefs, attitudes and emotional reactions) during the coaching session, which leads to a 'perspective transformation' for the client (Hawkins, 1994, 2005). Our transformational coaching model is based, in part, on the insights of Mezirow (1991) who clarified the processes by which adults learn and change their behaviours.

2 *Working on multiple levels at the same time*

To effect change with the client, the coach needs to be able to work on multiple levels at the same time (that is, to attend to the physical, psychological, emotional and purposive elements and how they combine in the present situation). The change in perspective has to be 'embodied' (i.e. the coachee needs to be able to think, feel *and* do differently) for it to be truly transformational.

3 *Shift in the room*

Transformational coaching therefore focuses strongly on freeing the coachee's 'stuck' perspective within the session, live in the room. The process, by which the coach helps the client to experience an integrated transformation of perspective, is termed 'creating shift in the room'. A method of first matching and then mismatching the coachee is used to create the transformational shift and use is made of the CLEAR model to achieve this.

4 *Four levels of engagement*

The change in perspective comes through a change in the coachee's assumptions, values and beliefs about the presenting issue. Transformational coaches may use the 'four levels of engagement' model to map the connection of these assumptions to the feelings that drive the behaviours, that then generate the specific responses which an executive is trying to modify.

In this chapter we explore the history and background of transformational coaching. We then illustrate how transformational coaching focuses on creating a shift in the thinking, feelings and behaviour of the coachee at each stage of the CLEAR process (**C**ontracting, **L**istening, **E**xploring, **A**ction, **R**eview). We end by showing how it differs from other coaching approaches and evaluate its use.

HISTORY AND ROOTS OF TRANSFORMATIONAL COACHING

As coaches, we have worked with senior executives exploring how they could be more effective at work. Most coaching sessions created new awareness and insight for the coachee. They would leave with good intentions to use this insight to create a better reality back at work. Often, however, they would return to the next session having 'failed' to follow through. They would use phrases such as: 'I was too busy'; 'other issues came up'; 'it was more difficult than I thought'. In supervision, we would share our frustration and blame the coachee or their organization for the lack of change.

After becoming aware of this pattern, we started to ask the more searching question: 'what could we change in our coaching practice that would increase the amount of follow through in the good intentions of our coachees?' We were reminded of Dr. Johnson's comment: 'the road to hell is paved with good intentions'. It reminded us of executive teams we worked with which had met regularly and agreed to do something, only to return several weeks later, collectively frustrated by the fact that nothing had happened. We realized that there was a fundamental difference between 'agreeing to act' and 'acting'. Intellectual agreement to an action is worlds away from an intense desire to make something happen. In the initial discussion however they can easily look the same.

Key methodologies behind transformational coaching

We went on to explore what we could do as coaches that would encourage 'embodied commitment' in the coachee, not just intellectual insight and good intention. We drew on a number of key theories and methodologies:

Psychodrama (Moreno, 1972) showed the importance of the 'cathartic moment' of emotional expression.

Gestalt psychology (Polster, 1973; Clarkson & Mackewn, 1993) underlined the focus on shifting how the client is aware of themselves and their relationship with the coach.

Gendlin's 'focusing' (Gendlin, 1978) explained the notion of the 'felt shift'. Gendlin discovered that success in psychotherapy is linked to how clients talk about the issue being addressed and how they focus on physical sensations in relation to the issue. Creating a 'felt shift' in the internal response to the issue creates a more sustained change than mere insight.

Systemic family therapy clarified the process of creating a systemic shift in interlinked relationships (Minuchin & Fishman, 1981).

Levels of Learning (Argyris & Schön, 1978; Bateson, 1985). Bateson distinguished four types of learning:

- *Zero Learning:* describes many processes that in common parlance are termed 'learning', but which are only about the receipt of data; these may lead on to 'learning' but are not learning events in themselves.
- *Learning Level I:* concerns skills learning, making choices within a simple set of alternatives, called single-loop learning by Argyris and Schön (1978).
- *Learning Level II:* happens when the assumptions within which Level I learning takes place are challenged, called double-loop learning by Argyris and Schön (1978).
- *Learning Level III:* 'Learning at Level III is likely to be rare in human beings' (Bateson, 1985). It involves seeing the world as it is, rather than how someone wants it to be. It is the realm which can be talked of only in symbolic and paradoxical language because it is stripped of personal colour and concern. According to Bateson (1985), to the degree that a person achieves Learning III, the 'self' will take on a sort of irrelevance.

Recent developments in neuroscience

Recently, there has been tremendous progress in discovering more about the brain and, in particular, the importance of the limbic or mammalian brain. Whereas most coaching works with the cognitive aspects of the neocortex brain, neuroscience is indicating that fundamental change requires a shift in the patterns of relating that are embedded in the limbic brain. Lewis, Amini and Lannon (2001) argue the need for those enabling change to focus on 'limbic resonance, regulation and revisioning'.

Outcomes of transformational coaching

From these explorations we started to experiment with developing a form of coaching that focused on two outcomes.

1. enabling 'Level II' learning (Argyris & Schön, 1978; Bateson, 1985), by creating a shift in the coachee's mindset and emotional framing of his/her reality, rather than changing choices within the current set of perceived possibilities.
2. moving beyond new awareness and insight, to create a 'felt shift' live in the room, where the coachee's whole way of engaging with the issue has changed, including: language and metaphors; body language (posture, breathing, tone, tempo, pitch and rhythm of voice); way of relating to the coach (such as engagement and eye contact); an increase in embodied, energetic commitment to action; and newly rehearsed ways of moving the presenting issue forward.

As we utilized this more in our coaching and supervision practice, we discovered that this approach created a more lasting impact than other approaches we had used. In supervision, where we started to use a similar transformational approach, coaches were returning to supervision sessions excited about the changes they had produced. Furthermore, some coaches were returning saying they did not even have to follow through with their plan for change, as it was almost as if the other parties had heard the supervision session and had anticipated the changes. At first this seemed rather magical, but then we realized, from a systemic perspective, that if one part of the system fundamentally changes, the rest of the system has to adapt to match it.

The conclusion from our explorations, and from those of our supervisees, was that if the change does not start in the coaching room, it is unlikely to happen back at work.

THE KEY ELEMENTS OF TRANSFORMATIONAL COACHING

1 The CLEAR model and relational skills

The CLEAR model is a core practice in transformational coaching. It has five stages, each requiring different relational skills. In CLEAR, the coach starts by *Contracting* with the coachee both on the boundaries and on the focus of the work. Then the coach *Listens* to the issues the coachee brings, listening not only to the content, but also to the feelings and ways of framing the story used by the coachee. The coach needs to let the coachee know that they have not only heard the story, but have 'got' what it feels like to be in that situation. Only then is it useful to move on to *Explore* with the coachee what is happening in the dynamics, both of the work relationships and the coaching relationship playing out in the room, before facilitating the coachee to explore new *Actions*. Finally, the coach *Reviews* the process and agrees next steps.

The use of CLEAR is necessary but not sufficient for practising transformational coaching. In order to get to the nub of the problem, coaches also need to have a 'compass' that steers them towards the critical area for change. New coaches often have a natural tendency to focus either on offering solutions or exploring feelings. This can influence how they react when they start listening to the client. Those coaches who are practical, logical and data focused feel comfortable in encouraging their client to go deeper into the detail, and then move swiftly to offer a solution. Others may immediately seek out the feelings in the situation, and try to bring those out more clearly, holding off from offering practical solutions. Neither is wrong, but context requires an ability to use both/either of these perspectives at the appropriate time.

Initial preferences therefore are not a useful guide for coaches in a coaching session. To be able to navigate from the initial data brought by the coachee to a transformation of the coachee's perspective on their issue in a way that allows them to be and act differently, coaches need some sort of 'map' showing how the issue is constructed and a notion of where they need to concentrate, in order to create this substantial shift in perspective.

2 *Exploring the four levels*

The 'four levels of engagement' model (Figure 16.1) explains how the coach can avoid 'problem solving' or ventilation of feelings as a default coaching outcome and helps create a developmental/transformational intervention for coachees. Awareness of the model allows the coach to see whether he/she is dealing with facts, patterns of behaviour, feelings or assumptions. If the entire content of the conversation has focused upon facts and behaviours, then the coach knows that, in order to help the coachee move on, it will be necessary to help

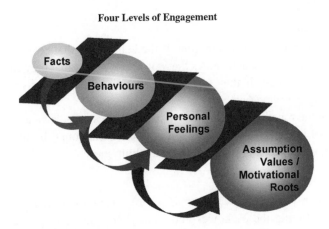

Figure 16.1   Four levels of engagement.

them look at the underlying feelings driving these events. It also shows that to create sustainable change, coachees need to understand their internal dialogue, which generates the dysfunctional feelings in the situation in which they find themselves (i.e. their assumptions).

Getting to the roots of the issue

This simple but profound model offers a map of where coach and coachee need to get to in their coaching conversations and how to decide which questions to ask next. It is a helpful map for all who wish to develop transformational coaching skills. In a world in which people seek out 'quick fixes' and formulae for success, this could be seen as another 'golden bullet', a recipe for transformation every time. It isn't. However, although it is not prescriptive in shaping a coaching conversation, it is indicative of the ground that needs to be covered. It is more art than science. We will explore below how this model fits with the CLEAR process for transformational coaching. To start, we explore the four levels to see how they might be used.

Level 1 data

When starting a new coaching conversation, most coaches want to gather data, asking, for example: 'What does the issue look like? How often does it happen? What are the consequences? Who is involved?' As experience is gained, coaches probably need a lot less detail before moving things forward for the coachee. Level 1 therefore focuses on the details of the events that are being discussed. It will generate a list of facts (this issue happened with this person, on this date, and yielded these results).

The detail, though, can be confusing. If coaches are being told about random events with no apparent connection, they have no means of helping coachees understand what is happening. If events are truly random, the coach and coachee cannot learn from them. To understand whether these facts are random or a habitual response, they need to go to Level 2 and ask questions about behaviours.

Level 2 patterns of behaviour

Behaviours are simply patterns of interaction. If the behaviours that create specific events start to show a familiar pattern, the coach knows that it is highly likely that they can help the coachee, first, to understand, and then, if they wish, to transform these reactions so that they are not locked into repeating the same outcomes.

Being clear what the repetitive behaviour looks like brings some awareness as to what might be happening but, of itself, will not help to shift 'stuck' behaviours. In our experience, insight alone does not create transformation. It needs something more.

Level 3 feelings

If people are constantly reacting in the same specific ways to similar triggers, they need to understand what is driving these choices and what pushes these responses. Seeing the habit patterns at play, they need to become aware of the feelings that fuel and drive these responses and give them the power to repeat them *ad infinitum*. The feelings at the root of why people behave as they do are part of the mechanism that supports 'homeostasis'. Homeostasis is the human body's hard-wired response for protecting it against random and potentially dangerous change. Our bodies are 'wired' to keep body temperature and heart rate within specific bounds and if our body goes outside those ranges, it employs a wide variety of 'physical' and 'emotional' means to get things back 'in the groove'. Thus, people can come to rely on certain habits (e.g. running away, eating too much, smoking) to calm their anxieties, and if they are denied these behaviours, there is a strong emotional response in trying to re-establish them.

Feelings can trap coach and coachee by their intensity and their engaging qualities. By uncovering the underlying feelings that drive a reaction, coaches are not necessarily nearer to creating the change that the coachee wants. We cannot change the emotions we experience by focusing on these emotions. We can only change the emotions by asking 'why?'

Level 4 assumptions

To change feelings, we need to look at assumptions, because these generate the feelings that drive the behaviours that create the type of event we are trying to change. At Level 4 it is possible to uncover and articulate the story being told by the coachee when faced with specific events. For example, if I have not had a very distinguished academic history, when faced with 'clever people', I might tell myself 'I need to constantly prove that I am as good as they are'. I might then come across as competitive and bombastic with colleagues and clients. These dysfunctional responses could hurt my credibility and that of my company.

Level 4 is populated by assumptions about:

- personal reality ('I am hopeless at confronting powerful people')
- strongly held values ('I am only here to serve others')
- guiding principles ('being competitive with others is the worst kind of pride').

By uncovering the narrative at this level, the coachee can check whether it is simply a fossilized remain from a previous era in their life (e.g. a now dysfunctional response to the trauma of being humiliated publicly in adolescence for offering a strongly held opinion) or whether it has current validity. To shine a light on this aspect of the coachee's beliefs, they can simply ask the question 'What is the assumption I make about this sort of situation?' If this question draws a blank, they can engage their creative faculties by asking 'In order to have the feelings I have in this situation, what sort of assumptions would I need to be making?'

Focusing on data (Level 1) and behaviour (Level 2) might serve if coaches are offering skills coaching. On their own they do not provide the traction to create transformational change. Performance coaching (i.e. focusing on improving the outcomes in the current role) will also need to look at feelings (Level 3) in order to understand the strength with which the current behaviours are maintained. In both developmental and transformational coaching, it is necessary for coaches to include all four levels. The difference between the two would be that in transformational coaching, the coach uses these four levels to work directly 'in the room' with the issues and immediately rehearse the shifts and changes that have been explored.

Mapping the CLEAR process onto the four levels

Taking a typical transformational coaching session, the CLEAR process can be mapped onto the four levels. This is not prescriptive, but shows a general intent and flow in the coaching session. If coaches are going to create a clear focus for a session, in order to create a shift in the room they must contract clearly as to the best outcome for the coachee. In transformational coaching the coach should look at how long the session is going to last and, rather than focusing on broader goals, encourage the coachee to think carefully about what specifically they want to have been changed by the end of the session.

'What would good look like, for this session to be a real success for you?' 'In the 40 minutes we have together, what is the real stretch that you need to make to move things forward?'

By working with the coachee to look at what a successful next step would require, the coach helps the coachee to visualize and/or rehearse the goal and therefore be more likely to achieve it.

Contracting: (Levels 1 and 2)

Effective executive coaching requires three-way contracting between the coach, the coachee and the organizational client. The coachee's sponsor is the representative of the organization and is responsible for the organization of learning, and benefiting from this coaching relationship. The sponsor is not just there to support the coachee's learning, but has an important role in locking the relevant bits of the coachee's learning back into the wider system's learning.

The Contracting phase in CLEAR is importantly different from, say, the GROW model (Whitmore, 1992) because it focuses upon the shift needed now in the room, as well as acknowledging the broader goals of the coaching process. This phase is not just relevant at the very beginning of each session, but whenever during a session the coach feels some shift has occurred that may have refocused what might be important to work on. Contracting is expected to be an iterative process within each session, as well as between sessions.

Listening: (Levels 2 and 3)

The Listening phase is used to uncover details of the situation to be worked upon. If coachees report issues in their usual way, it will not help them to see things differently and will not generate new possibilities for the coach or coachee to play with. It is important therefore to interrupt habitual responses at this early stage. While listening, the coach can also test the coachee's flexibility to think and behave differently, by interrupting the pattern of delivery. For example if the coachee appears to be going into 'automatic pilot' in their description of the problem, the coach might interject and either register an alternative view of the assumptions being made or ask a catalytic question (e.g. 'If that wasn't the reason, what else might have been going on?').

The coach needs to listen to what is happening in the situation, what is not being voiced, what has been tried, what has worked or not worked, but also to understand what this situation has 'cost' the coachee and others involved, and what is the degree of urgency in coming to a resolution. Effective listening builds trust and helps the coachee to develop greater levels of understanding and awareness. A primary objective of coach training is to help the coach use listening as an integral part of creating transformational change in the session.

By mapping the listening phase of CLEAR onto the four levels, it can be seen to use the facts (Level 1), the behaviours (Level 2) and the feelings generated (Level 3), in order to understand what has been done already and what the activity has cost the coachee emotionally.

Explore (Levels 3 and 4)

The Explore phase starts to build on what has already been discussed and searches for new possibilities for change. This stage of the coaching relationship is nurtured through a process of skilful questions and listening. Powerful questions are core, as they enable the coachee to explore the situation from different standpoints, generating new perspectives and possibilities. Useful types of coaching questions here include:

- **Closed questions** – seeking data ('How many apples do you have?')
- **Open questions** – seeking information ('Can you tell me about your apple trees?')
- **Leading questions** – seeking information and indirectly shaping the answer ('Why do you like apples best?')
- **Inquiry questions** – inviting active inquiry ('What are the criteria for judging the best apple?')
- **Transformational or mutative questions** – inviting active inquiry that not only assists the coachee in thinking outside their current frames and mindsets, but also creates an emotional shift in the person being asked ('What would it take for you to begin to like apples?')

At this point we often use Heron's Confronting, Catalytic and Cathartic interventions (see Hawkins & Smith, 2006: ch. 7) to move the coachee towards seeing the story they are telling themselves. The objective is to create a wider range of choices from which the coachee can choose a better way forward.

Action (Levels 4, 3 and 2)

Having decided on a course of action, it is vitally important that the transformational coach creates time and space for rehearsing what the coachee will say and do when they address the issue they have discussed.

If coachees do not rehearse the way in which they want to behave differently, and do not practise it, and get clear feedback on how they are coming over, they are less likely to do things differently outside the coaching session. So the action stage requires the relational skills of inviting the coachee to embody that change, live in the room. 'So you will confront this issue with your colleague when you meet with them next Tuesday. Show me how you will do that.

Talk to me as if I am the colleague'. This would be followed by direct feedback from the coach and an encouragement to do a second or third rehearsal. The coach focuses on the coachee creating an authentic, embodied shift in how they relate to the other person. This will manifest in new ways of breathing, posture, eye contact, and different energy, as well as new language and metaphor.

Review (Levels 1–4)

In the final part of the session, the objective is to help the coachee review what has worked and what would be more effective next time. It helps them to see the web of connections between different parts of the process and how different questions sharpened and focused the inquiry. This feedback is of huge benefit for the learning of both coach and coachee and allows both to 'bank' new found ways of doing things, and take confidence from the session, so that they have the opportunity to behave differently in new circumstances in the future.

The transformational coaching process

The craft of the coach is multilayered, requiring high levels of attention and awareness, and openness to using oneself in the service of what needs to change in the system. The coach begins by listening intensely (i.e. 'Level 4 listening' above, and in Hawkins & Smith, 2006: ch. 12) and responding with 'fearless compassion' to the client in the room and their wider system outside. The coach is silently holding the questions:

- 'What is the shift that needs to happen in this wider system?'
- 'What needs to shift in the relationship between this individual and the issue they are describing?'
- 'For those shifts to occur, what needs to shift right now in this individual?'

The coach then turns the focus back to the 'system that is live in the room' – themselves and their coachee and the relationship between them – all the while holding the following questions in mind:

- 'To be in service of those changes, what needs to shift in my relationship to this coachee right now?'
- 'What do I need to alter in my being to help bring that about?'

The coach holds these questions, not trying to work out an answer intellectually, but waiting for a felt sense of what is necessary for the intended transformative purposes.

Understanding of the coachee's situation starts with the larger view of the system of which they are a part. From here it moves to the specifics at play in the present relationship. However, the change *process* moves differently. It goes the other way round. It starts with the individual in the present moment, then reverberates through the relationship between coach and coachee, and later instigates a change in the coachee's relationship with the wider system.

What do the 'shifts' look like?

'Shift in the room' will, to differing degrees, impact all four levels of the coachee's engagement with the coach. If coachees have a moment where they realize that the way they had been thinking about things is not the only way, this triggers a set of reactions at all levels. These bits of evidence in the room support coaches in the direction they are taking. It is independent of whatever the coachee says and is further evidence in the room about what is happening.

Level 1

Physical appearance changes. The coachee might look brighter, more open and engaged, have livelier energy. People's posture, breathing, voice tone, etc. model a change in the way they relate physically in the situation.

Level 2

In the room, coachees adopt new behaviours in relation to the coach and the issue they brought. Their behaviour is less predictable and more experimental, and less reflective or 'in their head'.

Level 3

The feeling tone changes for the person – from locked and stuck to energized and hopeful of new possibilities. There is often a 'Derrrr!' response – the person laughs, hits palm of hand on forehead in disbelief that they have really believed this story for so long. That lightening of tone and laughter is a strong clue to the shift having taken place.

Level 4

The story being told is now clear to them and, because of that, it holds far less power. The mindset shifts and there appear to be possibilities that were not there before of doing things differently.

HOW IS TRANSFORMATIONAL COACHING DIFFERENT?

Transformational coaching is not the only useful form of coaching, but it is the most effective for trying to enable embodied, level two learning that creates a shift in consciousness and a sustained shift in how the coachee is engaging at work. In Hawkins and Smith (2006) we presented a continuum of coaching that showed the relationship of transformational coaching to skills, performance and developmental coaching (see Figure 16.2).

One end of the continuum focuses on developing new skills or competencies in the coachee. These skills could be specifically related to role or job, such as sales, IT or more general people management skills (e.g. appraisal of staff, giving and receiving feedback). Much of this sort of coaching is included in training courses and is a general part of on the job learning. We would

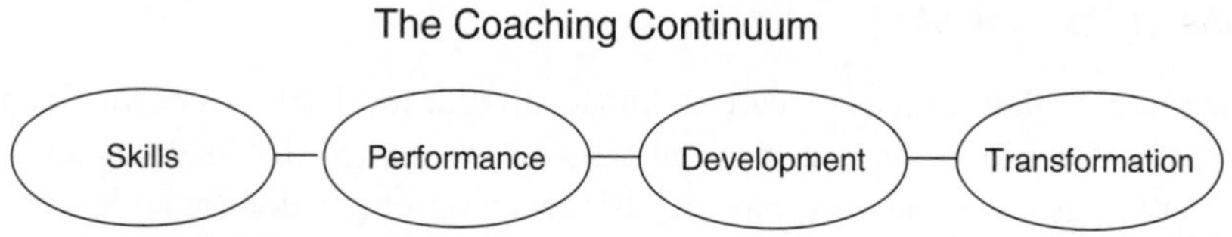

The Coaching Continuum

Figure 16.2   The coaching continuum.
Source: **Hawkins & Smith, 2006.**

contend that the majority of skills coaching does not require external or specialized coaching, it is a core aspect of a line manager's skills.

Performance coaching is less focused on the acquisition of skills (inputs) and more centred on raising levels of performance (outputs and outcomes) in a current role. It focuses more on applied capabilities than competence. This is the sort of coaching typically offered by a manager or internal coach in one-to-one sessions, and is a key part of good performance management.

Developmental coaching is less focused on the current role and more centred on longer-term development. Besides helping the coachee develop competencies and capabilities, it will include more focus on the development of the whole person and their broader human capacities, showing how they can use their current role to develop their capacity for future roles and challenges. Thus there is more focus on second order or double-loop learning (Argyris & Schön, 1978; Hawkins, 1991).

At the other end of the spectrum, *transformational coaching* focuses even more on 'second order' or Level 2 learning and change. Developmental learning will tend to focus on increasing capacity within one life stage and in what Torbert (2004) describes as a particular 'action logic', by which he means 'the way the coachee frames the world both cognitively and emotionally'. In contrast, transformational coaching will be more involved with enabling the coachee to shift levels or 'action logics' and thereby make a transition from one level of functioning to a higher one.

EVALUATION

It should be clear from what has been said so far that transformational coaching is not an answer to every coaching need. It is focused at one end of the coaching spectrum. Using a transformational approach in skills and performance coaching could, for instance, be experienced as intrusive and threatening, unless there was a contract with the coachee to take a much broader and deeper view of the issues at hand. Transformational coaching requires the coachee to have an active agenda of transformation, and an active need to change. The agenda for transformational coaching is second order change. First order change is simply the sort of change that requires addition or subtraction of what is already there. Therefore it works within the current bounds of existing assumptions. Second order change is achieved when there are radical changes in assumptions about significant elements of life. They are what Mezirow (1991) called perspective transformations. It is this type of change that transformational coaching addresses; if someone does not want or need to shift foundational assumptions in order to change, then this type of coaching could be experienced as intrusive.

Transformational coaching comes into its own when coachees need to create a radical shift in the way they operate, and the weight of pressure on them demands that the change is speedy. Transformational coaching looks at supporting a step change in someone's approach to a situation. It could be used where the person does not have the luxury of gradual personal development. This suggests that in the fast pace of today's corporate life, this type of coaching has strong relevance, particularly for those in senior positions, where the consequence of slow personal change is often quick dismissal.

When new or experienced coaches are trained in transformational coaching, the first stage is to help them learn the various models, both theoretically and practically. After they have created a strong practical foundation we remind them that ultimately transformational coaching is an attitude, based on a core belief that change starts with oneself and in the here and now. Following Ghandi, we believe it is important that 'We be the change we want to see'.

Although the underlying models can at first seem quite complex, transformational coaching focuses on three simple questions:

- What is disconnected that needs to be connected?
- What is the truth that needs to be spoken?
- What is the shift that needs to be enabled?

In asking these questions the coach applies them to all parts of the system: 'What is disconnected within the client organisation?'; 'What is the shift that needs to be enabled right here in the room?'; 'What is the truth that needs to be spoken by me, by the coachee, or in the organisation?'.

The world is changing faster than most humans are able to adapt. Learning ways of accelerating depth transformation in human beings is an urgent and important calling. Our hope is that Transformational Coaching will make a contribution to this challenge.

FURTHER READING

Bateson, G. (1985). *Steps to an ecology of mind*. New York: Ballantine Books. (This groundbreaking book explores how ideas interact and how systems of thought sustain themselves and evolve. It is not an easy read, but is a seminal work for this type of change.)

O'Neill, M.B. (2000). *Coaching with backbone and heart: A systems approach to engaging leaders with their challenges*. San Francisco, CA: Jossey-Bass. (Mary Beth O'Neill communicates the practicalities of the task of coaching leaders, the importance of a systemic understanding and the necessity of business understanding, and provides particular insight into what we have called 'fearless compassion'.)

Hawkins, P., & Smith, N. (2006). *Coaching, mentoring and organizational consultancy: Its supervision and development.* London: Open University Press. (This text sets systemic transformational coaching in a broader context and also looks at the way in which transformational coaching skills apply to the practice of executive coaching supervision.)

REFERENCES

Argyris, C., & Schön, D. (1978). *Organizational learning.* Reading, MA: Addison-Wesley.

Bateson, G. (1985). *Steps to an ecology of mind.* New York: Ballantine Books.

Clarkson, P., & Mackewn, J. (1993). *Fritz Perls.* London: Sage.

Gendlin, E.T. (1978). *Focusing* (1st ed.). New York: Everest House.

Hawkins, P. (1991). The spiritual dimension of the learning organisation. *Management Education and Development, 22*(3).

Hawkins, P. (1994). The changing view of learning. In J. Burgoyne, *Towards the learning company.* London: McGraw-Hill.

Hawkins, P. (2005). *The wise fool's guide to leadership.* Winchester: O Books.

Hawkins, P., & Smith, N. (2006). *Coaching, mentoring and organizational consultancy: Supervision and development.* Maidenhead: Open University Press.

Lewis, T., Amini, F., & Lannon, R. (2001). *A general theory of love.* New York: Vintage Books.

Mezirow, J. (1991). *Transformative dimensions of adult learning.* Oxford: Jossey-Bass.

Minuchin, S., & Fishman, H.C. (1981). *Family therapy techniques.* Cambridge, MA: Harvard University Press.

Moreno, J.L. (1972). *Psychodrama* (Vols. 1–3). Boston, MA: Beacon Press.

Polster, E., & Polster, M. (1973). *Gestalt therapy integrated.* New York: Random House.

Torbert, W. (2004). *Action inquiry: The secret of timely and transforming leadership.* San Francisco, CA: Berrett-Koehler.

Whitmore, J. (1992). *Coaching for performance.* London: Nicholas Brealey.

17

Executive and Leadership Coaching

Jon Stokes and Richard Jolly

INTRODUCTION

Executive Coaching is a term used broadly to cover work with executives from middle management upwards or sometimes even to those in junior roles deemed to have high potential. It is used most effectively with those individuals who have significant responsibility for the current and future success of the organization and who have the potential to develop and change. While sometimes used for individuals who are performing poorly or having a negative effect on those they lead, remedial work is not its primary focus.

The needs of such a diverse group vary considerably and thus so does the extent to which the coaching relationship needs to be one of teacher or trainer versus facilitator or consultant, or how much it should focus on management skills versus the leadership role. Too broad a definition renders the term Executive Coaching virtually meaningless since it can and sometimes is used to cover any form of training or development activity carried out on a one-to-one basis by a coach with an executive. Consequently we reserve the term for work with senior level executives that focuses on the executive becoming more self-aware in order to carry out their leadership role more effectively (Levinson, 1996; Peterson, 1996; Kilburg, 2000; Fitzgerald & Berger, 2002).

Executive coaching could therefore be defined as a form of personal learning and development consultation provided by someone external to the organization who focuses on improving an individual's performance in the quintessentially executive role of balancing the forces of cooperation and competition in an organization (Barnard, 1938). It can be distinguished from mentoring, which is typically a more informal relationship with a more experienced colleague (Clutterbuck, & Megginson, 2005) and from coaching received from an individual within the same organization, typically the individual's manager (Landsberg, 1997).

While a senior executive's role will include elements of both management and leadership, executive coaching focuses primarily on the latter. Management is essentially the skill of working with 'the known' within defined and existing parameters and constraints, and focuses on achieving controlled and quantifiable task objectives. Leadership focuses primarily on what is 'not known', the future and on what changes may be required. It is often about emotions rather than facts; it is about people and relationships rather than tasks. Whereas management aspires to be a science, leadership will always remain an art. What is required of those in senior roles in organizations is usually far more about leadership than management. Indeed, making the shift from manager to leader, from relying on an operational perspective to employing a strategic one, from a mindset of controlling events to a mindset of enabling others, and achieving a better understanding of the organization as a whole, are just some of the reasons individuals seek executive coaching.

In this chapter we recognize that leadership, as an activity rather than a role, is not something confined to the top of an organization. Leadership exists at all levels in an organization, and thus much of what we say will also have more general application.

BACKGROUND AND CONTEXT

Up until the mid-1980s, the coaching of executives (though that term was rarely used) was provided informally either by internal Human Resource professionals, usually with a remedial emphasis, or by an external professional whose primary role was that of trusted advisor from a legal, accounting or marketing background. It had no established theoretical framework and practitioners generally had little or no formal training. During the late 1970s and beyond, a combination of factors served to open up a demand for the specialist professional executive coach.

Changing attitudes to authority and the desire for more diversity at the top of organizations posed a challenge to accustomed ways of leading and managing (Drucker, 1993; Handy, 2002). This led to a demand for professionally trained coaches with expertise in human psychology and relationships in the workplace beyond simply being experienced HR professionals or trusted professional advisors (Kilburg, 2000). Four major factors drove these changes.

1 Less stress on formal hierarchy and more emphasis on the right to express individual views meant that leaders needed to learn a broader repertoire of skills for influencing and motivating,

especially with groups within society that had not previously had a place at the top (Hirschhorn, 1997). Although traditionally considered bastions of confidence and power, in which position in the hierarchy guaranteed a degree of respect and influence, the impact of social and economic changes made organizations increasingly unstable, fractured arrangements. Senior executives no longer felt they could trust the corporation to look after them and increasingly could not rely on alliances with their peers in a rapidly changing, highly competitive environment (Miller, 1993; Krantz, 1998). These demands combined to drive many senior executives to seek individual confidential relationships of counsel in which they could develop new skills and have the space and time to reflect on the increasing pressures of organizational leadership (Orenstein, 2007).

2   At the same time, and partly in response to the same factors, HR departments were enlarged and began placing a greater emphasis on development activities for staff. Development was not just for staff requiring remedial attention, but began to be seen as a right, as well as a way of retaining the best staff. It was also seen as a strategy for changing the culture of a whole firm via personal performance coaching across groups of leaders (Tichy, 2004).

3   The breakdown of traditional, hierarchical institutions in the west meant that individuals seeking success needed to do so by better managing themselves personally and professionally, and by improving their own performance through their own efforts and will. Because of this, the self-help book and self-development programme industries burgeoned at an astonishing rate. The expansion of executive coaching could be seen in the context of a more general expansion of a cultural norm of individualized personal development. This put the stress on personal effectiveness as the new, more meritocratic route to wealth, success and happiness (Wuthnow, 1996; Frey & Stitzer, 2002).

4   The rise of a more explicitly merit-based approach to the promotion of executives, rather than simply age or longevity in the organization, or whether they knew the right people, created new opportunities for achievement-oriented managers from different social and educational backgrounds. This also increased the pressures on individuals to perform. Such pressures have led to managers working increasingly long hours, thus changing the traditional culture where seniority meant fewer hours. Today, the more senior is an executive, the harder he or she has to work, and the more permeable the traditional work versus personal life boundaries have become (Reeves, 2001). Helping leaders to manage the continual challenges of finding some sort of balance between the various roles in their lives has become a recent additional important role for coaches.

Among the main proponents of executive coaching have been Marshall Goldsmith, Warren Bennis, Jim Kouzes and Tim Gallwey (Goldsmith, Lyons & Freas, 2000). Gallwey (2000) in particular revolutionized the field by suggesting, based on his experience as a tennis coach, that expertise as a manager was often a handicap to being an effective coach, since it encouraged the coach to 'tell' the 'trainee' how to do it, as opposed to using a facilitative approach to provide the conditions that enable the coachee to learn from their experiences of success and failure and to reach their own conclusions and devise their own responses. This is now the stated aim of most executive coaches.

The evolution of executive coaching has led to the field rapidly becoming professionalized, with specialist organizations being formed to promote the interests of executive coaches, such as in the Association for Professional Executive Coaching and Supervision (APECS), in the United Kingdom (www.apecs.org) and the Worldwide Association of Business Coaches(WABC) in the United States (www.wabccoaches.com).

WHY DO LEADERS SEEK EXECUTIVE COACHING?

Executives typically seek coaching during times of transition, when they are taking up a new position or joining a new organization, or when they are facing new personal challenges either from colleagues or subordinates within the organization, or when addressing difficult issues in their private lives.

Life at the top can be lonely and the higher the executive rises the less frequent and less reliable the feedback from colleagues becomes. Individual agendas multiply and conflict. Leaders need on occasion an independent sounding board; someone who can assist them in working through problems and potential solutions and to create a space for thinking in the executive's otherwise action-packed working life. A phrase sometimes used to describe this challenge is 'when you are fighting off the alligators, it's hard to remember you were trying to drain the swamp'. Some leaders, given their achievement orientation, get so preoccupied with 'fighting alligators' that they can fail to focus on the actions critical to achieving their own and the organization's ambitions. Leaders need to take responsibility for draining the swamp, and this involves the ability to set and follow through on their key priorities.

Those new to leadership roles, or who have recently moved into a new position, need to actively integrate themselves into the role and the organization. Senior leaders of the order of 30-50% fail or have left within 18 months of a new appointment (Watkins, 2003). Similarly, those facing new challenges in their role, such as how to exert influence on a broader stage as a consequence of organizational expansion, will need new capabilities in motivating and persuading. What has led to their success so far is unlikely to be sufficient going forward. Managers are not promoted to leaders because they were good at their previous role, but rather because there is a hope that they will be able to develop, learn and adapt their behaviour to be successful in the new role. Many managers derail because of their inability to change their behaviours as they become more senior (Van Velsor & Leslie, 1995). Executive coaching can help them adapt to the new role demanded of them by their organization.

Those who aspire to leadership generally have a strong drive towards power, achievement and success. Consequently, some common problems are:

- a need to dominate and control
- a focus on action, rather than thinking

- a need to be right
- impatience
- a need to be associated with success and to avoid failure
- a high need for self-determination
- a need to feel powerful
- a need to know
- overcommitment.

Topics such as these will be among the key agenda items for any leadership coaching assignment.

GOALS AND TASKS OF EXECUTIVE AND LEADERSHIP COACHING

Undoubtedly, executive coaching has at times been in danger of becoming an over-used management fad, particularly when it is being prescribed without a great deal of thought being given to its objectives (Berglas, 2002).

As mentioned earlier, executive coaching has a broad remit and will vary at one extreme from relatively superficial external goals to perhaps more profound internal change. Building on Argyris and Schön (1978) in relation to levels of learning, we identify three levels of activity.

Level 1 **Behaviour Change** – normally achievable in the relatively short-term. It requires focused feedback, a commitment to change, the development of alternative behaviours and practice as well as reinforcement.

Level 2 **Self-Image** – the stories we tell ourselves about ourselves and how we view ourselves both consciously and unconsciously, impact our self-confidence and our sense of ourselves as either victim or agent in the world. For example if a client is not able to imagine him or herself as a partner in a professional practice firm then it is highly unlikely that he or she will be promoted to such a position. Such questions go beyond mere professional identity. They generally touch on deep-rooted conflicts that all human beings face. Issues of self-confidence and personal self-doubt may need to be tackled.

Level 3 **Purpose and Meaning** – questions of personal purpose, as well as how to contribute to a greater organizational purpose, lie at the heart of a leader's motivations. The greatest leaders in history have acquired their commitment through the crucible of difficult experiences, turning these from potential trauma into sources of inspiration and courage. While executive and leadership coaching can benefit from studying such great leaders, it has been suggested that many leaders are in fact 'twice born' (Zaleznik, 1992), in the sense of having experienced events which have made them feel different from their peer group, leading them to step outside of focusing on their everyday living and to observe life audaciously, resulting in a new beginning in their attitude to life.

Four central dilemmas can be said to lie at the heart of effective leadership:

- the **strategic** longer term perspective versus the **operational** day-to-day perspective
- being **directive** versus **enabling** others
- **getting ahead** versus **getting along** with others
- **being empathic** versus being **ruthless**.

Successful leaders are rare because balancing and optimizing these conflicting tendencies requires great skill; human beings generally have a preference towards one or the other polarity. The executive coach's task is to help the leader to hold and bear the tension between the forces pulling in one direction or another, to provide a sounding-board and a container (Stokes, 1994), as well as a space in which the leader can reflect on personal preferences and ethical dilemmas. Thus the executive coach's task should be to strive to add value in the job of balancing and optimizing these dilemmas more than any particular quantitative business or management outcome.

Berglas (2002) suggests that the executive coach requires a degree of psychological training and sophistication and both Berglas (2002) and Peltier (2001) have identified areas where technical competence might reasonably be expected from an executive coach. These include:

- an understanding of personal, organizational and group psychology and dynamics, and their impact on individuals and teams
- appropriate business knowledge
- methods of leadership, team and organizational development
- leadership and team assessment methodologies
- certification with a range of psychometric instruments
- an understanding of how to promote the adult learning process.

With these dilemmas and competencies in mind, we have identified how coaching senior executives to lead effectively benefits from a sequence of four essential steps.

1. Know yourself   self-awareness is the first step. Typically, the coaching will ask: What motivates you? How do others perceive you? Why would anyone want to follow you?

2. Own yourself   being prepared to be accountable for the effect we have on others comes next. Coaching questions might include: What is the impact you have on others, both positive and negative? Who might find your style, attitudes or values motivating or difficult?

3. Be yourself   a lack of authenticity is often one of the first criticisms that will be made of a new leader. If there is a gap between 'talking the talk' and 'walking the walk' there is little chance of sustained support. Executives need to be clear about their own values and sticking to them also requires courage.

4. Help others to do the same   a key aspect of good leadership is bringing on and supporting other voices of leadership. The coach will ask such questions as: Does your leadership style enable others to take up leadership roles? Effective leaders empower others, not simply themselves.

These are matters and questions to which responses and decisions are not easy, or even possible to find without support. They require sustained effort, credible feedback and, on occasion a willingness to face painful emotional truths. Having the benefit of a period of reflection, with an executive coach who is independent of the organization and who has no personal or political agenda of his or her own, can enable a more balanced, objective and effective approach to these questions.

SPECIFIC FEATURES OF EXECUTIVE AND LEADERSHIP COACHING

Briefly summarized, executive coaching is a professional and confidential partnership relationship between a senior executive and coach involving:

- ongoing confidential meetings (lasting between one hour and a full day) organized on a regular basis for a period of six months or longer
- the primary goal of improving the executive's leadership skills
- some assessment of the individual's current effectiveness in the leadership role
- very often the use of data from psychometric and other assessment and feedback tools
- a relationship of challenge and support
- building on strengths as well as how to manage or change weaknesses
- an objective of both behavioural change and increased personal maturity and wisdom.

Opinions vary as to the extent to which the coach should be held responsible for ensuring that organizational goals are achieved. Arguably, the tension between personal self-interests and organizational group interests lies at the very heart of what a senior leader in a firm has to manage. Having the coach take sides on these questions could defeat the executive's challenge of taking up their authority effectively, and runs the risk of becoming a sophisticated form of staff supervision.

Certainly, clarity about accountability for how the coaching will contribute to organizational effectiveness must form a central part of the setting up of any executive coaching assignment. But it must remain the executive's task to interpret how best to achieve organizational goals as opposed to someone external to the organization. Having a coach who simply directs the coachee about the right and wrong course of action, though often a relief to both parties, may discourage executives from exploring the issues for themselves and from fully taking up their authority and accountability.

A coaching assignment should ideally be a partnership between the executive, the coach and the organization working together. However, in the real world of organizations, and especially large bureaucratic organizations in difficulty, such ideal goals are not always easily achieved. The executive may have multiple lines of accountability to persons with conflicting views and interests. The aims and strategies of an organization rarely remain uncontested for long among its senior executives. Nevertheless, the aim must be that the executive, the coach and other key stakeholders work to create a partnership that ensures that the executive's development advances the organization's overall business objectives.

EXECUTIVE AND LEADERSHIP COACHING AND OTHER COACHING GENRES

Several factors distinguish executive coaching from other forms of coaching.

- The primary client is the organization and its various stakeholders rather than simply the individual, who is seen as located and therefore to be understood within a wider system of roles and accountabilities.
- Executive Coaching always involves an intent to align the capabilities of the individual with the ambitions of the organization, and to work to support and achieve the organization's overall purpose and objectives.
- The aim of coaching will usually be informed by, and often agreed with, the individual's line manager, to whom some form of feedback before, sometimes during and generally at the end of a period of coaching is appropriate.
- Matters of purely private concern and interest, with no implications for the sponsoring organization, are not the primary focus of executive coaching, although they will often be a necessary component to address in order to help the executive improve his or her performance.
- The coach's fees are therefore generally paid by the organization and not personally by the executive.

These rules are not hard and fast, however, and require a degree of flexible interpretation. People are generally motivated at work by personal needs, not all of which are the concern of the organization. For example in the real world even the most committed and hard-working executive will go through periods of doubt and frustration with his organization and will inevitably at times consider a career elsewhere. Indeed, such reactions may be a normal response. It would be naïve to prohibit such conversations, as they are part of the process of helping executives develop greater self-awareness.

RELATIONSHIP TO THEORETICAL APPROACHES

Executive Coaching may draw on any of the theoretical approaches outlined in Section One of this Handbook, all of which may provide complementary insight into three of the essential functions of leadership.

- **Personal leadership** – what do I as a leader stand for in terms of my purpose and values in this organization?
- **Team leadership** – how do I influence and persuade others to follow me and to work together collaboratively?
- **Organizational leadership** – how are the external and internal structural and systemic factors best managed in a strategy that will achieve the organization's objectives?

The theoretical approaches outlined in Section One that executive coaches most commonly draw on include the following.

The psychodynamic approach

Those working within this tradition combine insights from psychoanalysis about the nature of emotional conflict and psychological defences in individuals and groups with the 'systems' perspective on organizations. An early example of applying systems thinking to coaching is the Organizational Role Consultancy methodology (Krantz & Maltz, 1997; Newton, Long, & Sievers, 2006) developed at the Tavistock Institute from the 1960s onwards. This is a relatively formal methodology and a precursor of executive coaching that emphasizes that executives are part of a system, rather than simply being individuals with specific personalities. The system needs to be taken into consideration during coaching if that individual is to take up his or her role effectively in the organization. To what extent the executive's personality influences the behaviour of the organization or alternatively how much the dynamics of the organization are determining the executive's feelings and behaviour are two questions central to this approach. Nowadays, most executive coaches would recognize that attention to the dynamics of the organizational system is as much part of executive coaching as is a focus on personal psychology.

The cognitive–behavioural approach

This approach focuses almost entirely on the individual rather than the group or the system and on the way in which certain cognitive assumptions are interfering with the executive's capacity to take a leadership role. It is particularly relevant where an individual leader is emotionally inhibited or overwhelmed by anxieties, for instance in situations of conflict, in large meetings or in informal social settings. Helping the executive replace dysfunctional thought patterns with more adaptive versions is vital to this approach.

The transactional analysis approach

The Parent-Adult-Child perspective of transactional analysis sheds light on the way in which scripts and games are played out in organizations between managers and staff; how a leader may be experienced as 'parental' and thereby provoke manipulative 'child' behavioural response in the behaviour of followers. The concept of 'life script' or repetitive patterns in relationships of dependency is key.

The existential approach

This approach stresses how each individual is the ultimate source of accountability and how members of organizations can easily lose sight of their capacity to make choices and become trapped in a victim mentality where they come to believe they are unable to change themselves or their circumstances. It focuses on the value of authenticity and the significance of trust and truth telling in organizational leadership.

EVALUATION OF EXECUTIVE AND LEADERSHIP COACHING

Measuring success as a leader is complex. Are external effectiveness criteria, such as the profitability or longevity of the business, most telling? Or is the judgment of followers, as measured by the responses of those who choose to follow - their 'approval rating' - most important? Studies of leadership often confuse these two very different questions. In fact, as a broad generalization, no substantial, generally accepted objective evidence has yet been put forward demonstrating that better leadership in and of itself yields better results, higher profits, or indeed any other objectively measurable organizational outcome. Indeed, it is highly unlikely that this could ever be demonstrated convincingly, since the number of variables determining profitability that would need to be controlled for any degree of scientific precision is effectively infinite. Such things as chance events, the history of the firm before the leader took office, the efforts of others, the failure of significant competitors, the recruitment of new personnel, and the ownership of previously undervalued technologies to name just a few, mean that leadership can only really be quantitatively measured by just one criterion - how many others wish to follow?

The nature of what constitutes 'good leadership', like beauty, can more be said to lie as much in the eye of the beholder as in any objective criterion. If this is accepted, then qualitative rather than quantitative analysis and evaluation will be more fruitful and revealing. Two fundamental reasons for this are:

Leadership is at root a relationship   between followers and the leader; the power of a leader comes from the followers. This is a fact that both leaders and followers often forget. The leader is dependent entirely on his or her followers who decide whether or not to follow. The leader is thus also a product of the group – it is the group that gives sanction and power to the leader. When, as is often the case with leaders who have been in power too long, these facts are forgotten the leader quickly loses power and often becomes accusatory towards his followers.

Leadership is about values   *Qualities of courage, self-sacrifice, judgment and character are significant.* These are not qualities which can be measured objectively or learned in management training. Whilst an element of these qualities may be genetically determined, generally they arise out of tough personal experiences turned to personal benefit, often through the mentorship of others more experienced than the novice leader. An entirely normal and untroubled life to date is generally a poor preparation for a leadership role. Such individuals are less likely to have the strong inner drive to change things, or to have developed a robust personal conviction that they are right when the going gets tough. As a consequence the executive coach will at times need to work with some powerful psychological dynamics in the coaching relationship.

Research on the outcome evaluation and efficacy of executive coaching is in its infancy (Kilburg, 2000; Orenstein, 2006). This is in part due to the limited quality of the studies (Kampa-Kokesch & Anderson, 2001) and partly the difficulty of measuring efficacy in an evolving field (Lowman, 2001). To ask 'does executive coaching work?' is too broad a question, better to ask 'what works, with whom, to achieve what aim, by what criterion?' Certainly many studies show that executives receiving coaching value it highly and do change (e.g. Jones, Rafferty, & Griffin, 2006) and this evidence is building (Passmore, 2006). Effective research in the future will need to focus on the more specific variables of aim, method, client and coach variables, amongst others.

The executive coach's primary purpose then, is to enable the senior executive to take up his or her leadership role more effectively, to manage the conflicting force of cooperation and competition within the organization, and to balance the competing interests of the long list of stakeholders who must be satisfied if the organization is to prosper. The executive coach's client relationship is inevitably twofold, comprising both the individual in the coaching session and the organization that provides that individual with their executive authority. Methods and theories of executive coaching may vary but all share a common aim of enabling the executive to grow, learn and develop. Few organizations that have the ability to sustain success are simple systems that can achieve complete alignment amongst all of their stakeholders. Rather, they are complex political, social and emotional systems that need to mirror the complexity of their environment (Ashby, 1956). Whilst this remains the case the purposes, methods and measures of Executive Coaching will remain equally and entirely properly debated and contested.

FURTHER READING

Goldsmith, M., Lyons, L., & Freas, A. (2000). *Coaching for leadership*. San Francisco, CA: Jossey-Bass. (A broad-brush introduction with contributions for many of the foremost figures in the field, though with a strong US bias.)

Heifetz, R.A. (1994). *Leadership without easy answers*. Cambridge, MA: Harvard University Press. (An original and penetrating analysis of leadership from the Kennedy School of Government at Harvard University that is relevant to anyone coaching someone in a leadership role.)

Kilburg, R.R. (2000). *Executive coaching*. Washington, DC: American Psychological Association. (An excellent and comprehensive review of the psychodynamics of individuals and organizations as applied to coaching.)

REFERENCES

Argyris, C., and Schön, D. (1978). *Organizational learning*. Reading, MA: Addison-Wesley.

Ashby, W.R. (1956). *An introduction to cybernetics*. London: Chapman & Hall.

Barnard, C.I. (1938). *The functions of the executive*. Cambridge, MA: Harvard University Press.

Berglas, S. (2002). The very real dangers of executive coaching. *Harvard Business Review, June*.

Clutterbuck, D., & Megginson, D. (2005). *Mentoring in action: A practical guide for managers*. London: Kogan Page.

Drucker, P. (1993). *Post-capitalist society.* Oxford: Butterworth-Heinemann.

Fitzgerald, C., & Berger, J. (2002). (Eds.). *Executive coaching: Practices & perspectives.* Palo Alto, CA: Davies-Black Publishing.

Frey, B., & Stitzer, A. (2002). *Happiness and economics.* Princeton, NJ: Princeton University Press.

Gallwey, T. (2000). *The inner game of work: Overcoming mental obstacles for maximum performance.* London: Orion Business Books.

Goldsmith, M., Lyons, L., & Freas, A. (2000). *Coaching for leadership.* San Francisco, CA: Jossey Bass.

Handy, C. (2002). *The age of unreason: New thinking for a new world.* London: Random House.

Hirschhorn, L. (1997). *Reworking authority.* Cambridge, MA: MIT Press.

Jones, R.A., Rafferty, A.E., & Griffin, M.A. (2006). The executive coaching trend: Towards more flexible executives. *Leadership & Organizational Development Journal, 27*(7): 584–96.

Kampa-Kokesch, S., & Anderson, M. (2001). Executive coaching: A comprehensive review of the literature. *Consulting Psychology Journal: Practice and Research, 53*: 205–28.

Kilburg, R.R. (2000). *Executive coaching.* Washington, DC: American Psychological Association.

Krantz, J. (1998). Anxiety and the new order. In E. Klein, F. Gabelnick & P. Herr (Eds.), *Leadership in the 21st century.* Madison, CT: International Universities Press.

Krantz, J., & Maltz, M. (1997). A framework for consulting to organizational role. *Consulting Psychology Journal, 49*(2): 137–51.

Landsberg, M. (1997). *The tao of coaching.* London: Harper Collins.

Levinson, H. (1996). Executive coaching. *Consulting Psychology Review, 48*(2): 115–23.

Lowman, R. (2001). Constructing a literature from case studies: Promises and limitations of the method. *Consulting Psychology Journal, 53*: 119–23.

Miller, E.J. (1993). *From dependency to autonomy: Studies in organization and change.* London: Karnac Books.

Newton, J., Long, S., & Sievers, B. (2006). *Coaching in depth – the organizational role analysis approach.* London: Karnac Books.

Orenstein, R. (2006). Measuring executive coaching efficacy? The answer was right here all along. *Consulting Psychology Journal, 58*: 106–16.

Orenstein, R. (2007). *Multidimensional executive coaching.* New York: Springer.

Passmore, J. (2006). Coaching psychology: Applying an integrated approach in education. *Journal of Leadership in Public Services, 2*(2): 27–33.

Peltier, B. (2001). *The psychology of executive coaching: Theory and application.* London: Brunner-Routledge.

Peterson, D. (1996). Executive coaching at work: The art of one-on-one change. *Consulting Psychology Journal, 48*: 78–86.

Reeves, R. (2001). *Happy Mondays – putting the pleasure back into work.* London: Momentum.

Stokes, J. (1994). Institutional chaos and personal crisis. In A. Obholzer & V. Roberts (Eds.), *The unconscious at work.* London: Routledge.

Tichy, N. (2004). *The leadership engine: How winning companies build leaders at every level.* London: Collins Business.

Van Velsor, E., & Leslie, J. (1995). Why executives derail: Perspectives across time and cultures. *Academy of Management Executive, 9*(5).

Watkins, M. (2003). *The first 90 days.* Boston, MA: Harvard Business School Press.

Wuthnow, R. (1996). *Poor Richard's principle.* Princeton, NJ: Princeton University Press.

Zaleznik, A. (1992). Managers and leaders: Are they different? *Harvard Business Review, March–April.*

18

The 'Manager as Coach'

Andrea D. Ellinger, Rona S. Beattie and Robert G. Hamlin

INTRODUCTION

The purpose of this chapter is to explore the concept of the 'manager as coach', and to integrate recent empirical research that has explored the efficacy of this form of coaching. In this chapter we examine the beliefs that exemplary managers serving as coaches have, the catalysts for managerial coaching, the requisite effective and ineffective behaviours of managerial coaches, and the contextual factors that may be influential in promoting a 'manager as coach' approach in organizations. The chapter also draws upon other theoretical perspectives associated with coaching, and examines their applicability to the 'manager as coach' approach. It concludes with an examination of empirical research that has explored the impact of coaching in workplace contexts.

The concept of the 'manager as coach' is not a new phenomenon. Past research on managerial behaviour and resulting taxonomies has identified 'instructing subordinates' (Kraut, Pedigo, McKenna, & Dunnette, 1989), 'training-coaching' (Yukl, 1994 [1981]), and 'providing growth and development' (Morse & Wagner, 1978; Yukl, 1989, 1994 [1981]) as components of managerial roles or as a subset of the leader role (Mintzberg, 1990, 1994). Ever since Evered and Selman (1989) first established coaching as a core managerial activity, it has progressively gained currency, as evidenced by a recent CIPD Learning and Development Survey (2006) that indicated that 47% of line managers are using coaching in their work.

Human resource practices have increasingly devolved to line managers, employee expectations have grown with respect to their development, and the importance of talent management has required that managers assume more predominant roles as coaches and developers of their employees. Yet, despite the growing interest in the manager as coach concept, and the apparent benefits associated with managerial coaching for employees, managers, and for the organization, empirical research on managerial coaching is still in its infancy. In fact, Peterson and Little (2005) have acknowledged that, 'there has been a relative paucity of resources aimed specifically at helping managers to coach people better' (2005: 179). Therefore, to address the criticism that managerial coaching is prescriptive and somewhat atheoretical, a further purpose of this chapter is to synthesize the empirical research on managerial coaching to inform academics, researchers, practitioners, and clients about this form of coaching.

SPECIAL FEATURES AND GOALS OF MANAGERIAL COACHING

Coaching has often been perceived as a remedy for poor performance (Fournies, 1987). However, more recent conceptions of coaching have moved beyond a deficit orientation to one of a developmental orientation, in which coaching is considered to be a day-to-day, hands-on process of helping employees recognize opportunities to improve their performance and capabilities (Orth, Wilkinson, & Benfari, 1987; Popper & Lipshitz, 1992), of empowering employees to exceed prior levels of performance (Burdett, 1998; Evered & Selman, 1989: Hargrove, 1995) and as a process of learning designed to provide guidance, encouragement, and support to the learner (coachee) (Redshaw, 2000). Mink, Owen and Mink (1993) have conceived coaching as a process in which the coach creates an enabling relationship with others to help them learn, so that improved performance is a by-product of learning. More contemporary perspectives have considered coaching as being synonymous with facilitating learning (Beattie, 2002; Ellinger, 1997; Ellinger & Bostrom, 1999).

While coaching is often provided by a coach external to the organization who provides contracted coaching services to the client, in contrast, the 'manager as coach' concept refers to a manager or supervisor serving as a coach or facilitator of learning in the workplace setting, in which he or she enacts specific behaviours that enable his/her employee (coachee) to learn and develop (Beattie, 2002; Ellinger & Bostrom, 1999; Talarico, 2002). The goals associated with managerial coaching are often to improve an employee's performance through learning, but may also be multifaceted. For example, promoting an understanding of the employee's strengths and weaknesses through the provision of extensive feedback, and encouraging self-awareness that may influence personal relationships and work behaviours may be additional goals associated with this form of coaching. In essence, managerial coaching refers to managers being coaching resources to their employees within their organizations.

Some scholars contend that the 'managerial coach' is a rare species, because managers lack the time or requisite skills and capabilities to coach, are not encouraged or rewarded for coaching, and may not perceive it to be an important managerial role (Goleman, 2000; Hunt & Weintraub, 2002a). Yet for those managers who do perceive themselves to be managerial coaches, a 'coaching mind-set' (Hunt & Weintraub, 2002b) or a set of beliefs about being a managerial coach (Ellinger & Bostrom, 2002) are considered to be necessary prerequisites, along with specific skills and capabilities that enable the manager to coach effectively.

The 'manager as coach' mindset

Managers who have become effective coaches have the following characteristics in common: an attitude of helpfulness; less need for control; empathy in dealing with others; openness to personal learning and receiving feedback; high standards; a desire to help others to develop; a theory of employee development that is not predicated on a 'sink or swim' approach; and a belief that most people do want to learn (Hunt & Weintraub, 2002b). Based upon their work with managers who have become coaching managers, Hunt and Weintraub consider these attitudes and beliefs to constitute the coaching mindset. Although empirical research on this aspect of coaching is limited, Ellinger and Bostrom (2002) identified three major categories of beliefs held by exemplary managerial coaches, namely beliefs about their managerial roles and capabilities, beliefs about learning and the learning process, and beliefs about learners. First and foremost, these managers believed that coaching employees and facilitating their development is their role and what they are expected to do. Furthermore, they drew distinctions between coaching, which is 'all about people – helping them grow and develop', and management, which is 'telling people what to do' (Ellinger & Bostrom, 2002: 156). For these managers, managing was often about telling, judging, controlling, and directing, whereas being in a 'coaching mindset' was about empowering, helping, developing, supporting, and removing obstacles. It was recognized that managers often had to switch between these roles because certain circumstances might require role switching.

In terms of their capabilities, these exemplary managers believed that they had skills, process capabilities, and experiences to coach their employees effectively. Their self-efficacy was evident, as was their ability to establish trust, rapport, and to build relationships with their employees, because they cared enough to want to help them. In terms of the beliefs about learning and the learning process, these managers considered learning to be important, ongoing, and shared. Furthermore, learning was most effective when it was integrated with work, when feedback was provided, and when learners (coachees) were encouraged to learn for themselves. The final category of beliefs identified in Ellinger and Bostrom's empirical study of exemplary managers reflected beliefs about learners. Such managers considered their coachees to be capable and willing to learn, and recognized the need for learners to possess a solid foundation of information, and a need to understand the whys.

The catalysts for coaching opportunities

Since coaching is often an informal learning strategy that is used by managers, understanding the catalysts for initiating a coaching dialogue with employees is also important. Mumford (1993) has acknowledged that any managerial activity contains the potential for learning, and may include some of the following: a new assignment; a new challenge; a new project; a shock or crisis; problem solving within a group; differing standards of performance; an unsuccessful piece of work. Similarly, research by Ellinger (2003) on the catalysts for coaching by managers revealed the following triggers: gaps and deficiencies of existing employee skills; political and high consequence issues; assignments; projects; employee transitions; and developmental opportunities.

The skills and behaviours required for coaching

The requisite skills associated with managerial coaching have been described in the practitioner-oriented literature and include: listening skills, analytical skills, interviewing skills, effective questioning techniques, and observation skills. The actual behaviours identified have typically included giving and receiving performance feedback, communicating and setting clear expectations, and creating a supportive environment conducive to coaching (Graham, Wedman, & Garvin-Kester, 1993, 1994; King & Eaton, 1999; Marsh, 1992; Mobley, 1999; Orth et al., 1987; Phillips, 1994, 1995; Zemke, 1996).

Recent research by McLean, Yang, Kuo, Tolbert and Larkin (2005) has yielded a self-assessment of coaching skills based upon a four-dimension coaching model. This model suggests that the 'manager as coach' reflects four aspects of managerial behaviour. The 'manager as coach' should: communicate openly with others; take a team approach instead of an individual approach with tasks; tend to value people over tasks; and should accept the ambiguous nature of the working environment. Their findings suggest that managerial coaching is a multidimensional construct that supports their four-dimension coaching model. In responding to this work, Peterson and Little (2005) have questioned whether the team approach is a primary component of effective coaching, since coaching is often considered a one-on-one managerial intervention. Further, they have noted that other factors associated with coaching skills should be considered, such as: developing a partnership, effective listening skills, and providing feedback, as well as capabilities for facilitating development. In response to Peterson and Little's criticism, Park, Mclean and Yang (2008) recently added a component related to facilitating development, and have subsequently tested this revised instrument which has evidence of validity.

Possessing coaching skills, and being able to translate such skills into practice, has been an area of research that has revealed consistent findings about managerial coaching behaviours. For example incorporating Schelling's eight behaviours associated with successful sales managers, Graham et al. (1994) interviewed account representatives and obtained ratings of their respective manager's coaching skills prior to the implementation of a manager coaching skills training programme. The findings supported the existing literature on coaching concerning the importance of providing feedback, setting clear expectations, and creating a climate for coaching that involves a positive trusting relationship. Ellinger's (1997) and Ellinger and

Table 18.1:   Behavioural taxonomies

Ellinger's (1997) and Ellinger and Bostrom's (2002) Behavioural Taxonomy	Beattie's (2002) Behavioural Taxonomy
The empowering cluster consisted of the following behaviours: • question framing to encourage employees to think through issues • being a resource – removing obstacles • transferring ownership to employees • holding back – not providing the answers. The facilitating cluster consisted of the following behaviours: • providing feedback to employees • soliciting feedback from employees • working it out together – talking it through • creating and promoting a learning environment • setting and communicating expectations • stepping into other to shift perspectives • broadening employees' perspectives – getting them to see things differently • using analogies, scenarios, and examples • engaging others to facilitate learning.	Beattie's behavioural categories consisted of: • thinking – reflective or prospective thinking • informing – sharing knowledge • empowering – delegation, trust • assessing – feedback and recognition, identifying developmental needs • advising – instruction, coaching, guidance, counselling • being professional – role model, standard setting, planning and preparation • caring – support, encouragement, approachable, reassurance, commitment/involvement, empathy • developing others • challenging employees to stretch themselves.

Bostrom's (1999) research identified a taxonomy of thirteen managerial coaching behaviours that included both facilitating and empowering behaviours (see Table 18.1). Similarly, Beattie's (2002) research on managerial coaching in the context of a social service organization revealed twenty-two discrete effective facilitative behaviours that were classified and allocated into one of nine identified behavioural categories, as also illustrated in Table 18.1.

Subsequent comparative analyses between the Ellinger and Beattie taxonomies have revealed a high degree of congruency in managerial coaching behaviours (Hamlin, Ellinger, & Beattie, 2006). More recent research by Longenecker and Neubert (2005), Powell and Doran (2003), Shaw and Knights (2005) and Amy (2005) have offered additional support for these behavioural findings. Additionally, Noer (2005) and Noer, Leupold and Valle (2007) have suggested that managerial coaching is a dynamic interaction between three sets of behaviour: *assessing*, *challenging*, and *supporting*.

Contextual factors influencing managerial coaching

Scholars have acknowledged that creating a culture of coaching is important in promoting managerial coaching behaviours (Evered & Selman, 1989; Hunt & Weintraub, 2002b, 2007). However, empirical research exploring such contextual influences on managerial coaching has been very limited. Beattie's (2006) research in the social service setting found that environmental factors such as political, economic, societal, and technological trends influenced the management framework and learning needs within the two organizations she studied. In terms of the organizational influences, she identified history, mission and strategy, structure, and culture as impacting the context for managerial coaching. Specifically, in these organizations, the aspirations to become learning organizations contributed to line managers' roles as coaches and developers. In terms of human resource development strategy, the provision of training for managers to assume developmental roles by supporting their learning needs was also a critical influence. These contextual influences favourably supported the managers to serve as coaches.

However, organizations that do not have the same employee development aspirations or infrastructures to adequately prepare managers to assume coaching roles, or to recognize, encourage, and reward employees often do not effectively leverage managers as coaches. Furthermore, there is a paradox when managers become coaching managers because they 'must both coach and evaluate direct reports' (Hunt & Weintraub, 2002b: 16). It is possible that the evaluative component of their position may detract from employees being open about their 'concerns, problems, and mistakes' (p. 17). As alluded to in Ellinger's (1997) research, the importance of managers being able to role switch and to recognize when they need to focus on developmental coaching, or when they need to wear a more directive managerial hat, is critical and requires 'significant emotional maturity' (Hunt & Weintraub, 2002b: 17).

THE ROLE OF MANAGER AS COACH AND THE RELATIONSHIP WITH THE COACHEE

In the absence of their wanting to be coached, it is often difficult if not virtually impossible for the manager to coach his or her employees. The coaching relationship established between the manager and employee (coachee) must be one that is based on mutual trust and openness. The manager must believe that he or she is capable of serving as a coach, can leverage coaching opportunities, and can effectively engage behaviours that facilitate the coachee's learning. The coachee, according to Hunt and Weintraub (2002b), should possess the following characteristics: an ability to reflect on his/her actions from an objective point of view; curiosity about his/her actions and those of others; acceptance that others may possess more knowledge; the ability to share his/her self-observations with the manager without shame; a willingness and capacity to listen and be receptive to feedback; and motivation to improve and learn through the process of coaching.

Although managerial coaching can be provided as a structured intervention, often, as Hunt and Weintraub (2002b) advocate, coaching should be 'slipped into' (2002b: 18) the manager's daily routine. Managers are often in the unique position of interacting with their employees on a regular basis, are responsible for their employees' performance, and often can leverage on-the-job learning. Therefore, managerial coaching often becomes an informal activity that is initiated through a dialogue with the coachee. In many cases, the coaching dialogue may begin as a result of a performance gap or performance deficiency, but a coaching dialogue may also be initiated as a result of a developmental opportunity that the manager has identified and which will promote the coachee's learning. It may also be a result of several of the other aforementioned catalysts for coaching. When the catalyst for coaching occurs, either as a result of the manager or coachee's initiative, it is then important for the manager to determine the most appropriate behaviours to engage. In many situations, the manager may engage in a conversation with the coachee that integrates question framing techniques to encourage the coachee to think for himself/herself. It might also be that the manager provides feedback to the coachee, or engages in a role-play activity. The manager may engage several behaviours or may determine that a select few are more relevant from those sets of behaviours identified in the empirical research.

RELATIONSHIP WITH THE THEORETICAL TRADITIONS AND ILLUSTRATIVE MANAGERIAL COACHING EXAMPLES

The managerial coaching literature base has been criticized for being atheoretical. However, as this handbook illustrates, there are many philosophical underpinnings associated with coaching in general and different forms of coaching in particular, and a review of these theoretical traditions offers some potential grounding for the 'manager as coach' concept.

Solution-focused coaching

Grant (2006) has acknowledged that 'solution-focused' coaching has its roots in Erikson's approach to strategic therapy. Therapists had become disenchanted with the diagnostic medical approach and began to 'simply ask questions that focused their clients' attention on building solutions' (Grant, 2006: 74). The application of this to workplace coaching, and particularly to the 'manager as coach' form of coaching, is predicated upon a number of key principles as follows:

- problems stem from a limited repertoire of behaviour
- the focus is on constructing solutions
- the notion that the coachee, rather than the coach, is the expert in his/her own life
- the coach can learn more about coaching from the coachee
- the coach helps the coachee to recognize resources
- there is an action orientation, specific goal setting
- change can occur in a short period of time, designed for each coachee, future oriented
- coaching engages the coachee
- the coach actively challenges the coachee to think in a new way.

Further, principles of self-directed learning influence the 'solution-focused' approach.

The following example illustrates the applicability of the 'solution-focused' coaching approach to the manager as coach form of coaching.

'An important presentation' – Scott and Amy

Scott, a senior information technology manager, had a female manager, Amy, reporting to him. Amy had put together a presentation based on some data that had been collected to develop a strategy for a new computer system. Amy sought Scott's assistance and review of her presentation because she knew that he had reasonably good experience with putting together presentations and communicating with the non-technical customer set. He and Amy sat down and went through her presentation. Scott realized that what Amy had prepared was so 'far from what I felt would work that we actually went through this three times over a ten-day period'. Scott encouraged Amy to go through the overheads but then he 'started asking her questions and making comments, and sharing with her as I looked at these slides how I would react as a potential audience. What I didn't do – and this was the hardest part for her because she didn't understand exactly what I was trying to explain – I refused to make the overheads for her.' Scott said that Amy initially didn't understand conceptually what he was trying to get across so he asked a lot of questions. 'It was a very incremental process and so as we went through it, it was more of a concept by concept and she would then come back with an overhead or series of overheads that were different based on that.' Scott indicated that his ability to challenge her, ask questions to stimulate her thinking and to 'let her think about it' also worked effectively with her in this coaching situation. In essence, through a question framing approach, Scott enabled Amy to discover the solution because she needed to develop the presentation herself.

Behavioural coaching

Coaching is about behaviour change, although not from a mechanistic, stimulus-response perspective, but rather from a whole person approach (Peterson, 2006). Classic behavioural change techniques often include modelling, feedback, shaping and successive approximation, self-management, rewards and reinforcers, and behavioural practice (Peterson, 2006). Peterson suggests that a behaviour-based approach to coaching 'starts with clarity around what really matters to people, and then helps them get there' (Peterson, 2006: 74).

The following example illustrates the applicability of the behaviour-based coaching approach to the 'manager as coach' form of coaching.

Spending time with an employee – Sean and Ted

Sean, a senior level manufacturing manager, described Ted, one of his employees, as a 'technically very smart person but personally underdeveloped ... very immature and rude.' Sean said that he sent Ted to seminars on communication, on resolving conflicts and that these different seminars 'didn't make an impact on his behaviour.' Sean said that he and Ted were 'always head butting on that because he always thought he should be promoted and I'd say I can't promote you until you develop these people skills.' Ted was resistant to Sean letting him know that he didn't possess the skills necessary for advancement and so Sean said, 'I went through a process of coach[ing] him.' Sean committed to doing a survey of Ted's internal and external customers, compiled the data, and then put the responses in a format so that Ted could better understand the things he does well and areas for improvement. The feedback indeed suggested that Ted was perceived to be technically competent but personally rude and overbearing. Sean took Ted to lunch and spent three hours reviewing the survey results. Ted was 'in denial that he had a personality issue' so they went through the whole process of 'if you don't change your personality to fit in with a team environment, you are basically gonna be mad the rest of your life and we went through the whole soul searching thing … asking questions.… During the course of that year you could see a noticeable change in his behaviour .' Sean acknowledged that it was a process of helping to convince a technical person that people skills are important and helping him to develop a corrective action plan that made this coaching intervention effective. Essentially, providing 'third-party feedback' about Ted's behaviour served as the catalyst for Ted to recognize that he did need to consider changing his behaviour so that he could interact more professionally with his internal and external customers.

Cognitive coaching and cognitive behavioural coaching

Cognitive coaching theory draws upon cognitive therapy which suggests that one's moods are strongly related to and triggered by one's cognitions or thoughts (Auerbach, 2006). Therefore, the cognitive therapist often assists clients 'in identifying errors in their thinking and aiding them in adopting more accurate, useful cognitions' (Auerbach, 2006: 104) and helps them to 'learn more realistic ways to approach the world' (105). Drawing upon the work done by Costa and Garmston (as cited in Auerbach, 2006), 'cognitive coaching enhances the ability of the person being coached to examine their patterns of thinking and behaviour, and to reconsider the underlying assumptions that precede actions' (Auerbach, 2006: 109). Similarly, according to Williams, Edgerton and Palmer (2009), the main goals of cognitive behavioural coaching are '(1) to facilitate self-awareness of underlying cognitive and emotional barriers; (2) to equip the individual with thinking skills; and (3) to build internal stability and self-acceptance in order to mobilize the individual to their choice of action' (refer to Chapter 2, this volume).

The following example illustrates the applicability of the cognitive coaching approach to the manager as coach form of coaching.

'Going against the company culture' – Edward and Sarah
Edward, a mid-level product research and development manager, described his employee, Sarah, who was working in a team environment but was behaving in a manner inconsistent within the culture of the team. Essentially, she was coming over very assertively and strongly, approaches that worked well and were valued by her previous employer, but were at odds

with her new team and organizational setting. Edward acknowledged that he 'could see the handwriting on the wall' regarding her behaviour so 'we sat down and really talked.' Edward acknowledged that he attended her meetings so that he could observe her. He acknowledged that his 'job as a manager is to remove barriers if I think you are not being as effective as you can be, whether those are barriers within you or external to you, I'm not doing you a favour by white washing anything.' He and Sarah met several times so he could share what he was seeing and hearing and she could share what she was thinking and feeling. They had several sessions of 'talk[ing] though what some of the [options] are – gain acceptance and then I might suggest some options, the employee might suggest some options, and then we might come up with a game plan about what might be an appropriate approach to do that.' For Sarah, this form of managerial coaching enabled her to become more self-aware of her own mental models that were influencing her behaviours and getting in her way. Ultimately, she was able to challenge her own thinking to determine how best to operate in her new organizational culture with guidance from her manager during several conversational 'talking it through' meetings.

The 'manager as coach' form of coaching can be informed by many perspectives, and a variety of approaches can be adopted so that managers can become optimally effective in coaching their employees. Many managers do not have counselling, psychology, or therapy backgrounds. Therefore, they need to be exposed to such approaches, and appropriately trained so that they can use tools and techniques that are theoretically grounded but practical.

EVALUATION

As a performance improvement strategy, it is often assumed that coaching positively impacts individual and team performance. For example research has suggested that specific coaching behaviours have been directly correlated with net increases in sales (Graham et al., 1994). Other research has suggested that improvements in systems, cost savings, and knowledge sharing may be directly attributed to coaching interventions when managers serve as coaches for individuals or teams of employees (Ellinger, 2003). Yet, beyond these studies, 'empirical research on the effects of coaching … by managers is still very limited' (Yukl, 1994 [1981]: 125). Thus, while scholars suggest that the benefits of coaching are enormous and associated with: producing long-lasting learning; contributing to high levels of motivation; and improving and enhancing employee performance, working relationships, job satisfaction, and organizational commitment (Anon, 2001; Redshaw, 2000); overall, the empirical research on the efficacy of managerial coaching is still underdeveloped.

Recently, a few studies have been conducted that report on the impact of managerial coaching. Ellinger, Ellinger and Keller (2003) found that warehouse employees' perceptions of the extent of their respective supervisors' coaching behaviours were significant predictors of job satisfaction and job performance. Hannah's (2004) case study on supervisory coaching within the British Rail context revealed that, with supervisory coaching, employee competence improved and the resulting service consistency increased passenger satisfaction with customer service received. Shaw and Knights (2005) also found that introducing a coaching style as a preferred leadership style within a small to medium sized enterprise (SME) resulted in enhanced knowledge and potential growth, along with improved communications and inter-personal relationships. Further evidence of the benefits of managerial coaching have been provided by Elmadag, Ellinger and Franke (2008), whose study found that managerial coaching had a stronger influence on frontline employee commitment to service quality than formal training or rewarding; and Park, McLean and Yang (2008) found a positive influence of mana-gerial coaching skills on employees' personal learning, organizational learning, and turnover intentions.

Although recent research has found that managerial coaching has been linked to many positive employee and organizational outcomes, it is important to acknowledge that not all managerial coaching is effective. Attention to ineffective managerial coaching behaviour has been equally underdeveloped; however, recent comparative analysis has revealed considerable consistency among ineffective managerial behaviour. Ellinger, Hamlin, and Beattie (2008) have found that the predominant ineffective behaviour held in common among all three studies was an autocratic, directive, controlling, dictatorial managerial style, which is often associated with a 'traditional bureaucratic management paradigm'. This paradigm has been characterized by command, control, compliance, and coercive styles of management, which is not considered appropriate for promoting a 'coaching management paradigm' that encourages empowerment, inclusion, and participation. Another commonality revealed in the research was the use of ineffective communication and poor dissemination of information, along with the use of inappropriate behaviours and approaches which included, among others, not spending enough time with employees.

Overall, this outcomes-based research has offered support for the efficacy of managerial coaching in workplace contexts. Although the apparent benefits of managerial coaching have been established, certainly there are likely drawbacks to managerial coaching, and additional research is needed to better understand the limitations of managerial coaching within workplace contexts.

FURTHER READING

Bianco-Mathis, V.E., Nabors, L.K., & Roman, C.H. (2002). *Leading from the inside out: A coaching model.* Thousand Oaks, CA: Sage. (This book presents a holistic view of coaching that provides leaders with a five-step framework that can be applied, for developing themselves, their teams, and their organizations.)

Hunt, J.M., & Weintraub, J.R. (2002b). *The coaching manager: Developing top talent in business.* Thousand Oaks, CA: Sage. (This book provides an overview of a model of developmental coaching by managers, based upon the authors' extensive interactions with coaching managers over the years. It includes cases, self-assessment tools, and checklists to guide practising managers in becoming more skilful coaches.)

Hunt, J.M., & Weintraub, J.R. (2007). *The coaching organization: A strategy for developing leaders.* Thousand Oaks, CA: Sage. (This book provides an overview of how leaders and human resource professionals can build organizational coaching capability by using developmental coaching and other forms of coaching to enhance organizational results.)

REFERENCES

Amy, A.H. (2005). Leaders as facilitators of organizational learning (unpublished Doctoral dissertation, Regent University at Virginia Beach, VA).

Anonymous (2001). Mentoring and coaching help employees grow. *HR Focus, 78*(9): 1–6.

Auerbach, J.E. (2006). Cognitive coaching. In D.R. Stober & A.M. Grant (Eds.), *Evidence based coaching handbook* (pp. 103–27). Hoboken, NJ: John Wiley & Sons.

Beattie, R.S. (2002). Line managers as facilitators of learning: Empirical evidence from voluntary sector. *Proceedings of 2002 Human Resource Development Research and Practice across Europe Conference.* Edinburgh: Napier University, January.

Beattie, R.S. (2006). HRD in the public sector: The case of health and social care. In S. Sambrook & J. Stewart (Eds.), *Human resource development in the health and social care context.* London: Routledge.

Burdett, J.O. (1998). Forty things every manager should know about coaching. *Journal of Management Development, 17*(2): 142–52.

Chartered Institute of Personnel and Development (CIPD). (2006). *Learning and development survey.* London: CIPD.

Ellinger, A.D. (2003). Antecedents and consequences of coaching behavior. *Performance Improvement Quarterly, 16*(1): 5–28.

Ellinger, A.D., & Bostrom, R.P. (1999). Managerial coaching behaviors in learning organizations. *Journal of Management Development, 18*(9): 752–71.

Ellinger, A.D., & Bostrom, R.P. (2002). An examination of managers' belief about their roles as facilitators of learning. *Management Learning, 33*(2): 147–79.

Ellinger, A.D., Ellinger, A.E., & Keller, S.B. (2003). Supervisory coaching behavior, employee satisfaction, and warehouse employee performance: A dyadic perspective in the distribution industry. *Human Resource Development Quarterly, 14*(4): 435–58.

Ellinger, A.D., Hamlin, R.G., & Beattie, R.S. (2008). Behavioural indicators of ineffective managerial coaching: A cross-national study. *Journal of European Industrial Training, 32*(4): 240–57.

Ellinger, A.M. (1997). Managers as facilitators of learning in learning organizations (unpublished Doctoral dissertation, University of Georgia at Athens, GA).

Elmadag, A.B., Ellinger, A.E., & Franke, G.R. (2008). Antecedents and consequences of frontline service employee commitment to service quality. *Journal of Marketing Theory and Practice, 16*(2): 95–110.

Evered, R.D., & Selman, J.C. (1989). Coaching and the art of management. *Organizational Dynamics, 18*: 16–32.

Fournies, F.F. (1987). *Coaching for improved work performance.* Kansas, MO: Liberty Hall Press.

Goleman, D. (2000). Leadership that gets results. *Harvard Business Review, March–April*: 78–90.

Graham, S., Wedman, J.F., & Garvin-Kester, B. (1993). Manager coaching skills: Development and application. *Performance Improvement Quarterly, 6*(1): 2–13.

Graham, S., Wedman, J.F., & Garvin-Kester, B. (1994). Manager coaching skills: What makes a good coach? *Performance Improvement Quarterly, 7*(2): 81–94.

Grant, A.M. (2006). Solution-focused coaching. In J. Passmore (Ed.), *Excellence in coaching: The industry guide* (pp. 73–90). London: Kogan Press.

Hamlin, R.G., Ellinger, A.D., & Beattie, R.S. (2006). Coaching at the heart of managerial effectiveness: A cross-cultural study of managerial behaviours. *Human Resource Development International, 9*(3): 305–331.

Hannah, C. (2004). Improving intermediate skills through workplace coaching: A case study within the UK rail industry. *International Journal of Evidence Based Coaching and Mentoring, 2*(1): 17–45.

Hargrove, R. (1995). *Masterful coaching*. San Diego, CA: Pfeiffer & Company.

Hunt, J.M., & Weintraub, J.R. (2002a). How coaching can enhance your brand as a manager. *Journal of Organizational Excellence, 21*(2): 39–44.

Hunt, J.M., & Weintraub, J.R. (2002b). *The coaching manager: Developing top talent in business*. Thousand Oaks, CA: Sage.

Hunt, J.M., & Weintraub, J.R. (2007). *The coaching organization: A strategy for developing leaders*. Thousand Oaks, CA: Sage.

King, P., & Eaton, J. (1999). Coaching for results. *Industrial and Commercial Training, 31*(4): 145–8.

Kraut, A.I., Pedigo, P.R., McKenna, D.D., & Dunnette, M.D. (1989). The role of the manager: What's really important in different management jobs. *The Academy of Management Executive, 3*(4): 286–93.

Longenecker, C.O., & Neubert, M.J. (2005). The practices of effective managerial coaches. *Business Horizons, 48*: 493–500.

Marsh, L. (1992). Good manager: Good coach? What is needed for effective coaching? *Industrial and Commercial Training, 24*(9): 3–8.

McLean, G.N., Yang, B., Kuo, M.C., Tolbert, A.S., & Larkin, C. (2005). Development and initial validation of an instrument measuring managerial coaching skill. *Human Resource Development Quarterly, 16*(2): 157–78.

Mink, O.G., Owen, K.Q., & Mink, B.P. (1993). *Developing high-performance people: The art of coaching*. Reading, MA: Addison-Wesley.

Mintzberg, H. (1990). The manager's job: Folklore and fact. *Harvard Business Review, March–April:* 163–73.

Mintzberg, H. (1994). Rounding out the manager's job. *Sloan Management Review, 36*(1): 11–26.

Mobley, S.A. (1999). Judge not: How coaches create healthy organizations. *The Journal for Quality and Participation, 22*(4): 57–60.

Morse, J.J., & Wagner, F.R. (1978). Measuring the process of managerial effectiveness. *Academy of Management Journal, 21*(1): 23–35.

Mumford, A. (1993). *How managers can develop managers* (2nd ed.). Aldershot: Gower.

Noer, D. (2005). Behaviorally based coaching: A cross-cultural case study. *International Journal of Coaching in Organizations, 3*: 14–23.

Noer, D.M., Leupold, C.R., & Valle, M. (2007). An analysis of Saudi Arabian and US managerial coaching behaviors. *Journal of Managerial Issues, 19*(2): 271–87.

Orth, C.D., Wilkinson, H.E., & Benfari, R.C. (1987). The manager's role as coach and mentor. *Organizational Dynamics, 15*(4): 66–74.

Park, S., McLean, G.N., & Yang, B. (2008). Revision and validation of an instrument measuring managerial coaching skills in organizations. In T.J. Chermack, J. Storberg-Walker & C.M. Graham (Eds.), *Proceedings of 2008 Academy of Human Resource Development Conference* (CD-ROM). Panama City Beach, FL, February.

Peterson, D.B. (2006). People are complex and the world is messy: A behavior-based approach to executive coaching. In D.R. Stober & A.M. Grant (Eds.), *Evidence based coaching handbook* (pp. 103–27). Hoboken, NJ: John Wiley & Sons.

Peterson, D.B., & Little, B. (2005). Invited reaction: Development and initial validation of an instrument measuring managerial coaching skill. *Human Resource Development Quarterly, 16*(2): 179–83.

Phillips, R. (1994). Coaching for higher performance. *Management Development Review, 7*(5): 19–22.

Phillips, R. (1995). Coaching for higher performance. *Executive Development, 8*(7): 5.

Popper, M., & Lipshitz, R. (1992). Coaching on leadership. *Leadership & Organization Development Journal, 13*(7): 15–18.

Powell, T., & Doran, M. (2003). Managers' perceptions of their role in facilitating employee learning. *Proceedings of 2003 International Academy of Human Resource Development conference,* University of Minnesota, Minneapolis, MN, June.

Redshaw, B. (2000). Do we really understand coaching? How can we make it work better? *Industrial and Commercial Training, 32*(3): 106–8.

Shaw, S., & Knights, J. (2005). Coaching in an SME: An investigation into the impact of a managerial coaching style on employees within a small firm. *Proceedings of the Sixth international conference on HRD research and practice across Europe,* Queens Hotel, Leeds, May.

Talarico, M. (2002). Manager as coach in a pharmacy benefit management organization: A critical incidents analysis (unpublished Doctoral dissertation, University of Minnesota at Minneapolis, MN).

Yukl, G. (1989). Managerial leadership: A review of theory and research. *Journal of Management, 15*(2): 251–89.

Yukl, G. (1994 [1981]). *Leadership in organizations* (3rd ed.). Upper Saddle River, NJ: Prentice Hall.

Zemke, R. (1996). The corporate coach. *Training, 33*(12): 24–8.

19

Team Coaching

David Clutterbuck

INTRODUCTION

The instinct to work in teams can be observed widely in social species, from apes to wolves. Through such collaborations, tasks can be accomplished more effectively (although there are significant exceptions) and individual learning rapidly shared with the rest of the team members.

Team coaching in the workplace is a relatively recent concept, although it is well-established within the world of sport. However, as discussed later, the structure, aims, processes and interdependencies of sports teams are significantly different from those in the workplace – to the extent that the validity and safety of transfer between the two worlds is low (Keidel, 1987).

Although a Google search indicates that Team Coaching is offered as a service by many training and consultancy organizations, there seems to be little consistency of definition or practice. The situation is not helped by the fact that the evidence-based literature on team coaching is woefully thin. The first substantive attempt to define team coaching was by Hackman and Wageman (2005), who describe it as a direct intervention with a team intended to help members make coordinated and task-appropriate use of their collective resources in accomplishing the team's work. My own definition, based on listening to how team coaches describe their role, is: 'a learning intervention designed to increase collective capability and performance of a group or team, through application of the coaching principles of assisted reflection, analysis and motivation for change'. The contrast in theoretical approach here is between short-term performance orientation and the concept of the team as a learning organism (Marsick, 1994; Clutterbuck, 1996, 2000).

Skiffington & Zeus (2000) present the team coach as someone who facilitates problem solving and conflict management, monitors team performance and coordinates between the team and a more senior management sponsor. This construct presupposes a very hands-on role for the team coach and a high level of responsibility for team performance, which is absent in both the Hackman/Wageman and Clutterbuck definitions.

There are therefore, as with coaching itself, several alternative perspectives about the role and function of team coaching. The common factors, however, include:

- an acceptance by the team and the team coach that a coaching approach is appropriate and beneficial
- a focus on performance (though whether this is a cause or effect of learning differs)
- an emphasis on conversations between team members, aimed at making more effective use of collective skills, knowledge and interests.

Proponents of team coaching argue that coaching an individual without attempting to influence the immediate human systems in which they operate reduces the impact of the coaching intervention. Teams develop habitual behaviours and norms, which exert considerable entropic energy to undermine individual and collective change (Valley & Thompson, 1998). An important component of this dynamic is the team's mental model, which becomes rigid and less likely to be challenged as circumstances change.

Like individuals, team effectiveness can also be undermined by quality of thinking. Addressing and improving the quality of thinking, for both individual issues and more broadly, is the core of coaching and this applies equally to individuals and the collective work group (Rogers & Blenko, 2006).

In addition, teams have many of the characteristics of organisms. Team personality, which has been widely studied (Van Vianen & de Dreu, 2001; Gustavsson & Baccman, 2005), appears to be a valid but under-explored concept and teams also develop collective norms about issues such as time orientation.

The context of team coaching is significantly different from that of one-to-one coaching. Among the principal differences are:

- Confidentiality: even with a high degree of psychological safety, team members may be reluctant to disclose to a group of colleagues, or to admit weaknesses to their boss.
- Pace of thinking and deciding: some members of the team may reach a conclusion faster than others. Where the coach in a one-to-one relationship can adjust pace to the speed of the coachee's mental processing, the team coach needs to be able to hold the attention and interest of the vanguard, while ensuring the rearguard are able to catch up at their own pace.
- Scope of topic: team coaching can only deal effectively with issues in which all the team members have a stake. Sometimes this involves helping team members recognize the mutual benefits and value of supporting a colleague.
- Building trust within the coaching relationship: while team members will vary in the level of trust they place in the coach, progress can normally only be made when the team as a whole is ready to trust both the coach and the process.

GOALS AND TASKS

The goals of team coaching are dependent on the stage of team development and on the specific characteristics of the team. Although it is common to refer, for example to *the leadership team*, the collective leadership may not be a team at all (Katzenbach, 1998). A group is distinguished from a team in various ways, but some of the most common (Hackman, 1990; Thompson, 2000) are:

- shared goals and purposes
- structured communications
- allocated responsibilities and accountabilities
- a level of interdependence
- willingness of members to place the collective goal above their own priorities
- clear boundaries (who is and is not included)
- operation within a social systems context (i.e. it is part of a larger organization, to whose goals it contributes).

Team coaching is also commonly used at the time of team formation, particularly when a project team is strategically or economically important for the organization. The process of transition through forming, storming, norming, performing and transforming (Tuckman and Jensen, 1977) benefits from some process management and team coaching is claimed to speed up the time it takes to reach the performing stage (Hackman & Wageman, 2005; Jackson & Taylor, 2008). Hackman and Wageman build on the work of Gersick (1988, 1989) to suggest that team coaching interventions should be structured to fit the stages of psychological and process development of the team. What this means in practice is that at the early stages of team formation, team coaching should be focused on clarifying the team task, setting norms of how to work together, defining boundaries and roles and gaining motivational momentum. At the mid-point of the team's development (or of a project assignment), it is ready to reflect on the task and the processes for achieving it. Towards the end of the project's assigned time, team members become open to a review of learning, both individual and collective.

Team coaching may also be remedial, in the sense that a team may need practical assistance in addressing specific issues of performance (e.g. achieving rapid improvements in productivity or customer service) or collective behaviour (e.g. managing conflict). The majority of case studies in Clutterbuck (2007) relate to these two categories, with building a team from a group as a common sub-theme. Wageman, Nine, Burruss and Hackman (2008) maintain strongly that focusing team coaching on interpersonal relations (the core of team building) does not reliably improve team performance, but that team coaching is most effective when focused on motivation (the effort people put in), strategies for performance and increasing the level of skills and knowledge within the team. However, case study evidence tends to suggest that increasing mutual trust and respect does have an impact on performance. A pragmatic perspective, suggested by Clutterbuck (2007), is that behavioural interventions are more likely to improve performance when aimed at specific team processes or objectives.

Where the group already exhibits most or all of the characteristics of a team, the coaching goals tend to relate to specific areas of performance. One way of categorizing these is as:

- interpersonal dynamics – issues such as recognizing and managing conflict, increasing collective emotional intelligence and building and sustaining an appropriate coaching climate
- temporal issues – for example how the team balances its emphasis on past, present and future; and time management
- managing key processes – goal setting and management, functional analysis, innovation, decision making and communication.

In all of these areas, the core task of the coach goes beyond making the team aware of problems and helping it develop solutions for the present – that is more typically a task for facilitation. Team coaching goes several steps further, helping the team to develop the capacity (skills, knowledge and capability) to manage these issues more effectively on its own.

FEATURES, PROCESSES, ROLE OF COACH
AND RELATIONSHIP WITH CLIENTS

Team coaches can operate from four perspectives or relationships with the team. At the simplest level, the team coach is also the team leader – by analogy, the team captain, who is both leading the team and engaging in the collective task. This is a role that involves multiple conflicts. Ferrar (2006) lists a number of barriers to effective line manager coaching, some of which apply equally to individual and collective coaching. These include difficulties in achieving full openness, pressure on the line manager to work to short-term agendas, groupthink, and the tendency of managers to adopt parent–child behaviours towards direct reports. Wageman, Nine, Burruss and Hackman (2008), in a recent study of 120 top teams, concluded that the role of line manager as coach is typically less effective than using a coach who is not engaged in the team task.

A second role for the team coach is the equivalent of the touchline manager, who is not part of the play, but can observe, give feedback and bring the team together for reflection. Ferrar's barriers to effectiveness still apply, but the coach is potentially able to apply a wider perspective from not being engaged in the task. Whether this actually happens may depend on how much of their attention is devoted to managing other stakeholders.

A third perspective is equivalent to being in the stands, unable to influence the play in real time, but able to help the team think strategically about what is its task and the processes it uses to achieve it. Here, Ferrar's barriers become less significant.

Finally, there is an external perspective – the coach, who does not observe the team at all, but who relies on evidence the team itself gathers, either intrinsically or from third parties (for example through customer surveys). This is qualitatively a very different role, as it involves helping the team to develop and pursue its own learning agenda.

An issue for the team coach in all these perspectives is how to balance collective coaching with additional, individual coaching. The team leader and team manager as coach will need to be careful not to alienate some individuals by being perceived as offering other team members proportionately more coaching (or by offering them too much!) A useful process in this context is the *team development plan* – an amalgam of personal development plans and the business plan. Clarity around individual coaching needs and opportunities for peer coaching are important elements of this working document.

Also important contextually is the nature of the team itself. There are several ways in which teams can be classified. For example the degree of task interdependence has a significant impact on the type and frequency of communication needed, the nature of relationships within the team and the potential for role conflict. The flow of work within the team provides another method of classification (Ratliff, Beckstead, & Hanke, 1999), from simple teams where everyone does the same task, to relay teams where tasks are different and sequential, through integrative teams where everyone does a different task at the same time (e.g. an operating theatre) and finally problem-solving teams where the process and procedures may be defined as the task progresses.

In a study of how teams learn (Clutterbuck, 2000), I identified six major team types, each of which had different issues in terms of their learning dynamics. These are basically:

- Stable teams – where membership and tasks are constant over a long period. Stable teams have advantages in terms of learning (strong learning partnerships can develop) but over time group norms tend to narrow creative thinking and reduce experimentation.
- Cabin crew teams – where the task remains the same but membership is constantly changing. Examples include film crews and some aspects of police work. The benefit of having lots of people to learn from may be outweighed by the lack of opportunity to form strong, long-term learning partnerships.
- Standing project teams – relatively stable new teams drawn from a variety of other teams and working on usually short term projects. By the time the team has gone from storming to performing, it has often reached the end of its lifetime, so the learning can easily be lost.
- Evolutionary teams – longer term projects, where the tasks and the membership change over time, with new people taking over as the project moves into new phases. A major problem for learning in this context is failure to educate newcomers in the history of the project.
- Developmental alliances – teams set up specifically for learning (for example action learning sets). An issue here is the relative priority given to membership of this team compared with other, task-focused teams, to which members may belong.
- Virtual teams – teams with fuzzy boundaries, or geographically dispersed. Here the learning problem may be creating opportunities for collective reflection.

Whatever method of team classification is chosen (and there are several more), team coaches need to be aware of the functional dynamics of the teams with which they work and adapt their approach accordingly. In many cases, the team itself may not be consciously aware of its functional dynamics, nor of the implications these may have in terms of performance management.

Similarly, the team coach needs to be aware of the extensive spectrum of influences on team performance and team learning. Some of the most significant include:

- **Diversity** – Homogenous teams tend to provide higher levels of customer service, but lower levels of creativity. Heterogeneous (diverse) teams vice versa. According to Early and Mosakowski (2000), mildly diverse teams perform least well, because they tend to fractionate into sub-teams; but highly diverse teams can perform exceptionally well when they spend time developing rules for personal and task communication, shared expectations about roles and performance, norms for conflict management and a sense of common identity. Although they do not specifically make a link with team coaching as a means of achieving these characteristics, it is likely to be much harder without external intervention.

- **Conflict management** – Not all forms of conflict are damaging. While conflict based on emotion and personality tends to undermine team performance, conflict of ideas and approaches can be highly efficacious. The key is for the team to develop language and protocols that recognize conflict at an early stage, steer it towards dialogue around ideas and approaches, and allow for collaborative, no-fault solution-finding (Jehn and Mannix, 2001).
- **Communication** – Communication within the team is critical in maintaining workflow, sharing learning and maintaining social identity. Teams may also adopt any or all of three strategies in communicating to key external audiences: ambassadorial (managing team reputation with top management); task-coordinating (liaising with other teams and stakeholders); and environmental scanning (Ancona and Caldwell, 1992). The effectiveness of these strategies in managing team reputation varies over time.

The range of tools and processes the team coach requires is therefore wide and arguably much wider than for one-to-one coaching.

A central issue in team coaching and essential in contracting is clarity of responsibility. There are typically four major stakeholders in externally resourced team coaching: the team; the team leader/manager; other team members (i.e. apart from the manager); and the sponsor. Issues that need to be foreseen and managed include:

- The team leader's behaviour or competence may be one of the primary reasons for poor team performance – hence there is a potential for conflict of loyalty.
- The team and the leader may have different agendas, as may the sponsor.
- Many teams are in fact composed of sub-teams, with considerable variation in their willingness and ability to collaborate.

HOW TEAM COACHING IS DIFFERENT

We have already explored how team coaching differs from individual coaching. However, it is often confused with team leading, team building and team facilitation. In each case, there are some overlaps in role, but also considerable distinguishing features. The following Tables (19.1 and 19.2) illustrate some of these overlaps.

Team coaching is also different from group therapy, although some of the same techniques may be used on occasion. Corey (2004: 4) describes some of the values of group therapy as 'practicing new skills … feedback and insights of other members as well as the practitioner … opportunities for modelling'. However, the members of a therapy group have few of the characteristics of a team; the aim of group counselling is to achieve individual improvements, rather than a common goal. A clue to the difference lies in Corey's explanation: 'The role of

Table 19.1: Differences between team leading and team coaching[1]

Issue	Leader-as-manager	Leader-as-coach
Task goals	Set goals for and with the team Develop commitment to the goals Review progress against the goals	Help establish processes for setting and reviewing goals Explore alignment between personal, sub-group and team goals Help explore the causes of setbacks/progress failures
Learning goals	Establish development needs of each team member Agree PDPs	Help establish processes for integrating individual and team development plans
Visioning	Articulating the team's ambitions internally and to external stakeholders (e.g. higher management) Contextualizing the vision within the corporate vision	Testing the quality and viability of the vision and how it influences day-to-day activity Helping the team articulate the *values* behind its vision
Coordination	Ensuring that everyone understands their roles and responsibilities Reviewing and improving work processes, in consultation with the team Planning and strategizing	Giving feedback on processes and procedures; and on how the human factor affects these Helping the team question its processes and approaches Developing strategy skills
Problem solving and decision making	Demonstrating effective decision-making and problem-solving behaviours, by involving team members and achieving consensus	Helping the team improve its problem-solving and decision-making processes
Conflict management	Pre-emptive action to identify, discuss and prevent potential conflict Mediating and agreeing rules that will reduce conflict	Giving feedback to ensure that conflict is recognized Improving the team's ability to manage conflict
Communication	Demonstrating effective communication Being available when needed Creating opportunities for communication to occur	Helping the team understand the theory and practice of communication Helping investigate and learn from communication failures
Learning processes	Ensuring the team takes time to reflect and review	Helping the team build the skills and processes of reflective dialogue
Boundary management	Protecting the team from external threats and interference Resource acquisition	Helping the team review and improve its boundary management
Performance management	Clarifying expectations of performance Appraisal Recognizing and rewarding performance	Exploring the influences on performance at both individual and team levels

[1] Reproduced with permission of the publisher and author (Clutterbuck, 2007).

the group counsellor is to facilitate interaction among the members, help them learn from each other, assist them in establishing *personal* goals, and encourage them to translate their insights into personal plans that involve taking action *outside* of the group' (Corey, 2004, emphasis added). Team coaching, by contrast, emphasizes *collective* goals and action *within* the team.

Table 19.2:   Team coaching v. team facilitation[1]

Attribute	Team coach	Team facilitator
Use/generation of feedback	Gives or helps team use & also receives feedback	Helps team generate mutual feedback
Engagement	Within the team or engaged with the team	Detached from the team
Learning process	Shares the learning process	Directs/manages the learning process
Action/monitoring	Intellectual, emotional and practical support through the changes	Process support for the changes
Relationship	Reagent	Catalyst
	Coach acquires learning or change through the process	Facilitator remains largely unchanged
Learning conversation	'Open' dialogue – structure generated from within	'Directed dialogue' – structure emerges from the facilitator's observations
Enablers	Working within team dynamics	Understanding team dynamics
Outcomes	Team and individual achievement	Agreement on team direction and method

[1] Reproduced by permission of the publisher and author (Clutterbuck, 2007).

RELATIONSHIP WITH THEORIES AND TRADITIONS

While team coaching in sport is closely associated with *sports psychology* as a source of evidential and philosophical grounding (Weinberg & Gould, 2007), these do not necessarily provide a basis for understanding team coaching in the workplace. The extent to which sports coaching approaches can be transferred to the workplace is hotly disputed. Katz (2001) points to a number of fundamental differences in context between the two roles:

- Sports coaching is about winning/ beating the competition; work teams place greater emphasis on co-operation and collaboration.
- Sports coaching involves a great deal of practice for periodic short bursts of exceptional performance; coaching in the workplace is typically about achieving consistent, long-term performance improvements. (Exceptions, where the analogy may work better, include emergency services and the military.)
- Coaching is only one of many influences on team performance in the workplace – resource availability, team structure and task design all play an equal or greater role.

According to Keidel (1987), there are three layers of interdependence in sports teams:

1) pooled, where team performance is the sum of individual performances (for example baseball or cricket)
2) sequential, where team performance relies on a mixture of individual and orchestrated performance (for example football)
3) reciprocal, where team performance is more than the sum of individuals (for example basketball).

The equivalent work teams might be: sales, where everyone works independently; assembly manufacture, where work is passed from one to the next; cross-functional task force, where there is continuous involvement by all team members. Using the wrong analogy, or an analogy that fits only partially, can be disruptive to team performance.

Team coaching relates to *performance coaching* in that teams have goals, which must be achieved. Goal clarity is typically seen as at the heart of performance coaching, although Megginson (2007) and Clutterbuck (2008) argue strongly that too narrow a focus of goals is dysfunctional. Like individuals, teams have a variety of potential or real barriers that prevent them achieving their performance potential. These include:

- the tendency towards social loafing (Ringelmann, 1913)
- poor prioritization of goals
- failings in leadership
- collective self-limiting beliefs.

The task of the team coach includes helping the team identify barriers to performance, designing appropriate strategies to overcome those barriers, and creating the time and motivation to implement those strategies. It also involves stimulating open dialogue around individual and collective behaviours, which contribute to good and poor performance.

All teams that have been in existence for more than a short period have a history. The members may also import into the team their own history (or baggage) from other teams, either within the organization or outside. Awareness of one's own and others' histories and their impact on collaborative behaviours may be low. Psychodynamic conversations can help the team recognize, accept or challenge, and manage these histories.

Cognitive behavioural approaches are sometimes associated in team coaching with motivational processes by identifying and eliminating behaviours, which are not conducive to achieving collective goals or collaboration, or by embedding new behaviours, which are. A specific application here is the development of coaching and co-coaching behaviours within the team. Because effective coaching is a consensual activity, it requires an attitudinal and behavioural shift on the part of the line manager as coach and on the part of other team members as coachees. (In practice, much of the coaching may also take place between peers within the team.) Agreeing and implementing appropriate feedback systems is integral to this behavioural change process.

However, cognitive behavioural approaches also have a role to play in helping the team develop more rigorous decision-making processes. 'Groupthink' is a constant danger in the team context (Janis, 1972). For teams at the top, the frequency of substantive decisions is also associated with team (and organizational) performance (Mankins & Steele, 2006). Effective decision making requires processes that challenge rationalizations and raise awareness of psychological traps in thinking – for example our tendency to attach higher significance to events that have strong emotional impact (Hammond, 2006).

Solutions-focused coaching and positive psychology

Such approaches provide an alternative perspective for team coaching methodology. The solutions focused team coach helps the team extract from its experience the strengths and characteristics of its behaviours and processes when things are going well. S/he uses questions such as:

- What positive moments were there in this gloomy period?
- What happened to make them different?
- What can we learn from these highlights that would help us tackle the issue differently?
- How could you create more of those moments – make them the dominant theme?
- If you had already resolved the problem, what would you and others have done?

The discipline of **_family therapy_** (Nichols & Schwartz, 1991) may also inform team coaching processes, by focusing attention on the systems within the team and in the team's interactions with the external world. Like the family therapist, the team coach helps the team recognize interaction patterns that might otherwise not have been apparent and helps the team establish new behavioural norms, which may have a positive impact on the entire team system. One of the most obvious applications here is overcoming a problem that team leaders, who have attended behavioural training programmes (for example in coaching skills), often encounter – the team members may be resistant to the new behaviours, with the result that the leader is rapidly rehabituated to behave as before. Viewing the change as a team change, rather than one of leadership style, and addressing the team from a systemic perspective, can provide a powerful means of ensuring that the intended new leader behaviours stick.

Team coaching can also apply much of the learning relating to **_group therapy_**. Therapy and coaching generally differ in that the former emphasizes cognitive and behavioural dysfunction and the latter emphasizes building on existing competencies; this broad differential can be observed between group therapy and team coaching. However, many teams do exhibit dysfunctional behaviours, especially in terms of conflict, groupthink, collective avoidance or delusion, resistance to change, defensive behaviour and so on (Corey, Covey, Callanan, & Russell, 1992). Group therapy has well-established processes for managing all of these issues.

In **_developmental coaching_**, the objective is self-awareness. Collective self-awareness is a more complex concept, which requires an integration of self-knowledge and knowledge about the fears, motivations, ambitions and emotions of other team members. By raising collective awareness – through dialogue and use of mutual feedback – the team coach equips the team to engage in systematic, sustainable change. Team coaching also shares with developmental coaching a focus on assisting transitions between developmental levels or stages. Where developmental coaching incorporates models of individual maturation (e.g. Erikson, 1974; Kegan, 1982), team coaching helps groups achieve transitions in collective maturation. The most common model for this is Tuckman and Jensen's (1965, 1977) forming, storming, norming, performing and adjourning. However, this model appears to relate only to project teams with a finite life, or to the early stages of new teams of other types. There does not seem to be a substantive model relevant to stable teams in their maturity (and possibly, decline).

EVALUATION

The paucity of evidence-based literature on team coaching makes it difficult to conduct a substantive evaluation.

Some observers contest the validity of team coaching as a genre, on the basis that it is no more than facilitation or team development, and that part of the essence of coaching is that it is an individual process. Taking these arguments in turn, we have already discussed a number of salient differences between team coaching and facilitation. The validity of these distinctions is still open to debate. An argument could be made, for example that there is enough similarity between the two roles to depict a sub-genre of a coaching style of facilitation, or alternatively, a facilitative style of coaching. As to whether coaching can only be an individual process, interesting forms of peer coaching in groups have been described by, among others, McNicoll (2008). Group supervision can also be seen as a well-established analogy of coaching (Hawkins & Smith, 2006).

Team coaching can be highly demanding of the coach since there is the need to manage simultaneously the coaching process and the interactions of team members. It requires considerable skill to avoid common pitfalls, such as:

- assuming the team leader's role or responsibilities. An ineffectual leader may abdicate difficult tasks or decisions to the coach.
- becoming subverted into existing group norms or thinking patterns
- creating dependency – the degree of intimacy and frequency of interaction can gradually create conditions where the team looks to the coach to solve its problems. Instead, the team coach should be focusing from the beginning on helping the team learn how to coach itself.

While one-to-one coaching now has broadly accepted codes of ethical practice, the ethics of team coaching, as a relatively new workplace discipline, are much less distinct. Some of the ethical issues that have emerged in workshops include:

- In individual coaching, the well-being of the client normally comes before that of the organization. But how does the coach balance the welfare of an individual versus that of the team as a whole?
- The team has been set very challenging goals, which demand long hours. The coach can see that this is having a negative affect on the home lives and health of some team members. The team say they are prepared to live with these conditions for a period, because the project is high-profile and will be beneficial in terms of their careers. However, the coach suspects that some people are going along with this view because they do not want to let down their colleagues.
- When is it appropriate to advise breaking up a dysfunctional team; and when should we try to fix it through coaching?
- When is it *not* appropriate to take on a team coaching assignment?
- The team leader is manipulative and dishonest towards the team. The coach knows his real intentions, but the team does not.
- It is clear to the coach that there is a serious issue, which the team is avoiding; (for example dysfunctional behaviour of a key member who has unique knowledge or special client relationships). The team leader has warned the coach against addressing this issue, but s/he knows the team cannot make real progress without dealing with it.

The answers to these dilemmas are not always straightforward, especially given that there are multiple stakeholders involved in a team coaching assignment.

The nature, context, content and skills base for team coaching are still evolving and it is difficult to predict what standards will eventually emerge. There is an urgent need for empirical research to determine the roles and boundaries of team coaching, the minimal competencies and experience required to be effective in the role and good practice in such areas as contracting, process management and evaluation. Team coaching may be the newest kid on the coaching block, but it is growing up fast!

FURTHER READING

The most comprehensive and approachable analysis of team dynamics is Leigh Thompson's *Making the team* (Prentice Hall, 2000). Wageman et al. (Harvard Business School, 2008) build on Gersick's (*Academy of Management Journal*, 1988) evidential analysis to draw conclusions about the timing of coaching interventions. Beyond this, there is currently little targeted literature on this topic, other than my own book, Clutterbuck's *Coaching the team at work* (Nicholas Brealey, 2006).

REFERENCES

Ancona, D.G., & Caldwell, D.F. (1992). Bridging the boundary: External activity and performance in organizational teams. *Administrative Science Quarterly, 37*: 634–65.

Clutterbuck, D. (1996). Developing learning teams. *Training Officer, July/August*.

Clutterbuck, D. (2000). *Learning teams report*. St Albans: Exemplas.

Clutterbuck, D. (2007). *Coaching the team at work*. London: Nicholas Brealey.

Clutterbuck, D. (2008). Are you a goal junkie? *Training Journal*, May: 43–6.

Corey, G. (2004). *Theory and practice of group counselling* (pp. 4–5). Florence, KY: Thomson Brooks/Cole.

Corey, G., Corey, M.S., Callanan, P., & Russell, J.M. (1992). *Group Techniques*. Pacific Grove, CA: Brooks/Cole.

Early, P.C., & Mosakowski, E. (2000). Creating hybrid team cultures: An empirical test of transnational team functioning. *Academy of Management Journal, 11*: 231–41.

Erikson, E.H. (1974). *Dimensions of a new identity*. New York: Norton.

Ferrar, P. (2006). The paradox of manager as coach: Does being a manager inhibit effective coaching? (Unpublished Masters dissertation, Oxford Brookes University.)

Gersick, C. (1988). Time and transition in work teams: Toward a new model of group development. *Academy of Management Journal, 31*: 9-41.

Gersick, C. (1989). Marking time: Predictable transitions in task groups. *Academy of Management Journal, 32*(2): 274–309.

Gustavsson, B., & Baccman, C. (2005). Team-personality: How to use relevant instruments to predict team performance. Paper presented at the 47th annual conference of the International Military Testing Association, Singapore, November.

Hackman, J.R. (1990). *Groups that work (and those that don't): Creating the high performance organization*. London, HarperBusiness.

Hackman, J.R., & Wageman, R. (2005). A theory of team coaching. *Academy of Management Review, 30*(2): 269–87.

Hammond, J. (2006). The hidden traps in decision-making. *Harvard Business Review, Jan*: 118–26.

Hawkins, P., & Smith, N. (2006). *Coaching, mentoring and organizational consultancy.* Maidenhead: McGraw-Hill.

Jackson, K., & Taylor, I. (2008). *The power of difference: Exploring the value and brilliance of diversity in teams.* London: Management Books 2000.

Janis, I.L. (1972). *Victims of groupthink.* Boston, MA: Houghton Miffin.

Jehn, K.A., & Mannix, E.A. (2001). The dynamic nature of conflict: A longitudinal study of intragroup conflict and group performance. *Academy of Management Journal, 44*(2): 238–51.

Katz, N. (2001). Sports teams as a model for workplace teams: Lessons and liabilities. *Academy of Management Executive, 15*(3).

Katzenbach, J.R. (1998). *Teams at the top.* Boston, MA: Harvard Business School Press.

Kegan, R. (1982). *The evolving self: Problem and process in human development.* London: Harvard University Press.

Keidel, R. (1987). Team sports as a generic organizational framework. *Human Relations, 40*: 591–612.

McNicoll, A. (2008). Learning at the leading edge. Paper presented at the bi-annual conference of the New Zealand Association of Training and Development, Auckland, May.

Mankins, M., & Steele, R. (2006). Stop making plans: Start making decisions. *Harvard Business Review, June:* 76–84.

Marsick, V. (1994). Trends in managerial reinvention. In *Management Learning* (pp. 11–13). London: Sage Publications.

Megginson, D. (2007). An own-goal for coaches. Paper presented to the European Mentoring and Coaching Council UK annual conference, Ashridge, April.

Nichols, M.P., & Schwartz, R.C. (1991). *Family therapy: Concepts and methods.* Upper Saddle River, NJ: Allyn and Bacon.

Ratliff, R., Beckstead, S.M., & Hanke, S.H. (1999). The use and management of teams: A how-to guide, *Quality Progress, June.*

Ringelmann, M. (1913). *Aménagement des fumeurs et des purins.* Paris: Librarie Agricole de la Maison Rusique.

Rogers, P., & Blenko, M. (2006). Who has the D? How clear decision roles enhance organizational performance. *Harvard Business Review, Jan*: 53–61.

Skiffington, S., & Zeus, P. (2000). *The complete guide to coaching at work.* New York: McGraw-Hill.

Thompson, L. (2000). *Making the team: A guide for managers,* Upper Saddle River, NJ: Prentice Hall.

Tuckman, B.W. (1965). Developmental sequence in small groups. *Psychological Bulletin, 63*: 384–99.

Tuckman, B.W., & Jensen, M. (1977). Stages of small group development revisited. *Group and Organizational Studies, 2*: 419–27.

Valley, K., & Thompson, T.A. (1998). Sticky ties and bad attitudes: Relational and individual bases of resistance to changes in organizational structure. In M.A. Neale & R. Kramer (Eds.), *Power and influence in organizations.* Thousand Oaks, CA: Sage Publications.

Van Vianen, A.E. and de Dreu, C.K. (2001). Personality in teams: Its relationship to social cohesion, cohesion and team performance. *European Journal of Work & Organizational Psychology, 10*(2): 97–120.

Wageman, R., Nine, D., Burruss, J., & Hackman, R. (2008). *Senior leadership teams: What it takes to make them great.* Boston, MA: Harvard Business School Press.

Weinberg, R.S., & Gould, D. (2007). *Foundations of sport and exercise psychology.* Champaign, IL: Human Kinetics.

20

Peer Coaching

Richard Ladyshewsky

INTRODUCTION

Peer coaching is a process involving a coach and a coachee, with relatively equal status, focusing on expanding, refining and building new skills and competencies in training and workplace situations. They normally have similar training or background preparation which enhances mutual support.

Peer coaching was developed extensively in the early 1980s as part of teacher development, where much of the earlier literature can be found (Ackland, 1991; Joyce & Showers, 1982; Showers, 1984; Skinner & Welch, 1996). It was seen as an effective strategy for class-room teachers to get non-evaluative feedback from a peer teacher regarding curriculum implementation and teaching effectiveness. Both teachers and health professionals have used this approach as a support strategy to improve professional practice (Ladyshewsky, 2004; Sekerka & Chao, 2003; Skinner & Welch, 1996; Waddell & Dunn, 2005; Wynn & Kromrey, 1999). In the business or organizational context, the approach has been used to build skills, to support people in leadership and management development programmes and to promote transfer of training (Ladyshewsky, 2007; Ladyshewsky & Ryan, 2006; Peters, 1996).

This chapter provides an overview of peer coaching with detailed information on what is necessary to ensure success of the coaching relationship. A framework is then provided that differentiates this developmental interaction from other coaching genres. Lastly, theoretical perspectives that underpin peer coaching are described. Examples are offered throughout to illustrate this genre in practice. Peer coaching can be applied to a wide range of peer groups, of any age and in many sectors, but for the purposes of this chapter, the focus is on its use in the training environment and workplace.

GOALS AND TASKS OF PEER COACHING

A key goal of a peer coaching relationship is to provide the coachee with a development experience that is built around trust and confidentiality. This experience is typically driven by the coachee, who recognizes a development need and seeks the support of a peer coach. The coaching is most often used to help the coachee achieve a specific set of skills that lead to competency, although the potential to assist in other areas is also a possibility, depending on the skill of the coach.

The efficiency and effectiveness of this coaching genre is enhanced when participants are given initial training in coaching skills, contracting and reflective journalling. Ongoing support to participants in formal peer coaching programmes also promotes ongoing success.

While peer coaching can occur naturally, failure to formalize the process and train participants may impact on rapport building, development of trust, confidentiality, status and power. Training ensures that the important features of equality and mutuality in the relationship are maintained (Damon, 1984; Damon & Phelps, 1989). Equality in the relationship is critical if self-disclosure is to be encouraged. This self-disclosure leads to a sense of mutuality or connectedness in the relationship. This in turn promotes deeper conversations about development and practice which are necessary for gaining the insights needed for escalating skill development.

Ideally, the coachee, in consultation with the coach, works collaboratively to create a development plan (Knowles, Holton, & Swanson, 1998) that specifies the goal to be achieved along with the resources and strategies that will be employed. Strategies for evaluating progress are also included in the plan along with key performance indicators that measure success. The collaborative creation of a development plan, driven largely by the coachee's needs, ensures that the plan is owned by the coachee. It maps out the accountability of the parties involved, and assists the coach and coachee to maintain focus during their sessions. Often, the arrangement is reciprocal, with each party alternating between the role of coach and coachee. Each coachee would have a specific development plan.

The task of the coach is to create a trust-filled open space for self-disclosure whereby the coachee can explore development needs in an experiential manner (Kolb, 1984). This goal is accomplished through regular meetings with the coachee whereby the coach uses open-ended and probing questions that encourage the coachee to explore his or her thinking and action. The goal of the coaching is to remain objective and non-evaluative in order for the coachee to make self-discoveries that progress development and skill.

Peer coaching is a laterally directed learning strategy in which individuals seek support from those whom they see as equals. This is different from a vertically directed learning strategy whereby a supervisor, for example, coaches the subordinate. This vertical strategy can be referred to as the 'manager as coach' and is fraught with status–solidarity issues and evaluation, which impact on equality and mutuality. This is absent or minimal when peers coach each other because of the equality in status and power.

Tasks that enhance the experience are the use of reflective journals (Kerka, 1996; Ladyshewsky, 2007). Reflective journaling requires the coachee to review their practice as part of their skill development. The coachee reviews these reflections so that they can bring them to the coaching session. The coach, through the use of open-ended and probing questions, assists the coachee to see patterns in their reflections and reviews. The coachee then gains greater insights into the knowledge, skills and attitudes that influence their progress.

FEATURES, PROCESSES AND ROLES IN PEER COACHING

D'Abate, Eddy and Tannenbaum (2003) conducted a comprehensive review of developmental interactions such as coaching, mentoring and tutoring, and were able to map specific features of these interventions. They classified these interactions into five areas: participant demographics; interaction characteristics; organizational distance/direction; purpose of the interaction; and degree of structure. Their research reveals a significant amount of inconsistency and overlap between peer coaching and other developmental interactions.

The defining features of peer coaching which manifest consistently in the literature are: a lateral organizational direction to the relationship; a focus on specific objectives; feedback as a central part of the development experience; and observation of practice (D'Abate et al., 2003). This observation can be direct or indirect. Other dimensions of the relationship which appear throughout the literature, but to a lesser extent, are interaction characteristics which have bidirectional benefit and a focus on short-term performance. Behaviours in peer coaching are directed towards achieving learning goals. Behaviours are highly collaborative, with mutual problem solving focused on achieving developmental outcomes. Further, aiding and befriending are also consistent behaviours which are designed to provide emotional support in the process (D'Abate et al., 2003).

As noted earlier, the peer coaching relationship develops in response to an identified learning need in the coachee. Hence engagement in the relationship is often a voluntary one; although more structured programmes can be implemented into the workplace and training environment. The coachee sees value in a strategic learning partnership, and the process of building a supportive relationship begins.

One model of peer coaching, although very clinically focused, is described as having five stages: forecasting; training with demonstration of new practice behaviours; opportunities for practice; non-evaluative feedback; questioning and self-assessment (Waddell & Dunn, 2005). An eight stage model that outlines the features, processes and roles in a peer coaching relationship has also been described (Ladyshewsky & Varey, 2005). These eight stages were

Table 20.1: Eight stage peer coaching model

Step	Description	Objective of Each Stage (Desired Outcome)	Impact of Stage if not Executed Properly
1	Assessment & Trust Building	Peers assess each other for personal compatibility and suitability of partnership.	Trust and understanding are not built into the relationship, mutuality and equality suffers and relationship fails.
2	Planning	Timing and place for peer coaching sessions are established. Commitment is made to a structured process.	If sessions are cancelled, inconvenient, inappropriately timed or consistently interrupted – sessions may be seen as unproductive and motivation to participate declines.
3	Formalizing Process & Scope	The coachee's particular needs and the scope of the sessions are determined, based on priority of interests and available time.	If the coachee's needs do not drive the process and scope – actions will not be relevant. Commitment wanes.
4	Defining Purpose & Goals	Coach explores with the coachee potential learning objective(s). Goals and objectives are further defined.	Unless both parties gain this understanding only symptomatic surface level solutions are discovered and main goals will not be achieved.
5	Clarifying Facts & Assumptions	Coach asks the coachee to separate assumptions from facts and offers non-evaluative feedback and perspectives to assist in gaining objective clarity.	If the coachee is not challenged, they may not develop self-awareness and insights into how to progress development.
6	Exploring Possibilities	Conversations move from correctly identifying the issue, event or dilemma to developing possibilities for solutions. The coachee finds their own path out of the learning development plan assisted by the coach who creates space for exploration of different scenarios. This creates commitment to the action.	If the range of solutions are not constructed by the coachee, they are disempowered and become dependent on the coach. Lack of exploration creates the risk of partial solutions being implemented due to lack of meta-cognitive reflection. Risk of constraints emerging, which block progress, due to lack of exploration.
7	Gaining Commitment to Actions	Conversation moves to creating verbal commitment to identified actions with clear outcomes.	If actions are vague they are difficult to act on with confidence and the assessment of directly attributable outcomes is difficult – reducing further reflection and learning.
8	Offering Support and Accountability	Coach offers follow-up support with genuine interest in coachee's results. Follow up is structured by the coach to assist in motivation, learning support and ongoing trust building.	Without authentic support in the relationship, follow up is seen purely as accountability. Relationship becomes strained and trust declines and is likely to stop with only one or two cycles.

conceptualized by comparing and contrasting different types of coaching relationships. They were then modified specifically to create and sustain the dynamics needed for a successful relationship by trialling them in practice. Each step in this eight stage model is directed towards achieving the specific and necessary outcome essential to the overall success of the development interaction. Failure to fulfil each stage of the process is likely to lead to negative consequences in the relationship. These factors are explained more fully in Table 20.1.

There are other specific features and processes of the peer coaching relationship which get less attention in the literature (D'Abate et al., 2003). The duration of the interaction can vary, depending on the needs of the coachee. For the most part, however, the literature suggests that the relationship is generally of a shorter term, as it is focused typically on developing a skill, after which the relationship ends. The schedule of meetings is typically regular, as this keeps the coachee engaged, motivated and supported during the change process.

Trust, confidentiality and matching

Trust and confidentiality are important cornerstones of a successful peer coaching interaction. Given that the relationship is housed within the training environment or workplace, the coach is often, but not exclusively, selected from within that sector. Hence, issues of trust and confidentiality are magnified. Coachees may approach coaches because of previous experience of working together, or through recognition of their skill sets being useful for their development. Coaches should be external to any line management or direct report relationship to ensure relationships are status and power neutral and therefore equal and open to mutual discourse. Otherwise, the relationship is no longer 'peer' based. These matching issues are important considerations for a successful engagement.

Formality

An element of formality to the peer coaching process is also helpful as it facilitates the achievement of outcomes by ensuring the coach and coachee stay focused on previously agreed goals. Formality involves having a regular meeting schedule, ensuring dialogue is focused on learning goals and the development plan, incorporating information from the learning journal, and keeping discussions non-evaluative through the use of open-ended and probing questions. It is critical that time is provided within the work and training environment for the coaching to take place.

This formality keeps the ownership and direction of the process conceptually in the hands of the coachee, even if the interaction has been suggested by the coachee's manager as a development strategy through the performance management process. The formality maps out an agreed upon process, the accountability of coach and coachee as well as others in the plan, such as the manager, the human resources professional or other experts. Issues of confidentiality, disclosure and trust become more central to the contracting process along with the scope and nature of the development plan. Having these mapped out in advance ensures the experience is focused on learning and development.

Non-evaluative feedback

Given that coaching is typically established to work on a development need or skill deficiency, some assessment of performance growth is needed. This assessment or feedback can be formal or informal, and is aligned to the goals and key performance indicators. The coachee needs this information to pace their learning and to map their progress. The role of the coach is to encourage the coachee, through the provision of 'non-evaluative' feedback on progress, to assist in confidence building, motivation and self-efficacy.

The coach must also be very sensitive to the feedback that is offered to the coachee, especially in the early part of the relationship. In order to preserve the equality and mutuality of the relationship, feedback should be non-evaluative (Showers, 1984). If feedback starts to become evaluative, then the status–solidarity dimension (Baker, Jensen, & Kolb, 2005) between the coach and coachee changes and equality disappears. This is because the coach has shifted role from peer coach to peer reviewer. This change in role, which often occurs insidiously without the coach realizing it, may strain the relationship. When evaluation enters the relationship, the coachee is less likely to self disclose, and the mutuality of the relationship suffers because underlying expectations of how the relationship is supposed to work become violated. Luft & Ingham (1955) describe changes in interpersonal interactions when these are influenced by issues such as evaluation or power.

The coach can ensure that the feedback is non-evaluative by using open-ended and probing questions. This type of questioning helps the coachee to reflect deeply on their experiences and skills – a critical component of experiential learning (Kolb, 1984) and deep learning (Boud, 1993; Marton & Saljo, 1976). Who, what, where and how questions are particularly useful as they help the coachee explore and self-evaluate their skills and performance (Zeus & Skiffington, 2002). For example in helping a coachee to develop conflict management experience following a negative experience where, for example they lost their temper in a group, a peer coach may ask, 'who do you think you could call upon in the group to help diffuse tension?'; 'what evidence do you have to support your claim that they don't like you?'; 'where could you implement changes in the meeting structure to manage conflict?'. 'Why' questions, in contrast, push the coachee towards having to justify action, which may strain the relationship. Using the same example, if the coach asks, 'why did you lose your temper in that meeting?' the coachee may become defensive.

Other important communication skills needed by the coach include active listening skills, the ability to use verbal and non-verbal communication strategically and also employ emotional intelligence (Goleman, 1995; Merlevede, Bridoux, & Vandamme, 2001).

Termination of the relationship occurs when the objectives of the development plan have been achieved or learning has reached a plateau and the parties agree to disband. This does not preclude the peers from coming together once again if a new development need arises, or the old plan needs revisiting.

DISTINCTIONS BETWEEN PEER COACHING AND OTHER GENRES

Peer coaching is distinct, yet symbiotic, with other forms of coaching such as: skills and performance coaching; executive and leadership coaching; and the 'manager as coach' models. It is often used synonymously with mentoring but is, in fact, quite distinct.

Skills and performance coaching

Peer coaching is focused largely on developing skills and performance as a result of the insights gained from collaboration with one another. It is a short term initiative driven by specific goals and development plans. On this level, it is very similar to skills and performance coaching where improving ability is the focus. However, the coach, in skills and performance coaching, usually has greater expertise and competence and is commissioned to help the coachee. This greater expertise is important in some forms of skills and performance coaching (Sue-Chan & Latham, 2004), as the coach is seen to be more credible. The loss of the 'peer' element, however, increases the likelihood of coachee movement into the 'hidden or private' window (Luft & Ingham, 1955) and the concomitant reduction in self-disclosure.

Executive and leadership coaching

Executive and leadership coaching can also be peer based, with the coach being internal or external to the training environment or workplace. This coaching engagement may be commissioned by the executive/leader as part of their development, be aligned to a leadership development programme, or assigned by superiors as a strategy to 'smooth out rusty edges' in an otherwise promising leader. When one gets to executive ranks, however, the availability of peer coaches within the organization is limited. Those that are available are often competing for the same position(s) one level above and are therefore not appropriate for peer coaching. The cooperative element that peers are able to use to build the learning partnership is difficult to achieve in this instance. Instead, the relationships are often competitive. Peer coaches for these executives need to be sought externally.

Mentoring

Mentoring and coaching are often used interchangeably in the literature. Some authors do not see a difference at all (Sperry, 1996) whereas others see definitive distinctions (Chao, 1999; Waddell & Dunn, 2005). Structured mentoring programmes in organizations are more often downward in orientation and often internal to the organization. Further, the object of development is often general or holistic and long term. The matching process is also quite formal and guided by the formality of the programme (D'Abate et al., 2003). The mentor is also in a higher status position, given their experience, age and seniority. This influences the solidarity between the parties (Baker et al., 2005) by the understanding that the mentor has a large role to play in driving the direction of the relationship. This same structure can also be seen in informal mentoring relationships that emerge serendipitously. These informal mentoring relationships are still downward in orientation, long term, and focused on holistic or general issues. Peer coaching is clearly based on equality, which has a differential impact on the status–solidarity relationship. As noted earlier, peer coaching is also more aligned to specific skill development, is of short term duration and driven by specific goals, which from the description above, is distinct from mentoring.

PEER COACHING AND ITS RELATIONSHIP TO THEORETICAL APPROACHES

Peer coaching can be linked to the following theoretical approaches: solution-focused coaching; person centred coaching; and cognitive behavioural approaches to coaching. The extent to which the coach is able to apply these theoretical approaches to the developmental interaction depends on the coach's knowledge and ability to practise within these theoretical frameworks.

Solution-focused approach to coaching

Given that peer coaching is directed towards achieving a specific skill or improving performance, guided by a goal and development plan, its forward development nature parallels the solution-focused approach to coaching (Greene & Grant, 2003). Solution-focused coaches encourage the coachee to focus on desired future states and then help them to discover how they might achieve these using skills they already possess (de Shazer, 2005).

The peer coach within the solution-focused approach would support the coachee in defining goals and exploring strengths that they already possess which might be used to reach these goals. By focusing on solutions and goals, rather than on problems, energy can be directed towards achieving targets, rather than trying to fix problems. This creates attention density (Rock & Schwartz, 2006) and strengthens learning pathways in the brain that facilitate learning. Goal setting theory (Locke, 1996), like solution-focused coaching, is geared towards helping the coachee focus on the outcomes they are seeking. Within this genre, the coach must help the coachee to frame the goals and tasks in a way that they can embrace and take ownership of them. For example in solution-focused coaching, a coachee who is frustrated with conflict in the workplace would be assisted by a peer coach to explore their strengths in managing conflict. These strengths would be harnessed to assist the coachee in developing a preferred conflict-free workplace; rather than focusing on the problems causing the conflict, solutions that remedy the situation receive energy.

Person centred approach to coaching

The person centred approach to coaching, sometimes referred to as the humanistic approach, flows from the work of Carl Rogers and focuses on helping the individual to develop their potential as a human being (Carlopio, Andrewartha, & Armstrong, 2005). Abraham Maslow, another proponent of the humanistic approach, referred to this as self-actualization (Carlopio et al., 2005).

A peer coach who embraces this humanistic philosophy would assist the coachee by using development interaction to first understand the human experience of the coachee. Through this understanding, the coach could then support the coachee to examine their unique context, to develop further self-awareness in the coachee and to help the coachee seek choices that have meaning and value. For example a peer coach may assist a coachee to discover how work events relate to life experience. Through this understanding, the coachee may gain insights into their behaviour and how this might link to workplace behaviour.

Cognitive behavioural approach to coaching

The cognitive behavioural approach to coaching is focused on helping the coachee become aware of thought processes, often contradictory or sabotaging, which have a negative impact on behaviour and skills achievement. Most behaviours have cognitive underpinnings (Urdan & Midgley, 2001) and in order to regulate behaviour more effectively, individuals need to consider the combination of the environment, thoughts, feelings and behaviours (Grant, 2001). Being able to self-regulate emotion and cognition in combination with training programmes that include coaching, has demonstrated significant long-term gains in performance (Grant, 2001).

The peer coach's role in this theoretical approach is to assist the coachee to examine thoughts, feelings and behaviours in a range of situations. Hopefully, the coachee gains new insights into how these factors link into their thinking and how this drives behaviour. Through these insights, the coachee can begin to manage the change process towards skill acquisition by managing the thought processes that block growth and development. Using a conflict management example, a peer coach may help a coachee to see how their thoughts about situations are lacking real evidence. This may free the coachee to move forward, realizing that fears or beliefs that they have held about conflict are inaccurate.

Learning theory approach to coaching

Peer coaching is particularly aligned to theories of learning that see cooperation among peers as an essential prerequisite for cognitive growth. The intellectual disagreements that occur during these discussions create conceptual conflicts that motivate individuals to seek out new information (Johnson & Johnson, 1978; Johnson, Johnson, & Smith, 1998; Johnson, Maruyama, Johnson, Nelson, & Skon, 1981). Most of the literature supporting peer assisted learning appears to fall within this theoretical dimension. Peers are a compelling source of conflict because they speak on levels which can be easily understood by one another (Damon, 1984; Foot & Howe, 1998). Further, the informal communication between peers is less threatening; hence, there is potential for deeper engagement in the learning experience.

Transfer of learning is also facilitated by a socio-cognitive learning approach and is paralleled by the discussions about training and application to work that take place during peer coaching.

Vygotsky (1978, 1986) reports that peers benefit from one another by internalizing the cognitive processes implicit in their interactions and communications. The peer dialogue that results emulates several critical features of rational thinking, in particular: the verification of ideas; the planning of strategies; the symbolic representation of intellectual acts; and the generation of new solutions. Vygotsky argues that social and cognitive interaction with a more capable peer allows a slightly less capable peer to enter new areas of potential. For example, the coach and coachee could be engaged in a debate about the roles and responsibilities of a manager to mediate conflict. The engagement of the two parties in this discussion, directed by the coachee's desire to improve their conflict management skills, may shift the coachee's perspective towards a more positive perspective.

These theoretical perspectives can all be applied within peer coaching. The application depends in part on the goals and objectives of the coachee, and the ability of the peer coach to work within the theoretical paradigm. In leadership development, the application of all of these theoretical perspectives would be important. First, a solution-focused approach would challenge the coachee to visualize themselves as an effective leader and work towards that vision. In order to move towards this goal, a person centred approach would be important to consider the human experience of the leader and how this is influencing their development. A cognitive behavioural approach would assist the leader in understanding thought processes that may have developed from their experience, which are limiting performance. Lastly, a learning theory approach would be applied to challenge the leader's thinking in order for them to consider other perspectives defining their actions.

EVALUATION

Through an evaluation of the tradition of peer coaching, it becomes apparent that this model is an excellent learning strategy for the development of skills and to enhance performance. This stems from the fact that individuals at comparable points in their professional development often make similar information processing errors. Hence, partnerships where individuals are at the same level can be of great assistance because both individuals see and experience their learning challenges in similar ways. For individuals at a novice level (Oldmeadow, 1996), problem solving typically involves the use of a backward or deductive reasoning process to sort through hypotheses (Patel & Kaufman, 1995). For example a novice physical therapist may have to explore six different hypotheses to arrive eventually at a decision about a client's physical diagnosis. This problem-solving process is quite different from ones used by those who are more advanced in their skills base (Oldmeadow, 1996). Individuals at this expert level use a forward or inductive reasoning process by applying previous knowledge frameworks (Patel & Kaufman, 1995). For example a senior physical therapist may recognize very early in the interaction that a client has a specific shoulder problem they have seen many times before. The strategies to manage this client are very clear because they fit the clinician's pattern of experience. Hence, the value of peer coaching for individuals who are at similar developmental levels is supported by information-processing theory.

Limitations related to peer coaching largely relate to the skills base of the coach in building the relationship, maintaining confidentiality, building trust, keeping the dialogue non-evaluative and applying the correct practice within a theoretical framework (e.g. solution focus). The ability to embed experiential learning principles into the coaching experience is also an important aspect that ensures a successful learning experience. Reflective questioning, theory building and reapplication of experience must be modelled in the coaching framework. The ability to build development plans around goals also influences success. Hence, the strength of this intervention rests on how well prepared are participants and how well the organization supports this learning strategy within the training or developmental process.

Strengths of the peer coaching model are its ability to promote deep reflection, to build understanding and application of knowledge, theory and skills in a non-threatening and non-evaluative manner. Peer support is a strong psychological factor in promoting and maintaining goal activity. A further strength of the approach is that it can be implemented at relatively low cost for an organization. As a result, it can be an effective organizational learning strategy that can be used to build learning within an organization, increase transfer of training (Baldwin & Ford, 1988) following training and development initiatives, and facilitate positive returns on training investments.

Peer coaching, while sharing many features of other forms of coaching, achieves its unique outcomes through the nature of the partnership which is based on equality and mutuality. This fosters self-disclosure and engagement in the learning process. The importance of keeping the relationship equal, by having clear developmental plans in place and keeping feedback non-evaluative, preserves the relationship and the benefits that ensue. Peer coaching can operate within several of the theoretical traditions provided the coach has the skill and understanding to practise within these frameworks. It is an excellent organizational learning tool.

FURTHER READING

Topping, K., & Ehly, S. (Eds.). (1998). *Peer Assisted Learning*. London: Lawrence Erlbaum and Associates. (Although focused on peer learning in school, this book overviews a range of peer assisted learning models that can be used with adults. It will help readers gain a deeper understanding of the range of peer learning support strategies that can be used to promote development.)

Zeus, P., & Skiffington, S. (2000). *The complete guide to coaching at work*. Sydney: McGraw-Hill. (This book provides a good overview of basic coaching skills and principles for application in the workplace. The ideas presented are very applicable to peer coaching. A range of different coaching relationships are also outlined.)

Boud, D., Cohen, R., & Sampson, J. (Eds.). (2001). *Peer learning in higher education*. London, Kogan Page. (This book focuses on peer learning in higher education. A range of peer-assisted learning strategies are outlined, which can be modelled within peer coaching contexts. The first four chapters are particularly useful for further exploration of how to design and implement effective peer interaction systems.)

REFERENCES

Ackland, R. (1991). A review of the peer coaching literature. *Journal of Staff Development, 12*(1): 22–6.

Baker, A., Jensen, P., & Kolb, D. (2005). Conversation as experiential learning. *Management Learning, 36*(4): 411–27.

Baldwin, T., & Ford, J. (1988). Transfer of training: A review and directions for future research. *Personnel Psychology, 41*(1): 63.

Boud, D. (1993). Experience as the base for learning. *Higher Education Research and Development, 12*(1): 33–44.

Carlopio, J., Andrewartha, G., & Armstrong, H. (2005). *Developing management skills* (3rd ed.). French's Forest, NSW: Pearson Australia Group.

Chao, R. (1999). Invited reaction: Challenging research in mentoring. *Human Resource Development Quarterly, 9*(4): 334–8.

D'Abate, C., Eddy, E., & Tannenbaum, S. (2003). What's in a name? A literature-based approach to understanding mentoring, coaching, and other constructs that describe developmental interactions. *Human Resource Development Review, 2*(4): 360–84.

Damon, W. (1984). Peer education: The untapped potential. *Journal of Applied Developmental Psychology, 5:* 331–43.

Damon, W., & Phelps, E. (1989). Critical distinctions among three approaches to peer education. *International Journal of Educational Research, 13:* 9–19.

de Shazer, S. (2005). *More than miracles: The state of the art of solution-focused therapy.* Binghamton, NY: Hawthorn Press.

Foot, H., & Howe, C. (1998). The psychoeducational basis of peer assisted learning. In K. Topping & S. Ehly (Eds.), *Peer assisted learning* (pp. 27–43). London: Lawrence Erlbaum and Associates.

Goleman, D. (1995). *Emotional intelligence.* New York: Bantam Books.

Grant, A. (2001). Coaching for enhanced performance: Comparing cognitive and behavioral approaches to coaching, 3rd International Spearman Seminar: Extending intelligence: Enhancement and new constructs. Sydney, November.

Greene, J., & Grant, A. (2003). *Solution-focused coaching: A manager's guide to getting the best from people.* London: Pearson Education.

Johnson, D., & Johnson, R. (1978). Cooperative, competitive, and individualistic learning. *Journal of Research and Development in Education, 12*(1): 3–15.

Johnson, D., Johnson, R., & Smith, K. (1998). Cooperative learning returns to college: What evidence is there that it works? *Change, 30*(4): 27–35.

Johnson, D., Maruyama, G., Johnson, R., Nelson, D., & Skon, L. (1981). Effects of cooperative, competitive, and individualistic goal structures on achievement: A meta-analysis. *Psychological Bulletin, 89*(1): 47–62.

Joyce, B., & Showers, B. (1982). The coaching of teaching. *Educational Leadership, 40*(1): 4–8.

Kerka, S. (1996). *Journal writing and adult learning* (Report No. EDO-CE- 96-174). (ERIC Document Reproduction Service No. ED399413).Washington, DC: Office of Educational Research and Improvement.

Knowles, M., Holton, E., & Swanson, R. (1998). *The adult learner* (5th ed.). Woburn, MA: Butterworth Heinemann.

Kolb, D. (1984). *Experiential learning.* Englewood Cliffs, NJ: Prentice-Hall.

Ladyshewsky, R. (2004). The impact of peer coaching on the clinical reasoning of the novice practitioner. *Physiotherapy Canada, 56*(1): 15–25.

Ladyshewsky, R. (2007). A strategic approach for integrating theory to practice in leadership development. *Leadership & Organization Development Journal, September.*

Ladyshewsky, R., & Ryan, J. (2006). Peer coaching and reflective practice in authentic business contexts: A strategy to enhance competency in post-graduate business students. In A. Herrington & J. Herrington (Eds.), *Authentic learning environments in higher education* (pp. 61–75). Hershey, PA: Idea Group Publishing.

Ladyshewsky, R., & Varey, W. (2005). Peer coaching: A practical model to support constructivist learning methods in the development of managerial competency. In M. Cavanagh, A. Grant & T. Kemp (Eds.), *Evidence-based coaching:* Vol. 1: *Theory, research and practice in the behavioural sciences* (pp. 171–82). Bowen Hills, QLD: Australian Academic Press.

Locke, E. (1996). Motivation through conscious goal setting. *Applied and Preventive Psychology, 5,* 117–24.

Luft, J., & Ingham, H. (1955). *The Johari window: A graphic model for interpersonal relations.* Los Angeles, CA: University of California Western Training Laboratory.

Marton, F., & Saljo, R. (1976). On qualitative differences in learning. I. Outcome and process. *British Journal of Educational Psychology, 46*: 4–11.

Merlevede, P., Bridoux, D., & Vandamme, R. (2001). *Seven steps to emotional intelligence.* Carmarthen: Crown House.

Oldmeadow, L. (1996). Developing clinical competence: A mastery pathway. *Australian Physiotherapy Journal, 42*(1): 37–44.

Patel, V., & Kaufman, D. (1995). Clinical reasoning and biomedical knowledge: Implications for teaching. In J. Higgs & M. Jones (Eds.), *Clinical reasoning and the health professions* (pp. 117–28). Oxford: Butterworth Heinemann.

Peters, H. (1996). Peer coaching for executives. *Training and Development Journal, 50*(3): 39.

Rock, D., & Schwartz, J. (2006). *The neuroscience of leadership.* Retrieved May 2006 from www.strategy-business.com/article/06207

Sekerka, L., & Chao, J. (2003). Peer coaching as a technique to foster professional development in clinical ambulatory settings. *Journal of Continuing Education in the Health Professions, 23*(1): 30–7.

Showers, B. (1984). *Peer coaching: A strategy for facilitating transfer of training.* Eugene, OR: Oregon University Center for Educational Policy and Management.

Skinner, M., & Welch, T. (1996). Peer coaching for better teaching. *College Teaching, 44*(4): 153–6.

Sperry, L. (1996). Executive consulting, psychotherapy, and coaching. In L. Sperry (Ed.), *Corporate therapy and consulting.* Philadelphia, PA: Brunner/Mazel.

Sue-Chan, C., & Latham, G. (2004). The relative effectiveness of external, peer and self-coaches. *Applied Psychology: An International Review, 53*(2): 260–78.

Topping, K., & Ehly, S. (Eds.). (1998). *Peer assisted learning.* London: Lawrence Erlbaum and Associates.

Urdan, T., & Midgley, C. (2001). Academic self-handicapping: What we know, what more there is to learn. *Educational Psychology Review, 13*(2): 115–38.

Vygotsky, L. (1978). *Mind in society.* Cambridge, MA: MIT Press.

Vygotsky, L. (1986). *Thought and language.* Cambridge, MA: MIT Press.

Waddell, D., & Dunn, N. (2005). Peer coaching: The next step in staff development. *Journal of Continuing Education in Nursing, 36*(2): 84–9.

Wynn, M., & Kromrey, J. (1999). Paired peer placement with peer coaching: In early field experiences: Results of a four-year study. *Teacher Education Quarterly, 26*(1): 21–38.

Zeus, P., & Skiffington, S. (2002). *The coaching at work tool kit.* Roseville, NSW: McGraw Hill.

21

Life Coaching

Anthony M. Grant and Michael J. Cavanagh

INTRODUCTION

One way to develop an understanding of life coaching is to contrast it with counselling and mentoring, and executive and workplace coaching. Counselling tends to focus on helping people regain functionality in their lives, whereas mentoring involves one person with expertise in a specific area helping another in making significant transitions in knowledge, work or thinking (Megginson & Clutterbuck, 1995). Executive coaching focuses on helping clients who have managerial responsibility in organizations to achieve goals that improve their professional performance, and consequently the effectiveness of the client's organization (Kilburg, 2000). Executive coaching is typically (but not always) paid for by the organization. Workplace coaching takes place in work settings with non-executive employees. It may include on-the-job coaching by line managers and supervisors, aimed at improving productivity and developing an individual worker's skill.

In contrast to the above, life coaching is less about restoring or improving functionality and more about enhancing existing well-being. It typically tends to focus on goals that fall within the personal sphere rather than the work or employment sphere. Thus the overarching aim of life coaching is sustained cognitive, emotional and behavioural changes that facilitate goal attainment and the enhancement of performance and well-being in one's life (Douglas & McCauley, 1999).

Life coaching takes a personal values-based, holistic approach to personal change and development: the coachee spends time examining and evaluating his or her life, and then systematically makes life-enhancing changes with the support of a coach. Key issues often focus on work–life balance, dealing with stress, managing finances, enhancing relationships and generally developing a more fulfilling and purposeful life. Some life coaches have specialities, such as a focus on helping people work through major life transitions or developing new career directions; others focus on helping people develop a clear sense of purpose and life direction. Life coaches tend to provide a service to individual clients, rather than organizations, and the clients themselves invariably pay for the coaching services.

The human potential movement and life coaching

The roots of contemporary life coaching appear to emerge from humanistic traditions of psychology (e.g. Maslow, 1954), and the practices of the Human Potential Movement (HPM) (for a detailed discussion, see Spence, 2007). One of the key influences were the Erhard Seminars Training or EST programmes developed by Werner Erhard (Kirsch & Glass, 1977). These were marketed as personal transformation, and as such can be considered as drawing on the same social impetus that later gave rise to life coaching. Indeed, one of the early pioneers of commercial life coach training, Thomas Leonard, drew heavily on these approaches in the life coach training programmes offered by his company, Coach U.

Parallel with the growth of HPM and the life coaching genre, psychologists were also drawing on validated clinical and counselling psychology and offering life coaching services. As far back as Filippi (1968) and Ponzo (1977) there have been discussions in the psychology literature about the need for counsellors to act as life-skills coaches. Albert Ellis (e.g. Ellis & Harper, 1961), one of the founders of the cognitive–behavioural approach, frequently prefigures life coaching, although he did not use the term in his work. Similarly, commentators such as Thompson (1980) predicted that by the year 2000 psychologists would have increased their emphasis on life quality enhancement as opposed to remedial therapy.

Despite these early trends, psychology as an academic discipline and a helping profession tended to be associated, at least in the public's mind, with mental illness and the treatment of distress, rather than the promotion of well-being. Psychology did not truly engage with life coaching until the early pioneers of commercial life coaching in the US, such as Thomas Leonard, had raised the profile of life coaching and life coach training during the late 1980s and early 1990s. However, at this time life coaching was still viewed by many as being faddish, theoretically incoherent, new-age and more of a network marketing opportunity than a solid helping modality.

However, as public interest in life coaching has developed there has been a significant shift towards a theoretically-grounded and empirically-validated approach to life coaching. Some of the drivers of this include interest from researchers and academics in the use of life coaching as a methodology for developing understanding of the processes underpinning human change and development (Grant, 2003); greater sophistication in the consumers of coaching services (both clients and trainee coaches) (Jarvis, 2003); and the increasing involvement of psychologists who offer life-coach training courses. In addition, a number of universities worldwide now offer postgraduate degrees in coaching.

The literature on life coaching also reflects this shift, with increasing numbers of life coaching books being published that are explicitly grounded in evidence-based methodologies (e.g. Grant & Greene, 2001; Neenan & Dryden, 2002). This trend toward a more professional approach is also reflected in the fact that professional bodies such as the Psychological Societies of Australia, Britain, Denmark, Ireland, South Africa and others have established groups focused on coaching.

Emergence of evidence-based approaches

An evidence-based approach to life coaching can be distinguished from approaches to coaching that are based on ad hoc adaptations of 'pop-psychology' or personal development programmes. Adapted from its use in medical settings, the term 'evidence-based coaching' refers to the intelligent and conscientious use of best current knowledge in making decisions about how to deliver coaching to coaching clients, and in designing and teaching coach training programmes (Sackett, Haynes, Guyatt, & Tugwell, 1996). Best current knowledge is up-to-date, empirically valid and conceptually coherent, from relevant areas such as behavioural science, adult education, business, and philosophy.

Evidence-based approaches to life coaching came to the fore with the establishment of peer-reviewed coaching-specific journals such as the *International Journal of Evidence-based Coaching and Mentoring* (2003), *the International Coaching Psychology Review* (2006), and *Coaching: An International Journal of Theory, Research and Practice* (2008). Indeed, the total number of peer-reviewed coaching-specific publications has increased dramatically. However, despite these recent developments and the increased flow of coaching-related research, research specifically into life coaching is surprisingly scarce. A literature search of the peer-reviewed literature, as presented in the data base PsycINFO in August 2008, using the key words 'life coaching', found a total of 59 citations. The majority of these were reviews of books on life coaching, or editorials or details of book chapters which were about life coaching. There was a total of only 23 peer-reviewed papers on life coaching.

The lack of life coaching research means that there is little solid empirical data to guide the conscientious professional life coach. Consequently, in order to design and deliver solid life coaching services, the professional life coach needs to be well-versed in identifying relevant knowledge from related areas such as counselling psychology, positive psychology, theories of adult learning and human development. Thus the scholar practitioner model may be a useful professional framework for life coaching. The scholar practitioner knows how to access, evaluate and adapt information in order to best meet the needs of their client. Such a stance towards professional practice requires constructive self-reflection (McGonagill, 2002) and an explicit articulation and examination of the assumptions, methods and techniques used in life coaching practice.

MAIN ASSUMPTIONS AND LINKS TO THEORETICAL TRADITIONS

Understandings of life coaching vary in the extent to which they focus on personal development compared to the achievement of performance targets. Approaches fall on a continuum between facilitation of self-directed learning at one end and the sort of direct instruction found in sport coaching or educational tutoring at the other. Most approaches to life coaching fall between these two ends of the continuum. The role of the life coach is seen as conducting coaching conversations in which the coach asks direct, personal and often challenging questions that help the coachee focus on clarifying and exploring ways to achieve their goals. In the life coaching relationship, the coach primarily plays the role of a facilitator of change; it is the client's responsibility to enact change (Whitworth, Kimsey-House, & Sandahl, 1998).

Underlying the practice of life coaching are the assumptions that:

- People have considerable latent potential.
- Significant human change is possible.
- The client is resourceful (although they may not be aware of such resources).
- There is an absence of serious mental health problems in the life coaching client.
- Life coaching is not focused on repairing psychopathologies.
- Life coaching is an inherently goal-focused process.
- Change can happen in a short period of time.
- The client is willing to do the work of change.

Such assumptions suggest that professional life coaching has very clear links to at least four established theoretical traditions. First, life coaching tends to make explicit the relationships between thinking, feelings, behavioural and the external situation or environment, echoing the central aspects of cognitive–behavioural approaches. Second, life coaching is solution-focused, focuses on goals rather than the past, and assumes that the client has resources, strengths and abilities hereto unrecognized. Third, life coaching draws very heavily on humanistic values central to the person-centred tradition. Finally, life coaching is increasingly aligned with positive psychology, with its emphasis on understanding the nature of the life well-lived and the use of a grounded systematic approach to achieving that life.

The notion that most people have latent potential dates back to Aristotle and can be followed through to Maslow (1968) and more recently into the Positive Psychology movement (Ryff & Singer, 2008). Indeed, there is substantial empirical evidence that people have considerable latent potential which can be brought to the fore in many areas of life, including sports, human performance broadly defined, education, business and mental health (for in-depth analysis, see Druckman & Bjork, 1991). Further, solution focused approaches to human change, which explicitly operationalize the assumption that people have unacknowledged resources, have been found to be effective ways of helping people in a wide range of settings (Kim, 2008; Stams, Dekovic, Buist, & de Vries, 2006).

However, the a priori assumption that clients who present for life coaching do not have clinically significant levels of mental health problems may not be justified. Green, Oades and

Grant (2006) surveyed a total of 107 potential life coaching clients from a community sample and found that 52% had clinically elevated scores (a score of two standard deviations above the mean) on the Brief Symptom Inventory (BSI) (Derogatis & Melisaratos, 1983). The BSI is a frequently used and well-validated screening tool that is designed to be used with both clinical and non-clinical populations. Spence and Grant (2007) found that 25% of 84 participants in life coaching had clinically elevated BSI scores. These findings suggest that some individuals who seek life coaching may have higher than average levels of psychopathology, and these findings clearly do not support the assumption that there is an absence of serious mental health problems in life coaching clients. These findings have important implications and challenges for the ethical practice of life coaching.

APPROACHES, PROCESSES AND THE COACH–CLIENT RELATIONSHIP

Much life coaching takes place over the telephone. Indeed, some life coaches never meet their clients face-to-face. There has been some controversy over whether face-to-face or phone life coaching is more effective, although some of this debate appears to have been fuelled by a need to promote specific proprietary coach training systems that use face-to-face coaching methodologies (see Corbett, 2006). In fact there is a growing body of evidence from the mental health area that phone coaching can be effective (Evans, Morgan, Hayward, & Gunnel, 1999), and it has been shown that peer coaching by phone can be very effective in enhancing professional skills in the workplace (Gattellari, Donnelly, Taylor, Meerkin, Hirst, & Ward, 2005), but there is little or no empirical outcome research in life coaching that compares phone with face-to-face coaching. Its exponents argue that phone coaching, when conducted properly, is very time efficient and facilitates a direct, honest, and intimate relationship in which the absence of physical cues actually enhances rapport through the need for in-depth listening (Hymer, 1984).

The internal structuring of life coaching sessions, whether by phone or face-to-face, is a key area in need of further research. There is evidence that highly structured interventions may be very effective. For example Howard, Kopta, Krause and Orlinsky (1986) found that the frequency of counselling sessions was not related to client improvements, rather the structure and intensity of sessions were the key important factors. Furthermore, there is good evidence that effective change requires scaffolding. Scaffolding is a strategy that involves supporting novice learners by making the initial learning context quite simple and this is done by initially limiting the complexities of the context and gradually removing those as learners gain the knowledge, skills and confidence to cope with the full complexity of learning target (Young, 1993). At the same time, an over-structured approach to life coaching may be alienating for some clients, particularly where the coach's relationship building skills are not sophisticated or where the coach is not able to tailor their approach to suit the needs of the individual client.

Individual approaches to life coaching will vary depending on factors such as the coach's training, theoretical approach, personal preferences and personality, and client needs and expectations. However, the degree to which life coaches adopt a systematic structured approach to coaching is unclear. What is clear is that many of the proprietary commercial life coach training programmes place great emphasis on structure. This is because highly structured, systemized life coaching programmes that emphasize technique and methodology are easier to teach to potential life coaches than programmes that require broad understanding of theoretical principles and empirical evidence. The 'seven steps to your ideal life' approach is easier to understand than programmes that teach from theory into practice. Thus a highly structured, systemized approach is well-suited to the teleclass teaching and the highly heterogonous student populations that are frequently found in commercial life coach training programmes (Grant & O'Hara, 2006).

Contracting and payment issues

The great majority of problems that might emerge in life coaching can be circumvented by having clear, detailed and explicit up-front contracting. Contracting is a core process in life coaching and is used to make explicit the nature of the coaching relationship, the expectations and responsibilities of all parties, including costs, confidentiality issues, legal disclaimers and payment procedures and cancellation fees. A life coaching contracting agreement typically also includes a mental health/illness disclosure clause along the lines of 'coaching is not therapy and does not aim to treat psychological problems. The client agrees to disclose full details of past or present psychological or psychiatric treatment. If such issues become salient during the coaching relationship the coach may recommend referral to an appropriate and qualified specialist'. Written contracting can also be an effective way of enhancing commitment to the change process (see for example, Leung, 1974; Neale, Singleton, Dupuis, & Hess, 1990).

Life coaching clients are often asked to pay for their coaching service in advance and this requirement may also be part of the written coaching agreement (Leshinsky, 2007). However, the issue of advance payment for coaching services is somewhat controversial. It is often justified to clients by claiming that it enhances commitment to the coaching process. But emphasis on advance payment may be distasteful for some life coaching clients, giving the impression that the life coach is more interested in running a smooth, coach focused business operation than focusing on client needs. Interestingly, executive coaching services, which are perceived as being more professional than life coaching services, are typically paid for following delivery.

A key difference between life coaching and executive or workplace coaching is that the life coaching client is typically paying for the coaching service themselves, and this can impact on the dynamics of the coach–client relationship. Where in executive coaching the coaching engagement is frequently overseen by an internal sponsor such as a human resources or learning and development professional, in life coaching the coachee is the paying client and there is no third party involved. This means that life coaching may be at greater risk of derailment, and life-coaching clients should always check to see if their life coach has a supervisor or mentor coach who oversees their life coaching practice.

GOAL SETTING IN LIFE COACHING

Little research has focused on the process of goal setting in life coaching, but anecdotal evidence suggests that the completion of some type of structured life inventory is often used as a precursor to goal setting in this context. These inventories can range from idiosyncratic 'ideal life' checklists to the use of scientifically validated inventories such as the Quality of Life Inventory (QOLI) (Frisch, 1994). Inventories such as the QOLI are well suited for goal setting in life coaching because of their clear non-pathological orientation and their emphasis on strengths as well as problems. The QOLI assesses life satisfaction in 16 domains of life including health, home, money, work, relationships and play and can be used as an outcome measure to assess the effectiveness of the coaching intervention.

The number of goals set in life coaching will vary. Some life coaches suggest that clients focus on only one or two goals, others encourage clients to set more and address whole of life issues (Williams & Davis, 2002). Often, life coaching clients will be encouraged to complete a written pre-prepared form detailing their goals, and possibly writing down the costs and benefits of goal attainment.

On the other hand, some life coaching programmes pay little attention to the quality of the goal identification process itself. Rather, the main focus of attention is placed on developing motivation to change, designing action plans, overcoming barriers to change and supporting the client in making these changes. While these are important facets of coaching, they are dependent on the quality of the goal. Motivation will pall, and the best action plan will ultimately fail to deliver what the coachee is looking for if the goal is inappropriate.

Many life coach training organizations teach relatively simplistic approaches to goal setting; for example goal setting approaches that stop at the notion of 'SMART' goals (specific and stretching, measurable, achievable, realistic and time-framed). While there is good evidence that goals that meet these criteria can be effective (Locke, 1996), other dimensions of goals are also important. For example goals should be self-concordant. That is, they should align with the client's personal values (see Sheldon, 2001). Similarly, locus of control and whether goals are approach goals or avoidance goals have a major impact on satisfaction and well-being. Some life coaching programmes do indeed place great emphasis on the explicit articulation of the client's values in the goal setting process. However, it is equally important that sufficient time be given to discussing the goals under consideration, rather than rushing to set a goal and quickly moving on to action: the 'rush to closure' can lead to derailment later in the coaching process.

Monitoring and evaluation between sessions

Good quality life coaching interventions place significant emphasis on pre-session preparation and the monitoring and evaluation of between-session action steps (sometimes called fieldwork or homework). Life coaching clients are often asked to complete a pre-session form in which they detail their progress to date, how they have been feeling since the last session, and what they want to get out of the upcoming session. Although such forms may appear simplistic, such pre-session work may help the client move from a contemplative to deliberative or action-focused mindset (Gollwitzer, 1999) and such mindset shifts can significantly impact on client engagement and goal attainment.

Following the life coaching session, many coaches ask their clients to complete a post-session self-evaluation form detailing the specific action steps to be completed before the next session, and asking the client to reflect on any insights or learnings that may have arisen in the coaching session. Such reflective practices are fundamental to creating purposeful change (Argyris, 2002) and are part of the self-regulation cycle of goal setting, action planning, acting, monitoring, evaluating and change that essentially underpins all forms of purposeful human change (Carver & Scheier, 1998).

A significant part of the life coach's role involves keeping the client on track for success. This is not always easy. Many people come to life coaching with the desire to create change. Fewer stay self-motivated as the work of change becomes real and difficult. For most people purposeful change is not easy. If it were easy then there would be no need for coaches or other professional change agents. Some life coaches request an email from the client each time the client completes one of the between-session action tasks. It can be helpful in maintaining motivation for the client to have to report their progress to the coach between coaching sessions. However, in their quest to help the client achieve their goals, novice or unskilled life coaches may seek too much between-session contact with the client and this may result in fostering dependency on the coach, a reduction in the client's sense of control and autonomy, or simply creating too much for the client to do, leading to feelings of overwhelm. In these cases goals set in coaching can begin to feel like gaols.

Ending the coaching relationship

Even with clear upfront contracting about the coaching relationship, the termination phase of the life coaching relationship, as in therapy and mentoring, can be a difficult process for both coach and client (for a detailed empirical analysis of relationship endings, see Clutterbuck & Lane, 2004). Where the coaching relationship has not been great, both parties may avoid discussing issues related to the termination of the coaching. In this situation at best there may be a brief 'thanks for your help, I'll be in touch' comment. Even worse, the client, feeling resentful and somewhat aggrieved, may simply keep cancelling meetings and let the coaching relationship drift away.

Where the coaching relationship has been good, both parties may avoid the question of whether the coaching engagement has reached a natural end-point and may seek to continue coaching beyond its usefulness. It is natural to feel sadness when an important relationship is coming to an end – such close relationships have typically been formed based on discussion of personal and often emotionally-laden material (Cavanagh & Grant, 2004). However, it is important for both coach and client to recognize that coaching is ultimately a professional relationship, not a personal one. The coach's role is to prepare the client for the termination phase from the beginning of the coaching engagement. After all, one key aim of coaching is that the client becomes their own coach!

Ideally the initial life coaching contract should detail how the coaching relationship will be reviewed and terminated. Many coaching contracts state a set period of time, or a fixed number of sessions following which the coaching will be reviewed, and a decision made to continue or not. The temptation for the inexperienced life coach may be to press for continuation in the pursuit of building their coaching business. The temptation for the client in this situation may be to avoid a discussion about the termination process, and carry on with the coaching in order not to upset the coach. The danger in this is that the client may come to feel that coaching (and the coach) is not serving their needs and at worst, come to resent the time and costs coaching places on them. Clearly this is an unsatisfactory outcome for both coach and coachee.

Given that coaching relationships per se can arouse significant emotions for both the coach and the client (Cox & Bachkirova, 2007), the professional coach has a responsibility to proactively manage the termination process. It is important to recognize that the coaching relationship is a multifaceted one with at least three sub-themes: (i) a valued relationship, (ii) trust and (iii) transparency (Gyllensten & Palmer, 2007). Termination should therefore be dealt with in a way that is transparent, builds trust, and recognizes the value of the past relationship.

Termination of a life coaching engagement may be brought about not only by a pre-agreed timeframe. It may happen quite organically. It should be recognized by the coach that the dynamics of the relationship will change significantly over time. When the client first starts coaching, and intimacy between the coach and client is relatively low, the coach's energy and enthusiasm may be high, and delivering tangible benefits may be at the forefront of the coach's mind in each session. As the relationship develops, greater intimacy between coach and client may lead to less focus on tangible benefits. In short, the coaching sessions become less about goal attainment and more like supportive counselling, or even friends having a nice chat. When this starts to happen, it may be a sign that the coaching relationship has run a natural course, irrespective of any predetermined timeframe. The coach needs to address this issue by holding an open and frank review session in which the client has the opportunity to talk about the coaching and then set new goals, make purposeful and specific changes in how the coaching is conducted, or take a break from coaching for a while.

Controversial points in life coaching: coach or couch?

Although the relationship between coaching and counselling is complex, one key difference between life coaching and therapeutic counselling or psychotherapy is that therapeutic counselling and psychotherapy mainly focus on helping people recover from psychological distresses, and life coaching is not focused on addressing this. Rather, life coaching is about fine-tuning one's life.

The reason for emphasizing the distinction between the therapeutic foci of counselling and the aim of life coaching is because most coaches are not trained, registered or licenced as mental health professionals (Bachkirova, 2007; Grant & Zackon, 2004). Clearly, the public is at risk when coaches who are untrained in mental health interventions attempt to treat psychological problems such as depression, acute anxiety, substance abuse or major relationship difficulties, or because they do not recognize or take into account the nature of the vulnerabilities of people with mental health problems (Cavanagh, 2005).

This is not to say that coaches cannot coach people who are suffering from such problems. There is emerging research suggesting that coaching in conjunction with medical interventions can be very successful. Indeed, a well-trained life coach who works in conjunction with a trained (mental) health professional may be able to significantly speed the client's recovery. Edelman et al. (2006) describe how a whole-person approach to treating and minimizing cardiovascular risk factors which used health coaches alongside medical practitioners was successful in terms of increased exercise, weight loss and decreased risk of coronary heart disease. The key issue here is that coaches should know the limits of their expertise and they should work with appropriately trained professionals in designing interventions with the client.

However, the boundaries between a life coaching relationship and a counselling or psycho-therapeutic relationship are not clearly defined. The conversation can easily turn from coaching to counselling. Given that it has been found that between 25% and 50% of people seeking life coaching have clinically significant levels of psychopathology (Green et al., 2006; Spence & Grant, 2007), it may well be that some clients are using life coaching as de facto forms of therapy. Thus, life coaches have an unequivocal duty of care to ensure that they can recognize the limits of their competencies and make appropriate referrals (Buckley, this volume; Spence, Cavanagh, & Grant, 2006).

THE CHALLENGES AND LIMITATIONS OF LIFE COACHING

From the perspective of practice, the lack of clear training guidelines, industry regulation and rigorous accreditation represent real risks to the emerging profession of coaching. At present there are no barriers to entry in life coaching. Anyone, with or without training, can offer life coaching services. It is this lack of standards that has led to the variability in quality of service offered by life coaches and in turn led to its poor reputation even within the wider coaching industry.

There is a further challenge that faces life coaching that is perhaps more worrying than the quality of service issues that arise with under-trained coaches. A basic tenet of all professional codes of ethics is the requirement that professionals know the limits of their expertise and operate within those limits. There are within the wider life coaching industry individuals who are offering services aimed at addressing serious difficulties for which the individual has no training or qualification beyond their own assertion of expertise. For example, untrained individuals are purporting to offer coaching for such conditions as ADHD, anorexia or relationship difficulties. Furthermore, some coaches make claims of efficacy unsupported by any data. Such behaviour threatens the very integrity of the coaching endeavour.

In the area of practice development, the grounding of practice in theoretically coherent and evidenced-based models is the major challenge facing life coaching. For the industry to develop into a recognized area of professional practice, the development of a research based body of knowledge is essential. This raises a further challenge for life coaching – namely moving from an individual proprietary approach to practice towards a community of practice approach. To date the coaching industry has tended strongly toward basing practice on commercially owned proprietary models of coaching – many claiming to be the most or even only effective coaching model available. For coaching to progress beyond a proprietary product model of service to a genuine profession, there needs to be greater openness to having one's models of practice held up to rigorous peer-reviewed evaluation. More importantly, the widespread sharing of this research for the information and development of industry-wide practice is a key element in the creation of a profession of life coaching. This is a significant challenge to the way the life coaching industry appears to be organized at the moment.

EVALUATION

Evidence-based life coaching conducted by properly trained coaches who work within a scholar–practitioner model has terrific potential to contribute to the well-being of individual clients and communities. In effect, evidence-based life coaching conducted by well-trained practitioners has the potential to offer a much needed service in our society, where people can take time to review their life directions, take stock, explore new life options, develop new directions and get support in creating purposeful change and enhancing their well-being.

An evidence-based approach to life coaching has great potential as a means of facilitating positive change. Yet life coaching is frequently undervalued as a human change methodology. Greater status appears to go to executive, business or workplace coaching. There is something of false distinction in this. Drawing strong boundaries between life coaching and other forms of coaching neglects the commonalities of practice among them. At present, there are few encouragements for practising life coaches to develop a stronger research and knowledge base. However, this is a challenge to the industry – to step into the power of its own change methodology – both in terms of practice development, and demonstration of the efficacy and value of that practice. Perhaps the last word on the relative value of life coaching compared to other applications of coaching should go to Dr Patrick Williams

(Williams & Davis, 2002): 'No matter what's on your business card, if you're coaching a breathing client, you're life coaching because they have a life'.

FURTHER READING

Grant, A.M., & Greene, J. (2004). *Coach yourself: Make real change in your life* (2nd ed.). London: Momentum Press.
Neenan, M., & Dryden, W. (2002). *Life coaching: A cognitive-behavioural approach.* New York: Brunner-Routledge.
Whitworth, L., Kimsey-House, H., & Sandahl, P. (1998). *Co-active coaching: New skills for coaching people towards success in work and life.* Palo Alto, CA: Davies-Black.
Williams, P., & Menendez, D.S. (2007). *Becoming a professional life coach: Lessons from the institute for life coach training.* New York: Norton & Co.

REFERENCES

Argyris, C. (2002). Double-loop learning, teaching and research. *Academy of Management Learning and Education, 1*(2): 206–18.
Bachkirova, T. (2007). Role of coaching psychology in defining boundaries between counselling and coaching. In S. Palmer & A. Whybrow (Eds.), *Handbook of coaching psychology* (pp. 325–50). London: Routledge.
Carver, C.S., & Scheier, M.F. (1998). *On the self-regulation of behavior.* Cambridge: Cambridge University Press.
Cavanagh, M. (2005). Mental-health issues and challenging clients in executive coaching. In M. Cavanagh, A.M. Grant & T. Kemp (Eds.), *Evidence-based coaching* (vol 1): *Contributions from the behavioural sciences* (pp. 21–36). Bowen Hills, QLD: Australian Academic Press.
Cavanagh, M., & Grant, A.M. (2004). Executive coaching in organisations: The personal is the professional. *International Journal of Coaching in Organisations,* 6: 6–15.
Clutterbuck, D., & Lane, G. (Eds.). (2004*). The situational mentor: An international review of competences and capabilities in mentoring.* Aldershot: Gower.
Corbett, K. (2006). *The Sherpa report.* Cincinnati, OH: Sasha Corp.
Cox, E., & Bachkirova, T. (2007). Coaching with emotion: How coaches deal with difficult emotional situations. *International Coaching Psychology Review, 2*(2): 178–90.
Derogatis, L.R., & Melisaratos, N. (1983). The brief symptom inventory: An introductory report. *Psychological Medicine, 13*: 595–605.
Douglas, C.A., & McCauley, C.D. (1999). Formal developmental relationships: A survey of organizational practices. *Human Resource Development Quarterly, 10*(3): 203–20.
Druckman, D., & Bjork, R.A. (1991). *In the mind's eye: Enhancing human performance.* Washington, DC: National Academy Press.
Edelman, D., Oddone, E.Z., Liebowitz, R.S., Yancy, W.S., Jr., Olsen, M.K., Jeffreys, A.S., et al. (2006). A multidimensional integrative medicine intervention to improve cardiovascular risk. *Journal of General Internal Medicine, 21*(7): 728–34.
Ellis, A., & Harper, R.A. (1961). *A new guide to rational living.* Englewood Cliffs, NJ: Prentice-Hall.
Evans, M.O., Morgan, H.G., Hayward, A., & Gunnel, D.J. (1999). Crisis telephone coaching for deliberate self-harm patients: Effects on repetition. *British Journal of Psychiatry, 175*: 23–7.
Filippi, R. (1968). Coaching: A therapy for people who do not seek help. *Zeitschrift Fuer Psychotherapie und Medizinische Psychologie, 18*(6): 225–9.
Frisch, M.B. (1994). *Quality of life inventory.* Minneapolis, MN: National Computer Systems.

Gattellari, M., Donnelly, N., Taylor, N., Meerkin, M., Hirst, G., & Ward, J. (2005). Does 'peer coaching' increase GP capacity to promote informed decision making about PSA screening? A cluster randomised trial. *Family Practice*, *22*(3): 253–65.

Gollwitzer, P.M. (1999). Implementation intentions: Simple effects of simple plans. *American Psychologist*, *54*(7): 493–503.

Grant, A.M. (2003). The impact of life coaching on goal attainment, metacognition and mental health. *Social Behavior and Personality*, *31*(3): 253–64.

Grant, A.M., & Greene, J. (2001). *Coach yourself*. Cambridge, MA: Perseus Publishing.

Grant, A.M., & O'Hara, B. (2006). The self-presentation of commercial Australian life coaching schools: Cause for concern? *International Coaching Psychology Review*, *1*(2): 20–32.

Grant, A.M., & Zackon, R. (2004). Executive, workplace and life coaching: Findings from a large-scale survey of International Coach Federation members. *International Journal of Evidence-based Coaching and Mentoring*, *2*(2): 1–15.

Green, L., Oades, L., & Grant, A. (2006). Cognitive-behavioral, solution-focused life coaching: Enhancing goal striving, well-being, and hope. *The Journal of Positive Psychology*, *1*(3): 142–9.

Gyllensten, K., & Palmer, S. (2007). The coaching relationship: An interpretative phenomenological analysis. *International Coaching Psychology Review*, *2*(2): 168–77.

Howard, K.I., Kopta, S., Krause, M.S., & Orlinsky, D.E. (1986). The dose-effect relationship in psychotherapy. *American Psychologist*, *41*(2): 159–64.

Hymer, S.M. (1984). The telephone session and the telephone between sessions. *Psychotherapy in Private Practice*, *2*(3): 51–65

Jarvis, J. (2003). *Coaching and buying coaching services*. London: Chartered Institute of Personnel and Development.

Kilburg, R.R. (2000). *Executive coaching: Developing managerial wisdom in a world of chaos* (pp. 53–67). Washington, DC: American Psychological Association.

Kim, J.S. (2008). Examining the effectiveness of solution-focused brief therapy: A meta-analysis. *Research on Social Work Practice*, *18*(2): 107–16.

Kirsch, M.A., & Glass, L.L. (1977). Psychiatric disturbances associated with Erhard Seminars Training: II. Additional cases and theoretical considerations. *American Journal of Psychiatry*, *134*(11): 1254–58.

Leshinsky, M. (2007). *Coaching millions: Help more people, make more money, live your ultimate lifestyle*. New York: Xeno Press.

Leung, P. (1974). The use of behavior contracts in employability development planning. *Journal of Employment Counseling*, *11*(4): 150–3.

Locke, E.A. (1996). Motivation through conscious goal setting. *Applied & Preventive Psychology*, *5*(2): 117–24.

McGonagill, G. (2002). The coach as reflective practitioner. In C. Fitzgerald & J.G. Berger (Eds.), *Executive coaching: Practices and perspectives* (pp. 59–88). Palo Alto, CA: Davies-Black.

Maslow, A.H. (1954). *Motivation and personality*. Oxford: Harpers.

Maslow, A.H. (1968). *Towards a psychology of being*. New York: Wiley & Sons.

Megginson, D., & Clutterbuck, D. (1995). *Mentoring in action: A practical guide for managers*. London: Kogan Page.

Neale, A.V., Singleton, S.P., Dupuis, M.H., & Hess, J.W. (1990). The use of behavioral contracting to increase exercise activity. *American Journal of Health Promotion*, *4*(6), 441–7.

Neenan, M., & Dryden, W. (2002). *Life coaching: A cognitive-behavioural approach*. New York: Brunner-Routledge.

Ponzo, Z. (1977). Back to basics: The counsellor-coach. *Canadian Counsellor*, *12*(1): 55–8.

Ryff, C., & Singer, B. (2008). Know thyself and become what you are: A eudaimonic approach to psychological well-being. *Journal of Happiness Studies*, *9*(1): 13–39.

Sackett, D.L., Haynes, R.B., Guyatt, G.H., & Tugwell, P. (1996). Evidenced based medicine: What it is and what is isn't. *British Medical Journal*, *13:* 71–2.

Sheldon, K.M. (2001). The self-concordance model of healthy goal striving: When personal goals correctly represent the person. In P. Schmuck & K.M. Sheldon (Eds.), *Life goals and well-being: Towards a positive psychology of human striving* (pp. 18–36). Kirkland, WA: Hogrefe & Huber.

Spence, G.B. (2007). Further development of evidence-based coaching: Lessons from the rise and fall of the human potential movement. *Australian Psychologist, 42*(2): 255–65.

Spence, G.B., & Grant, A.M. (2007). Professional and peer life coaching and the enhancement of goal striving and well-being: An exploratory study. *Journal of Positive Psychology, 2*(3): 185–94.

Spence, G.B., Cavanagh, M.J., & Grant, A.M. (2006). Duty of care in an unregulated industry: Initial findings on the diversity and practices of Australian coaches. *International Coaching Psychology Review, 1*(1): 71–85.

Stams, G.J., Dekovic, M., Buist, K., & de Vries, L. (2006). Efficacy of solution-focused brief therapy: A meta-analysis. *Gedragstherapie, 39*(2): 81–94.

Thompson, A.S. (1980*).* Counseling psychology in the year 2000. *Counseling Psychologist, 8*(4): 21–2.

Whitworth, L., Kimsey-House, H., & Sandahl, P. (1998). *Co-active coaching: New skills for coaching people towards success in work and life.* Palo Alto, CA: Davies-Black.

Williams, P., & Davis, D.C. (2002). *Therapist as life coach: Transforming your practice.* New York: Norton.

Young, M.F. (1993). Instructional design for situated learning. *Educational Technology Research & Development, 41*(1): 43–58.

22

Career Coaching

Bruce Hazen and Nicole A. Steckler

INTRODUCTION

Career management is a process that all workers engage in, consciously or unconsciously. Career coaches bring the advantage of insight, information and planned action to the pursuit of goals, such as:

1. choosing work (career decision making)
2. moving up in a profession, job or organization (development strategy)
3. moving out, by choice, of a form of work or an organization (career transition strategy to find work or create entrepreneurial work)
4. finding work after job loss (job search strategy)
5. planning for the end of paid work and the beginning of a period of generativity (focusing on the developmental issues of up-and-coming generations).

Insight is gained through a process of dialogue, appreciative inquiry, interpretation, reframing, assessment and other classic counselling techniques. Information and education is a product of the career coaching process as the coach adds both wisdom and knowledge about various work cultures, processes and styles that clients may lack. Career coaching is one of the most focused, result-oriented forms of coaching because of the clearly defined presence of work as an end goal. Achieving that goal also means a coach must prepare a client to enter the marketplace in a knowledgeable and astute way, exhibiting tactics and behaviours that are appropriate to that work culture.

The concept of 'vocational guidance' was developing within North American schools in the early 1900s, and during that timeframe Frank Parsons was credited with founding career guidance and starting the Vocation Bureau of Boston. Subsequent research and models of career theory and guidance were developed throughout the 20th century by such thinkers as John Holland, Edgar Schein, Donald Super (Blustein, 2006), and, more recently, Richard Bolles (2008), Charles Hakim (1994) and Ken Dychtwald (2005).

GOALS AND TASKS

Career coaching goals can range from the tactical and measurable (lost a job, find a new one) to the more intra-psychic and intangible. Coaches assist in the establishment of a satisfying marriage of work and current identity, where work fits the character, competencies, values and experiences of the coachee. At the same time, career coaching seeks to benignly disturb the current identity, then design and guide the experiments necessary to refine and develop that identity to its next stage of actualization.

Looking again at the five areas of career coaching work, there are key tasks that enable goals of coaching and career management to be realized (see Table 22.1). The goals in these areas are cognitive, emotional and behavioural.

Many of these career coaching goals and tasks are demonstrated by the case of a senior engineering manager in an international heavy manufacturing company who sought coaching

Table 22.1:   Goals, objectives and processes in career coaching

Goals of Career Coaching	Coachee objectives	Coaching processes
1. Choosing work	Gain self-insight and realistic knowledge of both self and the work culture coachee hopes to join. Learn the behavioural skills needed to study the market through networking. Feel confident enough to make a choice	Conduct assessments. Gather family and personal history of work. Educate about skills, jobs and work organizations. Direct field research. Conduct behavioural skills practice (networking, interviewing).
2. Moving up in profession or organization	Advance in competency, complexity of work, authority and status.	Development planning. Assess and measure current and desired future state and help coachee measure and close the gaps that exist. Action learning design. Mentor or sponsor identification. New job launch plan.
3. Moving out, by choice	Leave a job, organization or profession in a timely and judicious way. Find or create a job or an entrepreneurial endeavour.	Define exit strategy and timing issues. Create a job-search campaign. Assess entrepreneurial readiness and create a plan for starting a business. Create new job launch plan.
4. Finding work after job loss	Replace work lost due to poor performance, job elimination, retirement or other involuntary means.	Same as 'Moving Out' above with the addition of assessing and processing potential emotional, financial and skill deficit issues that temporarily lower client effectiveness. New job launch plan.
5. Ending current work	Retire (many definitions). Rehire into new or same roles / new or same organization. Volunteer. Mentor others.	Explore client values and framework for defining and living in retirement. Define roles, organizations and needs that contain work opportunities unfettered by the need for a full pay check or established 'job'.

as he anticipated the loss of his job when a product-line reached its projected end of life, and needed to define and choose among options, including:

- deciding to leave on his own by activating an early retirement
- considering unpaid work in retirement to fulfil sociopolitical values
- waiting to be laid off and receiving a severance package
- beginning a job search while currently working, so as to land a new job prior to job elimination.

The challenge for the coach was to utilize knowledge of work culture and client values to consider how age, gender, social class, language, family expectations, the larger culture and the economy all interact in career strategy design and execution. For example entrepreneurial options might abound for an engineer in California. A French engineer might have a socially sponsored financial system to lend predictability to retirement plans. A 28-year-old female engineer in Russia or Iran (or from similar cultures) might have cultural and family expectations that would weigh heavily in strategy design, even if the options under consideration were those listed above.

FEATURES, PROCESSES AND ROLES

Career coaching takes place in a wide range of contexts and life stages. High schools, colleges and universities offer career services including assessment and advising. Individuals who lose their jobs as part of lay-offs are often offered outplacement services, usually from an outplacement firm on contract with the downsizing organization. Experiences in these two contexts in particular may colour the potential coachee's expectations of what career coaching has to offer. Other coachees may arrive at career coaching along a similar path to those seeking life coaching or leadership/job effectiveness coaching. Coachees may be motivated by dissatisfaction with their current work situation, by wanting to contribute more and seek advancement, by attraction to a different line of work, by an upcoming planned retirement, and/or by experiencing transitions that could be described as 'mid-life crises'.

'Plan and implement' v. 'test and learn' approaches

Two guiding concepts of how career planning unfolds can be used to clarify the coaching process and the role of the career coach. The 'plan and implement' approach starts with analysis, followed by action, creating a linear path toward a clear goal; the 'test and learn' approach starts with action, followed by analysis, leading to other actions, creating a cycle of testing and learning (Ibarra, 2004).

Each of these approaches is based on different underlying assumptions about human personality. The 'plan and implement' philosophy builds on the notion that that each of us has a core 'true' self, and that personality is consistent if not immutable. In this tradition career planning and/or transition builds on introspection and assessment in order to uncover an appropriate career fit for that individual. In contrast, the 'test and learn' approach takes as its starting place notions of human personality as a collection of 'possible' selves, including those that repel us as well as those that attract us. Within this philosophy career transition then becomes a process of what Ibarra (2004) calls 'crafting experiments': trying out new actions, professional relationships, and stories that offer opportunities to explore 'possible selves' in a low-cost, low-risk way; then reflecting on the resulting experiences in terms of fit, and crafting the next round of experiment, progressing, over time, from lower-risk exploratory experiments to more confirmatory experiments that would require greater investment.

These are useful to the coach as guiding frameworks and particularly useful at different career stages. For example, plan and implement may be particularly useful for job search after lay-off, when the goal is immediate re-employment in a similar role; test and learn may be especially appropriate for a mid-career individual considering a significant change in profession.

Less obvious (but equally important) is the internal preference the coachee (and the coach) may have for these styles of engagement with career planning. Some coachees may prefer a more mechanistic, linear, structured 'engineering' approach, while others may prefer a more organic, exploratory 'experiment' process. The successful career coaching outcome depends on fit between the coachee's career situation and goals/needs, the coachee's style preference and personality, and the coach's strengths and preferences. The greater the breadth of skills and range of approaches offered by the coach, the greater the coach's flexibility and ability to meet the needs of a wide range of coachees.

The coach and coachee each come to the relationship with existing beliefs about career development and preferences for either a more organic or mechanistic process for coaching and for career exploration. Ideally, the coach is equipped to be able to work along the whole spectrum in order to match the coachee's needs, as well as expand the coachee's capacity to meet a real challenge that may not conform to their initial worldview. With a coachee whose natural preference is for a more linear, mechanistic process, the coach serves as a guide along the way in the more organic process of 'crafting experiments'. With a coachee whose natural preference is more evolutionary and organic, the coach provides guidance and structure as necessary for the coachee to reach his or her goals.

Life cycle of a career coaching relationship

Contracting

Contracting can be thought of as the coach and coachee coming together to decide what destination they are aiming for and what methods they want to use to get there. The coach must establish a connection and understanding of the coachee's current situation, and partner with the coachee around change. The contracting stage clarifies roles and goals: What is the coachee seeking to accomplish and what role is he or she looking for the coach to play? In this phase the coach gauges the sophistication of the coachee to see if he or she has accurately differentiated between how the coach might act as a consultant, networking facilitator, and/or introduction agent (likely roles) versus a talent agent, a publicist or recruiter (unlikely roles). Clarifying the role expectations of the coachee may lead to a referral for the type of service the coachee is seeking.

Sometimes contracting comes up again at a middle stage of a coaching engagement. For example with a coachee who loses an engineering job as part of a corporate downsizing, the initial contract may be for job search. Through the initial coaching sessions an underlying awareness emerges that the coachee does not want to return to the same type of large corporate setting. ('So, you don't know what you want to do, but you know you don't want to go back to the cubicle farm?' 'Yes!') The coach expands the initial contracting to clarify whether there is an immediate necessity to find work, or whether the coachee has the financial and emotional capacity to explore career change at this time. If the latter, the contract switches out of the initial plan and implement job search agreement to more of a test and learn career change exploration.

Assessment

The assessment phase of coaching goes deeper into goals: what depth of career exploration is the coachee seeking? A primary value of assessment is the ability to get at skills and preferences in a more value-neutral way, away from the job/company context. Coachees identify what parts of previous jobs they have liked and disliked, and what skills are personal strengths for them versus requirements of previous jobs. Multiple methods may be used: interviews (structured/open ended), psychometric instruments, and/or self-reflection exercises are all options. Assessment can offer the coachee both objectivity and movement early in the coaching process.

At this point the focus also shifts into deeper assessment of the individual: how congruent are they with the goal being articulated? The process is different from psychological assessment, although occasionally coaching assessment uncovers a psychological dynamic that is interfering with career and relationships at work, in which case the coach would refer the coachee for psychological work prior to proceeding with career coaching.

Action planning

The heart of the action-planning stage is to agree upon the behaviours that will get the coachee to the goal agreed upon in the assessment stage. The degree of structure or spontaneity may differ depending on whether the pair use a more plan and implement or test and learn approach. With either approach the coachee and coach must define, at least roughly, a professional objective. In the 'test and learn' approach the objective may change as a result of the very method being used, but the process is never a random curiosity search. For that, there is no need to pay a coach.

Market inquiry

Next, the coachee collects data from the employment market and sifts though the evidence, analysing it as market feedback. One successful method for this process starts with designing a 'focus of inquiry' (Hazen, 2007) by identifying a set of problems, issues, needs and trends (PINT) for analysis, relevant to the markets of interest, and about which the coachee would like to know more. This has the dual purpose of getting the coachee focused and knowledgeable about their job search or career change targets of interest in order to learn, and at the same time, position themselves as a somewhat knowledgeable peer in front of individuals who can start to get to know them as colleagues or 'tribe members'. This stage is the prelude to the employment stage, providing a chance to identify the areas in which coachees want to promote themselves. The career coach's role is both outward-focused and inward-focused in this stage; the coach is adding information and recommendations as to where to research (and with whom) and harnessing both their own knowledge and the knowledge and experience of previous clients to help in evaluating the results from the inquiry. The desired outcome is to narrow the inquiry down to the most fruitful areas of focus.

A critical point here is that the coach is chartered to hold awareness of the coachee's combined skills, values and interests and to be the constant reminder of their importance so the coachee is dissuaded from making an overly simplistic choice. For example a coachee whose strengths are not in sales discovers an exciting new product which can only be accessed through an entrepreneurial track. Here the role of the coach was to feed back the data and his/her own impressions that clearly pointed to a mismatch between the coachee's interests and skills, and the intense selling and marketing activity that would be required to start up this new business.

Respond and decide

A strong market inquiry stage leads naturally to responding to these discoveries or analyses with intensification of both focus and effort into a more select number of targets. While the market inquiry was more about outbound curiosity, the 'respond and decide' stage is more about responding to shared, mutual interest and intensifying efforts to promote yourself to the right audiences. If this stage is successful the ultimate result is an invitation or a contract to engage. An additional alternative at this stage is the entrepreneurial option, where coachees decide to become the owner–operator of their own business.

Entry plan

When the coachee is ready to accept a new position, the coach can act as corporate anthropologist to help the coachee anticipate the new roles, rules and expectations regarding entry into a new 'tribe'. This crucial stage is where the coachee learns the cultural customs of the newly chosen career and/or job in addition to acclimatizing to the new job responsibilities. A new job launch plan helps the coachee to harness the specific opportunities and resources available to them during the 'honeymoon' of the first few months in a new job.

When the coachee chooses the entrepreneurial option of starting a new business, the coach's role will differ, depending on the coach's background. One likely scenario may be that the coach guides or refers the coachee to someone who can guide the detailed construction of a business plan and or specialize in more quantitative analysis of financial aspects of their business idea (Horan, 1997, 2006).

Ending/disengagement

In the final phase of a career coaching engagement, the dual focus is both to help the coachee anticipate stages of future career development or distress, for which a career coach could be a resource. Disengagement can lay groundwork for prevention or early intervention if and when any bumps in the road present themselves.

In the phase immediately after a new job or artful career change, a not unexpected exhaustion often leaves coachees not very receptive to the notion of an 'always on' career management strategy. The coach can remind the coachee that if some unforeseen aspect of the new organization becomes problematic (and this is frequently the case), there is something they can do about it early on. The objective is to de-stigmatize and normalize the likely challenges that lie ahead, and to prepare the coachee to enter the next career phase with a greater sense of self-efficacy and empowerment.

DISTINCTIONS BETWEEN CAREER COACHING AND OTHER GENRES

There are numerous similarities between career coaching and the processes and goals of other forms of coaching. For example we have identified 'moving up' or development within a job, organization or profession as one of the arenas of work of the career coach. Clearly Performance Coaching could work on this same agenda and would contribute to the skills and behaviours needed to network or interview in a job search process. Life coaching and executive coaching would join with career coaching in the development of self-efficacy as a client takes on their personal, internal debate over a significant leadership role or promotion and the approach-avoidance which that might engender.

The following three genres of coaching discussed in this Handbook contrast more sharply with career coaching.

Manager as coach

On the surface one might suggest that a manager is in a perfect position to coach with regard to career goals and strategies. But the career coach is crucially different from a manager regarding assessment skills, objectivity and confidentiality. Managers who are managing in a coaching style are still charged with inspiring and creating business results. Their motivations and incentives are geared for the good of the organization, not the individual. Career coaching and career strategy is decidedly person-centered.

Team coaching

Again, this form of coaching has the good of the group (team), as opposed to the individual, in mind. While an individual may gain work-related insight from team coaching, the ultimate purpose is to better the performance and results produced by the team. Team coaching could, at times, be distracting from personal career strategy refinement. One of the persistent skill issues career coaches work on is their coachees' culturally learned inability to tell an accomplishment story that focuses on their own contribution and not on a nameless, faceless collection of people back in their former organization, called 'the team'. Remembering the goal of a job search strategy, the coach must be quite pragmatic about enabling their client to convey the team context but to focus on personal capabilities within that context.

Peer coaching

Career coaches must possess superior, broad knowledge of the world of work, and experience in the processes that govern the identification, recruitment, placement, development and movement of talent. Peers may only have this knowledge and training coincidentally. More dangerously, they may be unconscious of their limited scope of knowledge and experience but may generalize these perceptions, inappropriately, to their peer coachee's different areas of interest or inquiry.

One support used in job search can be built around a peer coaching model: the job search team. The job search team is chartered to supply peer support to encourage job search productivity, trade market intelligence, offer leads and networking introductions, and provide realistic feedback about individuals' search activity and communication style. Peers offer a form of 'street credibility' that can sometimes reset a misguided job search strategy faster than the professional language and demeanour of a typical coaching professional.

RELATIONSHIP BETWEEN CAREER COACHING AND THEORETICAL TRADITIONS

Career coaching uses a blend of different theoretical approaches. The following four are of particular relevance.

Cognitive–behavioural

Cognitive–behavioural approaches to coaching are particularly useful in working with two common career circumstances: coachees who have just been terminated or had their position eliminated, and coachees who are currently working through a conflict with their boss or have left an organization because of a conflict with their boss. This technique is particularly good for coachees who have anger or blame directed inward at themselves. For those individuals, the cognitive–behavioural model helps to clear the psychological obstacles before attempting to do career strategy work.

The coach's job is to listen for indicators of potentially irrational thinking such as the coachee's use of the phrases 'should', 'supposed to' and 'ought to'. For example a coachee was having difficulty accepting and moving beyond job loss in a lay-off situation. While expressing the (irrational) belief that she was incompetent, she didn't believe that any of the other 30 people who were laid off were incompetent. The coach used a cognitive–behavioural approach to confront the discrepancy, observing, 'You said these other 30 were competent professionals doing good work, so according to your "should", they should still have their jobs. So, since they don't have their jobs, let's look for some other rational explanation for why you don't have your job'.

Narrative

Narrative approaches to coaching link nicely with some of the theory of specialists in the field of occupational psychology. Holland (1997) refers to the Personal Career Theory (PCT) that individuals develop as a way to explain their perception of how their career choices and results play out. When the personal narrative that accompanies their PCT seems to fail to provide an adequate context for the events or strivings that are emerging in an individual's work life, help is often sought in the form of a coach.

We tend to screen out stories, facts, and even observations that are not congruent with the selective perception that accompanies our current story or theory. The career coach's role is to:

- assist the coachee with insight into current identity
- differentiate what Drake (2007) refers to as the available stories offered by our context, history, culture, family and even vocabulary, and the potential stories that can be created or co-created for a more congruent or fulfilling future
- explain or normalize the shifts in identity that occur with development, trauma, new relationships and age
- expand the possibilities to create new identities through the creation or co-creation of new narratives about work that respect the shifts or changes that are taking place and reflect the co-defined realities of the coachee's emerging context.

The recrafting of one's story can be particularly challenging for the individual who is shifting their working identity to a new career, not just a new job. Ibarra (2004) describes the three stages that require an individual to create new stories about themselves as seeker, in-between and 'ex'. The career coach can add value, speed and clarity to the creation of the new and various stories.

The coach can expedite the creation of new stories when working with coachees to interpret psychometric measures of their preferences and interests. Coaches can use the data as an opportunity to have coachees look at the other occupations that share the same interests and see these other occupations not as what they 'should become', but rather, as potential 'clients, customers or colleagues' in their future work. For example consider a coachee who is a history teacher and 20-year veteran of the classroom, and whose Strong Interest Inventory (2004) indicates similar interest patterns with occupations such as marketing executive, graphic artist, teacher, and technical writer. The coachee reacts negatively to the notion of becoming a marketing executive. The coach invites the coachee to transform that reaction by thinking of the marketing executive not as a career goal, but as a possible teammate. The coachee re-narrates a story as: 'Maybe I work for a textbook publisher and I'm on a team with a marketing executive, a graphic artist, and a technical writer, working together to design a textbook cover that will get students interested in learning history'.

When coachees complete this exercise, they have, essentially, created alternative stories about their working identities, starting with assessment-based data (as well as their coach's insights and observations) and projecting some of who they are or could be when inspired by some of that data.

Positive psychology

Career coaching draws many of its underlying assumptions from the theoretical perspective of positive psychology. A primary goal of career coaching is to assist the coachee in developing a nuanced understanding of his or her strengths and then translating or 'behaviouralizing' those strengths as they might be valued in the marketplace. A clear mutual understanding of the coachee's strengths is critical for constructing an answer to the question: 'What would success look like?'

Often, career coaches use approaches drawn from positive psychology to help coachees become aware of strengths that others perceive in them, as well as to revalue strengths of which they may already be aware. One approach used in leadership development contexts that may be adapted for use in career coaching is the 'reflected best self' exercise, in which individuals solicit feedback from a cross-section of colleagues, customers, friends and family members who know them well, asking them to 'tell me about a time when you saw me at my best: what did I say or do, and what was the impact you observed?' This is especially useful with coachees who are struggling to translate their accomplishments into summarized form for their résumés and/or examples to share during employment interviews.

Person-centred

Coaches and coachees often strive to bring analysis and data to their process but the coaching experience is often used more as a thinking-out-loud laboratory, which makes the person-centred approach to listening and deeply acknowledging the coachee's experience one of the most useful career coaching approaches.

In some instances, career coachees are aware of their strengths but their valuing of them has gone to neutral or negative. The neutral quality is created by the mental 'tornado' that they are in as they mentally spin around various key questions without coming to closure. For example, a coachee may find he/she starts conversations with him/herself about career change, maybe gathers a little information, gets distracted and moves on to other tasks, and then returns to the career question and starts the process all over again. The experience of many small whirlwinds throughout the day that never go anywhere is a depleting 'tornado' experience, creating zones of chaos and self-doubt as opposed to order or directionality.

Thinking of the career indecision 'tornado' as a set of run-on sentences, the person-centred coaching relationship inspires the coachee to better formulate the fragments and recursive thinking loops that have characterized their career change 'tornado' in order to present information to their coach. The process of creating and telling one's story often leads to insights – 'no, that's not quite how it happened' or 'I didn't realize I felt that way' – which create new awareness and understanding. Additional awareness and understanding often arise when the coach artfully acknowledges and/or reframes the patterns he or she is hearing in the coachee's story. The coach may at this juncture draw on narrative, cognitive–behavioural or other approaches for the next steps in the coaching process. All of them can be thought of as resting within the connectedness and trust created by the person-centred approach to listening and acknowledging the reality of the other person's experience.

EVALUATION

Career coaching is called for when coachees seek the benefit resulting from planned action, or when their personal career theories no longer seems to serve them in explaining the world of work and their place in it. Common constraints on the nature and success of career coaching include intra-psychic, interpersonal and socioeconomic constraints.

Intra-psychic and clinical issues may block client success. As coaches, we draw on psychological theories and traditions that are also the basis for therapy. When we assess the fabric of a coachee's life and start pulling a thread related to career, we can find ourselves unravelling marriage, family, alcoholism and depression issues that are not the purview of career coaches. Even with clinical background and training, the career coach has not entered into a therapeutic relationship and is not chartered to work in clinical areas and, therefore, runs the ethical risk of creating a 'dual relationship' with a coachee by engaging in psychotherapy in addition to career coaching. Psychological understanding is crucial so as to identify, but not treat, issues that are blocking progress. Referral knowledge is essential.

In other instances it is appropriate for the career coach to blend in other types of coaching. For example career and leadership coaching may be called for by coachees who are struggling within a management role. Coachees may prematurely flee a job or organization (and seek career coaching) due to discomfort with the role of manager. They may seek new jobs rather than address style, skill or knowledge shortcomings that could be addressed through coaching to enable them to successfully sustain the leadership role.

Being patient with the initial goal assessment may be difficult. It is crucial to sort out the differences between a career change strategy and a job search strategy early in the engagement. The lack of clarity or ambivalence of many clients will require patience and careful assessment on the part of the coach to determine the mission of their work together. Impatience can result from a poor match between a *goal-oriented* coach who is working with an *insight-oriented* client wanting to experiment with defining a new working identity. Alternatively, career coaching may be offered as part of an outplacement service that is time limited and driven by a sense of urgency or quality metrics that do not similarly compel the coachee.

The context of employer-paid career coaching can raise contextual issues. Coachees may question what is considered confidential and whether or not there is a real or perceived dual relationship when the coach is simultaneously operating as *corporate* 'HR professional' and an *individual* 'career coach' discussing personal development strategy with an employee.

Finally, there may be both cultural and economic constraints on career coaching. In more localized, tradition-driven, tribal or non-industrialized cultures, the few individuals that could use career coaching may find it lacking due to the fact that the majority of citizens have their career decisions defined and answered for them by the social context. Even in a more commercial or industrial culture, ability to pay for career coaching can be a constraint. There may also be a mismatch between the points in time when individuals are most in need of career coaching (job and income loss), coinciding with times when they may be least able to pay for a coach's services.

Work and the workplace are, for most of us, a compelling arena for our interest and investment. Career coaches are the 'investment advisors' of this part of our life portfolio. It is a form of coaching that is blessed with rich rewards for the coachee and the coach, due in no small part to the frequently measurable outcome of the coaching process: useful, observable work to which the talents of the coachee can be applied.

FURTHER READING

Farren, C. (1997). *Who's running your career? Creating stable work in unstable times.* Austin, TX: Bard. (For the coach seeking a market-facing view of career development and change, Farren offers tools to help a career strategist map the true origins of work and the contemporary viability of professional identity over job or organizational identity. In concert with her market-facing approach, she examines entrepreneurial career paths more than most career writings.)

Ibarra, H. (2004). *Working identity: Unconventional strategies for reinventing your career.* Boston, MA: Harvard Business School Press. (For the coach seeking unconventional strategies for career exploration, Ibarra offers a practical process for career reinvention based on inductive analysis of longitudinal observations of mid-life career changers. Ibarra honours the 'Plan and Implement' model of career development even as she expands beyond it to offer a rich and practical description of an alternative 'Test and Learn' approach, crafting experiments in order to iteratively learn from experience and gradually evolve next career moves. The many rich stories in this book illustrate how a series of low-cost, low-risk experiments over time can enable profound career shifts.)

Butler, T. (2007). *Getting unstuck: How dead ends become new paths.* Boston, MA: Harvard Business School Press. (For the coach seeking a nuanced approach to assessment of an individual's career development needs and change dynamics, Butler offers career coaching stories illuminating how his clients uncovered the underlying psychological dynamics behind their impasse and moved through a series of self-awareness exercises to clarity about next steps and action. Butler weaves the psychology of Carl Jung and David McClelland, among others, into a series of 'deep dive' exercises that culminate in a map of the individual's life interests, social motivators, themes, and dynamic tensions.)

REFERENCES

Blustein, D. (2006). *The psychology of working: A new perspective for career development, counseling, and public policy.* Mahwah, NJ: Lawrence Erlbaum Associates.

Bolles, R.N. (2008). *What color is your parachute? A practical manual for job-hunters and career changers* (rev. and updated annually). Berkeley, CA: Ten Speed Press.

Butler, T. (2007). *Getting unstuck: How dead ends become new paths.* Boston, MA: Harvard Business School Press.

Drake, D.B. (2007). The art of thinking narratively: Implications for coaching psychology and practice. *Australian Psychologist, 42*(4): 289.

Dychtwald, K. (2005). *The power years: Pursue your dreams, deepen your relationships, achieve financial freedom.* Hoboken, NY: John Wiley & Sons.

Farren, C. (1997). *Who's running your career? Creating stable work in unstable times.* Austin, TX: Bard.

Hakim, C. (1994). *We are all self-employed.* San Francisco, CA: Berrett-Koehler.

Hazen, B. (2007). Managing career self-reliance. Invited presentation, State of Oregon Training Summit, Salem, OR, May.

Holland, J.L. (1997). *Making vocational choices: A theory of vocational personalities and work environments* (3rd ed.). Odessa, FL: Psychological Assessment Resources.

Horan, J. (1997). The one page business plan (for the creative entrepreneur). Berkeley, CA: The One Page Business Plan Company.

Horan, J. (2006). The one page business plan (for the professional consultant). Berkeley, CA: The One Page Business Plan Company.

Ibarra, H. (2004). *Working identity: Unconventional strategies for reinventing your career.* Boston, MA: Harvard Business School Press.

Strong Interest Inventory (2004). Mountain View, CA: CPP.

23

Cross Cultural Coaching: A Paradoxical Perspective

Geoffrey Abbott

INTRODUCTION

Cross cultural (or intercultural) coaching has emerged as a distinct practice in situations where cultural influences have been identified as particularly relevant to the client's personal and professional development. A cultural issue that draws a cross cultural coaching intervention might be global in nature, such as in the expansion of a company across national boundaries into cultural environments that are 'foreign' on almost every indicator; or it might be as narrow as a shift of an employee from one department of a company to another. The practice of cross cultural coaching can happen on an individual, group or organizational level. This chapter describes how the practice of cross cultural coaching has emerged and examines the interrelationship with other forms or genres of coaching – noting, paradoxically, that all coaching is cross cultural – and none. Regarding the future, the main proposition is that high impact cross cultural coaching requires engagement with uncertainty, change and complexity in community, organizational and group contexts. In particular, coaching can assist clients in embracing and managing core paradoxes that have the capacity to derail positive change and growth.

Cross cultural coaching often occurs simply by way of the fact that the context is in some way 'cross-', 'multi-' or 'inter-' cultural. Some common examples include:

- mergers and acquisitions (cross-border or in-country)
- joint ventures and alliances (cross-border or in-country)
- expatriate assignments

- multicultural teams
- international projects (commercial, aid, educational, etc.)
- internal restructures
- job shifts from one company to another, or one department to another
- bi-cultural or mixed background coaching clients, and so on.

An assumption of cross cultural coaching is that there are multiple realities and that each situation within each of the above categories requires a unique approach. There is no 'Seven Steps – One Size Fits All' model. Coaching conversations become a means by which contextual forces can be given prominence – not discounted.

The mobility of people and capital through globalization has seen an increase in the number of situations where cultural issues come to the fore. The most recent manifestation of this shift towards cross cultural interaction is the rapid economic expansion of the so-called 'BRIC' countries of Brazil, Russia, India, and China (Goldman-Sachs, 2007) and other emerging economies. These countries are not only new players on the world stage (particularly in mergers and acquisitions), but they also have distinct cultures that are very different from those of the traditional economic powerhouses of the USA and Western Europe. In addition, the constant movement of peoples around the globe as refugees and migrants has added to the cultural diversity of workforces in many countries that were relatively monocultural through long periods of their history.

The result is that in the early 21st century, coaching – particularly executive and business coaching – has become a necessarily cross-cultural practice. Nevertheless, many coaches have little or no specific knowledge, models, techniques or assessment tools that can assist them to deal with the reality of the intercultural practice of which they are part. This is not surprising, as few established models exist for coaching across cultures. In 2003, Rosinski published *Coaching across Cultures* and invited coaches, organizations and individual clients to view culture as an advantage rather than as an obstacle. He provides tools and methodologies for coaches to use with clients to leverage cultural differences for individual, organizational, community and societal development. The freshness of his contribution is to place culture as a key influence in coaching effectiveness. He draws together knowledge from disparate disciplines to give coaches a solid foundation for their practice.

Since then, other texts have given some attention to the cultural perspective in coaching, usually by way of a dedicated chapter (for example Drake, Brennan, & Gørtz, 2008; Morgan, Harkins, & Goldsmith, 2005; Passmore, 2006; Stober & Grant, 2006). Another text that gives special attention to cultural issues in coaching is that of Law, Ireland, & Hussain (2007). Most recently, Moral and Abbott (2009) have given an organizational context to the practice of international coaching, seeking to intertwine culture within traditional and new coaching themes. Gradually then, coaching texts and coach training programmes are recognizing the importance of cultural perspectives.

Predating coaching-specific literature, interculturalists such as Bennett (1993, 1998); Hofstede (1997); Trompenaars and Hampden-Turner (1998) and others have provided a wealth of information upon which coaches who work internationally can and do draw. Adler (2008) has also provided rich resource material and models from an organizational perspective for coaches in the international business field, giving particular attention to gender issues.

Cross-cultural psychology and management researchers have given prominence to the interplay of cognitive, behavioural and emotional factors in understanding and managing the pressures and complexities of cross-cultural situations. Earley and Ang (2003) introduce and explore the concept of 'cultural intelligence' which describes a person's (1) knowledge of cultural difference; (2) capacity to change behaviour to accommodate difference; and (3) motivation to change behaviour in the light of knowledge of cultural differences and capacity to change. Similarly, Ward, Bochner and Furnham (2001) explain how psychological impact of interacting with new cultures can be conceptualized through the interplay of cognitive, behavioural and emotional aspects. This is useful knowledge for coaches who are assisting clients to deal with cultural complexity.

Many paradoxes have emerged in the expanding field of cross cultural coaching. One is that the choice of a cross cultural coaching intervention in itself reveals a level of awareness about culture that might render unnecessary such a culture-specific intervention. Another paradox is that to label the intervention as 'cross cultural' may potentially undermine its effectiveness because this might detract from attention being given to other powerful factors that are impacting on a change process.

Culture has been defined in so many ways that it is almost indefinable. Trompenaars and Hampden-Turner (1998: 6) suggest it is 'the way a group of people solve problems and reconcile dilemmas'. Schein (1999: 29) defines it as 'the sum total of all the shared, taken-for-granted assumptions that a group has learned through its history'. Hofstede (1997: 5) defines culture as 'the collective programming of the mind which distinguishes the members of one group or category of people from another'. Externally, it is manifested in symbols and artifacts. Internally, it resides in deeply embedded subconscious assumptions and patterns of thinking and feeling and acting. Culture is not static; cultural interaction inevitably results in some degree of change in the cultures of the interacting groups. Some changes are huge; others are imperceptible. The uncertain nature and practice of cross cultural coaching reflects the muddiness and wooliness of the concept of culture itself.

Another paradox is that all coaching is cross cultural; and yet no coaching is cross cultural. That is, the individual identity of each person is partly influenced by the cultures of the group with which he or she interacts. Thus, any kind of coaching work will touch either implicitly or explicitly on the various cultural influences involved (team, family, community and so on). At the other extreme, it could be said that coaching can never be labelled 'cross cultural' because so many influences impinge on the coaching engagement that to concentrate only on culture makes no sense.

A common implicit assumption in choosing 'cross cultural coaching' in place of other genres of coaching is that somehow it is possible to isolate culture as a variable and treat it separately in developing strategies for development and change. While to some extent it is possible, from another perspective it is not. A holistic, integrationist, situational view of coaching would suggest that culture is inextricably linked with various cognitive, emotional, behavioural, structural and other influences. There is no resolution to these dilemmas or contradictory truths. It is a question of accepting a fundamental paradox in cross cultural coaching:

1. It is sometimes necessary and possible to deal explicitly and primarily with culture as a variable and influence in coaching (including measuring it and making generalizations on the basis of culture) – in other words to 'do' cross cultural coaching;
2. Doing cross cultural coaching is theoretically dubious and can be highly perilous.

Holding on to this paradox is essential for effective cross cultural coaching. Difficulties arise when:

- The coach through his or her own expertise and interest in culture keeps the focus on culture when in fact there might be other issues and variables that need attention.
- A client or organization is blind to cultural factors and chooses a coaching intervention that is not culturally appropriate or is not able to take advantage of cultural perspectives and resources.
- The coach is not sufficiently skilled, experienced or knowledgeable around cultural issues to be able to identify, explore and leverage culture in the coaching engagement.
- Cultural stereotypes are mobilized and inadvertently reinforced in a form of sophisticated stereotyping (Osland, Bird, Delano, & Jacob, 2000). This point is critical and is covered below in the discussion of cultural measurement.

Coaching approaches that integrate culture into a holistic approach to individual and organizational change are finding favour. Ken Wilber's Integral Model (Armstrong, 2009; Wilber, 2000) has been effectively utilized to position cross cultural coaching. The Integral Model identifies four quadrants on a two-by-two matrix (see Figure 23.1). Culture is placed in the internal/ collective quadrant. In integral coaching, the coach will work the coaching conversation around the four quadrants.

SPECIFIC FEATURES AND GOALS

The defining feature of cross cultural coaching is an assumption that culture has a major (and potentially positive) influence on individual and group performance, development and

	Internal	External
Individual	Feelings Thoughts	Behaviour
Collective	**Culture**	Systems Structures

Figure 23.1   The integral model (Wilber, 2000).

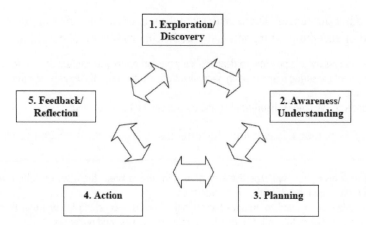

Figure 23.2   Action learning cycle.

satisfaction. The influences operate interactively across the cognitive, behavioural and affective domains and the task of the coach is to work holistically with the client in ways that will assist them towards more satisfying and productive futures (Abbott, Stening, Atkins, & Grant, 2006). Beyond this assumption, the practice can vary as to how culture is mobilized.

Cross cultural coaching that is integrated with other approaches, is contextual, and is grounded in action learning principles (Abbott & Grant, 2005), appears to provide opportunities for achieving personal and group development on many fronts. An action learning model is illustrated in Figure 23.2:

Though linear in stages one to five, in practice the model is much more fluid. In cross cultural coaching, a fluid and dynamic action cycle is paramount because it provides a mechanism for clients (individual, team, organizational) to adjust and adapt to complex and changing circumstances. Regular periods of reflection in coaching sessions can give clients invaluable opportunities to step back and examine themselves – their feelings, thoughts and behaviours – in the evolving cultural context. Such reflection is valuable fuel for planning and action towards desired outcomes.

Unlike training, cross cultural coaching provides ongoing opportunities to work through stages 3 and 4 of action learning – planned action based on enhanced awareness in context. Figuring out action strategies that foster the leveraging of difference through creative synergies takes time and in-depth discussion. Group training situations cannot always provide such opportunities. Following client action, coaching sessions provide further opportunities for clients to take action, then engage in creative dialogue about what happened (feedback and reflection – stage 5). Then, the ongoing process of coaching takes the client into further cycles of discovery, awareness-raising, action and feedback/reflection. Typically, a cross cultural coaching intervention would run over eight to twelve sessions over six to twelve months, perhaps longer. The reason for a relatively long timeframe is that culture is often an underlying variable that is entwined in all aspects of the client's experiences. Working at this level is complex and requires a high degree of experimentation through the various stages of the action learning cycle.

Coaching across cultures requires a language to assist clients to make sense of their stories and to discuss cultural influences with a degree of depth and sophistication. Establishing such a vocabulary early can be helpful in tackling complex situations later on. One aim of cultural measurement frameworks is to give a terminology for discussing differences. Culture values, dimensions and orientations have been measured in various ways by many different interculturalists and values researchers (e.g. Hofstede, 1997, 2001; Kluckhohn, 1967; Schwartz & Bilsky, 1987; Trompenaars & Hampden-Turner, 1998). Hofstede's five dimensions (formerly four) were derived from a survey of IBM offices in the 1960s. They are commonly used in the cross cultural area – including by coaches. The dimensions are:

1. power distance (high/low)
2. uncertainty avoidance (high/low)
3. individualism v. collectivism
4. masculinity v. femininity
5. long-term v. short-term orientations.

Similarly, Hampden-Turner and Trompenaars (2000) have identified seven common dimensions across which people tend to vary in response to common challenges faced by groups and communities:

1. universalism v. particularism
2. individualism v. communitarianism (social responsibility, harmonious relations, cooperation)
3. affective v. neutral cultures
4. specificity v. diffusion
5. achieved status v. ascribed status
6. inner direction v. outer direction
7. sequential time v. synchronous time.

They promote the concept of cultural synergies – seeking to reconcile the dichotomies rather than to see them as incompatible. Looking for synergies is a common approach in cross cultural training, yet in practice it is very difficult to achieve within limited timeframes and constructed training agendas.

Rosinski (2003) provides a Cultural Orientations Framework (COF) which distils various cultural measurement approaches into a 'coach-friendly' list of orientations. The questionnaire is straightforward and available online. Respondents simply rate what they believe their current orientation is against each item. For example a respondent may express a high individualistic orientation, rather than a collectivist orientation. They also express their preferred orientation; that is, the questionnaire splits on 'current' orientations (which are determined to some extent by the context) and 'preferred' orientations. Although the COF has fixed categories and dimensions, Rosinski explains that there is scope for coaches to work with clients in context to develop new and more appropriate dimensions that suit the time, place, people and issues at hand.

In constructing the various measurement tools, the approach was to collect data from large samples across different cultures and then to use advanced multivariate statistical analysis to identify factors that represent cultural dimensions, orientations or values. In theory, some measurement of group culture is then possible, which can subsequently be used to compare with other groups and as a baseline for change processes (e.g. through coaching programmes, organizational change processes). Another paradox emerges. Quantifying culture in this way carries the assumption that as an influence it can be isolated. Once isolated, it can then in theory be 'dealt with'. With this assumption, we can potentially miss or underestimate the embedded nature of culture.

There have been vigorous debates about 'the best' cultural measurement system. While interesting from an academic perspective, they are not overly useful for those working with culture in situ. Values and culture are vague concepts at best and there will never be a perfect system. However, cultural orientations and dimensions can be useful road maps for coaches and clients who are working across cultures, always remembering that the map is not the territory. Coaches working across cultures need to make their own decisions and be prepared to engage clients in creative, messy, tentative and ongoing dialogue to help make sense of what is going on.

A real risk in using cultural measurement is to unknowingly enter the territory of 'sophisticated stereotyping' (Osland et al., 2000) and inaccurately or inappropriately label people, groups or societies. This is one of the many paradoxes of coaching across cultures. The dimensions and orientations are invaluable in conceptualizing the world of the client – for the coach and for the client – but they can lead to negative outcomes if not dealt with very carefully. Inexperienced coaches may use results from a cultural measurement test to make predictions or interpretations that are 'sold' to the client as fact. These can then take on a life of their own in the client's thinking, feeling and behaving, and in the way the coach designs and implements the coaching intervention. It all may sound highly scientific at the time but is likely at best to be of little real value to the client and at worst to be totally misleading.

An associated limitation of the measurement systems is that they are usually presented as dichotomies. Although it is common for interculturalists and cross-cultural coaches to promote synergies between the opposites, the image of opposites remains – even in the use of Rosinski's COF with his emphasis on 'leveraging differences'. There remains a sense that by moving towards the other end of the scale from one's current orientations, there is a need to compromise or to somehow be 'less'. The outcome of a coaching conversation may result, for example, in a client believing that being 'more direct' in communication would be a wise strategy. Paradoxically, being diplomatic and indirect may be the client's major personal and professional strength. They may consciously or subconsciously pull back from using their core strength in a situation where even more rather than less of it may be required. In effect, the result, though not the coaching intention, could be that the client ends up as being somehow diminished.

Hampden-Turner and Trompenaars (2000) see different cultural approaches as mirror images of each other and as having very dynamic interaction. They plot their paired dimensions on 'x' and 'y' axes and suggest that the interaction of the variables is where the potential for growth and development resides. By further developing the idea of creative synergies it is possible to

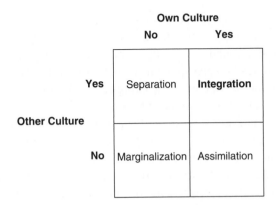

Figure 23.3   Identification with own and other cultures (Berry, 1997).

depict the orientations and dimensions in a way that promotes paradoxical thinking and leads clients towards more creative approaches. The use of the common two-by-two matrix assists in this process. An overarching two-by-two matrix by Berry (1997) illustrates the value of the matrix in supporting 'and' rather than 'either/or' approaches when dealing across cultures. Figure 23.3 illustrates the choices open to someone who is in contact with a different culture. Berry's context was acculturation across national borders; the model applies equally well in organizational mergers and other cross-cultural situations.

Berry (1997) observed that the best way of achieving smooth acculturation is usually through an integrationist approach, in contrast to assimilation, separation or marginalization.

Integration   occurs when there is an interest on behalf of the expatriate in both maintaining his or her original culture while being in daily interactions with other groups. Thus, some degree of cultural integrity is maintained, while at the same time the expatriate seeks to participate as an integral part of the larger social network.

Assimilation   contrasts with integration and is where the individual does not wish to maintain his or her own cultural identity and seeks identification with and assimilation into the host culture. With expatriates, this is sometimes referred to as 'going native'.

Separation   is when the individual places a value on holding on to his or her original culture and seeks to avoid interaction with the host culture. This stance is quite common with expatriate managers who may form enclaves (particularly in hardship posts). This was evident within a sample of expatriate managers in a recent coaching research study in Central America (Abbott, 2006).

Marginalization   is the strategy adopted when there is little possibility or interest in cultural maintenance (often for reasons of enforced cultural loss) and little interest in having relations with others (often for reasons of exclusion or discrimination).

Integration has been found to be the most successful strategy in studies of acculturation; marginalization is the least; and assimilation and separation strategies are intermediate (Berry, 1997). This pattern has been found in virtually every study, and is present for all types of acculturating groups. The findings in organizational contexts are similar. Though there will be exceptions, this is useful information for coaches working across cultures and assisting clients to raise awareness, make choices and design effective actions in their different contexts.

In a work context, the Harrison Assessment Paradox Graph (Harrison & Harrison, 2008) is a tool that attempts to promote a reconciliation of opposites through paradox theory. The tool is more designed for executive recruitment and job-fit purposes than for cross-cultural work per se, although the authors give weight to its cross-cultural application demonstrated through success in China. The tool also depicts apparently contradictory variables on two axes in a two-by-two matrix. The Harrison approach uses paradox theory, drawing on the work of Jung, Freud and others (Harrison & Harrison, 2008). According to paradox theory, our lives involve dealing with a series of paradoxes – twelve are listed. Each paradox is a relationship between two categories of traits, 'gentle' traits and 'dynamic' traits. Most of the trait paradoxes are similar to the paired dimensions listed in the cross-cultural measurements systems mentioned above. Six of the twelve traits are:

- certain v. open/reflective
- analytical v. intuitive
- enforcing v. warmth/empathy
- athoritative v. collaborative
- organized v. flexible
- frank v. diplomatic.

Being strong on both of the traits that make up the paradox is termed 'balanced versatility'. If the range of behaviour extends only to the 'dynamic' aspect of the paradox, it is called 'aggressive imbalance'. If the range extends only to the 'gentle' aspect of the paradox, it is called 'passive imbalance'. Imbalances have some counterproductive tendencies. A low range of behaviour on both aspects is called 'balanced deficiency' – with counterproductive tendencies (Figure 23.4).

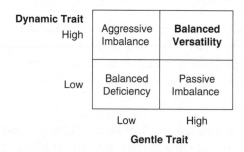

Figure 23.4   Trait interaction possibilities (Harrison & Harrison, 2008).

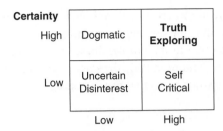

Figure 23.5   Certainty/reflectiveness paradox.

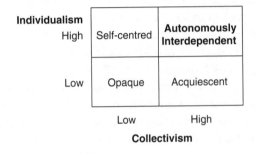

Figure 23.6   Individualism/collectivism paradox.

An example of balanced versatility in relation to the traits of 'certainty' and 'reflectiveness/openness' is given in Figure 23.5.

The point of presenting this tool is not to argue for its scientific accuracy regarding the identification of universal paradoxes. In fact, the 'multiverse' (James, 1907) position proposed for cross cultural coaching interventions would suggest that the concept of a fixed list of paradoxes makes little sense. Ideally, in each context the participants (clients and coaches) will construct relevant paradoxes through dialogue. The value is in suggesting to coaches that they use cultural dimensions measurements utilizing a paradoxical representational rather than a dichotomous depiction. For example the individualism/collectivism dichotomy could be represented (see Figure 23.6). An illustration of how this might be applied to a coaching situation will be presented later in the chapter.

With the assistance of paradox theory, the leveraging of differences through coaching can reframe cultural dimensions from dichotomies into orientations that can be held together and synthesized to develop approaches that are of most benefit to the client in specific contexts.

Even without measurement, a cross cultural coaching intervention can be powerful in introducing a language for uncovering and naming issues which may be culturally underpinned. A point made often in the cross cultural literature is that people are often blind to the nature and influence of culture in their lives and organizations. Coaches who are culturally savvy themselves can ask questions that can encourage clients to at least consider culture as a factor.

THE ROLE OF COACH AND RELATIONSHIP WITH CLIENTS

A key role of a coach working across cultures is to assist clients to notice the potential influence of culture in complex and changing environments. The action research framework positions the coach as an active participant in the relationship – not a passive observer or simply someone who mirrors the world of the client. The questions asked by the coach and the choices about the process and direction of the coaching will have their own cultural biases. It is therefore paramount that coaches engage in their own processes of self-discovery and development. They then need to be appropriately explicit about their preferences and biases as they work with clients, and be very self-analytical about the way in which these forces may be operating. Abbott et al. (2006: 306) suggested that coaches working across cultures should have (in addition to generally accepted coaching competencies):

1. sound appreciation of the cultures of the client and the host country
2. self-awareness of the coach's own cultural background
3. personal experience in cultural adaptation and acculturation
4. familiarity with cross-disciplinary intercultural theory and research.

As noted earlier, a coach working across cultures is likely to use a cultural measurement tool of some kind. In training programmes, participants gain an understanding of cultural differences and hopefully a heightened awareness and understanding of who they are in relation to where they are and who they are with. The role of the coach beyond this is to explore reframing and managing of paradoxes to generate creative synthesis and inform action. The work of the coach is mainly in encouraging clients to develop narratives that include cultural sense making and shape futures that capture as many different dimensions and angles as possible. Put simply, the coach can help shape clarity in complexity.

Case study: Rafael Luz

The following case study provides an illustration of how cross cultural coaching works in practice and also highlights how a paradox framework can assist in case conceptualization and development. The case study is of a Central American manager (Rafael Luz – not his real name) working in Central America with a European based multinational company. The coaching programme with Rafael was one of 15 conducted as an action research doctoral study, examining how executive coaching could facilitate expatriate acculturation (Abbott, 2006).

Rafael Luz commenced his coaching programme while working in a middle management project role in finance and information technology. Rafael was formerly manager of operations and administration at the national airline. He had an engineering degree from an American University and an MBA from the top business school in Central America. The coaching programme comprised seven sessions of one to two hours over eleven months.

Rafael was dissatisfied with his limitations as an expert in finance and information technology. He was interested in developing his career and eventually being a general manager. The early coaching conversations gave Rafael an opportunity to give voice to a narrative that drew on his past successes as a manager in the local culture, and his academic and technical successes in a new culture (USA). The evolving narrative included reshaping his career back into the management stream within the multinational, and perhaps extending beyond into management in local companies. Culture was deeply interwoven in each element of the coaching programme. No measurement tools were used.

Rafael clarified his goals, in particular his interest in improving his communication skills:

RL: One of the areas I don't really see as a weakness but one I would like to strengthen is communication. I don't see myself with problems on content. It is more externalizing those ideas to others.
GA (coach): You had feedback that you had too much detail and you also said you liked detail?
RL: But I would be willing to trade it off if I could transfer it.

This was the entry point for a discussion about the company culture, which extended into a more general discussion about national culture and communication styles. The company culture at senior levels favoured direct communication with minimal up-front detail. In fact, detail was a major strength for Rafael. In cross-cultural terms, this could be presented as a dichotomy of direct and indirect communication (very commonly listed as a cultural orientation). The coaching could potentially have focused on pushing Rafael towards directness and away from his preferred style of giving large amounts of information.

From a paradox framework, this could be conceptualized slightly differently – as two related and conflicting variables of directness and detail (see Figure 23.7). The coaching conversation is a place where the contextual variables can be teased out and explored and so the task was to unravel with Rafael what might be going on in the context and then to assist him to use his potential on each to maximize value from the other in a synergistic approach.

Rafael seemed high on detail but low on directness. When explored, it transpired that Rafael was actually quite comfortable with directness – but initially he saw it as a trade-off for his unique talents for managing enormous and complex detail across financial and technological fields. Although it was a trade-off he was prepared to enact, it was not attractive. In context, it emerged that Rafael was not asking enough direct questions to find out exactly how much detail was required at particular points in time. His challenge was to use directness at the front end of conversations to draw out the detail required in the context. The cultural issue was that in his previous management positions there had been an expectation that a presenter would provide

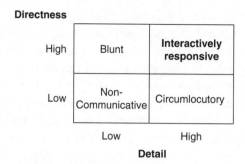

Figure 23.7   Rafael's communication paradox.

considerable detail. The new assumption, organizationally and to some degree culturally-based, was that people expected a relatively short up-front delivery, followed by multiple exchanges to move through layers of detail that were behind the initial presentation.

The emphasis in the coaching was not to detract from Rafael's strength in the detail but to validate and manage that strength through utilizing a different kind of directness. The coaching sessions were dedicated to managing detail in a way that allowed it to be delivered rapidly and with focus at points when it was best needed. This approach fostered the 'leveraging of differences' in a dynamic way that went beyond the traditional cultural synergy approaches.

RELATIONSHIP WITH THEORETICAL TRADITIONS

Cross cultural coaching cannot stand alone. Abbott and Rosinski (2007) have outlined how 'global coaching' incorporates the cross-cultural perspective and other perspectives, genres, or traditions of coaching. Following are four examples of how different genres were operating in the cross cultural coaching with Rafael Luz.

Psychodynamic coaching

Cultural influences are often embedded deep in the subconscious. The coaching relationship carried high potential for transference and countertransference – with cultural undertones. The coach was an expatriate with a profile not dissimilar to the expatriate management group in-country and therefore could potentially be viewed by the client as representative of the multinational company norm. The coach's challenge was to be as aware as possible of any transference that might be occurring and to deal with it in the coaching dialogue.

Cognitive–behavioural coaching

Fundamentally, the coaching programme with Rafael was a behavioural change process. Part of the process was in-session training with Rafael on responding to direct questions with direct answers and in generating direct questions to be used to sharpen his interaction with senior expatriate executive. Cognitive reframing was required with Rafael to assist him in a shift from an assumption that 'direct communication managing complex detail are incompatible', to a new assumption that 'direct interactive communication can be highly effective in managing and communicating complex detail'.

Cognitive–developmental coaching

The coaching process had a strong developmental aspect. The conversations encouraged Rafael to see himself more objectively – that is, to step out of his role as a technical financial specialist and to examine his potential and his future from a higher and wider perspective. The shift during the period of the coaching could be interpreted as typical of a manager expanding from Stage 3 to Stage 4 in Kegan's adult development model (Berger & Fitzgerald, 2002; Kegan, 1982, 1994). Berger and others have discussed how coaching programmes can be powerful in promoting experiential learning with associated cognitive developmental growth.

Positive psychology and solution-focused coaching

The coaching approach combined a focus on strengths with the opening up of new possibilities consistent with these coaching genres. Rafael's grasp of detail was portrayed as an asset to be managed rather than down-played. Similarly, coaching drew out strengths from Rafael's background in being direct in his communication. Then, a very pragmatic contextual process followed to work those two strengths together for a solution that in the end paid enormous dividends.

The coaching sessions were devoted to validating Rafael's uniqueness and to allow him to design a future of his own making. Initially, the company seemed to be viewing Rafael as stereotypical of someone from the region who was buried in detail and unable to work at a high level with rapid-pace decision making. The coach's validation and valuing of Rafael's past, present and future assisted him to overcome the perceptions and to craft a role for himself that few would have envisaged possible.

The coaching dialogue gave attention to Rafael's past successes in Latin business contexts and grounded his future development on a successful integration with the organizational culture within which he was operating (consistent with Berry's integrationist strategy). This approach gave flesh to Rosinski's position of viewing culture as an opportunity rather than an obstacle to personal and professional development and is very much consistent with positive psychology principles.

EVALUATION

Cross cultural coaching is difficult to evaluate as a context or a genre. When coaches integrate a cultural perspective using approaches consistent with Wilber's (2000) integral model, culture can be conceptualized and mobilized as a variable and be a powerful ally to coaches and their clients. However, culture can be unhelpful or even damaging when viewed as a separate or fixed variable that can be manipulated or altered. In this form, culture can be used to rationalize, excuse, dictate, glorify, or even dismiss aspects of client's development. The challenge is to be mindful of the potential for culture to be a major influence but to be very open-minded as to how it may be playing a part in the client's situation.

The successful managing of differences that often occur in cross-cultural contexts lies in the managing of paradox, and coaching can encourage clients towards synergistic approaches to these conflicting and confusing challenges. It can help them to find a degree of clarity in the complexity of their situations and equip them to make more effective decisions. At its worst, cross cultural coaching could marginalize culture and give attention to the 'problem' of cultural differences. It could unknowingly become a vehicle for perpetuating stereotyping through the introduction and validation of rigid measurement systems that allow and even encourage simplistic interpretations of how people differ on the basis of culture. At its best, cross cultural coaching is an inspired action-learning process that gives prominence to context where culture is explored and mobilized through conversations followed by client action. Appropriate terminologies are borrowed and constructed that give life to real issues that are playing out in the lives of clients. Clients are encouraged through narrative to take an expanding view of who they are and what they are doing on an individual, organizational, community and global scale.

As a final comment, the field of cross cultural research and cross cultural coaching has largely been driven by Western thinking and business practice. It is only recently that coaching has started to gain a strong presence in Asia, South America, the Middle East and in Eastern Europe. Also, the cross-cultural researchers cited in this chapter are generally people who have been educated in traditional Western education systems. Different voices are emerging in inter-cultural research and in coaching. The future of cross cultural coaching will be enhanced by this diversity. The direction is for stories to be created from inside cultural contexts by the participants, rather than interpretations overlaid by outside 'experts' who claim to carry knowledge of apparently universal cultural patterns or thinking, feeling and behaving.

FURTHER READING

Adler, N.J. & Gundersen, A. (2008). *International dimensions of organizational behavior* (4th ed.). Cincinnati, OH: South-Western. (Nancy Adler is a leading thinker, researcher and practitioner in international organizational behaviour and more recently in coaching. This book is an excellent resource for coaches working with international companies.)

Moral, M., & Abbott, G. (Eds.). (2009). *The Routledge companion to international business coaching.* London: Routledge. (Gives attention to coaching in an international business context. Each chapter contains theory, case studies, models and tools for coaches, executives and HR professionals. Issues covered include global virtual teams, international team coaching, collective intelligence, survival theory in international business, global nomads.)

Rosinski, P. (2003). *Coaching across cultures: New tools for leveraging national, corporate and professional differences.* London: Nicholas Brealey. (This book is well-researched and provides clear illustrations of how to leverage cultural differences. It also contains the Cultural Orientations Framework and a framework for Global Coaching. A 'must read' for any coaches working in intercultural environments.)

REFERENCES

Abbott, G.N. (2006). Exploring evidence-based executive coaching as an intervention to facilitate expatriate acculturation: Fifteen case studies (unpublished Doctoral dissertation, Australian National University, Canberra).

Abbott, G.N., & Grant, A.M. (2005). Evidence-based executive coaching and action research: A natural fit. In I.F. Stein, F. Campone, & L.J. Page (Eds.), *Proceedings of the Second ICF Coaching Research Symposium: 3 November 2004, Quebec City, Canada* (pp. 22–9). Washington, DC: International Coach Federation.

Abbott, G.N., & Rosinski, P. (2007). Global coaching and evidence based coaching: Multiple perspectives operating in a process of pragmatic humanism. *International Journal of Evidence Based Coaching and Mentoring, 5*(1): 58–77.

Abbott, G.N., Stening, B.W., Atkins, P.W.B., & Grant, A.J. (2006). Coaching expatriate managers for success: Adding value beyond training and mentoring. *Asia Pacific Journal of Human Resources, 44*(3): 295–317.

Adler, N.J. & Gundersen, A. (2008). *International dimensions of organizational behavior* (5th ed.). Cincinnati, OH: South-Western.

Armstrong, H.B. (2009). Integral coaching: Cultivating a cultural sensibility through executive coaching. In M. Moral & G. Abbott (Eds.), *The Routledge companion to international business coaching.* London: Routledge.

Bennett, M.J. (1993). Towards ethnorelativism: A developmental model of intercultural sensitivity. In *Education for the intercultural experience* (pp. 21–71). Yarmouth: Intercultural Press.

Bennett, M.J. (1998). Overcoming the golden rule: Sympathy and empathy. In M.J. Bennett (Ed.), *Basic concepts of intercultural communication: Selected readings* (pp. 191–214). Yarmouth: Intercultural Press.

Berger, J.G., & Fitzgerald, C. (2002). Leadership and complexity of mind: The role of executive coaching. In C. Fitzgerald & J.G. Berger (Eds.), *Executive coaching: Practices and perspectives* (pp. 27–57). Palo Alto, CA: Davies-Black Publishing.

Berry, J. (1997). Immigration, acculturation, and adaptation. *Applied Psychology, 46*(1): 5–34.

Drake, D.B., Brennan, D., & Gørtz, K. (Eds.). (2008). *The philosophy and practice of coaching: Insights and issues for a new era.* Chichester: Jossey-Bass.

Earley, P.C., & Ang, S. (2003). *Cultural intelligence: Individual interactions across cultures.* Stanford, CA: Stanford University Press.

Goldman-Sachs. (2007). *BRICs and beyond.* London: Goldman-Sachs Group.

Hampden-Turner, C., & Trompenaars, F. (2000). *Building cross-cultural competence: How to create wealth from conflicting values.* Chichester: John Wiley & Sons.

Harrison, A., & Harrison, D. (2008) *Assessment paradox graph.* Retrieved 26 July 2008 from http://www.harrisonassessments.com/

Hofstede, G. (1997). *Cultures and organizations: Software of the mind.* New York: McGraw-Hill.

Hofstede, G. (2001). *Culture's consequences: Comparing values, behaviors, institutions and organizations across nations* (2nd ed.). Thousand Oaks, CA: Sage.

James, W. (1907). A pluralistic universe. In L. Menand (Ed.), *Pragmatism: A reader* (pp. 132–8). New York: Random House.

Kegan, R. (1982). *The evolving self: Problem and process in human development.* Cambridge, MA: Harvard University Press.

Kegan, R. (1994). *In over our heads: The mental demands of modern Life*. Cambridge, MA: Harvard University Press.

Kluckhohn, C. (1967). Values and value-orientations in the theory of action: An exploration in definition and classification. In T.P.E.A. Shils (Ed.), *Towards a general theory of action*. Cambridge, MA: Harvard University Press.

Law, H., Ireland, S., & Hussain, Z. (2007). *The psychology of coaching, mentoring and learning*. Chichester: John Wiley and Sons.

Moral, M., & Abbott, G. (Eds.). (2009). *The Routledge companion to international business coaching*. London: Routledge.

Morgan, H., Harkins, P., & Goldsmith, M. (Eds.). (2005). *The art and practice of leadership coaching*. Hoboken, NJ: John Wiley and Sons.

Osland, J.S., Bird, A., Delano, J., & Jacob, M. (2000). Beyond sophisticated stereotyping: Cultural sensemaking in context. *Academy of Management Executive, 14*(1): 65–79.

Passmore, J. (Ed.). (2006). *Excellence in coaching: The industry guide*. London: Kogan Page.

Rosinski, P. (2003). *Coaching across cultures: New tools for leveraging national, corporate and professional differences*. London: Nicholas Brealey.

Schein, E.H. (1999). *The corporate culture survival guide: Sense and nonsense about culture change*. San Francisco, CA: John Wiley and Sons.

Schwartz, S.H., & Bilsky, W. (1987). Towards a universal psychological structure of human values. *Journal of Personality and Social Psychology, 53*(3): 550–62.

Stober, D.R., & Grant, A.M. (Eds.). (2006). *Evidence based coaching handbook: Putting best practices to work for your clients*. Hoboken, NJ: John Wiley & Sons.

Trompenaars, F., & Hampden-Turner, C. (1998). *Riding the waves of culture: Understanding cultural diversity in global business* (2nd ed.). New York: McGraw Hill.

Ward, C., Bochner, S., & Furnham, A. (2001). *The psychology of culture shock* (2nd ed.). Hove: Routledge.

Wilber, K. (2000). *Integral psychology: Consciousness, spirit, psychology, therapy*. Boston: Shambhala.

24

Mentoring in a Coaching World

Bob Garvey

INTRODUCTION

This chapter discusses the role, function and purpose of mentoring within a commercial world often dominated by talk of coaching. It draws on the literature of both mentoring and coaching and emphasizes the dynamics of dyadic developmental relationships. It also integrates mentoring and coaching practices into a broad category of one-to-one developmental dialogue.

The word 'mentor' comes directly from Ancient Greek and means 'of the mind'. The character, 'Mentor' was first introduced in Homer's epic poem, *The Odyssey*. According to *The Oxford Dictionary*, the term 'mentor' was first used in English to describe a developmental process in a letter from Lord Chesterfield to his son in 1750. It was later used by Lord Byron in his poems *The Curse of Minerva, Childe Harold's Pilgrimage* and *The Island* to describe characters of influence. However, probably the most significant volume on mentoring was Fénélon's (1651–1715) *Les aventures de Télémaque*.

Fénélon's (1808) work is a treatise on educational techniques. Based on Homer's epic poem, *The Odyssey* it is a comprehensive description of the holistic learning and development of young Telemachus. The work includes illustrative examples of learning from experience, reflective questioning, practical skills development, learning social awareness and self-awareness, role modelling and leadership development. Fénélon implied that leadership could be developed through guided experience. Louis XIV saw this as a challenge to his divine right, banished Fénélon to Cambrai and cancelled his pension. Nevertheless, Fénélon's work was very widely read throughout Europe and his influence is seen in the works of other writers on educational philosophy during the 18th century.

Caraccioli's book *Veritable le mentor ou l'education de la noblesse* published in 1759 was translated into English in 1760 and became *The true mentor, or, an essay on the education of young people in fashion.* This work describes mentoring from the perspective of the mentor. Caraccioli acknowledges the influence of Fénélon's work on his own and included a mentoring process model:

> observation leading to …
> toleration leading to …
> reprimands leading to …
> correction leading to …
> friendship leading to …
> awareness.

While the language in this model is archaic, it does contain some interesting parallels with both mentoring and coaching. For example, models of coaching for performance and mentoring in the education sector include 'Observation' as a key element of the process. 'Toleration' may be associated with patience and respect, perhaps even listening skills. 'Reprimands' and 'Correction' could be linked in modern thinking to feedback, demonstrations or searching for solutions to challenges. 'Friendship' is not normally an outcome of coaching but can be a natural consequence of mentoring. 'Awareness' is a key outcome for any coachee or mentee.

Another writer influenced by Fénélon was Rousseau. He was influenced by Fénélon's ideas on dialogue as an important vehicle for learning – we learn in conversation with others. It is no surprise then that Rousseau thought that the ideal model for learning effectively was one-to-one! Rousseau's *'Emile'* (1762) explores the learning and development of the central character, Emile, who is given a copy of *'Les aventures de Télémaque'* as a guide to his developmental journey. In *'Emile'*, Telemachus becomes a model for learning, growth and social development.

A third writer from the 18th century produced two volumes called *'The Female Mentor'*. These were published in London in 1793 with a third volume in 1796. The author, Honoria (probably a *nom de plume*) identifies and describes the characteristics of the female mentor through a commentary and series of asides made throughout the volumes. These characteristics include patience, virtue, listening, challenge and support. The books are dedicated to Fénélon for sharing his approach to education and life.

The term 'coaching' first appears in English literature in Thackeray's *Pendennis* in 1849. Thackeray used the term 'coaching' as a pun, blending the idea of travelling in a horse drawn carriage from A to B (Oxford University being B), and helping someone to improve their academic attainment. Later, the term 'coaching' became associated with performance enhancement in sport and life skills development.

Mentoring and coaching share similar features in history. Both can be linked to education and learning and both are described as one to one processes. Recent European Mentoring Coaching Council (EMCC) research (Willis, 2005) indicates that coaching and mentoring are indeed similar activities and clearly demonstrates that coaches and mentors, in the main, share the same practices, skills and processes.

THE PROBLEM OF DEFINING MENTORING AND COACHING

In the last 40 years, mentoring activity has gained much momentum in private sector businesses, the public sector, small and large businesses and in education and social welfare. A recent survey in the UK Health Service (Healthcare Commission, 2005) estimated that 230,000 people participated in mentoring activity during 2004. The UK Health Service is the largest employer in Europe, with an estimated 1.3 million employees. If extrapolated out to other sectors, this would mean that 17% of the UK workforce would have experienced mentoring activity and this does not include educational and social mentoring activity. Therefore, in numerical terms mentoring reaches a huge number of people.

Coaching activity across Europe is also considerable. The recent Bresser Report (2008) suggests that approximately 17,000 businesses engage in coaching activity and practices are very diverse.

The rapid rise of both mentoring (Healthcare Commission, 2005) and coaching activity (Bresser, 2008) over a relatively short period has led to definitional confusion of both. There is much debate among academics and practitioners as to the true and distinctive nature of each. For example, Rosinski (2004) states:

> Although leaders can act as coaches, I have found that this role is often confused with mentoring. Coaches act as facilitators. Mentors give advice and expert recommendations. Coaches listen, ask questions, and enable coachees to discover for themselves what is right for them. Mentors talk about their own personal experience, assuming this is relevant for the mentees. (Rosinski, 2004: 5)

I agree with Rosinski that mentoring is often associated with 'expert' knowledge sharing and advice giving, but it is also associated with listening, asking questions and enabling mentees to discover for themselves.

A further point of confusion comes later in the same book where Rosinski (2004) goes on to say: 'In my view coaches are also responsible for transferring knowledge. Coaches don't simply help resolve coachees' issues. They actually share their knowledge so that coachees can become better coaches. For example the coach will briefly explain his frame of reference' (2004: 245).

The above quote raises a problem because it is hard to distinguish between 'sharing knowledge' with the purpose of enabling someone to become a 'better coach' and talking, as a mentor, about one's 'own personal experience, assuming this is relevant to the mentee'. Rosinski's position raises the question of what the difference is between 'personal experience' and 'knowledge'. These points are discussed later in this chapter.

Gladstone (1988: 10) suggests that trying to define mentoring is difficult because 'it is as informal as pairing, as variable as the organizations in which mentors and *protégés* find themselves, and as idiosyncratic as the people involved'.

Definition, by its very nature, seeks to simplify and reduce. It also, as can be seen above, attempts to polarize. In a world arguably dominated by cause and effect thinking, clear definition has a simplistic appeal. With social phenomena as complex as mentoring and coaching, definitional simplification is unhelpful. Lack of definition need not, however, be a problem. An alternative perspective explores the subtleties and complexities of the phenomena within their social contexts (see Bruner, 1985). Geertz (1971) suggests that this is called a rich or 'thick description'.

The descriptions of mentoring offered below are not definitive but are a personal description of mentoring. There are four main elements:

First, mentoring is dependent on the human qualities of trust, commitment and emotional engagement. Often, in successful mentoring partnerships, the pair respect and like each other, and this may result in friendship.
Second, it includes the use of such skills as listening, questioning, challenging and supporting.
Third, central to mentoring is 'the mentee's dream' (Caruso, 1992). Mentoring is primarily for the mentee and the concept is therefore fundamentally associated with a desire to progress, to learn and understand and to achieve. People often engage in mentoring where the mentee is making a transition. For example a new job, a promotion, a new stage of life, setting up a business, facing retirement, moving from unemployment to employment, reorganization or change.
Fourth, mentoring is a relationship between two individuals with learning and development as its core purpose. This relationship is a core part of the dynamic and it is here that mentoring activity starts to depart from coaching. Some of the relationship issues will be discussed later in this chapter but the following quote from Hunt and Weintraub (2002: 10) supports this view and emphasizes the 'emotional bond' as a key difference between mentoring and coaching: 'we believe that coaching doesn't necessarily require the type of emotional bond usually associated with mentoring'.

SPECIFIC FEATURES OF MENTORING

This section briefly covers some of the main features of mentoring activity.

Relationship

Central to mentoring is the idea that the 'relationship' plays an important part in facilitating learning. The affective side of mentoring plays a role, particularly in the light of the tendency for interpretations of mentoring and coaching to polarize; for example to emphasize either the professional or the personal development of the mentee (Carruthers, 1993) or performance set against development or the long-term relationship versus short-term (Clutterbuck & Megginson, 2005).

De Haan (2008) also links coaching and mentoring activity and along with Sieler (2003) and Bluckert (2005) is one of the few authors to raise the importance of the relationship between coach and coachee. Hunt and Weintraub (2002: 9) stress the idea of a relationship over time as well as supporting the idea that coaching and mentoring are similar processes: 'Mentoring typically involves a more ongoing relationship. Effective mentors do use some of the same coaching practices' (Hunt & Weintraub, 2002: 9).

Ancient and modern mentoring literature has made the relationship point extensively (see for example, Homer, 1184 [1250] BC; Caraccioli, 1760; Honoria, 1796; De la Mothe-Fénélon, 1808; Levinson, 1978; Torrance,1984; Bennetts, 1995, 1996; Hurley & Fagenson-Eland, 1996;

Scandura, Tejeda, Werther, & Lankau, 1996; Hale, 2000; Samier, 2000; Friday, Shawnta, Friday, & Green, 2004). This literature either presents relationship building as key to achieving positive outcomes in mentoring or as problems associated with manipulation, favouritism or abuse.

Connor (1994) offers a rationale for integrating mentoring with the theory found in the kind of learning involved in counselling. Counselling practice highlights human qualities such as trust, openness, honesty and integrity. Additionally, notions crucial to workplace learning such as those of 'skills development', 'training for specific purposes', 'experiential learning' and 'situated learning' all relate to a model of learning which includes the concept of mentoring (Garvey, 1994c; Daloz, 1999). There are also connections here between those who view mentoring as a means to an end, such as learning for improved efficiency and effectiveness, and those who emphasize its wider psychosocial context (Kram, 1983) in which people are regarded as 'ends in themselves'.

Simmel (1950) explored issues of intimacy, secrecy, dependency, termination and triviality within dyads and observed that *two* is the maximum number of people needed for the security of a 'secret', suggesting that 'secrecy' places a mutual dependency on the relationship. In modern parlance, 'secrecy' could be replaced by the word 'confidentiality'. Confidentiality is fundamental to the success of both coaching and mentoring relationships (MacLennan, 1995; Clutterbuck & Megginson, 1999; Grodzki & Allen, 2005; Megginson, Clutterbuck, Garvey, Stokes, & Garrett-Harris, 2005). Modern writings on both mentoring and coaching regard dependency as a problem and also stress the allied notions of 'trust', 'commitment' and 'active involvement' as important elements of the relationship.

The certainty that any dyadic relationship may end can be a powerful influence on the partnership. Simmel suggests that the sense of the end can lead to either greater dependency or lack of trust. He also states that the sense of the end can bring the pair closer together. The coaching and mentoring literature discusses the issue of proper closures and endings of the relationship at some length (see Garvey, 1994b; Clutterbuck & Lane 2004; Grodzki & Allen, 2005).

'Triviality', Simmel suggests, is created by the initial expectations in the relationship failing to materialize in practice; and perhaps the frequency and sharing of experiences within the relationship contributes to a sense of 'triviality'. This can result in the dyad closing down as the pair or one of the pair runs out of things to say and gets bored! Consequently, there is a need for regular review and stimulation for it to deliver successful outcomes (see Neilson and Eisenbach, 2003).

Within any dyad there is potential for intimacy and the dyad provides the further potential for deep friendship with a tendency for intimacy and mutual dependence. Simmel makes it clear that this is not a consequence of the content of discussions but the uniqueness of the relationship. Intimacy exists 'if the 'internal' side of the relationship is felt to be essential; if its whole affective structure is based on what each of the two participants give or show only to the one other person and to nobody else' (Simmel, 1950: 126). In other words, the open nature and the confidentiality of the discussions provide the ingredients for intimacy.

Social context

Mentoring is a dynamic activity and the form it takes within a social setting influences its potential for success or failure as a developmental intervention. Mentoring has both the potential to be genuinely supportive and helpful to people and abusive and manipulative (see Carden, 1990). Mentoring relationships can be about the exercise of power and control over others. In the UK, some associate mentoring with gratuitous advice giving, the 'old boys' networks, 'sitting with Nellie' or straightforward and old fashioned nepotism. In part, this is because it is such an ordinary and natural human activity and difficulties in human relationships are a normal part of life. In addition, genuine practical and structural difficulties contribute to the success or failure of mentoring and on occasions, mentoring is subject to social and cultural pressures. Again, this is a departure from what is written about coaching, which is often positioned as 'clean' and 'objective'. Mentoring is potentially messy and therefore even less subject to strict definition.

Advice giving

The experienced mentor does not give gratuitous advice since, as Rosinski implies, knowledge sharing or advice given with an assumption of relevance or without respect for the receiver is unhelpful. However, we are social beings who learn in a social context.

In their notions of 'communities of practice' and 'legitimate peripheral participation', Lave and Wenger (1991) developed the idea of learning as a social activity within a social context. There seems little doubt that people learn by, through and with each other but there are various ways in which this can be done. Emler and Heather (1980) suggest that sharing knowledge is essential in human development: 'We are a successful species because we cheat; we tell each other the answers'. Knowledge or experience sharing and advice giving can be an essential part of learning: if we do not do this as a species, we commit the next generation to reinvent the wheel! As Sir Isaac Newton is deemed to have said 'If I have seen further, it is because I have stood on the shoulders of giants'. Knowledge is therefore a building process. If the mentor shares knowledge and experience with the intent of offering it up as options or choices for action or as a vehicle for further discussion, it establishes rapport, empathy, credibility and additionally, accelerates learning.

Mentoring in a knowledge economy

Mentoring helps the individual to discover what sort of person she or he could be. Sometimes this involves learning and acquiring specific knowledge, specific skills and more often gaining inspiration, challenge, encouragement and support so that understanding develops and appropriate behaviour is acquired. Gladstone (1988: 21) suggests that 'successful mentors accept change willingly' and that 'mentorees are encouraged to devote their talents and energies to attainable goals and as a result they develop self-confidence'. Within the context of a knowledge economy, confident people are an important asset.

Additionally, the dominant rhetoric in economic life is the accelerating pace of change, influenced by technological and political initiatives. If believed, the implications of this rhetoric for individuals are considerable. The need for people who are able to adapt to change rapidly, learn quickly and apply their knowledge to a range of situations has increased. In this climate, it is crucial for employees to have 'strong and stable personalities' (Kessels, 1996: 4).

APPLICATIONS

There are different views about the purpose and function of mentoring. People across the world recognize mentoring as a highly effective developmental process and there are many examples of mentoring activity in many diverse settings.

Although contexts and practices vary, the relational aspects between mentor and mentee help to create and support professional and academic development, personal development and learning. Mentoring makes a crucial contribution as the mentee integrates prior and current experience through meaningful and deep dialogue with the mentor. Mentoring is effective when learners are making transitions at key points in their educational or occupational careers. It helps, for example, in the following contexts:

*Induction   *Developing strategic capability
*Support to development   *Career progression and job change
*Social integration and cultural change   *Support for learning on the job
*Diversity programmes   *Redundancy support
*Talent management   *Leadership development

Organizational context and mentoring

Any honest investigation of mentoring will recognize its potential to become part of the 'shadow-side':

The shadow-side activities have two distinct characteristics: they are outside ordinary management processes because they are covert, informal, or even unable to be discussed; and they are economically significant, in that they very often add direct or indirect costs, including lost opportunity costs, that escape ordinary accounting procedures (Egan, 1993: 33). This is not to say that their contribution is negative; on the contrary, as Egan puts it, 'Some shadow-side activities add value rather than cost' (1993: 33).

In a recent presentation about mentoring given by a human resource director, a fellow director remarked: 'All this mentoring stuff sounds a bit airy-fairy to me. I'm not having it in my department.' The HR director replied, 'Well, you have it in your department whether you like it or not, you just can't stop it.'

Mentoring has the potential to offer value whether or not it is recognized as a formal process or system. This is because mentoring is a normal human activity and whether or not it is constructed as a formal scheme, it will exist because it links strongly to Erikson's (1995) 'generativity' concept. Erikson links generativity to the strong human desire to procreate but it is also about bringing on, influencing and supporting the next generation. As Garvey, Alred and Smith (1996: 13) point out: 'Mentoring is one way to satisfy the deep-seated desire to "*leave an impression on the world*", which is recognized as a characteristic of mature adulthood'.

Levinson (1978) also associates mentoring with the generativity concept and suggests that this contributes to the motivation to mentor. Generativity and the desire to influence is often observed when senior managers in organizations talk about '*giving something back to the organization*'.

In sum, mentoring as a learning and supportive relationship has a vital part to play in developing learning in a whole variety of conditions.

THE MENTOR ROLE AND THE RELATIONSHIP WITH MENTEES

In early research (Garvey, 1994a) a range of different people from different backgrounds described the 'quality' of their mentoring relationship in terms of:

1. the wide ranging topics discussed in the partnership
2. how many people within the organization knew that a mentoring relationship existed
3. a 'tacitly understood' or 'explicitly understood' partnership at work
4. the degree of activity within the partnership
5. security and stability within the partnership.

These descriptions translated into a framework (Garvey, 1994c) that helps to describe the mentoring relationship and is referred to as the 'dimensions framework'. The participants in the research viewed these descriptions as important aspects of their natural and informal mentoring relationships. These dimensions offer the basis for a new approach to understanding both coaching and mentoring (Garvey, Stokes, & Megginson, 2009). This approach is not underpinned by simplifying definitions but, rather, by flexible description. The original descriptions were developed into the dimensions as follows.

Description 1, translated into the *OPEN/CLOSED* dimension. This dimension is about the content of the discussions. In an OPEN discussion, anything is on the agenda. If it is CLOSED, the discussion may focus on specific issues.

Description 2, translated into the *PUBLIC/PRIVATE* dimension. This is about who knows mentoring is going on in an organizational context and who ought to know.

Description 3, translated into the *FORMAL/INFORMAL* dimension. This is about the administration and management of the relationship. In a FORMAL arrangement, the mentoring pair may agree meetings in advance, take notes, time limit the discussion, agree to meet in a regular venue at regular intervals. If it is INFORMAL they will meet on an 'as required basis' and generally work on a 'go with the flow' basis.

Description 4, translated into the *ACTIVE/PASSIVE* dimension. This is about 'Who does what in the relationship?'

Description 5, translated into the *STABLE/UNSTABLE* dimension. This is about trust and consistency. It is about sticking to the ground rules while being prepared jointly to review them.

These dimensions represent points on a continuum. They are not fixed points but rather dynamic and subject to change over time as the relationship develops and matures. The research also identified that mentor and mentee often had a different perspective on their relationship and so, although these dimensions may be negotiated at the start of a mentoring relationship, they will require regular review over time. In this way, the rapport in the relationship is strengthened and this often leads to improved outcomes, as noted by Neilson and Eisenbach (2003).

The dimensions not only describe the dynamics of a mentoring relationship but also provide the basis of the ground rules and may help to develop mutual understanding between mentor and mentee. No one set of dimensions represent the ideal relationship.

The mentor's role therefore, is to listen, support and challenge and to do this in the context of:

- change and transition
- leadership development
- time management and work–life balance
- performance and behaviour
- motivation and confidence
- personal and people related issues
- thoughts and feelings on a range of issues.

The mentor will do this by:

- sensitively drawing on relevant experience and skills
- employing well developed interpersonal skills
- relating well with people who want to learn
- having a desire to help and develop mentees
- being open-minded, flexible and recognizing his or her own need for support
- giving time and being willing to develop the relationship.

Given the similarities between coaching and mentoring practice discussed earlier in this chapter, this framework could be applied to either. I am convinced that many writers on coaching would agree with the above points but call the activity 'coaching' instead!

RELATIONSHIP WITH THEORETICAL TRADITIONS

O'Brien (1995) describes a mentoring process embedded within change and development, and draws on psychodynamic principles for its ethical framework, while McAuley (2003) employs the psychoanalytic notion of transference and countertransference to develop and extend our understanding of the mentor/mentee relationship. Bennetts (1996) and Garvey (2004) link mentoring to Rogerian philosophy, and other writers (Gibb, 2004) consider ethical and boundary issues which relate to psychological frameworks. Baum (1992) applies Freudian psychology to mentoring relationships in the US, suggesting that within mentoring there is potential for narcissistic fantasy and Oedipal reality in mentoring relationships as the mentee pursues his or her 'dream'.

However, the coaching literature seems to be concerned with psychology far more than does the mentoring literature. An example is found in Lee (2003), where he refers to 'psychological mindedness' as an important element of a coach's practice and Bluckert (2006: 87) describes this as 'people's capacity to reflect on themselves, others, and the relationship in between'. He suggests that this is best done with an understanding and awareness of psychological processes. These ideas suggest that an understanding of psychology and therapeutic practice is a necessary requirement for mentors as well as coaches. Berglas (2002) in relation to coaching would agree. He considers that knowledge of psychology is necessary and asserts that only trained therapists should coach; but his position is not clear when he states:

> My misgivings about executive coaching are not a clarion call for psychotherapy and psychoanalysis [...] My goal, as somebody with a doctorate in psychology as well as serving as an executive coach, is to heighten awareness of the difference between a problem executive, who can be trained to function effectively, and an executive with a problem who can best be helped by psychotherapy. (Berglas, 2002: 89)

This quotation offers further insight into the complex and overlapping practices of mentoring, coaching and counselling. Alternative views suggest that mentoring is essentially two colleagues engaged in a purposeful conversation and therefore knowledge of psychology is not necessary for mentors.

Unlike coaching, where psychological methods often migrate to informing practice and brands of coaching (see for example Solution Focused Coaching or Cognitive–Behavioural Coaching), mentoring draws on this literature to inform and challenge rather than create practice and here is another distinction between the two. Coaching is increasingly viewed as a profession with codes of practice and standards. This has the potential to exclude the practicing manager who wants to use coaching as a way of managing. Mentoring is seen as a supportive activity available to anyone and requires only minimum training and some ongoing support.

EVALUATION

As with coaching, within mentoring there are opportunities for the organization, the mentor and the mentee to benefit from mentoring or purposeful conversations. In broad terms, this might be as follows:

For the mentee:

- improved performance and productivity
- career opportunity and advancement
- improved knowledge and skills
- greater confidence and well-being.

For the mentor:

- improved performance
- greater satisfaction, loyalty and self-awareness
- new knowledge and skills
- leadership development.

For the organization:

- staff retention and improved communication
- improved morale, motivation and relationships (less conflict)
- improved learning.

As human beings, we have the potential to be truly magnificent at relationships as well as to be exceptionally bad at them! Mentoring relationships are no different. Because it is a natural activity, as a practice within an organization it will be present either by default or by design. If the best is to be achieved, mentoring activity does need some 'light touch' design and some core conditions need to be considered, such as:

- voluntarism and choice
- clear recruitment strategy
- training of mentors and mentees
- ongoing support for mentors and mentees if they require it
- a clear and transparent matching policy
- establishing reviewable ground rules
- ongoing review
- working with the mentee's agenda
- accepting mentoring as legitimate work (Alred, Garvey, & Smith, 2006).

However, as Garvey (2004) suggests, caution is necessary because:

> The real danger for mentoring is the tendency to adopt mentoring as a strategy for facilitating learning and change without due consideration for the social setting or the cultural context. All too often, mentoring is used as the 'fixer' of problems, a fast tracker to success, a 'cure-all' without due consideration for the wider social, political and economic context. An organisation can talk development as much as it likes but without real commitment to the notion then it is just another initiative to squeeze a little more out of people. (Garvey, 2004: 176)

Genuine and authentic intent is an essential ingredient for mentoring and coaching within an organization because holistic development is only achievable in a wholesome and honest environment.

Mentoring has a longer tradition than coaching but both activities share many of the same practices, applications and values. In the end, it comes down to a choice of terminology and the meaning associated with that terminology. Meanings, as Bruner (1985; 1990) tells us, are dependent on the social context so it is inevitable that the terms mentoring and coaching will mean different things to different people in different contexts. For me, the problem comes when either mentoring or coaching writers attempt to position one as fundamentally different from the other. Coaching has in recent times become the dominant term and the one with greater and more direct commercial interest. However, coaching as a concept is derived from mentoring, and perhaps an argument is beginning to emerge for a multiple perspective approach to mentoring and coaching through description rather than definition. For the future, maybe a new term will emerge that will satisfy all interested parties.

FURTHER READING

Garvey, B., Stokes, P., & Megginson, D. (2008). *Coaching and mentoring theory and practice*. London: Sage. (A comprehensive and critical discussion of many aspects of mentoring and coaching.)

Alred, J., Garvey, B., & Smith, R. (2006). *The mentoring pocket book*. Arlesford: Management Pocket Books. (A practical, no nonsense guide to mentoring.)

Riley, P. (1994). *Fenelon: Telemachus*. New York: Cambridge University Press. (Insights into historical perspectives on mentoring.)

REFERENCES

Alred, J., Garvey, B., & Smith, R. (2006). *The mentoring pocket book*. Arlesford: Management Pocket Books.

Baum, H., (1992). Mentoring: Narcissistic fantasies and oedipal realities. *Human Relations, 45*(3): 223–45.

Bennetts, C. (1995). Interpersonal aspects of informal mentor/learner relationships: A research perspective. Paper in proceedings at the European Mentoring Centre Conference, London, October.

Bennetts, C. (1996). Mentor/learner relationships – A research perspective, Making it happen. South West Conference, Torquay, January.

Berglas, S. (2002). The very real dangers of executive coaching. *Harvard Business Review, 80*(6): 86–92.

Bluckert, P. (2005). Critical factors in executive coaching – the coaching relationship. *Industrial and Commercial Training, 37*(7): 336–40.

Bluckert, P (2006). *Psychological dimensions of executive coac*hing. Maidenhead: Open University Press.

Bresser (2008). *Results of the European coaching survey*. Cologne: Bresser Consulting.

Bruner, J. (1985). Vygotsky: A historical and conceptual perspective. In J.V. Wertsch, *Culture, communication and cognition: Vygotskian perspectives*. Cambridge: Cambridge University Press.

Bruner, J. (1990). *Acts of meaning*. Cambridge, MA: Harvard University Press.

Caraccioli, L.A. (1760). *The true mentor, or, an essay on the education of young people in fashion*. London: J. Coote.

Carden, A. (1990). Mentoring and adult career development. *Counselling Psychologist, 18*(2, April): 275–99.

Carruthers, J. (1993). The principles and practice of mentoring. In B. Caldwell & E. Carter (Eds.), *The return of the mentor: Strategies for workplace learning*. Bristol: Falmer.

Caruso, R.E. (1992). *Mentoring and the business environment: Asset or liability?* Aldershot: Dartmouth.

Clutterbuck, D., & Lane, G. (2004). *The situational mentor*. Aldershot: Gower Publishing.

Clutterbuck, D., & Megginson, D. (1999). *Mentoring executives and directors*. Oxford: Butterworth Heinemann.

Clutterbuck, D., & Megginson, D. (2005). *Making coaching work: Creating a coaching culture*. London: CIPD.

Connor, M. (1994). *Counsellor training: An integrated approach*. London: Kogan Page.

Daloz, L. (1999). *Mentor: Guiding the journey of adult learners*. San-Francisco, CA: Jossey-Bass.

de Haan, E. (2008). *Relational coaching: Journeys towards mastering one-to-one learning*. Chichester: John Wiley.

De la Mothe-Fénélon, F.S. (1808). *The adventures of Telemachus* (Vols. 1 & 2) (trans. J. Hawkesworth). London: Union Printing Office.

Egan, G., (1993). The shadow side. *Management Today,* September: 33–8.

Emler, N., & Heather, N. (1980). Intelligence: An ideological bias of conventional psychology. In P. Salmon (Ed.), *Coming to know.* London: Routledge and Kegan Paul.

Erikson, E. (1995). *Childhood and society.* London: Vintage.

Friday, E., Shawnta, S., Friday, A., & Green, L. (2004). A reconceptualization of mentoring and sponsoring. *Management Decision, 42*(5).

Garvey, B. (1994a). Mentoring in the market place: Studies of learning at work (unpublished Doctoral dissertation, University of Durham).

Garvey, B., (1994b). Ancient Greece, MBAs, the Health Service and Georg. *Education and Training, 36*(2): 18–26.

Garvey, B. (1994c). A dose of mentoring. *Education and Training, 36*(4): 18–26.

Garvey, B. (2004). When mentoring goes wrong. In D. Clutterbuck & G. Lane, *Situational mentoring.* Aldershot: Gower Publishing.

Garvey, B., Alred, G., & Smith, R., (1996). First person mentoring. *Career Development International, 1*(5): 10–14.

Garvey, B., Stokes, P., & Megginson, D. (2009). *Coaching and mentoring theory and practice.* London: Sage.

Geertz, C. (Ed.). (1971). *Myth, symbol and culture.* New York: Norton.

Gibb, S. (2004). The moral dimension of mentoring. In D. Clutterbuck & G. Lane, *Situational mentoring.* Aldershot: Gower Publishing.

Gladstone, M.S. (1988). *Mentoring: A strategy for learning in a rapidly changing society.* Research Document CEGEP. Quebec: John Abbott College.

Grodzki, L., & Allen, W. (2005). *The business and practice of coaching.* London: Norton.

Hale, R. (2000). To match or mis-match? The dynamics of mentoring as a route to personal and organizational learning. *Career Development International, 5*(4/5).

Healthcare Commission. (2005). *NHS national staff survey 2004 – Summary of key findings.* London: Healthcare Commission.

Homer (1184 [1250] BC). *The Odyssey.* In R. Lattimore (1965), *The Odyssey of Homer.* New York: Harper Perennial.

Honoria (1793). *The female mentor or select conversations* (Vols. 1 & 2). London: T. Cadell.

Honoria (1796). *The female mentor or select conversations* (Vol. 3). London: T. Cadell.

Hunt, J.M., & Weintraub, J.R. (2002). *The coaching manager: Developing top talent in business.* Thousand Oaks, CA: Sage.

Hurley, A.E., & Fagenson-Eland, E.A. (1996). Challenges in cross-gender mentoring relationships: Psychological intimacy, myths, rumours, innuendoes and sexual harassment. *Leadership and Organisation Development Journal, 17*(3): 42–9.

Kessels, J.W.M. (1996). Knowledge productivity and the corporate curriculum in knowledge management: Organization, competence and methodology. Proceedings of the Fourth international ISMICK Symposium, Rotterdam, October.

Kram, K.E. (1983). Phases of the mentor relationship. *Academy of Management Journal, 26*(4): 608–25.

Lave, J., & Wenger, E. (1991). *Situated learning: Legitimate peripheral participation.* Cambridge: Cambridge University Press.

Lee, G. (2003). *Leadership coaching: From personal insight to organisational performance.* London: CIPD.

Levinson, D. (1978). *The seasons of a man's life.* New York: Alfred Knopf.

McAuley, J. (2003). Transference, countertransference and mentoring: The ghost in the process. *British Journal of Guidance and Counselling, 31*(1): 11–23.

MacLennan, N. (1995). *Coaching and mentoring.* Aldershot: Gower Publishing.

Megginson, D., Clutterbuck, D., Garvey, B., Stokes, P., & Garrett-Harris, R. (Eds.). (2005). *Mentoring in action.* London: Kogan Page.

Neilson, T., & Eisenbach, R. (2003). Not all relationships are created equal: Critical factors of high-quality mentoring relationships. *International Journal of Mentoring and Coaching, 1*(1). Retrieved from www.emccouncil.org

O'Brien, J. (1995). Mentoring as change agency: A psychodynamic approach. *Counselling,* February: 51–4.

Rosinski, P. (2004). *Coaching across cultures.* London: Nicholas Brealey.

Rousseau, J. (1762). *Émile ou de l'éducation* [Emile: or, on education]. Geneva: A La Haye, Chez Jean Néaulme.

Samier, E. (2000). Public administration mentorship: Conceptual and pragmatic considerations. *Journal of Educational Administration, 38.*

Scandura, T., Tejeda, M., Werther, B., & Lankau, M. (1996). Perspectives on mentoring. *Leadership & Organization Development Journal, 17*(3).

Sieler, A. (2003). *Coaching to the human soul: Ontological coaching and deep change.* Newfield, VIC: Newfield-Australia.

Simmel, G. (1950). *The sociology of Georg Simmel* (trans. and ed. K. H. Wolff). Glencoe, IL: Free Press.

Thackeray, W.M. (1849). *The history of Pendennis.* Harmondsworth: Penguin.

Torrance, E.P. (1984). *Mentor relationships: How they aid creative achievement, endure, change and die.* Buffalo, NY: Bearly.

Willis, P. (2005). *EMCC competency research project: Phase 2.* Watford: European Mentoring and Coaching Council.

Professional Practice Issues

25

The Future of Coaching as a Profession

David A. Lane, Reinhard Stelter and
Sunny Stout Rostron

INTRODUCTION

The popularity of coaching is seen in an array of international coaching conferences, burgeoning coach training and education, and emergent professional bodies for coach practitioners. This escalating demand has motivated coach practitioners, consumers and educators of coaching to advocate the professionalization of the industry to ensure the quality of coaching services.

Coaching as a form of practice is now widely adopted, although recognition as a profession remains contentious and patchy, with different jurisdictions taking contrary views on its legitimacy. A growing awareness of the potential benefits to the industry of professional status has led to participation in international dialogues, such the Global Convention on Coaching (GCC) and the International Coaching Research Forum (ICRF). The GCC was established with the explicit aim of promoting consultation and exploration of areas such as the professionalization of coaching, and the ICRF has begun work to promote the value of research, critical self-reflective practice, and the development of a coaching knowledge base. There are nevertheless lessons that coaching can learn from other professions who have already trodden this path.

This chapter outlines the criteria for a discipline to be accepted as a profession, briefly assessing the extent to which coaching complies. Potential lessons for coaching from the development of psychotherapy into a profession are then summarized, highlighting the fragility of the term 'profession' in contemporary society. The chapter goes on to outline key observations on professionalization, as distinct from 'professionalism'. Feasible options regarding the status of coaching as a true profession, or alternatively as an occupation maintaining professionalism are compared, and ongoing concerns and challenges are underlined.

Criteria for a profession

Generally accepted core features of a profession include the requirement for members to have formal academic qualifications; adherence to an enforceable code of ethics; practice licensed only to qualified members; compliance with applicable state-sanctioned regulation; and a common body of knowledge and skills (Spence, 2007: 261). This is a highly contentious area and there are many ways of viewing a profession.

From a legalistic perspective, a profession is established if some of the following criteria are embodied in a law or similar statues (DBVC, 2007):

- societal mandate (monopoly for professional practice)
- formalized curriculum/professional education
- plurality of theory and methods as the basis for the curriculum
- research foundation in relation to the professional practice
- governmental accreditation, professional licence
- quality assurance
- reflective professional competence
- standards of ethics
- specific career paths, professional trajectories and passages
- professional body – association with formalized rights and duties for their members
- financial independence of the single professional (employment, scale of fees).

Bennett (2006: 241–2) has reviewed the relevant literature and summarized the criteria to enable coaching to be determined a profession as follows:

1. *Identifiable and distinct skills* – i.e. skills that are widely accepted as required for the performance of skilled coaching.
2. *Education and training required to acquire proficiency* – for example the minimum initial and ongoing training required to coach; generally accepted competences required for coaches; means of assessing competence.
3. *Recognition outside the community as a profession* – for example recognition by established professions as a profession; government classification of coaching as a profession.
4. *Code of ethics* – a code of ethics for coaches defined, implemented, monitored and effectively enforced by a governing body, making coaching a self-disciplined industry.
5. *Public service* – public service by coaches that is motivated by altruism rather than financial gain.
6. *Formalized organization* – widely accepted and established professional association(s) representing the profession and those practising coaching.
7. *Evaluation of merit (credentialling) and self-regulation of service* – for example definition of accepted requirements for coaches; systems for assessing competence; systems for monitoring and regulating service delivery by coaches; mechanisms for encouraging thought and discussion about the practice of coaching.
8. *Established community of practitioners* – for example forums where coaches can network and exchange ideas on coaching; publications supporting the community of practitioners.

9. *Status of membership in a profession* – for example recognition of coaches by their clients and the general public as members of a profession.
10. *Public recognition* – recognition by the general public that coaching is a distinct and established profession.
11. *Knowledge base* – coaching practice founded in theoretical and factual research and knowledge, with a defined body of knowledge, a defined theoretical foundation, and ongoing evidence–based theoretical and practical research.

However, there is a long way to go before coaching can be defined as a profession in the narrowest sense. In the list of the criteria above none of these is fully realized in the professional field of coaching, either nationally or internationally. Bennett (2006: 242) highlighted the following critical gaps between the criteria listed above for a profession and the current practice of coaching.

- There are currently no generally accepted, identifiable and distinct skills for coaches.
- Training and/or education are not required before a person can practise as a coach, although various coach-training programmes are available.
- The general public and related professions do not recognize coaching as a profession.
- There is not an established community of practitioners; for example less than half the estimated coaches in the world belong to representative bodies such as the International Coach Federation (ICF).
- There is a lack of defined theory on which coaches base their practice.

Lessons from psychotherapy

In some ways the current position and disputes about status in the field of coaching mirror those around parallel fields such as psychotherapy. Indeed, the position of psychotherapy is illustrative of the type of problems coaching may face unless it adopts a strongly collaborative approach.

Various schools of psychotherapy have developed with their own philosophy, model of causation and intervention. Candidates were trained within one modality (i.e. speciality) and as standards developed each modality claimed its own standards body. Splits between members within single bodies led to even more forms of 'accreditation' and as new methods emerged additional accreditation bodies were formed. This is in contrast to physical medicine where the invention of a new treatment did not lead to multiple accrediting bodies with a single theory as the basis for registration and licence to practise. Practitioners are regulated as medics first, and second by their specialism rather than their theories about human illness. In psychotherapy (and perhaps in coaching) any new theory, whether evidence-based or not, could gain adherents, thus creating new accrediting bodies.

As psychotherapy sought to gain 'respectability' in the form of statutory regulation, the problem was compounded by disputes between professional bodies as to which one represented the appropriate truth. Since the basis for practice was either theory and competences that had not been agreed, or an agreed knowledge base shared across all practitioners, it was difficult for statutory authorities to regulate. A 'Psychotherapy Regulation Act' could require 450 different models of practice to be listed, each with differing standards to cover the range of current practice. No jurisdiction would contemplate such complex legislation.

Eventually, attempts by the various groups to collaborate resulted in agreement to at least the hours of training and some common areas of knowledge (e.g. through the United Kingdom Council for Psychotherapy (UKCP). This has only been partly successful, with ongoing disputes between the members of these collaborative bodies and with members leaving, rejoining, leaving again and others forming their own new competitive collaboration. In Europe this confusion has lead to some countries restricting practice to medical practitioners and psychologists, as a sub-function within those professions, thereby denying psychotherapy as a separate profession. In others psychotherapy can be practised but only in a limited number of modalities. Forms of practice common (in the unregulated profession) in the UK would not be allowed in Germany or Spain. In the UK, the government is currently considering the regulation of psychotherapy and is also going down the restricted modality route with cognitive–behavioural, analytic, humanist and systems models being the preferred routes. The alternative favoured by the European Federation of Psychologists Associations (www.efpa.eu) is to determine the guiding principles for practice (as for all other professions) rather than to treat psychotherapy as a practice of limited modalities.

In some countries where regulation has been attempted these issues have emerged and consequently some jurisdictions have restricted the rights to practise to a limited number of modalities or specific types of psychotherapy practice. Germany, for example recognizes three modalities, whereas others have yet to regulate the psychotherapy profession at all. In the UK, there are multiple competing bodies which exist without a statutory framework although the authorities are currently considering regulation within four modalities. Thus a form of practice accepted in the UK (existential psychotherapy which has its own accrediting society) is not a permissible modality in Germany. In the USA, the position varies from state to state; what is included within the field also varies widely. This leads to considerable confusion about what is in and what is out, and has led to debates in some countries about how wide the field should be.

While psychotherapists worldwide fight among themselves about what is the best form of practice, others in the better established professions of psychiatry (which is state regulated in most jurisdictions) and psychology (which is regulated in many) claim ownership of the field. Some influential voices in these fields fully deny that coaching is a separate profession, and claim that it is an area of practice for their speciality rather than a separate field in its own right. As psychotherapists find themselves in territorial disputes with psychologists and psychiatrists they are also seeking to embrace the newer emerging fields, such as coaching, as their territory, arguing that coaching is a field that requires practice by a psychotherapist (Berglas, 2002).

The question is whether we wish to use this model for coaching. Even though it is acknowledged by the Global Coaching Community (GCC) that coaching is a unique synthesis of a range of disciplines (GCC, 2008: 5), attempts within coaching to seek professional standing have been hampered by its lack of conformity to the precedented basis for granting a right to be a profession. Given that each of the professional bodies within the coaching field take a different view of the criteria for professional status, gaining agreement as to what constitutes the 'profession' of coaching is difficult. Although different from psychotherapy, professional bodies in the coaching field are not accrediting bodies in themselves; they simply provide guidelines for 'professional' practice. Unless coaching can agree on the core principles (as for example in the EFPA model discussed above) then the negative effects of the regulation in psychotherapy may apply: either coaching is excluded from practice as in some European countries, or state regulators will determine which forms of practice are allowed or not, thereby excluding many practitioners.

Fragility of the term 'profession' in late modern society

During the last few decades, the concept of the profession has itself become fragile. The main reason for this process of disintegration is that professionals have been losing their monopoly of knowledge. This loss, in fact, is one of the fundamental reasons for the rapid development of the coaching industry: knowledge has become something that evolves in specific communities of practice. Knowledge is not a list of facts that is stable, but it is contextualized and relational – that is, it depends upon how and where it is being used and by whom. Furthermore, knowledge is democratized by being accessible through channels open to everybody, mainly through the internet. In that sense there is no profession that has exclusive ownership over the knowledge base in specific areas of expertise. Even within traditional fields such as medicine there is growing competition from alternative practitioners such as herbalists and homeopaths. The development in recent decades has shown that traditional professions, because of fast and diversified knowledge production and dissemination, no longer enjoy automatic respect from clients based on their superior access to information.

Consequently, it is crucial to think about an alternative understanding of the concept of profession. Drake (2007), for example has argued that we have moved beyond the traditional profession towards a craftsperson's view of professional practice, blending science and art in what he terms the 'pursuit of conscious mastery'. This has clear implications for the professionalism of coaching. Drake (2009) has argued further that coaches need to move beyond their biases for their specialized, professional knowledge to make sufficient room for other forms of knowledge and toward an engagement in a mutual and co-creative process to formulate what is happening in the coaching conversation. Others have pointed to the client becoming their own 'self-coach'. Corrie (2009) provides a framework for the coach to share tools with the client.

It seems to be challenging and unhelpful to attempt a degree of conformance in the coaching field where coaching is established as a traditional profession, since:

- Coaching is not based on societal mandate or a monopoly for professional practice.
- Coaching is not subject to governmental accreditation or a professional license.
- Coaching has no quality assurance.

- Coaching has only voluntarily accepted standards of ethics.
- Coaching has no specific career paths, professional trajectories and passages.
- Coaching has no association with formalized rights and duties for their members.
- Coaching does not guarantee financial independence for the single professional (employment, scale of fees).

However, that does not prevent coaches working towards interdisciplinary cooperation, towards a multidisciplined professional or alternative perspective, towards agreeing key elements that might enhance the quality of the coaching offering to clients.

Traditional and alternative perspectives

Issues similar to those that have formed part of debates in other professions are emerging (Lane & Corrie, 2006). Some strongly support the view that coaching should conform to the traditional view of a profession. However, an alternative view states that professions should be recognized as institutionalized forms of power, and that adopting the traditional approach could be detrimental to the future of coaching. In the literature on the sociology of the professions there are significant critiques of professions (see for example Larson, 1977; Johnson, 1995; Lo, 2004). These views are similar to those discussed by Lane and Corrie (2006), who argue that the knowledge to which professionals lay claim is arrived at and sustained through relationships with the state and the marketplace. Professions in general can also be seen as interest groups engaged in a collective mobility project to improve their economic and social standing. Power is gained through the attainment of professional autonomy by state licensing, which enables monopoly supply. This means that those who can most closely align themselves with power in the marketplace (for example through gaining acceptance for their form of practice from health insurers or corporates), or align with the interests of the state (in the form of practice in public institutions), seek to dominate supply and exclude others – thus collaboration is only favoured by those with power to award contracts to supply.

The integration of the interests of coaching and the market or the state could result in the prioritizing of certain forms of knowledge over others. The market may favour short-term, cost-effective interventions which might demonstrate value to the client, but primarily to the fee-paying manager. In this scenario, the state will also favour approaches that are legitimized by evidence-based practice. There are those who see this route as detrimental to the interests of both clients and coaching as a profession.

It could be argued that the practice of some specific types of coaching is divisive, because of the ways in which priority is given to certain forms of knowledge over others, asserting that these represent the 'truth'. These separate approaches create regimes that lead to forms of knowledge, competences and values that are impervious to other ideas and create isolation between different practitioners in the field. Thus coaches come to work, think and act within narrow areas of practice set by others because they have internalized what Foucault (1983) would call 'regimes of truth'. There can be seen in the behaviour of some organizations an attempt to dominate based on a limited set of ideas rather than an attempt to enrich the field through collaboration.

The global convention on coaching

Each of the GCC's 10 working groups (in collaboration with their respective consultative bodies) developed white papers with the intention of defining the possible future of coaching worldwide. These were presented and debated at the GCC's Dublin convention (7–11 July 2008). The result was the *Dublin declaration on coaching* (GCC, 2008), which recommended:

1. the establishment of a common understanding of the profession through creation of a shared core code of ethics, standards of practice, and educational guidelines;
2. acknowledgement and affirmation of the multi-disciplinary roots and nature of coaching as a unique synthesis of a range of disciplines that creates a new and distinctive value to individuals, organizations and society;
3. using coaching to respond to a world beset by challenges with no predetermined answers by using coaching to create a space wherein new solutions can emerge; and
4. moving beyond self-interest to address the critical issues identified by the 10 working groups in an ongoing dialogue. (GCC, 2008: 5)

Significantly, a number of those consulted throughout the GCC process want to draw upon a much wider range of evidence to inform coaching practice than has traditionally been the case. In doing so they are contesting the power that professional coaching bodies are seeking. They argue that many forms of evidence should inform the work of coaches, including more implicit or 'intuitive' knowledge, as well as greater creativity in our practice.

Another group want to emphasize relationships with clients as the primary basis on which coaches should think about their identity as a profession. While they accept the claim that our solutions to human problems are grounded in evidence, they want to recognize that we have to understand how they are shaped through social networks. Lane and Corrie (2006) have looked at how such networks operate, and argue that an expert cannot exist without a lay public recognizing and engaging the badge of expertise. The lay public is expert in other ways to which we have often failed to give sufficient credence, and this, they argue, has limited professional understanding. For example by failing to legitimize clients' stories (or rather, by requiring clients to conform to our way of telling them), we have come to favour technical solutions that do not challenge those in authority. In so doing, we are not recognizing how we might become part of the problem, rather than the solution. We fix problems defined by those in power rather than really hear the voice of the client (see Corrie & Lane, 2009 for a more detailed account of the use of the client's voice). Also, the coach becomes a part of the organizational system and unable to see the real issues as defined by the client. The use of fixed-agenda coaching determined by a sponsor following a 360° feedback process is an example of this problem-fixing approach (Jarvis, Lane, & Fillery-Travis, 2006).

A further example of this hegemony is the way in which the client, in some approaches to coaching, is asked to provide data in the format required by the client's coaching process or methodology. This situation is evidenced by the number of textbooks in the field which point to a step-by-step process in which the client is asked questions in a specific order and maybe even in a specific way – the assumption of the 'miracle coaching question' being a case in point.

Many practitioners working in diverse and complex settings have adopted a more broadly-based definition of coaching, and argue that this should lead us into a reconceptualization of what it means at the current time to embrace a 'coaching' identity. The members of the working and consultation groups and those present at the GCC in Dublin raised many different questions. It was generally felt that the recommendations of the Dublin process were focused and action-oriented; the entire process identified five key areas for immediate attention: research, ethics, coach education and development, standards of competence and supervision.

Profession or occupation?

Common concerns of GCC participants around the professional status of coaching focused on whether it should become a profession or remain an occupation. Not all coaching is facilitated by a 'professional coach'; the 'coach' might be engaged in another profession, e.g. a teacher coaching his colleague, a nurse coaching a trainee, or a line manager coaching another manager or employee. Coaching in this context is part of continuous professional development, where everybody in an organization or company can potentially be coach or coachee, and where employees acquire coaching competencies through specific coaching training programmes (see Law, Ireland, & Hussain, 2007). Thus coaching might be seen as a dialogical tool for continuous professional development rather than as a professional area of practice.

So, although coaching draws on multiple disciplines and is used by many types of people in many environments, it is not necessarily the case that everyone in the coaching community wants to see the creation of a profession. An occupation can be defined as (1) an activity that serves as one's regular source of livelihood; a vocation; or (2) the principal activity in your life that one practises to earn money. To have an occupation does not – by its definition – require a special education to be able to handle the vocational tasks at hand.

On the other hand, if a profession is deemed desirable it means that a number of specific criteria such as those outlined by Bennett (2006) have to be fulfilled. It might be necessary to go further and consider the narrower position of state-regulated professions, as defined by DBVC (2007), if coaches really want to legitimize their practice. This is probably a step too far for coaching, but voluntary agreements exist currently for many bodies in the field. They share some minimal commitment to standards covering:

- voluntary commitment to possible professional standards and code of ethics
- vocational training in coaching (competence- or skills-based, rather than based on an agreed knowledge base)

- voluntary organizations making some minimal degree of commitment to safeguarding the interests of the field, including coaches and clients.

Individually, many of the nascent professional bodies in the field go beyond this.

Professionalism rather than a profession

It might be a long and, in the traditional sense, possibly a never-ending path to establish the coaching profession. It might be more fruitful to make explicit that coaching has some of its roots in different disciplines and professions (for example HR management, psychology, organizational systems, social work, education, counselling); but that coaching expertise is further enhanced by vocational training and further education in the field of coaching – enterprises led by institutions of higher education, coach training bodies and in-house courses that can ensure that the training received is based on research and on a high degree of theoretical and empirical evidence. The existing bodies in the field which have made commitments to research-led models (Worldwide Association of Business Coaches (WABC) in the USA and the European Mentoring and Coaching Council (EMCC) in the UK/Europe among others) also represent part of that drive towards professionalism.

In respect of professionalism, the Dublin meeting of the GCC concluded as follows.

(a) Coaching is an emerging profession.
(b) Coaching draws on multiple disciplines, which in combination create its own knowledge base and professional practice. The multiple disciplines and knowledge bases include learning theories, adult development, behavioural/ social sciences, leadership and management sciences, communication techniques.
(c) Coaching in its broadest form is also a process or technique increasingly used by different types of people in many environments, and may not always be formally recognized as such.
(d) The quality of the coaching engagement is dependent on the standard, consistency and rigour of the education, development, ethics and core competencies of the emerging profession.

As such a number of questions emerge.

(a) As things stand, there are no barriers to entry; anyone can call themselves a coach, and there is a community which likes that freedom.
(b) The integration of 'coaching' into the wider community, particularly as a style of communication, does not mean that everyone is a 'professional' coach.
(c) Will other professions and associations see a coaching profession as a threat?
(d) Do all parts of the coaching community want to see the creation of a coaching profession?
(e) Will the politics of the coaching community get in the way of creating a profession?

Concerns and questions

A variety of questions and concerns have arisen throughout the GCC process that require shared dialogue, research, recommendations and action to be taken. If coaching is to emerge as a discipline with a professional future, a wide variety of difficult conversations need to take place in such forums as the GCC and other professional body events, where stakeholders can share their expertise and work collaboratively.

It has been recommended as a result of the GCC process that we need empirical evidence that coaching can make a difference on an individual, organizational and societal level. There still remains a lack of clarity and consensus as to what is professional coaching, what makes for an effective and reputable coach, whether coaching should in effect become a profession and if coaching works (Fillery-Travis & Lane, 2006). Globally, research needs to be conducted to determine what competences are necessary for the education and development of coaches worldwide, and what will be a definition of coaching that the global community will accept.

One substantial concern is whether the international coaching bodies are committed to working together, and in collaboration with coach education and development organizations, and with other coaching stakeholders to define and regulate the profession.

Other concerns relate to the role of supervision in the education and development of coaches; the distinctions between the curricula across different levels of coach education and practice; and whether a universal ethical code can be developed with the various professional bodies being willing to adapt a code that reaches across borders.

It is important that there is some kind of synthesis between the professional coaching bodies, the educational institutions developing academic and practitioner programmes, and the organizations who are currently buying coaching interventions. In seeking to clarify what is coaching, and what role practitioners, academics and all stakeholders have to play, the dialogue has begun.

There are serious issues of power and diversity which may impact on how and which initiatives are taken forward. What are the issues of power that we need to address in order to be willing to listen to each other, and how can we use the dialogue process to do so? The successful professional development of coaching is going to take commitment, perseverance, and a willingness to let go of power, control, ego and territoriality.

Although we live and work in a diverse world, we still mistrust differences. In the coaching community, there is the beginning of dialogue, events and collaboration to understand the status of coaching within each country and culture, and an understanding that our common needs are similar. It is only through a continuation of concerted dialogue that we can begin to shift the status quo and move coaching towards becoming a more rigorous field.

We are a fair distance from becoming a profession. The current status of coaching is reliant on self-regulation through various professional bodies such as the ICF, EMCC, WABC, Association for Coaching (AC), and Coaches and Mentors Association of South Africa (COMENSA)). Self-regulation is supported by their underlying principles and values, voluntary codes of ethics, recommended standards of competence, complaints procedures and other guidelines. Despite these recommended guidelines, for example most practitioners do not carry liability insurance as do such other professions as medicine and psychology. The Dublin Declaration recommends 'regulating ourselves' before someone else does: 'In the absence of us defining ourselves the market will do it for us' (GCC, 2008: 9).

EVALUATION

While we take the view that it is an appropriate aim to strive for more professionalism in the field of coaching, we should be aware of a number of obstacles or conditions that hinder the establishment of coaching as a profession in the traditional sense. We would argue that it might not even be in the best interests of coaching or its clients to pursue the traditional route to legitimization. The concept of a 'profession' is under attack and it may be that coach practitioners need to think about different forms of association, perhaps along the following lines:

1. Coaching is a beneficial and useful enterprise as part of other professions.
2. The concept of profession has changed. In that sense, it might not even be realistic to establish coaching as a profession in a traditional sense.
3. The professionalism of coaches can be developed through interdisciplinary efforts based on research and evidence-based practice.
4. To be able to work professionally as a coach means to be aware of specific antinomies and tensions in the coaching process.
5. Voluntary bodies in collaboration can begin to define new models of association that sit outside of traditional professions which retain their virtues but avoid their vices.

REFERENCES

Bennett, J.L. (2006). An agenda for coaching-related research: A challenge for researchers. *Coaching Psychology Journal: Practice and Research, 58*(4): 240–49.

Berglas, S. (2002). The very real dangers of executive coaching. *Harvard Business Review,* June.

Corrie, S. (2009). *The art of inspired living: Coach yourself with positive psychology.* London: Karnac Books.

Corrie, S., & Lane, D.A. (2009). *Constructing stories, telling tales: Case formulation in psychology.* London: Karnac Books.

Deutscher Bundesverband Coaching [Federal Association of Coaching in Germany] (DBVC) (Ed.). (2007). *Leitlinien und Empfehlungen für die Entwicklung von Coaching als Profession* [Guidelines and recommendations for the development of coaching as a profession]. Osnabrück: DBVC.

Drake, D.B. (2007). The art of thinking narratively: Implications for coaching psychology and practice. *Australian Psychologist, 42*(4): 283–94.

Drake, D.B. (2009). What story are you in? Four elements of a narrative approach to formulation in coaching. In S. Corrie & D.A. Lane, *Constructing stories, telling tales: Case formulation in psychology.* London: Karnac Books.

Fillery-Travis, A., & Lane, D. (2006). How to develop your research interests. In S. Palmer & R. Bor (Eds.), *The practitioner's handbook: A guide for counsellors, psychotherapists and counselling psychologists.* London: Sage.

Foucault, M. (1983). The subject and power. In H. Dreyus & P. Rabinow (Eds.), *Michael Foucault: Beyond structuralism and hermeneutics.* Chicago, IL: University of Chicago Press.

Global Coaching Community (GCC). (2008). Dublin declaration on coaching. Paper presented at the Global Convention on Coaching, Dublin, August.

Jarvis, J., Lane, D.A., & Fillery-Travis, A. (2006). *The case for coaching: Making evidence based decisions on coaching.* Wimbledon: Chartered Institute of Personnel and Development.

Johnson, T.J. (1995). Governmentality and the institutionalization of expertise. In T. Johnson, G. Larkin & M. Saks (Eds.), *Health professions and the state in Europe* (pp. 7–24). New York: Routledge.

Lane, D.A., & Corrie, S. (2006). *The modern scientist-practitioner: A guide to practice in psychology.* Hove: Routledge.

Larson, M.S. (1977). *The rise of professionalism: A sociological analysis.* Berkeley, CA: University of California Press.

Law, H., Ireland, S., & Hussain, Z. (2007). *The psychology of coaching, mentoring and learning.* Chichester: John Wiley.

Lo, M-C.M. (2004). The professions: Prodigal daughters of modernity. In J. Adams, E.S. Clemens & A.S. Orloff (Eds.), *Remaking modernity: Politics, history, and sociology* (pp. 381–406). Durham, NC: Duke University Press.

Spence, G.B. (2007). Further development of evidence-based coaching: Lessons from the rise and fall of the human potential movement. *Australian Psychologist, 42*(4): 255–65.

26

Ethics in Coaching

Diane Brennan and Leni Wildflower

INTRODUCTION

The issue of ethical standards is critical in any profession. Coaching is no exception. The increasing success of coaching since 1995 in North America, Europe, Australia and more recently, Asia, has prompted a rapid growth of coaching programmes and coaches entering the field world-wide (PwC, 2007). With this success comes a measure of notoriety. Coaching has grown widely in acceptance in business and professional organizations, and there are few barriers to individuals wishing to establish themselves as coaches: coaching operates independently of oversight by any one professional body or government.

Various professional coaching bodies, however, have established standards of ethical practice for their members, including:

- European Mentoring and Coaching Council (EMCC)
- International Coach Federation (ICF)
- Association for Coaching (AC)
- Association for Professional Executive Coaching and Supervision (APECS)
- International Association of Coaching (IAC)
- Worldwide Association of Business Coaches (WABC).

In addition to the various coaching bodies, the British Psychological Society (BPS), Australian Psychological Society (APS) and the American Psychological Association (APA) have established special interest groups in coaching psychology.

These bodies work independently, but there are commonalities across the codes that will be explored within this chapter. Each provides a code of ethics and a complaints process to encourage compliance with professional standards and ethical practice among their membership. The opportunity to join and be held accountable for ethical conduct builds public confidence for practitioners in this relatively young emerging profession (Garlo & Prior, 2003). Considering the Pricewaterhouse Coopers estimate of 30,000 coaches worldwide in the 2006 benchmarking study (PwC, 2007), a conservative estimate of perhaps 65% of coaches could belong to one or more of the professional bodies. Those who do are assumed to demonstrate commitment to some definition of ethical practice.

This chapter includes a discussion and comparison of the ethical standards of coaching, psychological, law and education organizations, and a discussion of the ethical issues that currently face professional coaches including contracting, confidentiality, conflict of interest, dual and multiple relationships and boundary management. The issues will be considered for independent coaches as well as for those who are employed within organizations.

EVOLUTION OF ETHICS IN COACHING

A code of ethics provides foundational guidelines in relation to what to expect from those within the profession (Gert, 1988). Ethical codes are standards of conduct that define the essentials of honourable behaviour within the particular field or organization. Upon joining, a member of a professional body agrees to abide by the organization's code, and acknowledgement of the code creates a feeling of community and mutual obligation among the members toward each other and the overall profession (Khurana & Nohria, 2008). For example physicians, psychologists, counsellors, lawyers, teachers and human resource professionals all follow a code of conduct and meet the standards established for their particular profession. Acknowledging the code demonstrates commitment to high standards of practice for those they serve.

In relation to coaching, de Jong considers sound ethics to be the essence and underpinning of good coaching (de Jong, 2006). Coaching pioneers such as Thomas Leonard and Laura Whitworth (Brennan, 2008) came from various professions including accounting, finance, psychology, law, management and education, and also saw the need for an ethical framework early on in the development of the field (Garlo & Prior, 2003).

Looking at codes of ethics across various disciplines, the common themes are:

1. Do no harm: Do not cause needless injury or harm to others.
2. Duty of care: Act in ways that promote the welfare of other people.
3. Know your limits: Competence and practice within your scope.
4. Respect the interests of the client.
5. Respect the law.

COMPARISON OF COACHING CODES

The ethical codes from organizations, including ICF, the EMCC, the AC, the APECS, the IAC and the WABC, are strikingly similar. Even what appear at first as differences tend to reveal themselves, on closer inspection, as regroupings of familiar principles – variations in taxonomy rather than content. For example the EMCC code of ethics references competence, context, boundary management, integrity and professionalism, while ICF describes professional conduct at large, conduct with clients, conflicts of interest and confidentiality. The similarities are not surprising, given that some of these codes have been modelled on others, and all of them derive from a limited number of common sources. On the other hand, such bodies as have taken the trouble to draw up new codes for coaching have clearly been motivated to look afresh, and with conscientious attention, at the ethical pressures that an individual in this emerging profession is likely to encounter. We can rule out careless or uncritical borrowing.

The degree of similarity in the resulting formulations is a reminder of the extent to which these codes are based not only on earlier professional codes drawn up by other professional groups such as psychologists and medics but, beyond them, on more basic societal codes. They spring, in other words, from a deeper source (Weiner, 2006). The major areas of professional concern expressed in these codes, which include not exploiting positions of power or status, avoiding conflicts of interest and keeping confidences, could be applied directly to people in general as they function in work and in relationships. These codes seem to give expression to an emerging consensus of what constitutes conscientious behaviour that goes beyond the limits of coaching or any other specialized activity. The consensus underlying these modern codes is aspirational, pragmatic and humane, concerning itself with the ways in which our behaviour impacts other people.

These values are expressed with particular thoroughness and attempted precision in professional codes of ethics for several reasons. First, it is in the nature of being a professional that one functions with a particular level of consciousness of the effect of one's behaviour. Second, professional bodies have the power, to a greater or lesser extent, to enforce high standards of behaviour on a group of individuals who have chosen to abide by a particular code, in return for which they can enjoy the status and benefits of membership.

Coaching here is in a significantly different position from medicine, where qualifications and membership are far more tightly defined, and removing someone from the profession is difficult. In coaching, standards of behaviour are largely self-imposed. Even in this unregulated environment, however, the existence of a code is crucial, serving as a set of descriptors against which a client or colleague can measure a coach's performance, or as a system of prompts for self-evaluation.

Codes of ethics in coaching, based though they are on the codes of older more established professions, also tend to differ in emphasis, tilting somewhat in their overall effect towards the positive and balancing prohibition with exhortation. At the same time they focus more attention on the subtle psychological interaction between coach and client which is both the context of the work and a significant part of its content and, in doing so, they emphasize the autonomy and dignity of the client.

In the nuanced exchanges that form the basis of the coaching relationship, codes of ethics, however elaborate and however strictly enforced, will never be sufficient. The coach will always be called upon, by the nature of the work, to be acutely conscious of its ethical dimension.

In July 2008, the Global Convention on Coaching (GCC), a gathering of individuals representing some 40 countries around the world, came together to continue a dialogue about the future of coaching. Ethics was one of the ten topics covered in the dialogue process. Key findings and recommendations from the GCC were published in a summary document (GCC, 2008) and confirmed:

1. After twelve months of open discussions world-wide, it has become evident that a strong code of ethics is of paramount importance.
2. The code underpins the emergence of coaching as a profession, its status, education and development and core competencies.
3. A strong code will help sustain the profession. It is also evident that such a code needs accountability mechanisms.

The common elements among the existing codes point the way towards a shared code of conduct for the emerging profession. Several of the organizations are already in conversations to explore carrying this process forward for the overall good of the profession.

ETHICAL BEHAVIOUR IN A COACHING RELATIONSHIP

Ethical codes, though they attempt to define a set of behaviours, are necessarily limited. The process of abstracting moral principles leaves out the tacit frameworks that inform one's self understanding, sense of self-worth and sense of moral behaviour (Taylor, 1989). It is a fair assumption that most coaches act within the code of ethics drawn up by their coaching organization: they do not explicitly cross boundaries between the personal and the professional; they do not knowingly lie to clients; and they do not become sexually involved with them. But what about transgressions that are sufficiently subtle that they might not even be recognized by the coach responsible for them?

One of the areas of ethical concern often stated by respected coaches is the concern over competence. In an effort to win over clients, coaches may promise unrealistic outcomes. They might assume that they can help create changes or provide insights for clients which are beyond their level of ability.

In a profession where the very act of engagement has emotional and moral ramifications, it is more necessary and more difficult to describe correct ethical behaviour. It is in precisely this zone of subtle moral judgment that the most important dimension of an ethical practice lies. It is also where adult development and moral competencies overlap with ethical guidelines. Unfortunately, behaviour at this level cannot be legislated for, or controlled with consequences for infractions. In every coaching situation, we must count on the coach's impulse not only to 'do no harm', but to work conscientiously towards positive results for the client.

Circumstances where unethical behaviour might pass under the radar of a code of ethics might include situations where the coach:

1. misrepresents his or her ability to deliver an outcome in order to keep a client or, more innocently, to make the client feel better
2. becomes emotionally involved in the client's issues and indirectly or inadvertently manipulates the client in order to meet his or her own needs
3. retains a client who loves being coached but makes no progress in his/her coaching work.

The aspiration to act ethically cannot be separated from the ability of individuals to separate themselves from others and to have developed a sophisticated level of moral reasoning. Professional practice as a coach requires ongoing commitment to ethics with continuous awareness and learning in the process.

ETHICAL ISSUES

The coaching organizations with established codes of ethics and standards also have complaint processes should concerns arise. These provide for self-monitoring in a field that has no overarching monitoring or regulation. They are not intended to remediate damage caused to clients, but rather to steer the future actions of the coach.

The complaint processes, while distinct within the framework of each organization's operation, consistently include a request for a written complaint with the identification of the individual initiating the concern. The processes are complex and intended to provide an independent and objective review of the situation. If the coach is found to have breached the code of ethics, remedies or sanctions are determined in accordance with the seriousness of the breach. Remedies might be mentoring, supervision, and/or additional education specific to the area of concern. Sanctions may include a loss of certification in or membership of the organization.

In 2006, the ICF summarized the situations generating the most frequent inquiries in four categories at an ethics presentation at the annual international conference (Rubenstein, 2006). The four identified are Contracting, Confidentiality, Misrepresentation and Conflict of interest.

1. *Contracting*

Contracting issues included concerns about compensation, where a coach might require a percentage of the client's increase in gross profit in addition to the coaching fee. This type of arrangement is not uncommon in consulting. Tying the coach's compensation to the client's outcome, however, creates an attachment that is contrary to the foundational competencies in coaching and could be viewed as exploiting the client.

In some parts of the world it is not uncommon for coaches to request payment for services in advance. This can cause concern if a client ends a coaching relationship prematurely. The coach is responsible for ensuring there is a clear agreement that defines services and financial terms that are in alignment with area business practices. It is the responsibility of coaches to be aware of differences that may be relevant within their region.

Other inquiries reported around compensation involve coaches receiving income from affiliate relationships and referrals to other services, programmes or products. While it may seem profitable to engage in these types of relationships to generate revenue, it is important to investigate fully and determine if they are indeed fit for the business and are acceptable practice in the particular area of the world. Any relationships of this type need to be clearly disclosed.

2. *Confidentiality/boundary management*

The confidential nature of the relationship between coach and client forms the basis for trust within the relationship. Brock states that the expectation for confidentiality in coaching is to 'Respect confidentiality of all client information (including company and/or client name) except as authorized by client or required by law' (2006). The question of a breach in confidentiality can arise among coaches as they share stories or examples of work with clients. However, sharing an anonymized coaching situation with a supervisor or coaching group as part of reflective practice (Hay, 2007) is encouraged, and is beneficial for ongoing professional development and learning. Concern arises when a coach uses a client's name without permission or describes a situation in a manner that promotes the coach and disregards the client.

Coaches working in organizations, either internally as employees, or externally as contractors, face an added dimension of complexity around confidentiality. Organizations funding coaching for an individual or team often require, at least initially, a periodic report on the value of the coaching experience. The organization is often referred to as the 'sponsor' of the coaching. Sponsors with a formal coaching programme or past experience with coaching generally understand the importance of a clear agreement to define the reporting process at the beginning of the relationship. To avoid an unintentional breach of confidentiality, the coach should not be in a position to prepare or present a report. The coach can support the client in this process, although the communication is best done by the client.

Boundary management is important to note here. Coaching clients are healthy and whole in their lives. They are coming to coaching to move forward in their goals and development. Clients may be unknown prior to beginning the coaching relationship or they may be acquaintances, business associates, colleagues, friends and sometimes even family. Coach and client may develop a friendship over time. It is important to have a clear coaching relationship and not allow personal bias to influence professional actions. Blurring the lines between coach and friend, family, colleague, etc., creates a potential for ethical concern and poor outcome. It is critical to stay mindful of the ethical responsibility to the client and to maintain confidentiality, objectivity and equal partnership. Should there be any concerns the coach has a responsibility to raise the issue, act in the best interest of the client and, if necessary, end the coaching relationship.

Coaches working within organizations may have the opportunity to work with individuals and teams crossing lines throughout the company. The confidential space created between client and coach allows for openness and honesty that may not occur anywhere else in the individual's life. It is not uncommon for the coach to hear sensitive and personal information about the individual, or about others within the organization or the organization itself. With the privilege of coaching comes great responsibility to maintain client confidentiality.

3. *Misrepresentation*

The desire to attain a competitive edge in the market place can drive coaches to embellish their qualifications, credentials or value to the client.

They might also be tempted to extend their activities beyond coaching. Coaches come from a variety of backgrounds and bring a wealth of knowledge and expertise from previous professions. It is advisable for coaches to acknowledge these areas of expertise, and to be clear on what coaching is and what it offers. What separates coaching from other professional services is the belief in the client's resourcefulness and potential. Consulting or training should be identified as distinct activities.

Another area where concerns of misrepresentation arise is with marketing and presentation materials. Members of the coaching community are generous and supportive of individuals entering the emerging profession. The international composition of the community creates opportunity for ideas and materials to be shared around the world. However, just as in any other profession, coaches need to respect copyright law, ask permission for use of materials and acknowledge creators.

4. *Conflict of interest*

The success of coaching has prompted many to enter the market in various ways. There are new training programmes, products and services marketed to coaches daily. In turn, coaches market these products to clients. There is little to measure one programme, product or service against another or to ensure that all truly bring value to the buyer. It is up to the coach involved in these types of arrangements to stay aware and 'not knowingly exploit any aspect of the coach–client relationship for personal, professional or monetary advantage or benefit' (ICF, 2005).

Brock (2006) succinctly summarizes the responsibility of the coach: 'Seek to avoid conflicts between my interests and the interests of my clients; whenever any actual conflict of interest or the potential for a conflict arises, I will openly disclose it and fully discuss with my client how to deal with it in whatever way best serves my client'.

Additional areas that are of importance as we consider ethical issues include: Dual and Multiple Relationships, Competence, and Self-management.

5. *Dual and multiple relationships*

Brickey (2002) defines the dual relationship as one where the relationship with someone has more than one role or interest. Relative to coaching, this may be a client who is also the spouse of a friend or the cousin of another client, etc. Thinking further, the client may additionally be the coach's accountant, lawyer or physician. Full disclosure of any conflict of interest, clearly defined roles, responsibilities and boundaries, client-focus, reflective practice and supervision are key to successfully navigating dual or multiple relationships (Zur & Anderson, 2006).

6. *Competence*

Competence is defined in human resources terms as meeting the standard requirement to properly perform a particular job. Competence in coaching includes a combination of knowledge, skills and behaviour. While there is not a universally accepted measure of competence, what is held consistent among coach professionals is the support for coach-specific education, skill development, practice and ongoing professional development. In the absence of a universal standard, anyone can call themselves a coach, and they do. Proliferation of the open field poses the possibility of damaging the reputation of coaching.

Coaches need to be conscious of their own limits, understand the requirements of coaching competence, be coached on their coaching and engage in reflective practice for ongoing professional development. They should not try to be all-encompassing or fit to what the client needs. Even if they have a background in psychology or counselling, it is best to stay out of the counselling realm when contracted to coach with the client (Rogers, 2004). In coaching situations where counselling appears to be needed, the issue should be raised with the client and an offer of referral made.

7. *Self-management*

Self-management as defined here is recognizing bias, preconceived ideas, initial impressions, opinions or stereotypes that can influence the ability to be fully focused and present with the client. Distractions can occur in any coaching relationship, though within the corporate environment the internal coach faces this challenge with more intensity. A coach may have knowledge of the client's reputation within the company or through coaching with the client's peers before the coaching partnership began (Rogers, 2004). The coach needs to recognize any bias and to self-manage in order to be focused and present with the client. If coaches cannot achieve the level of self-management to fully support the client, they should remove themselves from the engagement and assist the client in finding another coach. Firing oneself as a coach, whether within a company or in a private coaching business, is sometimes necessary in the service of the client.

The role of the coach is to facilitate the client's learning to find his/her own answers. There may be times when the coach strategizes or brainstorms with the client or offers an idea for consideration. The idea is not the client's solution but rather one possibility. If the client's expectation is that the coach will have the solution to their concern, perhaps the client does not understand the coaching relationship. If coaches feel they need to offer advice to give value to the client, they may need to step back to examine the relationship with the client and their own understanding of coaching.

THE FUTURE: AN ETHICAL COACHING COMMUNITY

Coaching is a powerful process that is increasingly evolving in research, understanding of theories, practice and professional qualification (Brennan, 2008). Coaches have a responsibility to engage as professionals and to recognize their responsibility and contribution to their clients, colleagues and society as a whole. The Canadian Psychological Association (CPA) provides definition and language to describe the responsibility that applies to the professional coach and the coaching community.

> Every discipline that has relatively autonomous control over its entry requirements, training, development of knowledge, standards, methods, and practices does so only within the context of a contract with the society in which it functions. This social contract is based on attitudes of mutual respect and trust, with society granting support for the autonomy of a discipline in exchange for a commitment by the discipline to do everything it can to assure that its members act ethically in conducting the affairs of the discipline within society. (CPA, 2000: Preamble)

As critical as practising ethical behaviour within a coaching relationship, is the ability of coaches to create, maintain and foster an ethical community of coaches. Ethical behaviour among coaches would include the practice of sharing information and best practices; being open to new knowledge; respecting diversity and cultural difference and collaborating with a range of coaches and organizations to help strengthen the profession as a whole.

Many coaching organizations and training schools are run as businesses and have to succeed in a competitive market place. But, in conflict with the economic pressure to compete, is the professional impetus to cooperate. It is clear that coaching will only progress towards full professional status if the many parties involved find common ground. This will involve a shared understanding that the communal benefits of a free exchange of ideas and knowledge, and a willingness to refer clients outweigh the dangers of giving up areas of control and sources of income. It will require a degree of mutual trust that is not so different from the trust that as coaches we ask of our clients.

If, as suggested by Kohlberg (1981), we assume that ethical behaviour depends on a level of individual maturity then the work of the developmental theorists is important to consider.

According to Robert Kegan, individuals pass through developmental stages throughout their lives (Kegan, 1982, 1994). As they move to higher stages, their ability to make meaning in life becomes more complex and multifaceted:

- At stage 3, people are 'other dependent'. They are able to see themselves as part of something larger than themselves, but cannot resolve conflicting viewpoints of others or between themselves and others.
- At stage 4, people are able to own their own work and make their own decisions, and are internally motivated. They are able to see different points of view, yet are ultimately driven by their own sense of mission and values.
- At stage 5, people are capable of seeing their own and others' points of view simultaneously. They are able to view an issue from multiple perspectives.

Kegan's and Kohlberg's models share several qualities. In both, one must progress through each successive stage. It is not possible to skip over a developmental stage. Furthermore, individuals seldom regress into less complex stages.

The ability to understand others in more complex terms is a critical component of ethical behaviour (Laske, 2006: 11). An important outcome of a coach functioning at a higher stage of development is the nuanced ability to view the client's situation, and to act ethically in service of the client.

Kegan and Kohlberg provide two theoretical lenses through which to view moral and ethical development. There are many others. What we learn from these theories is that the acquisition of values and ethical behaviour is, at least in part, a developmentally driven process and not something handed to people from parents, churches or schools. How we respond to a moral or ethical dilemma is a function of a range of complex factors. Understanding our own and others' moral behaviour is an intricate process.

Ethical behaviour among coaches might include the following.

1. Recommending a competing coach training school to a prospective student, when one's own school is not a good match for that individual.
2. Recommending a competing coach or coaching organization to a prospective client, who would benefit from a specific area of expertise.
3. Competing coach training schools offering to hold joint or collaborative conferences or seminars.
4. Reaching out to coaches with different coaching methods offering to share ideas, knowledge, and new research.

EVALUATION

There is a growing movement in America, Europe and around the world, to form a coherent identity for the practice of coaching in order to move it towards full professional status. An agreed ethical framework governing the relationship between the coach and the client would be an essential element of this new professional identity. The professional coaching bodies have an opportunity to work together for the benefit of the overall profession.

It is a challenge to go beyond the isolation of individual organizations and strengthen the foundation for the future. Of equal importance is a coming together of a community of coaches who all share a level of trust and respect in their dealings with each other. Only when coaching can move beyond preconceived notions and limitations and integrate into the fabric of society will there be a sustainable and measurable impact on the future.

REFERENCES

Brennan, D. (2008). Coaching in the US: Trends and challenges. *Coaching: An International Journal of Theory, Research and Practice, 1*(2).

Brickey, M. (2002). Dual relations: Can coaches be pragmatic? *Division 42 Professional Practice, Spring*. http://www.division42.org/MembersArea/IPfiles/IPSprg_2002/articles/prof_practice/duel_relations.html

Brock, V. (2006). Where do we align our ethical code? Learning from other professions. *Choice, 4*(3).

Canadian Psychological Association (CPA). (2000). Retrieved June 2009, from http://ethics.iit.edu/codes/coe/can.psychological.assoc.2000.html#intro

de Jong, A. (2006). Coaching ethics: Integrity in the moment of choice. In J. Passmore (Ed.), *Excellence in coaching* (pp. 191–202). London: Association for Coaching.

Garlo, D.M., & Prior, D.M. (2003). Committing to an ethical framework: A powerful Choice. *Choice, Fall*.

Gert, B. (1988). *Morality: A new justification of the moral rules*. New York: Oxford University Press.

Global Convention on Coaching (GCC). (2008). *Dublin declaration and appendices*. International Coach Federation Research Portal www.coachfederation.org

Hay, J. (2007). *Reflective practice and supervision for coaches*. New York: Open University Press.

International Coach Federation (ICF). 2005 [2008]) *Ethics code*. Retrieved from http://www.coachfederation.org/about-icf/ethics-%26-regulation/icf-code-of-ethics/

Kegan, R. (1982). *The evolving self: Problem and process in human development*. Cambridge, MA: Harvard University Press.

Kegan, R. (1994). *In over our heads: The mental demands of modern life*. Cambridge, MA: Harvard University Press.

Khurana, R., & Nohria, N. (2008). It's time to make management a true profession. *Harvard Business Review, October*: 70–7.

Kohlberg, L. (1981). *Essays on moral development* (Vol 1): *The philosophy of moral development*. San Francisco, CA: Harper and Row.

Laske, O. (2006). Why does your maturity matter? *Choice, 4*(3).

PricewaterhouseCoopers (PwC) (2007). *International Coach Federation global coaching study*. Lexington, KY: International Coach Federation. www.coachfederation.org

Rogers, J. (2004). *Coaching skills: A handbook* (ch. 7, pp. 163–8). New York: Open University Press.

Rubenstein, D. (2006). Cracking the code: Unveiling the mystery – beta test and walk away with the new ICF ethics education program. Paper presented at the International Coach Federation Annual Conference, St. Louis, Missouri, November.

Taylor, C. (1989). *Sources of the self: The making of modern identity*. Cambridge, MA: Harvard University Press.

Weiner, K.C. (2006). Foundations of professional ethics. In P. Williams & S.K. Anderson (Eds.), *Law and ethics in coaching: How to solve and avoid difficult problems in your practice* (pp. 21–38). Hoboken, NJ: John Wiley & Sons.

Zur, O., & Anderson, S.K. (2006). Multiple-role relationships in coaching. In P. Williams & S.K. Anderson (Eds.), *Law and ethics in coaching: How to solve and avoid difficult problems in your practice* (pp. 126–9). Hoboken, NJ: John Wiley & Sons.

PROFESSIONAL BODIES' CODES OF ETHICS CONSULTED (RETRIEVED OCTOBER 2008)

- American Psychological Association (APA) http://www.apa.org
- Association for Coaching (AC) http://www.associationforcoaching.com
- Association for Professional Executive Coaching and Supervision(APECS) http://www.apecs.org
- Australian Psychological Society (APS) http://www.psychology.org.au
- British Psychological Society (BPS) http://www.bps.org
- European Mentoring and Coaching Council (EMCC) http://www.emccouncil.org.uk
- International Association of Coaching (IAC) http://www.certifiedcoach.org
- International Coach Federation (ICF) http://www.coachfederation.org
- Worldwide Association of Business Coaches (WABC) http://www.wabccoaches.com

27

Coaching Supervision

Peter Hawkins

INTRODUCTION

At the core of continuing professional development is continual personal development, where our own development is weaved through every aspect of our practice. When this happens every coachee becomes a teacher, every piece of feedback an opportunity for new learning, producing practices that support the balanced cycle of action, reflection, new understanding and new practice. Elsewhere (Hawkins, 2006; Hawkins & Smith, 2006) we have shown why we believe that having supervision is a fundamental aspect of continuing personal and professional development for coaches, mentors and consultants. Supervision provides a protected and disciplined space in which the coach can reflect on particular client situations and relationships, the reactivity and patterns they evoke in them and, by transforming these live in supervision, can profoundly benefit the coachee, the client organization and their own professional practice.

Coaching and mentoring have been areas of enormous growth in the last ten years (Jarvis, 2004). Berglas (2000) estimated that there were at least 10,000 professional coaches working for businesses in the US and predicted that the figure would exceed 50,000 in 2007. Despite this, coaching supervision was noticeable by its absence in the first 20 years of the growth of this new profession, but at the turn of the century it began to be advocated by a number of key writers (see Flaherty, 1999; Downey, 1999).

In the early part of the twenty-first century very few coaches were receiving supervision, and those who did so were approaching supervisors trained in psychotherapy or counselling. While there is much we can learn from these and other people professions, where quality supervision has been practised for longer than coaching, there are also dangers as outlined below.

It was not until 2003 that the first specific training was offered for coaching supervisors and 2006 that the first book on coaching supervision was published (Hawkins and Smith, 2006).

In carrying out research into supervision for The Chartered Institute of Personnel and Development (CIPD) in the UK, we explored the reasons for the lack of development of coaching supervision (Hawkins & Schwenk, 2006). In interviews and focus groups with experienced coaches we were given a number of different explanations:

1. lack of clarity about what supervision involves
2. lack of well trained supervisors
3. lack of commitment to personal development as it makes us vulnerable
4. lack of discipline among coaches
5. addiction to being in the role of the person enabling others, rather than receiving enablement.

Probably all of these have some degree of truth, and a full answer needs to include these and other factors. In the absence of a body of good theories, trainings and practitioners, many coaches have turned to counsellors, psychologists and psychotherapists for supervision or supervisory models.

There is much that the helping professions can learn from each other, but it is also important to recognize the difference between the fundamental work of each professional group, and hence the dangers of over-applying the theories and models of one group to the work of another. One of the dangers of a coach visiting a counsellor or counselling psychologist for supervision is that a supervisor's professional focus may tend towards understanding the psychology of the coachee. Depending on their orientation the supervisor might also focus on the relationship of coach and coachee and may have a tendency to focus more on pathology than on health! The biggest danger is when a fundamental orientation that is more interested in individuals than organizations tips over into an unrecognized tendency to see individuals as victims of 'bad' or 'unfeeling' organizations. At worst this can create a classic drama triangle of 'organization as persecutor; coachee as victim and coach as rescuer'. One of the key challenges of coaching supervision is for it to develop its own approach and methodology for supervision, which, while learning from what has been developed elsewhere, can address the challenge of coaching having multiple stakeholders.

COACHING SUPERVISION RESEARCH

The research for the CIPD mentioned above (Hawkins & Schwenk, 2006) focused on a number of key questions:

- What is coaching supervision?
- Why should HR professionals be interested in it?

- What do HR professionals need to know about coaching supervision?
- What does good practice look like?
- How can supervision help coaching to be more effective?

The research was conducted through a variety of methods: a web survey, where we had responses from over 500 individual coaches and over 120 organizations; four focus groups in various parts of the UK, which included both buyers of coaching and experienced providers; and six best practice case studies of organizations that had committed to incorporating supervision into both their internal and external coaching provision.

What we found was that:

- Coaching supervision was much advocated but poorly practised.
- According to the surveys, 88% of organizers of coaching and 86% of coaches believed that coaches should have regular ongoing supervision of their coaching.
- Only 44% of coaches receive regular ongoing supervision and only 23% of organizations provided regular ongoing coaching supervision.
- Of the coaches receiving supervision only 58% had started within the last two years.
- Many of those who were receiving supervision were consulting with supervisors of counselling or psychotherapy and some with peers without supervision training.
- There was a shortage of training courses in coaching supervision.
- This was the first research in the field of coaching supervision.
- There was an absence of specific models and methodologies for coaching supervision.

WHAT IS SUPERVISION?

In 2006, Hawkins and Smith defined supervision as 'the process by which a coach with the help of a supervisor, can attend to understanding better both the client system and themselves as part of the client-coach system, and by so doing transform their work and develop their craft' (Hawkins & Smith, 2006).

To this could be added: 'Supervision also does this by attending to the transformation of the relationship between the supervisor and coach and to the wider contexts in which the work is happening'.

We believe that coaching supervision has three elements:

1. coaching the coach on their coaching
2. mentoring the coach on their development in the profession
3. providing an external perspective to ensure quality of practice.

This three-function model parallels the three functions that Kadushin put forward for social work supervision in the 1970s and that Proctor espoused for counselling supervision in the 1980s. Kadushin (1992) talked of the 'managerial, educative and supportive' aspects of supervision and Proctor (1988) of supervision being 'normative, formative and restorative'.

Having worked with these two models for many years we have found both to be rather confined to their own fields, and so have developed our own model that defines the three main functions as developmental, resourcing and qualitative. Kadushin focuses on the role of the supervisor, Proctor on the supervisee benefit and our new distinctions on the process in which both supervisor and supervisee are engaged.

ROLE AND PURPOSE OF SUPERVISION

I believe that the role and purpose of the supervision of coaches is to build strongly upon the work carried out in the field of supervision by those in the helping professions, but some important changes are necessary in order to really support the executive coaching agenda.

Supervision is a key element in both the training process for coaches and for their lifetime continuing professional development. In training it is the process of rigorous supervision that helps the trainee link the theory and skills they learn on courses to the realtime experience of working with coachees. On workshops we can absorb models and develop competencies, but these do not by themselves produce an excellent coach. Supervision provides the reflective container for the trainee to turn their competencies into capabilities and to develop their personal and coaching capacities.

Importantly, supervision is there to serve not only the profession, but also the developmental needs of the coach/supervisee, the individual coachees that the coach is coaching, and the client organizations that employ the coach.

Some key outcomes on which supervision should be focused include:

- provision of the key part of continuous professional development and action learning of the coach or mentor (D);
- help for the coach or mentor to develop their internal supervisor and become a better reflective practitioner (D);
- provision of a supportive space for the coach or mentor to process what they have absorbed from their clients and their clients' systems (R);
- help to keep the coach and mentor honest and courageous, attending to what they are: not seeing, not hearing, not allowing themselves to feel, or not saying (Q);
- a chance to look at where and how the coach or mentor may need to refer the client on for more specialized help (Q).

Bracketed letters indicate how these outcomes link back to the three functions of Qualitative (Q), Developmental (D) and Resourcing (R) – see Table 27.1.

Table 27.1: Three main functions of supervision

Hawkins	Proctor (1988)	Kadushin (1992)
Developmental	Formative	Educational
Resourcing	Restorative	Supportive
Qualitative	Normative	Managerial

The Coaching Continuum

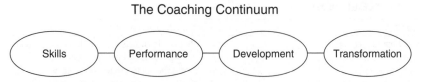

Figure 27.1 The coaching continuum (Hawkins & Smith, 2006).

STAGES IN A SUPERVISION SESSION

The five-stage coaching model CLEAR (*Contract, Listen, Explore, Action, Review*), that was discussed in Chapter 16 can also be applied to the stages of supervision, or coaching the coach.

In this model the supervisor starts by *Contracting* with the supervisee on both the boundaries and focus of the work. Then the supervisor *Listens* to the issues that the coach wishes to bring, listening not only to the content, but also to the feelings and the ways of framing the story that the coach is using. Before moving on, it is important that supervisors let the coach know that they have not only heard the story, but have 'got' what it feels like to be in their situation. Only then is it useful to move on to the next stage; to *Explore* with the coach what is happening in the dynamics of both the coaching relationship and also in the live supervisory relationship, before facilitating the coach to explore new *Action*. Finally, *Review* the process and what has been agreed about next steps.

This model can be developed and utilized differentially depending on the nature of the coaching. In Hawkins and Smith (2006) we outlined a continuum of coaching (see Figure 27.1). We argued that the form of supervision being utilized needs to match the coaching approach, thus performance coaches need performance supervision and transformational coaching needs transformational supervision. To illustrate this I have put below the different types of interventions that may be made by a supervisor at each of the CLEAR stages, depending on whether they were doing performance or transformational supervision (see Table 27.2).

Contracting for supervision

All forms of supervision relationship need to begin with a clear contract, which is created and formed by both parties, and also reflects the expectations of the organizations and professions involved. Supervision contracts need to include:

a. practicalities, such as times, frequency, and place; anything that might be allowed to interrupt or postpone the session; and clarification of any payment involved;
b. boundaries, including how supervision is different from coaching or counselling; and any confidentiality arrangements;
c. working alliance – how the relationship needs to work for the supervisee to get the most benefit from the supervision;
d. The session format – how the process will work;

Table 27.2:   The CLEAR model

Performance coaching	Transformational coaching
C. What do you want to focus on?	C. What would success look like from this session?
L. Tell me about the situation	L. What I am sensing from your story is …
E. What else might you try?	E. What is the wildest thing you could do?
A. So what are you going to do and when?	A. Imagine I am that person and rehearse your opening line.
R. When will we meet to review it?	R. My appreciation is …
	My encouragement is …

e. The organizational and professional context – who else the supervision needs to serve, including the organization that employs the coach, their coachees and their organization; the professional bodies to which the coach belongs; and anyone who might accredit the coach.

THE SEVEN-EYED COACHING MODEL: A PROCESS MODEL OF SUPERVISION

In 1985 a more in-depth model of supervision was created (Hawkins, 1985), which later became known as the seven-eyed supervision model. This has been used across many different people professions and in many countries around the world (Hawkins & Shohet, 2006). Since 1995, with colleagues at Bath Consultancy Group, the model has been further developed for the world of coaching, mentoring and organizational consultancy (Hawkins, 1995; Hawkins & Smith, 2006). The purpose of the model is to provide a complete range of different areas in supervision that can be focused on and the range of styles necessary. It is based on a systems understanding of the ways things connect, interrelate and drive behaviour. It points out the way in which the systemic context of the coachee can be mirrored in the coaching relationship and how the dynamics of the coaching relationship can be mirrored in the supervisory relationship (see Figure 27.2). These seven areas of potential focus can be useful to both supervisor and supervisee in reviewing the supervision they give and receive and help them discover ways in which they can expand their supervision practice (see Figure 27.3).

1. The coachee's system

Here the focus is on the coachee and the content of the issues they have brought to the coaching as well as the wider issues of their organization. It includes not only the problem with which the coachee and the client organization want help, but also how the issues are being presented and framed.

Mode one skill   The supervisor's skill in this mode is to help the coach return accurately to what actually happened with the coachee – what they saw, what they heard and what they felt – and to try and separate this actual data from their preconceptions, assumptions and interpretations. It is useful for the coach to be helped to take notice of what happened at the boundaries of their

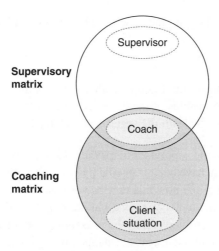

Figure 27.2 The seven-eyed model of coaching supervision.

time with the coachee, including their arrival and departure, for it is often at the boundaries that the richest unconscious material is most active.

2. The coach's interventions

Here the focus is on any interventions the coach may have made and alternative choices that might have been used. Focus may, for example, be on a situation in which the coach is about to intervene and explore possible options, including the likely impact of each.

Mode two skill Often coaches will ask for help with an impasse they have arrived at in facilitating the change process. They will often present this impasse in the form of an 'either/or', such as: 'Should I collude with this situation or confront the issue?' The skill of the supervisor is to avoid the trap of debating the either/or options, and instead enable the coach to realize how they are limiting their choices to two polarized possibilities. They could facilitate a shared brainstorming session that frees up energy and enables the creation of new options. The benefits and difficulties of these new options can be explored and some possible interventions tried out in role-play.

3. The relationship between the coach and the coachee

Here the focus is neither solely on the coachee and their system, nor on the coach, but on the relationship that they are creating together.

Mode three skill The supervisor has to facilitate a situation where the coach can stand outside the coach/coachee relationship to see it afresh and from a new angle. The Chinese have a proverb: the last to know about the sea are the fish, because they are constantly immersed within it.

In this way the supervisor is helping the coach to be a flying fish, so they can see the water in which they normally swim.

4. The coach

Here the focus is on the coach, highlighting both what is being re-stimulated in them by the coachee's material and the dynamics of the client system, and themselves as an instrument for registering what is happening beneath the surface of the coaching relationship.

Mode four skill In this mode the supervisor helps the coach to work through any re-stimulation of their own feelings that may have been triggered by working with this client. Having done this the coach can be helped to explore how this may be very useful data for understanding what the coachee and the client system are experiencing but are unable to directly articulate. The coach can then explore how their own blocks may be preventing them from facilitating the coachee and their system to change, and what needs to happen to enable a shift in the coachee and the client organization.

5. The supervisory relationship

Here the focus is on the live relationship between the supervisor and the coach. The focus needs to include what the coach has unconsciously absorbed from the coachee system and how that may be being played out in the relationship with the supervisor. The coach can inadvertently treat the supervisor in the way their coachee treated them.

Mode five skill   Here the supervisor needs to be able to attend not only to what they are being told about the coaching system, but also to what is happening in the relationship in the room. Having acquired this skill, the supervisor can then at times offer their tentative reflections on the impact of the coaching relationship of the presented material to illuminate the coaching dynamic. When done skilfully this process can help the coach bridge the gap between their conscious understanding of the coaching relationship and the emotional impact it has had upon them.

6. The supervisor self-reflection

The focus for mode six is the supervisor's 'here and now' experience while with the coach and what can be learnt about the coach/coachee/client relationship from the supervisor's response to the coach and the material they present.

Mode six skill In this mode the supervisor has to attend, not only to the presented material and the impact on the 'here and now' relationship, but also their own internal processes. The supervisor can discover the presence of unconscious material related to the coaching relationship by attending to and reflecting on their own feelings, thoughts and fantasies while listening to the presentation of the coaching situation. These can be tentatively commented on and made available as possible indicators of what lies buried in the relationship with the coachee. The additional skill is to explore the means of sharing this with the coach in a non-judgmental and speculative way.

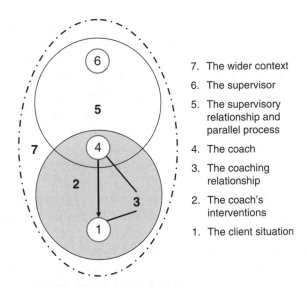

7. The wider context

6. The supervisor

5. The supervisory relationship and parallel process

4. The coach

3. The coaching relationship

2. The coach's interventions

1. The client situation

Figure 27.3   The seven modes of coaching supervision.

7. The wider context

The focus of mode seven is on the organizational, social, cultural, ethical and contractual context in which the coaching is taking place. This includes being aware of the wider group of stakeholders in the process that is being focused upon. This may include the client organization and its stakeholders, the coach's organization and its stakeholders, and the organization or professional network of the supervisor

Mode seven skill   The supervisor has to be able to bring a whole systems perspective to the understanding of how the systemic context is affecting not only the behaviour, mindsets, emotional ground and motivations of the coach and coachee, but also themselves. The skill is to attend appropriately to the needs of the critical stakeholders in the wider systems and to understand how the culture of the systemic context might be creating illusions, delusions and collusions in the coach and supervisor. To attend to mode seven also requires a high level of transcultural competence (Hawkins & Shohet, 2006; Hawkins & Smith, 2006).

Using all seven modes

In talking with both supervisors and coaches who have gone to others in search of help in exploring coaching situations, we have discovered that different supervisors are often stuck in the groove of predominantly using one of the seven modes of working. Some focus entirely on the situation out there with the coachee and adopt a pose of pseudo-objectivity (mode one).

Others see their job as coming up with better interventions than the coach managed to produce (mode two). This can often leave the coach feeling inadequate or determined to show that these suggested interventions are as useless as the ones they had previously tried. Other coaches have reported taking up a problem with a coachee and having left supervision feeling that the problem was entirely due to their own shortcomings (mode four).

'Single-eyed vision', which focuses on only one aspect of the process, will always lead to partial and limited perspectives. This model suggests a way of engaging in an exploration that looks at the same situation from many different perspectives and can thus create a critical subjectivity, where subjective awareness from one perspective is tested against other subjective data.

Each mode of supervision can be carried out in a skilful and elegant manner or ineffectively, but no matter how skilful one is in one mode, the skill will prove inadequate without the ability to move from mode to mode.

The most common order for moving through the modes is to start with mode one, talking about specific coaching situations, then to move into modes three and four to explore what is happening both in the coaching relationship and for the coach/supervisee. This may well lead to exploring the here and now relationship in the room between the coach and the supervisor (modes five and six), and/or bring into awareness the wider context (mode seven). Finally, having gained new insights and created a shift in the supervisory matrix, the attention may turn back to mode two, to explore what different interventions the coach might use in their next session to create the necessary shift in the coaching matrix. The coach might even try out some of these interventions in what is termed a 'fast-forward rehearsal' (see Chapter 16). From our experience we have learnt that if the change starts to happen live in the supervision, it is far more likely to happen back in the coaching.

The model has also been used as a way of empowering the coach, who is the customer of the supervision, to enable feedback on the help they are being given and to request a change in focus. It can be used as a framework for a joint review of the supervision process by the coach and supervisor.

TRAINING AS A SUPERVISOR

In 2002, the debate about the need for supervision in coaching began to change. Some of the professional coaching bodies, particularly in the UK but also in the USA, started to argue that all coaches should receive supervision from trained and qualified supervisors. In response, Bath Consultancy Group led the way in the development of a certified training programme in the supervision of coaches and mentors.

Our starting belief was that these professions had much in common with other helping professions when it came to supervision, but were also significantly different, particularly as their work was focused primarily on an individual client. In contrast, work-based coaches and mentors always have a minimum of three clients:

1. the coachee
2. the organization they work in and for
3. the relationship between them and their organization.

Our second belief is that learning to be a supervisor is best undertaken through cycles of action learning, not by sitting in a classroom. Thus the training involves a great deal of supervision practice in threes, comprising a supervisor, supervisee and shadow supervisor, who gives feedback to the supervisor, sometimes at the end of the practice session, and sometimes in the middle, in structured 'time-outs'. The trainee supervisors, as well as undertaking the modules, receive 10 hours of supervision from an experienced supervisor on their supervision, and two tutorials to help them maximize their individual learning.

In the Bath Consultancy Group we are constantly learning from each cohort of new trainees about the fascinating craft of supervising coaches and the lifelong journey to develop this craft. Increasingly, we are reminded that at the heart of being a good coach or a good coaching supervisor is not academic knowledge, a collection of theories and models, or an armoury of tools and techniques, but constant dedication to developing one's human capacity to be fully present for another, acting with what we term 'ruthless compassion'. For it is the ruthless compassion we can bring, not only to our client, but also to the work they do in the world and to our craft, that ultimately allows the fears and anxieties that pervade so many work situations to be overcome, and for our clients to find new strength to act courageously.

CONCLUSION

It is important that supervision is not seen as an activity carried out by a supervisor, supposedly with super vision! Rather, it should be seen as a joint activity between coach and supervisor that ensures that the quality of practice constantly develops the capacity and capability of the coach and makes sure they are resourcing themselves adequately for the work they are undertaking.

It is important that supervision is not just a process for experienced supervisors to pass on their way of practising to other coaches. In Hawkins and Shohet (2006) the way in which supervision needs to play an important role in facilitating a learning profession is described. It is argued that:

For too long we have reduced the concept of supervision to a cultural socialisation process where the elders of the professional community shape the practice, behaviours, understanding, perceptions, feelings and motivations of the apprentices and noviciates.

This approach to supervision can restrict the learning to that of the supervisee learning what has already been discovered by the supervisor and more senior members of the coaching profession. This in turn can lead to the profession becoming more constrained in well established practices, rather than constantly refreshing itself from the regular new challenges both that clients bring to coaches and coaches bring to their supervisor. (Hawkins & Shohet, 2006: 205)

and go on to advocate that:

If we are to create learning professions that constantly renew their cultures, then supervision needs to become the learning lungs that assist the professional body in its learning, development and cultural evolution. This entails not only focusing on both the supervisee and supervisor learning, but providing a dialogical container in which new learning can emerge in the space between the supervisor and supervisee. Supervision needs to be practised in a way that allows learning to emerge in the interaction between the three unique areas of experience that are brought into relationship:

- The client situation and context
- The supervisee's experience and understanding
- The supervisor's experience and understanding

Too often we have seen supervision reduced to the exchange of pre-existent 'thoughts' and knowledge. The supervisee tells their supervisor what they already have thought and know about their client, and the supervisor shares their pre-existent knowledge about *similar clients*. (Hawkins & Shohet, 2006: 206)

Supervision needs to be a place of co-creative and generative thinking where new learning is being forged for clients, coach and supervisor, and for the profession.

The author would like to acknowledge contributions from colleagues and fellow authors Nick Smith and Gil Schwenk in the writing of this chapter. The author can be contacted at peter. hawkins@bathconsultancygroup.com.

FURTHER READING

The principal book focusing specifically on coaching supervision is:
Hawkins, P., & Smith, N. (2006). *Coaching, mentoring and organizational consultancy: Supervision and development.* Maidenhead: McGraw-Hill/Open University Press.

REFERENCES

Berglas, B. (2000). The very real dangers of executive coaching. *Harvard Business Review,* June 2002: 86–92.
Downey, M. (1999). *Effective coaching.* London: Orion Publishing Group.
Flaherty, J. (1999). *Coaching: Evoking excellence in others.* Woburn, MA: Butterworth-Heinemann.
Hawkins, P. (1985). Humanistic psychotherapy supervision. A conceptual framework: Self and society. *European Journal of Humanistic Psychology, 13*(2): 69–77.
Hawkins, P. (1995). *Shadow consultancy.* Bath: Bath Consultancy Group.
Hawkins, P. (2006). Coaching supervision. In J. Passmore (Ed.), *Excellence in coaching: The industry guide.* London: Kogan Page.
Hawkins P., & Schwenk, G. (2006). *Coaching supervision.* London: CIPD Change Agenda.

Hawkins, P., & Shohet, R. (2006). *Supervision in the helping profession* (3rd ed.). Maidenhead: Open University Press.

Hawkins, P., & Smith, N. (2006). *Coaching, mentoring and organizational consultancy: Supervision and development.* Maidenhead: McGraw-Hill/Open University Press.

Jarvis, J. (2004). *Coaching and buying coaching services: A guide.* London: Chartered Institute of Personnel Development.

Kadushin, A. (1992[1976]). *Supervision in social work.* New York: Columbia University Press.

Proctor, B. (1988). Supervision: A working alliance (videotape training manual). St Leonards-on-Sea, East Sussex: Alexia Publications.

28

Coaching and Mental Health

Andrew Buckley

INTRODUCTION

Coaching is normally seen as an activity to enhance performance and achievement of goals. Whether these goals are work related, or have a focus to enhance life in general, coaching is not seen as remedial. Grant states 'the assumption [is] that clients are from a population without significant levels of psychopathology or emotional distress' (Grant, 2005: 2). This assumption limits the coachee population by excluding those people who do have significant levels of emotional distress or psychopathology and will include both those with a diagnosed mental illness and those who have not sought medical help with problems.

This chapter is about the recognition and management of this non-coaching population; individuals for whom coaching will prove ineffective, inappropriate or potentially harmful due to their mental state. Starting with an exploration of mental ill health in its broadest sense and the relevance of this to the coachee population, this chapter goes on to explore warning signs that may indicate a problem, exploration with the coachee to help build a more complete picture of what may be happening and a discussion of the law, ethics and practicalities that need consideration by the coach before deciding on the most appropriate action.

Case studies are used to highlight ways that coachees could behave and to raise questions for the coach; none of these examples show clear signs of mental illness but illustrate the more borderline cases that may occur as part of anyone's coaching practice.

MENTAL ILL HEALTH AND THE COACHEE POPULATION

The extent to which individuals suffer temporary and more permanent mental health problems has become clearer over recent years. Anyone who thinks that mental ill health happens to 'them', those 'poor souls' that need hospitalization or have 'inadequate personalities' is hiding from the real situation. The fact that 'mental illness accounts for over a third of the burden of illness in Britain' (CEP, 2006: 3) highlights just how widespread are the problems.

Mental health issues in the working population are widespread, with figures such as one in six employees suffering problems at any one time often quoted (SCMH, 2007). Issues range from the less common, but severe and enduring, conditions such as schizophrenia and bipolar affective disorder at less than 1 in 100 people of working age, to the very common but less severe and often transitory problems of depression and anxiety. Evidence highlights that problems are by no means contained just within those employees who take sickness absence. In what is becoming known as 'presenteeism' employees attend work but struggle with a mental health issue. Presenteeism accounts for a higher cost to business than that of employees taking formal sickness absence and is more of an issue with executive, technical and managerial grades than other staff (SCMH, 2007). This is highly relevant to the coaching profession, as it is at the higher grades that coaching tends to be focused in many organizations.

Whether seen as an 'illness' or a psychosocial problem mental health issues are extremely common among all of the population, including coachees.

Information on the extent of mental illness or psychopathology among coachees is limited. Green, Oades and Grant (2005) found that just over 23% of applicants for a life-coaching programme in Australia had clinically elevated scores of symptoms of mental health problems pre-coaching. This is similar to the findings of Spence and Grant (2007), where 25% of participants in a life-coaching programme had elevated scores. The results of these and other studies suggest that coachees are as likely to be experiencing mental health problems as the general population (see Grant, 2007: 251, for a summary), and that the coach can expect to meet coachees who are experiencing mental health problems.

Recognizing and managing the boundary around mental health issues is a key skill for all coaches. 'Given that a proportion of clients presenting for coaching will have mental health problems' (Grant 2007: 251), coaches, as Clutterbuck suggests 'need to be aware of the boundaries that it is dangerous to cross' (Clutterbuck, 2007: 19); and 'the coach does need the ability to be able to judge when not to coach' (Buckley, 2007: 20).

When faced with a mental health issue the coach must be able to answer the questions 'Can my coaching help?', 'What are my limitations with this issue?' and 'Should my coaching continue?' before deciding what to do. Any diagnosis, treatment, ways to help or exploration of underlying issues is the province of mental health specialists and is best avoided. Coaches whose background is in psychology or the psychological therapies may have the skills, training and experience to be able to come to an informed decision as to what is wrong and may be well placed to offer effective 'therapy', but should still ask the question 'can my coaching help?' rather than 'can I help?'

To be able ethically, professionally and effectively to manage these clients, there is a four-stage route to guide the coach.

1 recognition that some people will have mental health problems that make coaching inappropriate
2 an understanding of the signs and symptoms of mental ill health and an ability to question further when needed
3 an ability to reflect on the wider circumstances of ethics, the law, professional standards and practicalities
4 ask 'What next?' Continue coaching, stop coaching or refer for medical help?

UNDERSTANDING MENTAL ILL HEALTH

UK based consultant psychiatrist Mike Nowers says 'mental illnesses lie on a spectrum between health and illness and an individual may slide from health into illness over a period of time and in a way that may be hard to identify. You do not catch mental illness ...' (Buckley & Buckley, 2006: x). This difficulty of clearly observing, measuring, testing for and understanding the very nature of what is meant by mental illness presents anyone who may need to take into consideration the relative nature of a person's mental state with challenges.

Case Study 1

A coach is pleased to be put in contact with a Chief Executive (CE) and there is an optimistic telephone conversation.

During the first meeting, the coachee appears flat and tired and shows little interest in coaching. During the next session, everything seems a struggle for the CE. The coach mentions what has been noticed and asks how long it has been like this. There is a trigger point, a personal loss with which the CE is trying to come to terms.

The coach is able to help the CE to work out a temporary plan, and coaching is delayed to enable the CE to come to terms with the loss.

When the coach and coachee meet next, some months later, the CE appears completely different, and coaching continues in a very positive way towards a successful outcome.

In this example, coaching is delayed until the coachee is able to benefit from the experience. Coaching through the period needed to come to terms with the loss would have been questionable from a contractual perspective, as real coaching could not take place, and ethically any help needed may have been more appropriately met by another type of 'helping by talking', such as a psychological therapist.

No one is immune from suffering mental health problems; issues, distress and clear illness can appear as if from nowhere. Most people will understand that an event in life can lead to distress and changes in outlook and behaviour. The chief executive in Case Study 1 is an example; the loss mentioned could be the death of someone close; changes in how he sees himself due to age; or even the realization that personal aspirations can no longer be met. The key is the trigger event that offers a cause for the suffering.

Case Study 2

John has been responsible for the IT needs of a fast-growing company for several years. He seemed the obvious choice to develop a team as the company grew in size. The CEO was convinced of the benefits of coaching and organized a coach to help John in his new role.

The coach found that John would talk passionately and knowledgably about the IT infrastructure but not about his new team. The sense was that the team was just there to do tasks that John did not have time for. John appears to be managing the growing needs of the IT department by working longer hours and getting more frustrated. Coaching could help with this through discussions of delegation and team working. John gets visibly upset, as the IT system is not working well and, although he has the skills to fix the problems, he cannot manage the workload. He says that only he can do the tasks; he has no trust in his team members. Although John was highly capable of managing the IT needs of a small company he is not able to manage a team and has become very distressed as this became more evident.

Coaching has proved unable to help John with the contracted task, that of transitioning to manager. From the organization's perspective a positive coaching outcome could be to recognize this and to take steps to manage the business needs of the IT team. John may gain insight and realization that managing people is not for him. Should he choose to try to address this then it is likely that a therapeutic way of working would be indicated.

There are many similarities to Case Study 1 in the problems faced by John, the IT manager, in Case Study 2. Again, there is a trigger event; his 'environment' at work changed from dealing with the IT system to facilitating the system management. Coaching to support a change in work focus has proved ineffective. Any underlying cause is unclear, and likely to remain so for the coach

Mike Nowers suggests,

It is the context within which people are living their lives that is the key. How their individual personalities can manage the pressures and stresses of everyday living and the occurrence of negative or sometimes seemingly positive life events will dictate whether and when people cross the threshold from health into mental illness. (Buckley & Buckley, 2006: xi)

The variable nature of mental health and the effect of environmental changes is one of the reasons why a mental health problem is so difficult to predict, and often to identify.

For the coach, understanding mental ill health, mental illness and other terms such as psychopathology is more than deciding if a coachee has a mental illness. An ability to recognize unusual signs and relate these to an individual's circumstances is the task when deciding how to answer the question 'is my coaching appropriate?'

RECOGNIZING MENTAL HEALTH ISSUES

Table 28.1 lists the signs of mental ill health and is based upon a mental state examination that could be conducted by a mental health specialist. None of these signs or symptoms will demonstrate, unequivocally, that the coachee has a mental health problem; rather, it is the accumulation of signs and linked behaviour that would lead the clinician to diagnose a

Table 28.1:   Warning signs of mental ill health

Appearance	Is there anything unexpected with respect to dress and personal care?
	Are there any clues in how the coachee moves, or doesn't?
	Is there any unusual body language?
Behaviour	Is there any agitation or nervousness?
	Is the coachee lethargic or uninterested?
	Repetitive behaviours can be a sign of problems.
	Is there incongruence between what is being discussed and expressions and body language?
Mood	Overly optimistic or pessimistic – especially if this doesn't correlate with other information?
	Does the coachee appear fixed emotionally or inactive, possibly apathetic?
Thoughts	Any preoccupations or fixations?
	Are thoughts, as expressed, reasonably rational or are there some signs of irrationality, possibly delusions?
Perception	Are there any signs that the coachee is not experiencing the world 'normally'?
Intellect	Any changes in intellect over time?
	Does the coachee appear as expected intellectually?
	Are there any signs that the coachee is 'not here' today, not present and not taking part in the session?
Insight	Can the client offer an explanation for these unusual signs?
	Does the explanation or how the client attributes the unusual signs seem reasonable?

mental illness. When taken in isolation many of these signs form part of normal behaviour for all of us at one time or another.

Most mental illnesses lie on a spectrum between health and illness, and individuals may slide from health to illness in ways that are hard to identify and of which the coachee may be unaware.

Identifying any changes in behaviour, thoughts or feelings is central to the recognition of a mental health problem and may present as a challenge to the coach. Friends, family and work colleagues have the advantage of knowing someone over a period of time and in different situations, whereas the coach will usually have only limited knowledge of what could be considered usual behaviour for the coachee. Once puzzling behaviours have been noticed, reflecting on all that is known of the coachee can give helpful clues.

- First contact: are there any incongruous differences between how the coachee is during sessions and how they described themselves initially?
- Information from a third party: has the coach any information from a third party that hints at changes over time? In work-based coaching, for example is there a difference between what has been described and what the coach finds when talking to the coachee? The chief executive in Case Study 1 is a good example of the coachee not appearing as first expected.
- Changes over time: Mike in Case Study 4 seems to be sliding towards problems, as does John in Case Study 2. For John the changes are an increasing frustration; perhaps he is feeling out of control while struggling to manage a team; and Mike seems to be struggling to cope with changes in his personal circumstances.

Unless the behaviour that causes concern is something so worrying that immediate action is needed, reflecting on the situation, ideally with a supervisor, and exploring the background with the coachee before deciding what to do is important. Once the coach has noticed something unusual or possibly worrying, thinking through all that is known of the coachee is an important step. Jumping to conclusions, possibly deciding on a 'diagnosis' based on a fragment of evidence, is known as 'spot labelling' and needs avoiding. Seemingly bizarre behaviour may indicate nothing more than an unusual personality, the goal is to consider what may be happening rather than to ignore the behaviours before continuing coaching.

There are three key areas where more information can help the coach.

- The past: how long has the coachee been feeling or behaving like this? This helps the coach to find out if there are long-term issues or if there has been a trigger point that is leading to distress.
- Pervasiveness: is the present distress affecting all of the coachee's life or just part? The distress or worrying behaviour may have a focus at work, for example, but not at home. If all of life is involved then the implications for any coaching are different, as discussed later in this chapter.
- A plan: A plan to deal with the issues is very positive in two ways. A plan suggests recognition of problems or issues and shows personal insight; a plan offers hope of action to help the coachee to return to normal.

Exploring emerging concerns with the coachee enables the coach to be in a much clearer position to decide the next step and is as important as knowledge of the signs of mental ill health. The answers to questions help to complete a picture. How this impacts on the future of any coaching depends, though, on several other factors, such as the coaching context, the contract and the specific skills of the coach, as well as the wishes of the coachee.

THE COACHING CONTEXT

The relationship between coachee and coach is essentially private but can never take place in isolation. The next part of the decision-making journey towards answering the question 'can my coaching help?' or 'should my coaching continue?' looks at the factors and views to be considered as part of the wider context. There is a boundary overlap between three parties; the coachee, the coach and the system within which they are operating. When a coachee has shown signs that may indicate a mental health problem or if a coachee has a diagnosed mental illness (whether temporary or lifelong) coaching should only take place when all three parties are in agreement.

The main consideration is the system within which the coaching is taking place. Primarily this is society as a whole. Society influences the boundaries between coaching and other activities, between the coach and other professionals, through both the general understanding of what coaching is and is not, and any laws currently in place. It is beyond the scope of this chapter to detail the laws in individual countries. It is, however, imperative that the individual coach has an understanding of the legal framework in which they work. Of most relevance will be those laws pertaining to the status of coaching in relationship with other 'helping-by-talking' activities such as counselling, psychotherapy and the psychologies. The legal status of the psychological therapies has real relevance and potential impact on, with whom, and under what circumstances the coach may work.

The codes of ethics and good practice of membership organizations such as the Association for Coaching, the International Coach Federation and the European Mentoring and Coaching Council are relevant to those who may be coached. Membership of one of these bodies implies acceptance of these codes and, while they will have no legally binding implications, complaints about malpractice could result. Linked to this is the provision of indemnity insurance. The insurance provider will have insured the activity of coaching, and the onus is on an individual coach to show both that coaching (and not another activity) was undertaken, and to show that the client was suitable to be coached within the competences of the coach and the laws and practices in force.

The final part to be considered in the coaching context or 'system' is the involvement of any third party. Primarily this will be an organization paying for some form of business coaching. Should the coachee maintain an overwhelming focus on personal issues, the organization may well consider this a poor use of resources, as business benefits are not being addressed. If the coachee shows signs of a possible mental health issue, or has a history of mental illness, then it is possible there may be legal implications around the duty of care owed to an employee. Misusing coaching as a more socially acceptable route to help with an employee who would be best placed by seeing a therapist does have legal implications; this area should include coaching for work-based stress as well as for defined and diagnosable illness.

So far, the contextual considerations around the advisability of starting or continuing coaching have focused on those cases where the system suggests coaching should not continue. One other possible conflict is the potential coachee who has little, if any, understanding of what coaching is. Should an individual approach a coach for help with a psychological problem or mental illness that is likely to be outside the legal and social norms of what coaching is, then the coach is advised not to offer coaching and should suggest a more appropriate route to help, such as a visit to the individual's family doctor in the first instance.

Case Study 3

Mary contacted a coach to ask for help in putting her life back on track. She said that it had stalled after her husband had left her, and her two children had chosen to live with him rather than her.

At first, lots of plans come out at; ideas for a new and invigorating life including friends, trips, relationships and work. But, as coaching continues, nothing seems to change. Mary always has a reason why none of her goals are met. During the sessions Mary agrees enthusiastically with the coach and makes plans, but by the next session these have all failed and a new set of ideas is talked about.

The coach notices an emerging pattern; failure is always someone else's fault.

Mary appears to have a barrier to taking control and responsibility for her life and it is unlikely that coaching will help in this case. Coaching has been unable to help Mary, but there are no signs of mental ill health. In this example ending the coaching would be appropriate; looking for help elsewhere is her own responsibility.

As in any profession, the range of skills and experience of individual coaches varies widely and there will be times when it is the competency of the coach that decides the best thing to do next. A skilled coach, possibly with a therapeutic background, may be able to continue with a coachee who has some specific problem areas that can be avoided. Knowing how to avoid this 'can of worms' requires training and experience. Inadvertently opening up deep-seated psychological problems may cause considerable hardship for the coachee. It is difficult to pack away psychological problems once they have been exposed. The example of Mary in Case Study 3 highlights the unknown.

Time available also plays a part in these decisions. If the coaching contract is for only three or four sessions then there is a greater need to avoid issues than if there were a much longer expected relationship when it would be considered reasonable that the coachee could work around or through any problem areas.

WHAT TO DO?

Any coaching relationship will be evaluated by the visible actions taken. In the context of those coachees, whose behaviour may lead the coach to suspect that a psychological issue is impacting, or likely to impact, on the course or outcome of the coaching, the steps taken by the coach to manage the situation will be the actions visible to an outside party, whether this is society as a whole or an organization that is paying for coaching.

The options available are:

- Delay coaching – put coaching on hold for a period to see if the coachee is able to resolve any problems. Functional suffering, such as grieving a loss, may well pass and the coachee could benefit from coaching in a few weeks or months.
- Continue coaching – perhaps with extra care. Most likely appropriate if the focus of any mental health issue is clearly separate from the coaching focus. Coaching may also be possible while the coachee receives treatment or support from a mental health specialist, although the coach would need to be careful; first and above any coaching goals must come the overall health of the coachee.
- Stop coaching – the safest option is to draw a line under any coaching once mental ill health is suspected.

Table 28.2 will help when deciding 'what next?' If the decision is taken that coaching is inappropriate the coach may need to offer some support to the coachee to find appropriate help. This ranges from suggesting a visit to the family doctor, suggesting therapy as more appropriate and, in rare and extreme cases, taking action on behalf of the coachee, such as calling an ambulance or emergency services. Supervision may provide the coach with the opportunity to clarify any suspicions and to reflect on courses of action before any decision and discussion takes place with the coachee.

The ethics of coaching is discussed in its wider context elsewhere in this handbook as well as by de Jong (de Jong, 2006) and Buckley and Buckley (2006). An understanding of the ethics

Table 28.2: Deciding 'What next?'

- Can the expected focus of coaching be seen as clearly separate from the issues giving concern?
  - If the coachee's problems seem separate from the coaching focus, continuing may be appropriate.
  - If all of the coachee's life seems affected by the issues, then stop.
- Are the coachee's problems likely to pass?
  - Functional suffering will, often, pass; consider continuing.
  - If long term or a recurring pattern, stop.
- Has the coachee received appropriate help elsewhere?
  - If the coachee is supported elsewhere then consider continuing.
  - Emotional suport is not the province of coaching; if the coachee is unsupported, then stop.
- How emotionally resilient or robust does the coachee appear?
  - An emotionally robust person may be able to benefit from coaching while struggling through problems in part of their life; consider continuing.
  - A coachee who struggles emotionally is less likely to benefit from coaching; stop.
- How self-aware of the issues is the client?
  - Self-awareness is linked to emotional resilience; a self-aware coachee may be able to separate coaching from their issues; consider continuing.
  - An inability on the part of the coachee to recognize issues and problems probably precludes coaching as a sensible approach; stop.
- Issues in others can have personal impact on any of us.
  - If, as coach, you are affected by the coachee's issues, then stop.

and good practice of coaching, irrespective of membership of, and agreement to any codes from, coaching organizations, is important for any coach. The efficacy of any coaching will be viewed with these standards in mind. One of the most important ethical considerations for the coach when considering whether to offer coaching to someone is non-malfeasance – a term which means a commitment to taking actions that do not harm the coachee. This suggests that a cautious approach will be best when a coach meets anyone with possible mental health problems.

Case Study 4

Mike phones a coach whose number he has been given by his wife. He says he has to change his behaviour, as he has become quite aggressive and angry with both his wife and daughter. His daughter has left home to live with a boyfriend who 'is a waster'. Mike was made redundant some months ago and is spending more and more time in the bar, where he says he can relax and unwind.

Mike appears upset at how his life has changed and seems keen to try to make some changes.

He misses an appointment and then phones to say he still wants to see the coach, even though his wife has left and gone to stay with her mother. He is tearful on the phone and the coach wonders if he has been drinking, even though it is morning.

Mike's life is unravelling in many ways and he probably needs professional support. If he refuses to accept this view and wants to continue seeing the coach s/he would be best advised to refuse. Help cannot be forced on anyone; inappropriate help may well do more harm than good.

Mike in Case Study 4 may not be showing clear signs of mental illness yet, but he is experiencing real difficulties. What is normally meant by coaching could cause harm in this example. So much of his life has changed and there is a hint that his choice of behaviour, in increasingly using alcohol to mask feelings and problems, may be a contributory factor. It may appear harsh to refuse to support someone who is so obviously struggling, but there is a real risk of doing more harm by continuing.

EVALUATION

For the coach, understanding when not to coach is a vital skill. It is important for the coach as well as for the coachee, who may be encouraged to seek more appropriate help; 'after all most people who suffer from a mental illness will make a full recovery with appropriate diagnosis, management and treatment' (Buckley & Buckley 2006: xii). Effective management of the boundary between psychologically 'healthy' coachees and those with problems is equally important for any purchaser of coaching services, for the ongoing professionalism of the coaching industry and for relationships, both legal and professional, with others who work in the 'helping by talking' professions.

If one in four or five coachees have elevated levels of psychological distress, then hopefully it can be seen how important it is that all coaches are appropriately trained in the recognition and management of mental health and psychological problems. As the coach training industry continues to mature, and coach training standards become increasingly available, I believe that specific training in the recognition of those coachees with psychological problems or mental illness will become the norm. Developing training that meets the needs of individual coaches, including those with a background in psychology or psychological therapies, may present challenges. The most obvious type of training may be an adaptation of the diagnostic model as used in medicine and much of psychology. This would present challenges, due to the length of training needed for the coach to gain an understanding of this complex area. There is a growing body of evidence suggesting that short courses in the recognition of mental illnesses following this medical model may be problematic for the non-medical professional (Kitchener & Jorm, 2004; Moor, Maguire, et al., 2007; Read, 2007).

Although there are some who advocate the advantages to the coach of an awareness of the categorical approaches to diagnosis (Cavanagh, 2005: 23), I believe that an approach based on a psychosocial model is appropriate and more likely to provide effective outcomes to the coaching relationship when signs of mental health problems occur, as the primary question then is not 'is the coachee mentally ill?' but 'can my coaching help?'

Coaching cannot help everyone; for such people, knowing how to recognize the signs and what to do is part of good coaching practice.

FURTHER READING

Buckley, A., & Buckley, C. (2006). *A guide to coaching and mental health; The recognition and management of psychological issues.* London: Routledge.

Cavanagh, M., Grant, A.M., & Kemp, T. (Eds.). (2005). *Evidence-based coaching,* Vol. 1: *Theory, research and practice from the behavioural sciences* (pp. 21–36). Bowen Hills, QLD: Australian Academic Press.

Davies, T., & Craig, T.K.J. (1998). ABC of mental health. London: BMJ Books.

REFERENCES

Buckley, A. (2007). The mental health boundary in relationship to coaching and other activities. *International Journal of Evidence-based Coaching and Mentoring,* Special Issue, Summer.

Buckley, A., & Buckley, C. (2006). *A guide to coaching and mental health: The recognition and management of psychological issues.* London: Routledge.

Cavanagh, M. (2005). Mental-health issues and challenging clients in executive coaching. In M. Cavanagh, A.M. Grant & T. Kemp (Eds.), *Evidence-based coaching,* Vol. 1: *Theory, research and practice from the behavioural sciences* (pp. 21–36). Bowen Hills, QLD: Australian Academic Press.

Centre for Economic Performance (CEP). (2006). *The depression report: A new deal for depression and anxiety disorders.* London: London School of Economics.

Clutterbuck, D. (2007). *Coaching the team at work.* London: Nicholas Brealey.

de Jong, A. (2006). Coaching ethics: Integrity in the moment of choice. In J. Passmore (Ed.), *Excellence in coaching, the industry guide* (pp.191–202). London: Kogan Page.

Grant, A.M. (2005). What is evidence-based executive, workplace and life coaching? In M. Cavanagh, A.M. Grant & T. Kemp (Eds.), *Evidence-based coaching,* Vol. 1: *Theory, research and practice from the behavioural sciences* (pp. 1–12). Bowen Hills, QLD: Australian Academic Press.

Grant, A.M. (2007). A model of goal striving and mental health for coaching populations. *International Coaching Psychology Review, 2*(3): 248–62.

Green, S., Oades, L., & Grant,A.M. (2005). An evaluation of a life-coaching group programme: Initial findings from a waitlist control study. In M. Cavanagh, A.M. Grant & T. Kemp (Eds.), *Evidence-based coaching,* Vol. 1: *Theory, research and practice from the behavioural sciences* (pp. 127–41). Bowen Hills, QLD: Australian Academic Press.

Kitchener, B.A., & Jorm, A.F. (2004). Mental health first aid in a workplace setting: A randomized controlled trial. *BMC Psychiatry, 4*: 23.

Moor, S., Maguire, A., McQueen, H., Wells, E.J., Elton, R., Wrate, R., Blair, C. (2007). Improving the recognition of depression in adolescence: Can we teach the teachers? *Journal of Adolescence, 30*: 81–95.

Read, J. (2007). Why promoting biological ideology increases prejudice against people labelled schizophrenic. *Australian Psychologist, 42*(2): 118–28.

Sainsbury Centre for Mental Health (SCMH). (2007). *Mental health at work: Developing the business case.* Policy Paper 8, retrieved June 2008 from www.scmh.org.uk

Spence, G., & Grant, A.M. (2007). Professional and peer life coaching and the enhancement of goal striving and well-being: An exploratory study. *Journal of Positive Psychology, 2*(3): 185–94.

29

Continuing Professional Development for Coaches

Dianne R. Stober

INTRODUCTION

Since 2000, conversations regarding what is required for a professional practice of coaching have expanded from discussions within informal networks of individuals to global dialogues among coaching bodies and other stakeholder groups. While coaching is still emerging as a profession and consensus is lacking among the coaching community, developments have occurred in what are options for education and training, efforts are underway to delineate what are the requisite bodies of knowledge, and initial forays have been made in identifying coaching competencies. Given the lack of coherence at this point in time, one suggestion has been to adopt an evidence-based practice philosophy as a guide for professional development. This calls on coaches to integrate the best available knowledge with their own expertise in the service of individual coachees and their contexts.

This chapter explores the challenges for coaches' professional development going forward from this current scenario.

Initial challenges for professional development

Coaching has emerged over the past 20 years into silos of communities and information has proliferated from approaches to established practice in fields as diverse as psychology, management, and education to grassroots approaches to personal development such as life coaching. These networks have varied from organized interest groups within professional associations, such as the British and Australian Psychological Societies, to topics of interest within divisions of other associations like the Academy of Management and the American Psychological Association, the National Education Association, and many others, to coaching-specific organizations such as the International Coach Federation (ICF), the European Mentoring and Coaching Council (EMCC), the Worldwide Association of Business Coaches (WABC), the International Association of Coaches (IAC), and many others. While this rapid development of various organizations and groups is a reflection of the interest in coaching, this same development means that there are a multitude of simultaneous challenges to a coherent view of professional development.

Probably the biggest challenge lies in the fact that coaching is not as yet an established profession. Coaching, as an emerging profession, is still in the early stages of defining itself. In particular, there are a number of criteria which distinguish a profession that have not yet been fulfilled in coaching, although progress has been made. Some of these criteria include (Bennett, 2006):

- minimum levels of education and training required to become proficient; accepted competencies and skill sets
- practice grounded in identified bodies of knowledge and avenues of communication and idea exchange
- an agreed set of ethical standards by which coaching can self-discipline practice, including avenues of enforcement
- widely accepted professional organizations that represent the profession and those practising it
- systems for evaluating merit or certifying competence that are widely accepted and allow for further development of the profession
- external recognition of coaching's professional status by those served and the general public.

Several of these criteria directly relate to the challenges facing professional development in coaching. The education and training required for practice, the competencies needed, and grounding in the bodies of knowledge which comprise the profession all have direct ties to professional development. We will look at each of these criteria in terms of professional development in turn.

A second challenge is how the various stakeholders view professional development itself. Some professions, such as psychology, management, and education, have communities that have developed a speciality or focus in coaching. These professions have established structures for development through continuing training and education, supervision, and outlets such as peer-reviewed journals and conferences that serve as recognized forums for discussion of new areas of practice like coaching. Generally speaking, there are assumptions within these professions that newer practices will be developed through the formulation of theory and practice and then tested through research methods. Coaching, as a new area of practice among these professions, is developing within the established structures of these professions.

Meanwhile, grassroots coaching organizations that have sprung up outside established professions and academic circles have recognized the need for standards of professional development and have begun developing programmes and criteria of their own. Some of these organizations have professionals from various backgrounds involved in their development, who bring with them previous history of what constitutes professional development. However, while undoubtedly the development of training and ethical standards, along with standards of qualification, are informed by various professionals' educational histories, many grassroots organizations take a somewhat *tabula rasa* approach to professional development. What it means to be a coach has been founded on common sense and observed experience rather than tightly tied to existing theories or empirical data.

As a result of these varied approaches to coaching, at this point in time we have a chaotic and uneven landscape of professional development. We have different established professions with their own particular views of coaching as a subset of their discipline, others formulating coaching as a cross-disciplinary endeavour, and industry organizations proposing coaching as a unique and distinct arena of practice. These different approaches result in different pictures of what a coaching professional needs in terms of development.

Areas of focus for professional development

There a several areas within professional development that warrant special focus, both at the individual level and at the professional community level. For individual coaches, it is important to assess where they might need to seek additional experience, skills, or knowledge. For the coaching community, there is a distinct need to focus on those areas which are not agreed upon nor fully developed.

Education and training as professional development
The landscape of coach education and training is a diverse terrain. If we include initial education and training as an important part of the professional development of individuals as coaches, as yet there is no widely agreed upon body of knowledge, set of skills, or core competencies that would reflect what is required to educate a coach. This means there is no established clarity or consensus about what constitutes the initial professional development of coaches, much less what would entail continuing professional development of practising coaches. There are industry training organizations of widely varying quality; programmes within graduate schools of business, psychology, education, etc. offering everything from individual courses to continuing education certificates to specializations within doctoral programmes; special interest groups within existing professions that offer workshops, conferences, and publications; and coaching-specific associations that offer various certifications in coaching. The plethora of options, groups, claims made, and territory staked out can be an overwhelming and difficult wilderness to navigate for the individual coach seeking education, training, and ongoing development.

Industry training organizations   One option for training and professional development in coaching lies within the various industry training organizations. A typical Google search (in 2009) of coach training organizations yields 593,000 hits. Types of training run the gamut from workshop intensives that teach coaching skills to programmes with multiple courses over many months. Some are face-to-face and many have a distance-based aspect whether online or via teleconferencing. The background of those providing the training may vary from those who base their expertise in work and life experience to those who have PhDs in fields that overlap with coaching.

As coaching has grown towards a potential profession, an uncomfortable question arises in a 'live and let live' context regarding education and training. At this point, there are so many different training programmes, certifications, and such a lack of consensus about what even defines coaching that it begs the question of what the educational requirements should be for a coach. In looking at this issue, there is an underlying question of scope of practice. Are we talking about someone who applies coaching skills within a particular context, whether it is managers who use coaching as part of their management approach, or teachers who coach students, or healthcare professionals who apply coaching skills to supporting patients making positive health behaviour change? Or are these individuals who work with others coming for coaching as the main service? In the former, coaching skills training may be the primary need in order to use coaching as a tool within the practice of another profession or occupation. In the latter, there is a fundamental question of what knowledge is required for the professional practice of coaching. For those who are practising as coaching professionals, skills training is not enough (Drake & Stober, 2007). Professional coaches should ground their practice in theoretical and research knowledge.

Graduate schools   Another source of education, training, and professional development is higher educational institutions. As coaching has continued to develop, colleges and universities have entered the coaching education arena. In 2006, the Graduate School Alliance in Executive Coaching identified 123 colleges and universities providing a variety of types of coaching education within the United States alone (Starr, 2006). Overlapping somewhat with coach training organizations, some of the university programmes focus more on coaching skills; others are full-blown programmes linked with graduate degrees with specializations in coaching. Those that are linked with existing degrees tend to have explicit requirements for the study of relevant theoretical and empirical bodies of knowledge along with supervised experiences of coaching practice. Because higher education institutions have been through recognized accreditation processes for education, they tend to have more uniform requirements for coursework and practicum experiences. Graduate programmes also require some education and training in research methods, which brings us to another key issue in professional development for coaches.

The question of research competency for coaches

As coach education and training has taken root within academic circles at the graduate level, and more research on coaching has been undertaken, the issue of research competency arises. One of the hallmarks of a profession includes establishing a body of knowledge (Bennett, 2006). At this time, much of the coaching-specific research is being conducted within universities by graduate students. These students are often housed within departments such as psychology or organizational development that have areas of overlap with an emerging discipline of coaching. As these students move on to other academic positions or out into practice, and continue research, they will continue to grow and develop a coaching-specific literature and body of knowledge. A challenge will be whether these efforts remain splintered among many different disciplines, or whether they coalesce into a coherent and distinct discipline of coaching.

Returning to the development of individual coaches, an important distinction is that between formal and informal research. While coaches are often encouraged to 'do their own research' in terms of assessing progress with clients with questions regarding outcomes that coachees are realizing, this is not to be confused with formal research. With access to tools such as Survey Monkey, it can be tempting to put together a list of questions, which, while potentially valuable in gathering feedback, most likely will not constitute an assessment with validity or reliability. Formal research requires an explicit methodology, whether that is a qualitative or quantitative method. Such methodologies require a particular set of knowledge, skills, and abilities.

However, this does not mean that all coaches must be empirical researchers. Rather than insisting that all coaching practitioners must be trained to do original research, a scholar–practitioner approach would enable coaches to critically evaluate and apply evidence to their practice with coachees. The goal of such an approach is to give coaches enough grounding to become critical consumers of research (Stober, 2005). In order to be a critical consumer, coaches need to have a basic understanding of research methods and analysis. Being able to assess whether a particular piece of research has been conducted well and whether the results have been interpreted fairly is the aim of a scholar–practitioner model. As an example, let us assume that a journal article reported results that suggested that a certain approach to goal-setting was highly effective in facilitating high potential coachees transitioning from lower ranks of leadership to the executive level within organizations. The coaching intervention was given to fifteen coachees and results for five different assessments were analysed. A scholar–practitioner might be quite sceptical of the results based only on this description, as there would probably be serious questions raised as to the adequacy of the sample size in drawing conclusions about the results, especially if this was intended as a quantitative study. Without a basic understanding of research, there can be a temptation to assume that because a piece of research has been published, then the research is valid.

Having an adequate understanding of research methods enables professional coaches to assess what are accurate and fair applications of research results to practise and within what contexts. Would it be legitimate to apply a life coaching approach to values setting that was found to be effective for early career coachees to a sample of college students? A coach who can read such a research report and recognize points of overlap between the two types of coachees and any critical areas of difference is likely to be able to assess more effectively the validity of applying the results from one group to another.

In terms of professional development and research competency, a scholar–practitioner model will serve coaches well. This means that coaches who may not have a background that includes education in research methods will want to obtain some additional education, and those that do will need to apply those skills to coaching-specific research.

Grounding coaching in existing bodies of knowledge and
professional development

One of the areas with both high points and gaps is the grounding of coaching in existing bodies of knowledge. Within a number of fields, notably psychology, management, and education, there have been concerted efforts to tie coaching practice directly to knowledge of human growth, development, and interaction. This volume, along with a number of others (e.g. Peltier, 2001; Skiffington & Zeus, 2003; Stober & Grant, 2006; Palmer & Whybrow, 2007) reflects development in linking coaching to bodies of knowledge. There are also a growing number of journals, special issues, and literature reviews that have been devoted explicitly to coaching. Coaching-specific journals include the *International Coaching Psychology Review; Coaching: An International Journal of Theory, Research, and Practice;* the *International Journal of Evidence-based Coaching and Mentoring;* and the *International Journal of Coaching in Organizations.* Other journals that have had special issues on coaching or an ongoing stream of articles on coaching include the *Consulting Psychology Journal: Practice and Research;* the *Academy of Management Review;* and the *Journal for Supervision and Curriculum Development.*

Along with developments in producing explicit links between coaching and existing bodies of knowledge, attention is being paid to what bodies of knowledge are required for coaching professionals. For example the Graduate School Alliance for Executive Coaching in North America has developed a comprehensive set of guidelines for academic programmes (see http://www.gsaec.org/curriculum.html). These guidelines include the following broad bases of knowledge for executive coaches: (1) individual differences and development; (2) interpersonal dynamics and communication; (3) group and inter-group dynamics; (4) organizational systems and dynamics; (5) social systems and dynamics; (6) change management; (7) adult learning; (8) coaching theory and principles. Within each of these areas, there are many theories and approaches for coaches to understand and with which to become familiar.

Given that many coaches are coming from a particular background of expertise and knowledge, whether it be from psychology, healthcare, management, or other professions, it is important that they take stock of where gaps in their knowledge base might lie. For example someone who is a clinical psychologist and seeking to practise as an executive coach might need to seek out ways to develop their knowledge and skills relating to organizations or business. Likewise, someone coming from a corporate background would probably need to obtain expertise in psychological theories and practice as they pertain to coaching. Until there is agreement (and regulation) within the coaching industry regarding which knowledge bases with which professionals must have familiarity, it is up to individuals to come to decisions about their own development and what is required for competent practice.

It will be helpful to outline a few questions which can aid in that decision process:

- What type of coaching is the goal?
- What knowledge bases are relevant for ethical practice in this area?

- Out of those knowledge bases, which have I mastered and which require further study in order to be mastered?
- Where can I obtain exposure and education to bases of knowledge with which I lack familiarity?
- Do I need to seek formal education or training in these areas? Or in supervision?

In answering these questions, coaches and potential coaches are able to outline what gaps exist in their background and what education or training they need to seek out. However, until the coaching industry has developed consensus regarding what bases of knowledge are needed for professional, ethical practice, wide variation will remain in this area among the various coaching associations, coach training organizations, academic programmes, and related professional associations.

Competencies for coaching

Central to the question of what education and training for coaches is required is the clarification of what coaching competencies are needed. Calls for competencies have been made over the past decade and as yet there are no generally agreed upon competency models (Brotman, Liberi and Wasylyshyn, 1998; Ennis et al., 2005; Bennett, 2006). A number of coaching industry associations have listed competencies that are linked to their credentialing criteria, including the ICF, the EMCC, and the WABC (see organization websites for full descriptions). There are commonalities among the various competency descriptions which generally fall within the following:

- ethical standards which promote 'do no harm' and respect for the coachee
- effective establishment of the coaching relationship and its boundaries, including building trust, rapport, effective communication
- effective promotion of growth and change for the coachee including increased awareness, reaching goals, leveraging strengths, etc.
- continuing education and skill development by the coach linked to the area of practice within coaching (e.g. business coaching, life coaching, executive coaching).

Implications for professional development of coaches The various competencies listed within coaching organizations have yet to be researched or systematically evaluated, so, as with many other areas of professional development in coaching, it is up to the individual to assess the face validity of these competency areas. Similar to the questions regarding bodies of knowledge, it is important for the individual coach to assess the range of intended practice of coaching, what competencies they already have, and how they might seek further development for competencies they may not yet have mastered. Specific educational or training courses may fit the bill, and in other situations, seeking out a supervisor might enable a coach to further develop their professional identity.

In looking at the professional development realities of an emerging profession of coaching, it is clear that the varied options for education and training and lack of agreement on required bodies of knowledge and coaching competencies complicate any straightforward approach to coach development. At this point, a model of how coaches could implement a scholar–practitioner philosophy may at least give the individual coach a point of focus in their professional development.

The call for evidence-based coaching

An initial step forward towards a profession lies in agreeing a philosophy of practice, and therefore an understanding of what contributes to the professional development of coaches. If establishing coaching as a profession requires a specified body of knowledge and minimum levels of education and training, then the professional development of coaches, both initially and continuing, will need to be grounded in that knowledge. Evidence-based practice (EBP) is a philosophy of practice that can provide a guide to the professional development of coaches as we strive to bring both structure and flexibility to the emerging profession. EBP grew out of a recognition within the field of medicine that there was research that had implications for clinical practice, but that much of that research was never taken up by practitioners and used with patients. For coaching, EBP offers great potential for how coaches can learn from the development of other professions. So what does EBP actually mean? Evidence-based practice, in medicine, is: 'the conscientious, explicit, and judicious use of current best evidence in making decisions about the care of individual patients, [which] means integrating individual clinical expertise with the best available external clinical evidence from systematic research' (Sackett, Haynes, Guyatt, & Tugwell, 1996: 71).

Sackett et al. (1996) go on to say that neither individual practitioner expertise nor external evidence is enough. Research evidence gives us new knowledge, yet it is the practitioner who needs to decide how and when that evidence applies. And without the input of new evidence, practitioners miss out on knowledge that can improve their skills or indicate a particular approach is no longer valid. As discussed earlier, this has implications for the need for coaches to have a basic understanding of research in order to critically evaluate and apply research evidence. However, EBP is not about dry, academic texts and journals; rather EBP is an approach 'where "artful" practice and "scientific" evidence meet' (Stober, Wildflower, & Drake, 2006: 1).

The benefit of using an EBP framework is that it can provide an overarching guide to the coach as he or she works with each individual coachee. Regardless of approach or orientation of the coach, EBP can help guide how coaches structure and think about the coachee, the relationship, and indeed themselves in that context. This is done by paying attention to the integration of three main components of an evidence-based approach: (1) best available knowledge; (2) the coach's expertise; and (3) the individual coachee's preferences, personality, values, etc. If coaches pay attention to each of these areas and look to add to their knowledge and expertise in a reflective manner, using EBP will support continuous professional development.

Best available knowledge   Without stipulated bases of knowledge for competent coaching, it is important for coaches to look at what background knowledge they have from previous work and what knowledge they still need to seek out. Professional development for coaches means being familiar with the coaching-specific literature while also knowing relevant literature from other established disciplines. Much of the coaching-specific evidence is exploratory or descriptive (Stober, 2005). These approaches are sources of hypotheses and can inform theory development, however they do not demonstrate cause and effect nor explain underlying mechanisms at work. While coaching-specific evidence is still in early stages of explanatory research, there is quite a bit of evidence to be found in related disciplines that is applicable. We can extrapolate evidence from other practices aimed at growth and development, such as humanistic approaches (Stober, 2006); cognitive–behavioral approaches (Costa & Garmston, 2002; Edwards, 2003; Auerbach, 2006; Peterson, 2006); developmental theory (Berger, 2006); adult learning (Cox, 2006); psychoanalytic theories (Kilburg, 2003; Allcorn, 2006; Orenstein, 2007); systems approaches (O'Neill, 2000; Cavanagh, 2006); and goal-setting research (Grant, 2006), among many others.

As a result, in terms of professional development, coaches will have the significant task of casting a wide net across related fields in order to gain disparate knowledge that is relevant to coaching practice. As education and training guidelines for coaching continue to develop, this task is likely to become more codified and circumscribed within educational programmes. Along with the need to identify relevant knowledge, coaches may also need to seek out education regarding research methods and develop skills in critically evaluating relevant research in order to identify that best available knowledge. An EBP approach does not mean that coaches blindly follow any particular published evidence, theory, or practice; rather, coaches are able to apply critical thinking skills to what knowledge is relevant, useful, and applicable to practise (Grant & Stober, 2006).

The coach's expertise Along with acquiring relevant bases of knowledge and identifying the best available, professional practice also means coaches need to be able to apply that knowledge of evidence appropriately. We have already discussed the lack of agreed competencies for coaching and have laid out broad areas of competency that seem to be represented by various coaching associations. Beyond mastering the necessary skills for delivering coaching, coaches, it is suggested, will through the EBP approach become more expert; they will be able to draw upon the depth and breadth of their accumulated knowledge and use themselves as effective instruments of change, and to apply that knowledge within the fluid environment of various coaching conversations and contexts. Given the wide range of backgrounds different coaches bring to their practice, it is paramount that they pay attention to the sources of information and knowledge upon which they can draw. It is also important in the development of coaches that awareness of the limits of skill and practice is sharp and that coaches do not go beyond those boundaries while seeking to gain the expertise that might be needed.

An EBP approach is an integrative approach, urging coaches to blend the best available knowledge with their own expertise and background in the service of their coachees. This requires a deep appreciation for each individual coachee and the selection of appropriate methods and models that fit the particular context. Next we turn to the third component of an EBP approach.

Individual coachee preferences and characteristics   Given that each client has a unique personality, situation, and goals, EBP requires the coach to pull together the best available knowledge and his or her own expertise within the particular context of that coachee. Each client's values, outlook, expectations, and situation must be considered if coaching is to be effective. Thus coaches will also need to assess a variety of characteristics of each coachee such as age, developmental stage, sociocultural contexts (e.g. gender, culture, socioeconomic status, etc.), current environmental factors such as job and career status, individual and personality factors, and expectations for coaching (Stober et al., 2006). The implication for professional development is that coaches will seek to develop structures and frameworks for gathering and evaluating important characteristics of the coachees with whom they work. Developing competencies in conceptualizing coaching contexts is vital for effective coaching. Some questions to consider include:

- Do I have a structure or protocol for gathering important characteristics of coachees?
- What assessments would generally be most helpful, and which in particular individual contexts?
- How can the collected knowledge be integrated with knowledge and expertise?

In terms of professional development within the coaching industry as a whole, an EBP approach gives grounding for education and training and for ongoing development of practising coaches. There is a wide range of coach training programmes; some base training primarily on skills development and some also emphasize the need for grounding in bodies of knowledge that inform the practice of coaching. There are professional development needs and opportunities for these organizations and for individual coaches wherever they might be along this EBP continuum. For coaches and training organizations that have focused primarily on skills development, there is a huge professional development opportunity to seek out the connections between 'what we do' and the theory and evidence that provides the 'why we do what we do'. For training organizations, there is a need for honest assessment of whether current programmes adequately educate coaching professionals in bodies of knowledge. Likewise, coaching programmes need to evaluate how robust their education and training is in terms of assisting individual coaches to assess their own expertise and to develop effective frameworks for evaluating the individual coachee's characteristics and context. By taking an EBP approach to education and training, we have the possibility of integrating relevant evidence and expertise from various root disciplines of coaching and moving into an era of synthesis and solidification of what constitutes the practice and profession of coaching.

EVALUATION

At this point in the emergence of coaching as a potential profession, what constitutes professional development is as varied as the wide range of coaching organizations, stakeholders, and education and training programmes. Until there is agreement on what is required for educating and training coaching professionals, what the requisite bodies of knowledge are, and establishing a distinct coaching-specific literature, professional development will remain a fuzzy area. However, individual coaches certainly can evaluate the state of practice and look for opportunities to address any gaps in their own development. An evidence-based approach can guide coaches in this endeavour by outlining three broad areas of concern: their familiarity with the best available knowledge, their awareness of their own expertise and the boundaries of that expertise, and their ability to assess the individual characteristics of each coachee. If coaches work towards integrating these three key components, their own continuing professional development will surely grow.

REFERENCES

Allcorn, S. (2006). Psychoanalytically informed executive coaching. In D.S. Stober & A.M. Grant (Eds.), *Evidence based coaching handbook: Putting best practices to work for your clients* (pp. 129–52). New York: Wiley.

Auerbach, J.E. (2006). Cognitive coaching. In D.S. Stober & A.M. Grant (Eds.), *Evidence based coaching handbook: Putting best practices to work for your clients* (pp. 103–28). New York: Wiley.

Bennett, J.L. (2006). An agenda for coaching-related research: A challenge for researchers. *Consulting Psychology Journal: Practice and Research, 58*: 240–9.

Berger, J.G. (2006). Adult development theory and executive coaching practice. In D.S. Stober & A.M. Grant (Eds.), *Evidence based coaching handbook: Putting best practices to work for your clients* (pp. 77–102). New York: Wiley.

Brotman, L.E., Liberi, W.P., & Wasylyshyn, K.M. (1998). Executive coaching: The need for standards of competence. *Consulting Psychology Journal: Practice and Research, 50*: 40–6.

Cavanagh, M. (2006). Coaching from a systemic perspective: A complex adaptive conversation. In D.S. Stober & A.M. Grant (Eds.), *Evidence based coaching handbook: Putting best practices to work for your clients* (pp. 313–54). New York: Wiley.

Costa, A.L., & Garmston, R.J. (2002). *Cognitive coaching: A foundation for Renaissance schools* (2nd ed.). Norwood, MA: Christopher-Gordon.

Cox, E. (2006). An adult learning approach to coaching. In D.S. Stober & A.M. Grant (Eds.), *Evidence based coaching handbook: Putting best practices to work for your clients* (pp. 193–218). New York: Wiley.

Drake, D., & Stober, D.R. (2007). The rise of the post-professional: Lessons learned in thinking about coaching as an evidence-based practice. In M. Cavanagh, A. Grant, & T. Kemp (Eds.), *Evidence-based coaching* (Vol. 2): *Cross-disciplinary perspectives.* Sydney, NSW: Australian Academic Press.

Edwards, J. (2003). Cognitive coaching: Research on outcomes and recommendations for implementation. In I. F. Stein & L. A. Belsten (Eds.), *Proceedings of the 1st ICF Coaching Research Symposium* (pp. 20–32). Mooresville, NC: International Coach Federation.

Ennis, S., Goodman, R., Hodgetts, W., Hunt, J.M., Mansfield, R., Otto, J., et al. (2005). Core competencies of the executive coach. Retrieved 8 September 2008 from http://ww.theexecutivecoachingforum/ECFCompetencyModel905.pdf.

Grant, A.M. (2006). An integrative goal-focused approach to executive coaching. In D.S. Stober & A.M. Grant (Eds.), *Evidence based coaching handbook: Putting best practices to work for your clients* (pp. 153–92). New York: Wiley.

Grant, A.M., & Stober, D.R. (2006). Introduction. In D.S. Stober & A.M. Grant (Eds.), *Evidence based coaching handbook: Putting best practices to work for your clients* (pp. 1–14). New York: Wiley.

Kilburg, R.R. (2003). *Executive coaching: Developing managerial wisdom in a world of chaos.* Washington, DC: American Psychological Association.

O'Neill, M.B. (2000). *Executive coaching with backbone and heart: A systems approach to engaging leaders with their challenges.* San Francisco, CA: Jossey-Bass.

Orenstein, R.L. (2007). *Multidimensional executive coaching.* New York: Springer.

Palmer, S. & Whybrow, A. (2007). *Handbook of coaching psychology.* New York: Routledge.

Peltier, B. (2001). *The psychology of executive coaching: Theory and application.* New York: Brunner-Routledge.

Peterson, D.B. (2006). People are complex and the world is messy: A behavior-based approach to executive coaching. In D.S. Stober & A.M. Grant (Eds.) *Evidence based coaching handbook: Putting best practices to work for your clients* (pp. 51–76). New York: Wiley.

Sackett, D.L., Haynes, R.B., Guyatt, G.H., & Tugwell, P. (1996). Evidence-based medicine: What it is and what it isn't. *British Medical Journal, 13*: 71–2.

Skiffington, S., & Zeus, P. (2003). *Behavioral coaching: How to build sustainable personal and organizational strength.* Sydney, NSW: McGraw-Hill.

Starr, L.M. (2006). *Academic guidelines distribution project.* Retrieved 6 September 2008 from http://www.gsaec.org/research.html.

Stober, D.R. (2005). Approaches to research on executive and organizational coaching outcomes. *International Journal of Coaching in Organizations, 3*: 6–13.

Stober, D.R. (2006). Coaching from the humanistic perspective. In D.S. Stober & A.M. Grant (Eds.), *Evidence based coaching handbook: Putting best practices to work for your clients* (pp. 17–50). New York: Wiley.

Stober , D.R., & Grant, A.M. (2006). *Evidence based coaching handbook: Putting best practices to work for your clients.* New York: Wiley.

Stober, D.R., Wildflower, L., & Drake, D. (2006). Evidence-based practice: A potential approach for effective coaching. *International Journal of Evidence Based Coaching and Mentoring, 4*(1): 1–8.

Conclusion

Tatiana Bachkirova, David Clutterbuck and Elaine Cox

To conclude this book we want to comment on several themes that emerged from the spectrum of approaches, genres and contexts of coaching that we have presented. We will then set out our personal reflection on the work done and a view that has been formed as a result of working on this book. We will finish with our perception of the current knowledge base of coaching and the potential implications of this view for coaches.

The four main themes that we want to comment on are:

1   the role of constructivism in considering a variety of approaches in coaching practice
2   the role of personal theories or models of coaching
3   the dynamics of change in the coaching field and the need for experimentation
4   eclecticism in relation to the use of techniques in coaching.

THE ROLE OF CONSTRUCTIVISM IN CONSIDERING APPROACHES TO COACHING PRACTICE

We noticed that the perspective of constructivism was prominent in the writing of several authors in this book, probably reflecting the active stance of coaches not only to their actual role in the world but also to the way they construct this world in terms of knowledge and perception. Constructivism is a theory of knowledge formation that involves an internal process of interpretation and experimentation. People are active sense-makers of their experiences, or as Kelly (1955) argued, they are 'personal scientists'. In the constructivist view of the world, the knowledge that we each create and use is personal to us, and our current perspectives are created through a fusion of our existing knowledge and frames of reference and any new material and experience presented to us.

This train of thought has left us with the realization that the impact and usefulness of this book will be different for every reader; each person will assimilate the content according to his/her values, beliefs and current worldview. Every reader of this book will use the information contained here differently according to the way he/she interprets the chapters and how he/she presently interprets the world. However, as interpretations are always open to change, we hope that the range of perspectives in this book will invite readers to affirm or challenge their constructed worlds of coaching in different ways at different points in their life.

THE ROLE OF A PERSONAL THEORY OR MODEL OF COACHING

In this book we have brought together the theories and influences on coaching that form the picture of the field as we, the editors, see it – from a particular perspective and at a particular point in time. Our intention was to be the most inclusive we could be in terms of the theoretical perspectives, contexts, genres and professional issues that currently relate to the coaching field. We are hoping that such a wide picture will serve as a comprehensive knowledge base with which readers can engage, and from it begin to create (or recreate) their own model of coaching. The value of having a personal theory or model is that it allows practitioners to examine their practice, to be aware of what is important for them, to know what they ultimately want to achieve in their work and the means they use in this process. We hope that this book provides sufficient input to enable readers to identify or to construct their own model of coaching practice.

Building on Lane and Corrie (2006) we suggest that a personal model of coaching practice may include three essential elements:

- a philosophy that underpins coaching practice
- the main purpose of coaching: What is it for? What is the coach trying to achieve?
- a coherent process: what tools, methods and procedures are needed and appropriate for working towards this purpose, and are congruent with this philosophy.

We believe that a personal model should start from a philosophy, that is, a coherent framework that encompasses our own worldview and what is important for us in the way we practise. It also includes a rationale for why this framework is as it is, in the context relevant to our particular practice. The task of creating this element of the model would be well served by gaining a good understanding of the traditions and approaches discussed in this book. For example a coach's philosophy may be one that fits perfectly with one of the approaches or traditions introduced in Section One of the book. In this case, it is quite possible that what that coach tries to achieve in his/her practice will be identical or closely aligned with the main goals and tasks of this approach. The process described in this approach could also fit with the procedures that are followed and with the tools that are used. If coaches already have a model of their coaching practice, then the book may offer ways of questioning or confirming it from different perspectives.

Our experience shows, however, that often coaches do not have an explicit model of their practice. Sometimes this is a reflection of the pragmatic stance that coaches take towards their role of helping clients to achieve their goals, without recognition that it is not really a value-free position. Sometimes they explain the lack of an explicit model by defending the flexibility of their approach and the fact that they change the model according to the needs of the client or appropriateness of the situation. Such flexibility, however justified, may cover a reluctance to explore potential frameworks and their own underlying values and intentions, leaving the coach without a clear rationale for why they do what they do. In such cases, a particular commitment or view about this does not mean a rigid position, but may indicate a starting point that reflects the current state in the coach's personal journey as a professional. This current state is important as a point of reasonable consistency from which a coach might choose to increase awareness and to experiment in enhancing their practice.

THE DYNAMICS OF CHANGE IN THE COACHING FIELD AND THE NEED FOR EXPERIMENTATION

Given that the knowledge base for coaching is still emerging, it is valuable for coaches to experiment with approaches within their coaching relationships, both in terms of techniques and their own learning processes. Some approaches (for example Gestalt) actively encourage experimentation; others (for example clean language, or GROW) tend to lead the practitioner towards a relatively fixed logic and process. However, even in the latter case, confident coaches will seek opportunities to expand their skills through experimentation. It is unfortunate that so little of this learning is captured and recorded. We perceive one of the major roles of supervision, particularly at this point in the establishment of the profession, to be the collation and exposition of the experience of experiment. The creation of a coaching supervision community, representing the profession as a whole rather than competing professional bodies, could be a useful place for this knowledge-gathering to begin. In addition to making good use of supervision, coaches would also benefit from participating in learning communities that encourage experimentation, sharing experiences and potentially developing new approaches in coaching practice.

ECLECTICISM IN RELATION TO THE USE OF TECHNIQUES IN COACHING

An argument, which we have only lightly addressed, is whether a narrowly-based approach to coaching (for example a practice based primarily within transactional analysis (TA), or the cognitive–behavioural tradition) is more effective and/or more ethical than one which draws upon a more eclectic portfolio of philosophies and bodies of knowledge – in other words, depth versus breadth. On the one hand it could be argued that using techniques and procedures from one school of knowledge enables the coach to operate at a greater depth of understanding, and that consistency of approach then develops the routines of the client's experience, so that they can work *with* the coach in the application of process. It can equally be argued that a single-philosophy approach is incompatible with the variety of needs and receptivity of the client; that a wider portfolio of potential responses and methods from the coach offers greater flexibility to design approaches specific to the individual. From this latter perspective, the single-approach coach is inevitably more coach-centred (as opposed to client-centred), because the coach's assumptions about the issues and process of solution create a boundary to the coaching conversation. At the other extreme, excessive breadth – knowing a little about a lot of approaches – may be equally questionable if the coach is only able to use these at a relatively superficial level.

There are no simple conclusions to draw from this debate, but we believe in the value of a well-formulated philosophy that incorporates one, two or more theoretical perspectives that do not clash in terms of their main assumptions. Such a foundation could withstand a pull in a different direction from the inspiring variety of other well-supported perspectives on coaching. It would be able to support 'a managed eclecticism' in terms of the tools, techniques and knowledge that other approaches offer.

At a more pragmatic level there are some useful basic suggestions for situations that call for the use of tools and techniques that are not embedded in any one perspective or approach to coaching (Megginson & Clutterbuck, 2005):

- Use only what you know from the inside: practice first – if necessary on yourself.
- Use them within a loose model of helping.
- Have many, so that you are not offering a solution in search of a problem.
- Make explicit the intention of the coach in using the technique – apply them *with* the client, not *to* the client.

OUR REFLECTION ON THE PROCESS OF WORKING WITH THIS BOOK

What we have presented here is a shared body of theoretical and contextual knowledge built on the research and experience of a large number of experts in the field. It was a privilege and a challenge to work with a book of such scope and with so many recognized, experienced professionals who generously shared their knowledge and ideas for coaching practice. Also it was an opportunity to put into practice our view of the field as a matrix – the only structure that made sense for us in trying to capture and conceptualize the diversity of the coaching field. It was also a challenge because of the difficulty in keeping authors within the proposed structure: all had much more to say than could be accommodated in a single chapter.

Although we are aware that much more needs to be done to create a solid knowledge base for coaching, working on this book made us aware again of how vast is the pool of knowledge that is potentially useful for coaching and of how wide is the range of ideas brought to coaching from other disciplines. It made us very hopeful about the future of coaching to see how rigorous and sometimes ingenious we as coaches are at distilling from the immensely wide and deep subject areas of knowledge the focused and practical ways necessary for understanding and enriching the coaching process for the benefit of our clients.

HAVE WE ACHIEVED OUR PURPOSE FOR THE BOOK?

In a sense, there cannot be a conclusion to this Handbook, because the variety of chapters on approaches, genres and contexts that we have brought together here can only ever be a partial picture of the field of coaching. Indeed, between the time of writing and when this book is published, there will almost certainly be a variety of new approaches and new applications. Similarly, the professional issues that are discussed are constantly shifting in nature and emphasis.

As a natural consequence we can say that coaches, who are trying to create an integrated perspective (whether they call it a personal theory or a model of coaching practice) that includes the value of diverse approaches and genres, will be wise to constantly reform, refine, re-examine and rebuild that perspective. Therefore, a final thought that we would like to share at the end of this book is that the integration of approaches should never be the result or consummation of such an endeavour; rather it should be an ongoing and meaningful process.

REFERENCES

Kelly, G.A. (1955). *The psychology of personal constructs.* New York: Norton.
Lane, D.A., & Corrie, S. (2006). *The modern scientist-practitioner: A guide to practice in psychology.* Hove: Routledge.
Megginson, D., & Clutterbuck, D. (2005). *Techniques for coaching and mentoring.* Oxford: Butterworth Heinemann.

Author Index

Abbott, G.N. 331, 335
Abbott and Grant 328
Abbott and Rosinski 336
Abbott et al. 328
Ackland, R. 284
Adler, N.J. 325
Alexander, G. 206
Alexander and Renshaw 206
Allan and Whybrow 89
Allcorn, S. 413
Allen, J.R. 173, 179
Allen, J.R. and Allen, B. 179
Alred, Garvey and Smith 351
Amy, A.H. 261
Anderson, J.P. 37
Anderson, T. 127
Angus, Levitt and Hardtke 123
Argyris, C. 304
Argyris and Schön 233, 234, 242, 249
Aristotle 300
Armstrong, H.B. 327
Auerbach, J.E. 265, 413
Austin, J.L. 107, 108

Bachkirova, T. 3, 218, 306
Bachkirova and Cox 141, 227
Baker, Jensen and Kolb 289, 290
Baldwin and Ford 294
Bandler, R. 187, 189, 195
Bandler and Grinder 188, 189
Bandura, A. 38, 166, 167, 204
Barnard, C.I. 246
Barrett, F. 55
Barrett-Leonard, G.T. 68, 69
Barrow, G. 179
Basseches, M. 227
Bateson, G. 55, 189, 196, 233, 234
Baum, H. 350
Baumeister and Vohs 168
Bayer and Gollwitzer 61
Beattie, R.S. 258, 261

Beck, A.T. 38
Beck, D. and Cowan 133
Beck, J. 38
Beisser, A.R. 83
Bennett, J.L. 358, 359, 364, 406, 408, 411
Bennett, M.J. 325
Bennetts, C. 344, 349
Bennis, W. 247
Bentz and Shapiro 156
Berg, I.K. 55
Berg and Szabo 55, 56, 58, 63
Berger, J. 140, 143, 337, 413
Berger, J. and Fitzgerald 137, 140, 225, 337
Berger, P.L. and Luckmann 121
Berglas, B. 381
Berglas, S. 64, 249, 250, 350
Berman and Bradt 218
Berne, E. 172–3, 174, 175, 177, 184, 185
Berry, J. 331, 332, 337
Bion, W. 28, 33
Bluckert, P. 82, 101, 350
Blustein, D. 312
Boje, D.M. 129
Bolles, R. 312
Boniwell, I. 159
Boscolo and Bertrando 124
Bostic St Clair, C. 188
Bostic St Clair and Grinder 188, 190–1
Botella and Herrero 123
Boud, D. 289
Bowlby, J. 23
Bozarth and Motomasa 73
Braud and Anderson 156
Brennan, D. 370, 377
Brickey, M. 376
Brock, V. 374, 375
Brodley, B.T. 70
Brookfield, S. 228
Brooks, C.H. 193, 195
Brotman, Liberi and Wasylyshyn 411
Bruner, J. 120, 123, 125, 344, 351

Bryant and Veroff 163
Buber, M. 81, 89
Buckley, A. 306, 395
Buckley and Buckley 396, 397, 401, 403
Burdett, J.O. 258
Burke, K. 120
Byron 341

Cameron, R. 156
Cameron, Dutton and Quinn 167
Campbell, J. 121
Caraccioli, L.A. 342, 344
Carden, A. 346
Carlopio, Andrewartha and Armstrong 291
Carter, J. 83
Caruso, R.E. 344
Carver and Scheier 61, 304
Cavanagh, M. 65, 403, 413
Cavanagh and Grant 60, 305, 306
Chao, R. 290
Cherniss, J. 101
Chou, Y.-C. 60
Choy, A. 178
Clarke and Dawson 181
Clarkson, P. 81
Clarkson and Mackewn 233
Clutterbuck, D. 272, 273, 275, 277, 278, 279, 395
Clutterbuck and Lane 304, 345
Clutterbuck and Megginson 246, 345
Cohn, H.W. 94, 101
Coldman, D. 154
Connor, M. 345
Cook-Greuter, S. 133, 134–5, 137, 140
Cooper, M. 95
Cooperrider et al. 162
Corbett, K. 301
Corcoran, J. 206
Corcoran and Stephenson 55
Corey, G. 276, 277
Corey et al. 280
Cornell, W. 178
Corrie, S. 361
Corrie and Lane 363
Cortright, B. 146, 154
Costa and Garmston 37, 265, 413
Couch, U. 298
Coue, E. 193
Coulehan, Friedlander and Heatherington 126
Cox, E. 7, 206, 413
Cox and Bachkirova 305
Curry et al. 166
Curwen, Palmer and Ruddell 38
Czarniawska, B. 120

D'Abate, Eddy and Tannenbaum 286, 287, 290
Dahl, Bathel and Carreon 55
Dahlsgaard, Peterson and Seligman 160
Daloz, L. 345
Damon, W. 285, 292
Damon and Phelps 285
d'Ansembourg, T. 208
Davidson, C. 175
Davies and Harré 122
de Jong, A. 370, 401
De la Mothe-Fénélon, F.S. 341, 342, 344
de Shazer, S. 55, 56, 60, 61, 64, 291
Deci and Ryan 76
Deci and Vansteenkiste 77
Derogatis and Melisaratos 301
Descartes, R. 114
Dewey, J. 8, 107, 108
Diener, E. 158
Dilts and DeLozier 195
Dilts et al. 188, 196
DiMattia and Mennen 37
Douglas and McCauley 297
Downey, M. 381
Drake, D.B. 122, 123, 124, 126, 127, 129, 361
Drake, Brennan and Gørtz 325
Drake and Stober 408
Drath, W. 137
Drucker, P. 246
Duncan and Miller 73
Dutton and Heaphy 167
Dychtwald, K. 312
D'Zurilla, T.J. 38

Eakin, P.J. 123
Earley and Ang 325
Early and Mosakowski 275
Edelman et al. 306
Edgerton, N. 42
Edgerton and Palmer 37, 42, 43
Edwards, J. 413
Egan, G. 347
Ellinger, A.D. 266
Ellinger, A.D. and Bostrom 258, 259, 260–1
Ellinger, A.D., Ellinger, A.E. and Keller 266
Ellinger, A.D., Hamlin and Beattie 267
Ellinger, A.M. 258, 260–1, 262
Ellis, A. 38, 42, 64, 298
Ellis, A. and Blum 40
Ellis, A. and Harper 298
Ellis, A. et al. 42
Ellis, D. 151
Elmadag, Ellinger, A.E. and Franke 267
Emler and Heather 346

English, F. 174
Ennis et al. 411
Epston, D. 121
Erhard, W. 298
Erickson, M. 189, 195, 219
Erikson, E.H. 280, 348
Evered and Selman 257, 258, 261

Favell, I. 40
Ferrar, P. 3, 274
Ferrer, J. 146
Filippi, R. 298
Fillery-Travis and Lane 73, 366
Fitzgerald and Berger 245
Flaherty, J. 381
Flores, F. 107
Foot and Howe 292
Ford, J.G. 72
Foucault, M. 123, 362
Fournies, F.F. 258
Fowler, J.W. 133
Freedman and Combs 124, 127
Fredrickson, B. 159, 164, 167
Fredrickson and Losada 162
Freud, S. 23, 80–1, 350
Frey and Stitzer 247
Friday et al. 345
Frisch, M.B. 303

Gable and Haidt 159
Gadamer, H.-G. 107
Gallwey, W.T. 204, 206, 212, 247
Garlo and Prior 370
Garvey, B. 345, 348, 349, 351
Garvey, Stokes and Megginson 348
Gattellari et al. 301
Geertz, C. 121, 344
Gergen and Gergen 122
Gerhardt, S. 24, 179
Gersick, C. 273
Gert, B. 370
Gibb, S. 349
Gladstone, M.S. 343, 346
Goldberg, Muir and Kerr 24
Goldsmith, M. 247
Goldsmith, Lyons and Freas 247
Goldstein, K. 82
Goleman, D. 133, 258, 289
Gollwitzer, P.M. 304
Goodman, P. 80
Goodman, R. 223–4
Graham, Wedman and
    Garvin-Kester 260, 266

Grant, A.M. 3, 38, 49, 61, 70, 76, 159, 263,
    292, 298, 394, 395, 413
Grant, A.M. and Greens 299
Grant, A.M. and O'Hara 302
Grant, A.M. and Palmer 3
Grant, A.M. and Zackon 306
Grant, B. 70
Graves, C. 133
Gray, J. 101
Grbcic, S. 50
Grbcic and Palmer 50
Green, A. and E. 147
Green, L.S., Oades and Grant 38, 49, 55, 300–1,
    306, 395
Green, S., Grant and Rynsaardt 49, 55
Greenberg and Mitchell 23
Greenberger and Padesky 42
Greene and Grant 57, 60, 291
Grendlin, E.T. 233
Grinder, J. 187, 188, 189, 195
Grinder, DeLozier and Bandler 189
Grodzki and Allen 345
Gustavsson and Baccman 272
Gyllensten and Palmer 305

Hackim, C. 312
Hackman, J.R. 273
Hackman and Wageman 271, 272, 273
Hale, R. 345
Hall and Lindzey 82
Hamlin, Ellinger and Beattie 261
Hampden-Turner and Tromenaars 330
Handy, C. 246
Hannah, C. 266–7
Hargrove, R. 258
Harrison, A. and Harrison, D. 332
Hart, B. 129
Hart, T. 156
Hawkins, P. 242, 381, 384, 386
Hawkins and Schwenk 382
Hawkins and Shohet 389, 391, 392
Hawkins and Smith 239, 240, 241, 242, 281,
    381, 382, 383, 385, 386, 389
Hay, J. 174, 185, 374
Hazen, B. 316
Heidegger, M. 81, 107, 108
Held, B.S. 65, 168
Hermans, H.J.M. 121, 122, 127, 154
Hermans and Kempen 123
Heron, J. 156, 239
Hewson, D. 121
Hillman, J. 125, 154
Hirschhorn, L. 247

Hofstede, G. 325, 326, 329
Holland, J. 312, 319
Homer 341, 344
Honderich, T. 107
Honey, K. 226
Honoria 342, 344
Horvath and Symonds 60
Howard et al. 301
Hunt and Weintraub 220, 258, 259, 261, 262, 344
Hurley and Fagenson-Eland 344
Hymer, S.M. 301

Ibarra, H. 313, 314, 319
Ihde, D. 99

Jackson, K. and Taylor 273
Jackson, P. 222, 223
Jackson, P. and McKergow 54, 55, 59, 62
Jacobsen, B. 94
James, W. 121, 333
Janis, I.L. 279
Jaques, E. 227
Jarvis, J. 298, 381
Jarvis, Lane and Fillery-Travis 363
Johnson, D. and Johnson, R. 292
Johnson, D., Johnson, R. and Smith 292
Johnson, D. et al. 292
Johnson, T.J. 362
Joseph, S. 46, 70, 77
Joseph and Bryant-Jefferies 72
Joseph and Linley 72, 73, 76
Joseph and Worsley 72
Joyce and Showers 284
Jung, C.G. 23

Kadushin, A. 383, 384
Kampa-Kokesch and Anderson 255
Katz, N. 278
Katzenbach, J.R. 273
Kauffman, C. 159, 162
Kauffman and Scoular 73
Kearns, Forbes and Gardiner 49
Kegan, R. 63, 133, 135, 136–41, 137, 143,
    144, 218, 224, 227, 228, 280, 337, 378
Keidel, R. 271, 278
Kelly, G.A. 188, 417
Kerka, S. 286
Kessels, J.W.M. 347
Khurana and Nohria 370
Kierkegaard, S.A. 81
Kilburg, R.R. 64, 245, 246, 255, 297, 413
Kim, J.S. 300
King and Eaton 260

King and Kitchener 133
Kirsch and Glass 298
Kirschenbaum, H. 68
Kitchener and Jorm 403
Klein, M. 23, 27
Kluckhohn, C. 329
Knowles, M. 7, 212
Knowles, Holton and Swanson 6, 7, 8, 203, 218,
    219, 220, 285
Kodish, S.P. 38
Koffka, K. 81
Kohlberg, L. 132, 377, 378
Köhler, W. 81
Kohn, A. 213
Kolb, D. 7, 8, 219, 220, 223, 285, 289
Korzybski, A. 188
Kouzes, J. 247
Kram, K.E. 345
Krantz, J. 247
Krantz and Maltz 253
Kraut et al. 257
Kroger, W.S. 193

Ladyshewsky, R. 284, 286
Ladyshewsky and Ryan 284
Ladyshewsky and Varey 286
Lahey et al. 140
Landsberg, M. 246
Lane and Corrie 362, 363, 418
Larson, M.S. 362
Laske, O. 140, 227, 228, 378
Latham, G. 167
Latner, J. 81
Lave and Wenger 346
Law, Ireland and Hussain 325, 364
Lazarus, A.A. 40, 41, 42, 43, 44
Lazarus, R. 168
Lee, G. 31, 32, 100, 350
Leonard, T. 298, 370
Leshinsky, M. 302
Lethem, J. 55
Lettvin et al. 108
Leung, P. 302
Levinson, D. 219, 344
Levinson, H. 245
Levitt, B.E. 70
Lewin, K. 81
Lewin, R. 65
Lewis, Amini and Lannon 234
Lindeman, E. 7, 212
Lindez-Pelz and Hall 187
Linley and Harrington 159
Lo, M.-C.M. 362

Locke, E.A. 291, 303
Locke and Latham 38, 40
Loehr, J. 207
Loevinger, J. 133, 140, 220
Longenecker and Neubert 261
Lopez, S. 166
Lopez and Snyder 161
Lowman, R. 255
Lucius and Kuhnert 227
Luft and Ingham 289, 290
Lyubomirsky, S. 166, 167
Lyubomirsky, King and Diener 159

MacLennan, N. 345
Maddux, J.R. 166
Mancuso and Sarbin 121
Marsh, L. 260
Marsick, V. 272
Marton and Saljo 289
Maslow, A. 133, 220, 300
Mathison, J. 197
Mattingly, C. 123
Maturana, H.R. 108
Maturana and Varela 107
Maturana et al. 108
May, R. 97
McGonagill, G. 299
McKee, R. 124
McLean et al. 260
McMahon, G. 37, 39, 45
McNicoll, A. 281
Megginson, D. 279
Megginson and Clutterbuck 297, 420
Megginson et al. 345
Melnick and Nevis 82
Merleau-Ponty, M. 107, 108
Merlevede, Bridoux and Vandamme 289
Merriam and Clark 220
Merry, T. 73
Mezirow, J. 7, 8–9, 243
Mezirow et al. 220, 223
Micholt, N. 174
Miller, E.J. 247
Miller, W.R. and Rollnick 49
Mink, Owen and Mink 258
Mintzberg, H. 257
Minuchin and Fishman 233
Mishler, E.G. 123
Mobley, S.A. 260
Mohr, G. 182
Moor et al. 403
Moral and Abbott 325
Moreno, J.L. 233

Morgan, Harkins and Goldsmith 325
Morse and Wagner 257
Mumford, A. 259–60
Murray and Murray 55

Napper and Newton 178
Neale et al. 302
Neenan and Dryden 37, 38, 42
Neenan and Palmer 37, 39, 40, 42, 44, 73
Neilson and Eisenbach 349
Newton, I. 346
Newton, J., Long and Sievers 253
Newton, T. 178
Newton, T. and Napper 185
Nevis, E.C. 88
Nietzsche, F. 108
Noer, D. 261
Noer, Leupold and Valle 261
Nowers, M. 396, 397

O'Broin and Palmer 73
Ochs and Capps 122
O'Connell, B. 54, 55, 56, 61
O'Connor and Lages 225, 227
O'Connor and Seymour 190
Oettingen and Gollwitzer 61
O'Hanlon, W. 38
O'Hanlon and Beadle 58, 59, 60, 204
Oldmeadow, L. 293
O'Neill, M.B. 413
Orenstein, R. 247, 255, 413
Orth, Wilkinson and Benfari 258, 260
Osland et al. 327, 330

Palmer, S. 38, 40–1, 42, 43, 48, 49
Palmer and Burton 37
Palmer and Cooper 40, 44
Palmer, Cooper and Thomas 44
Palmer and Gyllensten 37, 38
Palmer and Neenan 43
Palmer and Puri 43
Palmer and Szymanska 37, 38, 39, 42, 45, 50
Palmer, Tubbs and Whybrow 48
Palmer and Whybrow 49, 70, 159, 410
Park, McLean and Yang 260, 267
Parsons, F. 311
Passmore, J. 255, 325
Passmore and Marianetti 155
Passmore and Whybrow 73
Patel and Kaufman 293
Patterson and Joseph 77
Pavlov, I.I. 213
Peltier, B. 105, 250, 410

Perls, F. 80–1, 187, 188
Perls, L. 80–1
Perls, F, Hefferline and Goodman 81
Perry, W.G. 218, 224
Peters, H. 284
Peterson, C. and Seligman 160
Peterson, D. 245, 264, 413
Peterson, D. and Little 258, 260
Phillips, R. 260
Piaget, J. 132
Polster and Polster 233
Ponzo, Z. 298
Popovic and Boniwell 168
Poppen, R. 41
Popper and Lipshitz 258
Powell and Doran 261
Prochaska et al. 160
Proctor, B. 383, 384

Rafferty and Griffin 255
Ratliff, Beckstead and Hanke 275
Read, J. 403
Redshaw, B. 258, 266
Riegel, K. 220
Riessman, C.K. 127
Roberts and Billings 44
Rock and Schwartz 291
Rogers, C.R. 68, 69–70, 226, 291, 249
Rogers, J. 376
Rogers, P. and Blenko 272
Rosenberg, M.B. 207
Rosinski, P. 325, 329, 330, 337, 343
Rousseau, J.-J. 342
Rowan, J. 30, 146, 148
Rowan and Jacobs 156
Rubenstein, D. 373
Ryan and Deci 76, 77, 165
Ryff and Singer 300

Sackett et al. 299, 412
Samier, E. 345
Sanders, P. 73
Saner, R. 83
Sartre, J.-P. 81, 97
Satir, V. 188
Scandura et al. 345
Schaie and Zanjani 218
Schank, R.A. 121
Schein, E. 221, 312, 326
Schelling, T. 260
Schmid, B. 181, 182
Schmid, P. 76
Schore, A.N. 24, 27

Schwalbe, K. 40
Schwartz and Bilsky 329
Searle, J.R. 107, 108, 112
Sekerka and Chao
Seligman, M.E.P. 162
Seligman and Csikszentmihalyi 76
Seligman, Rashid and Parkes 159
Seligman et al. 159, 162
Senge, P. 197
Senge et al. 150
Shaw and Knights 261, 267
Sheldon, K.M. 303
Sheldon and Elliot 77
Sheldon and Lyubomirsky 163
Shlien, J.M. 77
Showers, B. 284, 289
Sieler, A. 105, 107, 112
Sills, C. 172
Sills and Hargaden 173
Siminovitch and Van Eron 83, 84, 85, 87, 91
Simmel, G. 345
Skiffington and Zeus 272, 410
Skinner, B.F. 213
Skinner, M. and Welch 284
Smith, Morton and Oakley 193
Snyder, R. 166
Snyder, Rand and Sigmon 166
Snyder et al. 166
Socrates 39, 44
Solms, M. 24
Spence, G.B. 298, 358
Spence, Cavanagh and Grant 306
Spence and Grant 55, 301, 306, 395
Sperry, L. 47, 217, 290
Spinelli, E. 95, 97, 99, 100, 101, 103, 104
Stacey, R.D. 65
Stams et al. 300
Starr, L.M. 408
Stevenson, H. 83
Stewart, I. 172, 184
Stober, D.R. 409, 413
Stober and Grant 73, 325, 410
Stober, Wildflower and Drake 412, 414
Strasser, F. and Strasser, A. 101
Sue-Chan and Latham 290
Sugarman, L. 217, 219, 228
Summers and Tudor 173, 178
Super, D. 312

Talarico, M. 258
Taylor, C. 372
Tedeschi and Calhoun 168
Temple, S. 177, 184

Tennant and Pogson 220
Thackeray, W.M. 342
Thompson, A.S. 298
Thompson, L. 273
Tichy, N. 247
Torbert, W. 133, 242
Torbert et al. 133, 140
Torrance, E.P. 344
Tosey, P. 197
Trompenaars and Hampden-Turner 326
Tuckman and Jensen 273, 280
Tugade and Fredrickson 164
Tulving and Thompson 193
Turner, V. 121
Twain, M. 148

Urdan and Midgley 292

Valle and King 95
Valley and Thompson 272
Van Belle, H. 226
van Gennep, A. 121
Van Velsor and Leslie 248
Van Vianen and de Dreu 272
Vansteenkiste and Sheldon 77
Vygotsky, L. 293

Waddell and Dunn 284, 286, 290
Wageman et al. 273, 274
Wallen and Nevis 82
Wampold, B.E. 73
Ward, Bochner and Furnham 326
Watkins, M. 248
Watson, J.B. 213
Weinberg and Gould 278
Weiner, K.C. 371
Wertheimer, M. 81

West, L. and Milan 223
West, W. 146
White, M. 121, 124, 125
White and Epston 121, 124
Whitehead and Russell 196
Whitmore, J. 148, 149, 160, 206, 238
Whitmore and Einzig 148, 149, 152,
    153, 154, 155
Whitworth, L. 370
Whitworth, Kimsey-House and Sandahl 162, 300
Wicklund, J. 55
Wilber, K. 5, 6, 133–4, 135, 141, 146, 147, 148, 149,
    154, 327, 338
Wilkins, P. 72
Williams, H., Palmer and Edgerton 265
Williams, P. 307–8
Williams, P. and Davis 303, 308
Williams, P. and Menendez 151, 152, 155
Winnicott, D. 23, 25, 28, 29
Winograd and Flores 107
Wittgenstein, L. 107, 108
Wolpe, J. 41, 47
Wolpe and Lazarus 41, 47
Woolger, R.J. 151
Worsley, R. 73
Wuthnow, R. 247
Wynn and Kromrey 284

Yalom, I. 95
Yontef, G. 88, 89
Young, M.F. 301
Yukl, G. 257, 266

Zaleznik, A. 249
Zemke, R. 260
Zeus and Skiffington 289
Zur and Anderson 376

General Index

ABCDEF model 42, 43
  G-ABCDEF 42, 47
Academy of Management Review 410
ACE patterns 31, 43
action learning cycle 328–9
action plans 40, 45, 57, 63, 91, 161, 265, 303, 315
  entry into new roles 316–17
actualizing tendency 12, 69, 72, 101, 165, 226
  see also self-actualization
ADHD 307
agency beliefs 166
American Psychological Association (APA)
  369, 406
anchoring 191, 195
andragogy 7–8
anger reducing imagery 43
APECS 248
appreciative inquiry (AI) 213
assessment phase, career coaching 315
assimilation, cultural 331, 332
Association for Coaching (AC) 366, 369, 371, 400
Association for Professional Executive Coaching
  and Supervision (APECS) 369, 371
Association for Transpersonal
  Psychology (ATP) 146
Australian Psychological Society (APS) 369, 406
authentic dialogue, Gestalt approach 88–90
authority of the coach 114
autonomy 7, 69, 136, 165, 173, 183, 189, 190, 212,
  304, 362, 372

Bath Consultancy Group 386, 390, 391
behavioural coaching 205, 249, 264–5
behavioural models, tools and techniques 40–1
behavioural taxonomies, table of 261
behaviourist psychology 18–19
best possible future self, exercise 164
body, domain of, in ontological coaching 109, 110,
  111, 113–14, 115, 117, 118
boundary management 374–5, 385
brainstorming 205, 209
Bresser Report 343

Brief Family Therapy Centre, Milwaukee 55
Brief Symptom Inventory (BSI) 50, 301
British Psychological Society (BPS) 146, 369, 406
British Rail 267

Canadian Psychological Association (CPA) 377
career coaching 17, 48, 74, 311–23
  distinctions between other genres and 317–18
  evaluation of 321–2
  features, processes and roles 313–17
  goals and tasks 312–13
  relationship with theoretical traditions 318–21
Centre for Economic Performance (CEP) 395
certainty/reflectiveness paradox, cross cultural
  coaching 333
Chartered Institute of Personnel and Development
  (CIPD), UK 382
  Learning and Development Survey 257
children 7, 30, 55, 58, 86, 99, 138, 146, 176, 179,
  180, 181, 183, 203, 253, 274, 400
chunk size 193
CLEAR process 16, 232, 234–5, 236, 238–9, 285
  table of performance and transformational
  coaching 286
co-active coaching model 162
Coaches and Mentors Association of South Africa
  (COMENSA) 366
*Coaching: An International Journal of Theory, Research
  and Practice* 299, 410
cognitive approach 29
cognitive-behavioural coaching (CBC) 11–12,
  30, 37–53, 73, 114, 141, 165, 213, 226–7,
  253, 265–6, 279, 292, 318–19, 321, 337,
  350, 419
  assumptions of 38
  comparisons of traditions 45–6
  contexts 46–9
  evaluation of 49–51
  goals and tasks 38–40
  role of the coach 44–5
  special features, processes and the role of
  the coach 40–5

cognitive-developmental coaching 9, 13–14, 132–45,
227–8, 337
    comparisons with other traditions 141
    concepts and assumptions 133–5
    contexts 141–2
    development lines in an individual,
        diagram of 134
    evaluation of 142–4
    goals and tasks 135–41
    history of 132–3
    Kegan's theory 136–41; five stages of
        development, table of 138–9
cognitive models, tools and techniques 42–4
cognitivism 188–9
communication, context of team coaching 276
communication paradox, cross cultural
    coaching 334–6, 337
competence 4, 372, 373, 376, 408–9, 411–12,
    413–14
confidentiality 288, 345, 374–5, 385
conflict management 276, 292
conflict of interest 375
constructivist approach 8, 55, 179, 188, 218, 213,
    220, 221, 417–18
*Consulting Psychology Journal: Practice and
    Research* 410
contact, Gestalt approach 81, 83
    interruptions to 84–7; introjection 85, 86;
        retroflection 85, 86–7
continuing professional development 19, 405–16
    areas of focus 407–12
    evaluation 414–15
    evidence-based practice 412–14, 415
    initial challenges 405–7
contracting
    career coaching 314–15
    ethics of 373–4
    life coaching 302–3, 305
    person-centred approach 74
    supervision 385–6
    transformational coaching 238
coping imagery 43–4
Coping Inventory for Stressful Situations (CISS) 50
counselling 3, 34, 41, 55, 69, 72, 73, 76, 77, 90, 140,
    141, 173, 184, 222, 261, 266, 276, 297, 298,
    299, 301, 305–6, 311, 345, 350, 365, 376,
    381, 382, 383, 385, 399
counter transference 27–8
creative living 29
cross-cultural coaching 17, 116–17, 182–3,
    211–12, 324–40
    evaluation 338; integral model and management
        of paradox 338

cross-cultural coaching *cont.*
    features and goals 327–34; action learning cycle
        328–9; certainty/reflectiveness paradox 333;
        identification with own and other cultures 331;
        individualism/collectivism paradox 333; integral
        model 327; trait interaction possibilities 332
    relationship with theoretical traditions 336–7
    role of coach and relationship with clients 334–6,
        337; communication paradox diagram 336
crystallizing 151
cultural blindness 137
Cultural Orientations Framework (COF) 329, 330
Cycle of Experience, Gestalt approach 83–4, 85, 88

defence mechanisms 26–7
descriptive questioning 103
Deutscher Bundesverband Coaching (DBVC) 354, 358
developmental coaching 4, 16, 31–2, 47, 63, 128,
    141–2, 217–30, 242, 280
    assumptions 219–20
    background 218–19
    benefits and limitations 228–9
    comparison with other genres 224–6
    goals and tasks 220–1
    relationship with theoretical traditions 226–8
    role of coach and relationship with clients 221–4
    skills performance and developmental coaching,
        an evolution 211, 217–18
dialogical space 127
discourse, power of, narrative coaching 123–4
diversity of teams 275–6
drama triangle roles 177, 178, 180, 183, 382
dreams, role in transpersonal coaching 151
dual relationship 376

eclecticism, use of coaching techniques 419–20
ecology 194
education and training as professional
    development 407–8, 411
ego 129, 133, 134, 220, 227, 366
    ego states 14, 30, 176–7, 179, 181, 183
emotions
    relational regulation of 24–5
    role of in ontological coaching 108, 109, 110, 111,
        112–13, 114, 115, 117
empathy 207–8, 211, 214
encoding specificity principle 193
ending the coaching relationship 62, 304, 317
engagement, four levels of, transformational
    coaching 232, 235–41
    assumptions 235, 237
    CLEAR and 236, 238–9
    data (facts) 235, 236

engagement *cont.*
  feelings 235, 236–7
  patterns of behaviours 235, 236
  see also ending the coaching relationship;
    learning, levels of, transformational
    coaching
Erhard Seminars Training (EST) programmes 298
ethics 18, 369–80, 400, 401–2, 411
  comparison of coaching codes 371–2
  ethical behaviour in a coaching
    relationship 372–3
  ethical issues 373–7
  evaluation 378–9
  evolution of 370
  future: an ethical coaching community 377–8
European Federation of Psychologists Associations
    (EFPA) 360, 361, 400
European Mentoring Coaching Council (EMCC) 342,
    365, 366, 369, 371, 406, 411
evidence-based approaches 299, 412–14, 415
executive and leadership coaching 16, 32, 47,
    63–4, 75, 89, 91, 94, 100, 104, 115–16,
    161, 167, 197, 211–12, 225–6, 245–56,
    290, 297, 302
  background and context 246–8
  comparison with other genres 252
  evaluation of 254–5
  features of 251–2
  goals and tasks 249–51
  need for 248–9
  relationship with theoretical approaches 252
  see also manager as coach; managers
existential anxiety 96
existential coaching 6, 81, 94–106, 253–4
  applications of 103–4
  evaluation of 104–5
  key assumptions of 95–6
  methods and techniques for facilitation of
    change 101–3
  processes and dynamics 97–9
  role of coach 100–1
  tasks and goals 101
experimentation, need for 419
extrapersonal, the 147
eye-accessing cues 196

family therapy, systemic 233, 280
feedback, non-evaluative 288–9
five aspect model, Greenberger and Padesky 42
five dimensions model, Hofstede 329
fixed-agenda coaching 363
focusing, Gendlin's 232
formality 288

future of coaching 18, 357–67
  concerns 365–6
  evaluation 367
  fragility of concept of profession 361–2
  professionalism 365
  professional criteria 358–9
  professional status 364–5
  psychotherapy, influence of 359–61
  traditional and alternative perspectives 362–3

games, transactions and script, transactional
    analysis 177–8, 179
  diagram of drama and winners triangles 178
Germany, psychotherapy in 360
Gestalt approach 12, 29, 30, 71, 80–92, 114, 115,
    128, 179, 187, 213, 233, 419
  applications of 90–1
  assumptions and beliefs 82–3
  defining features of 83–90
  evaluation of 91–2
  perspective of human functioning 81–2
  theoretical tradition 80–1
Global Convention on Coaching (GCC) 357, 360,
    363–4, 365–6, 372
globalization 324, 325, 336, 338, 405
goal imagery 43
goal setting theory 38, 167
  see also individual coaching genres; QOLI;
    SMART goals; time-bound goals
Goldman-Sachs Group 325
Graduate School Alliance in Executive
    Coaching 408, 410
graduate schools 408
gratitude visits 163
group therapy 276–7, 280, 328
GROW model 90, 160–1, 190, 206, 223–4,
    238, 419
growth, concept of, narrative coaching 123
growth-fostering psychologies in relation to SPC
    213–14

Harrison Assessment Paradox Graph 332
health coaching 12, 46, 48–9, 179, 306
  medical model 69, 72, 75, 76, 77
  see also mental health
Health Enhancing Thinking (HETs) 49
Health Inhibiting Thinking (HITs) 49
health professionals 284, 305, 401, 408
Health Service, UK 343
Healthcare Commission 343
holarchy 133
holding environment, creation of a 25–6
hope theory 166

human potential movement (HPM) 298–9
human resources (HR) 4, 174, 175, 180, 246, 247, 257, 289, 302, 322, 347, 365, 376, 382–3
humanistic approach 81, 92, 141, 165, 179, 213, 291, 292, 298
humility, need for in coaching 114

IBM 329
identity, concept of situated, narrative coaching 122–3
identity of coaching 2–4, 378
    transitions from traditional coaching 3
    see also future of coaching; personal model of coaching
imagery, role in transpersonal coaching 151, 153
IMPACT 206
improvement, celebrating 205
individualism/collectivism paradox, cross cultural coaching 333
industry training organizations 407–8
inner-game model 206
inquiry 208, 211, 214
institutionalizing 151
integral model, Wilber's 327, 338
integration, cultural 331, 332, 337
internal professional coach 4
International Association of Coaching (IAC) 369, 371, 406
International Coach Federation (ICF) 366, 369, 371, 373, 375, 400, 406, 411
International Coaching Psychology Review 299, 410
International Coaching Research Forum (ICRF) 357
International Journal of Coaching in Organizations 410
International Journal of Evidence-based Coaching and Mentoring 299, 410
intimacy 345

Job Stress Survey (JSS) 50
Journal for Supervision and Curriculum Development 410
Journal of Rational-Emotive and Cognitive-Behaviour Therapy 38
Journal of Transpersonal Psychology 146

Kegan's theory 136–41
    five stages of development, table of 138–9
Kellog Europe 4
knowledge base of coaching 4–9, 410–11, 420
    best available knowledge 412–13
    four dimensions of coaching 5
    tensions in coach/client knowledge bases 65
knowledge base of mentoring 346–7

language, role in ontological coaching 108, 109, 111–12, 114, 115, 117
leadership, good 250, 251, 252, 254
    see executive and leadership coaching for detailed analysis
Leadership Development Profile (LPD) 140, 143
leading 192
learning, dynamics of team 275
learning, experiential 8
learning, levels of
    executive and leadership coaching 249
    transformational coaching 233, 234, 242
    see also engagement, four levels of; transformational coaching
learning, self-directed 57, 220
learning cycle, action 328–9
learning need, identifying 204–5
learning strategies 209, 211, 214
learning theories 5–9, 212, 223–4, 292–3, 299
letting come 150
letting go 150
life coaching 15, 17, 46, 49, 71, 72, 74, 90, 165–6, 181–2, 297–310
    approaches, processes and coach–client relationship 301–3
    assumptions and links to theoretical traditions 300–1
    challenges and limitations of 306–7
    counselling or coaching? 305–6
    ending coaching relationship 304–5
    evaluation of 307–8
    evidence-based approaches 299
    goal setting 303, 304
    human potential movement 298–9
    life positions and flow 181, 182
    monitoring and evaluation between sessions 304
links, making 28–9
listening 126–7, 205, 207, 238–9, 241, 301
logical levels model 195–6

manager as coach 15, 16, 90, 115, 128, 211–12, 225, 257–70, 274, 279, 286, 289, 316, 317
    evaluation 266–7
    features and goals 258–62; catalysts for coaching opportunities 259–60; contextual factors 261–2; mindset 259; skills and behaviours required 260–1
    relationship with theoretical traditions 263–6; going against company culture example 265–6; spending time with an employee example 264–5
    role of manager as coach and relationship with coachee 262–3

managers 48, 103, 113, 174, 175, 181, 183, 312–13,
    337, 408
  chief executive (CE) 396, 397
  expatriate managers 331
  human resources (HR) 4, 174, 175, 180, 246, 247,
    257, 289, 302, 322, 347, 365, 376, 382–3
  line managers 3, 4
  managing directors (MDs) 27, 28, 115–16
  middle managers 50, 265–6
  paradox framework for cross-cultural coaching,
    case study 334–6, 337
  role models 4
  sales managers 260
  see also executive and leadership coaching;
    manager as coach
marginalization, cultural 331, 332
market inquiry 315–17
  responses and decisions 217
matching and pacing 191–2, 195
matching, trust and confidentiality 288
matrix, table of genres and contexts of coaching 10
meaning and meaninglessness 97–9
meaning scheme, shift in 231
mental health 18–19, 301, 306, 394–404
  action needed 401–3; table of decisions to
    make 402
  coaching context 399–401
  evaluation 403–4
  recognizing mental health issues 397–9;
    table of warning signs 398
  understanding mental ill health 396–7
  see also health coaching
Mental Health Institute, Palo Alto 55
mentoring 3, 17–18, 74, 90, 211–12, 246, 286,
    289, 290–1, 297, 299, 304, 341–54, 365,
    369, 373, 380, 381, 383, 386, 400, 406, 410
  applications 347–8
  defining 343–4
  evaluation of 350–2
  features 344–7; advice giving 346; knowledge
    economy 346–7; relationship 346–7; social
    context 346
  relationship with theoretical traditions 349–50
  role of mentor and relationship with
    client 348–9
Meta Model 188, 190, 191, 194, 198
metaphor 195
Milton Model 189, 191, 195, 198
miracle question 58, 61
misrepresentation 375
Mobius-strip model 206, 211, 212, 213
moods, role in ontological coaching 112–13
motivation imagery 43

motivational interviewing 48, 73, 213
multimodal therapy 42, 73
multiple contracts, transactional
    analysis 174, 175
multiple levels, working on 231–2
multiple relationships 376
Myers-Briggs typology 223

narrative coaching 13, 120–31, 179, 227, 319–20
  assumptions of 121–2
  comparisons and applications 127–8
  evaluation of 129
  goals and tasks 126–7
  history of 120–1
  processes and dynamics of 122–5
  role of coach 125–6
Narrative Diamond model 127
National Education Association 406
National Union of Teachers 47
need-fulfilment process, Gestalt model 83–7
neuroscience, recent developments in 233–4
New Age 147, 153
NLP approach (neuro-linguistic programming) 15, 114,
    115, 187–99, 213
  applications of 197–8
  evaluation of 197
  origins of 187–8
  processes and dynamics 190–1
  role of coach and relationship with clients 191
  tasks and goals 189–90
  techniques for facilitating change 191–7;
    case study 196–7
non-violent communication model 207

ontological coaching 13, 107–19, 128
  applicability of 115–17
  comparison with other coaching genres 114–15
  evaluation of 117–18
  goals and tasks 109–10
  processes and features of 110–14
  theoretical basis of 108–9
Ontology of the Human Observer 107
orders of mind see Kegan's theory
Organization Development Center, Gestalt Institute
    of Cleveland
Organizational Role Consultancy methodology 253
outcomes, well-formed 192–4
  stated in the positive 192–3
ownership 194, 250

PAC (parent adult child) 30, 176, 179, 181, 253
  see also ego states
PACE model 43

paradox theory 333, 338
  paradox framework for cross-cultural coaching, case study 334–6, 337
pathways thinking 166
payment issues life coaching 302–3
peer coaching 17, 47, 75, 211–12, 275, 281, 284–96, 318
  distinctions between other genres and 289–91
  features, processes and roles 286–9; eight stage model 286–7
  goals and tasks 285–6
  relationship with theoretical approaches 291–3
person-centred approach 12, 46, 68–79, 127, 226, 291–2, 317, 320–1
  assumptions 69–70
  comparison of traditions 71–2
  contexts 74–5
  evaluation of 75–7
  features, processes, role of the coach 72–4; contracting 74
  goals and tasks 70–1
  history and theoretical tradition 68–9
  PETS 42
Personal Career Theory (PCT) 319
personal model of coaching 418–19
phenomenological method 102–3, 128
phone coaching 301
PINT analysis 316
PITS 42
plan and implement 313–14
positive psychology coaching (PPC) 14, 30, 34, 50, 71, 76, 77, 115, 158–71, 213, 280, 300, 320, 337
  applications of 165–7
  comparison with other theories 165
  evaluation of 167–9
  examples 162–5; positive emotion about the future 164; positive emotion about the past 163; positive emotion about the present 163–4
  goals and tasks 159–60
  GROW model and 160–1
  processes of 161–2; assessment 161; coaching relationship 162; expectations and coaching orientation 161–2
PRACTICE model 40–1, 47, 48
presence, Gestalt approach 81, 84, 87–8, 89, 91, 92
PricewaterhouseCoopers (PwC) 369, 370
Process Consultation 221
prototyping 151
psychoanalysis 23, 68, 81, 141, 165, 179, 253, 350, 413
psychodrama 233
  see also drama triangle roles

psychodynamic approach 11, 23–36, 114, 127, 179, 253, 279, 336
  comparisons with other traditions 29–30
  contexts 30–3
  definition of term 23
  distinctive features of 25–9
  evaluation of 33–5; best use 35; limitations 34–5; strengths 33–4
  relational regulation of emotions 24–5
psychosynthesis 148, 154
psychotherapy 34, 41, 68, 73, 92, 154, 162, 173, 184, 185, 233, 305–6, 321, 350, 358, 359–61, 381, 382, 383, 395, 399
psycINFO 299
purpose and meaning, executive leadership 249

QOLI (Quality of Life Inventory) 303

race 183
rational emotive behavioural approach 37–8, 42
re-decision 178
re-storying, process of, narrative coaching 124–5
redirecting 150
reframing 59, 191
relatedness, principle of 95, 165–6
relational-cultural theory 213
relaxation 41
  relaxation imagery 44
religion and the transpersonal 147
resources, highlighting 59
right brain 147
room, coaching 232, 241

Sainsbury Centre for Mental Health (SCMH) 395
savouring 163–4
scaffolding 301
scaling 58–9, 61
self, concept of in existential coaching 95, 96, 100, 101, 104, 105
self, how to use the, Gestalt approach 87–8, 91
self, Kegan's theory of *see* Kegan's theory
self-acceptance 40, 250
self-actualization 63, 69, 70, 72, 176, 291
  see also actualizing tendency
self-awareness 38–9, 250, 252, 292
self-concordance theory (SCT) 165, 166
self-determination theory (STD) 76–7, 165
self-directed learning 57, 220
self-disclosure 285, 290
self-efficacy 166–7, 204, 214
self-image 249
self-management 376–7

self-regulation 57, 81–2, 292
sensory based goals 193
separation, cultural 331, 332
seven-eyed coaching model 386–90
seven-step model, Hampden-Turner and
    Trompenaars 329
seven-step model, Wasik's 40
skills and performance coaching (SPC) 4, 15–16,
    31, 46, 62–3, 166–7, 203–16, 217–18, 225,
    242, 290, 317, 386
    distinction between other genres and 211–12
    evaluation of 214
    features, processes and roles 204–11;
        case study 209–11
    goals and tasks of 203–4, 279
    relationship with theoretical approaches 212–14
small to medium sized enterprise (SME) 267
SMART goals 40, 41, 193, 194, 303
social-cognitive theory 38, 213
social context 346
solution-focused approach (SF) 12, 29, 38, 54–67, 73,
    213, 263–4, 279–80, 291, 294, 337, 350
    applications of 62–4
    assumptions 55–6
    characteristics of 56–7
    coaching engagement 60–2
    evaluation of 64–5
    history of 55
    techniques for change 57–60
SPACE model 42–3, 45, 47, 48
spiral dynamics 133
spirituality and the transpersonal 147, 149
sports psychology 278
story 206–7, 211, 214
strengths 164, 205
Strong Interest Inventory 320
subject-object interview (SOI) 140, 143
subject to object mechanism *see* Kegan's theory
successful accomplishment, observing examples
    of 205
supervision 18, 174, 281, 381–93
    definition of 383–4
    research 382–3
    role and purpose 384; table of three main
        functions 384
    seven-eyed coaching model 386–90
    stages in a supervision session 385; diagram of
        coaching continuum 385; table of CLEAR
        model 386
    training 390–1
Survey Monkey 409
suspending 150
Symptom Assessment-45 (SA45) 50

Tavistock Institute 253
teachers 284
team coaching 16–17, 33, 47–8, 128, 142, 167,
    180–1, 271–83, 318
    differences between team coaching and: group
        therapy 276–7; individual coaching 272, 276;
        team facilitation 278; team leadership 276, 277
    evaluation 281–2
    features, process, role of coach and relationship with
        client 274–6
    goals and tasks 273–4
    relationship with theories and traditions 278–80
test and learn approaches 313–14
thinking skills 39–40
    example of thinking errors 39
    thinking and the good enough coach 28
three-cornered contract, transactional analysis 174, 175
three good things, concept of 163
time-bound goals 40
time frame 194
time projection imagery 44
trait interaction possibilities 332
transactional analysis and coaching (TA) 14–15, 29,
    172–86, 253, 419
    aim of 173
    comparison with other traditions 179
    contexts 179–83
    evaluation of 183–5; limitations 184,
        strengths 184–5
    theory and processes of 174–8
transference 27
    see also counter transference
transformational coaching 9, 15, 16, 104, 130, 142,
    155, 211, 225, 231–44, 386
    distinctive features of 241–2; coaching
        continuum 242
    evaluation 242–3
    history and roots of 232–4
    key elements of 234–51
    outcomes 234
transformational grammar 189
transformative learning 8–9
transpersonal approach 14, 30, 141, 146–57
    application of 155
    clarification of term 147–8
    conditions and obstacles for development 148–9
    evaluation of 155–6
    methods and techniques for facilitating
        change and development 154–5
    processes/dynamics of 150–1
    role of the coach and relationship with the
        client 152–3
    tasks and goals of 153–4

Transpersonal Psychology Review 146
triviality 345
trust 288
two videos question 61

UK, psychotherapy in 360
UKCP (United Kingdom Council for
    Psychotherapy) 360
uncertainty, principle of 95–6
University of Santa Cruz 187
University of Surrey 187
USA psychotherapy in 360

Values in Action Institute Inventory of Strengths
    (VIA-IS) 160–1
Vocation Bureau of Boston 311

Washington University Sentence
    Completion Test 140
Wasik's model 40
way of being 13, 109, 110, 111, 114, 117, 118
Willis, P. 342
willpower 166
Worldwide Association of Business Coaches (WABC)
    248, 365, 366, 369, 371, 406, 411

The Qualitative Research Kit

Edited by Uwe Flick

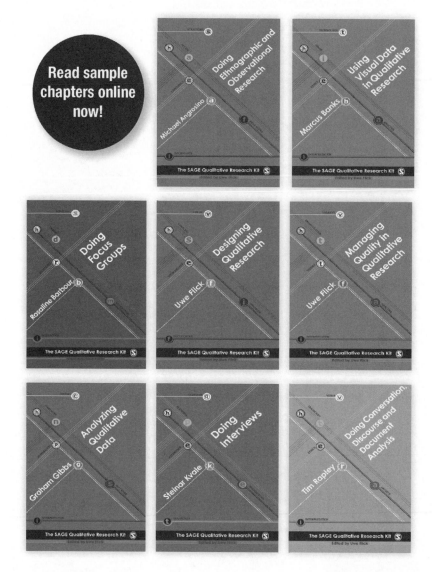

Read sample chapters online now!

Doing Ethnographic and Observational Research — Michael Angrosino — The SAGE Qualitative Research Kit

Using Visual Data in Qualitative Research — Marcus Banks — The SAGE Qualitative Research Kit

Doing Focus Groups — Rosaline Barbour — The SAGE Qualitative Research Kit

Designing Qualitative Research — Uwe Flick — The SAGE Qualitative Research Kit

Managing Quality in Qualitative Research — Uwe Flick — The SAGE Qualitative Research Kit

Analyzing Qualitative Data — Graham Gibbs — The SAGE Qualitative Research Kit

Doing Interviews — Steinar Kvale — The SAGE Qualitative Research Kit

Doing Conversation, Discourse and Document Analysis — Tim Rapley — The SAGE Qualitative Research Kit

www.sagepub.co.uk

Research Methods Books from SAGE

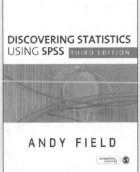
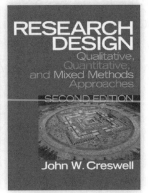

Supporting researchers for more than forty years

Research methods have always been at the core of SAGE's publishing. Sara Miller McCune founded SAGE in 1965 and soon after she published SAGE's first methods book, *Public Policy Evaluation*. A few years later, she launched the Quantitative Applications in the Social Sciences series – affectionately known as the 'little green books'.

Always at the forefront of developing and supporting new approaches in methods, SAGE published early groundbreaking texts and journals in the fields of qualitative methods and evaluation.

Today, more than forty years and two million little green books later, SAGE continues to push the boundaries with a growing list of more than 1,200 research methods books, journals, and reference works across the social, behavioural, and health sciences.

From qualitative, quantitative and mixed methods to evaluation, SAGE is the essential resource for academics and practitioners looking for the latest in methods by leading scholars.

www.sagepublications.com